SPORTS IN AMERICAN LIFE

Cover illustration:
Defending champion Muhammad Ali glares at a fallen Sonny Liston midway through the first round of their second bout held in Lewiston, Maine, on May 25, 1965. Ali himself was uncertain whether he had hit Liston with a "right cross or a left hook," and Liston said that Ali caught him with a "sharp punch" that he did not see coming. Many skeptics contended Liston took a dive; most spectators at ringside and those watching on television never saw the punch. Compounding the confusion, referee Jersey Joe Wolcott failed to start a count, but then declared Ali the winner by knockout only after the two fighters had resumed throwing punches 17 seconds after the "phantom punch" had sent Liston to the canvas. Announcer Howard Cosell told a national television audience that "bedlam, chaos and confusion" surrounded this surreal ending to the title bout. This photograph was taken by Associated Press photographer John Rooney.

SPORTS IN AMERICAN LIFE

A HISTORY

SECOND EDITION

Richard O. Davies

WILEY-BLACKWELL

A John Wiley & Sons, Ltd., Publication

This edition first published 2012
© 2012 John Wiley & Sons, Inc.

Wiley-Blackwell is an imprint of John Wiley & Sons, formed by the merger of Wiley's global Scientific, Technical and Medical business with Blackwell Publishing.

Registered Office
John Wiley & Sons Ltd, The Atrium, Southern Gate, Chichester, West Sussex, PO19 8SQ, United Kingdom

Editorial Offices
350 Main Street, Malden, MA 02148-5020, USA
9600 Garsington Road, Oxford, OX4 2DQ, UK
The Atrium, Southern Gate, Chichester, West Sussex, PO19 8SQ, UK

For details of our global editorial offices, for customer services, and for information about how to apply for permission to reuse the copyright material in this book please see our website at www.wiley.com/wiley-blackwell.

The right of Richard O. Davies to be identified as the author of this work has been asserted in accordance with the UK Copyright, Designs and Patents Act 1988.

Wiley also publishes its books in a variety of electronic formats. Some content that appears in print may not be available in electronic books.

Designations used by companies to distinguish their products are often claimed as trademarks. All brand names and product names used in this book are trade names, service marks, trademarks or registered trademarks of their respective owners. The publisher is not associated with any product or vendor mentioned in this book. This publication is designed to provide accurate and authoritative information in regard to the subject matter covered. It is sold on the understanding that the publisher is not engaged in rendering professional services. If professional advice or other expert assistance is required, the services of a competent professional should be sought.

Library of Congress Cataloging-in-Publication Data

Davies, Richard O., 1937–
    Sports in American life : a history / Richard O. Davies. – 2nd ed.
        p.   cm.
    Includes bibliographical references and index.
    ISBN 978-0-470-65546-7 (alk. paper)
1. Sports–United States–History.   I. Title.
    GV583.D39 2011
    796–dc23

                                                            2011018169

A catalogue record for this book is available from the British Library.

This book is published in the following electronic formats: ePDFs 9781118121368; ePub 9781118121375; mobi 9781118121382

Set in 10/13pt Minion by SPi Publisher Services, Pondicherry, India
Printed in Singapore by Ho Printing Singapore Pte Ltd

3   2014

For Jayme, Mackenzie, and Katie

Contents

List of Illustrations

Preface

During the early years of the nineteenth century, the word "sport" carried a much different connotation than it does today. To be a sporting man in the mid nineteenth century was to be someone who flouted the rules of social acceptability by gravitating toward activities deemed inappropriate for a proper gentleman. The term "sport" was, in fact, used to identify men who embraced the bachelor culture of the tavern, where amid a haze of cigar smoke and the odor of stale beer and cheap whiskey, they watched cockfights and dogfights, bet on an upcoming horse race or baseball match, and won or lost money on the toss of the dice or the turn of a card. Upon special occasions they might even watch pugilists bloody each other in a bare-knuckle prizefight.

There also emerged during the same time period a group of men referred to as sportsmen. These were men of good social standing who found outlets from their pressing business and professional lives as participants and spectators in such activities as sailing, swimming, horse racing, foot racing, rowing, and baseball. By century's end they likely had also gravitated toward popular new activities such as tennis, bicycle racing, football, golf, basketball, and volleyball. As these sports grew in popularity, sportsmen (now joined by a small but growing number of sportswomen) mimicked trends within the professional and business worlds by striving to achieve order and stability. They established amateur and professional leagues and associations, published statistics, developed and marketed specialized equipment, and enforced written rules governing athletic competition.

Although sports and games revealed a distinctly provincial quality in 1800, by the beginning of the twentieth century spontaneity and informality had been replaced by formalized structures, written rules, and bureaucratic organization. Befitting the growing specialization within the emerging national marketplace, a small number of skilled athletes were even able to work at play, earning their living as professional athletes. Several of the new sports provided women opportunities to participate, although under carefully guarded conditions. In this rapidly changing environment, the word "sport" lost much of its negative connotation. Now, to be a sporting man or woman was to be involved in a robust new American lifestyle. By the early twentieth century, organized sports had assumed a prominent place in American life, reflective of the exuberant capitalistic and democratic spirit of a rapidly maturing society.

This book traces the evolution of American sports, from its unorganized and quaint origins to the present time. The narrative is organized around the argument that sports, for good or for ill, have been a significant, if often overlooked, social force throughout the history of the United States. In recent years, historians have come to recognize that throughout the history of mankind, games have revealed many of the underlying values of society. Rather than being irrelevant diversions of little consequence, such activities provide important insights into fundamental values and beliefs. The games people played may have provided a convenient means of releasing tension or a means of escaping the realities of the day, but they also provided rituals that linked generations and united communities.

The essential assumption of this book is that throughout American history the form and purpose of sporting events have been closely connected to the larger society from which they arose. As but one recent example: during the days immediately following the terrorist attack upon the World Trade Center in New York City and the Pentagon in Washington, DC, on September 11, 2001, Americans found reassurance in expressing their national unity and resolve through highly symbolic patriotic exercises conducted prior to the start of baseball and football games. National leaders urged the resumption of sports schedules as soon as it became apparent that no more attacks were imminent, viewing the playing of games as an emphatic statement of national resolve that the terrorists would not disturb the rhythms of everyday life.

Sports in American Culture

Organized sports in the nineteenth century grew naturally with the new systems of transportation, manufacturing, and commercial organization. They took hold primarily in the cities that were created by the new modern America, and during the twentieth century they grew exponentially, propelled to prominence by the new communications media of radio, motion pictures, newspapers, and television. In contemporary America, sports have become an enormous multibillion-dollar enterprise. Professional football and baseball franchises are valued at between $400 million and $1 billion, and nearly every major American city has in recent years spent hundreds of millions of dollars to build sports arenas and stadiums to accommodate professional teams. Most major professional teams operate on annual budgets that exceed $200 million, and major college athletic programs have annual budgets ranging between $30 million and $100 million, with a growing number exceeding that figure. An oft-overlooked ancillary economic activity attests to the importance Americans place upon sporting events: conservative estimates are that gamblers bet at least $4 billion a year on sporting events, a figure larger than the gross national product of some Third World countries. At least 20 percent of the news reported in any daily urban newspaper is devoted to the activities of a small handful of that city's prominent residents who dribble basketballs, hit baseballs, or knock each other to the ground with intense ferocity. Radio and television networks provide 24 hour coverage of America's sports to a seemingly insatiable audience. A vast assortment of consumer items – automobiles, clothing, and beverages – are marketed in close relationship with sports teams and athletes.

My first effort to examine the role of sports in American life presented the argument that a broad swath of the American people were obsessed with sports; at the time I thought my interpretation would engender considerable criticism, but instead it resonated with general readers as well as those in academia.[1] In many ways, America's obsession with sports and the men and women who play the games has intersected in unsuspected ways with larger issues of public policy. For example, in many cities students attend public schools in dilapidated buildings with leaking roofs and outmoded classrooms and laboratories, and are taught by underpaid teachers using tattered out-of-date textbooks. City streets go unrepaired, libraries close, and hospitals struggle to deal with their patient loads, but in these same cities, civic leaders eagerly cater to the demands of professional teams. The owners – multimillionaires all – enjoy a special kind of public welfare through their lucrative agreements with local governments. Crucial social services might go untended, but time and again, taxpayers vote in favor of a tax increase to build a new arena or stadium and public officials placate team owners by granting tax breaks, sweetheart deals on rental fees, and control of concessions and parking.

Between 1980 and 2010, nearly every major American city constructed lavish new sports venues for several professional teams, often to the serious neglect of other community needs. Just as the citizenry of medieval European communities revealed their essential values by constructing imposing cathedrals in the town square, so too have modern American cities given expression to their priorities and values by erecting enormous sports facilities.

Sports and American History

The issue of stadium construction and operation is but one example of how sports and larger community issues intersect. The pages that follow examine the role of sports within the broader context of the major themes of American history. This book is an extension of major trends of the last quarter-century that have reshaped the way historians look at the past. The historical profession, which had long focused its attention on political, economic, and diplomatic themes, was fundamentally affected by the social upheavals of the 1960s. As part of the fallout of that turbulent period, the traditional historical approach that focused on the achievements and failures of a white, male political and economic establishment was challenged. A new generation of students, who questioned many of the existing myths about the "establishment," demanded courses in African American, Hispanic, and Native American history, classes on the history of environmental issues, and fresh perspectives on the American experience written from the vantage point of the poor, women, and the working class.

It was within this period of intellectual ferment that scholars first began a serious examination of the role of sports in American history. The extensive body of literature upon which this book is based reveals that most of the writing on the history of American sports before the mid 1970s was done outside the academy, but since then professional historians have begun to produce books and articles that explore the relationship of American sports with larger social issues. In 1972, the first professional society in the United States devoted to the field of sports history was established, and several pioneering scholars made laudable efforts to provide a meaningful synthesis.[2] A few courses on the history of baseball had been taught previously, but in the ensuing decades more inclusive histories of American sports were introduced. Academic publishers began releasing a growing number of scholarly monographs on the subject of sports. History survey textbooks now included pictures of early baseball parks or college football games along with the more conventional images of soldiers, presidents, and reformers. But resistance, or at least persistent apathy, has slowed the integration of sports into broader cultural contexts in the curricula of the humanities and social sciences.

The emergence of sports history as a serious scholarly endeavor is no small achievement, because within any college or university there are faculty members who decry the existence of intercollegiate sports programs. A national survey I conducted in 1999 indicated that the overwhelming number of specialized upper-division and graduate-level American courses in social history still do not include the role of sports, and that history departments remained reluctant to conduct searches for faculty with sports as a focus of their teaching and research.

The rationale for this resistance is not surprising. Many faculty members have rightfully objected to gargantuan athletic department budgets and the simultaneous exploitation and coddling of athletes on their campuses, and have been outraged by the many scandals that have time-and-again besmirched the image of American higher education. Tenured faculty who offer seminars in American social history have built their research programs on other important cultural connections – the arts, labor, motion pictures, literature, immigration, class, gender – and the list goes on. Few graduate programs provide encouragement to graduate students to undertake serious research in sports-related topics, and those that select them are routinely warned that their placement in the academic marketplace could easily be jeopardized. Such was the case of Yale doctoral student Warren Goldstein in the 1970s who opted to present a dissertation on the history of baseball. His "Playing for Keeps: A History of Early Baseball" became a landmark study that opened up scholarly potentials for future scholars. Nonetheless, he reports that his dissertation topic made his search for a tenure-track university position a difficult and prolonged exercise.[3]

This text will examine many themes, but throughout, the roles of gender and race are pervasive. Writing in 1994, two scholars who have made major contributions to the literature exploring the cultural context of American sports, Elliott J. Gorn and Michael Oriard, called for scholars engaged in sociology, literature, psychology, philosophy, anthropology, and history to explore the many ways their cultural studies intersect with sports: "Where is there a cultural activity more freighted with constructions of masculinity than football, more deeply inscribed with race than boxing, more tied in the public mind to the hopes and hopelessness of inner-city youth than basketball?" Taking note of the heavy emphasis being placed upon multiculturalism in contemporary college curricula, they pointed to the pervasive role of sports in the mass media. "It is almost a cliché," they wrote, "to mention that sports are the lingua franca of men talking across divisions of class and race. Sports can reveal just how interdependent particular subcultures and the larger consumer culture can be. Think, for example, of the symbiotic ties between inner-city playground basketball and the National Basketball Association."[4]

On a superficial level, from the colonial period to the present, sporting events have provided a useful diversion from the pressures of daily life. Just as colonists tossed a ball or watched a horse race to enliven their lives, so too do contemporary Americans follow the ups and downs of their favorite teams, put $10 in the office pool on the NCAA basketball tournament, and play on their church's co-ed slow-pitch softball team. On a more serious level, parents, religious leaders, educators, and moral reformers have used sports to teach new generations the values of fair play, honesty, perseverance, and cooperation. Presidents from Theodore Roosevelt to Barack Obama have interjected themselves into the public debate over pressing sports issues. President George W. Bush was part owner and managing partner of a major-league baseball team, the Texas Rangers, before his election as governor of Texas in 1994. Sporting venues have often provided a stage on which Americans have dealt with the paramount issues of race and sexual discrimination. Students can learn much about the nature of American race relations by examining the Negro Baseball Leagues, the "fight of the century" between Jack Johnson and Jim Jeffries, the triumphs and tragedies of track star Jessie Owens, or the courage and resolution of Jackie Robinson in challenging the unwritten exclusionary racial covenant of organized baseball. Students interested in the dynamics of the women's rights movement can similarly draw insights from the struggles against entrenched sexism in both amateur and professional sports by such gifted athletes as Gertrude Ederle, Babe Didrikson Zaharias, Wilma Rudolph, and Billie Jean King. Political battles over the development of athletic programs for schoolgirls and college women during the past four decades have been, and remain, an integral part of a much larger national struggle against gender discrimination.

For the purpose of this book, the word "sport" entails an organized competitive activity between participants that requires some combination of skill and physical prowess. Thus, such games as baseball, volleyball, and tennis are considered sports; chess, backgammon, and bridge are not. Some competitive games played primarily for pleasure or exercise, such as croquet, badminton, jogging, aerobics, and racquetball, are likewise excluded from this definition, but stock car and marathon races fit comfortably within it. Professional wrestling, despite its popularity, is excluded because it is a loosely scripted entertainment spectacle rather than a competitive contest. Similarly, junk sports such as roller derby and motocross are excluded, along with choreographed performance spectacles such as water ballet, figure skating, and ice dancing. In recent years, new sports have emerged out of what were originally recreational pursuits: snowboarding, skateboarding, and mixed martial arts. Although hunters and fishermen refer to themselves as "sportsmen" and while professional fishermen sometimes engage in tournaments, those activities are considered here to be of a recreational nature.

This is an examination of the world of sports as it intersects with the larger themes and issues of American life. American sports, at their best, have provided us with inspiring stories of courage, grace, drama, excitement, and accomplishment. Conversely, they have also brought out, for all to see, depressing examples of brutality, cruelty, racism, sexism, stupidity, intolerance, homophobia, xenophobia, nationalism, greed, and hypocrisy. Both extremes are on display in the pages that follow. In many respects, these pages present my personal take on the role of sports in American history, a culmination of a lifetime spent as a participant in and close observer of the American sports scene, and, for the past 20 years, as a professor exploring the fascinating saga of sports in the American experience as a researcher and classroom instructor.

For better or for worse, sports have played an integral part in the history of the United States, providing Americans with a venue in which major cultural and social issues have been debated, contested, and, in some notable instances, resolved. In a sense, this book seeks to examine the American past through the prism of sports. It is not simply a story of the winners and losers, nor is it a chronicle of the individual achievements of athletes. This is a book intended for the serious student interested in examining the American past from the perspective of sports.

Richard O. Davies
University of Nevada, Reno

Acknowledgments

No book of this magnitude can be brought to publication without the assistance of many individuals. This second edition has sought to sharpen the focus of the original text and incorporate important developments that have occurred in the past five years. Ever since I began work on the first edition I have benefited from the encouragement and guidance of Wiley-Blackwell Senior Editor Peter Coveney. His enthusiastic support for the project, coupled with his guidance and good humor, made the effort rewarding. The details of editing and production have been overseen with efficiency and understanding by Editorial Assistant Galen Smith. I gratefully acknowledge her assistance throughout the process.

Several student assistants provided essential help for the first edition: Jennifer Valenzuela, Seth Flatley, Eric Bender, Jayme Hoy, and Yulia Kalnaus. I am especially grateful for the contributions of graduate students Kimberly Esse and Andrew McGregor for this second edition. I appreciate the careful reading given the manuscript by Dr Dee Kille and Professor Thomas E. Smith of the University of Nevada, Reno, Professor Ronald A. Smith of Pennsylvania State University, and Professor Frank Mitchell of the University of Southern California. I am deeply indebted to Professor Scott Casper, chair of the Department of History of the University of Nevada, Reno for his many years of friendship and support of my work. He provides leadership for a department of 15 teacher-scholars that is exceptional because of the spirit of collegiality and professionalism that characterizes the way it functions. The department is the beneficiary of a very generous endowment that supports the research of its members. I gratefully acknowledge the assistance provided by the John Noble Endowment for Historical Research and posthumously thank my good friend for his generosity that will provide for years to come substantial support for the research of each department member.

Throughout my career Sharon has been unfailingly supportive of my various academic roles as teacher, researcher, and administrator. Undertaking to write a book as broad and complex as this entails a multiyear commitment. This book is dedicated to our three granddaughters who have enriched our lives. It is our hope that their futures are filled with the joys provided by playing the games they enjoy and supporting the teams and athletes they respect.

1

The Emergence of Organized Sports, 1607–1860

Although there is substantial evidence to indicate that folk games and contests were an integral part of everyday life in colonial America, it was not until the nineteenth century that the playing of games began to reflect the structure and organization that we associate with modern American sports. Colonists participated in a myriad of activities that are best described as folk games, meaning that they were characterized by their spontaneity and absence of standardized rules and bureaucratic organization. Many varied games were played in the English colonies, but the most popular spectator event in colonial America was horse racing, much of which occurred in the Tidewater region of Maryland and Virginia. Colonial games and recreations were characterized by their casual nature, more or less governed by informal rules of local origin and subject to constant revision and argument. Team games were unheard of, and participation in any activity that included physical competition was limited to a small percentage of the colonial population.

Although the many games and contests that absorbed the attention of colonial America incorporated many New World variations – including adaptation of Native American games – their roots could be found in rural England. Immigrants to the New World naturally brought with them the customs, values, and vices of the Old World. The Puritan leaders who came to Massachusetts Bay Colony were determined to build a new order – a shining "city on a hill," as John Winthrop eloquently expressed it in 1630 – that placed emphasis on the creation of a theocratic state in which pious men and women responded to God's calling to a life of discipline and productivity as farmers, seamen, and craftsmen. Similarly, the Anglicans who gravitated to the Chesapeake Bay region were equally determined to replicate the social norms of the landed gentry of rural England, replete with the pleasures of lavish balls and banquets, riding to hounds, the playing of billiards and card games, and hell-bent-for-leather quarter horse races, all of which were accompanied by gambling.

Sports in American Life: A History, Second Edition. Richard O. Davies.
© 2012 John Wiley & Sons, Inc. Published 2012 by John Wiley & Sons, Inc.

The era of folk games began to give way to a new era of organized sports in the decades following the American Revolution, but it was not until the 1850s that organized team games, complete with written rules, structured play, and measurable outcomes, became commonplace. These changes reflected the vast technological and economic changes that trended towards urbanization, manufacturing, and heavily capitalized commercial development. By 1860, a vast network of canals and 30,000 miles of railroads had connected a burgeoning urban network that stretched from Boston and New York to as far west as Chicago and St Louis. Telegraph lines made it possible to send and receive messages with incredible speed, and coal-powered ships carried raw materials and finished products up and down America's rivers and across the Great Lakes.

The Census of 1860 revealed just how far the young nation had come since the presidency of George Washington. In 1790, over 95 percent of the people derived their livelihood from agriculture, and New York City and Philadelphia were the two largest cities with populations of 33,000 and 28,500 respectively. By 1860, 20 percent of the American people lived in urban places and New York City had a population in excess of 1 million. In 1830, fully 80 percent of the American people were classified as farmers, a figure that fell to just 53 percent 30 years later. The urban and industrial transformation of America, however, was barely visible in the South, a region hamstrung by the "peculiar institution" of slavery that slowed social and economic innovation and discouraged the development of manufacturing and the building of vibrant urban centers. The United States had entered the new modern era characterized by standardization, organization, hierarchical decision-making, mass production, efficiency, and electronic communications.

Games in Colonial New England

The harsh environment of colonial America was not conducive to playing games. Mere survival was an everyday fact of life. Inherent Puritan skepticism about the worth of non-productive games was inevitably intensified by the unrelenting frontier environment in which colonists found themselves. What they referred to as the "howling wilderness" proved to be a powerful influence upon their thoughts and actions; in such an environment, the development of a substantial leisure ethic was necessarily circumscribed. If a game encouraged participants to shirk their essential obligations for work and worship, then it definitely was deemed inappropriate. Focus on the serious nature of life was especially pronounced in New England where powerful public pressure gave primacy to the importance of an individual's dedication to a life of productive labor and worship. The Puritans did not abolish games and recreational activities, but they made clear distinctions between games and other diversions that tended to restore clarity of mind and refresh the body so that one could return to the field or shop reinvigorated. Actually, much of the Puritans' concerns about games and play grew out of memories of England, where unseemly social behavior routinely occurred in conjunction with activities that were closely associated with rowdy behavior, excessive drinking, and gambling. As historian Bruce Daniels concludes, "colonies did not pass laws against ball and blood sports; public contempt sufficed to bar them." As he notes, the pervasive lack of attention to ball games by New Englanders in their sermons, diaries, correspondence, and newspapers throughout the entire colonial period "speaks volumes" about their absence from the daily lives of colonists of New England.[1]

To their credit, the Puritans adamantly sought to suppress "butcherly sports" such as the brutalizing of animals that regularly occurred in England. Puritans struggled to control and even abolish animal baitings, cockfighting, and violent human competitions such as pugilism and a primitive game of "foot ball" that revolved around the advancement of an inflated pig's bladder across a goal by means of kicking or running. These contests sometimes involved hundreds of participants and serious injuries were not uncommon. New England leaders, however, permitted practical activities that promoted fitness and health, such as hunting and fishing. New England's massive forests contained a bounteous array of game that provided food for the family table. However, the successful hunting of big game – bear, deer, and moose – proved a difficult task due to the lack of accurate firearms, so New Englanders tended to focus their attention on the many ponds, lakes, and streams that teemed with fish. Fishing enjoyed widespread popularity as an approved recreational activity; it was, in fact, one of a small number of recreations that Harvard College officially sanctioned for students. Given the considerable attention devoted to fishing in the writings of colonial New Englanders, it is safe to conclude that most males at one time or another cast a line into the streams and lakes of the region. And of course many adults made their living as commercial fishermen in the waters of the North Atlantic. Fishing was, as Daniels concludes, the "ideal pastime for men and boys" because of its utility and lack of association with untoward social behaviors.[2]

The relatively diverse and cosmopolitan population of the New York City region dictated a less constrictive view of games and recreation. Originally settled by the Dutch, the city of New York provided an environment in which residents found time to relax and play games suggestive of modern-day croquet, cricket, tennis, lawn bowling, and badminton. To the anguish of many, animal baitings and cockfights were also instituted – often at fairs and other community-wide social events – and they enjoyed widespread popularity among the lower classes in part because these sports were conducive to wagering.

The dominant Quaker population of Philadelphia and its environs resulted in the banning of most forms of leisure activity, including dancing, card playing, animal baiting, and maypole celebrations. Young people were encouraged to learn to hunt and fish as part of the struggle for subsistence in the rugged colonial environment, and such activities as running and swimming were seen as helpful to the physical development of young girls and boys. Like the Puritans, the Quakers of Pennsylvania viewed the playing of games within the larger context of whether the activity promoted general community welfare, economic growth, military skills, physical fitness, and spiritual growth.

Thus recreational activities in the colonies north of the Chesapeake Bay region generally had to be rationalized within the context of the larger issues of protecting the Sabbath, preventing cruelty to animals, responding to one's secular calling, providing food for the table, or maintaining health and fitness. Gambling in the regions controlled by the Puritans and Quakers was generally minimal and not a matter for serious concern. In fact, churches, schools, colleges, and other public agencies themselves encouraged a widely accepted form of gambling to finance major projects. Public lotteries were frequently offered by authorities to raise monies to build new churches, school buildings, or other public facilities, a practice that local governments would abandon early in the nineteenth century after a wave of scandals discredited the honesty of such lotteries. In the latter half of the twentieth century, political leaders in 37 states resurrected the lottery as a means of raising revenue for such purposes as funding public education as a means to avoid increasing taxes.

In both New England and the Middle Colonies, colonists interacted regularly with Native Americans. This interaction, however, does not seem to have greatly influenced the development of games and recreations engaged in by the colonists, although some of the games played by Indians were similar to those enjoyed by the colonists, and included ample symbolism related to fertility, healing, and warfare. Often the games played by Native Americans included preparation through elaborate rituals, dances, and sacred chants intended to ward off evil spirits and to help ensure victory in the upcoming contest. The most common of the games played by the natives was a game involving the use of a small ball and sticks equipped with small leather nets. The Cherokee called their version of the game "the little brother of war" because it involved hundreds of players engaged in advancing the ball over several miles of rugged terrain. Some games could last for days. Because of the vast numbers of players it was difficult for many of them even to get close to the ball, so they contented themselves with attempts to injure their opponents with their sticks. In what is now upper New York and Ontario, early French explorers witnessed a similar game being played by the Iroquois, although typical sides numbered about 20 with two goals set up about 120 feet apart. The French thought that the sticks resembled a bishop's crozier, spelled *la crosse* in French, so the name of the game that remains yet today an important sport in the Eastern United States carries the name given to it by the French.

Recreations in Southern Colonies

In 1686, an aristocratic Frenchman visited Virginia and recorded his observations of everyday life in his diary. Durand de Dauphine noted that in Jamestown many members of the House of Burgesses began to play high-stakes card games immediately after dinner. About midnight, one of the players noticed the visitor from France intently watching the action and suggested that he might want to retire for the evening, "For it is quite possible that we shall be here all night."[3] Sure enough, the next morning, Durand found the same card game still in session. As historian T. H. Breen has explained, what Durand observed was certainly not an aberration but rather a normal aspect of life among the Virginia elite. In sharp contrast to social norms in the North, the planter class that controlled life in colonial Virginia and Maryland was strongly committed to high-stakes gambling as a form of entertainment; gentlemen regularly bet on cards, backgammon, dice, and horses.[4]

The tobacco planters in Maryland and Virginia found special meaning in their gambling obsession, which seemed to fit well into the culture in which they lived and worked. Gambling enabled them to translate into their lives the values by which they operated their plantations, where risk taking, competitiveness, individuality, and materialism were paramount. During the seventeenth century, the first generations of planters utilized white indentured servants to help solve their need for unskilled labor in the tobacco fields, but that system proved unreliable. In order to assure an adequate and continual supply of field hands, they readily adopted the alternative of human slavery. The widespread use of black slaves – the first group of 19 being brought to Virginia in 1619 – shaped the social order of the South forever, creating a complex social mosaic that commingled the emotionally charged issues of class and race.[5]

As a result of the increasing number of slaves imported from the Caribbean and Africa, white males assumed a social status that was determined by whether or not they owned slaves, and if so, how many. Whites who did not own slaves and had to work in the fields themselves were considered commoners with whom true Southern gentlemen – slave owners all – did not associate on a social basis. A gentleman of a high social level supervised the operation of his plantation and his slave labor force, but physical labor was considered beneath his social status. This new Virginia upper class naturally gravitated toward a life that demanded expression of their social ranking – in their proclivity for large and richly appointed houses, their stylish clothes, their lavish entertainment style, and their expensive material possessions. Because both men and women of the elite were considered to be above the performance of manual labor, they were inevitably forced into a situation where they were expected to work very hard at serious leisure activities. For women this meant a constant social whirl of teas, receptions, and visits, while their men's lives were punctuated by high-stakes gambling, a widely accepted avocation that in and of itself connoted wealth and stature within Virginia society.[6]

These men were fiercely driven. Caught up in the immense uncertainties of the tobacco trade characterized by widely fluctuating markets, the planters often found themselves helpless pawns in an intensely competitive and turbulent economic environment. Simply put, in the tobacco-growing regions of Maryland and eastern Virginia, one could only improve one's social standing by increasing one's wealth. Truth be known, the planters' high status was often at risk, and their lives and financial wellbeing were often imperiled by forces beyond their control. Too much or too little rain wreaked havoc with harvests; ships carrying their precious annual crops to European markets sometimes disappeared in the storms of the Atlantic Ocean; a succession of good harvests could drive down the market price; and poor harvests carried serious economic consequences. White indentured servants and black slaves remained an uncertain, unreliable, and often troublesome source of labor. Prone to work slowdowns, their numbers were often decimated by devastating epidemics and short life expectancies. A prominent Virginia planter, William Fitzhugh, warned an English correspondent whose son was contemplating migrating to Virginia to take up the life of a tobacco planter, that "even if the best husbandry and the greatest forecast and skill were used, yet ill luck at sea, a fall of a Market, or twenty other accidents may ruin and overthrow the best industry."[7]

In such a precarious environment, gambling became a natural expression for men caught up in the system. For some of the more desperate, perhaps, it held out the hope of improving their financial status, but for most it was an essential form of social interaction that was consistent with the lifestyle they pursued. Their willingness to risk large sums on horse races, cockfights, or table games provided tangible evidence that they had sufficient affluence to withstand heavy gambling losses, as befitting people of high social status. While table games provided popular indoor recreation – and many a fortune often hung on the turn of a card or the toss of the dice – it was horse racing that held the greatest fascination for the Southern gentry. In this rural environment, horses were held in high esteem because they provided the essential means of transportation. Ownership of an elegant, high-spirited horse was not unlike ownership of an expensive, sporty automobile in twentieth-century America: it set a gentleman apart from the middling and lower classes. As a tangible extension of the planter's ego, a powerful and handsome horse was a source of pride and a symbol of lofty status. Virginians bred muscular horses with strong hindquarters that enabled them to run at high speeds for a relatively short distance. Popularly called quarter horses, they were trained to run all out in races measured to a quarter mile in length.[8]

While some races, such as those held in conjunction with fairs or the convening of the local courts, were scheduled weeks or months in advance, many were impromptu affairs that resulted from the offering and acceptance of a challenge between gentlemen. Stakes in these races were often high: sometimes an entire year's tobacco crop might ride on a single mad dash by two horses down a dirt road. Spectators eagerly flocked to these exciting events and made their own bets. While many commoners as well as slaves might attend, they were normally excluded from entering their horses. For one thing, the high stakes involved usually precluded their participation. But more importantly, horse racing was a sport largely reserved for the gentry, and it simply was not acceptable for a gentleman to lower himself to compete with a commoner, let alone be the loser in such a competition.

In these races, the owner sometimes rode his own horse, thereby intensifying the competitive factors at play; others might have one of their slaves trained as a jockey. Devious tactics – attempts to bump a rival horse off his stride, for example – were commonplace, or at least frequently alleged. The races were brief, exciting events, with the two horses often crossing the finish line neck-to-neck, thereby producing many a dispute as to the winner. Because of such disagreements and charges of unsportsmanlike riding, the outcome of a race could be the beginning of a rapidly escalating argument. The accepted method of resolution, however, dictated that the dispute be settled without recourse to dueling pistols. Rather, the courts of Virginia developed a substantial body of case law regulating the payment of horse race wagers. Custom required that large wagers be made in writing, and colonial courts considered these documents legally binding. Often these agreements included promises by both parties to affirm that they would not attempt to bump the rival horse, unseat his mount, trip or cut off a rival's horse, or otherwise employ dangerous or devious tactics. As T. H. Breen observes, these high-stakes races provided an apt metaphor for the highly speculative business in which the tobacco planters found themselves.[9]

By the eighteenth century, the Virginia racing culture had matured sufficiently enough that a few oval racetracks began to appear. Some of the more affluent sportsmen now imported thoroughbred horses. These elegant horses, capable of running long distances, slowly but surely replaced the quarter horse in popularity. These expensive horses were handled by skilled trainers, ridden by professional jockeys (not uncommonly slaves) wearing the bright-colored apparel signifying the owner, and raced at week-long events scheduled for special occasions at the colonial capital of Williamsburg. Historian Elliott Gorn aptly summarizes the value system of the Southern gentry who "set the tone" for this "fiercely competitive style of living." In a constantly fluid social and economic system, he contends,

Individual status was never permanently fixed, so men frantically sought to assert their prowess – by grand boasts over tavern gaming tables laden with money, by whipping and tripping each other's horses in violent quarter-races, by wagering one-half year's earnings on the flash of a fighting cock's gaff. Great planters and small shared an ethos that extolled courage bordering on foolhardiness and cherished magnificent, if irrational, displays of largess.[10]

While the Tidewater gentry went about their gentlemanly pastimes, the lesser members of Southern society participated in a leisure culture that revolved around tavern life. Taverns were located in towns and along country roads where they offered shelter for travelers, plain food, and plenty of drink. Here locals mingled with travelers for conversation and played a wide range of card games, pitched quoits, and displayed their talents at lawn bowling. The games were inevitably made more spirited by wagering. As in England, blood sports were quite popular, and enterprising innkeepers promoted these events as a means of attracting business; most popular were cockfights and animal baitings, as well as an occasional bare-knuckle prizefight. The most popular sport by far was the cockfight, and these events often attracted an audience that saw men of all social stations lining the pit elbow-to-elbow while cheering, drinking, and gambling. Occasionally reformers, more often in Northern colonies, sought to regulate these businesses by fining innkeepers who permitted gambling, revoking licenses of repeat offenders, and making it difficult for individuals to recover gambling losses in local courts. In 1760, for example, the Massachusetts General Court passed a resolution that stipulated, "Games and Exercises although lawful, should not be otherwise used than as innocent and moderate Recreations," and proceeded to outlaw gambling that occurred in taverns. Whatever the law, gambling remained an integral part of the life of American people of all social stations; the single variable seemed to be that the larger one's income, the greater the wager.[11]

Along the colonial Virginia frontier and extending into the trans-Appalachian area of Kentucky and Tennessee, the realities of daily life were reflected in the preference of recreations. Shooting contests that determined local marksman champions were popular, reflecting the importance of hunting in securing meat for the dinner table. Fairs and other social gatherings often featured running and jumping contests. Of course cockfighting and dog-baiting contests were favorites, as was quarter horse racing. The Southern back country, however, was known for its emphasis on a particularly violent form of human combat that was part wrestling, part fisticuffs, with a couple of particularly gruesome elements thrown in for good measure – eye gouging and attempts at severing various body parts. These gruesome fights, called "rough-and-tumble," were occasionally held at community celebrations, but they also occurred as a means of concluding an argument or obtaining satisfaction for a perceived personal insult. Spectators placed wagers on the combatants, and the contest was conducted with a pronounced absence of rules; any tactic to gain an advantage was acceptable, including hitting, biting, kicking downed opponents, kneeing in the groin, and scratching with sharply filed fingernails. In the rugged male-dominated environment of the frontier, personal "respect" was of great importance. For young men, historian Elliott Gorn concludes, "rough-and-tumble fighting demonstrated unflinching willingness to inflict pain, while risking mutilation – all to defend one's standing among peers."[12]

In the years after the American Revolution, this no-holds-barred form of fighting emphasized the gouging of an opponent's eye as the ultimate objective. Among those most likely to participate were uncultured young males who lived on the fringes of civilization along the trans-Appalachian frontier – hunters, trappers, stevedores, drifters, unskilled laborers, hardscrabble farmers. Rough-and-tumble grew in popularity during the late eighteenth century in the sparsely settled regions of western Virginia and the Carolinas, Kentucky, and Tennessee. The emphasis of these fights was, Gorn writes, "on maximum disfigurement, on severing body parts." The primary objective was to extract an opponent's eyeball by the use of sharply filed and heavily waxed fingernails. Teeth were sometimes filed to severe points as another means of attack, although some local champions specialized in other brutal tactics. One traveler noted, "these wretches in their combat endeavor to their utmost to tear out the other's testicles."[13] Travelers through the region after the Civil War reported their shock at seeing a large number of aging men with missing eyes or rough facial scars from fights held in the distant past. Rough-and-tumble – a phenomenon in a frontier region where life was frequently harsh and brief – was a widespread practice that slowly died out as a more genteel civilization slowly encroached upon the backwoods towns of the mountain country of the Southeast.

The Revolutionary Era and Beyond

The patterns of informal sporting events and leisure activities that existed in colonial America continued essentially unchanged well into the nineteenth century. These traditions, however, began to give way to a much more organized and formalized structure of sport. The emotional fervor associated with the Revolution tended to dampen interest in recreation because it was widely believed that the future of the new country depended upon a hard-working, serious-minded people who were not easily distracted by idle amusements. In fact, on the eve of the American Revolution the Continental Congress took official notice of this sentiment, urging the various colonies by resolution to "encourage frugality, economy, and discourage every species of extravagance and dissipation, especially all horse-racing, and all kinds of gaming, cock fighting, exhibition of shows, plays, and other expensive diversions and amusements."[14]

Following the War of 1812, the American economy entered a period of rapid expansion, fueled in part by the introduction of steam-powered shipping on internal waterways and the construction of a large network of canals and toll roads. The introduction of railroads during the 1830s set off a period of frenetic construction of new lines, producing what historians have called the "transportation revolution." In the decades before the Civil War, the United States was transformed by innovations in mining and manufacturing, mass merchandising, heavy immigration, sustained urban growth, expansion of international trade, and the establishment of companies that served regional and even national markets. It was within this context that sports – which for more than two centuries had been a localized and unorganized phenomenon – took on the structured appearance that would be recognizable to the American sports fan of the early twenty-first century.

Indications of significant changes in patterns of leisure activities were visible by the 1830s, especially in Northern cities. Individuals interested in playing competitive games often insisted upon the use of agreed standards and rules of play. These rules were frequently the product of committees working within the structure of clubs and other organizations designed to bring order and conformity to the rules governing a particular sport. It was inevitable that the first major reforms leading toward standardization of rules and policies would apply to the most popular of sports – horse racing. Throughout the South and into the frontier West, informal racing remained popular, but in and around New York City, men interested in the turf introduced reforms that pushed the sport toward a modern identity. In 1821, the New York legislature voted to legalize horse racing, prompting the creation of formal organizations designed to bring consistency within the sport. Rules governing races were adopted and enforced, and construction of oval tracks with wooden grandstands soon followed that permitted patrons to watch the races from elevated seats.

Improved flow of information provided a significant precursor of changes to come. In 1831, the popular *Spirit of the Times* was first published by sportsman William T. Porter. Although he reported on many activities, Porter focused his attention upon horse racing. He established and published odds, encouraged equitable betting policies, advocated the adoption of standardized rules regarding the conduct of races, promoted prominent racing meets, and, most important for gamblers, reported in detail the records of individual horses. The growing popularity of the turf was revealed in the rapid increase in annual racing meets, which normally lasted three days: 56 such events were reported in 1830 but that number more than tripled in the next two decades.[15]

Concurrently there emerged a movement to encourage standardization of the sport through the creation of jockey clubs. The premier antebellum organization was the New York Jockey Club. Its hefty $10 annual membership fee meant that only men of substantial social consequence applied for membership. For its spring and autumn meetings at Union Course on Long Island, the club established rules that would assure fair competition and prevent the sport from being manipulated by "sharps."[16] The club's announcement of its fall 1842 meeting, for example, contained a detailed list of 64 rules, including the appointment of four stewards who were required to wear an "appropriate badge of distinction" and were responsible "to preserve order, clear the track, keep it clear, keep off the crowd of persons from the horses coming to the stand." Three judges were charged with overseeing the start and finish of each race. Even the uniform worn by jockeys was covered: rule 35 stated, "No rider shall be permitted to ride unless well dressed in Jockey style. To wit, Jockey cap, colored jacket, pantaloons, and boots."[17]

Porter championed order and efficiency, writing at one point that it was the responsibility of "gentlemen of standing, wealth, and intelligence" to provide leadership of this sport so that it would not be overtaken by "lower-class ruffians and ne'er-do-wells."[18] One person who heeded Porter's clarion call to "the very Corinthian columns of the community" was the scion of a wealthy Hoboken family, John Cox Stevens. In 1823, he and his brother Robert Livingston Stevens helped produce one of the first great sporting spectacles in American history: a match race between a powerful nine-year-old thoroughbred, Eclipse, which had for several years dominated the New York City racing circuit, and the leading Southern thoroughbred, Sir Henry, a premier horse out of the stable of James J. Harrison of Petersburg, Virginia. Each horse was backed by the large sum of $20,000. The nation's attention became riveted upon the race, with the growing political conflict over slavery providing an ominous backdrop. The two horses ran three 4 mile heats before a cheering crowd estimated to be in excess of 50,000 at the Long Island Union Course, with Eclipse winning the third and deciding heat and taking home the prize money. Substantial sums of money changed hands between gamblers that exciting day. The *Niles Register* estimated $1 million in wagers, although that large sum and the size of the crowd were probably overstated.[19]

As tensions between the slave states and the North intensified, promoters took advantage of sectional feelings and promoted other races with strong North–South overtones. One of the more memorable of these was the 1842 match between a Virginia horse owned by Colonel William R. Johnson, which was curiously named Boston, and the pride of the New York area, the sensational filly Fashion. She won the first 4 mile heat by less than a length and in the process set a record of 7:32.5 minutes. The second heat was close until the nine-year-old Boston showed his age and faded during the last mile, losing by some 60 lengths to the filly. The Northerners' joy in their horse's victory, however, was muted by post-race criticism led by William T. Porter in his *Spirit of the Times*. He directed his ire at the Union Course promoters, who charged what Porter (and many others) viewed as an exorbitant $10 admission charge.[20]

Another North–South challenge occurred in 1845 at the Union Course before a large and enthusiastic crowd "of race-going blades" who created a scene of "tumult, disorder, and confusion," according to one newspaper account. In addition, the *New York Herald* reported that the audience included a motley collection of "indescribable camp followers, sutlers, loungers, rowdies, gamblers, and twenty other species." Before a crowd estimated to number 30,000, probably once more in substantial exaggeration, since the grandstands only seated 3,000, the Southern filly Peytonia narrowly defeated Fashion in two heats. Again, strong sectional sentiments provided a dramatic backdrop to the race, as reported by the *New York Herald*: "In addition to the sectional feeling and the strong rivalry of sportsmen, and in no sense partisans – the vast sums of money pending on the race, attached a degree of absorbing interest in the result."[21]

The Democratization of Racing: The Trotters

Although the general public took great interest in the occasional high-profile thoroughbred race, the sport was largely dominated by the wealthy – slave holders in Virginia and mercantile leaders in New York City. The less affluent found other outlets to engage their passion for racing. Although it has received relatively little attention, prior to the Civil War large numbers of working- and middle-class Americans became fascinated by harness racing. This uniquely American sport began early in the nineteenth century along the urban corridor between Baltimore and Boston. Informal races between horse-drawn buggies over public roads and streets gained popularity in Northern cities, especially New York City. According to historian Dwight Akers, the 5 mile stretch of Third Avenue that ran northward from the Bowery was "consecrated ground" for the "roadites."[22]

There emerged a large, informal fraternity that raced their "roadsters" in the evening hours after work. The horses, which the men used for their daily business travel, came from the common stock and lacked the bloodlines of the thoroughbreds. Central to the popularity of harness racing was that it permitted wide participation; anyone with a horse and buggy could try his hand, and unlike thoroughbred racing where professional jockeys were utilized, the owner and the driver were one and the same. Along Third Avenue, competition naturally grew, especially among the younger "blades" who enjoyed a spirited race. One lady, however, observed that some of these young men "spent their afternoons trotting from tavern to tavern along the highways." Apparently, she sniffed, "they live for alcohol and horses!"[23] The appeal of harness racing was that it was open to all comers. Oliver Wendell Holmes noted that the trotting horse served a useful purpose as an everyday source of transportation, while the thoroughbred did not: "Horse racing is not a republican institution; horse-trotting is."[24]

By 1850, harness racing had become an organized sport that surpassed thoroughbred racing in popularity. The first enclosed racing oval for trotters was constructed in 1815 on the north side of Manhattan. In 1824, the New York Trotting Club was established and another oval track was constructed on Long Island. Over the next quarter-century, the sport continued to grow in popularity, but its common roots precluded the newspaper coverage reserved for thoroughbreds. Because the trotting horse came from common stock, rapid commercialization was feasible. Promoters recognized that the investment in such a horse was minimal when compared to the thoroughbred, a fact that enabled them to offer much smaller purses (often less than $50, sometimes as little as $10) and still attract a competitive field. The sturdy composition of the trotting horse also meant that they could be entered in races more often than a thoroughbred.[25]

Harness racing engendered widespread public interest. Its unpretentious aura appealed to spectators who were put off by the snobbery and exclusiveness associated with the thoroughbreds. In 1856, a journalist observed that thoroughbred racing "will never succeed in New York until it and its attended arrangements are put on a more democratic basis – something approaching the order of the first class trotting races. Then like the trots, it will get the support of the people." Oliver Wendell Holmes was struck by the bond between harness racing and everyday American workers: "Wherever the trotting horse goes, he carries in his train brisk omnibuses, lively bakers' carts, and therefore hot rolls, the jolly butcher's wagon, the cheerful gig, the wholesome afternoon drive with wife and child – all the forms of moral excellence."[26]

The popularity of trotters spread across the United States. Seven tracks operated with regularity in the New York City area by the mid 1850s, and an additional 70 tracks had opened elsewhere. The operators of county fairs found harness racing an appealing attraction, and the relationship of the sport with state and county fairs remains an American tradition in the twenty-first century.

The unlikely exploits of a four-year-old gray mare, purchased by an Irish peddler in 1837 for $12.50, spurred the sport's popularity. For a time Lady Suffolk pulled David Bryan's butcher cart through the streets of New York City, but in 1838 Bryan entered her in a harness race on Long Island. She won her first race in a flat 3 minutes along with a purse of $11. Over the next 14 years, Lady Suffolk was entered in 162 races and won an estimated $50,000 for her owner. She was eventually retired at the age of 19, but even then demonstrated her amazing strength by participating in 12 races during her final year on the track.[27] She was memorialized by the popular song, "The Old Gray Mare." By the eve of the Civil War,

Figure 1.1   Trotters Mountain Boy and Lady Thorn head for the finish line at Prospect Park in Brooklyn in 1869. Trotters and pacers captured the imagination of working- and middle-class Americans during the mid nineteenth century as a democratic alternative to the perceptions of thoroughbred racing as elitist. The sport developed strong roots throughout America and became a main attraction at state and county fairs.
Image © Bettmann/Corbis

harness racing had moved from an informal means of entertainment on the streets of New York to a successful commercial enterprise that was national in scope. As such, harness racing set the pace, so to speak, for many other commercial sporting ventures soon to come.

Racing by Land and Sea

Horse racing was not the only form of racing to capture the public's fancy. For several decades prior to the Civil War, long-distance human foot races captured widespread interest. Popularly called "pedestrianism," these races appealed to the gambling instincts of Americans. Between 1820 and 1835, several such races held in the New York City area received minor notice in the newspapers, but in 1835 the area's leading sportsman, John Cox Stevens, attracted widespread attention when he announced a prize of $1,000 to any person who could run 10 miles in less than 1 hour. On race day, nine men toed the starting line and took off to the cheers of a large crowd. A 24-year-old Connecticut farmer, Henry Stannard, was the only runner to cross the finish line under the 1 hour mark, and he did so with only 12 seconds to spare.[28]

The novelty of that race inspired many others in the years to come, with promoters of the Beacon Course racetrack even holding foot race competitions as a means of recovering some of their financial losses from the lack of public support for thoroughbred meets. One of the underlying themes of these races was competition between Americans and runners from Ireland and England. An estimated 30,000 spectators turned out in 1844 at Beacon Course to watch a field of 12 Americans (including John Steeprock, a Seneca Indian) fend off the challenges of three Englishmen and three Irishmen. America's pride was severely threatened as the runners approached the final mile with two Englishmen in the lead, but a New York carpenter, John Gildersleeve, took the lead during the final lap and inspired cheers from American spectators. One newsman, probing the reasons for the great interest in the race beyond its sheer novelty, found his answer in conversations with members of the audience: "It was a trial of the Indian against the white man, on the point in which the red man most boasts his superiority. It was the trial of the peculiar American physique against the long held supremacy of the English muscular endurance." As historian Melvin Adelman concludes, "The excitement derived from the fact that the white man beat the red man and the American defeated the Englishmen."[29] Future promoters of sporting events would find racial, ethnic, and nationalistic rivalries to be a reliable gimmick to attract paying customers.

The interest in pedestrianism prompted many promoters to stage races, most of which were long-distance affairs with men competing against each other and the clock for prize money. A few professional runners emerged who often put up their own challenge money before match races, and while Gildersleeve ended up accepting invitations to run in many parts of the country, most runners were content to compete in their own locale. The sport did not endure, falling victim to the rise of track and field and the introduction of the bicycle and bicycle racing by the 1880s.[30]

Americans also showed considerable interest in various forms of rowing contests. As with other sports, informal contests had been held between locals in various American ports during the colonial and early national period; races between longshoremen and local boat owners, sparked by a wager or two, determined local bragging rights. As early as 1824, a rowing contest with a $1,000 prize was held on the Hudson River between a group of young Americans organized into a rowing club called the Whitehallers and a crew from a British frigate. Newspapers reported that a crowd of upwards of 20,000 watched the 4 mile race from the shoreline. An American victory produced a flurry of national pride and encouraged the conduct of races elsewhere.[31]

By the mid 1830s, more than 20 rowing clubs were active in the New York City area, and similar clubs were established in cities stretching from Boston to Savannah. Interest was particularly high in Philadelphia, where the Schuylkill River beckoned generations of dedicated oarsmen. In 1872, the National Association of Amateur Oarsmen was established with some 200 clubs in existence.[32]

Rowing appealed to a wide spectrum of men interested in vigorous exercise and competition, but only the very wealthy could afford to participate in yachting. One of the first yacht races on record involved the wealthy sportsman John Cox Stevens, whose yacht *Wave* sped to victory over John Cushing's *Sylph* in a highly publicized race across New York Harbor in 1835. In 1844, Cox played a key role in establishing the New York Yacht Club for the express purpose of promoting "health and pleasure, combined with a laudable desire to improve our almost perfect naval architecture." Just as various jockey clubs asserted their goal in holding racing meets was to "improve the breed," so too did the yachtsmen seek to produce faster ships. In 1846, the New York Yacht Club held its first regatta, producing great interest throughout the city.[33]

The New York Yacht Club soon became recognized for a membership representing the *crème de la crème* of New York society. Stevens constructed a large clubhouse in Hoboken at Elysian Fields where club members and their spouses and friends enjoyed exclusive social events. The clubhouse was described by New York City mayor, Philip Hone, as "a handsome Gothic cottage in a pleasant grove in the Elysian fields, presided over by that prince of good fellows, John Cox Stevens, who makes the punch, superintends the cooking and presides at the table." The club's annual regatta at exclusive Newport, Rhode Island, became a highlight of the summer social calendar for New York City's high society.[34]

The club attracted international attention in 1851 when Stevens formed a syndicate to build a sailing ship specifically designed to challenge the best that England could offer. After Stevens retired from his role as a prominent owner of thoroughbreds in the late 1830s, he turned his attention to his "first love," the sea. The son of a wealthy entrepreneur, he had been raised along the water's edge where he developed lifelong hobbies of swimming and sailing. He owned a succession of private vessels, including *Trouble*, built in 1816 of dimensions (56 feet in length) sufficient to be recognized as the first authentic American yacht. Now 65 years of age in 1851, Stevens had come to appreciate the talents of a young ship architect, George Steers, whom he commissioned to build a yacht designed for racing. The result was the *America*, a vessel that Stevens dispatched to Great Britain to challenge the best the English could muster. Initially the English yachting crowd held *America* in contempt because they "did not regard it as of the slightest consequence, or as at all likely to interfere with their monopoly of the glory." When *America* arrived at the Isle of Wight several days before the August 23 race date, however, its sleek profile made Englishmen nervous. One journalist noted, "She sits upon the water like a duck," but was possessed of "a clean build and saucy raking masts." He feared that *America* "evidently looks bent on mischief."[35]

Indeed. After a slow start against 18 English ships, *America* began to pass the competition, "leaping over, not against the water." Two hours into the 60 mile course around the Isle of Wight, *America* held a 2 mile lead against its closest rival, and at the 7 hour mark led the British favorite, *Aurora*, by 7 miles! Queen Victoria and the royal family waited at the finish line aboard the Royal Yacht *Victoria and Albert*, and as the first sails came into view, she inquired of a signal master peering through binoculars, "Which yacht is first?" He replied, "The *America*, your majesty." "Which is second?" the Queen asked. "Your majesty, there is no second."[36]

The next day, the Queen boarded *America* to present Stevens and his crew with a hideously ornate cup that came to be called the America's Cup. It remains yet today the most coveted prize in yachting. In a most unsentimental move, Stevens soon thereafter sold *America* to English interests and returned to the United States aboard a steam-powered

ship while American newspapers trumpeted the supremacy of Yankee shipbuilding. New York lawyer George T. Strong believed the exuberant nationalistic celebration disturbing: "Newspapers [are] crowing over the victory of Stevens' yacht which has beat everything in the British seas," he wrote in his diary, "quite creditable to Yankee ship-building, certainly, but not worthy the intolerable, vainglorious vaporings that make every newspaper I take up now ridiculous. One would think yacht-building were the end of man's existence on earth."[37]

The Formative Years of Prizefighting

While some Americans were thrilled by yachting, a larger and much more diverse group followed the races of men and horses. Bare-knuckle prizefighting also attracted widespread interest despite being illegal and the subject of considerable public condemnation. During the 1820s and 1830s, however, a group of professional pugilists did battle in public places, most often large saloons where the atmosphere was raucous, the air filled with cigar smoke, and the language coarse as beer and whiskey flowed freely. Money also changed hands as bets on the contestants were settled. Unlike the rough-and-tumble fights on

Figure 1.2   The sleek yacht *America* is captured by artist J. E. Buttersworth as it leaves Boston harbor on its way to England for the great race of 1851. Its stunning triumph over the best the British could muster set off a long and loud outburst of American braggadocio. Yet today, the garish trophy – now named the America's Cup – presented to owner John Cox Stevens by Queen Victoria remains the most prestigious in sailing. *Image © Bettmann/Corbis*

the frontier, these bouts were conducted according to established rules. A downed opponent could not be kicked or hit; a round ended whenever a contestant was knocked or wrestled down; a contestant had 30 seconds after being downed to resume the contest by "coming to scratch" or "toeing the mark," which meant resuming the fight by standing along a line drawn through the center of the ring. A bout ended whenever a fighter failed to toe the mark or conceded defeat. Consequently, bouts between evenly matched foes could go for scores of rounds, with some bouts lasting more than an hour's duration.

Promoters found they could attract large crowds if they matched fighters representative of rival ethnic groups; pairing an Englishman against an Irishman assured a large and boisterous crowd. As with other spectator sports, New York City became the center of pugilistic activities, although prizefighting also flourished in such cities as New Orleans, Philadelphia, Baltimore, and Boston. It was in New York City and its immediate environs that most major bouts were held. Although illegal, prizefighting captured the attention of a wide spectrum of male New Yorkers. Public attitudes on pugilism were distinctly divided. As historian Elliott Gorn describes the situation, on the one hand boxing appealed to the democratic sensibilities of the nation: two men enter the ring with equal opportunity to achieve victory by dint of their skill, strength, endurance, fortitude, and guile. On the other hand, the fact that men were encouraged to engage in a violent contest that could produce severe physical injury, even death, called into question the underlying humane and civic values of the young democracy. As one critic wrote, pugilism produced "nothing but brutality, ferociousness, and cowardess [*sic*]" that served to "debase the mind, deaden the feelings and extinguish every spark of benevolence." The violence of the sport stood in stark contrast to the widespread belief that democracy was capable of uplifting the moral character of the American people and, in particular, of eliminating violence from the social order. Consequently, as Gorn observes, boxing was a "denial of mankind's moral progress" that "mocked the more optimistic ideologies ascendant in the early nineteenth century." Prizefighting seemed to contradict "romantic assumptions of man's reason triumphing over his passions, of the moral progress of humankind."[38]

Violence was only one of many factors that motivated pugilism's critics. They contended that prizefights encouraged public disorder, heavy drinking, and gambling. Further, it was a sport that appealed to man's worse instincts that critics contended flourished among the lower echelons of urban society, especially immigrants from Germany and Ireland. The prim and proper middle- and upper-class Victorians viewed the new urban working classes as violent and dangerous – a serious threat to civic order. They believed prizefighting brought out the worst of man's nature – brutality, cruelty, passion, drunkenness, and gambling. In handing down sentences to three Irishmen in 1842 who had promoted a fight that led to the death of one contestant, New York City Judge Charles R. Ruggles gave vent to this perspective:

> A prizefight brings together a vast concourse of people: and I believe it is not speaking improperly of such assemblages, to say that the gamblers, and the bullies, and the swearers, and the blacklegs, and the pickpockets and the thieves, and the burglars are there. It brings together a large assemblage of the idle, disorderly, vicious, dissolute people – people who live by violence – people who live by crime – their tastes run that way.[39]

This condemnation came at the sentencing of immigrant Yankee Sullivan, who was the primary promoter for a notorious fight between Christopher Lilly and Tommy McCoy held on a bluff overlooking the Hudson River near the small town of Hastings, located 25 miles north of New York City. On September 13, 1842, an estimated 2,000 spectators witnessed this bout, which had attracted considerable interest. Both fighters weighed scarcely 140 pounds. For a time, the Irishman McCoy seemed to have the advantage, but as the fight progressed past an hour's duration his endurance waned as his opponent carved his face into a bloody mess. Following the rules of the day that acknowledged a knockdown ended a round, the match reached 70 rounds. By this time, McCoy was bravely enduring a merciless pounding. "Both eyes were black – the left one nearly closed, and indeed that whole cheek presented a shocking appearance," one spectator wrote. "His very forehead was black and blue; his lips were swollen to an incredible size, and the blood streamed profusely down his chest. My heart sickened at the sorry sight." As McCoy gasped for breath, many spectators called out to the referee and McCoy's handlers to halt the fight as "blow upon blow came raining in upon him." The courageous – if foolish – McCoy refused to quit despite being knocked down 80 times, but at the end of round 119 and 2 hours and 41 minutes later the fight ended when McCoy collapsed and died. The cause of death was later determined to have been from drowning in his own blood.[40]

No wonder many civic leaders were appalled by the popularity that pugilism commanded. One such proponent of Victorian sensibilities – Horace Greeley, publisher of the *New York Tribune* – denounced the "gamblers, brothel-masters and keepers of flesh groggeries who had perpetrated this frightful spectacle." According to this famed journalist, the end of American civilization was at hand unless the new urban working classes were brought under control. Philip Hone, a former mayor, took note in his diary that the sport of pugilism threatened American civilization: "The amusement of prizefighting, the disgrace of which was formerly confined to England … has become one of the fashionable abominations of our loafer-ridden city," he complained.[41] For critics such as Greeley and Hone, prizefighting not only reflected the dangers posed by the new urban working class, but also undercut the essential truth of the Protestant work ethic: with merely a lucky punch or two, a prizefighter could earn more money in one afternoon than a hardworking artisan or clerk could make in a year. Even more egregious, a gambler who bet heavily on that fighter could walk off with large sums without having to expend any effort, rewarded mightily for his endorsement of an antisocial activity that benefited saloonkeepers and other social misfits.

By the time of Tommy McCoy's demise, the Victorian element in the nation's leading cities had come to view with apprehension the steady growth and influence of what has been described as the "sporting fraternity," a segment of the larger urban bachelor culture that had developed in American cities. The sporting fraternity, known as the "Fancy," existed largely within the context of the many saloons that lined the streets of American cities. It was here that men could escape their wives and girlfriends and participate in an all-male subculture that focused on drinking, gambling, swapping stories, telling crude jokes, and discussing (and arguing over) matters of great import: sports, politics, and sex. Many of the saloons that catered to this crowd sponsored a variety of events to attract clients. These variously included such popular blood sports as dogfights, rat baitings, and cockfights. Occasionally a prizefight was the feature attraction.

Most professional fighters and their handlers were closely identified with saloons, and future bouts were often arranged at the bar. Cards, billiards, and dice games were a constant in this loosely organized urban brotherhood, and an evening might be topped off with a visit to a nearby brothel. Participation in this urban subculture provided young men with a special sense of individual identity within the larger, impersonal urban complex, bringing with it a modicum of social status and a sense of belonging to a group of one's peers.

For several years, the death of Tommy McCoy put a damper on prizefighting, but it inevitably made a comeback. Newspapers and magazines found a wide reading audience for their graphic stories about the pugilistic scene, and bouts between popular ethnic battlers began attracting large crowds. Such was the case when Yankee Sullivan challenged the top American heavyweight Tom Hyer. Hyer had beaten Country McCleester in 1841 and was popularly proclaimed the first American heavyweight champion. When Hyer and Sullivan encountered each other in a New York City bar in 1848, they got into an argument that became a scuffle, which led inevitably to a challenge. Each man agreed to put up $5,000 and for months the match was the talk of the town. Newspapers reported upon the challengers' training sessions, and betting was intense.

Despite widespread public interest, only a few hundred spectators actually witnessed the bout, which was held in a secluded area on Chesapeake Bay. Maryland law enforcement officials attempted to prevent the fight from taking place, but while in pursuit of the boat carrying the pugilists and their entourage, the police boat ran aground. Thus on a cold February day, with a dusting of snow on the ground, a ring was hastily constructed from tree limbs and some rope, and in mid-afternoon the much-hyped battle was on. It lasted less than 10 minutes, as the much larger Hyer knocked his opponent senseless with a barrage of blows to the head. Although the fight was fought in near isolation, fight fans in New York and other major cities eagerly awaited news of the outcome. Foreshadowing the role that communications would play in the growing popularity of sporting events, news from Chesapeake Bay arrived in newspaper offices across the country by the new technology of telegraph lines.[42]

The Hyer victory stimulated a demand for boxing matches, and many young men from the lower echelons of urban society attempted to fight their way to fame and fortune. Most, of course, failed, but one marvelous Irishman found that the sport provided his entrée to a celebrity's life of prestige and wealth. John "Old Smoke" Morrissey was born in Ireland in 1831 and brought to America by his parents when he was three. Growing up in Troy, New York, he became notorious for his violent temper, his frequent scrapes with the law, and his ability to use his fists. He moved to New York City about 1850 and became an enforcer for local politicians who found his services useful in breaking up opponents' meetings and intimidating voters. He also began earning money prizefighting. In one noteworthy saloon encounter, he was pinned atop a hot wood-burning stove by his adversary. The resulting stench from his severely burned flesh produced his nickname of "Old Smoke."

On September 1, 1853, Old Smoke fought Yankee Sullivan at Boston Corners, a small community where the state lines of Massachusetts, Connecticut, and New York converge. The sponsors selected this site because they hoped the uncertainty about the state in which the ring was actually located would prevent law enforcement officials from stopping the affair. A crowd estimated between 3,000 and 6,000 converged by railroad and horse and buggy on the town. Serious money was wagered at ringside, but also in cities across the United States. One newspaper estimated that at least $200,000 rested on the fight's outcome. By far the superior boxer, Sullivan bludgeoned Morrissey for 37 brutal rounds – Old Smoke's eyes were nearly swollen shut and his face was a bloody mess – but then various allegations were shouted between the two men's supporters and a free-for-all brawl broke out among the spectators. When the referee called for round 38 to begin, Morrissey staggered to scratch but Sullivan was busily punching away at one of Morrissey's supporters. The referee thereupon awarded the bout to Morrissey.

Predictably, most prominent urban newspapers denounced the fight as immoral and the behavior of the spectators outrageous, but they also provided their eager readers with detailed descriptions of the event. Morrissey's greatest asset as a fighter apparently was his ability to take enormous punishment. The bizarre ending to the fight added to his growing reputation as a romantic rogue, and he proceeded to win several fights over challengers of lesser ability than Yankee Sullivan. His reputation as someone not to be meddled with was greatly enhanced when one of his associates shot and killed a rival, William "Bill the Butcher" Poole (of English ancestry), who had once whipped Morrissey in a street fight; this shooting intensified anti-Irish sentiment throughout the city.

Morrissey's last prizefight was in 1858 against John Heenan, a formidable up-and-coming boxer from San Francisco. Although both were of Irish descent, the intense pre-fight ballyhoo portrayed Morrissey as a near-savage Irishman while Heenan, himself no saint, was somehow cast as a respectable middle-class gentleman. The fight was held on a lonely spit off the Canadian coast of Lake Erie, with both men putting up $5,000 as prize money. Large numbers of sportsmen traveled by rail or boat to Buffalo and boarded special excursion vessels to sail to the "secret" location near the town of Long Point. Fight fans everywhere waited for news of the outcome because serious money rested thereon. Relying upon his ability to absorb punishment, Morrissey slowly wore down the resistance of his opponent. By round 11, both men were bruised and battered. Only Morrissey had the strength to withstand a punch, however, and when he nailed his opponent's jaw with a punch, Heenan collapsed in a heap.

Thus ended the checkered pugilistic career of John "Old Smoke" Morrissey. But after he retired from the ring his fortunes took an amazing upward trajectory. He owned two popular saloons through which he became intimately involved with political figures in New York City. Morrissey opened a popular gambling hall at 8 Barclay Street that attracted an elite clientele, and his political connections within the Democratic Tammany Hall machine provided protection from law enforcement. He also was part owner of a citywide numbers racket that paid handsomely. In the summer of 1863, he opened a racetrack in Saratoga to attract high-roller customers to his lavish new hotel and casino, the Saratoga House. This resort in the Adirondack Mountains soon became recognized as the premier gambling establishment in the United States, often favorably compared to the best that Europe could offer. Morrissey's political career essentially ran parallel to his gambling enterprises; in 1866, he was elected to the United States House of Representatives; he later served two terms in the New York State Senate. Morrissey's funeral in 1878 was one of biggest the city had seen up to that time and was reported on the front pages of city newspapers.[43]

The story of Old Smoke was truly amazing. He had what the *New York Times* called "a checkered career" in its front-page obituary. The connections he made between his pugilistic, gambling, and political careers provided an early and telling example of an emerging pattern for American sportsmen. Not only did prizefighting open up avenues to immediate financial success for those with the ability and willingness to make the sacrifices demanded by the blood sport, but pugilism's close connections to urban politicos, gamblers, and the bachelor culture pointed to the direction that organized sports would take in the decades to come. The main thrust of the emerging pattern of American sports would be to counter the Victorian message of self-restraint and social control with a heavy emphasis on unrestrained masculine expression through sports, questionable political machinations, and gambling.

Baseball: The Creation of "America's Game"

Throughout much of the American colonial era young boys played a simple game that utilized a small ball and a wooden stick. Historians have long contended that the game was descended from the traditional English game of "rounders," but historian David Block has demonstrated this to be another baseball myth. He persuasively argues that games played in America well before 1800 which used a stick and ball, and were variously called "base-ball," "old cat," "tut ball," "barn ball," "trap ball," and "tip-cat," were the true predecessors of the American game. Block writes persuasively, "Given that the name 'base-ball' predated 'rounders' in England by nearly a hundred years, it is time to finally put to rest that tired old axiom that baseball descended from that 'ancient' English pastime." Whatever its origins, the impromptu game as played in America had an infinite variety of informal and ever-changing rules. Boiled down to fundamentals, however, a "feeder" tossed a small ball in an underhanded fashion to the "striker," who, upon hitting the ball, ran in a counter-clockwise fashion around four or five stakes driven into the ground. The runner sought to avoid being "put out," which occurred when his batted ball was caught on the fly or first bounce, or when he was "soaked" by a defensive player, that is, hit with a thrown ball before reaching the safety of a base.[44]

By the 1850s, however, the game had been transformed by the strong drive for organization and structure that was central to the emerging modern era. Although still popular with youngsters, what was now called "base-ball" appealed to young male adults, and informality gave way to written rules and policies, organized competition, statistical analysis of outcomes, and eventually the formation of regional and even national organizations. The game resonated with the urban bachelor set. Young adult males who held positions in the expanding urban middle class – artisans, bankers, agents, lawyers, physicians, shopkeepers, accountants, clerks, salesmen, teachers, businessmen – sought both physical exercise and social connections with like-minded men through organized clubs. Among the many activities sponsored by these clubs was playing the game that members recalled from their childhood.

In part, the game caught on so rapidly because of its simplicity. It could be played in a corner of a city park or on a vacant lot; the only equipment required was a wooden bat and a ball. Unlike the more complex English game of cricket, which enjoyed a popularity during the 1850s among a relatively small number of affluent urbanites, baseball did not require a lengthy time commitment and it was not encumbered with complex rules. The game could be played in a relatively short time, which fit busy schedules of upwardly bound urban professionals. As one commentator noted, as compared to the rival sport of cricket, baseball "comprises all the necessary elements for affording a pleasing and harmless excitement … yet can be regularly practiced and even played in the shape of formal matches without interfering unduly with business hours."[45] Although the game came easily to those endowed with natural athleticism, it also rewarded individuals who strived to improve their limited skills with diligent practice.

For many years, rules were determined locally. When teams traveled to other cities, the rules to be followed became an issue. Knowledgeable followers of the game during its formative years understood that there was a distinct Massachusetts Game as compared to the Philadelphia Game. The number of bases and the distance between them fluctuated considerably, as did the specifications of the distance that separated the "bowler" or "feeder" from the "striker." The catcher usually stood 10 feet or so behind the batter and none of the players used protective equipment of any kind, including gloves. The number of participants on a team also fluctuated, sometimes rising to as high as 14. In all versions of the organized game, however, the bowler was expected to help put the ball into play, and not deceive the striker; he was required to toss the ball gently in an underhanded fashion. Team captains normally arbitrated disputes over close calls, and the use of an umpire was resisted because the game was expected to be played fairly by gentlemen who could arbitrate disputes without rancor.[46]

The pioneering baseball club was the New York Knickerbockers, a fraternal group organized in 1842. Apparently some of its founding members had been playing ball for several years on a vacant lot at the corner of 27th Street and Fourth Avenue. In 1845, Knickerbocker Alexander Joy Cartwright, a young bookkeeper by trade, suggested the creation of a formal baseball club, complete with bylaws and a $5 annual membership fee. He also presented to his friends a written set of rules for the game, which were readily accepted most likely because they incorporated many concepts already in use. With Cartwright's rules providing a foundation for play, the popularity of the game soared in the New York City metropolitan area; this particular version of the game spread rapidly up and down the Atlantic coast. By the eve of the Civil War, most teams had adopted the Knickerbocker rules for what had become commonly known as the "New York Game."

Cartwright's prescience is startling. The only major things he left out that are central to today's game were the nine-inning rule, the use of umpires, and the base on balls. Cartwright placed four bases – now canvas bags instead of stakes – 90 feet apart in a unique diamond configuration, with the "bowler" required to release his underhanded pitch from a distance of 45 feet. The bowler's responsibility was to give the batter a ball that could readily be hit; it would take several decades before the role of the pitcher became that of trying to get the batter to make out with an assortment of overhanded pitches thrown at high velocity. Cartwright established the size of each team at nine. A batter was declared "out" if his batted ball was caught on the first bounce or on the fly, if he swung three times without making contact, or if the ball arrived securely at base before he arrived. He also abolished the painful practice of "soaking." Cartwright also established that three outs ended a team's "at-bat" and that the first team to score 21 "aces" was the winner.[47]

In keeping with their intent to be seen as gentlemen, the Knickerbockers also adopted rules to encourage good sportsmanship, including fines for appearing at games intoxicated ($1), criticizing umpires (25 cents), and using profanity (6 cents). The Knickerbockers presented a sprightly appearance when they played their games, outfitted in blue and white flannel uniforms topped by fashionable straw hats, making a sartorial statement consistent with their intent to be viewed as sportsmen of high moral character and considerable social standing. For a time the games were viewed as part of a pleasant social outing with young ladies that might be followed by a picnic or banquet.

It did not take long, however, for the competitive spirit to kick in. Within a few years, many teams had been formed in the New York City area, including those from the laboring classes. Teams increasingly played to win, even if this meant engaging in dubious tactics, and the language heard at games was anything but gentlemanly. The Brooklyn Eckfords, for example, became a top team by the mid 1850s and was composed of workers engaged in the shipbuilding trade. Baseball clubs sometimes had strong political connections; the powerful Brooklyn Atlantics was made up of players closely connected to the Democratic Party, and several members of the New York Mutuals were recognized as enforcers for the growing political machine directed by the notoriously corrupt city "Boss," William Marcy Tweed.[48]

With incredible swiftness, the game took on a new level of seriousness. Competition became more intense and the importance of victory replaced the social aspects of the game. Encouraged by the speed and convenience of railroad and steamboat transportation, the best teams traveled considerable distances to play challengers – to Boston, Baltimore, Buffalo, and Philadelphia, and many smaller towns in between. Improved communications provided by the telegraph also made it possible to send game results rapidly across great distances. Although the game was now played as far west as San Francisco, the hotbed remained the New York City metropolitan region. Several dozen teams now competed regularly for top billing, carrying such colorful names as the Eckfords, Atlantics, Eagles, Mutuals, Morrisianas, Gothams, Empires, Excelsiors, and of course, the Knickerbockers. The quality of play and the development of a spectator base led to the first enclosed field being established on a former ice skating rink in Brooklyn in 1862.[49]

In order to ensure uniformity of rules and patterns of play, 14 prominent baseball clubs joined together in 1858 to form the National Association of Base Ball Players (NABBP). Its membership grew at an impressive rate as more teams joined each year. The organization adopted a standard set of rules (derived largely from the rules of Alexander Cartwright), but change was inherent as the game developed. The 21-"ace" rule was dropped in favor of a nine-inning contest, although it was not until 1864 that the organization acceded to the Knickerbocker club's new rule proposal that a one-bounce catch did not constitute an out. In 1858, the New York fans were captivated by a much-anticipated game featuring the best players from Brooklyn pitted against the best of Manhattan (New York, 22; Brooklyn, 18); excitement was so high that promoters for the first time in history charged an admission fee, and rumors abounded that some teams were engaged in the nefarious business of paying top players.

By the eve of the Civil War, the game had reached the cusp of becoming a competitive, modern sport, complete with a formal controlling national organization, compensation of talented players, written rules, a team manager, and the keeping of formal statistical records of games, seasons, and individual player performances. Journalistic coverage continued to expand, and instructional manuals on playing the game were published. Businessmen naturally contemplated various approaches to exploit the game for financial profit; the concept of a professional team was not much distant. In just 15 years, the game had clearly outgrown the modest expectations of Alexander Cartwright and his pioneering band of Knickerbockers. Like other folk games that had been subjected to the powerful forces of modernism, baseball was becoming an integral part of the development of modern America.

2

Baseball: "This Noble and Envigorating Game"

The American game of baseball has long been the subject of speculation and scrutiny. Mark Twain suggested that the game was "the very symbol, the outward and visible expression of the drive and push and rush and struggle of the raging, tearing booming nineteenth century." Poet Walt Whitman famously described it as "Our Game, America's Game." Historian Allan Nevins commented that baseball is "a true expression of the American spirit." One scholar noted that baseball is a reflection of the aggressiveness of the American business culture, while another suggested that the game provided a symbolic transition from the rural America of Jefferson's time to the frenetic industrial and urban society of the modern era. Others were drawn to the fact that baseball was a "timeless" game played without the constrictive influence of a clock, an essentially urban game heavily laden with symbolic rural imagery, and a "scientific" game in which technique and cerebral strategies were rewarded over raw strength and power.

Bartlett Giamatti, former president of Yale University, a distinguished Shakespearean scholar and, for a brief time, commissioner of organized baseball, came to view baseball as a powerful metaphor for the American experience, expressing a fascination with the "love affair between America and baseball that has matured and changed but never died." Giamatti wrote, "For so much of expanding and expansive America, the game was a free institution with something for everyone." A lifelong Boston Red Sox fan, Giamatti acutely understood the many disappointments that come from a close identification with one team: "It breaks your heart. It is designed to break your heart. The game begins in spring, when everything else begins again, and it blossoms in the summer, filling the afternoons and evenings, and then as soon as the chill rains come, it stops and leaves you in fall alone."[1]

Throughout its more than 150-year history, baseball has remained a simple game, easily learned by boys everywhere. In its essential form, the game can be reduced simply to throwing, hitting, and catching a small ball. It was a game schoolboys played in a backyard or vacant lot, a game that became laced with symbolism that fathers passed on to sons in an American version

Sports in American Life: A History, Second Edition. Richard O. Davies.
© 2012 John Wiley & Sons, Inc. Published 2012 by John Wiley & Sons, Inc.

of the rites of passage. Over the years, baseball became intimately embedded in the American consciousness through the arts – theater, newspaper, song, film, radio, television, poetry, and novel. It also provided the medium for animated conversations (and arguments) in the daily flow of public and private discourse, and its images became embedded in the common language. One historian described it as "a complex of memories, associations, longings, focusing on things clean and aesthetically pure, things infinitely more pure, things infinitely more fun to think about, than the mournful political, economic, social realities, tensions, and discords afflicting the real world out there." Thus, most Americans have readily concurred with French scholar Jacques Barzun, who ventured this exaggerated observation: "Whoever would know the mind and heart of America had better learn baseball." Baseball, as the *New York Times* editorialized in the nineteenth century, was "this noble and envigorating game."[2]

Baseball's special place in American life was indelibly established in 1907, when a commission charged with identifying the origins of the game went so far as to ignore obvious facts to create an enduring mythology that still hovers over the game. The commission, created on the recommendation of one of the game's leading figures, former pitcher and sporting goods entrepreneur Albert Spalding, sought to establish the "fact" that the game originated in America and refute the contention that it had evolved from the English game of "rounders." The seven-man commission (whose membership included two United States senators) based its conclusion on the most dubious of evidence: a handwritten letter received from an elderly man who recalled an event that had occurred 68 years earlier in 1839 in the small upstate town of Cooperstown, New York. Abner Graves affirmed that his teenage friend Abner Doubleday had presented to his friends a written set of rules for the game of baseball. Case closed. The commission declared that "Our Game" had no European roots and that Doubleday was its creator.[3]

This fabrication was accepted as Gospel because the American people wished it so. One of the compelling factors in accepting Graves's incredible recollection was that Doubleday had served as a general in the Union Army, thereby establishing for the game a compelling patriotic context. However, when General Doubleday died in 1893, his obituary did not mention any role he might have had in creating the game of baseball. That is, of course, because he had no role in it. In 1839, he was already a second-year cadet at West Point and presumably beyond playing childhood games, let alone having the time to invent a new one. Although several generations of historians have resolutely exposed the Doubleday–Cooperstown fable for the hoax it is, it has nonetheless maintained a strong hold on the American consciousness because it provides an aura of uniqueness to the nation's "pastime." On the 100th anniversary of Doubleday's imagined revelation, the Baseball Hall of Fame opened in Cooperstown. Every year, hundreds of thousands of Americans make a "pilgrimage" to baseball's "Mecca" located in that sleepy tree-lined town to pay homage to the game's historical "legacy," where "immortal" players have been "enshrined" in the game's "pantheon."

The Early Professional Era

The Civil War did little to slow the growth of the game's popularity. During the conflict, many prominent New York clubs continued to play matches, although military obligations decimated the membership of some teams. Large crowds continued to attend games between the top clubs; in New York City, some 15,000 spectators watched the Atlantics and Excelsiors play on the same September day in 1862 that thousands of young men died at the Battle of Antietam in western Maryland.[4]

The war may have temporarily slowed baseball's growth, but in the last analysis it greatly stimulated the game's popularity. Union and Confederate soldiers played baseball to pass the time, and when they returned home after the war they took with them an appreciation of the game. These young men would become the heart of the development of "town ball," a phenomenon that swept the country during the late nineteenth century. Employers saw value in sponsoring teams for their workers and recognized the commercial benefits of sponsoring a winning nine. Competition for "amateur" players was often intense as employers in need of a pitcher would recruit one to their firm with an offer of higher pay. Shrewd employers recognized that the types of behavior that baseball promoted – teamwork, perseverance, dedication, diligence, effort – were consistent with those they desired in their employees. At the local level of amateur and semiprofessional play, baseball became, as one historian concluded, "an ally in the constant battle to maintain a satisfied and productive work force."[5]

Town ball flourished in the late nineteenth century, drawing upon the intense rivalries that developed between neighboring communities. It became a staple of everyday life in towns large and small and remained so well into the mid twentieth century. Competition often brought out the worst in many participants; team managers routinely accused each other of hiring "ringers," using crooked umpires, and employing unruly and unsportsmanlike tactics on the field of battle.[6]

The most significant development of the post-Civil War era, however, was the establishment of professional teams. Promoters and boosters envisioned a winning team as a means of promoting civic pride and national recognition for their city, and wily businessmen saw the potential of profits from owning a team. Grown men now were openly paid to play a boy's game. Specialized skills and services were much in demand in all sectors of the expanding economy, including organized commercial recreations and amusements that saw the opening of vaudeville theaters, music pavilions, public beaches, amusement parks, and the like. Professional baseball filled a niche in the expanding entertainment business. The burst of popularity resulted from the impact of new technologies: railroads made possible efficient team travel; telegraph companies sent game results across the nation with incredible speed; and new printing presses ground out information that stimulated demand for even more.[7]

For a time, the issue of paying players was vigorously debated. Founded in 1858, the National Association of Base Ball Players (NABBP) staunchly defended the concept of amateurism, and for a time enjoyed the support of most baseball journalists. The NABBP tenaciously clung to its view that "the custom of publicly hiring men to play the game of Base Ball [is] reprehensible and injurious to the best interests of the game." This position was probably grounded in the growing uneasiness about the increased numbers of professional players who were of Irish and German immigrant stock. As one sportswriter bluntly wrote, these players were "not men of moral habits or integrity of character."[8]

The construction of fenced ballparks stimulated the sale of tickets, which in turn meant that players wanted a share of gate receipts. In 1868, the *New York Times* reported that the nation's top eight teams had collected more than $100,000 in ticket sales. The drive for supremacy led clubs to search for top talent and to pay the best players for their efforts. Although only a handful of the estimated 100,000 adult ballplayers in 1870 were being paid directly for their skills, some were making in the neighborhood of $1,000 a year, about twice the annual income of a clerk or skilled manual worker. Any pretense about professionalism ended in 1869, when a club in Cincinnati fielded the first all-professional team. Management hired one of the best players from the East Coast and charged him with assembling a strong team. Born in England in 1835, Harry Wright initially became an outstanding cricket player for the Dragonslayers of the St George Cricket Club of New York City. He also became a leading baseball player for the Knickerbockers. In taking command of the Cincinnati club, Wright accepted the same salary he had earned playing cricket – $1,200 a year – and proceeded to sign several leading Eastern players. In Wright's initial season at Cincinnati in 1868, his team won 41 and lost only seven games, touring the East and Midwest by train in search of competition.[9]

Wright introduced several innovations that became a staple of the professional game. By assuming complete control of the team, he conducted vigorous practices, schooled his players in various strategies and tactics, demanded that they stay in good physical condition, and preached the gospel of sobriety. In so doing, he created a template for the position of "manager." In addition to his on-the-field duties, Wright scheduled games, handled travel arrangements, and oversaw ticket sales and business transactions. He also created the design of a team uniform that would be worn by millions of ballplayers thereafter. He outfitted his team in knee-length flannel knickers, with the calf covered by bright red stockings. Wright also abandoned the popular brimmed straw hats in favor of more practical campaign caps with front bills, and placed a red *C* on the front of woolen shirts to denote the team as representative of Cincinnati. Footwear featured black high-top shoes with metal cleats to increase traction. Reporters took to calling the team the Red Stockings, thus creating the tradition of teams being identified by a nickname. More than a century later, the uniform introduced by the Cincinnati Red Stockings had not changed much; the current Cincinnati Reds wear white home uniforms, red stockings, with a time-honored *C* embroidered on the shirt and cap.[10]

Wright's Red Stockings went undefeated in 1869, winning 57 games and tying one; many of the games were lopsided affairs as his professionals not only demonstrated good fielding skills but dazzled spectators with their well-honed ability to hit line drives and sharp ground balls called "daisy cutters." The star player was Wright's younger brother George, whose strong throwing arm enabled him to play a deep shortstop rather than along the base path as was customary. Harry Wright paid his brother the munificent salary of $1,400. The Red Stockings traveled an estimated 12,000 miles by train that year in search of worthy opponents, at one point riding the new transcontinental line to show their stuff in San Francisco. President Ulysses S. Grant invited them to the nation's capital to play a local all-star team. An estimated 200,000 fans watched the Red Stockings play. When the team arrived home at season's end, appreciative fans hosted a dinner in their honor, which the *Cincinnati Gazette* termed "one of the most elegant ever seen" in the Queen City. Thrilled by the team's record, club president Aaron Champion proclaimed at the banquet that he would rather be president of the Red Stockings than of the United States.[11]

Figure 2.1   The Knickerbocker team of 1858 is captured in this rare photograph. In 1845, club member Alexander Cartwright wrote a set of 20 rules that established the foundation for the American game of baseball. In 1849 Cartwright joined the gold rush in California and ultimately became a leading citizen of Honolulu where he died in 1892. *National Baseball Hall of Fame Library, Cooperstown, NY, USA © NBL*

The following year, the mighty Red Stockings won their first 27 games before losing an extra inning contest to the Brooklyn Athletics 8–7 before 15,000 New York fans who paid the substantial admission fee of 50 cents each to watch the game. Because their home field could seat only 2,500 fans, the Cincinnati club lost money, and its stockholders (anticipating future trends in professional team management) rebelled against high player salaries and fired President Champion (who sadly learned that his was not the ideal job). The team was shredded. Manager Harry Wright, with several of his top players in tow, left town for a better offer – to create a new team, the Boston Red Stockings, for the 1871 season.[12]

Wright's leadership radically transformed the game. Questions about the ethics of paying men to play a boy's game largely disappeared from public dialogue. Once-skeptical journalists seldom thereafter questioned the propriety of play-for-pay. Wright left no doubt that this was a business, at one point writing to an aspiring young prospect, "Professional ball playing is business, and as such I trust you will regard it while the season lasts."[13] The nature of the game was transformed by the all-consuming factor of professionalism. Players commanding substantial salaries were expected by their employers to win games, an objective that managers and players interpreted as empowering them to use any means possible to that end. Clean, honest, fair play was for suckers. Instead, all types of cunning, intimidation, rough play, and skullduggery were encouraged, including bending or breaking rules and physically and psychologically intimidating opponents and umpires. Tough, aggressive play became the norm as players sought to fend off challengers for their positions as well as defeat the opposition. Competition on the baseball diamond thus mirrored the cutthroat competition that raged in the business world of the Gilded Age.[14]

Henry Chadwick and a Game of Numbers

One individual who never played the game professionally stands out for helping produce the groundswell of popularity for baseball. Henry Chadwick was born in Exeter, England, in 1824, and arrived in America with his parents at the age of 12. Tall, slender, and possessed of considerable natural athletic ability, he gained local fame in New York City as a talented cricket player. He became a newspaper reporter for several New York newspapers, initially covering local sporting events, cricket in particular. One day in 1856, however, while leaving a cricket match, he came upon a baseball game being played by two topnotch teams, the Eagles of Brooklyn and the New York Gothams. He later recalled, "The game was being sharply played on both sides and I watched it with deeper interest than any previous base ball match that I had seen. It was not long before I was struck with the idea that base ball was just the game for a national sport for Americans."[15]

Chadwick's conversion from cricket was indicative of the rapid decline of the traditional English game among the American people. In 1860, he wrote convincingly on the origins of the new game, noting that although it was clearly derived from the timeless English game of rounders (which he himself had played as a boy in England), it was a remarkable reflection of the American spirit. He went on to attest to the game's virtues as molding high character and promoting good health, proclaiming that "this invigorating exercise and manly pastime may be now justly termed the American game of Ball" despite its "English origin."[16]

The new game became Chadwick's lifetime passion. Like other intellectuals of the Victorian era, he sought to find in competitive sports a transcendent set of values that could elevate a game to a position of social utility. He now proclaimed baseball "a moral recreation" and a "powerful lever ... by which our people could be lifted into a position of more devotion to physical exercise and healthful out-door recreation." As such, the game deserved "the endorsement of every clergyman in the country ... [as] a remedy for the many evils resulting from the immoral associations [that] boys and young men of our cities are apt to become connected with."[17]

Chadwick's contribution was twofold. Foremost, he introduced the extensive use of statistics to explain the game to his readers. Over several decades he experimented with various methods to reduce each game and season to statistical analysis. By the late 1860s, he had devised the composite box score as a means of summarizing the story of a game that revealed in numbers the contributions of each player – runs, hits, walks, put-outs, wild pitches, passed balls, strikeouts, assists, and errors. His box score also presented an inning-by-inning line score. He introduced the batting average as a means of assessing a player's value. In Chadwick's world, even an entire season could be compressed into an assemblage of numbers detailing the accomplishments of teams and individual players.

Chadwick's statistical crusade was in tune with the times. Baseball, if it were to become truly the national game, had to meet the standards of the new age: comprehensive and precise rules and policies, standardization, a uniform method of statistical breakdown and analysis, and ways to chart and analyze trends over time. He thus devised a complex system of symbols that he demanded become the standard for scoring a game (including the ubiquitous use of the letter *K* to denote a strikeout). His methods thus became the basis for the evaluation and comparison of the game over generations. "It is requisite that all first nine contests should be recorded in a uniform manner," he wrote in 1861, explaining the manner in which his new score sheets should be employed uniformly across the entire United States.[18] Thus Chadwick created a means for fans to communicate (and argue) with each other, in real time and over the decades, about the subtleties of the game. The cold figures of a batting average enabled fans to compare the relative merits of a pitcher like Cy Young with a Sandy Koufax, and the base stealing exploits of Ty Cobb with a Maury Wills. What this apostle for the new American game created during the early years of baseball was analogous to the innovations simultaneously occurring in industry. One scholar has noted, "Standardizing the rules of scoring was the equivalent of an industrial magnate's standardizing the weight, shape, and purity of a steel bar. If the statistics of performance were to have the meaning intended for them, it was absolutely essential that the playing situation for all teams and players be nearly comparable as possible."[19]

Chadwick's second contribution was to create through his extensive publications a national dialogue about the game and its merits. A Victorian moralist to the core, Chadwick in part used statistics to establish the value of each player and to hold him accountable for his efforts on the diamond. Repeatedly, however, his writings revealed him to be somewhat of a scold. He continually argued for rule changes that placed value on "clean," "manly," and "scientific" play. His urged the issuance of fines for players who argued with the umpire, used profanity, or spurned the instructions of their manager. In a typical Victorian revulsion against behavior that encouraged the use of raw strength over the powers of the mind, he railed against the innovation of fast pitches to overpower batters, and his ever-evolving box score formats never quite found a place to record the singular event of a ball being knocked over a distant fence. Home runs were, to Chadwick, an aberration in a game that should be played "scientifically" – that is, with emphasis placed upon the sacrifice bunt, stolen base, hit-and-run play, and the like. His moral sensibilities were never clearer than when he attacked the proclivity of many professional players – who tended to be young and unmarried – to gravitate toward gambling, drinking, and chasing women. In 1889, he wrote with consternation, "The saloon and brothel are the evils of the base ball world at the present day."[20]

Chadwick not only published his thoughts in New York newspapers but also contributed regularly to national journals. Chadwick's 1868 booklet, *The Game of Base Ball: How to Learn It, How to Play It, and How to Teach It*, was the first serious published effort to describe the fundamentals, strategies, theories, and rules of the game. Although his strident moralizing offended some, he maintained his role as critic-in-chief until his death in 1908, using his editorship of the unofficial baseball manual, *Spalding's Baseball Guide*, for the last 25 years of his long life to deliver his pronouncements on the state of the game. Although baseball historians have criticized Chadwick's work on many counts, his was a crucial role in creating a moral rationale and a statistical basis for the game that he believed held one of the keys to the nation's moral improvement.[21]

Growing Pains

During the 1870s, the game continued to change to meet the standards of the emerging modern era. It was being played in nearly every town and city across the land. The game provided a common ground for conversations everywhere. It yielded to the forces of standardization as national organizations supervised the establishment of rules and the maintenance of records and statistics. Propelled by the growth of print journalism, the game grew rapidly in popularity. No longer merely a pleasant game that boys and young men played for fun, baseball had also become the property of businessmen who created professional teams and leagues.

Rules were routinely changed to accommodate the special needs of spectators who wanted to watch an ever more exciting brand of ball. By the time the Cincinnati Red Stockings became the talk of the nation, the game had come to resemble today's game of fast-pitch softball. No longer was the "thrower" expected merely to lob up a fat pitch to the batter with a soft underhanded toss. "Throwers" now were called pitchers, and managers expected them to employ all sorts of different speeds to fool the batter. Among other things, they learned to snap the ball so that it would variously curve, drop, or rise. Until the 1870s, batters could request a pitch be tossed either "high" or "low." Umpires – usually local citizens willing to put themselves in harm's way – were now stationed off to the side from the batter and empowered to call a pitch as "strike" when the batter permitted a well-placed pitch to go by. Harry Wright became famous for his "dew-drop" pitch – a slow change of pace pitch intended to put the batter off balance after seeing several fast tosses. In order to keep the game moving at a rapid pace, the number of "balls" required to advance the batter to first base was reduced over the years from nine to four. The size of the ball – made with a hard rubber core, wrapped with woolen string, and covered with a sewn piece of horsehide – was reduced to about the size of today's ball, about 5½ ounces in weight and 9¼ inches in circumference. By 1880, standardized balls were being manufactured by several companies and marketed nationally through the first generation of sporting goods stores. The nineteenth-century ball did not rocket off the bat like today's "juiced" balls, and because they were kept in play for several innings they lost much of their bounce. These so-called "dead" balls remained the standard until the 1920s, when they were replaced with a more tightly wound ball that left the bat with greater velocity and traveled greater distances. The new "live ball era" produced a more exciting, fan-pleasing game that emphasized power hitting, which was underscored by the enormous popularity of home run slugger Babe Ruth.

The ethics of the game also changed dramatically. Although the games played by the early clubs were occasionally marred by arguments, for the most part they sought to emulate the decorum and behavior standards expected of cricket players. "It isn't cricket," was a popular American expression indicating a lack of adherence to the spirit of the rules. Unlike the sportsmen who played cricket, those who came to dominate the "American game" were mirror images of the hard-driving and often unscrupulous buccaneers who dominated the American economy during the raucous Gilded Age. The dominant ethic of the baseball player was to find ways to bend, break, or otherwise subvert the rules to gain an edge on the opposition. Leo Durocher's famous comment of a later time, "Nice guys finish last," was a throwback to this era when mental and physical toughness, sharpened spikes, bean balls, and hard slides into basemen were hailed as "manly" play. Especially at the higher professional levels, winning was indeed everything, and it mattered little how victory was achieved.

With that ethic in place, the role of the umpire became crucial and his powers were greatly increased to control the game. The quality of umpiring presented league officials with a difficult problem that defied easy solution. In local town ball encounters, the umpire was usually picked out of the crowd and often lacked adequate knowledge of the rules or the mechanics of umpiring. The quality of umpiring apparently was not much better in the professional leagues. Verbal abuse of umpires was commonplace and physical intimidation occurred frequently. In 1876, the new National League sought to address the issue by mandating a substantial wage of $5 per game in hopes of securing quality umpires; but with only one man assigned to a game it was impossible for him to cover the entire field adequately. Umpires, of course, were expected to be fair and impartial in all their decisions, or as Henry Chadwick eloquently put it, "The position of an Umpire is an honorable one, but his duties are anything but agreeable, as it is next to impossible to give entire satisfaction to all parties concerned in a match." Nonetheless, Chadwick said, "The moment he assumes his position on the ground," the umpire has "to close his eyes to the fact of there being any one player, among the contestants, that is not an entire stranger to him; by this means he will free his mind from any friendly bias."[22] But the truth was that the standards for selection and training were inadequate and the cost of multiple umpires prohibitive. Thus the tradition of baiting and intimidating the umpire became ingrained as a means by which players and managers would forever attempt to gain an advantage.

Enthusiastic spectators – aptly called "cranks" and later "fanatics" (later shortened to "fans") – joined in the fun and sought to assist their favorite team by seeking to distract the opposition and intimidate the umpire. In 1860, after fans of the Brooklyn Atlantics peppered the opposing Excelsiors with rocks and epithets, the young writer Albert Spalding denounced them as "utterly uncontrollable … thugs, gamblers, thieves, plug-uglies, and rioters." In California, reports indicated that fans upon occasion would shoot off a round or two into the air from a revolver when an opposing outfielder was settling under a fly ball. A *New York Times* writer observed in the early 1870s that the game had deteriorated from one "witnessed by crowds of ladies, and governed only by those incentives of an honorable effort to win the trophy," to "[a] game patronized by the worst classes of the community … characterized by the presence of a regular gambling horde, while oaths and obscenity have prevailed and fraudulent combinations of one kind or another have marked the arrangements connected with some of the prominent contests."[23]

The behavior of players and fans alike was disconcerting to the proper Victorians who cherished above all proper decorum and suppression of antisocial behavior. One of the most disheartening practices associated with baseball to these right-thinking respectable citizens was gambling by spectators in the grandstands despite the posting of signs prohibiting such practice. By the late 1860s, gambling on baseball had become so widespread that some feared the game would be destroyed if it was not curtailed. Some gamblers preferred a sure thing to the thrill of watching a close game upon which they had money invested, and they were widely suspected of bribing players to throw games. This practice – popularly known as "hippodroming" – first hit the news in 1865 when it was discovered that three players for the New York Mutuals had agreed to divvy up $100 offered by a gambler if they lost a championship series with the Excelsiors. In 1867, *Harper's Weekly* editorialized against baseball gambling, noting that, "The most respectable clubs in the country indulge in it to a highly culpable degree, and so common [are] … the tricks by which games have been 'sold' for the benefit of gamblers that the most respected participants have been suspected of baseness."[24] In other words, the fix was in, and players were engaged in losing games in return for payoffs from gamblers.

By the mid 1870s, baseball had developed a serious image problem. Gambling, unseemly spectators, and unsportsmanlike behavior by players and managers gave the game a coarse, even corrupt image. It was under this substantial cloud that some investors decided the time had come to create a professional league that would become known for its integrity and good citizenship.

Early Years of the Professional Game

The success of the 1869 Cincinnati Red Stockings essentially decided the issue. Amateur and semiprofessional baseball would continue to thrive, but the attention of the average sports fan would be directed increasingly toward the "major" leagues. The development of professional leagues was in no small way stimulated by intense competition between large Northeastern and Midwestern cities to attract railroad lines and to encourage industrial and commercial development within their borders. These intense, no-holds-barred, eco-nomic and political urban rivalries sparked interest in fielding winning baseball teams as part of the larger urban competition. In the early 1870s, boosters formed clubs, often by issuance of stock, to field professional teams in hopes of emulating the glorious example of Cincinnati's triumph. Club managers raised capital to build wooden grandstands and enclose fields. They hired a manager to scour the country in search of the best talent. Perceptive observers of the juggernaut that was the 1869 Red Stockings took note of the fact that only one member of the team was a native Cincinnatian, the remaining players having been imported from Eastern cities.[25]

A case in point was Chicago. Leaders in this booming railroad hub had looked jealously upon the publicity that the Queen City of Cincinnati had received from its undefeated Red Stockings, and they decided to emulate that achievement. In late 1869, team founders induced investors to purchase $20,000 in stock, and the Chicago White Stockings ball club was launched. They admitted they did not want to "see our commercial rival on the Ohio [River] bearing off the honors of the national game, especially when there was money to be made by beating her."[26] The importance of having a team "that would beat the world" was evident to these businessmen, whom the *Chicago Tribune* praised for "organizing a baseball club with the same energy as they would build a tunnel or construct a railroad."[27] These boosters, however, had assumed that the creation of a team would produce winning seasons and championships, bringing fame and fortune to the Windy City. That teams lost as well as won was driven home to White Stockings fans in 1875, when their team lost the champi-onship to the Browns, a team representing one of Chicago's primary urban rivals, the river city of St Louis. In the wake of that inglorious defeat, one Chicago newspaper sadly noted that "a deep gloom" now pervaded the city. In a substantial exaggeration, the reporter wrote, "friends refused to recognize friends, lovers became estranged, and business was suspended. All Chicago went to a funeral, and the time, since then, has dragged wearily along, as though it were no object to live longer in this world."[28]

High levels of financial success, however, did not mark the early years of professional baseball. Economic recessions, losing teams, disturbing reports of antisocial behavior by fans and players, the vexatious moral issue of playing games on Sunday, and the sale of alcohol all posed challenges to team owners. Teams played in the loosely organized National Association of Professional Base Ball Players (NAPBBP), which was dominated by Wright's Boston team. Several thinly capitalized teams were swept away in a tide of red ink, and the effort to establish regional "minor-league" teams was even more hazardous. Not unlike the heavy number of business failures of this turbulent economic era, the frequent liquidation of teams, even entire leagues, marked the early history of baseball. As but one example, the Southern League had 18 different team franchises between 1880 and 1900, had seven seasons suspended prematurely due to financial exigency, and did not play at all in 1890, 1891, and 1897. Of all the professional teams established in the late nineteenth century, fully three-fourths lasted less than three years before folding.

That dismal record in large part resulted from the fact that well-established, respected businessmen of considerable wealth viewed baseball – with its many rough edges – with contempt, leaving the field to marginal investors. Prim-and-proper bank officials naturally viewed baseball teams seeking loans with justifiable skepticism. Thus it was not surprising that many team owners came from the shadowy edges of the urban business community, including gamblers, saloon owners, brewers, and machine politicians.

The first organized "major league" was established in 1876. The driving force behind the creation of the National League of Professional Base Ball Clubs was Chicago coal magnate and civic booster William A. Hulbert, who had watched first hand the futile efforts of the NAPBBP as president of the Chicago White Stockings. A strong-willed man of considerable girth, Hulbert imposed his vision of the future of baseball upon the league that he controlled until his death in 1882. Comprising eight teams representing the cities of Chicago, Boston, New York, Hartford, Cincinnati, Louisville, St Louis, and Philadelphia, the National League easily displaced the poorly organized and inefficiently operated National Association of Professional Base Ball Players. With half of its teams located in the Midwest and the other half in the East, Hulbert's new league presented an image of a truly "national" league.

Hulbert limited the number of teams to eight and introduced a system to prevent the "revolving" of players from one team to another. Players could not negotiate a new contract and move to a rival team once a season began. Each member city was required to have a minimum population of 75,000, and no city could field multiple teams. Hulbert championed policies designed to appease social critics who had attacked baseball for its flouting of accepted social conventions. He banned Sunday games, prohibited the sale of beer and other alcoholic beverages at games, encouraged female attendance by offering reduced ticket prices for ladies on special days, and launched a strong anti-gambling crusade. In an effort to discourage the attendance of lower-class spectators most likely to engage in rowdy behavior, ticket prices were pegged at a formidable 50 cents (approximately one-half of an average laborer's full day's pay), which Hulbert hoped would entice "the better classes [to] patronize the game a great deal more." He even stipulated that weekday games begin at 3 p.m., a time when most laboring-class persons were still at work.[29]

Despite this strategy, the new league did not get off to an auspicious start. Several poorly capitalized teams folded during the early years, and others were kicked out of the league for defying Hulbert's authority. Controversy and rumors about the influence of gamblers were endemic. Nonetheless, from the outset Hulbert demonstrated his toughness when confronted with a challenge to his authority. Near the end of the initial season, when the financially hard-pressed New York and Philadelphia teams, both having suffered through losing seasons, refused to make a scheduled late-season swing to the Midwest, Hulbert expelled them from the league.

The following season, Hulbert responded decisively to the gambling issue when reports were published in the *Louisville Courier-Journal* that several leading players of the Louisville Grays had taken bribes to throw games that cost the team the league championship. Four players were summarily banished from the league for conspiring with a New York City gambler to split his winnings (which amounted to about $300).[30] Despite Hulbert's decisive action, the dark specter of gambling lurked over the game for several more decades. It would not be adequately addressed until after revelations surfaced that Chicago White Sox players had taken substantial bribes from gamblers to lose the 1919 World Series.

Before the 1880 season, club presidents took the position that players were employees – not skilled professionals – and approved a policy designed to halt the practice of "revolving." Each team, the owners agreed, could identify five players whose services were "reserved" to a particular club for as long as that club wished to retain their services; the policy was soon extended to all team members. The "reserve rule" proved to be everything the owners wished, stripping players of the right to shop their skills on the open market. This essentially eliminated any bargaining power the players might have used to increase their salaries. The "reserve clause" became a powerful tool of ownership, keeping player's salaries in check until the late 1970s when a series of legal challenges ended the policy that enabled management to keep salaries surprisingly low.

During the initial years, the White Stockings dominated the National League. Led by manager and pitcher Albert Spalding, Chicago easily won the first championship in 1876. Spalding was the compelling baseball figure of his time, and he made successive career moves from star pitcher to team executive to sporting goods entrepreneur and ultimately to baseball writer, historian, and publisher. After he retired from the field in 1878 due to an injured pitching arm, he devoted his attention to the commercial side of the game. His fledgling sporting goods manufacturing business got a huge boost when he snagged the contract to provide all balls for the National League. By 1890, his sporting goods manufacturing and sales company had become the nation's largest. Spalding also established himself as the major spokesman for the National League, publishing its official annual handbook, which included team and individual records, official rules and league policies, along with his own commentary on the state of the game. In a successful effort to co-opt a leading critic of the league, he appointed the opinionated Henry Chadwick editor of *Spalding's Official Base Ball Guide*. Chadwick's searing criticisms of the game were effectively silenced, and the annual publication became required reading for anyone seriously interested in professional baseball. Spalding also increased his financial investment in the White Stockings, and he not only assumed the presidency of the club when Hulbert died in 1882 but also became the primary spokesman for the league.[31]

During the 1880s, Chicago won several consecutive pennants, led by first baseman Adrian "Cap" Anson, who also served as manager. Standing 6 feet 2 inches and weighing 220 pounds, this rawboned Iowan towered above most players of his time. He was a powerful hitter, among the best of his generation. Although his managerial acumen was questionable, he won four consecutive championships because management provided him with the best talent in the league. As a player-manager, he set a high example on the field for his players, routinely leading the league in batting average and home runs. Over a 22-year career in the National League, Anson batted a stellar .334.[32]

While Anson provided the White Stockings with the necessary power, the colorful Mike "King" Kelly, who played every position but pitcher, produced the fireworks for the Chicago team. Kelly was a flamboyant Irishman with a knack for stealing bases, using exaggerated high-flying hook slides as one of his special crowd-pleasing ploys. Fans loved to chant "Slide, Kelly, Slide" as he cavorted on the base paths, and as the first great Irish American ballplayer, he helped lure many Irish spectators to the ballpark. Even a popular hit tune entitled "Slide, Kelly, Slide!" swept the nation. He also found ways to frustrate his opponents, some of them quite humorous. He especially enjoyed outfoxing the solitary umpire (who had many things to watch simultaneously). Among Kelly's many tricks were holding opposing base runners by grabbing their belt, cutting inside bases to reduce the distance he had to run to beat an incoming throw from the outfield, and faking being hit by a pitch. In 1887, club president Spalding shocked the baseball world when he sold Kelly's contract to the Boston Red Stockings for the enormous sum of $10,000. This sensational player transaction provided a major statement about the power that owners now wielded over players through the reserve clause. The purchase of Kelly's contract delighted Boston fans, who raised funds to purchase for their new star player a pair of matching horses and a bright carriage as a demonstration of their affection. Unfortunately, Kelly could not control his serious drinking problem – he showed up for many games intoxicated or seriously hung over – and his level of play deteriorated rapidly. This early fan favorite – arguably the first true "star" baseball player – died of alcohol-related symptoms a few weeks before he reached his 37th birthday.[33]

Emergence of the Modern Game

Despite its heavy emphasis on continuity and tradition, baseball has undergone major changes over the years. By the late 1880s, however, the type of play had become such that it would be quite familiar to fans in the twenty-first century. Of major significance were the changing rules regarding pitching. Over the years, the requirement that the pitcher softly lob an underhand toss to the batter was undercut by pitchers who began to throw the ball with considerable velocity, first three-quarter and then side-armed. One source indicates that the first overhand pitches were introduced in 1875, although that bit of trivia is open to question. In any case, the overhand pitch grew in popularity during the late 1870s and was formally accepted in the rulebooks by all professional leagues by 1885. In response to the increased velocity of pitches, the distance between batter and pitcher was lengthened from 45 feet to 50, and then to today's distance of 60 feet 6 inches. The dimensions and composition of the official ball were also standardized. New rules also called for a five-sided home plate made of hard rubber to replace the more dangerous metal plate.

It was during this period that gloves and other protective equipment were introduced. Previously, players had to handle sharply hit balls with their bare hands, which of course led to many errors and painful bruises. Games with 10 or even 20 errors being charged were not

unusual. Spalding recalls that the first glove he ever saw used was in 1875, but the player, Charles Waite, apparently was so embarrassed by his "unmanly" use of a skin-tight glove to protect his hand that he had the glove colored in flesh tones. During the 1880s, an increasing number of players began wearing small gloves to protect their hands, and this early experimentation led to the creation of a rounded glove designed by Harry Decker, a player of modest abilities who appeared in both the National League and the American Association. His glove eventually was modified into the oversized mitt worn by first basemen and catchers, but the other fielders adopted a smaller model that featured padding at the thumb and heel and light padding on the four fingers. These original fielders' gloves were made of hand-sewn leather – little more than 8 or 9 inches in diameter. For years, catchers had suffered painful injuries from foul balls and wild pitches; broken fingers were a particular occupational hazard. To provide reasonable protection of catchers who were moving ever closer to the batter so that they could throw out base runners, chest protectors, shin guards, protective

Figure 2.2 A standing-room crowd packs the Baltimore Orioles ballpark in 1897 for an important game with Boston. As was the custom, when the bleacher seats were filled, fans were permitted to stand in the outfield, sometimes creating confusion when a batted ball rolled into the crowd. *Image © Corbis*

cups, and padded wire masks were introduced in addition to the larger padded mitt. With the introduction of the glove, the practice of using one's hat to catch fly balls was declared illegal.[34]

The grandstands were initially constructed of wood, and most seating consisted of unfinished planks that were bleached out by the sun (hence the term "bleachers"). The small stadiums proved vulnerable to fires, and it was not unusual for play to be interrupted while workers rebuilt burned-out grandstands. In 1871, as but one sensational example, the Chicago White Sox had to cancel the end of their season when their stadium was leveled by the great Chicago Fire in early October. Seating for the major-league teams ranged normally from 7,000 to 10,000, although some clubs permitted fans to stand along the foul lines and to ring the outfield inside the fences, leading to exciting times when a ball in play ended up in the crowd. Most ballparks were constructed near the central city to make them accessible by walking or trolley. On special days, red-white-and-blue bunting draped from the grandstand created a patriotic aura, and small bands provided entertainment between innings. If local laws were amenable, vendors hawked beer to the thirsty crowd, an influence that often intensified the fans' vocal support of the home team. Some clubs even offered a full-service bar for the convenience of fans.[35]

The 1880s: A Decade of Rancor

William Hulbert attempted to raise the image of baseball in the eyes of Victorian America, but his efforts created many problems with team owners. His policy forbidding the sale of alcoholic beverages at games became a major point of contention, and he expelled the Cincinnati franchise from the league in 1880 for its insistence on selling beer. In 1881, critics rebelled against Hulbert's dictatorial ways and formed a new league, the American Association of Base Ball Clubs, and proclaimed itself "major league." Franchises were awarded to clubs in Philadelphia, St Louis, Cincinnati, Pittsburgh, Baltimore, and Louisville. Brewery owners were prominent among investors. Supporters of Hulbert derisively denounced the rival as the "beer league," but the leaders of the American Association were determined to fill the vacuum created by Hulbert's morality crusade. Ticket prices were set at just 25 cents to attract working-class fans – most of whom viewed prevailing Victorian moral standards with disdain and were delighted to learn that not only would games be played on Sundays (where legal) but also beer would flow freely at the ballpark. American Association teams secured the services of several of the top National League players with inducements of higher pay.[36]

For a time, the rival leagues seemed on the verge of a major fight when the National League placed a team in Philadelphia to challenge the Athletics of the rival American Association. Open warfare was avoided when the two leagues joined in a "National Agreement." Among other things, they agreed to respect each team's 11 "reserved" players, to pay each player at least a minimum annual salary of $1,000, and to play the game by the same set of rules while using the same game ball sold by Albert Spalding's company. Shortly after the basic agreement was in place, the management of the two leagues also agreed to "blacklist" any player dismissed by another team, and they established salary classifications that capped players' compensation.[37]

On the playing field, the level of play in both leagues seemed about equal. The St Louis Browns in the American Association emerged as a team to be reckoned with under the strong ownership of Christian von der Ahe and the able field leadership of youthful manager and first baseman, Charles Comiskey. The Browns won four consecutive titles and defeated the National League champions in two informal postseason "World Championship Series," precursors to what would become the annual World Series in 1903. Meanwhile, under Cap Anson, the Chicago White Stockings continued their domination of the National League by capturing five pennants during 1880–6.

Anson was also a primary force in the development of an informal agreement that barred African American players. African Americans had embraced the game with the same enthusiasm as whites, and amateur and semiprofessional teams representing black communities were commonplace. However, in keeping with the racial standards of the day, the formation of interracial teams was discouraged. In 1867, the National Association of Base Ball Players issued a policy statement that it would not admit teams of color or biracial clubs, ostensibly to reduce conflict on the field of play. In 1884, the Toledo team in the American Association signed a former University of Michigan player, Moses Fleetwood Walker, who became the first black to play for a major-league team. He batted a respectable .263 in 104 games, but Toledo dropped out of the Association in 1885. By that year, leadership in both leagues had reached an informal "gentlemen's agreement" not to sign black players. Although a few African Americans played for various minor-league teams into the 1890s, none were signed to play for a team in either the National League or the American Association.[38]

In 1887, Cap Anson refused to permit his White Stockings to take the field for an exhibition game against the Newark team if a hard-throwing African American pitched. Newark's management capitulated to this threat, and the media were informed that George Stovey was unavailable due to "illness." However, the event was seen for what it was: a definitive statement by one of baseball's leading figures that racial segregation practices, now widespread in other sectors of American society, also extended to the national game. This informal and unwritten policy of racial exclusion would last for more than 50 years until challenged by the Brooklyn Dodgers when Jackie Robinson was signed to a minor-league contract in 1945.[39]

The National Agreement respecting rival league contracts helped keep the peace between the two major leagues, although many contentious episodes had to be contained as teams jockeyed for an advantage. Despite the expanding economy of the 1880s, teams in both leagues were locked in a difficult struggle for financial survival. Despite its best efforts, the National League found itself losing the battle to create a more wholesome, family-oriented image because of the behavior of many of its players, who came from working-class backgrounds where heavy drinking, brawling, and general hell-raising were commonplace. Management was frequently embarrassed by published reports of player misconduct. Mostly young and unmarried, players were often seen during evening hours frequenting saloons, brothels, and gambling halls. Despite the best efforts of management, the image of the game continued to suffer.

With the owners now fully in control of the game and armed with the reserve clause, players became increasingly dissatisfied with their conditions of employment. In 1885, the two leagues concluded another "National Agreement," this time capping players' salaries at

$2,000 a year. Once a player signed a binding contract, he had few options if he was dissatisfied with a contract offer. Essentially, he could accept it, hold out in hopes of getting a more lucrative offer (an option realistically available to only a few top players), or quit the game.[40]

Consequently, when New York Giants infielder John Montgomery Ward, who possessed a Columbia University law degree, established the Brotherhood of Professional Base Ball Players in 1887 to represent the interests of players, the prospect of an all-out confrontation between management and labor loomed. In 1890, Ward's organization boldly formed a new Players' League, and more than 100 National League or American Association players moved to the new circuit. Management of the Players' League made the fateful decision to challenge the National League directly, placing seven of its teams in cities already hosting National League clubs.

With players now distributed among 24 teams in three rival leagues, the quality of play naturally suffered, and fans went elsewhere for entertainment. Attendance slumped badly, and all three leagues suffered losses that year. Investors who had funded the Players' League backed away from the possibility of another disastrous season and folded the league after only one season. As Spalding, who actively participated in the struggle against the Players' League, later wrote, the season of 1890 "caused serious financial loss to the moneyed backers of the Brotherhood … It occasioned the utmost bitterness of feeling between players and club owners … and it utterly disgusted the public with the whole Base Ball business. It set Base Ball back from five to ten years in its natural development."[41]

This struggle also devastated the American Association, which unceremoniously folded in 1892. And so, following a decade of conflict, intrigue, and endless struggle, the National League found itself alone as a "major league." Club owners then did what came naturally: they slashed players' salaries and otherwise imposed their will upon their workers who had no other option than taking up real jobs instead of playing a boy's game for pay. As the Brotherhood's adamant foe, Albert Spalding, explained, the aftermath of the struggle of 1890 "settled forever the theory that professional ball players can at the same time direct both the business and the playing ends of the game."[42] Just as most management–labor struggles of the late nineteenth century ended in defeat for labor, so too did the effort of John Montgomery Ward on behalf of baseball's version of the working man's cooperative result in another triumph for capitalism.

Between the 1840s and the end of the nineteenth century, a simple child's game was transformed into a sophisticated professional game with which American society would be forever identified. Initially made popular as a pastime for young adults living in Eastern cities, following the Civil War baseball was played in towns and cities across the land. Its popularity led to the creation of professional teams and leagues and of a national game that captured the imagination of the American people. As historian Harold Seymour observed, by the onset of the twentieth century "baseball not only reflected American life, it had made an indelible mark upon it."[43]

3

The Formative Years of College Football

The American system of higher education is unique for its commitment to athletic competition. No other country has anything approaching the massive sports enterprise that is supported by America's colleges and universities. Intercollegiate sports for those institutions competing at the highest levels of the National Collegiate Athletic Association (NCAA) command high visibility in the public eye. It is very big business, with individual campus budgets supporting a few hundred "student-athletes" reaching astronomical sums. Many major university athletic programs have annual budgets that exceed $100 million.

Every March, American sports fans become fixated upon the annual NCAA basketball tournament, a made-for-television bonanza that annually produces $800 million in broadcasting rights, and millions of dollars in ticket sales and ancillary enterprises, while generating an estimated $125 million in office pools and wagers. The Christmas and New Year's season has become a time for the playing of more than 30 college football bowl games – the culmination of a five-month season in which teams play a normal 12-game schedule – each of which generates millions of dollars in revenue. In addition to the 120 institutions that play football and the 313 that compete in basketball at the highest competitive classification, there are some 3,000 community colleges, four-year liberal arts colleges, and universities that field athletic teams for men and women who compete throughout the academic year at lower classifications.

From their inception in the late nineteenth century, intercollegiate athletics have sparked controversy. Although the size and scope of programs have grown enormously, the underlying issues remain essentially what they were a century ago. Critics and reformers have sought to eliminate intercollegiate sports, or at least reduce their importance, but those efforts have been largely unsuccessful. At the heart of the intercollegiate enterprise is the unique American game of football.

Sports in American Life: A History, Second Edition. Richard O. Davies.
© 2012 John Wiley & Sons, Inc. Published 2012 by John Wiley & Sons, Inc.

The Early Years of College Athletics

The earliest intercollegiate competition did not occur on a football field. Rather, the first instances of competition emerged among elite Northeastern colleges that tested each other's mettle in rowing. Crew races became popular before the Civil War as rowing clubs were formed on several Northeastern campuses. A highly publicized race between Yale and Harvard held on Lake Winnipesaukee in New Hampshire in 1852 drew a crowd of over 1,000 spectators, including presidential candidate Franklin Pierce. By the end of the decade, the College Regatta Association had been formed, complete with written rules and regulations to guide its member institutions. Several of its regattas held in the late 1850s drew crowds estimated as high as 20,000.

College track and field teams were also organized, and spring meets became widespread during the post-Civil War decades. College men also competed in the nation's most popular team sport, baseball. The first recorded college baseball game was played in 1859 between Amherst and Williams, with the better-trained Amherst team (it held practices before the contest) recording a victory by the improbable score of 73–32. For a time, baseball was the most widely played game on American campuses, until it was eclipsed by football.

One of the striking characteristics of the early stages of intercollegiate sports was that they were organized and operated by the students with little if any guidance from faculty or administrators. College sports grew out of campus competitions held between classes. Because most male students enrolled as freshmen and graduated in four years, the symbolic importance of each class was great. For many decades, students had engaged in informal intramural games that casually mixed the rules of rugby and soccer. Upon occasion, these games turned into rugged physical contests that resembled more a barroom brawl than an athletic contest. These interclass contests were often held as part of the annual fall hazing of freshmen by upperclassmen during the so-called "rush" week preceding a new academic year.

When the game of football began to attract interest, contests between classes were initiated, out of which slowly emerged the concept of the student body fielding a team to challenge nearby rivals. Today's sports fans are accustomed to the dominant role played in college sports by the professional coach. The phenomenon of "coachers," as they were originally called, evolved slowly out of the growth of the college sports enterprise between 1880 and 1920. Originally, however, college teams were student-financed and -operated affairs with an experienced student captain running the show and elected by his teammates. The captain's responsibilities combined those of today's coach and athletic director, and included organizing the team, arranging a schedule, selecting team members, supervising drills and practices, and providing leadership during games.

It was under this informal structure that football made its appearance during the final decades of the nineteenth century. According to most accounts, the first intercollegiate football game was played on November 6, 1869, when a group of Princeton students visited the College of Rutgers in New Brunswick. To ascribe to this event an important historical first, however, is a stretch. The game played that day scarcely resembled anything akin to American football, and the informality was a far cry from the emotion-laden spectacles of contemporary college contests. Instead, what transpired was merely a game vaguely resembling somewhat a modern-day soccer match. Each side placed 25 players on the field who were cheered on by a few hundred onlookers. The final score was 6–4 in favor of the home team; a banquet followed as each team toasted the other in a wholesome display of sportsmanship. Within three decades of the Princeton–Rutgers contest, however, this informal activity had evolved into a major spectator sport that trailed only horse racing and baseball in public appeal.

Football American Style

Following the Rutgers–Princeton encounter, various forms of "foot ball" appeared irregularly on the campuses of elite private colleges in the Northeast. Rules varied widely and were subject to constant revision. Scoring systems changed frequently, but initially the largest number of points was awarded for drop kicking the fat, somewhat oblong inflated ball through a goalpost, not by advancing it across the goal line. As the game became increasingly physical in the 1880s, with blocking and tackling becoming part of the game, some administrators and faculty members sought its abolition because of the serious injuries absorbed by participants. Until the creation of formal governing boards and conferences, player eligibility was left up to individual schools. This led to many flagrant abuses. It did not take long for skilled, physically adept "tramp" athletes to appear magically on a college campus in time for the fall season, and quietly disappear after the final game. "Proselytizing" (recruiting with financial inducements) of top players produced many a controversy. Occasionally, some itinerant athletes actually played for more than one school in the same season. Professors and deans questioned the dismal academic records of this migrant class of athletes, while also lamenting that many students exhibited far more interest in the games than they did in their studies.

The violent nature of the game – played initially without protective padding, governed by rules (or the lack thereof) that encouraged physical mayhem, and often poorly officiated by untrained referees – contributed to several highly publicized deaths and a long list of serious injuries each autumn. These casualties predictably produced demands that the rules be modified to make the game safer, while others, often academics, demanded the game be abolished. As an example, for many years one permissive rule stipulated that a player could be disqualified from a game *only after* he had slugged an opponent three times.

The new college game also had its legions of supporters. Many college administrators were pleased that the game was physical in nature, a fact they believed helped dispel the widespread myth current at the time that male college students lacked adequate masculine attributes, that as a group they were sissified, effeminate souls who shunned physical challenges and cowered behind their books. At a time when the dominant Victorian culture was emphasizing the importance of "Muscular Christianity" – a fusion of high levels of physical activity and religious devotion – football seemed to its advocates an obvious way to counter the notion that college men were not real men. Football demonstrated that college students were indeed brave men strong of body and willing to risk limb (and even life) on the football field for the glory of their alma mater.

College administrators recognized that journalists devoted considerable attention to the new game, which provided a means of getting an institution's name before the general public on a regular basis. Journalists were pleased to provide that coverage because the game filled a major sports void after the baseball season ended in early fall. Campus administrators also recognized that a strong football team brought many benefits to their institutions, among them the ability to attract financial contributions from non-alumni (a practice elevated to a high art form by the University of Notre Dame) and a means of encouraging the continued loyalty and giving by alumni.

On campus, the impact of football was palpable – at least to the game's supporters. The existence of a football team tended to decrease the troublesome conflicts between classes because it created a common focus for all students. Campus leaders – students, faculty, and administrators alike – now stressed the importance of encouraging "school spirit." Administrators also noted the positive impact on student behavior; the rioting and drunkenness that had for so long plagued college campuses seemed to taper off during the football season (although later generations of deans of student life, confronted with the phenomenon of tailgating, would strongly disagree with this assessment).

Thus did higher education embrace football. When the founding president of the new University of Chicago set up shop in 1891, one of his first decisions was to hire Amos Alonzo Stagg, a former Yale standout, and charge him with building a winning team to attract favorable publicity to the new institution. When it came to college sports, President William Rainey Harper was enthusiastic: "I am most heartily in favor of them," he said. He assured Stagg that he would provide him with the financial resources to build a powerful team. In return, Harper wanted immediate national recognition, something that normally takes decades to achieve if based upon the academic accomplishments of faculty and students.

At the same time, in a much different and more modest academic setting, the individual hired away from Ohio Wesleyan University to lead the small, struggling University of Nevada similarly turned to sports as a means of publicizing his remote institution located in the small town of Reno. Early in his tenure, President Joseph Stubbs established a football team complete with a professional coach to help attract attention to the new university. The editor of the student newspaper embraced Stubbs's vision, noting optimistically that it would soon be possible to send Nevada's teams to "Berkeley and Stanford to demonstrate our athletic supremacy." What presidents Harper and Stubbs perceived as a convenient strategy to help establish the foundation of a new university – fielding a powerful football team – provided a formula that would often be emulated by ambitious college presidents in years to come.

Yale and the Creation of Football

Today, the Yale Bulldogs play a modest Football Championship Subdivision (formerly I-AA) schedule in the Ivy League. The few thousand spectators who show up for games rattle around the mammoth Yale Bowl with its seating capacity of 65,000. Completed in 1914, this was one of the first mega stadiums to be constructed on a college campus. During the 1920s, similar monuments to the importance of football appeared on campuses as college football mania swept the nation. The construction of the Yale Bowl capped an incredible era of football domination at the New Haven campus beginning in 1876, during which time Yale's teams enjoyed several undefeated seasons and won over 95 percent of their games.

The primary factor in Yale's domination of the early college football scene was one man, rightly acknowledged as the "Father of American football." Walter Chauncey Camp's influence was not limited to his various roles at Yale as an outstanding athlete, team advisor, sometimes coach, and informal director of athletics. His influence extended to creating a set of rules that clearly distinguished the American game of "foot ball" from English soccer and rugby. Just as Americans embraced baseball rather than cricket, the spirit of American nationalism contributed to the creation of a game unique to the United States. Beyond his coaching and rules making, Camp helped popularize the new game by writing books on how to play and coach the game as well as some 250 articles that appeared in such widely circulated national magazines as *Harper's Weekly* and *Outlook*. As but one example of his flair for public relations, in 1889 Camp personally selected the first "All-American" team and did so each year until his death in 1925. That initial team comprised 11 players all of whom played for Princeton, Harvard, Columbia, and Yale, but by the early 1900s Camp's annual selections included standouts from Midwestern powerhouses such as Chicago, Wisconsin, Michigan, and Minnesota.

Born to middle-class parents and raised in New Haven, Camp was already well known locally as a skilled teenage rugby and baseball player before he first took the field for Yale in 1876. By the time he was a junior he had been elected football captain, and he immediately began to implement concepts that he would develop and refine throughout his lifetime. Essentially, Camp sought ways to encourage synchronized team play over the individual skills and spontaneous action that occurred in soccer and rugby. Over the years, as captain, team advisor, occasional coach, rules maker, author, and lecturer, Camp spearheaded the creation of a game in which the players became pawns controlled by the coach.

Camp became a successful business executive as president of a New Haven clock factory, and was an unabashed admirer of the "time-and-motion" theories of scientific management and production analysis being preached by engineering/manufacturing guru Frederick Winslow Taylor. Just as Camp utilized the efficiency concepts of "Taylorism" in his clock factory, he also applied them to the game of football. As he wrote in his *The Book of Football*,

> the object must be to use each man to the full extent of his capacity without exhausting any. To do this scientifically involves placing men in such position in the field that each may perform the work for which he is best fitted, and yet not be forced to do any of the work toward which his qualifications and training do not point.[1]

Throughout his career, Camp emphasized such telling phrases as "scientific planning" and "strategy and tactics." Essentially, he wanted to create a game in which chance and spontaneity were reduced by rules requiring team discipline and organized patterns of play. This was what he called "scientific foot ball." Players came to be viewed merely as cogs in an organized human machine, doing what industrial manager Camp liked to call the "work" of football.[2]

After his playing days ended, Camp continued to advise the team even as he developed his business career. He never held a position analogous to that of today's professional "coach." Instead, he served as an informal advisor to the team captain, occasionally showing up at team practices but for the most part relying upon his wife to report on practice results. He regularly met with team leaders to suggest strategies for the upcoming game. Between 1876, when he led Yale to its first football victory as a running back, and 1909 when he stepped away from his advisory position due to demands of business (and his declining influence on the evolving game), Yale lost only 14 games.[3]

Camp's lasting influence was as rules maker. During the formative years of the game, he was the dominant member of the Intercollegiate Football Rules Committee. His concepts were often insightful, if not brilliant. As he often said, his emphasis was upon "method not men," by which he meant that the game was best played when each member of the team carried out specific responsibilities as part of a larger whole. His views mirrored innovations in American industry, where intricate systems of manufacturing and distribution were being implemented in factories. Just as manufacturing executives wanted to leave nothing to chance in their factories and mills, where each worker had a specific assignment in the production process, so too did Camp seek to reduce the spontaneity of the game and the uncertainty of free (or "open") play so that the coach could effectively control the flow of the game.

Even during his playing days, Camp was thinking about the larger issues of the game. As team captain in 1878, he first proposed the reduction in team size from 15 to 11, a reform that was soon implemented. In 1880, his proposal to eliminate the rugby-type "scrum" was adopted. Instead of teams gaining possession after the referee tossed the ball into a frenzied melee of players, Camp introduced the concepts of the kickoff and the line of scrimmage. Originally, the team in possession of the ball retained it unless it was fumbled or punted away, or a field goal or touchdown was scored. After a fiasco in the 1881 Princeton–Yale game, when each team merely downed the ball throughout the entire two halves (both teams believed that a 0–0 tie would give them the championship), Camp introduced the concept that a team could retain possession only if it advanced the ball 5 yards in three "fairs" (a term later changed to "down"). This fundamental change in the rules led to the necessity of marking the field at 5 yard intervals, leading to comments that the playing field looked like a "gridiron."[4]

These innovations produced precisely what Camp sought: a much less spontaneous and more controlled game in which players became instruments for carrying out their coach's strategies. Consequently, there soon emerged the revolutionary concept of scripted plays in which each player on offense had a particular role to play. In 1888, Camp introduced a rules change that proved to be of major import. His new rule made it permissible to tackle the ball carrier below the waist, a change that Camp correctly believed would reduce wide-open running plays around the end of the line because it would lessen the ability of agile runners to avoid being brought down in the open field. With tackling below the waist in effect, what little "wide-open" play that existed gave way to a careful, methodical game that placed primary emphasis upon what was called "mass momentum play" – which meant a heavy concentration of struggling and slugging players in the center of the line. In an effort to grind out the necessary 5 yards in three attempts without fumbling, teams tended to

concentrate upon moving the ball forward by sheer brute force. Players closed ranks, often interlocking their arms, and pushed and pulled the ball carrier forward through similarly massed defensive players.[5] Significantly, Camp's rules prohibited the throwing of the ball by a running back to a teammate downfield, although backward tosses (called "laterals") were permitted. The introduction of the forward pass in 1906 was cause for great controversy because it created in the view of proponents of mass momentum play an undesirable element of uncertainty.

"Mass momentum" play reached its apex in 1892, when Harvard introduced the "flying wedge" formation against a surprised Yale team. The play was designed so that the offensive players lined up several yards behind the line of scrimmage in a V-shaped formation and simultaneously rushed toward one stationary defense lineman. When this mass of closely knit players neared the line of scrimmage, the center snapped the ball to a running back inside the wedge. The resulting collision with a stationary, isolated lineman produced many a concussion, broken bone, or worse. "What a grand play!" a *New York Times* reporter enthused. "A half ton of bone and muscle coming into collision with a man weighing 160 or 170 pounds."[6] The flying wedge lasted only one season

Figure 3.1 This typical formation employed by the 1893 Yale football team illustrates the theory of mass momentum advocated by Walter Camp. Rules permitted the linking of arms and the pushing and pulling of the ball carrier. Widespread criticism regarding injuries produced by this style of play led to major rules modifications in 1906 that included the forward pass. *Yale University Archives*

before the outcry against its brutality led to its being declared illegal by Camp's rules committee in 1894. Nonetheless, for the growing band of critics of the game, the short-lived flying wedge became a convenient symbol of the violence now associated with the game. Although many criticized the brutal play, others found it reassuring that American college students were up to the challenge of rugged physical combat. In an age when Social Darwinism, with its emphasis upon "survival of the fittest," was influencing public policy and academic inquiry, the game became a symbol of a resurgent national strength and virility. One observer said football "furnishes good ideals of courageous manhood." Or, as the president of Notre Dame, John Cavanaugh, commented, he would prefer to see his students suffer "a broken collar bone occasionally than to see them dedicated to croquet." After the University of Pennsylvania won a hard-fought Thanksgiving Day game against Columbia, played in a cold rain and a driving wind that made the field "a quagmire of ice-cold mud," the team physician was effusive in his praise: "Those frozen eleven, purple, shivering, chattering players" were to be praised because "every one of them loves manliness and courage."[7]

Even with the abolition of the flying wedge, the game remained particularly dangerous. Newspapers sometimes printed a "hospital list" of major injuries as part of their game reports. Concussions became routine as players collided at full speed without benefit of helmet or padding; most players took to letting their hair grow long as a means of providing some natural protection, but it was a sign of one's manliness not to wear a leather "head harness" after they were introduced at the turn of the twentieth century. (Curiously, it was not until 1939 that NCAA rules actually required the wearing of a helmet.)[8] Although athletes of a century ago were well conditioned, they were much smaller than today's players. Seldom did even the largest of linemen weigh over 180 pounds, and most running backs weighed between 130 and 160 pounds. Walter Eckersall, the famed All-American quarterback at Chicago who completed his eligibility in 1905, played at 135 pounds, and even as late as the 1924 season no member of the famed Notre Dame "Four Horsemen" backfield weighed over 165 pounds.

Mass momentum play resulted in a game in which injuries were more or less commonplace and deaths not all that uncommon. The president of Cornell University, Andrew Dickson White, denounced the game as a "vestige of barbarity," and Harvard president Charles Eliot caustically identified the problem as being "deliberately planned and deliberately maintained": that is, deaths and injuries resulted not by accident but from young men playing a violent game *according* to the rules. By permitting tackling below the waist, unprotected heads were thrust into hard-pumping knees. With the rules permitting teammates to push, pull, or even catapult running backs through or over the line, the emphasis upon raw strength was magnified and the potential for serious injury high.[9]

By the mid 1890s, the game having spread rapidly across the country, several college and high school players died each year. These deaths were widely reported by newspapers, producing a national controversy over the merits of the game that lasted for more than a decade. Although the rules permitted rough play, critics were also correct in their assertion that referees (often poorly trained for their task) were reluctant to issue penalties. With 22 players concentrated at the line of scrimmage, slugging, biting, kneeing, and gouging opponents was commonplace. Fistfights often disrupted play, and it was not unusual for police to have to intervene during a game to restore order. Football clearly was no place for the faint of heart, and many coaches reputedly taught tactics to "take out" opposing players. In 1893, President Grover Cleveland, having studied a report on the injury list at the two military academies, canceled the 1893 Army–Navy game. Well into the new century, the ongoing debate over the violence inherent in the game waxed and waned, depending upon the annual death rate.[10]

From the earliest days, it was evident that the game was played by young men intent upon one goal: victory. Critics asked the fundamental question: if the game supposedly built character and encouraged clean play and good sportsmanship as its advocates argued, why were referees required? If the game was played by sportsmen, why did the rules prohibit kicking, biting, or even choking one's opponent? Harvard president Charles Eliot, one of the game's consistent critics, never received an adequate response to his 1892 comments that the physical nature of the game encouraged devious and dirty play, or as he elegantly put it, the use of "tricks, surprises and habitual violations of the rules ... [that are] inordinate and excessive [in] an unwholesome desire of victory by whatever means." Three years later, Eliot was even less charitable to a game that he believed perverted the essential mission of his university. In a commentary to his alumni on "the evils of intercollegiate sports," he singled out football because it "grows worse and worse as regards foul and violent play, and the number and gravity of injuries the players suffer."[11]

Football Moves West

Despite its critics on and off campus, football continued to grow in popularity. During the 1890s, it spread rapidly to colleges throughout the Midwest and the South. Even in the sparsely populated Far West, the game caught on at such small institutions as the state universities of Idaho, Montana, Arizona, Oregon, and Nevada, although Stanford and California were recognized as the dominant Western football powers. Colleges large and small took up the game in response to student demands and the game's growing popularity. By the early twentieth century the dominance of Eastern elite schools was being threatened by powerful "Western" teams, namely the Universities of Michigan, Minnesota, and Chicago.

There is a timeless joke told by college presidents that their primary goal is to build an academic reputation for their institutions worthy of the stature of the football teams. The origins of that wry comment probably rest with the University of Chicago and its ambitious founding president, William Rainey Harper. As a Yale professor, Harper had watched Amos Alonzo Stagg perform as a star end for the undefeated Yale Eleven of 1888. Harper knew Stagg to be a deeply religious individual, someone who had considered a career in the ministry. Deciding against that option, Stagg became an instructor and coach at the YMCA school in Massachusetts, where students were trained to foster Christianity through the medium of sports. Stagg – named by Walter Camp in his inaugural All-American team of 1889 – was the epitome of the "Muscular Christian."[12] This hard-driving young man became one of the first professional college football coaches, and worked continuously at his profession as a head coach until he was 83 years old, and then as an assistant until his mid 90s.

In order to hire Stagg, who had other offers, Harper lured his new coach with a salary comparable to that of senior professors and deans. He even granted his coach an associate professorship with academic tenure before he set foot on campus. In making this appointment, Harper showed his fellow presidents the way to circumvent student control of athletics: he created the Department of Physical Culture and Athletics, one of the first of its kind in American higher education, and named Stagg as department head. This decision created a friendly academic environment to which Stagg could recruit top-flight prospective athletes.

Harper believed that a great university required a great football team. "The University of Chicago believes in football," he said with emphasis in 1895. "We shall encourage it here." Writing to his new coach, Harper told Stagg, "I want you to develop teams which we can send around the country and knock out all the colleges." In a prescient comment about the importance of financial and other incentives necessary to attract to the Chicago campus the quality of athlete necessary to accomplish that objective, he added, "We will give them a palace car and a vacation too."[13]

Although the football program was theoretically placed under the control of a faculty board, Stagg implemented his building program with little interference from the faculty. It did not take Stagg long to assemble the powerful football team that his president envisioned. From the beginning, some faculty carped about the dubious academic qualifications of his athletes, many of whom took their courses in the Department of Physical Culture. As director of that department, Stagg determined their eligibility to play football. Whenever his authority or his program was challenged, he successfully appealed to Harper for support. After Harper's premature death in 1905, Stagg used his many connections with alumni, boosters, and wealthy Chicago businessmen – such as the legendary meat-packer Walter Swift and department store magnate Marshall Field – to beat back efforts that threatened his empire.

It did not take the aggressive, innovative young coach long to demonstrate the public relations potential that a big-time football program possessed. At the end of his second season, Stagg created a stir throughout the Windy City when he brought in the University of Michigan team to play his Maroons on Thanksgiving Day. The "big game" had arrived in Chicago. President Harper seized upon this opportunity to invite many prestigious citizens (and potential donors) to be his guests at the game. A series of receptions and dinners was arranged around the spectacle. "For the last week nothing but football has been discussed at the University on the South Side," one newspaper commented.[14] Michigan proved to be the dominant team in the West as the Wolverines trounced Stagg's inexperienced squad 28–10. But that loss did nothing to dampen football spirit in Chicago; it only served to increase interest. The following year, Chicago fielded a powerful team that capped a successful season with a much-publicized train trip to the West Coast to play Stanford that included the ambience of an elegantly appointed palace car (as Harper had promised).

Stagg relentlessly built his program. He received a donation of land from Chicago mercantile giant Marshall Field upon which there arose a 25,000-seat stadium. President Harper's dream of football putting his young institution on the front pages of Chicago newspapers culminated in 1905. On Thanksgiving Day, two undefeated teams met at Marshall Field before an overflow crowd of 27,000. Michigan came into the game reputed to be one of the nation's top teams. Indeed, the Wolverines were on a 55-game winning streak that resulted from the innovative coaching (and aggressive recruiting) of Fielding Yost. During his first season of 1901, "Hurry Up" Yost's squad outscored its opponents by the staggering figure of 550–0 and had annihilated Stanford 49–0 in the first Rose Bowl game. Coming into the big Thanksgiving game in 1905, Yost's undefeated teams had overwhelmed their opponents by 2,821 points to 42, but the quality of Stagg's program was on display as the Maroons won the game 2–0 on a fourth-quarter safety.[15]

For the next two decades, Stagg continued to field powerful teams, but ultimately his program fell on hard times. As late as 1924, Chicago remained a national power; that fall the Maroons tied rival Illinois 21–21 in an epic contest that featured the exciting play of Illinois running back Harold "Red" Grange, the famed "Galloping Ghost" of All-American fame, and captured the Western Conference (Big Ten) championship. Stagg was pleased that a new attendance record was set and he began pushing plans to expand the stadium to a double-decked structure of 60,000 seats. However, his program soon fell into a sharp decline. Faculty criticism of his program had intensified, and he no longer had a sympathetic president for support. Competing programs in the Chicago area (Illinois, Northwestern, Notre Dame) drew away fans, as did the professional Chicago Bears; perhaps most telling was that the administration approved stringent entrance and eligibility requirements that made it increasingly difficult for Stagg to attract top athletes.[16]

The result was a string of losing seasons that began in 1925, and the number of lopsided losses mounted. Stagg recognized that the university's new president, Robert Maynard Hutchins, was unenthusiastic about football. Burdened with nine consecutive losing seasons, and embarrassed by defeats to teams he had once dominated, the 71-year-old Stagg resigned after the 1933 season and moved to the College of the Pacific where he coached for 12 more years, producing several winning seasons. In 1939, in the wake of continued losing seasons and a humiliating 85–0 pasting by Michigan, President Hutchins announced that the governing board had approved his recommendation to drop football as an intercollegiate sport. In 1942, the team locker rooms at Marshall Field became the location of a secret laboratory that produced the first successful controlled nuclear chain reaction, a critical scientific breakthrough that contributed to the development of the atomic bomb. The stadium was later demolished to make way for a library, and in 1969 a modest football program was reinstated and the University has since that time competed in Divisions III, the lowest rung of the NCAA hierarchy that does not permit the granting of athletic scholarships.

Football as Spectacle

By the turn of the new century, large crowds had become routine at elite programs. Increased interest led to the enclosure of fields, the construction of permanent seating, and (naturally) the selling of tickets. Attendance ranged between 20,000 and 40,000 for major contests. The surge in circulation of daily newspapers contributed significantly to football's growing popularity. Aggressive editors sought dramatic stories that would sell newspapers and enable them to outpace their competitors. As horse racing and baseball seasons were coming to an end in September, editors lacked much in the way of sports to report, and they turned to the emerging sport of college football. To read accounts of the games of this period is to be transported into a romanticized world of heroic players, brilliant coaches, and superhuman accomplishment. Large headlines proclaimed the amazing deeds of bigger-than-life players, and reporters wrote breathtaking accounts of epic gridiron battles. Important games between major rivals were reported on the front pages of the newspapers, complete with pen drawings depicting some of the action. Michael Oriard observes in his study of the early years of football that "by the mid-1890s, both the quantity and quality of the football coverage in the daily papers in New York, Philadelphia, and Boston were staggering: front-page, full-page, several-page accounts of big games, accompanied by sometimes dozens of sensationalized illustrations." Oriard concludes, "The late nineteenth-century daily newspaper 'created' college football to an even greater degree [than television during the 1950s], transforming an extracurricular activity into a national spectacle."[17]

Newspapers also took note of the social aspects of the game, reporting on famous persons in attendance, even describing the clothing worn by socially prominent ladies at the exclusive receptions and parties they attended before and after the game. Hard-charging rival newspaper publishers Joseph Pulitzer and William Randolph Hearst created separate sports sections for their New York newspapers, the *World* and the *Journal*, and staffed them with specialized reporters and columnists in a furious drive to expand readership. The extensive coverage of football stimulated increased newspaper sales, which boosted attendance, which in turn created a demand for even more newspaper coverage. Well before 1900, football had become more than a game played by a few college students; it had become a popular spectator sport. Played on Saturday afternoons, the game produced a public spectacle and a unique social setting that captured the public imagination.

The ripple effect was staggering. Almost overnight, important traditions were established. Organized student cheering sections were formed, and cleverly scripted cheers rang out along the sidelines. Sometimes students were coerced into participation. Prior to a big game with Indiana in 1901, the *South Bend Tribune* reported that on the Notre Dame campus "rooter preparations are on a strong scale. Every student will be there whether he likes it or not and take part in organized cheering."[18] To be elected a "cheer leader" became a mark of distinction, almost as important as being a star player on the varsity. At some institutions, separate seating sections were established for men and women; on many campuses, only men could be elected to the cheer squad (a tradition that only slowly broke down in the decades following the First World War). Pep bands added to the festivities, and soon each school had its own "fight song"; "On Wisconsin," "Across the Field" (Ohio State), "Hail to the Victors" (Michigan), and "The Notre Dame Victory March" are among many such memorable inspiring tunes written during football's formative years.

The tradition of homecoming was also established during this period. Fearing a slender turnout for the big game against archrival Kansas University scheduled in the small college town of Columbia, coach C. L. Brewer of the University of Missouri in 1911 issued an urgent public invitation to all alumni to "come back home, Tigers" to cheer on his team against the Jayhawks. Much to his surprise, a record-setting overflow crowd of 10,000 showed up to watch a hard-fought 3–3 tie. Shortly thereafter, the Missouri alumni director reported on the benefits of the event to a convention of his peers, and within a few years homecoming had become a signal autumn event on campuses across the country. Elaborate week-long events were held, including parades, banquets, songfests, fraternity and sorority parties, decorated dormitories, alumni luncheons, and bonfire rallies. All of these events were capped off with the Saturday afternoon football game and the big dance in the campus gymnasium that evening. University officials recognized that homecoming week provided an effective way to maintain sentimental connections between alumni and their alma maters.[19] It also helped if the home team won the homecoming game.

Football thus became more than a game, providing an important connection between students, alumni, community leaders, and the university. For prominent businessmen and politicians, it was considered advantageous to become recognized as a major "booster" of the local team (no matter if one was an alumnus or not), a supporter who contributed generously to the athletic fund and bought a block of tickets to distribute to business or political associates. For their wives, it was important to be seen at games and to host pre- and post-game social events. For students, it provided an exciting diversion from studies and a focal point for student social events.

Other parts of the unfolding spectacle naturally fell into place. For example, there was the matter of the color of uniforms that would distinguish one team from another. Student bodies held contests to select school colors, nearly all of which have remained unchanged to the present day. Similarly, students adopted various mascots or nicknames by which their team would be known. Ferocious animals were among the most popular (the Tigers of Missouri, Louisiana State, and Princeton; the Bulldogs of Georgia, Yale, and Mississippi State; the Wildcats of Kentucky, Northwestern, and Arizona; the Bears of Maine, Baylor, and California). Other schools sought to establish an identity with their state's heritage (the Tennessee Volunteers; the Ohio State Buckeyes; the Virginia Cavaliers; the Tar Heels of North Carolina; the Indiana Hoosiers; the Texas Longhorns; the Sooners of Oklahoma; the Rebels of Ole Miss; the Mountaineers of West Virginia; the Florida Gators). Less imaginative team monikers were derived from school colors: Alabama's Crimson Tide, the Green Wave of Tulane, and the Crimson of Harvard.

Conversely, some mascots were simply puzzling or even humorous: the Ephs of Williams College named after its founder Ephraim Williams; the Sage Brushers and/or Sage Hens of Nevada (changed to a more ferocious Wolf Pack by a student vote in 1921, although no wolves lived in the region); the Blue Hens of Delaware; the Golden Gophers of Minnesota; the Bug Eaters of the University of Nebraska (later renamed Cornhuskers in a nod to the state's dominant agricultural economy). Several land grant institutions with prominent agricultural colleges naturally became the Aggies (Texas A&M, New Mexico State, Oklahoma State College, University of California–Davis). As a reflection of the widely accepted racial stereotypes popular at the time, many institutions opted for the ferocious imagery of Native Americans: Miami (Ohio) Redskins, Fighting Illini of Illinois, Fighting Sioux of North Dakota, Running Utes of Utah, Marquette Warriors, Florida State Seminoles, Central Michigan Chippewas, St John's Redmen, and the Stanford Indians. The contentious issue of such mascots being demeaning to Native Americans would not appear until the latter years of the twentieth century. Somewhat curiously, Notre Dame adopted what easily could have been considered a disparaging ethnic slur: the "Fighting Irish." Murray Sperber notes in his history of Notre Dame football that the name had been widely bandied about by journalists for years before the campus community enthusiastically embraced it in the 1920s.[20]

Football in Crisis

In 1884, a New York reporter included this vivid description of the Yale–Princeton game staged at the Polo Grounds: "The elevens hurl themselves together and build themselves in kicking, writhing heaps." Spectators cheered as they witnessed

> a general vision of threatening attitudes, fists shaken before noses, darting hither and thither, throttling, wrestling and the pitching of individuals headlong to earth … They saw real fighting, savage blows that drew blood, and falls that seemed as if they must crack all the bones and drive the life from those who sustained them.

Finally, there "came a crush about midway of the field. All the maddened giants of both teams were in it, and they lay there heaped, choking, kicking, gouging and howling."[21]

Considering the mayhem that characterized early play, it is surprising that football managed to survive as a game played on college campuses. Widespread social acceptance helped the game survive a major crisis that threatened its existence early in the twentieth century. Concerns about physical dangers to players became conflated with criticisms about a wide range of abuses concerning academic integrity. Some outspoken critics simply wanted the game driven off campus, while a larger number insisted upon major reforms on two fronts: changing (and enforcing) the rules to eliminate the dangerous mass momentum style of play, and establishing rigorous controls on player recruitment and assurances that only bona fide students took part.

The most prominent person in the reform movement was the president of Harvard, Charles Eliot. He was both deeply concerned about the violent nature of football and fearful that the heavy emphasis upon victory threatened the integrity of higher education. In his crusade to abolish the game, Eliot found allies among his own faculty and elsewhere, but he was ultimately thwarted by a combination of student support for the game and pressures from prominent alumni. Twice between 1886 and 1906, the Harvard faculty succeeded in abolishing the sport for single seasons, but the game's popularity eventually overcame on-campus opposition. One of the primary reasons Harvard eventually opted for reform and not abolition was that two of its major competitors, Yale and Princeton, continued to encourage the game's development and in so doing attracted to themselves considerable public support and the loyalty of wealthy contributors.

At Princeton, a popular political science professor and faculty leader, soon to become president of the university, used his considerable prestige on campus to promote the game. A devout Presbyterian who enthusiastically embraced the doctrines of Muscular Christianity, Professor Woodrow Wilson firmly believed that the game built character by teaching players important lessons about discipline, teamwork, perseverance, and dealing with adversity and pressure. In a telling comment about the repeated failure of Harvard to defeat Yale or Princeton, he once caustically observed that Harvard had instituted an academic program built around elective courses, which he said suggested a lack of rigor, organization, and discipline – particular ingredients he believed important to a successful football program. As Princeton's president between 1902 and 1910, Wilson was known upon occasion to leap out of the stands to lead cheers during games; as one historian has written of the man who would become president of the United States, "Wilson glorified victory, lambasted those who failed to support athletics, criticized the team's failures, and carped about victorious rivals."[22]

Eliot, who built Harvard into an academic powerhouse during his long tenure as president (1869–1909), was dedicated to the premise that the university was a place where academic values must be paramount. In his drive to make Harvard into the nation's preeminent private institution, he repeatedly confronted the negative influence of football, whose values he believed were a denial of all that his academic agenda sought to accomplish. In a highly publicized report released in late 1894, Eliot condemned the concept of an institution of higher learning becoming engaged in entertaining the public:

> The evils of the intercollegiate sports … continue without real redress and diminution. In particular the game of football grows worse and worse as regards foul and violent play, and the number and gravity of injuries which the players suffer. It has become perfectly clear that the game as now played is unfit for college use … The state of mind of the spectators at a hard-fought football match at Springfield, New York, or Philadelphia cannot but suggest the query how far these assemblages differ at heart from the throngs which enjoy the prize-fight, cock-fight, or bull-fight, or which in other centuries delighted in the sports of the Roman arena.[23]

Eliot viewed athletics through a Victorian prism that emphasized amateurism, fair play, sportsmanship, and character building. That football teams (and their professional "coaches") often employed dubious ways to win games – relying as he said upon "tricks, surprises and habitual violation of the rules" – indicated to him that the game did not encourage sportsmanship but in fact produced the opposite effect. Noting that some reformers wanted to increase the number of officials on the field from the current one or two, he sniffed:

> It is often said that by employing more men to watch the players, with authority to punish instantly infractions of the rules, foul and vicious playing could be stopped. The sufficient answer to this suggestion is that a game which needs to be so watched is not fit for genuine sportsmen.

And in a comment about the integrity or competence of game officials that would routinely resonate with partisan fans down to the present time, Eliot noted that "experience indicates that it would be hard to find trustworthy watchers."[24] Ultimately, Eliot believed the game diverted students from their primary role as scholars.[25] Eliot was also appalled by the number of serious injuries that occurred even when rules were enforced: "The rules of the game are at present such as to cause inevitably a large number of broken bones, sprains, and wrenches, even during trial or practice games played legitimately, and they also permit those who play with reckless violence or with shrewd violations of the rules to gain thereby great advantages."[26]

This is not to say that Eliot was opposed to all sports. He supported the playing of games that provided healthful exercise and wholesome recreation. Reflective of a widespread perception of the time, Eliot also believed that vigorous exercise and competition offered the college man "a new and effective motive for resisting all sins which weaken or corrupt the body" – that is, premarital sex.[27]

President Eliot's crusade failed to produce tangible results, but public discussion of the issues he raised grew in intensity in the early 1900s. Despite mounting criticism, football continued to grow in popularity, its proponents greatly outnumbering the critics. University administrators, taking due note of gate receipts being collected by student sponsors and aware of the public relations benefits that could accrue in terms of student recruitment, alumni relations, and fundraising, took control away from student groups, as athletic departments made their appearance on campus, complete with athletic directors, professional coaches, support staff, and annual budgets.

In 1905, the long-simmering debate over dangerous play came to a head. That year three college and 18 high school football players died, and 167 collegians suffered serious injuries. University of Chicago professor Shailer Mathews summarized the criticism when he denounced the game as "a social obsession – a boy-killing, education-prostituting, gladiatorial sport."[28] Despite a decade of mounting criticism and modest reforms, the game had changed very little from the notorious flying wedge era. It remained as violent as ever, with play concentrated along the line of scrimmage.

It was not without significance that one of the players who sustained a painful injury that season was the son of the president of the United States, Theodore Roosevelt, Jr. At just 5 feet 7 inches and 150 pounds, "Teedie" played on the line for the Harvard junior varsity; during a hard-fought game with Yale, he received a severely broken nose that required reconstructive surgery. Spectators reported that the Blues concentrated their attack at the president's son, who bravely held his ground; some said the Bulldogs concentrated their offense at Teedie's position because of his famous father, while others noted he was the smallest man on the Harvard line.[29]

His son's shattered nose focused the president's attention on the issue of rough play, something that had concerned him for years. The game of football – with its rigorous physical and psychological demands – naturally appealed to this rambunctious president who often spoke glowingly of those brave men who chose to demonstrate their mettle in the "arena." What seems to have bothered Roosevelt most about the state of the game were persistent reports of unsportsmanlike behavior, or what TR called "mucker play." The president appreciated the rugged nature of the game; his concern was that it be played fairly and by the rules. In letters to Walter Camp he expressed his fear that President Eliot was about to take a "foolish course" to eliminate football at Harvard. "I want to take up the football situation," he told Camp, "and try to get the game played on a thoroughly clean basis."[30]

Roosevelt had little argument with the aggressive physical nature of the game. His political conversations and correspondence were often punctuated with comments about "hitting the line hard" on behalf of a particular issue. Although it was widely believed that Roosevelt threatened to abolish the game if substantive reform did not occur, there is no evidence to support that contention. He had, in fact, no authority to force its abolition. What he did have at his command was his "bully pulpit" which he used to draw public attention to the issue of unnecessary rough play when he called a conference at the White House on October 9, 1905. He invited representatives from three major football schools – Harvard, Yale, and Princeton. The representatives readily agreed to cooperate in effecting reasonable rules changes and improving the quality of officiating. Roosevelt declared himself satisfied and considered the matter closed.[31]

A few weeks following the White House conference, however, the president once more became engaged in the issue: Teedie suffered his badly broken nose, and a particularly gruesome play occurred in the big game between Harvard and Yale. Crimson freshman Francis Burr called for a fair catch on a punt but was hit high and low by two Yale men, one of them smashing him in the nose. The blow unleashed a torrent of blood as Burr collapsed to the ground. The vicious hit received considerable national attention and drew negative comments about incompetent officiating from Roosevelt. That event, however, was soon overshadowed by the death of a Union College player who suffered a blow to the head in a game at New York University. Charles Eliot was moved to demand the end of football once more: "Deaths and injuries are not the strongest argument against football," he growled. "That cheating and brutality are profitable is the main evil."[32]

Football thus confronted a major crisis as the 1905 season came to a close. Columbia president Nicholas Butler announced the abolition of football despite angry protests from students, and the *Harvard Graduates' Magazine* vigorously attacked Yale for refusing to cooperate with Harvard's plans for reform, charging that an anti-academic "athletocracy" controlled the Yale campus. Another threat appeared on the Pacific Coast, where the presidents of California and Stanford abolished football and replaced it with the English game of rugby. Other universities and many high schools in Oregon, Nevada, and California followed suit, although there was little student and alumni enthusiasm and much dissatisfaction. The small population in the Western tier of states tended to mute the impact of this threat to the game that had originated on the East Coast, but it was not lost on the game's defenders.

A combination of pressure – an agitated occupant of the White House, fear that more institutions would abolish the game, irritation with Walter Camp's influence on the rules committee, and general public outrage – prompted a series of meetings of concerned coaches and administrators. In late 1905, the National Inter-Collegiate Athletic Association was formed and its leaders immediately set about revising the rules of football. Their target was the control of the rules committee by Walter Camp and his cronies. Assuming leadership of the reformers was Captain Palmer Pierce, athletic manager of West Point, who later said, "The game of football was under a special fire of criticism," because under Camp's leadership it had been controlled by "a self-constituted, self-perpetuating and irresponsible body, which had degraded a once noble sport to the plane of a gladiatorial contest."[33]

Captain Pierce had a strong ally in Bill Reid of Harvard, and many younger coaches were anxious to create a more exciting brand of football in order to attract more spectators. They advocated a more "open" game that would emphasize innovative offensive tactics rather than the power run into the middle of the line preferred by Camp. The shrewd Reid used the rhetoric of his president to underscore the fact that the game would be abolished at Harvard if substantive reforms were not enacted; it was widely feared that the withdrawal of Harvard from the field of play would prompt other universities to follow suit. The result was that the new rules book made it illegal for teammates to push or pull the ball carrier through the defense; required the offense to begin each play with a minimum of seven men on the line of scrimmage (to eliminate linemen from lining up several yards behind the line of scrimmage and gaining momentum before crashing into a defensive player);

and eliminated the interlocking of arms by blockers. To encourage the use of more deceptive running plays in the open field, they lengthened the distance required to make a first down from 5 to 10 yards. Most significantly, the committee introduced the forward pass. Two years later, as but another means of encouraging the forward pass, the committee required that the ball be "tightly inflated" and changed its shape to make it more elongated so it could be thrown further and with greater accuracy. The committee also outlawed one of the major sources of excessive violence: the pushing or pulling of a ball carrier through the line by teammates. The ball carrier would now have to rely upon his teammates' skill as blockers.[34]

A new and exciting era was at hand. In the ensuing years coaches began to emphasize speed, deception, timing, and precisely executed plays designed to make long yardage. Emphasis upon raw power was reduced, although definitely not eliminated. Annual rules changes continued: the length of the field was established at 100 yards, with 10 yard end zones added (to encourage passes into touchdown territory); the value of a touchdown was increased to six points; and the extra-point kick after a touchdown was introduced. Protective headgear and shoulder padding were added to team uniforms, and officiating became more standardized with major conferences requiring training, rules testing, certification and evaluation of the performance of officials.

Most coaches approached the new rules gingerly. They were reluctant to abandon time-tested techniques, but innovative coaches received favorable publicity with the introduction of crowd-pleasing offensive innovations that opened up the game. The impact of the new rules was forcefully demonstrated in two games that involved the powerful team from the Academy at West Point. Near the close of the 1912 season, the Cadets hosted the upstart Carlisle Indian School team coached by Glenn "Pop" Warner. The game was played just 22 years after the US Army slaughtered an estimated 150 to 200 Lakota Sioux at Wounded Knee in South Dakota. Warner did not need a pep talk to inspire his team; as quarterback Gus Welch said later, "He reminded the boys that it was the fathers and grandfathers of these Army players who fought the Indians. That was enough." The much smaller Indians came into the game 10–0–1, and their offense that emphasized speed and finesse averaged nearly 50 points a game. The Cadets had only one loss, a 6–0 squeaker to Yale. Warner, arguably the most innovative and creative coach of his generation, had introduced a no-huddle offense and new formations that sought to take advantage of his squad's speed and lack of size. Running back Jim Thorpe, fresh off his summer Olympic triumph, was but one of many quality athletes that Warner had at his disposal. Newspaper accounts gave the Indians little chance against the powerful Cadets, and tended to emphasize that the game would be a renewal of the deadly battles in the American West just one generation removed. "Indians to Battle with Soldiers," the *New York Times* headlined. This time the soldiers, led by halfback Dwight Eisenhower and All-American tackle Leland Devore, got ambushed. "The shifting, puzzling, and dazzling attack of the Carlisle Indians had the Cadets bordering on panic," the *New York Tribune* reported of the convincing 27–6 Carlisle triumph.[35]

Warner's team had demonstrated the advantages of speed, innovative formations, and running plays. The following year the Cadets got a bitter lesson about an attack through the air. In October of 1913, the University of Notre Dame from South Bend, Indiana, now recognized as a rising football program under coach Jesse Harper, traveled east and stunned

the football world when it upset a powerful Army team 35–13 by using the forward pass combination of quarterback Gus Dorias and end Knute Rockne to befuddle the Cadets. These two athletes had spent the previous summer working at Cedar Point resort along Lake Erie perfecting their pass-and-catch timing on a wide expanse of sandy beach. In the wake of this game, coaches increasingly incorporated the forward pass into their offenses, and fans responded enthusiastically. The potentials of a completed forward pass or a run around end for a long gain produced a new level of excitement at games. Touchdowns could occur on any play from any place on the field. Stories of entire games spent with both teams pounding away at each other in the middle of the line became a thing of the past.[36]

Despite the rules changes, the game remained a game of controlled violence. Memories of the crisis of 1905 soon dimmed. When eight college players died in 1909, no concerted effort to abolish football re-emerged. Between 1910 and 1950, more than 500 high school and college players would die from football injuries, but the existence of the game was never again seriously threatened. By the time the United States entered the Great War in 1917, football had become firmly entrenched on college campuses as an integral part of American higher education.

Figure 3.2 The trend away from mass momentum play received a boost from the offensive play of the Carlisle Indians coached by the innovative Glenn "Pop" Warner. Carlisle emphasized speed and deception rather than raw power. This rare photograph is of the 1912 team that stunned the powerful West Point team in a confrontation the *New York Times* anticipated with the headline, "Indians to Battle Soldiers." Lined up in the backfield at the far right is the legendary athlete Jim Thorpe. *Cumberland County Historical Society, Carlisle, Pennsylvania, photo A. A. Line*

4

The Modernization of American Sports, 1865–1920

Organized sports became an increasingly important part of American life in the decades following the Civil War. Employers found team sports to be useful in controlling worker attitudes and behavior, and politicians and social workers believed organized play a useful tool to help "Americanize" immigrant children. Religious leaders believed sports properly played would create better Christians, while newspapers used college and professional sports as a means of reaching wider audiences. Affluent urbanites in need of physical activity were attracted to new private clubs that offered gymnasiums and swimming pools, as well as to country clubs that offered golf, tennis, swimming, and equestrian activities.

Between 1860 and 1920, the United States entered a new era that was shaped by investment banks and corporations that capitalized upon a wide range of scientific and technological advances. Driven by heavy immigration from Europe and Asia, the population increased from 31 million to 120 million. Far-reaching advances in manufacturing and transportation contributed to the spectacular growth of cities. By 1920, over half of the American people lived in urban areas. On the farm, innovations in planting and harvesting equipment as well as advances in crop and animal science meant that the average farmer produced 15 times the amount of food or fiber in 1920 than his predecessor did 50 years earlier. This agricultural revolution drove marginal farmers off the land and into the towns and cities in search of employment. Those who remained on the land were caught up in a new and often baffling economy controlled by central banks, commodities exchanges, foreign competition, and national railroad systems. America left its agrarian past behind and entered a more complex modern age. As a consequence of this far-reaching economic transformation, American sports took on a distinctly new look.

Sports in American Life: A History, Second Edition. Richard O. Davies.
© 2012 John Wiley & Sons, Inc. Published 2012 by John Wiley & Sons, Inc.

Prizefighting Enters the Mainstream

Prizefighting fell into sharp decline in the years after the Civil War because public officials felt the heat of Victorian moralists. Offended by the brutality of the sport, and concerned about its apparent encouragement of disorderly behavior, consumption of alcoholic beverages, and gambling, these stern guardians of public morality demanded enforcement of anti-prizefighting laws. By the 1870s, however, men's athletic clubs began providing instruction in "the manly art of self-defense" and conducted "public exhibitions" under the Marquis of Queensberry rules that required padded gloves, 3 minute rounds, 10 second knockouts, a limit on the number of rounds, and the abolition of wrestling, hitting below the belt, holding, and eye gouging. Boxing consequently began a comeback that would lead to its legalization in some states by the 1920s.

Prizefighting received a major boost when a young entrepreneur recently arrived from Ireland purchased the struggling *National Police Gazette* in 1877. The brash Richard Kyle Fox increased circulation by featuring stories emphasizing sin and sex. Drawings of sensuous women often appeared on page one. Printed on pink newsprint, the *National Police Gazette* became known as "the Bible of the Barber Shop." It was seen everywhere men gathered – saloons, hotel lobbies, pool halls, tobacco shops, gambling dens, barber shops. Fox turned the weekly into one of the great financial success stories of the publications industry. In so doing he set a new low for the lewd and bizarre, never hesitating to exploit racist and nativist themes along with the standard fare of sex and crime.[1]

Fox also relentlessly promoted prizefighting. In part, he did so because he enjoyed bedeviling ministers and social reformers, but he recognized heavy coverage of "the manly art" increased readership. In 1880, circulation jumped from 150,000 to 400,000 when the *Gazette* provided heavy coverage of the Joe Goss–Paddy Ryan fight. Fox even became a promoter of prizefights, creating six weight classifications and providing handsome championship belts for each. He sponsored bouts, negotiated with fighters and their managers, challenged anti-boxing laws in the courts, and imported pugilistic talent from Europe. His reporters cranked out an endless stream of enthusiastic accounts of major prizefights accompanied by artists' impressions of action in the ring.

Fox's crusade on behalf of boxing became intricately entwined with the career of the "Boston Strong Boy," John L. Sullivan. Throughout the 1880s, Fox carried on a lively feud with the popular heavyweight, belittling his pugilistic ability while futilely promoting one unsuccessful challenger after another who might topple the popular champion. Although Fox feigned personal animosity toward Sullivan, he knew that the public quarrel sold newspapers. Fox's petulance helped create America's first sports "star."

Legend has it that the feud began one spring evening in 1881 in Harry Hill's Saloon, a popular New York City watering hole for the sporting crowd. As Fox took his seat, he noticed a boisterous group at a nearby table where the well-known heavy drinker John L. Sullivan was surrounded by an entourage and a cluster of empty whiskey bottles. Fox reportedly said to the waiter, "Tell Sullivan to come over here. I want to talk to him." Well into his cups, Sullivan loudly retorted so everyone in the club could hear, "You tell Fox, that if he wants to see me he can goddamn well come over to my table." Fox subsequently spent the next decade attempting to teach the ill-mannered Bostonian a lesson by finding someone who could defeat him in the ring.[2]

Fox may have been truly offended by Sullivan's boorish behavior, but he also saw in the charismatic Irish brawler an adversary made in heaven. Just a month after the confrontation, he sent reporters to cover the championship fight between Sullivan and a longshoreman by the name of John Flood. In order to avoid the authorities, this fight was held on a barge floating in the Hudson River. Sullivan easily defeated his opponent and Fox was soon promoting a new challenger in the person of Paddy Ryan. He posted a $2,500 purse on Ryan's behalf and then trumpeted the challenger's prowess. No prizefight had previously received such buildup as the *Gazette* featured a steady stream of reports from secret training camps. The fight was scheduled for New Orleans but was moved to Mississippi City when Louisiana authorities threatened to arrest the participants.[3]

Fox prematurely dubbed Ryan the "Champion of America," but Sullivan easily dispatched his opponent in minutes with his "sledgehammer smashes." The best Fox's writers could report was that Ryan had demonstrated "vigor and gameness." Sullivan knocked Ryan senseless in round 9. "When Sullivan struck me," a woeful Paddy later said, "I thought that a telephone pole had been shoved against me endways." Disappointed, perhaps, but undaunted, Fox recognized that the man he despised was nonetheless his meal ticket, and put up $5,000 for a rematch (which produced a similar result). Fox had commissioned a glittering diamond-studded championship belt for the winner, but Sullivan dismissed it as "a dog collar" and set out on an eight-month carnival tour during which he fought any local challenger willing to take his chances for a $1,000 prize if he lasted four rounds against the champion. Few did.[4]

Determined to unseat the "The Great John L.," Fox came up with yet another challenger. Jake Kilrain had defeated several prominent fighters and seemed to be Fox's man. When Sullivan refused to agree to a match, Fox proclaimed that Sullivan had forfeited his crown and Kilrain was the new champion. Sullivan left for a six-month exhibition tour of Europe, and upon his return went on a prolonged drinking and eating binge that saw him balloon up from his 195 pound fighting weight to 240 pounds. His health deteriorated, and the *Gazette* reported that Sullivan was at death's door while simultaneously goading him with barbs that he was using his illness to avoid Kilrain. Finally, Sullivan agreed to a fight. Fox's reporters provided the "advance dope" from the training camps, much of which highlighted Sullivan's poor condition and Kilrain's strength and endurance.[5]

The nation's attention was glued to the upcoming confrontation as the melodrama unfolded in comic proportions. Louisiana authorities proclaimed their intention to arrest and prosecute the fighters and promoters, and the state police of Alabama, Mississippi, Louisiana, and Texas went on alert. For two months, promoters sold tickets even though they did not know where the fight would be held. On July 7, 1889, the day before the fight, Mississippi sawmill operator Charles Rich had a crew assemble a makeshift wooden grandstand of newly cut pine in a clearing on his heavily wooded 30,000 acre spread near the town of Richburg. Promoters had three chartered trains at the ready, and when they gave the word ticket-holders piled aboard and headed for parts unknown.

The original plan was for the showdown to occur shortly after dawn in order to avoid the oppressive heat, but the start was delayed several hours to permit arriving fans to take their places on the freshly cut boards that were now oozing pitch in the hot sun. By fight time, the temperature neared 100 degrees. A future mayor of New Orleans, John Fitzpatrick, served as referee, and precisely at 10:13 a.m. he drew a line in the dirt and called the fighters to scratch. What would be the last bare-knuckle championship fight thus commenced. It proved to be an epic struggle. Within the first 15 seconds Kilrain tossed Sullivan to the ground, and it became evident that his strategy was to take advantage of the perception that Sullivan had not recovered from his illness. Kilrain intended to wear him down under the hot sun that poured down on the makeshift ring. Round 4 lasted 15 minutes and revealed that it was Kilrain who was not in the best of condition as he absorbed a barrage of powerful blows. Kilrain bravely persevered as the rounds went by, absorbing a terrific pounding but somehow managing to prevent Sullivan from landing a knockout blow. By round 30, Kilrain had to be carried back to his corner after each round and pushed out to the scratch line when Fitzpatrick shouted "time." During the 30 second intervals between rounds, Sullivan gulped down copious amounts of whiskey, which apparently produced a violent vomiting spell in the midst of round 44. By round 60, Sullivan's eyes were nearly swollen shut, but an exhausted Kilrain could barely stand. Both men were bloodied, their ribs red and swollen, their faces splotched with ugly bruises, their skins bright red from the blistering sun. Finally, the carnage ended in round 75 as Sullivan pounded a defenseless Kilrain, whose manager tossed a sponge into the ring signaling concession. The brutal contest had lasted 2 hours and 16 minutes.[6]

Controversy surrounding this historic match would remain in the nation's newspapers for more than a year. Both fighters were arrested on the East Coast and extradited to Mississippi to stand trial. Separate trials in the small town of Purvis led to convictions, substantial fines, and jail sentences (one year for Sullivan, two months for Kilrain). But the Mississippi justice system proved lenient. For one thing, several of the jurors had attended the fight, public sentiment supported the two fighters, and the judge seemed starstruck in the presence of the famous John L. Convoluted legal reasoning from the bench made a mockery of Mississippi's anti-prizefighting statute, and upon appeal both defendants avoided jail time. The epic battle became an instant legend that grew ever larger with the passage of time. It proved to be the last bare-knuckle championship fight. The new age of "scientific" boxing was at hand, complete with padded gloves and Queensberry rules.[7]

After escaping the clutches of the Mississippi legal system, Sullivan lost interest in fighting and did not defend his crown for three years. He spent time on the vaudeville stage, toured the United States and Australia as the male lead in the melodrama *Honest Hearts and Willing Hands*, and flirted with the idea of running for Congress. He also continued his lifelong love affair with alcohol, and his weight reached 250 pounds. In 1892, at age 34 and faced with financial problems, Sullivan returned to the ring once more to defend his crown for a big payday. He did so in his typical flamboyant style by issuing a national challenge to anyone (excluding African Americans, he was quick to make clear) willing to put up a $10,000 side bet and fight for a winner-takes-all purse of $50,000 offered by New Orleans promoters eager to take advantage of a new city ordinance permitting boxing under the Marquis of Queensberry rules.[8]

Sullivan's last title defense ended one era and began another. It was fought under bright electric lights in a public arena before an audience of 10,000 of New Orleans' leading citizens. It was the first gloved championship bout. The man who challenged Sullivan was a young San Franciscan, "Gentleman Jim" Corbett, who had defeated Jake Kilrain in 1890.

Sullivan trained sporadically for the bout and continued his drinking. Meanwhile, Corbett reduced his smoking to just two cigars a day while getting himself into fighting trim. Following months of pre-fight hype, the actual bout proved anticlimactic, as the 26-year-old Corbett systematically bludgeoned the aging champion. In round 3 he broke Sullivan's nose with a solid left jab and blood spurted spectacularly across the ring. By round 10, Sullivan was barely able to defend himself. Finally, in round 20, Gentleman Jim decided it was time to end the one-sided contest and he caught John L. with a vicious right cross. Sullivan collapsed to the canvas "like an ox." The next day, Sullivan met the press, suffering from a broken nose, a closed eye, and badly swollen lips and tongue. His black and blue face was laced with ugly stitches. He also suffered from a hangover, the result of a long night of drinking to console himself on the loss of his crown.[9]

Prizefighting had entered a new era. The defeat ended Sullivan's professional boxing career, and he headed back to the vaudeville stage. The most popular sports star of the nineteenth century, Sullivan remained a national figure until felled by a heart attack in 1918. His boxing career had spanned two distinct epochs. The ability of the media to create sports stars had been demonstrated by Richard Kyle Fox. When Fox died in 1922, the *New York Times* identified him as a "Patron of Sports," although acknowledging, "he knew nothing of any game or sport, except boxing."[10]

Sports and Social Class

Following the Civil War, athletic clubs appeared in most American cities, attracting male members engaged in business and professional careers. One of their prominent features was exercise facilities, usually gymnasiums and swimming pools, sometimes indoor running tracks. These clubs tended to mimic the famous Union Club that first opened its doors in New York City in 1836, offering the amenities of the good life: an elegant bar and restaurant, billiards tables, and lounges where like-minded civic leaders could engage in conversation while puffing on expensive cigars.[11]

In the vanguard of this movement was the New York Athletic Club (NYAC), established in 1868 by three young businessmen to provide a gymnasium where members could exercise. Its major contributions were in track and field, and over the years the club established itself as the leader in the keeping of national records. Its rulebook set standardized weights and distances for various events. William Travers was elected president in 1882 with a mandate to build a suitably luxurious facility, and in 1885 the club opened an elaborate structure in midtown New York that housed a rifle range, an indoor swimming pool, a gymnasium, a bowling alley, and billiards tables, along with commodious dining and drinking facilities. In 1888, the NYAC acquired land outside the city, where it built a boathouse, an outdoor running track, and tennis courts. Membership in the NYAC became a tangible sign that a man had arrived at a high level of New York society.[12]

The NYAC was but one of several athletic clubs that operated in New York City, and similar clubs were established across the country. By the late nineteenth century, nearly every American city of 100,000 or more residents boasted of at least one athletic club that offered members social exclusivity along with athletic facilities. As the New York clubs engaged rival clubs in athletic competitions, the more aggressive clubs began to admit members whose social standing and income level were suspect but whose athletic talents were exceptional. Others found it expedient simply to pay outstanding performers to represent them in competitions, or to grant them free memberships. These efforts meant that young men of working-class status were often representing exclusive social clubs in their track and field competitions. This development naturally came into conflict with sentiment within the membership that expected social exclusivity. This led to the adoption, at least in principle, of the British concept of amateurism which emphasized the philosophy that true sportsmen participated in sports for the sheer joy of the competition, never cheated or sought unfair advantage over an opponent, devoted little time to practice or physical training, and most certainly never accepted gratuities for their athletic performance. The best sportsmen were those young men who considered competitive sports as a symbol of high social standing; only men of lesser social standing would consider playing for pay. Walter Camp, the football pioneer at Yale, put it bluntly: "You don't want your boy 'hired' by anyone. If he plays, he plays for victory, not for money … And he can look you in the eye as a gentleman should."[13] In 1876, the NYAC adopted a policy restricting its track meets to "any person who has never competed … for public or admission money, or with professionals for a prize … nor has at any period in his life taught or assisted in the pursuit of athletic exercises as a means of livelihood."[14]

Three years later, several athletic clubs joined together to form the National Association of Amateur Athletics of America, which adopted the NYAC amateur policy almost verbatim. But rancor and controversy revolving around various interpretations of the amateur code continued, and in protest the NYAC resigned its membership in 1886 and founded the Amateur Athletic Union. This organization would exert enormous influence over the domain of American track and field competition. Until the 1970s, the NYAC's annual indoor track meet held at Madison Square Garden was considered the premier event of its kind in the country.

In reality, these clubs often failed to live up to their commitment to the code of amateurism. Too many members were hard-driving businessmen who lacked the detached perspective and social self-assuredness of the hereditary British elite. Few had inherited their wealth; rather, most had obtained it in the aggressive business world. They tended to apply the same competitive attitude toward sports as they did to their economic environment. Nonetheless, they invoked the amateur concept when it suited their needs. It became deeply imbedded in the fabric of American sports, and in particular, dominated the thinking of the United States Olympic Committee. Colleges and universities also found amateurism useful as the rationale for developing a system that evolved into a multibillion-dollar enterprise but did not pay the performers beyond their minimal academic expenses.

An offshoot of the urban men's clubs was the private suburban clubs that provided affluent families with social separation from the middle and working classes and encouraged them to pursue the growing popularity of tennis and golf. The first example of the new "country club" was the Myopia Club, established in the 1870s and built on a 200 acre private estate 8 miles north of Boston. A clubhouse provided card and billiards rooms, dining facilities, and sleeping quarters, and several lawn tennis courts were constructed along with a baseball field. The primary interest of members was horseback riding and foxhunting. The Myopia Club set the pattern for future developments by providing a wide range of activities in a bucolic setting. However, commuting by train from Boston was inconvenient, so several members, having resettled in the elite suburb of Brookline on the west edge of Boston, organized a new country club at Clyde Park. The prospectus released by founder J. Murray Forbes in 1882 stated that the Brookline Club's "general idea is to have a comfortable club-house for the use of members with their families, a simple restaurant, bed-rooms, bowling-alley, lawn tennis grounds, etc."[15]

Similar clubs sprung up around major cities in the next three decades and often featured tennis. In Newport, Rhode Island, several wealthy families built their own private tennis courts in the 1880s. Here, at the location of the future National Tennis Center, the manicured grass courts provided tangible evidence of the club's exclusivity. The new game fitted well into an outdoor setting; significantly, it was a game that women could play despite the restrictions on movement imposed by long dresses. Tennis was a game suitable for both men and women, and it tended to enhance the family atmosphere the new clubs sought to encourage. However, tennis did not remain the primary focus of the new country clubs because both men and women were attracted to another game that seemed perfectly suited to the leafy suburban environment.

Golf became part of the American sports picture during the 1890s. It was a game that could be played by men and women of all ages. It provided moderate exercise in the open air, held out a variety of mental as well as physical challenges, was conducive to handicapping and betting, and seldom produced serious physical injury. The St Andrews Golf Club of

Yonkers was opened in 1888 and provided the American prototype of a private club that offered a golf course as its primary attraction. The popularity of the ancient game that had originated during the late Middle Ages in Scotland grew rapidly in the United States. By 1900 there were 1,040 courses in operation. The number of holes varied widely, from four to 12, but following the leadership of the Shinnecock Hills Country Club of Southampton, New York, a nine-hole challenge became the norm by 1900. During the early decades of the twentieth century, many nine-hole courses were increased to 18 holes, a number that became the standard for tournaments by the 1920s.[16]

The appeal of the country club to those who could afford its costs was great. Membership usually established one's elite social status and provided opportunities for socialization and conducting business on an informal basis. They also provided members with a clear social separation from the common citizen: "Getting into a club became important not so much as because it constituted a positive accomplishment in itself but because it gave the new member the right to participate in the exclusion of the unworthy," Robert J. Moss has observed. "Country clubs … existed to create unequal access, to draw a boundary between the elect and the unwanted."[17] The typical course, with verdant fairways and putting greens set among trees, ponds, and streams, appealed to the agrarian frontier nostalgia that percolated through the American subconscious. Golf provided relief from the congestion of the city in which members lived and worked. As the movement spread, some critics naturally worried that the clubs were exacerbating social divisions within communities; others simply condemned the perceived snooty elitism of the clubs. Consequently, golf acquired an image of elitism that would only slowly dissipate during the twentieth century.

During this formative period, however, a few perceptive social commentators took notice of the tendency of the country club to provide greater avenues for growth and participation in sports for women. As one writer, perhaps looking through rose-colored glasses, noted, "The Country Club has brought our women out of stuffy houses and out of their hopeless, aimless selves, has given color to their cheeks, vivacity to their movements, charm and intelligence to their conversation." However limited its impact upon society at large, the county club nonetheless helped advance the role of women in sports. "The country club has taken its legitimate position in the social cosmos. A place has been found outside the restricted possibilities of the home where men and women may meet on equal footing."[18] This, of course, was not accurate. In many instances the presence and participation of women on the golf course were barely tolerated. Men controlled the boards of directors, set the policies, hired the staff, and often decreed that women could play only on designated "ladies days" (scheduled midweek when the men were in their offices). Equality of the sexes would remain an issue for decades to come.

Without the popularity of golf, most of these clubs would not have survived. Those that were originally intended for equestrian sports, hunting, baseball, tennis, or cricket learned that by adding golf they could attract and keep members. Journalist E. S. Martin aptly summarized the essence of the movement:

> Country clubs are the result of the centralization of population, the increase of wealth, and the discovery of the game of golf by America … Country clubs could hardly flourish in great numbers without golf. To a majority of the active male members golf is the great attraction. Golf keeps up the membership and makes the club strong.

Figure 4.2   Golf provided women with a new opportunity to develop their athletic skills as private country clubs were established at the turn of the twentieth century. This young lady was captured by a photographer at the Portrush Club in New Jersey in 1911 as she demonstrated a proper follow-through on her fairway wood shot. *Image © Hulton-Deutsch Collection/Corbis*

Another writer put it more succinctly: "If sport has not been the *raison d'être* of every club's establishment it is at all events, with extremely few exceptions, the chief means of their existence."[19] It was not until the 1920s that the game of golf gained momentum with the general population when local governments began to construct and operate public courses. By 1930, there were 5,856 courses in the United States, the majority operated by city parks and recreation departments.

Strong Bodies and Devout Souls

When Englishman Thomas Hughes published *Tom Brown's Schooldays* in 1857, few Americans had ever considered that there might be a powerful relationship between strenuous exertion on the playing field and the development of devout Christian youth. Hughes captured the imaginations of young boys on both sides of the Atlantic with his sparkling story of young Tom's heroic behavior on the playing fields of Rugby School, and his stirring narrative prompted educators and clergy to recognize the connection between effective religious education and healthy athletic endeavor. Hughes's book had a profound impact upon middle-class America; it sold nearly a quarter million copies in the United States within a year of its publication. The novel contributed substantively to the powerful movement that came to be called "Muscular Christianity." Its central message was quite simple: participation in vigorous sports competition would produce a young man who understood the values of fair play, good sportsmanship, and an appreciation of the Ten Commandments. It molded the mind, the body, and the spirit into an attractive evangelical package. In the next half-century, many American writers sought to emulate Hughes's message of the importance of vigorous but fair play. Among the leaders of this new popular genre of teenage literature was Gilbert Patten, who cranked out more than 200 books and short stories between 1896 and 1912 detailing the breathtaking feats of the heroic Frank Merriwell on the football and baseball fields at Fardale Academy and Yale University. When he was not overcoming great obstacles and triumphing over poor sports, the dashing Merriwell was touring the world to find adventure, even helping a horse win the English Derby. "He never drinks," says one of his Yale classmates. "That's how he keeps himself in such fine condition all the time. He will not smoke, either, and he takes his exercise regularly. He is really a remarkable freshie."[20]

Muscular Christianity appealed to a wide range of Americans because it addressed serious questions that concerned American leaders. In urban America, increasing numbers of men worked behind counters or desks rather than doing strenuous outdoor physical labor. Some social commentators feared that the office-bound male was becoming less masculine. Some medical professionals even believed that the middle-class male was suffering from a newly discovered disease called "neurasthenia," a malady that sapped urban males of their vitality and virility. The perceived existence of neurasthenia led many to believe that the American male had become a liability in the competitive world in which Darwinian struggles for survival were believed to be a constant.[21]

Even more threatening was the perception that life in the cities was undermining the vitality of American men. Expanded and mandatory public school programs meant that boys were now required to spend up to nine months a year sitting at a school desk, limiting their opportunities to build their physiques. Fears also spread that young boys were being "feminized" by overly protective mothers. Other dangers to the future of American masculinity also lurked in the cities: the morals of young men were believed under attack by the urban bachelor subculture with its unsavory amusements. The solution to resist these threats was regular, vigorous exercise conducted in a wholesome Christian atmosphere. The influential mid-century Presbyterian minister Henry Ward Beecher was convinced that there existed a close connection between a vigorous life and moral development. He argued that activities such as swimming, rowing, horseback riding, gymnastics, and baseball were conducive to moral as well as physical development, and he urged religious and civic leaders to "give to the young men of our cities the means of physical vigor and health, separated from temptations of vice."[22]

A chorus of voices arising from leading intellectuals and the Protestant clergy embraced Beecher's call for reform. Ralph Waldo Emerson, Henry David Thoreau, Oliver Wendell Holmes, Nathaniel Hawthorne, and Henry Longfellow were but a few of the prominent individuals who were among the first to encourage boys and young men to pursue a vigorous lifestyle. As this movement gained momentum, no voice was heard more clearly than that of the Reverend Thomas Wentworth Higginson, a graduate of Harvard Divinity School. Writing in *Atlantic Monthly* in 1858, he denounced the perception that "physical vigor and spiritual sanctity are incompatible." Higginson argued that good health was "a necessary condition of all permanent success" because it enabled men to confront the challenges of life. He expressed his fear that in the new urban environment, young boys were greatly influenced by overly protective mothers because working fathers had little time to spend with them; the result was a growing softness, even effeminacy, among young American males. He chided parents whose sons were "puny, pallid, sedentary" for encouraging them to elect a career in the ministry or other nurturing professions. Acknowledging that girls also benefited from exercise, Higginson nonetheless said that only strong men could build a strong nation and that protective mothers could do lasting damage to their sons by sheltering them from the dangers of childhood:

> As the urchin is undoubtedly physically safer for having learned to turn a somerset, and fire a gun, perilous though these feats appear to mothers, – so his soul is made healthier, larger, freer, stronger, by hours and days of manly exercise and copious droughts of open air, at whatever risk of idle habits and bad companions.[23]

Muscular Christianity enjoyed substantial growth in popularity with the passing of the years. One tangible result was to increase the role and scope of physical education and competitive sports programs in the public schools and to sustain the creation of such new institutions as the Young Men's Christian Association (YMCA) and the Boy and Girl Scouts. The YMCA movement was founded in England in 1844 and spread to the United States before the Civil War. Initially, its primary target was young men who had left rural America for the city in search of better opportunities. The "Y" offered inexpensive housing in a Christian atmosphere as an alternative to the seductive influences of working-class boardinghouses and the tawdry amusements of the city. It was believed that the gymnasium and swimming pool provided positive alternatives to the many negative influences of the city that tempted unmarried young men. The movement spread rapidly across the United States after the Civil War. By 1900, some 350 separate facilities were operating in cities large and small, teaching the virtues of self-control, mental toughness, personal discipline, and good personal hygiene, concepts widely assumed to be prerequisites to success in America's competitive economic system. The organization's needs for professional leadership were so great that a special school was established in Springfield, Massachusetts. As the YMCA movement expanded, it focused increasingly on physical fitness and less on religious education. Its clientele also became more diverse as men were attracted to its swimming pools, squash courts, gymnasiums, and running tracks rather than its moral instruction.[24]

A parallel movement established a Young Women's Christian Association (YWCA), but its emphasis lay largely outside the Muscular Christianity movement. The YWCA emerged out of a confluence of many organizations intended to protect the welfare and morals of unmarried urban women. Consequently, the heavy emphasis of the YMCA upon physical fitness was not reflected in the YWCA, which offered educational and career programs for its adult membership. Consequently the burden of working with young girls fell to the Camp Fire Girls and the Girl Scouts.[25]

Like the YMCA, the Boy Scouts movement had its origins in England, and was introduced in the United States in 1910. Its program personified the Muscular Christian philosophy with its encouragement of such traits as honesty, trustworthiness, reverence, cheerfulness, obedience, bravery, and kindness. Scouting's emphasis upon learning these traits in the great outdoors – hiking, climbing, boating, swimming, camping, and learning wilderness survival skills – met with widespread approval, prompting Theodore Roosevelt to become an active advisor. Roosevelt praised the program's potential for "the development of efficiency, virility, and good citizenship," because he believed it essential that future leaders "be men of strong, wholesome character, of unmistakable devotion to our country, its customs and ideals." Vigorous sports and related outdoor activities provided growing boys with the necessary preparation for success in business, politics, and the military, enabling them to become vigorous leaders with sound moral principles firmly ingrained.[26]

By the early twentieth century, the several ideological strands of Muscular Christianity had permeated American life. Although many scholars, educators, social commentators, and clergymen contributed to the cause, no one person better symbolized the movement than Theodore Roosevelt. His own life was a testament to the importance of physical conditioning. As a child, he was asthmatic and endured other debilitating illnesses. He was nearsighted and had to wear thick glasses, which made the frail son of socially prominent parents ripe pickings for neighborhood bullies. When he was 14, after having been roughed up by two young toughs, his father introduced him to physical training, telling him that it was time to "build your body." The youngster received instruction in the manly arts from a former professional boxer and enthusiastically plunged into a regimen of weightlifting and calisthenics. Summers were spent on the family's estate on Long Island where he took to hiking, horseback riding, and swimming. He continued that regimen at Harvard, transforming himself into a sturdy young man possessed of considerable physical prowess and an enormous enthusiasm for rigorous physical activity. At Harvard, he boxed, wrestled, and rowed on class teams, and during the summers took long arduous backpacking trips into the backwoods of Maine and upstate New York. In 1883, in an effort to escape the concurrent personal tragedy of the deaths of his young wife and his mother, he bought a ranch in the Badlands of South Dakota and spent a year working the line with regular cowboys. Among other adventures, he had the delightful experiences of capturing a gang of rustlers at gunpoint and thrashing a thug in a barroom fight who made the mistake of poking fun at his eyeglasses.

Roosevelt became an enthusiastic proponent of "the strenuous life." Greatly influenced by the doctrines of Social Darwinism, Roosevelt believed that enemies abroad and weakness at home threatened America's future. In 1895, he confided to Walter Camp his fear that "we are tending steadily in America to produce in our leisure and sedentary classes a type of man not much above the Bengalee baboo."[27] He feared that men did not become warriors by working indoors, and lamented the decline in rural population because fewer soldiers would have the benefits of growing up in the outdoors, which included learning to shoot a rifle. What was needed, he said, were strong men who understood that a leader "in the arena" required the courage, endurance, and strength that came from a vigorous life. Strenuous sports, such as boxing, rowing, and football, provided the training and experiences necessary for leadership. In 1893, Roosevelt wrote that in modern America it was natural to put too little stress upon the virtues which go to make up a race of statesmen and soldiers, of pioneers and explorers by land and sea, of bridge builders and road-makers, of commonwealth builders – in short, upon those virtues for the lack of which, whether in an individual or in a nation, no amount of refinement and learning, of gentleness and culture, can possibly atone.[28]

The solution, he said, was "the very qualities which are fostered by vigorous, manly out-of-door sports." In 1902, in his book *The Strenuous Life*, Roosevelt noted that during his own childhood it was acceptable for boys born to wealthy parents to ignore their physical development, but that the new thinking required that they participate in "the rough sports which call for pluck, endurance, and physical address." In his widely read essay on "The American Boy," TR urged parents and educators to focus upon both the physical and the moral development of boys:

Now, the chances are he won't be much of a man unless he is a good deal of a boy. He must not be a coward or a weakling, a bully, a shirk, or a prig. He must work hard and play hard. He must be clean-minded and clean-lived, and able to hold his own under all circumstances and against all comers.

Because today's boys would become tomorrow's soldiers and statesmen, "A boy needs both physical and moral courage," and he emphasized that the traits that boys develop in their youth would shape their conduct as men "in the field." Roosevelt concluded his message to the young men of America with an oft-quoted exhortation: "In short, in life, as in a football game, the principle to follow is: Hit the line hard; don't foul and don't shirk, but hit the line hard!"[29]

America's Greatest Athlete

Those proclaiming the virtues of Muscular Christianity had an unwritten, perhaps even subconscious audience in mind: white, middle-class, male, Protestant Americans. Consequently, when the first American to attract national and international acclaim as a world-class athlete happened to be an impoverished Native American, mainstream America reacted with considerable ambivalence. As a student at Carlisle Indian School, Jim Thorpe was a track and field star who also demonstrated superior talent on the football field, earning All-American honors. He could run, he could tackle, he could kick, and he did so in competition with the best teams. He was also a superb baseball player who later spent six seasons in the National League. In 1912, he achieved world acclaim for an unprecedented gold medal display of athleticism and endurance at the Stockholm Olympics. Because he was a Native American, however, the mainstream media treated him with circumspection, although Thorpe was viewed by many Americans as something of a curiosity. When his status as an amateur was called into question in 1913, he was summarily stripped of his Olympic gold medals by a joint decision of the Amateur Athletic Union and the American Olympic Committee.

In 1879, the United States government established a boarding school in Pennsylvania to provide educational programs designed to assimilate Native American youth into mainstream American life. The founder of the Carlisle Indian Industrial Training School was a career military officer, Richard Henry Pratt, who wanted to educate Native Americans about the dominant white culture and prepare them for jobs in industry. The intent was to eradicate traditional Indian culture because Pratt believed that only by so doing could the Native American people avoid extinction. It was from this educational environment that Jim Thorpe burst onto the American consciousness in the early twentieth century as a phenomenal multisport athlete. Descended from Native Americans who belonged to the Sac and Fox, Potawatomi, and Kickapoo tribes, Thorpe was born in 1887 and grew up on a reservation east of Oklahoma City. In 1904, he was sent to Carlisle, where he came to the attention of the famed coach Glenn "Pop" Warner. He first gained recognition in track and field, and Warner was reluctant to play Thorpe on the football team for fear of injuring his top track star. At 6 feet 1 inch and weighing a muscular 190 pounds, Thorpe was too good an athlete to keep off the gridiron. In 1911 he received national attention when he led the football team – naturally called the Indians – to an upset victory over unbeaten Harvard. His punting ability – he kicked an 83 yard punt against Brown – and his skill as a running back and sure-handed tackler led to All-American honors. The American people became infatuated with what the press called "The Indian."[30]

In the 1912 Olympics Thorpe became an international sports figure when he won both the pentathlon and the decathlon at the Stockholm Olympics. In the five-event pentathlon he won four first places (broad jump, 200 meter dash, javelin throw, and 1,500 meter race), and in the 10-event decathlon he scored 8,413 points out of a possible 10,000, some 700 points ahead of his nearest competitor. King Gustav of Sweden told him upon presenting his gold medals, "Sir, you are the greatest athlete in the world." Thorpe reportedly responded, "Thanks, King."[31] Upon returning to the United States, Thorpe found himself a national hero and was greeted in New York City with a tickertape parade. He further enhanced his reputation as a multisport phenomenon by leading Carlisle's football team to a consensus national championship with a 12–1 record against the top teams in the East, including the shocking upset against Army. Walter Camp again named him an All-American. The American people considered Thorpe a national treasure, but his ethnicity was always mentioned prominently in newspaper accounts.

Thorpe's high standing with the public did not last for long. In January of 1913, just two months after he starred in the upset against West Point, a Massachusetts newspaper revealed that during the summers of 1909 and 1910 he had played for a Class D minor-league baseball team in Fayetteville, North Carolina, where he earned between $2 and $5 a game. The all-white male members of the American Amateur Union (AAU) and the American Olympic Committee (AOC) moved with incredible speed; they ordered that Thorpe return his Olympic medals and that his name and records be struck from the Olympic record book. Public opinion on this harsh and arbitrary decision to uphold a pristine concept of amateurism was sharply divided. Some felt betrayed by Thorpe's violation of the strict amateur code, while others, including Warner, contended that he was being harshly punished because he was Native American. A white champion, they suggested, would have been treated differently. This controversy brought into sharp public focus the relationship between sports and race. In his letter of apology to the AAU, Thorpe subtly pointed to the double standard by which he had been summarily judged:

Figure 4.3   Jim Thorpe is shown here during the shot put competition in the decathlon at the 1912 Olympic Games in Stockholm. Thorpe had his gold medal and records taken away the following year by the American Athletic Union when it was revealed he had previously played professional baseball. Many critics believed the action was based upon either racism, or an unrealistic interpretation of the concept of amateurism, or both. *Image © Bettman/Corbis*

"I was not very wise to the ways of the world and did not realize that this was wrong and it would make me a professional in track sports, although I learned from the other players that it would be better for me not to let any one know that I was playing." Pointing out that most of his professional baseball teammates were college athletes who maintained their amateur standing, he noted, "I did not know that I was doing wrong because I was doing what I knew several other college men had done; except that they did not use their own names."[32]

Thorpe was dumbfounded by his "disgrace" that the newspapers reported, asking Warner "I don't understand, Pop. What's that two months of baseball got to do with all the jumping and running and field-work I did in Stockholm? I never got paid for any of that, did I?" Having lost his amateur status, Thorpe left Carlisle without a diploma and decided to play professional baseball. Warner later expressed his suspicions that a baseball scout had orchestrated the scandal so that Thorpe would have to play baseball. Thorpe signed with the New York

Giants for $5,000 and jumped right to the major leagues on April 14, 1913. He played sparingly in the outfield for the Giants and the Cincinnati Reds for six seasons and concluded his baseball career with the Boston Braves in 1919. He played in 289 games and had a lifetime batting average of .252.

He began his professional football career with the Canton Bulldogs in 1915 and later played with several other teams over a career that extended to 1928. He was an outstanding punter and thrilled spectators with his hard-hitting play on both offense and defense. In 1920 he served in the mostly honorific role of president of the American Professional Football Association. For two seasons he coached and played for the most unusual team to appear in the National Football League. The Oorang Indians – a team composed solely of Native Americans – was improbably sponsored by a dog breeding company located in the crossroads town of LaRue, Ohio. Interestingly, team owner Walter Lingo created what are believed to be football's first half-time shows when he put his trained Airedales through a series of stunts. Thorpe's team lacked adequate personnel and suffered through two losing seasons, and Lingo thereupon returned his franchise to the fragile NFL. Thorpe ended his football career at the age of 41 when he made a brief appearance with the Chicago Cardinals in 1928.

By the time his playing days ended, Thorpe was already losing his battle with alcoholism. He moved from job to job, working variously as deck hand, painter, carpenter, barroom bouncer, factory guard, and ditch digger, and died in 1953 in Lomita, California. He was named by various media organizations as America's top athlete of the first half-century, and in 2000 was frequently identified as the greatest athlete of the entire century. In 1955, the NFL named their annual Most Valuable Player award for Thorpe, and he was among the initial class admitted to its Hall of Fame in 1963. In 1983, the United States Olympic Committee posthumously restored Thorpe's medals and placed his name back in the record books.

Organized Play for the Modern Era

As the United States strode confidently into the modern era, the importance of an enhanced educational system to serve the needs of business and industry became a high national priority. Consequently legislatures mandated school attendance until age 16, and state education boards established a network of teachers' colleges (originally called "normal schools") whose role it was to produce professional classroom teachers and administrators. Universities and colleges developed new curricula to prepare teachers, engineers, physicians, lawyers, and businessmen.

One of the leaders of the overhaul of the educational system was Dr Luther H. Gulick. While attending Oberlin College in the early 1880s, this serious young man fell under the influence of a pioneering professor of physical education, Delphine Hanna, whose inspired teaching led him to abandon his plans to become a medical missionary. His new mission in life was to design meaningful physical education programs to encourage the development of the physical and moral dimensions of the individual. After obtaining his medical degree from New York University in 1887, Gulick joined the faculty of the International Young Men's Christian Association Training School in Springfield, Massachusetts, a special school that offered training for future YMCA instructors and directors. Gulick became a leading spokesman for competitive games and had to overcome strong resistance from older YMCA leaders who had been trained in conducting repetitive calisthenics drills.

Joining Gulick on the faculty at Springfield were two other young men who were strong advocates of vigorous exercise and a strong religious faith. Amos Alonzo Stagg and James Naismith were committed to the YMCA's motto of a "fourfold program of fitness: physical, social, mental, and spiritual." Stagg had decided that because of a stutter he could better serve his God on the football field than in the pulpit. Naismith, an ordained Presbyterian minister recently graduated from McGill University, had arrived from Canada in 1890 as an instructor. Both young men saw a close relationship between matters of the spirit and the body. Stagg won the attention of the sports world when he molded a new football team out of the Springfield student body and faculty and nearly upset his alma mater. His star center on the team that lost to Yale 16–10 was the 160 pound Naismith, who upon inquiring as to the reason he was selected to anchor the center of the line, was told by Stagg: "Jim, I play you at center because you can do the meanest things in the most gentlemanly way."[33]

Stagg soon departed for the green pastures of the new University of Chicago where he would build a powerful football team, but Naismith remained on the Springfield faculty for several years. During his first year at Springfield, Naismith volunteered to teach a class of adult males who were in the final stages of their two-year program to become YMCA administrators. Although they gladly took to fall football and spring baseball, they found the mindless routine of winter calisthenics a terrible bore and expressed their dissatisfaction in such vigorous ways that they intimidated their instructors. Gulick asked Naismith to undertake the challenge:

> This new generation of young men wants the pleasure and thrills of games rather than the body-building benefits of exercise. They rebel at tumbling, push-ups, working out with Indian clubs, and other calisthenics. I want you to come up with a game that will give them the exercise they need in the gym during the winter months when we can't go outdoors for football or baseball.[34]

For two weeks, Naismith pondered the challenge and experimented with indoor versions of soccer and lacrosse, which led to too many bruises and bloodied heads. Then one day he recalled a game he had played as a child called "duck on a rock," which had emphasized tossing a rock at a target. The next day, he nailed two peach baskets to serve as targets precisely 10 feet above the floor at each end of the gym. When his students arrived for their class, their instructor was bouncing a soccer ball. He proceeded to explain to them 13 basic rules for the new game. Within minutes their happy shouts had echoed down the hall and a crowd of curious students and faculty had assembled to watch the action. With 18 men maneuvering around the small floor, it became evident that finesse, good passing, skilled marksmanship, and sound physical conditioning were essential qualities for this new game.[35]

Unlike football and baseball, the origins of which can be traced back several centuries, Naismith's new game had no historical precedent. The popularity of basketball spread across the United States with amazing rapidity through the YMCA network. College women embraced the game with the same enthusiasm as men. Emphasis on agility and skill rather than on pure physical strength made basketball an ideal indoor winter game for modern America. Social workers encouraged the game as a means of socializing immigrant children, and it became the dominant sport of many new ethnic groups in cities, but it also appealed equally to youngsters in small towns and rural areas. Soon basketball hoops were being nailed above barn and garage doors across the land so that youngsters could hone their skills outside formal team practices. As one enthusiast wrote in 1902, "In playing it comes the joy of a quickened pulse and fast-working lungs, the health-giving exercise to all our muscles, the forgetting of all troubles. There is no game which requires more wind or endurance nor which needs greater agility and deftness."[36]

Naismith never benefited financially from his invention. He left Springfield in 1895 to attend medical school in Denver, and upon graduation took a position as the first professor of health and physical education at Kansas University, where he remained until his death in 1939. He seldom played the game himself, although he was the first basketball coach at KU. Ironically, with a nine-year record of 55–60, the inventor of the game of basketball compiled the only career losing record in the school's history. True to his convictions, Dr Naismith was much more interested in teaching health and exercise science to undergraduate students and in encouraging participation in the intramural program than in promoting the game he invented.

Basketball was not the only contribution made to American sports by the Springfield YMCA school. In 1895, one of Dr Gulick's former students created another sport. At the YMCA in Holyoke, Massachusetts, William G. Morgan strung a tennis net 6 feet 6 inches above a gymnasium floor and had the players bat a soccer ball back and forth over the net. With a nod to the game of badminton, Morgan called his game "mintonette," but when an onlooker observed that the players were volleying the ball back and forth, the name of "volley ball" was adopted.

In 1900, Gulick became principal of Pratt High School in Brooklyn, where he introduced physical education classes into the formal curriculum; in 1903, he became director of physical education for the New York City school system. He added physical education classes to the system curriculum and established competitive athletic leagues. Gulick's message that physical activity encouraged better learning by relieving muscles cramped from long hours of sitting at a desk and by stimulating blood flow to the brain was widely hailed as a major advance in progressive education theory. His Public Schools Athletic League (PSAL), founded in 1903, was the nation's first competitive sports league for schoolboys, and he added a comparable program for girls in 1905. The PSAL was a conscious effort to use the attractiveness of competitive sports to assist the large number of immigrant children to embrace American values. The PSAL's motto of "Duty, Thoroughness, Patriotism, Honor and Obedience" spoke to the league's underlying socialization objectives. The PSAL became the model for interscholastic sports programs that were established throughout the United States in the years immediately preceding and following the First World War.[37]

Interscholastic Sports

It was only a matter of time until public schools began to field teams and form leagues. Having learned from leaders of the progressive education movement the importance of fostering the physical as well as the intellectual and spiritual lives of their charges, school administrators created competitive team sports programs in basketball, football, baseball, and track and field. By the 1920s basketball had become arguably the most popular sport at the high school level, played by both boys and girls. Basketball simultaneously developed deep roots in the urban cores of American cities and in the nation's rural areas. In thousands of small rural high schools that lacked sufficient number of boys to field a competitive football team, basketball became the sport that bonded the school with the community. Friday nights all across Main Street America saw small gymnasiums packed with cheering spectators. Even the smallest rural schools could field a team of five boys relatively adept at the game. Following the First World War, many state athletic associations were established to create eligibility standards, agree to game rules, and conduct championship tournaments. At the end of the regular season in February, county school districts conducted tournaments with the winners advancing sequentially to district, regional, and state championship tournaments.

In larger schools football also flourished, and in some states schools with small enrollments formed six- and eight-man teams. Just as Indiana and Iowa formed a strong bond with basketball, the states of Pennsylvania, Ohio, and Texas became known for their enthusiasm for high school football. The widespread introduction of physical education classes and interscholastic sports programs provided the logical culmination of the advocacy of the strenuous life. Such advocates of Muscular Christianity as Luther Gulick and James Naismith might have spoken eloquently about sports enhancing the spiritual nature of man, but for the average American the appeal was the excitement produced by spirited competition in the quest for victory.

Winning, even at considerable ethical cost, was easily rationalized, especially when a bitter rival was on the losing end. Just as college football became riddled with corruption that touched players, coaches, administrators, trustees, and alumni, so too did the same victory-at-any-price ethic surface in high school sports. The pressure to win meant that academic eligibility requirements were sometimes subverted; successful coaches were paid higher salaries than other faculty; and public opinion often forced well-meaning coaches with losing records to resign. The importance of sports programs, it was often argued, consumed more of the time of school boards than the academic side of the school system. Although physical education was trumpeted as an integral part of education reform, those classes were often given short shrift by teachers and administrators alike, with the real emphasis being placed upon fielding competitive teams. Within the social structure of the schools themselves, a special elite status was reserved for skilled athletes. Had Luther Gulick not died an early death in 1918, it is altogether conceivable that he would have led a national movement to reverse these powerful trends which subverted the moral and ethical objectives that he held so dear.

5

Baseball Ascendant, 1890–1930

Between 1890 and 1930, baseball was indisputedly the most popular sport in America. The game attracted millions of amateur participants and even the smallest of communities proudly fielded a "town team." In the cities, YMCA leagues and semiprofessional leagues were popular. Employers sponsored teams to play in industrial and commercial leagues, sometimes hiring employees whose primary function was to win ball games for the company team. In an age of pervasive racial segregation, African Americans formed their own amateur and semiprofessional teams and leagues and only on special occasions played white teams in "exhibition" games. Wherever there was a vacant city lot or an open field in a small town, boys of all ages "chose up sides" and played informal games to their hearts' content.

The game's popularity was evidenced by construction of modern stadiums for major-league teams that seated between 20,000 and 35,000 spectators. Because many wooden stadiums had been destroyed by fire over the years, double-decked structures of brick, concrete, and structural steel were erected in their place. The first of these new stadiums, Shibe Park, was constructed in 1909 in Philadelphia, and in the following year a similar structure opened in Pittsburgh. Within the next five years there appeared Navin Field in Detroit (later named Briggs and then Tiger Stadium), League Park in Cleveland, Redland Field in Cincinnati (later renamed Crosley Field), Ebbets Field in Brooklyn, National Park in Washington, DC (renamed Griffith Stadium in 1920), Braves Field and Fenway Park in Boston, Weeghman Park (renamed Wrigley Field in 1926) and Comiskey Park in Chicago. The New York Giants replaced their burned-out Polo Grounds in 1911 with a new horseshoe-shaped double-deck stadium that seated 35,000, the largest seating capacity of the new stadiums. In 1923, however, the Yankees opened the most famous ballpark in America which eclipsed that capacity. Located in the lower Bronx, Yankee Stadium had a capacity of

Sports in American Life: A History, Second Edition. Richard O. Davies.
© 2012 John Wiley & Sons, Inc. Published 2012 by John Wiley & Sons, Inc.

nearly 70,000, a monument to the game's increased popularity and management's vision of a prosperous future.

Unlike most sports venues built since 1960, these ballparks were not financed by local governments, but were paid for by team ownership. Nearly a century after they were constructed, only two of these venerable ballparks remain in use: Wrigley Field and Fenway Park. These structures are precious historical landmarks, symbols of the special place that baseball enjoys in American life and culture, providing connections to teams and players of years gone by. Baseball's hold on the American mind has been repeatedly revealed in literature and the theater. Schoolboys for the past 100 years have listened to readings of Ernest Thayer's poem written in 1888, "Casey at the Bat," and in 1908 the American people first heard a song destined to become an American favorite. "Take Me Out to the Ball Game" was first sung on the vaudeville stage by a young lady imploring her male friend to escort her to a game. Over the years baseball has been featured in many Hollywood films and has even entered our everyday conversations; every American knows the meaning of "strike out," "can't get to first base," "home run," "grandstander," "out in left field," "grand slam," and "booted that one."

The 1890s: Years of Discord

The demise of the Players' League after only one year of operation in 1890 left the National League unchallenged as the nation's only "major league." The American Association made a feeble effort to continue, but disbanded after the 1891 season, with the franchises in Washington, St Louis, Louisville, and Baltimore joining the National League. This meant that the league had expanded to 12 teams. No longer confronted by competition from other leagues, the owners demonstrated the arrogance and power consistent with the best of America's robber barons of the day and put a tight lid on player salaries. But the monopoly they now controlled did not guarantee financial success. Attendance fell to just 1,800,000 in 1894, due to a severe economic downturn.

The Baltimore Orioles and Boston Beaneaters were the indisputed best teams of the 1890s, with one of the two teams winning the championship each year until the Brooklyn Superbas broke their domination in 1899. The Orioles set the standard for what was known as "scientific" or "inside" baseball. This style of play emphasized low-scoring games, sacrifice bunts, base stealing, hit-and-run plays, slapping ground balls through holes in the infield, solid pitching, and strong defense. A home run was an infrequent occurrence. The scientific game was crafted to take advantage of the "dead" ball with which they played. The Orioles also played the game with a raucous attitude that emphasized a win-at-any-cost mentality. They routinely employed roughhouse tactics in an attempt to intimidate their opponents. Spikes were sharpened and used as weapons on the base paths against vulnerable infielders. Base runners were held by the belt when unobserved by the single umpire, and catchers interfered with batters. Pitchers sought to intimidate batters with high and inside fast balls. A veteran Boston sportswriter commented that the Orioles played "the dirtiest ball ever seen in this country," and did not hesitate to "maim a fellow for life." Umpire baiting was constant. Under player-manager John McGraw, the Orioles used every tactic possible – including physical and verbal attacks – to intimidate umpires. McGraw frequently encouraged

Baltimore fans to unleash a barrage of verbal abuse upon the umpire when a call went against the home team.[1] The prim and proper Connie Mack once commented that there were "no gentlemen" on the feisty Baltimore team, and umpire John Heydler (who later became a president of the National League) said that their brand of play was destructive to the game:

> They were mean, vicious, ready at any time to maim a rival player or an umpire if it helped their cause. The things they said to an umpire were unbelievably vile … The worst of it was they got by with much of their brow beating and hooliganism. Other clubs patterned after them and I feel the lot of umpire never was worse than in the years when the Orioles were flying high.[2]

Turbulence on the field was not restricted to the Orioles, however. Many believed that the Boston Beaneaters were just as fierce and perhaps a better ball club than the Orioles. As historian Charles Alexander points out, rowdy behavior was endemic in a game dominated by poorly educated young men who came from working-class backgrounds. Anti-Catholic sentiment of the time often led to accusations that rowdiness was the result of the presence of a large number of Irish Americans. Alexander suggests that the brawling Cleveland Spiders under the leadership of Oliver "Patsy" Tebeau might have been the worst of a bad lot; in one notable brawl-marred game in Louisville, the entire Cleveland team was arrested for disturbing the peace and thrown into jail. Games were frequently punctuated by violence: beer bottles were thrown out of the stands at umpires or opposing players; angry players physically assaulted the lone umpire; foul language spewed out of the stands and the dugouts; fights between players were frequent, and occasionally players would charge into the grandstands after a fan whose criticisms became too personal. Even the umpires sometimes got into the action. In 1892, umpire Tim Hurst smacked a fan seated in the front row with his mask after being called "a monkey-faced dub." When a policeman came to the fan's assistance, he too was smacked. Critics of the game feared that unless the incessant umpire baiting, foul language, and brawling were curbed, the game would never win over the middle-class fan.[3]

The players had good reason for taking the field with a sour outlook because team owners responded to falling attendance by slashing salaries. By 1895, average paychecks had declined about 30 percent from the days of the Players' League. In 1893, the owners put in place an unwritten policy limiting team payrolls to $30,000. Players grumbled but had no viable option other than to accept what management was willing to pay – or quit the game. Despite cuts in payrolls, most teams lost money during the Depression years. Although no firm evidence was forthcoming, the low salaries led to repeated rumors that some players sought to improve their income by consorting with gamblers to throw games, as well as betting on games in which they themselves played.[4]

Ban Johnson and the American League

The precarious condition of the game, exacerbated by shortsighted owners, virtually invited the intervention of new leadership. That person was a hard-charging, heavy-drinking, chain-smoking, overweight journalist from Cincinnati, Byron Bancroft Johnson. A college dropout, Ban Johnson had learned the intricacies of the game as a sports writer and editor for the *Cincinnati Commercial Gazette*, and then as president of the Western League, a top minor league that consisted of teams located across the Midwest. In 1899, he took advantage of the patriotic fervor produced by the Spanish–American War and announced the establishment of an American League. In 1901, he approached the National League asking that his new league be recognized as a co-equal major-league organization, but he was predictably rebuffed.[5]

Johnson thereupon declared war, announcing that he would not honor the National League's reserved players. He placed franchises in several cities already occupied by National League teams. Inept management and bitter feuds between National League club owners helped Johnson succeed in launching his new league. By offering a mere $500 more per player, the American League lured more than 100 players away from its rival. With the economy booming, Johnson had little difficulty in finding good leadership for his league's franchises. Clark Griffith established a team in Washington, wealthy Philadelphia businessmen Ben and Tom Shibe joined with Connie Mack to create the Athletics, and Charles Comiskey moved his St Paul team of the Western League to Chicago and appropriated the name of White Sox. Cleveland coal magnate Charles Somers established a team in his home city, and reportedly put up $5 million to finance Johnson's new league. In return, Johnson fondly referred to his financial angel as a man "of the daring soul, courageous heart, and a vast fortune." As Johnson's biographer Eugene Murdock concludes, "Ban Johnson built the American League, but Charles Somers paid the bills."[6]

The American League did well at the box office, attracting more than 1,600,000 fans in its first year of operation in 1901, just 5 percent behind the National League. The National League hierarchy responded to the challenge by sulking and filing an occasional lawsuit, none of which went far. The 1902 season made even the most obdurate National League owner recognize that Johnson's new league was for real. While the National League was dominated by the Pittsburgh Pirates, who had finished a boring 27 games ahead of second-place Brooklyn, the American League tantalized fans with a close pennant race ultimately won by Connie Mack's Philadelphia Athletics. Not surprisingly, the Athletics outdrew the Phillies by 140,000 spectators and the American League attracted 237,000 more fans than its rival.[7]

Clearly, the National League had to make peace with its rival. That occurred with unexpected swiftness during winter 1902–3. They agreed in principle to "co-exist peacefully and to abstain from signing the other league's players." Both leagues could field teams in Chicago, Philadelphia, New York, and St Louis, and they would be considered equal "major leagues." A National Commission was created to supervise operations, consisting of the presidents of the two leagues and a third person whom the two leagues could mutually accept. That person turned out to be the politically well-connected Gary Herrmann, the jovial owner of the Cincinnati Reds. Herrmann, however, was no equal in jousting with the domineering Ban Johnson, and neither was National League president Harry Pulliam. From the beginning, Johnson dominated the policy-making and administrative decisions of the National Commission.[8]

It did not take long for Ban Johnson to be recognized as "Baseball's Czar." With Johnson calling the shots, the commission established a stable and orderly climate in which the game became the focus of the fans' attention rather than distracting legal struggles, player defections, labor disputes, franchise moves, and the collapse of entire leagues that had characterized the previous quarter-century of professional baseball. The two leagues entered into a 50-year period where there were no franchise moves and relatively few turnovers in team ownership.

Consequently, the game enjoyed a half-century in which it was the unchallenged premier professional sport in the United States. To his credit, Johnson focused upon establishing the game's integrity. He pushed hard for "ladies day" games whereby women would be admitted at reduced charge, in hopes that their presence would help reduce antisocial behavior in the stands and on the field. He cracked down on players and managers who abused umpires, and launched an anti-gambling crusade. His effort to eliminate the influence of gamblers ultimately failed because many team owners did not share his apprehension, but his instincts were definitely on target.

One of the innovations Johnson orchestrated was the creation of a postseason playoff between the champions of the two leagues. In October 1903, the National League champion Pittsburgh Pirates, led by shortstop Honus Wagner, took on Boston, then known variously as the Americans, Pilgrims, and Puritans. Wagner fielded his position with grace and flair seldom matched thereafter, and hit for high percentage, winning eight batting titles. He retired in 1917 after 21 seasons with a handsome .327 average. However, Wagner batted only .222 in the World Series and the American Leaguers upset the favored Pirates five games to three. Louis Masur concluded his absorbing study of the first World Series by noting that "Ban Johnson took special joy in the victory. By force of will he had created the American League and went to war against the National. He had helped fashion a peace that looked as though it would last, and a circuit that attracted fans and played, in the parlance of the times, 'a fast game.'"[9]

The last echoes of that inter-league war, however, had not completely faded. The following year, the New York Giants won the National League pennant but manager John McGraw refused to play the American League champions from Boston. McGraw disliked Ban Johnson because he had repeatedly suspended McGraw in 1901 and 1902 for his umpire baiting when he managed the Orioles. McGraw had moved on to the Giants for a stupendous $11,000 salary in 1903. The hiatus of 1904 would not be repeated until a prolonged players' strike forced organized baseball to cancel the 1994 "fall classic."[10]

The following year, however, McGraw felt compelled to play the World Series because his players remained upset that they had lost out on a postseason payday the previous autumn. The 1905 confrontation between two excellent teams established the World Series as an important event in the minds of baseball fans everywhere. McGraw's Giants played his patented style of scientific baseball behind pitcher Christy Mathewson to win the series over Connie Mack's Philadelphia Athletics. When Mathewson shut out the Athletics to clinch the series, a reporter said the 27,000 fans who overflowed the Polo Grounds let out a "reverberating roar that lifted Manhattan's soil from the base."[11]

The Cyclone and the Georgia Peach

Under the leadership of Ban Johnson, baseball became respectable. Exciting pennant races and the emergence of a large number of outstanding "star" players lured spectators to the ballparks in ever-increasing numbers. In 1909, attendance exceeded 7 million. The value of franchises escalated as the game grew in stature and attendance soared. In 1906, the Boston National League franchise sold for $75,000, but five years later it was resold for $187,000, a very large sum for the day. The Chicago Cubs were purchased for $105,000 in 1905 but resold for $500,000 in 1915. When John McGraw joined the Giants in 1902, the team had just been purchased for $125,000, but in 1919 investment broker Charles Stoneham paid the astounding sum of $1,820,000 for the team. League stability meant that strong loyalties were established with fans, producing an aura surrounding the game that even a serious gambling scandal could not destroy.

One of the surest signs that baseball had achieved a special place in American life occurred on opening day in 1910, when President William Howard Taft – all 310 pounds of him – threw out the first ball of the season from the presidential box that Washington Senators owner Clark Griffith had installed by the team's first-base dugout. Taft is also credited with creating one of baseball's important traditions. During the middle of the seventh inning of a game he stood up to stretch, and the entire stands, in deference to their president, also rose. The seventh-inning stretch was thus, at least according to this tale, added to baseball's many traditions. In 1915, Woodrow Wilson became the first president to attend a World Series game when he traveled to Philadelphia to watch the Phillies tangle with the Boston Red Sox.

Improved quality of play – and the emergence of "star" players – enhanced the game's popularity. One of the early sensations was pitcher Denton True "Cy" Young. Born and raised on a farm in northeastern Ohio, as a teenager he was given the nickname "Cyclone" because of the velocity of his fastball. In 1890, at the age of 23, he reached the major leagues with the Cleveland Spiders. He pitched in the major leagues for 22 years, an amazing feat at a time when starting pitchers were expected to take to the mound every four days. As his career unfolded, Young expanded his repertoire of pitches by developing two distinct curve balls and a change-up. Like his contemporaries, he also used a spitball, which when properly loaded would swerve wildly as it approached the plate. (The spitball was declared illegal in 1920.)

Young pitched for 10 seasons with the Spiders, winning more than 20 games each season; three times he recorded 30 or more wins. In 1901, Young was one of the more than 100 players who joined the Boston club of the American League and registered back-to-back 30-win seasons. In 1904, Young pitched 24 consecutive hitless innings – a record still unmatched – and threw the first perfect game from the longer pitching distance of 60 feet 6 inches against Connie Mack's potent Philadelphia Athletics. Young continued to pitch effectively until retiring at age 45 in 1911 with a career won–lost record of 511–316 (both totals remain all-time records and surely will never be equaled).[12]

The unquestioned superstar of the prewar era was the tempestuous Tyrus Raymond Cobb, a fixture in center field for the Detroit Tigers. Beginning with his first at-bat in August 1905, when he slapped a double to right-center field, the "Georgia Peach" proceeded to dominate the game. A native of a small town in northern Georgia, Ty Cobb was intensely driven to succeed at his chosen craft. Cobb drove himself to become the game's top player by mastering the subtleties of the "scientific" strategies of the dead ball era. Everything about Cobb was in excess: his ferocious base running, sliding into base with spikes flashing; his continual verbal warfare with teammates, opponents, umpires, and even fans in the stands that featured an unending flow of vulgarity and venom; and his focused intensity in the batter's box. His style of play, a Detroit sportswriter observed, was "daring bordering on dementia." As Cobb once instructed a young player about batting:

> Always have a belligerent, take-charge attitude up there. You can cultivate quite a "mad on" while awaiting your turn at bat, a cold determination to ram the ball down the pitcher's throat. You'd be surprised how effective it is. It will show up in your walk, in your eyes, in the way you hold your head, the stance you take. Now the pitcher is fearing *you*.[13]

Cobb feared no one and, exhibiting an exaggerated sense of personal honor tinged with a mean streak of racism, was always ready for a fight. In more than one instance he beat adversaries senseless, and on several occasions went into the stands to attack hecklers. In one infamous encounter he assaulted a physically handicapped fan. He later recalled, "When I played ball, I didn't play for fun … It's no pink tea, and mollycoddles had better stay out. It's a contest and everything that implies, a struggle for supremacy, a survival of the fittest." When he retired as a player at age 43 in 1928, Cobb held an incredible 43 records. He won 12 American League batting titles, including nine in a row, and had a lofty .366 lifetime batting average that has never been equaled. His career base hit record of 4,191 lasted until 1985 when surpassed by Pete Rose. Blessed with above average speed, Cobb terrorized the opposition with his cagey and aggressive base running. He led the American League in stolen bases six times; in 1915, he stole 96 bases, a record that stood until 1962. It was not until 1977 that Lou Brock eclipsed Cobb's career total of 897 stolen bases.

Cobb's personal life was a reflection of his on-the-field ferocity. Clearly racist, he seemed to single out African Americans for abuse. He repeatedly got into scrapes with private citizens – bellmen, laborers, whomever. In 1914 he made the headlines when he pulled a revolver – he routinely carried a pistol off the field – on a neighborhood butcher he believed had shortchanged his wife. Cobb was detested by his teammates, some of whom demanded trades to get away from him. On the road he preferred to live and eat alone. His behavior did not change after he retired in 1928. His two marriages failed, his children shunned him, and he lived out his life alone and angry as psychological problems become more pronounced. When Cobb died in 1961, only three persons associated with baseball attended his funeral. Yet his impact upon the game was fundamental; one of the initial five players elected to the Hall of Fame, he garnered more votes than any other candidate, including Babe Ruth. As biographer Charles Alexander concludes, "He was never an easy man to know, never easy to get along with in or out of uniform, never really at peace with himself or the world around him. Ty Cobb was the most volatile, the most fear-inspiring presence ever to appear on a baseball field."[14]

Masters of Strategy

The role of manager evolved steadily after Harry Wright created the position with the Cincinnati Red Stockings. Two men with distinctly different personalities established and refined the role of manager: the pugnacious John J. McGraw and the gentlemanly Connie Mack. Both men

Figure 5.1   Ty Cobb slides into third base with his spikes flying. His pugnacious style of play was aggressive even for an era known for rough tactics. Cobb's mastery of the "scientific" style of play which emphasized speed and defense rather than power hitting set a high standard for the "dead ball" era. *National Baseball Hall of Fame Library, Cooperstown, NY, USA (Public Domain)*

enjoyed extraordinarily long tenures in their positions. McGraw managed the New York Giants from 1902 until he retired in 1932, and Mack sat quietly in the dugout orchestrating the play of his Philadelphia Athletics from 1901 until 1950.

McGraw had begun his career as a third baseman in 1891 with the rowdy Baltimore Orioles, and quickly became recognized as someone who would use whatever means necessary to win a game. One journalist condemned him as "the toughest of toughs and an abomination of the diamond," while another said he was a

> rough, unruly man, who is constantly playing dirty ball. He has the vilest tongue of any ball-player … He has demonstrated his low training, and his own manager knows that, while he is a fine ball-player, yet he adopts every low and contemptible method that his erratic brain can conceive to win a play by a dirty trick.[15]

From the beginning of his professional career, McGraw was recognized as a canny student of the game, a trait that led to his being named player-manager of the Orioles in 1899 at the age of 26. Throughout his career, the aptly named "Muggsy" (a name he detested and no one dared use in his presence) approached the game as if his very life depended upon winning. He was a master at intimidating umpires. He viewed them as his natural enemy and continuously and often ruthlessly sought to bend them to his will. Although he never hit an umpire, he did become a master of what he called "judicious kicking" during his many nose-to-nose confrontations with his adversaries in blue. One umpire once said that McGraw "eats gunpowder every morning and washes it down with warm blood."[16] His teams reflected the personality of their manager, and his record spoke for itself: 10 league championships, 11 second-place finishes, and three World Series championships. Pitcher Christy Mathewson, his favorite player, summarized his impact when he said, "The club is McGraw."[17]

McGraw was a perfect fit for New York, his temperamental Irish personality readily embraced by Giants fans. When the Giants defeated the Philadelphia Athletics in the 1905 World Series, fans stormed the field at the old Polo Grounds and carried the manager off on their shoulders. The hard-drinking McGraw became one of New York's most popular residents, and when not at the Polo Grounds ripping the umpires, could be found at the racetrack betting on the horses, or at one of his favorite watering holes buying a round for the boys.

If ever there was a polar opposite of McGraw, it was Connie Mack. Born in 1864 to Irish immigrant parents, Cornelius McGillicuddy grew into a tall, slender man with a talent for baseball. He changed his name to Connie Mack, perhaps in deference to the strong anti-Irish sentiment of the day, but according to baseball lore it was to assure that his name fitted into newspaper box scores. Although he played at every position but pitcher, he was primarily a catcher with the Washington club of the American Association. In 1901, Mack joined the Philadelphia entry in the American League as general manager, purchasing 25 percent of the ownership. Over the years, Mack acquired all outstanding shares, thus becoming sole owner of the Athletics. For 50 years, Mack served simultaneously as owner, general manager, and field manager. His record included nine pennants but 17 finishes in the cellar; he won 3,776 games and lost a record high 4,925. Competing in a relatively small market with the Phillies, he had to deal with limited budgets. Twice he built teams that won a total of seven league championships and four World Series titles (1911–15, 1929–32), but both times he was forced to sell off his star players to keep his club solvent.[18]

Connie Mack sat quietly in the dugout during games, a picture of calm reserve. He did not wear a uniform, favoring a three-piece suit complete with white dress shirt and necktie. Instead of the traditional baseball cap, he wore a derby. Win or lose, Mack embodied the best of baseball's virtues, demanding clean play and good behavior from his players on and off the field. He rarely argued with or shouted at the umpires, and off the field he was the cautious, quiet businessman who did not swear, smoke, gamble, or drink – four traits common to players and managers of the day. Mack's quiet demeanor and personal integrity would become his hallmark.

In 1922, the United States Supreme Court ruled that organized baseball was a sport and not a business and thereby was exempt from federal antitrust statutes, but to Connie Mack baseball was all business. It was his sole source of income and he had to rely upon gate receipts and concession sales to pay the bills. At one point he revealed his businesslike approach to the game: "It is more profitable for me to have a team that is in contention for most of the season but finishes about fourth. A team like that will draw well enough during the first part of the season to show a profit for the year, and when they don't win you don't have to give them a raise for the next year."[19]

No friend of Ban Johnson's new league, John McGraw sarcastically commented that Mack's team would soon be a big loser, or in the parlance of the day, a "white elephant." Mack playfully seized upon McGraw's comment and adopted the elephant as the team's mascot, putting a cute pachyderm on the team's uniform (where it remains to this day in Oakland). He even acquired a live elephant that cavorted around the ballpark to the fans' delight. In 1905, Mack and McGraw met head-on in the World Series, complete with one elephant. Powered by Christy Mathewson's pitching, McGraw prevailed in their first meeting, but he lost to the Athletics in the World Series of 1911 and 1913. During Mack's early years, the Athletics were a dominant force, winning six of the American League's first 14 pennants, before the team fell on hard financial times due to the salary wars created by the Federal League in 1914–15.[20]

Mack's second run at baseball fame occurred when he was nearing the age of 70 and many sportswriters were questioning his ability to manage in the new era of power baseball. Featuring catcher Mickey Cochrane, slugger Jimmie Foxx, hard-hitting outfielder Al Simmons, and one of baseball's all-time great pitchers, Robert "Lefty" Grove, between 1925 and 1933 the Athletics finished no lower than third, dethroning the powerful New York Yankees for three consecutive seasons between 1929 and 1931, and defeating the Chicago Cubs and the St Louis Cardinals in the World Series of 1929 and 1930. Once again, financial problems forced Mack to sell off his team's stars. This time the culprit was the Great Depression; despite success on the field, attendance dropped by more than 200,000 between 1929 and 1932. Things never got better for Mack and his Athletics. Over his last 17 years, until he retired at age 86 in 1950, the Athletics had only one first-division finish, a distant fourth in 1948.

The Federal League Challenge

Under the leadership of Ban Johnson, baseball became a stable and profitable enterprise and its popularity grew apace. Between 1903 and 1914, player salaries gradually inched upward, while the profits of team owners improved substantially. In 1910, the average major-league player earned about $3,000, which compared favorably to the annual salary of a factory worker of $700 or a skilled laborer of $1,200. Nonetheless, the players looked at the large crowds in the grandstands and concluded that they were not getting their fair share of the revenue. Because they were captives of the reserve clause, players had little choice but to accept what management offered. A few brave souls each year attracted attention by "holding out" during spring training in hopes of obtaining a more lucrative offer. When that occurred, the owners easily stirred up negative fan reaction against the recalcitrant player for being disloyal. Even such stars as Ty Cobb had little leverage. In 1913, the owner of the Detroit Tigers bluntly told him during a holdout, "You will play for Detroit or you won't play for anybody."[21] Cobb caved shortly before the season began.

The profits being earned by successful franchises naturally attracted the attention of big investors. Thus there appeared yet another new league in 1914–15. The short-lived Federal League contributed to a financial disaster for the management of all three leagues while giving players only a temporary boost in pay. In 1913, the Federal League was organized but it initially seemed of little significance since it pledged not to sign any player who was reserved by an existing team. But before the 1914 season, Chicago businessman James

A. Gilmore agreed to take over the struggling league. He created an eight-team league that placed teams in cities where major-league franchises already existed (Brooklyn, Chicago, St Louis and Pittsburgh) and in four others that were home to minor-league clubs (Kansas City, Indianapolis, Baltimore, and Buffalo). His request to have the Federal League designated as a third major league was summarily rebuffed by Ban Johnson, who attacked the new league for what it was – a significant threat to the peace and prosperity of the Nationals and Americans. Some thought Johnson guilty of hypocrisy because it was he who had created a new league a decade earlier.[22]

Gilmore's league signed 81 major leaguers and 140 minor-league prospects with substantially increased salaries. The turbulence created by the heavy turnover in team rosters greatly alienated fans, who stayed away from the ballparks of all three leagues. This put all owners in a squeeze: just as their labor costs were more then doubling, their income was in freefall. In 1914, only 1.7 million persons paid their way into one of the three leagues' parks, a figure that was comparable to attendance in 1903. It is estimated that at least half of the teams lost money in 1914, and those that had a profit were only marginally in the black. Connie Mack lost an estimated $80,000 despite winning the 1914 American League pennant; consequently, shortly after running the championship flag up the Shibe Park flagpole, he held his famous fire sale that resulted in either trading or releasing several star players.

For a time it seemed that the situation would be resolved in the courts when the Federal League brought suit alleging that organized baseball constituted a cartel in restraint of trade. The case ended up in the court of a federal district judge whose future would be intricately intertwined with baseball – Judge Kenesaw Mountain Landis. At the hearing, Landis left little doubt that his sympathies lay with the game itself and neither adversary. Instead of issuing a ruling, Landis simply sat on the case as the season of 1915 unfolded, giving off not-so-subtle hints that he preferred the two sides come to a settlement.

Escalating deficits dictated that the impasse could not continue. Complex negotiations resulted in the folding of the Federal League after the 1915 season. Chicago restaurant owner Charles Weeghman, who had operated the Chicago Whales, was permitted to purchase the National League Cubs, and he moved them into his new stadium on the north side of the city, where they remain to this day. Gilmore ruefully commented upon the conclusion of this turbulent episode of baseball history: "I thought there was plenty of room for three major leagues. I admit I had the wrong perspective … There is no room for three major leagues."[23]

Although most parties were reasonably satisfied with the complex settlement, it left the owners of the Baltimore franchise of the Federal League out in the cold. They thereupon filed suit in federal court alleging a violation of the Sherman Antitrust Act. The case eventually ended up before the United States Supreme Court, resulting in one of the most curious decisions ever issued by the high court. In 1922, the justices handed baseball unprecedented "umbrella" protection from antitrust provisions of federal law. Associate Justice Oliver Wendell Holmes wrote the majority decision declaring that although baseball was a for-profit business, it nonetheless was not "trade or commerce in the commonly accepted use of those words." Players did not produce a product, only "effort," and the court ruled that this "product" was only "incidental" to interstate commerce. Although millions of dollars were tied up in the overall enterprise and 16 teams played in seven states and the

District of Columbia, the tight cartel that was now organized baseball was nonetheless declared exempt from antitrust laws. As a result of this friendly decision, baseball became, and remains yet today, the only professional sport to enjoy such an extraordinary exemption from federal oversight, an advantage that its leadership has exploited ever since.[24]

Crisis: Gamblers Fix the World Series of 1919

Once peace was restored, owners cut players salaries back to pre-Federal League levels. Although the players groused over their reduced income, they put on a good show in 1916 with two close pennant races, and attendance jumped 30 percent. The Brooklyn Robins (so named after their manager Wilbert Robinson) brought the first league championship to Flatbush since 1899, but lost the World Series in five games to the Boston Red Sox. The Bostonians were led by a rising star, left-handed pitcher George Herman Ruth, Jr, who won 23 games during the regular season. In the second game of the World Series the 22-year-old phenomenon everyone called "Babe" pitched all 14 innings in a 2–1 Red Sox victory.

The season of 1916 restored baseball's popularity, but two major crises loomed around the corner. The first of these was how to respond to the entrance of the United States into the Great War in April 1917. Baseball was a game largely played by young men of military age, and baseball's leaders feared team rosters would be depleted. Those fears initially proved unfounded as mobilization occurred relatively slowly. The 1917 season was completed without serious disruption. By the time the Chicago White Sox defeated the New York Giants in the World Series, only 40 players had departed for military service.

American League president Ban Johnson responded shrewdly to the war effort, making several popular patriotic gestures. He ordered that the American flag be flown at all games, required that bands be on hand to play the national anthem, plastered stadiums with posters urging fans to purchase war bonds, and granted free admission to men in uniform. He even required his American League teams to take part in military drill, offering a prize to the league's best marching team. While National League players enjoyed a good laugh, the American League teams underwent regular instruction in close-order marching drills that culminated in a much-hyped patriotic marching contest. The St Louis Browns marched off with the grand prize of $500, one of the few triumphs in their long and dreary history.[25]

The season of 1918, however, was a disaster. The departure of 227 major leaguers for military duty or assignment to defense factories made a shambles out of the season. Retired players were hustled back onto the field of play. In May 1918, Secretary of War Newton Baker further complicated things for baseball by requiring all able-bodied men between the ages of 18 and 45 to either serve in the military or work in defense industries. Team owners voted to reduce the season to 140 games and attendance plummeted. The Boston Red Sox defeated the Chicago Cubs in a poorly attended World Series that saw Babe Ruth star both on the mound and at the bat. Had the war not ended, the 1919 season would undoubtedly have been cancelled.[26]

In retrospect, it might have been best *had* Johnson cancelled the season, because 1919 became the year that would forever connect baseball to serious scandal. The World Series pitted the heavily favored Chicago White Sox against a gritty but seemingly outclassed Cincinnati team. The Reds, however, romped to a 5–3 game triumph (the World Series had

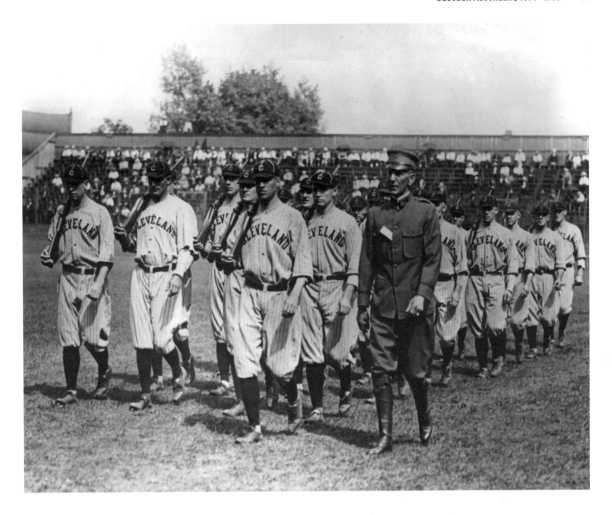

reverted to a best-of-nine format for this and the next two seasons), but the glory of that upset victory was dashed when it was revealed that eight Chicago players had pocketed $110,000 from gamblers to lose the series. The American people did not learn about this fraud until a year after the fact, and the story was only kept alive by the dogged reporting of Chicago newspaperman Hugh Fullerton, who published a series of allegations about a fix. Fullerton's charges were denied by baseball's leadership and he irritated them by charging that a conspiracy to cover up the scandal was in place.[27]

The cover-up crumbled after the end of the 1920s season. Philadelphia gambler Billy Maharg created a stir when he was quoted in the *Philadelphia North American* under the sensational headline, "Gamblers Promised White Sox $100,000 to Lose." The next day two rattled White Sox players, star slugger Joe Jackson and ace left-hander Eddie Cicotte, admitted to throwing the series under oath before a federal grand jury in Chicago. They also implicated several teammates. Maharg was part of a small group of Philadelphia gamblers that

Figure 5.2 Forward March! The Cleveland Indians participate in marching drills ordered for all American League teams during the 1918 season by league president Ban Johnson. For the duration of the Great War, Johnson ordered that the American flag be flown at every ballpark and that the National Anthem be played before the first pitch – traditions that endure to this day. *National Baseball Hall of Fame Library, Cooperstown, NY, USA (Public Domain)*

had promised the players $100,000 to dump the series, although they only managed to fork over $10,000. In 2 hours of testimony, with tears streaming down his face, Cicotte described how he had made two defensive errors in one inning that gave game 4 to the Reds, and how he had "grooved" the ball down the middle of the plate in game 1 so that the Cincinnati batters could "read the label on it." He and other witnesses then explained how pitcher Claude Williams had lost game 2 with an uncharacteristic streak of wildness, and why the normally reliable outfielder Happy Felsch managed to botch two easy plays in the sixth inning of game 5. When star hitter "Shoeless Joe" Jackson entered the federal courthouse to testify before the grand jury, a young boy reportedly said, "Say it ain't so, Joe! Say it ain't so!" And Jackson is reported to have quietly responded, "I'm afraid it is, son." Indictments were handed down by the grand jury charging the eight Chicago White Sox players with conspiracy, but legal maneuvering prevented the trial from taking place until August 1921.

Baseball executives quickly went into full-scale damage control, expressing both incredulity and outrage. They denied any knowledge of gambling influences in their game, a tale that knowledgeable baseball men found amusing. Baseball executives plaintively pointed out that even the best of hitters have slumps, that top pitchers sometimes get shelled, and that excellent fielders occasionally bobble a ground ball or make a bad throw. Detecting whether a player is deliberately attempting to make a misplay is no easy task. As Ban Johnson later recalled, he watched every game and had no inkling that the fix was in: "It all unfolded naturally to us in the grandstand. It seemed just hard luck that the great southpaw [Claude Williams] should be visited by a streak of wildness in two vital innings when all the remainder of the game he was steady as a clock."[28] Johnson's comment was indeed ironic! He had long been one of the few executives who had warned of the dangers of gambling only to have his fears rebuffed by complacent team owners.

The corrosive influence of gamblers had been bubbling near the surface, as Charles Alexander explains in his history of baseball. Charles Seymour concludes along the same vein as Alexander: "The evidence is abundantly clear … that the groundwork for the crooked 1919 World Series, like most striking events, was long prepared." The scandal, he writes, was "not an aberration brought about solely by a handful of villainous players. It was a culmination of corruption and attempts at corruption that reached back nearly twenty years."[29]

Beginning in 1908, rumors about gamblers influencing games percolated throughout the baseball world. In particular, these rumblings involved a hard-hitting and good-fielding first baseman, Hal Chase, who became infamous for his efforts to fix games and bribe players. Charges were even filed against him by his manager at Cincinnati in 1918, the highly respected Christy Mathewson. Yet the team owner and the president of the National League ignored the evidence and permitted Chase to move on to play for the Giants. Rumors surfaced that gamblers had a hand in deciding the 1917 World Series. Baseball executives, in particular National League president John Heydler, opted to ignore the many warning signs out of fears that a crackdown would hurt the image of the game and diminish ticket sales. They preferred to leave well enough alone, with the ultimate result being a public relations disaster that for a time seemed to have the potential to severely damage organized baseball.

The details of baseball's worst scandal are incredibly complex and the full story probably will never be known. Suffice it to say that the episode is replete with enough duplicity, corruption, double crosses, and broken promises to fill many a book – as indeed it has. As Alexander makes clear, it was a "conspiracy [that] had been a remarkably open secret."[30] Yet the essential story is relatively simple. Chicago pitcher Ed Cicotte hatched the idea to sell the series for about $100,000, and he made contact with two separate groups of gamblers. Several of his teammates agreed to participate, apparently angry about their low paychecks handed out by the unpopular, autocratic White Sox owner, the "Old Roman" Charles Comiskey. One group of gamblers was headed by Abe Attell, a former featherweight boxing champion and co-conspirator with Billy Maharg. The other group was headed by well-known New York City gambler and underworld figure, Arnold Rothstein, who apparently was in cahoots with gamblers from Boston. Two days before the series began, unknown to the Philadelphia crowd, Rothstein's agents met with the players in a south side Chicago hotel and handed over $40,000 with the remaining $60,000 to be paid after the deed was done. The plan called for the White Sox to throw only selected games so as to avoid suspicion, with Rothstein placing his bets on the outcome of the series and individual games accordingly. He even bet in a very public manner on the White Sox so as to cover his tracks. Rothstein's biographer estimates that after all expenses were paid, New York's premier gambler pocketed about $350,000.[31]

On November 6, 1920, a grand jury filed indictments against the "Chicago Eight" and three gamblers. Notably missing from the list was Arnold Rothstein, who professed complete innocence. The subsequent trial was a farce. Shortly before it opened, the district attorney discovered that all of the grand jury records and physical evidence in the case had been stolen! Even transcripts of the players' confessions before the grand jury had been lost. Inspired by this development, Cicotte and Jackson recanted their confessions and developed serious cases of amnesia. Without evidence or credible witnesses, the district attorney dropped the case in February 1921. Several months later, new indictments were handed down and the trial finally occurred in mid July of 1921. Once again the fix was in. The essential evidence was still missing and several new witnesses had fled to Canada, where they successfully fought extradition. Other witnesses suffered a simultaneous loss of memory and the judge was forced to issue a narrow set of instructions to the jury, which made the verdict inevitable. The jury found all parties innocent, and the Chicago Eight spent that evening celebrating.

Even before their hangovers had lifted, however, they learned that organized baseball now had a new sheriff in town. He was Kenesaw Mountain Landis, a former federal judge whose reputation as a jurist was nothing out of the ordinary but whose reputation for personal integrity was unquestioned. Most important, Landis's love of baseball had been demonstrated by his handling of the Federal League lawsuit. With the scandal raging all around them, in January of 1921 the owners rushed to put the best face on their beleaguered enterprise, and offered Landis a lofty salary of $50,000 per year to become its first commissioner (his salary as federal district judge was $7,500). In appointing Landis, the owners abandoned the three-man commission that had run things since 1903, effectively ending the autocratic rule of Ban Johnson, whose arrogance and domineering personality had alienated several key owners. But in so doing, the owners granted their new savior virtually unlimited authority. They agreed that he would have absolute power to take action against any person or any club he "suspected" of doing anything "detrimental to the best interests of the national game." The owners agreed "to loyally support their commissioner" and to "acquiesce in his decisions even when they believed them mistaken," and not to criticize him or his actions publicly. They had in fact created a new "czar" with unlimited power over their own enterprise.

Thus six months after Landis assumed office, the Chicago Eight awoke the day after their acquittal to learn that the commissioner had little appreciation for the Chicago system of justice. He had banned them from baseball for life. Landis bluntly wielded his powers as commissioner when he announced:

> Regardless of the verdict of juries, no player who throws a ball game, no player who undertakes or promises to throw a ball game, no player that sits in conference with a bunch of crooked players and gamblers where the ways and means of throwing a game are discussed and does not promptly tell his club about it, will ever play professional baseball.

Landis even tossed third baseman George "Buck" Weaver out of the game despite the fact he took none of the gamblers' money and did not participate in throwing any of the games. His sin? He had originally agreed to the scam but changed his mind before the first game. His crime was that he should have reported the conspiracy. "Birds of a feather flock together," Landis told the press. "Men associating with gamblers and crooks should expect no leniency."[32] Baseball fans would forever after refer to the team that besmirched the game's reputation as the Chicago "Black Sox."

Armed with unlimited powers, and superbly confident in his own judgment, Landis sacked the players and won widespread public acclaim. The scandal was put to rest. Soon baseball was soaring to new heights of popularity.

The Babe

Historians have often referred to the 1920s as the "Golden Age" of American sports. Sports became very big business as fans flocked to stadiums to watch their favorite teams and "star" players perform. Motion pictures, radio, and greatly expanded print media contributed to this growing sports frenzy. As the United States returned to what President Warren G. Harding called a time of "normalcy," the stage was set for the coronation of Babe Ruth as the most popular sports figure of the twentieth century.[33]

Ironically, the man who would be known for his home run hitting prowess had first attracted the attention of serious baseball fans as a young pitcher with the Boston Red Sox in 1916 when he won 23 games. However, his ability to handle a bat could not be ignored, and manager Ed Barrow began inserting him in the lineup at first base or in right field when he was not on the mound. Until Ruth burst on the baseball scene, the home run was a relatively infrequent event. Baseball purists preferred the scientific game of well-placed singles ("hit 'em where they ain't," as Wee Willie Keeler said), stolen bases, and well-executed hit-and-run plays. Now fans were enthralled by the power game and flocked to see Ruth swing from his heels, thrusting his 6 foot 2 inch frame into the ball with enormous power.

Ruth's last year in a Red Sox uniform was 1919. That year Ruth was a mainstay of the Red Sox pitching staff, but he nonetheless set a major-league record of 29 home runs. In his

truncated career as a pitcher, Ruth won 85 games and had a sparkling career earned run average of 2.70. Ruth's pitching and hitting, coupled with his youthful exuberance and flamboyant personality, attracted large crowds. Reporters loved his accessibility and knew he was good for a lively comment.

The owner of the Red Sox was the heavily indebted Harry Frazee, who regularly lost large sums producing bad Broadway musicals and making unwise stock investments. When Ruth demanded a doubling of his salary to $20,000, Frazee, confronted by large debts, sold Ruth's contract to the New York Yankees for $100,000. The sale of Ruth was but the first of a veritable fire sale of Red Sox stars to the Yankees as Frazee unloaded 13 additional players over the next three years, providing the Yankees with the backbone of one of the most fearsome teams in history. Ruth's pitching and hitting had enabled the Red Sox to defeat the Chicago Cubs in the 1918 World Series, and it would be the last such triumph to be enjoyed by the baseball fans of New England for almost a century. After Ruth's departure, the Red Sox went into a tailspin, finishing in last place in nine of the next 11 seasons. Although the Sox won four American League pennants between 1946 and 1986, they failed to win the World Series. Following the loss in 1986 to the New York Mets – when a crucial error by first baseman Bill

Figure 5.3 Commissioner Kenesaw Mountain Landis tosses out the first ball at an unknown game during the 1920s. Fans credited Landis with "saving" baseball when he banned eight Chicago White Sox players the day after they were acquitted by a Chicago jury, but baseball historians have criticized him for making erratic and bigoted decisions, including defending organized baseball's unwritten policy of excluding African American players. *National Baseball Hall of Fame Library, Cooperstown, NY, USA (Public Domain)*

Buckner on a routine ground ball proved disastrous – Boston sportswriter Dan Shaughnessy published a book claiming that by shipping Ruth to the detested rivals, Frazee had brought a terrible curse down upon the club. The "Curse of the Bambino" became part of baseball folklore.[34] In fact, the Sox were condemned to their fate by a combination of poor management and some genuine strokes of bad luck. Finally, after 86 long seasons, the Sox exorcised the curse in fall 2004 with a dramatic victory over the Yankees in the playoffs after being down three games to none, and then swept the powerful St Louis Cardinals in the World Series.

Babe Ruth thus landed in the nation's largest and most exciting city at the very time when sports were in ascendancy. In 1920, he became the unquestioned toast of New York when he smashed 54 home runs while batting .376. The Babe was the biggest show in the town that was the center of the entertainment business and hub of the national media. His on- and off-the-field exploits made him seem bigger than life, swatting towering home runs by day and enjoying the city's nightlife afterwards. His hearty appetite for vast quantities of food and alcohol became the stuff of legend, and his sexual energies were equally prodigious as he spent many a night with a seemingly endless parade of willing women. His roommate on road trips, Hall of Fame pitcher Waite Hoyt, later recalled that he seldom saw Ruth until after the sun came up in the morning.

Shortly after arriving in New York, Ruth joined up with publicist Christy Walsh who helped mold Ruth's public image as benefactor of the downtrodden and friend of children. Walsh made his client a national icon of mythic proportions, and his efforts made it difficult to separate fact from fiction. He especially played up Ruth's many visits to children's hospitals – an activity that Ruth in fact enjoyed. Walsh secured lucrative motion-picture appearances, demanded and got his client a prodigious $8,000 a week on the vaudeville circuit, generated many opportunities for endorsements (Babe Ruth Gum, Babe Ruth baseball caps, Babe Ruth Home Run Shoes, Bambino Smoking Tobacco), and published instructional baseball books, children's stories, and a long-running weekly syndicated newspaper column that was ghostwritten by Walsh or one of his associates. Ruth simultaneously endorsed Reo automobiles in St Louis, Packards in Boston, and Cadillacs in New York. At one point Walsh had four writers working overtime cranking out the Babe's many publications. (Ruth once commented that one of those anonymous journalists "writes more like me than anyone I know.")[35]

With Walsh calling the shots and prudently managing his client's investments, Ruth amassed a substantial fortune despite his penchant for spending money as rapidly as he consumed food and beer. Thus he easily survived the Great Depression and lived comfortably until his death in 1948. Ruth was the first of the great sports celebrities of a celebrity-saturated era. As historian Jules Tygiel aptly summarizes Ruth's life:

> He symbolized not only the exuberance and excesses of the 1920s, but the emergent triumph of personality and image in a modern America suddenly positioned to glorify these attributes. Lavishly chronicled on radio and in print, memorialized in photos and film, elevated to a new form of adoration in testimonial advertising, and molded by shrewd public relations, Ruth fulfilled people's fantasies and embodied their new reality.[36]

His performance on the field was equal to his public image. In his second year in New York, taking advantage of a more lively ball, Ruth hammered 59 home runs – an astonishing

number for the time – and drove in 170 runs while leading the Yankees to their first World Series appearance. His salary jumped to an unprecedented $52,000, a fact that only intensified public adoration in this materialistic age when the "self-made man" myth enjoyed wide acceptance. His production fell off in 1922 when he sat out a 39-game suspension imposed by Landis for playing in unsanctioned postseason exhibition games, hit "only" 35 home runs, and began to acquire a sizeable girth. It was only fitting that in the inaugural game played at Yankee Stadium in 1923 he smashed a home run in the ballpark already being called "the House that Ruth Built." Before record crowds, Ruth hit 41 home runs and enjoyed a .544 on-base percentage. He was selected unanimously as the American League's Most Valuable Player, and capped off that glorious year by hitting three home runs in leading the Yankees to their first World Series championship in an exciting matchup with John McGraw's Giants.

Ruth continued his assault upon American League pitching throughout the rest of the decade, averaging 49 home runs a season and 152 runs batted in,

Figure 5.4 Babe Ruth burnished his public image by reaching out to youngsters. His visits to children's hospital units and other charitable activities were heavily publicized by public relations aide Christy Walsh. Here Ruth poses for the camera giving batting tips to members of a youth team. *National Baseball Hall of Fame Library, Cooperstown, NY, USA © NBL*

while batting .353. The Yankees became baseball's most fearsome franchise, wining four pennants and three World Series championships during the 1920s. Ruth smashed 60 home runs in 1927, a record that would stand for 34 years. In 1930, his salary topped out at $80,000, which was more than double that of any other major-league player. Many Americans marveled that his salary that year was $5,000 higher than that of President Herbert Hoover. Asked how he could justify making more than the depression-besieged president, Ruth responded, "Why not? I had a better year than he did."[37]

By the early 1930s, however, Ruth's excessive weight and legendary all-night binges had taken their toll. He did rise to one final myth-making moment. Facing pitcher Charlie Root of the Chicago Cubs in the 1932 World Series, he stepped out of the batter's box and, according to legend, pointed toward the right-center field stands where he promptly hit the next pitch. Initial newspaper reports of the game failed to mention the "called shot," but in the years that followed, many versions of that dramatic moment made their way into print. Whether or not the incident actually occurred is beside the point; once it was reported it became part of the bigger-than-life aura that surrounded the Babe. Pitcher Charlie Root later insisted that Ruth never pointed to the stands: "Ruth did not point at the fence before he swung. If he had made a gesture like that, well, anybody who knows me knows that Ruth would have ended up on his ass."[38]

Ruth's performance thereupon began to fall off rapidly as he approached his 40th birthday, and he was traded to the Boston Braves before the 1935 season. Overweight and out of shape, suffering from a bum knee and an assortment of other ailments, he wanted to become a manager. When he realized that the Braves were not about to make him their new manager and had signed him only to boost attendance, he slugged three home runs in one game against Pittsburgh in late May, and promptly retired. He had the satisfaction of hitting his last home run – a seventh-inning blast of monumental proportions – off journeyman pitcher Guy Bush. The ball was the first ever to be hit over the second deck of the right-field stands in Forbes Field; the head usher attempted to measure the distance and concluded Ruth's last home run had traveled 600 feet. Although the measurement was imprecise, Pittsburgh baseball fans claimed it was the longest home run in the history of the town. Even pitcher Bush, who loved to harass the Babe from the bench, was amazed at the homer he had given up:

> I never saw a ball hit so hard before or since. He was fat and old, but he still had that great swing. Even when he missed you could hear the bat go swish. I can't remember anything about the first home run he hit off me that day. I guess it was just another homer. But I can't forget that last one. It's probably still going.[39]

That blast – number 714 – fittingly was the last hit of the Babe's incomparable career.

Baseball's Golden Age

Babe Ruth towered like a colossus over baseball during the 1920s, his spectacular exploits often obscuring the substantial accomplishments of many other outstanding players. During the 1920s, the Yankees were clearly the dominant team, but they always had strong competition. Yankee owner Jacob Ruppert and general manager Ed Barrow assembled a powerful supporting cast to complement their superstar. Hard-hitting first baseman Lou Gehrig joined the team in 1925 off the campus of Columbia University and, along with Earle Combs, Bob Meusel, Tony Lazzeri, and Ruth, formed one of the most formidable batting lineups in baseball history. The press aptly called it "Murderers Row." However, at decade's end, this powerful juggernaut was surpassed by the power aggregation Connie Mack assembled in Philadelphia. Over in the National League, John McGraw's Giants were always in the pennant chase, winning the flag four times in succession (1921–4), but gave way to the talented teams that general manager Branch Rickey assembled in St Louis. In 1926 the Cardinals, led by pitcher Jesse Haines and the league's best hitter, second baseman Rogers Hornsby, defeated the Yankees in a dramatic seventh game of the World Series when veteran pitcher Grover Cleveland Alexander struck out Lazzeri with the bases loaded in the seventh inning to preserve the championship. Hornsby led the league in hitting for six consecutive seasons and averaged an incredible .397 during that stretch; but indicative of the new style of play, Hornsby also hit for power, including 42 homers in 1922.

Over the next two decades, the Cardinals won nine pennants and six World Series championships. Central to their success was the front office leadership of Branch Rickey. He was a former catcher possessed of modest major-league skills, a graduate of Ohio Wesleyan University, and held a law degree from the University of Michigan. When injuries and tuberculosis cut short his major-league career with the New York Highlanders (later renamed the Yankees), he assumed the position of general manager of the St Louis Browns in 1913 and in the next two seasons also served as field manager. He emphasized proper off-field conduct by his players and drilled them in the fundamentals of the game during spring training. His sessions on the fundamentals of hitting, fielding, sliding, base running, and game strategies earned him the title "Professor of Baseball." In 1917, he transferred to the other St Louis team as field manager and moved into their front office later that year as general manager. Although holding several different titles, he astutely oversaw the Cardinals until 1941.[40]

Operating in a small market that had two major-league teams, Rickey realized he had to find a way of building pennant contending teams without following the standard practice of buying the contracts of top prospects from independent minor-league teams. He created a feeder system by acquiring minor-league teams and filling their rosters by signing large numbers of young prospects at low cost. He assembled a coaching staff that was charged with grounding the young players in sound fundamentals. Rickey reasoned that over the years this "farm system" would provide the Cardinals with a steady stream of major leaguers. And indeed it did. Rickey later commented that his farm system was not so much the work of a creative baseball executive as it was "the result of stark necessity."

Other teams had tinkered with the concept, but Rickey perfected it. In 1919, the Cardinals purchased the contract of future Hall of Fame pitcher Jesse Haines for $10,000, but would not buy another player contract for nearly 30 years. Rickey began building his system in 1919 when the Cardinals purchased the Class D Ft Smith, Arkansas, club, and in 1921 acquired the Syracuse franchise of the International League and Houston of the Texas League. As the years went by, more teams were added, to the point that in 1940 the Cardinals owned 32 minor-league franchises and had working agreements with eight more teams. The Cardinals had affiliated teams playing at the lowest Class D level all the way to AAA.

The result was that the Cardinals received a continuous flow of talent that made them a perennially contending team. Between 1930 and 1949, the Cardinals finished in first or second place 15 times. The Cardinals also were able to make a large profit by selling players' contracts to other teams. Because his own contract called for him to receive 10 percent of those sales, Rickey amassed a considerable personal fortune in the process.

Rickey's approach, however, did not meet with the approval of Commissioner Landis, who believed it kept many players with major-league talent tied up in the Cardinals farm system. He viewed Rickey's system as a means of stifling competition and undercutting the independence of minor-league teams. His several efforts to dismantle the Cardinals farm system, however, were rebuffed. During the Depression years of the 1930s, hard-pressed minor-league teams discovered that an affiliation with a major-league team helped stabilize their finances. Further, several other teams, most notably the Yankees, began to emulate the Cardinals and created their own farm club system.[41]

Rickey and Landis became engaged in an ongoing feud that often saw these two headstrong men in open conflict. Landis was given credit for his forceful handling of the Black Sox scandal, but often his actions revealed a man whose policies were neither consistent nor always in the best interests of baseball. Although he made headlines by forbidding some prominent owners to own stock in racetracks, he never took decisive action against Giants owner Horace Stoneham who was indicted on federal charges of bribery and mail fraud in the mid 1920s and who was a close friend of gambler and alleged fixer Arnold Rothstein. Although Landis banned an additional 12 players for gambling indiscretions after concluding the Black Sox episode, he wavered in dealing with top name players. Landis reportedly had in his possession strong evidence that implicated Ty Cobb and Cleveland's Tris Speaker of gambling on baseball games, but he did not take action, permitting them to retire quietly while issuing a public statement exonerating them of all allegations. Likewise, he refused to act on information pointing toward the dumping of games between Detroit and Chicago in 1917, and later issued a statute of limitations on any impropriety that might have occurred prior to his taking office in 1921. But he did ban for life base-stealing whiz Benny Kauff, charged with (but found innocent of) involvement in a car theft ring. His real crime seems to have been jumping to the Federal League in 1915.[42]

In 1923, several of the owners, now sorry that they had given Landis vast power over their game, become disenchanted with his imperial attitude and arbitrary decision-making. Landis confronted them with a well-publicized demand: either support him or fire him. The rebellion fizzled because Landis had won over the media, which repeatedly praised him as the staunch defender of America's Game. As the historian Eugene Murdock sardonically puts it, "In the annals of 'lost opportunities' the failure to accept Landis at his word and terminate his contract must rank near the top."[43] With his opposition in retreat, Landis consolidated his control and the owners lacked the gumption to challenge his decisions, inconsistent and arbitrary as they frequently were. He died in office in 1944 at the age of 78, engaged at the time in a determined effort to derail steps to end the racial segregation of organized baseball. Wrong as he was on this and other matters, Landis truly was the "czar" of baseball. When this headstrong and determined commissioner died, the owners made certain that they never employed another commissioner with such a dominant personality.

Historian Harold Seymour accurately concludes that by the end of the 1920s, a "close association and identification" had developed between the millions of baseball fans and their favorite teams as well as with the game itself. Americans took their baseball seriously and accorded it a special place in the life of the nation. Baseball's appeal, Seymour writes, had produced "a profound emotional grip on the public that gave the game genuine vitality."[44]

6

Playing Nice: Women and Sports, 1860–1945

Throughout much of American history, women have often been considered unwelcome intruders when they attempted to participate in organized sports. Even as late as the 1960s, opportunities for females to participate in sponsored competition were severely limited. When women began to take up competitive sports in a limited way in the latter years of the nineteenth century, they engendered a wide range of criticism. The early opponents of women's participation argued that women could succeed in sports only if they sacrificed their femininity and adopted masculine traits. Reproductive organs could be damaged, and aggressive play could unleash uncontrollable emotions capable of producing acute nervousness, a hypersexual appetite, and serious bodily injury. These attitudes prevailed to the point in the 1920s that female physical education leaders felt compelled to adopt a defensive position that embraced "moderation" to the point where they urged the abolition of competitive sports programs in the public schools and universities. The march toward equality of opportunity was long and difficult and consumed the entire twentieth century. Enormous cultural obstacles had to be overcome because, on the one hand, resistance by leading male athletic figures was persistent and powerful, and on the other hand, many female physical education leaders were opposed to the male competitive athletic model.

Female athletes faced a tangled web of opposition. During the nineteenth century, restrictions were imposed by a society that held distinctively different gender roles for men and women. Middle- and upper-middle class women were expected to devote their lives to the pursuit of domestic responsibilities as wife, homemaker, and mother, while working class and minority women were excluded from athletics simply by their social status. Dominant social conventions held that it simply was unacceptable behavior for women to exert themselves in competitive games. Young girls were expected to play with dolls, not balls. Parents worried that their daughters, upon reaching puberty, might become "muscle bound," "tomboys," or worse if they engaged in vigorous physical activity. Fears that athletic

Sports in American Life: A History, Second Edition. Richard O. Davies.
© 2012 John Wiley & Sons, Inc. Published 2012 by John Wiley & Sons, Inc.

competition would encourage masculine behavior meant that schools and colleges provided scant encouragement while not offering organized sports programs.

By the 1880s, a concerted effort by a small number of reformers began to chip away at the massive wall of discrimination. These pioneers began to rethink centuries-old assumptions and challenge the belief that vigorous exercise was dangerous for young women. Physical education classes were introduced, and by the twentieth century, schools and colleges offered limited programs in such sports as basketball, volleyball, tennis, and swimming. By the 1910s, popular magazines had discovered a new American, the "athletic woman," who enjoyed and excelled in sports. The Victorian image of women as frail and deferential was replaced by this new image. She was a confident and assertive individual who participated not only in athletics but also in business, education, politics and the professions.

These trends swept across American society during the 1920s. Clothing styles were revolutionized. Gone were the cumbersome long dresses, layers of petticoats, and restrictive corsets, along with outrageously large and ornate hats and elaborate hairstyles, to be replaced by knee-length skirts and short bobbed hairdos. Women openly expressed their equality with their male counterparts; they voted, held public office, attended college, smoked cigarettes, defied the Eighteenth Amendment, danced the Charleston, and generally exulted in their newfound liberation from the restrictive gender conventions of an earlier era. And for the first time, a few of the most famous sports figures were women.

The Early Years of Women's Sports

By 1910, far-reaching changes had occurred in the role and status of women. Popular magazines featured the "New American Woman" who embraced an active lifestyle. This welcome image resulted from over fifty years of reform efforts. Until the end of the nineteenth century, the dominant thinking of physical culturalists was that only a regimen of light-to-moderate exercise was appropriate for females. It was widely believed that the human body possessed a set amount of energy and that the mental exertion required by a rigorous higher-education program would diminish a female's physical capacity. As late as 1912, physician Dudley A. Sargent summarized these views when he tackled the question, "Are Athletics Making Girls Masculine?" His conclusion was definitely in the affirmative: "Physically all forms of athletic sports and most physical exercises tend to make women's figures more masculine, inasmuch as they tend to broaden the shoulders, deepen the chest, narrow the hips, and develop the muscles of the arms, back and legs, which are all masculine characteristics." The good doctor went on to summarize his research thusly: "Any one who has had much experience in teaching or training women must have observed these facts in regard to them: Women as a class cannot stand a prolonged mental or physical strain as well as men." He went on to urge that leaders make certain to limit the playing of basketball because of many reports of high school girls suffering from "nervous collapse" and "breaking down with heart trouble" due to excessive exercise.[1]

Such nonsense, of course, would not stand in the long run. But its influence endured well into the second half of the twentieth century. As early as the 1840s, education reformer Catharine Beecher had begun attacking such stereotypes. She lamented that while parents

Figure 6.1 Vassar College students demonstrate that they did not necessarily always "play nice" when they took to the basketball court. Fears that young women would display overly aggressive tactics, as evidenced here, led to the adoption of rules that sought to greatly reduce rough play. The referee in the white dress apparently survived this jump ball. *Special Collections, Vassar College Libraries, photo Walven*

of young girls sought to educate their minds, they tended to discourage active play and exercise: "They have done almost every thing they could do to train their children to become feeble, sickly, and ugly." She urged parents to encourage exercise for girls as an essential step in the development of healthy adult women. "Next to pure air," she wrote in 1855, "healthful exercise and amusements are the most important remedies."[2]

In 1861, philanthropist Matthew Vassar established a women's college in Poughkeepsie, New York, that featured a physical education program at the heart of the curriculum. The initial planning document for Vassar College stated, "Good health is essential to the successful prosecution of study, and to the vigorous development of either mental or moral powers." One of the first buildings constructed on campus was the "Calisthenium," where physical education and recreational activities were held. It also housed the School of Physical Training, where faculty implemented Matthew Vassar's vision of fusing rigorous physical and intellectual activity for women students.[3]

Vassar's ideas were slow to be replicated elsewhere, but by the 1880s in Boston at the Sargent School and the Normal School of Gymnastics, programs designed to produce teachers of physical education were attracting attention. Graduates of these two pioneering programs greatly influenced the development of women's athletic and physical education programs throughout the public schools and higher education. Although appreciative of the importance of physical activity, these educators nonetheless were greatly influenced by Victorian standards, so they emphasized the importance of "moderation." It was expected that female students reflect the "proper behavior" expected of ladies and not engage in activities "in excess." This cautious philosophy resulted in a prescription of calisthenics and dance classes, the playing of relatively sedate games such as badminton, croquet, and bowling, and the pursuit of such activities as horseback riding, boating, and skating. Weightlifting, long-distance running, and aggressive games definitely were not permissible.[4]

By the early 1900s, courses in physical education had become an integral part of the curriculum in American colleges and universities. Graduates of these programs took the message into public schools where they put girls through a regimen of exercises and games in physical education classes. Nonetheless, traditional attitudes lingered. In 1911, *Lippincott's Magazine* published an article entitled "The Masculinization of Girls," which explored the pros and cons of the new "athletic girl." The magazine reported, "She loves to walk, to row, to ride, to motor, to jump and run … just as Man walks, jumps, rows, rides, motors, and runs." The article called attention to an enormous ambiguity that hovered over women participating in sports. The article concluded that the "athletic girl" was in general a positive development: "With muscles tense and blood aflame, she plays the manly role." And that raised important questions. Did female athletes have to become "masculine" in order to participate in competitive athletics? Were a finely honed physique and a competitive instinct "unfeminine?" Would competitive sports unleash repressed sexual desires? Or worse, would girls become too "manly" and lose their femininity?[5]

A major impetus to increased physical activity for women was the bicycle craze that swept across America in the 1890s. The "safety bicycle" offered women a unique opportunity to expand their mobility and increase physical activity. The introduction of rear wheel chain drive, diamond-shaped frame construction, pneumatic tires, and reliable steering and braking mechanisms made bicycling a safe form of transportation as well as a source of amusement and exercise. The bicycle provided women with a new sense of freedom, prompting Susan B. Anthony to call it the "freedom machine." In 1895, having learned the joy of riding in her mid 50s, the well-known temperance and suffrage advocate Frances Willard published a humorous book describing her liberating experience. *A Wheel within a Wheel: How I Learned to Ride a Bicycle* emphasized the importance of exercise as contributing to better health, a heightened sense of individual worth, and an enhanced sense of mobility and freedom. She urged parents to permit their daughters to learn to ride if they were "normally constituted and dressed hygienically," reassuring them that "Many physicians are now coming to regard the 'wheel' as beneficial to the health of women as well as men."[6]

The impact of the bicycle was seen almost immediately in women's clothing. Long flowing skirts tended to get caught in the spokes and chain drive, and soon women were seen wearing stylish new types of riding pants or shorter, divided skirts. As *Life* magazine noted lightly in 1897,

Be it recorded that a large proportion of the bicycle girls look exceedingly well in bicycle clothes. Whether they wear stockings or leggings, whether they wear divided skirts, they adorn creation. Not the least good thing that the bicycle has done has been to demonstrate publicly that women have legs. Their legs are unquestionably becoming to them. So are their shirt-waists. Long may they wave.[7]

Although the cycling craze faded before the onslaught of the automobile culture during the early years of the new century, untold millions of women joined in the fun. This experience contributed significantly to the emerging new mindset regarding exercise for women.

Simultaneously with the bicycle craze, basketball created an exciting opportunity for women to participate in a competitive team sport. Women were fascinated by the game. They formed class teams in schools and colleges, and by 1900 varsity teams were challenging those of other institutions. Women discovered that on the court they could play with a newfound abandon. Exuberant play on the court, however, led to physical contact and contortions that challenged traditional rules of decorum. School and college administrators at times decreed that games be played behind closed doors so as to exclude wide-eyed male spectators. The challenge to traditional gender roles was readily evident in 1904 in the village of Camden, Ohio, when the high school put its first girls' team on the floor. The town's weekly newspaper reported that the school's "fair maidens" were defeated in a game because their "feminine sweetness" was no match for the "rough and tumble" visitors from a nearby city who "used other than lady-like tactics."[8]

Female physical education instructors were quick to observe what one termed "mad play," in which the participants became "bitter in feeling and lose self-control." Senda Berenson, a physical education instructor at Smith College, wrote approvingly in 1903 that, "games for women are meeting less and less opposition, and gaining larger numbers of warm supporters because our younger generation of women are already showing the good results that may be obtained … in better physiques and greater strength and endurance." She also took note that basketball, in particular, encouraged "rough and vicious play" that "seems worse in women than in men. A certain amount of roughness is deemed necessary to bring out manliness in our young men. Surely rough play can have no possible excuse in our young women." Reflecting popular assumptions about women's nature, Berenson wrote,

> It is a well known fact that women abandon themselves more readily to an impulse than men … This shows us that unless we guard our athletics carefully in the beginning many objectionable elements will come in. It also shows us that unless a game as exciting as basketball is carefully guided by such rules as will eliminate roughness, the great desire to win and the excitement of the game will make our women do sadly unwomanly things.[9]

Consequently, Berenson introduced what became widely known as the "Smith Rules" for women's basketball. Members of the six-player teams were restricted to separate areas on the court, physical contact was forbidden, and a player could dribble the ball only once. Defenders could neither "snatch" the ball from an opponent nor attempt to prevent an opponent from shooting for a goal. Although many girls' teams played the five-person "boys' rules," the Berenson model gained in popularity and stifled the development of rigorous play. Berenson's leadership set the tone for a growing movement by leading women physical educators and coaches to abolish the competitiveness of women's sports on the campus.

Berenson's influence was pervasive in shaping the game for women, and high schools readily adopted variations of the Smith Rules. In Iowa high schools, a special variation of the game that required three girls to play on the defensive end of the court and three on the offensive end became a state obsession; it was a game that had particular appeal in the small rural schools that were prevalent throughout the state. When most state athletic associations dropped interscholastic competition for girls during the 1920s and 1930s, the public schools in Iowa persisted with it – and continued to sponsor the six-player game. The latter remained in place until conformity with the now standard five-person game was imposed by the Iowa Girls High School Athletic Union amid a firestorm of controversy in 1993.

The new "athletic woman" caught the attention of popular artist Charles Dana Gibson, whose stunning drawings of tall, attractive upper-class young women enjoyed wide popularity from 1895 until the First World War. His popular "Gibson Girl" sketches appeared frequently in such magazines as *Collier's Weekly*, *Cosmopolitan*, and *The Outlook*. Gibson often took his subjects outdoors, where they would be seen astride a bicycle, on the tennis court, swinging a niblick on the golf course, or driving an automobile. When she went swimming, the Gibson Girl wore a modest bathing suit complete with stockings. The stunning Gibson Girl was tall and slender, of ample female form, smartly dressed, her upswept hair impeccably set, her face attractive but haughty. Clearly Gibson was not advocating an independent woman. To the contrary, he seemed preoccupied with romance and courtship, and his subjects were subtly portrayed as discreetly but resolutely flirting with handsome men. The message was clear: these attractive new-age women were headed in the acceptable direction of marriage. Whenever they appeared holding a tennis racquet or golf club, a suitably handsome male companion was somewhere in the picture. In one of Gibson's most popular drawings, entitled "Is a Caddy Always Necessary?" a couple is pictured seated unhappily on the edge of a sand trap while their teenage caddy stands by, oblivious to their desire to be alone on the wooded back nine. When the Great War broke out in 1914, Gibson was attracted to military subjects and largely abandoned his popular Gibson Girls. Within a few years, the alluring but aloof Gibson Girl gave way to the daring flapper of the 1920s.[10]

The Demise of Women's Athletics

While athletic programs for men gained in size and prestige on the campus during the 1920s, the opposite was the case for women. From the perspective of the twenty-first century, the dominant philosophy of women physical education professors and coaches prior to the 1970s is surprising. Although many colleges sponsored intercollegiate programs for women between the 1890s and the First World War, during the 1920s women educators led a concerted attack upon competitive programs to the point where most were abolished. Like a falling domino, interscholastic programs for high school girls also were axed. They would not be re-established for almost a half-century. The primary motivation was an awareness of the many unsavory aspects of men's intercollegiate sports. Allegations of recruiting and academic scandals became rampant during the 1920s, and a win-at-any-cost mentality raised many ethical questions among women educators about the value of competition. As Berenson explained, "The greatest element of evil in the spirit of athletics in this country is the idea that one must win at any cost – that defeat is an unspeakable disgrace." The win-at-any-cost syndrome was corrupting men's programs, especially football, and women educators did not want to encourage its replication in their programs.[11]

The result was a powerful movement to de-emphasize competitive sports for women. Replacing it was an effort to provide healthy recreation outside the realm of competition. "Sports for all" became the popular refrain, and the most prominent result was the creation of the "play day." Instead of competitive athletic contests being provided between rival schools, young women from several schools would meet for a day of games and activities, usually without the benefit of prior practice or instruction in the games to be played. Play day neatly fused the traditional – but declining – Victorian image of proper womanhood with prevailing medical theories on female physiology and a growing disgust over the reputation of college football. As Berenson said, "We [women] can profit by the experience of our brothers and therefore save ourselves from allowing those objectionable features to creep into our athletics."[12] Thus the prevailing image was that women were set apart both physiologically and morally from men.

Play days did not feature teams competing under their school colors. Instead, teams were created that mingled students from the participating institutions and a day was spent playing basketball, softball, soccer, field hockey, volleyball, and tennis, and perhaps engaging in some track and field events. Emphasis was upon participation rather than competition. The concepts of teamwork, training, and practice, and the implementation of strategies, were downgraded in favor of socializing and enhancing the individuality of the participants. Play day was thus both anti-competition and anti-varsity; it was formalized in the 1923 Platform adopted by the Women's Division of the National Amateur Athletic Federation at a Conference on Athletics and Physical Recreation for Women and Girls, which emphasized the objective of "a sport for every girl and every girl in a sport."[13]

Although the great majority of women coaches and physical educators were firmly committed to the anti-competitive model, there were naturally those who viewed the concept as inherently wrong. The leader of this minority group was Ina Gittings, a physical education professor at the University of Arizona. "Play days," she wrote in 1931

> are extremely weak and offer little or none of the joy and values of real games played skillfully, willingly, intelligently, and eagerly by well-matched teams. I picture the girls in a Play Day as sheep, huddled and bleating in their little Play meadow, whereas they should be young mustangs exultantly racing together across vast prairies.[14]

Gittings may have represented the minority view among women physical educators, but her critique of the anti-competitive model would resonate loud and clear in the 1970s when the women's rights movement discovered the great inequities in the college athletic experience:

> Have we not postponed this legitimate phase of physical activity and recreation long enough? There is nothing wrong with the games, competition, the girls, or travel, but there is something wrong with the Directors, who have phobias at the thought of making the same mistakes in

intercollegiates as men have made. And there is something wrong with the physical education instructors who cannot coach and conduct such activities without letting them get beyond control. Why not graciously concede and be in on the inevitable – the return of intercollegiate competition for women?[15]

Thus, much to Ina Gittings's dismay, and largely at the behest of women physical education professionals, all across the United States colleges and public schools dropped competitive athletic programs for women and girls. Perhaps Gittings did not appreciate the fears held by many of her contemporary women instructors that, should women's sports continue to grow, males would swoop in and take control to the point they would lose control of their athletes. These programs would not return for nearly a half-century and they would do so amid much controversy and conflict that required the firm intervention of the federal government.

Helen and Trudy: America's First Women Sports Stars

Images of the New American Woman and the Gibson Girl helped prepare American society to embrace its first female sports figures. The superb tennis skills of a young woman from California, Helen Wills, created awareness of what women athletes could accomplish. After struggling with debilitating childhood illnesses, she turned to tennis as a means of enhancing her physical condition. Standing 5 feet 7 inches, Wills cut a sharp figure on the court in her simple but stylish white skirt and sun visor. Seldom showing any emotion, she was dubbed "Little Miss Poker Face" by the press. Wills hit with incredible power and displayed uncanny accuracy in placing her shots. One leading tennis player and authority, Don Budge, recalled that he had never seen a woman hit a tennis ball with such power until Steffi Graf came on the scene in the 1980s.[16]

In 1926, Wills traveled to France to meet the reigning Wimbledon women's champion, Frenchwoman Suzanne Lenglen. That match, held at Cannes, produced considerable public interest. Scalpers were getting the astronomical sum of $50 apiece for tickets. Wills ultimately lost in a close and dramatic match, with many games going to multiple deuces and featuring long rallies. Wills dominated American women's tennis from 1927 until the mid 1930s. Her record of six US Open singles titles would last until eclipsed by Chris Evert in the 1980s; she also won two championships on the clay courts at the French Open, and four Wimbledon titles. Between 1927 and 1933, Wills won 180 straight matches without losing a single set.

One of the more improbable sports heroes of the 1920s was the daughter of a New York City butcher. Gertrude Ederle learned to swim at an early age while spending summers on the Jersey shore. She later recalled that she was "a water baby" who was "happiest between the waves." When Ederle was five, she developed a problem with her hearing after suffering a bout with measles. She later recalled, "The doctors told me my hearing would get worse if I continued swimming, but I loved the water so much, I just couldn't stop." By her late teens, she was winning freestyle races ranging between 100 and 800 meters, setting several world records. One day in 1922 she set seven world records in the waters off Brighton Beach in Brooklyn. Between 1921 and 1925 she held 25 amateur national and world swimming records, and she attracted national attention when she swam 16 miles from the Battery to Sandy Hook, New Jersey, through turbulent waters. At the 1924 Olympics, which for the first time held limited competitions for women, she won a gold medal and two bronzes.[17]

On August 6, 1926, Ederle thrilled the world when she became the first woman to swim the English Channel. When she entered the water at Cap Gris-Nez, France, she noticed a warning sign about high waves and choppy water, but after a brief prayer she plunged into the cold waters, her body slathered with heavy grease. If she had been able to swim in a straight line, her distance would have been 21 miles, but the high winds and waves were so rough that it is estimated she swam 35 miles to reach the English coast.

Ederle immediately became an American celebrity. She was welcomed back to the United States by a tickertape parade through the New York City financial district as an estimated 2 million people waved and cheered "Trudy! Trudy! Trudy!" She was even invited to the White House, where President Calvin Coolidge, not known for his social sensitivities and in typical form, laconically commented, "I am amazed that a woman … should be able to swim the English Channel." For a brief time Ederle rivaled Bill Tilden, Babe Ruth, and Red Grange as a national sports figure, but she discovered that fame was fleeting. She made a Hollywood movie about her life, took a stab at vaudeville, and was deluged with marriage proposals from unknown suitors. Her stint in vaudeville fell flat: "I was just a bundle of nerves. I had to quit the tour because I was stone deaf." In 1929, she suffered what was then called a "nervous breakdown," and in 1933 fell down an apartment stairwell, suffered a broken back, and was confined to a body cast for four years. She lived a long but lonely life, supporting herself during the 1950s and the 1960s giving swimming lessons at the Lexington School for the Deaf in New York City. Although the press occasionally recalled her Channel swim, she dropped from public view and lived quietly in New York, her moment of glory during the 1920s long forgotten by most Americans. She died alone in 2003 at the age of 98.[18]

The triumphs of women such as Helen Wills and Gertrude Ederle raised concerns that they exhibited traits that exceeded the conventional image of femininity. Ederle's stout 145 pound physique drew some comment, but the fact that she had crossed the English Channel 2 hours faster than any of the five men who had previously made the arduous trip raised many questions. When the dominant European tennis player Suzanne Lenglen came to the United States in 1920 to play America's top women players, she startled the sensibilities of many when she told *Collier's Magazine* that she and other serious women players "are out to win. No mercy is shown … There is no such thing as 'ladies first.'" Helen Wills's domination of her era of women's tennis produced considerable ambivalence. Tennis fans appreciated the speed, agility, and power that she exhibited, prompting journalists to use such terms as "killer," "ruthless," and "heartless" to describe the cold efficiency she displayed in dispatching her opponents. Such women were pursuing athletic excellence by exhibiting the same traits as male athletes – strength, speed, endurance, and agility enhanced by a fierce competitiveness. This image delighted feminists but disturbed traditionalists who feared that the new woman athlete portended the arrival of a generation of women who were neither fragile nor vulnerable and who would not need the protective care of men. Beyond question, the female athlete as exemplified by these women no longer accepted the traditional virtue of "moderation" in pursuit of their athletic dreams.[19]

Babe: The Texas Tomboy

Ederle and Wills gained acceptance as athletes because they did not openly challenge traditional images of women. However, when a woman of prodigious skill and strength openly flaunted prevailing values, public opinion was decidedly mixed. The American people viewed Mildred "Babe" Didrikson with a mixture of incredulity, uneasiness, and awe. Even years after her premature death in 1956, the ambiguity surrounding her life and career was palpable.

Didrikson appeared on the sports scene as the exuberant Twenties were winding down and the Great Depression beginning. By 1932, when Didrikson became a media sensation with her record-setting exploits at the Los Angeles Olympics, the unemployment rate had reached 25 percent. The collapse of the economy – highlighted by thousands of closed banks, a drop of the Dow Jones stock index of over 80 percent, long lines waiting for soup kitchens to open, and bewildered political and business leaders futilely attempting to find solutions – provided a somber environment for all athletes during the decade-long depression.

The fanfare of publicity that surrounded star athletes of the 1920s dimmed when the national mood turned gloomy as the economy tanked. Thus when Didrikson captured headlines with her record-shattering exploits in several sports, the public response was appreciative but subdued. The muted reaction was not simply due to the economy. It was also the result of an uncertainty of how to respond to a female athlete of incredible skill, whose multisport accomplishments overshadowed the best male athletes of the time. As biographer Susan Cayleff suggests, Didrikson "was caught in the midst of conflicting and rapidly changing notions of ideal womanhood" that were sweeping through American society. The new ideas were leading "to growing participation by women in the economy and politics, yet the dominant ideology asked them to remain housewives." Cayleff notes that "Babe defied norms. Unmarried, self-supporting, and earning big money, she implicitly rejected the economically-dependent status expected of women."[20]

The hesitancy with which the general public viewed Didrikson resulted in part from her refusal to conform to established standards. Her public comments about her lack of interest in boyfriends raised suspicions, which were accentuated by her physical appearance. A chiseled muscular body, what one mean-spirited journalist called a "hatchet face," and an unstylish short hairdo produced apprehension about her femininity and sexual orientation. Another journalist expounded on her image: "This chin of the Babe's, the thin, set lips, the straight sharp profile, the sallow suntan, undisguised by rouge, regarded in connection with her amazing athletic prowess at first acquaintance are likely to do her no justice." Many a writer referred to her as "freakish." Her exceptional physical strength and fluid body motions, her frequent participation in men's baseball and basketball games where her skill level was unquestioned, and her casual use of profanity added to public discomfort. Leading journalist Paul Gallico criticized her repeatedly, giving her the unfortunate nickname of "muscle moll." He wrote that Didrikson's appearance and behavior raised the question as to whether she "should be addressed as Miss, Mrs, Mr, or It." Didrikson's undisguised disdain for things feminine and her overpowering athleticism naturally inflamed the fears of parents that their daughters would adopt her as a role model and become "tomboys." Cayleff observes, "Her physique, her trousers and plain shirts, her short-cropped hair, and her sheer competence in the male realm of competitive sports presented an intimidating image to a culture recently attuned to the medical definitions of female homosexuality … Sportswriters and social commentators spent ink on all of these fears as they met its embodiment in Babe." After Babe's death, one women's physical education professor at Lamar University recalled, "My mother cried when I played softball," because she said, "I just don't want you to grow up to be like Babe Didrikson."[21]

Didrikson was born in 1911 to working-class immigrant Norwegian parents in the tough seaport town of Port Arthur, Texas. She claimed that her nickname was given to her by schoolmates who admired her ability to hit a baseball like Babe Ruth. As a youngster, she exhibited a fondness for contests and hard-nosed play at which she excelled. Her parents actively encouraged her competitive nature, including her unusual practice of repeatedly jumping the front-yard hedge (a skill she later said helped her win an Olympic gold medal in the hurdles). When the family moved to Beaumont, Babe's raucous behavior soon led to the designation as "the worst kid on Doucette Street" because she got into frequent fights with neighborhood boys. In the ninth grade, she knocked cold a football player who challenged her to hit him on the chin. In high school, she became known as a multisport overachiever as she excelled in basketball, softball, volleyball, swimming and diving, tennis, and track.

Even before graduating from Beaumont High, Didrikson accepted a position to become a "secretary" for a Dallas insurance company at the munificent sum of $75 per month (a very high starting clerical wage for the Depression era). She typed few letters and took no shorthand because her job was to play on the firm's industrial women's basketball team that owner and sports enthusiast Melvin J. McCombs had assembled. She led the Employer's Casualty Insurance Company Golden Cyclones basketball team to national titles in 1930 and 1931. Didrikson added to her reputation as a rebel by spurning the customary loose-flowing pantaloons for a skintight orange satin uniform that shocked everyone; her teammates soon adopted the same style, and other teams followed suit. In the summers she played on the firm's softball team, slugging many a home run, and at McCombs's urging, competed on the company's track and field entry in Amateur Athletic Union (AAU) tournaments.

Didrikson pushed herself to excel in track and field, putting in long hours every day on physical conditioning and practice. In the summer of 1930, despite suffering from a badly cut foot, she set an American record in the high jump and won first place in the shot put, baseball throw, and javelin. She then set her sights on the 1932 Olympics, a dream she had held since childhood. At the 1932 AAU national meet, which also served as the Olympic qualifier, she was entered by McCombs as a one-person team, which enabled her to compete in all events – a daunting physical challenge. In one 3 hour period, she won six of 10 events, setting world records in the baseball throw (272 feet), the javelin (139 feet 3 inches), and the 80 meter hurdles (12.1 seconds), and national records in the shot put (39 feet 6.5 inches) and the high jump (5 feet 3/16 inches), while also winning the long jump (17 feet 6 inches). She also finished fourth in the discus. This effort produced 30 points; the second-place team chalked up 22 points.

Now a highly publicized sports figure, Didrikson was frustrated to learn that Olympic rules restricted women to just three events. She thereupon set two world records, winning the javelin with a 143 feet effort, and the 80 meter hurdles at 11.7 seconds. Her effort in the high jump also should have produced a gold medal, but she was "penalized" by the judges for using an unorthodox and unladylike jumping style, her own modification of the western roll technique. The perplexed judges delayed a decision for 30 minutes while they reviewed film of her jumps, and thereupon ruled that, although she and Jean Shiley had tied at 5 feet 5 inches, Didrikson had committed a foul when her head crossed the bar before her feet. But instead of disqualifying her, they awarded Didrikson the silver medal. This bizarre turn of events aptly symbolized the controversy and confusion about gender roles that her athleticism provoked.

Didrikson attempted to capitalize on her Olympic fame, receiving a nice raise from McCombs and earning substantial sums on the vaudeville circuit (telling corny jokes, singing, jumping hurdles, running a treadmill, and playing a harmonica). She appeared as a pitcher in 200 games with the popular men's touring baseball team, the House of David, which required its players to wear long beards as part of their promotional gimmickry. She even pitched an inning of a 1934 exhibition game for the St Louis Cardinals against Connie Mack's

Figure 6.2   A determined Babe Didrikson is shown preparing for the 1932 Olympic Games. She thrilled American sports fans when she dominated the three events she was permitted to enter. Controversy followed the blunt-spoken athlete throughout a career that ended tragically with her death from cancer at the age of 45. In 1999, she was the overwhelming selection in various polls as the greatest female athlete of the twentieth century.
Image © Bettmann/CORBIS

Philadelphia Athletics (getting slugger Jimmy Foxx to fly out), played basketball for the barnstorming Babe Didrikson's All-Americans, and would have taken up tennis competitively except for a chronic right shoulder injury. These activities, while bringing in much-needed dollars because she was now supporting her parents, were essentially gimmicks and smacked of hucksterism.

In search of a serious competitive outlet, Didrikson turned to a game she had played only casually a few times previously – golf. For several months, she hit an estimated 1,500 practice balls a day. She won the prestigious Texas State Women's Golf Championship in 1935, but on the top amateur circuit Didrikson found herself treated as a pariah by her fellow golfers, largely women from genteel social circles who found her appearance, penchant for self-promotion, and questionable use of language beneath their expectations of a lady golfer. These criticisms stung, and Didrikson determined to undergo an image change. She wore more fashionable clothes, had her hair done in the latest styles, began wearing makeup and high heels, and was even seen carrying a dainty monogrammed purse. In 1938, she met a leading professional wrestler at a golf exhibition in California, fell in love, and 11 months later married George Zaharias. The rumors about her sexual orientation diminished but did not disappear.

Didrikson's status as an amateur golfer was questioned because she had received compensation for her basketball and baseball exploits. Rumors suggested that some of her fellow golfers filed a protest with the United States Golf Association because they were unable to beat her. Beyond question, she had used her Olympic fame to earn money, had been paid well by the House of David, and had received part of the gate as a barnstorming basketball player. But she had never played golf for money. Nonetheless, she was given a three-year suspension with the understanding that her amateur status would be restored if she did not play any sport for pay for three years. She served the three-year suspension and returned to competition in 1943.

In 1945, her victory at the Western tournament began a 10-year streak of golf that has never been equaled. Her game featured long drives; she was routinely 225 to 240 yards off the tee (one day with a brisk wind to her back she nailed a drive 442 yards); she often out-drove top male professionals in exhibition matches. She played the game shrewdly and intelligently, although at times she struggled on the green. In a reversal of her earlier effort to preserve her amateur status, she played a pivotal role in establishing the Ladies Professional Golf Association (LPGA). In 1946–7, she won 17 consecutive tournaments. She was now earning $100,000 a year in product endorsements and, despite many spats with her peers, was elected president of the LPGA three times and did much to elevate public awareness of the women's game. Nonetheless, the prize money for the LPGA tour was paltry in comparison with the men's tour; the largest single payday she received for a victory was $2,100. In 1951, she earned $15,087 when she won eight tournaments and finished second in five others; it was the largest annual amount won by a woman golfer up to that time.

Didrikson continued her dominance of women's golf until spring 1953, when she was diagnosed with colon cancer. At a time when even the mention of the word "cancer" was generally avoided, she publicly announced the nature of her disease and devoted herself to raising monies for research and treatments. Incredibly, she returned to golf four months after major abdominal surgery and quickly regained championship form, winning nine more tournaments and finishing in the money in 20 others. She had to combat fatigue and pain, but her competitive fires still burned brightly. However, the disease returned, and in September 1956 the woman who was overwhelmingly elected the top female athlete of the first half-century died at 45 years of age.

News coverage of the last 10 years of Babe Didrikson Zaharias's life should have concentrated upon her unprecedented success as a professional golfer. Her string of golfing triumphs, however, provoked an ongoing discussion about her transformation from "muscle moll" to a loving wife and homemaker who, the press never seemed tired of reporting, was an expert cook, loved to work in her flower garden, and slept in an 8 foot square bed with her husband. *Life Magazine* announced her transformation into a "real woman" with a headline: "Babe Is a Lady Now: The World's Most Amazing Athlete Has Learned to Wear Nylons and Cook for Her Huge Husband." The fact that she eventually concentrated upon a sport with high social standing, one that seemed more "feminine," seemed to mollify critics.[22] The *Saturday Evening Post* proclaimed that although she was once rumored to be a male, she now definitely had large breasts and a slender waist. The article noted with approval her "cooking, interior decorating, curtain making, gardening and other housewifely arts." The once-hypercritical Paul Gallico even commented favorably upon her "transition from the man-girl who hated sissies to a feminine woman." After her death, journalists were prone to say that she would be remembered not just for her many athletic accomplishments but, as Gallico wrote, "likewise in the hearts of all of us who loved her for what she was, a splendid woman."[23]

As the life of Babe Didrikson Zaharias illustrates, even at mid-century the status of women athletes was tenuous at best. They could not be recognized simply as athletes but were subject to scrutiny for the level of their "tomboyishness," their attention to domestic responsibilities, and their athletic performances. As Cindy Himes concludes,

> Babe Didrikson Zaharias, more than any female athlete of her day, embodied the new female athlete. Zaharias changed cultural perceptions of the physical limitations of womanhood using her body as a weapon … And, although she eventually knuckled under to society's dictates, for many years she stood in direct defiance of sex and class prejudice in the world of sport and in society at large. Babe Didrikson Zaharias became the standard for excellence in women's sports for several decades.[24]

Women Play Hardball: The Peaches and the Chicks

When the United States entered the Second World War in December of 1941, many leaders of organized baseball believed that the loss of players to military service would lead to a cancellation of the professional game. This perception inspired two baseball executives, Branch Rickey and Phil Wrigley, to create the All-American Girls Baseball League. With women assuming non-traditional roles in the military and in defense factories, they reasoned, why should women not assume a role on the ball field? With the infusion of $100,000 from Wrigley, four franchises were established in small Midwestern cities: the Racine Belles, Kenosha Comets, South Bend Blue Sox, and Rockford Peaches. Each team

Figure 6.3 A professional women's baseball player slides hard into third base. Players in the All-American Girls Professional Baseball League were required to adhere to high standards of decorum and fashion. They thrilled large crowds across the Midwest with their skill and exuberant style of play. *National Baseball Hall of Fame Library, Cooperstown, NY, USA © NBL*

had a male manager (including some ex-major leaguers) and a female chaperone. The teams initially played fast-pitch softball, drawing upon a large pool of talent from urban industrial leagues. Players earned between $55 and $150 a week and played a 108-game season, providing entertainment for more than 200,000 fans. While spectators came initially out of curiosity, many returned because of the high quality of play. The league – now called the All-American Girls Professional Baseball League – survived after the war and in 1948 expanded to 10 teams, including the Grand Rapids Chicks, the Kalamazoo Lassies and the Minneapolis Millerettes. The most successful team was the Ft Wayne Daisies. The league changed its rules in 1948 to create a modified form of baseball, complete with overhand pitching and a smaller ball. That year attendance approached 1 million, the appeal being a tough brand of baseball complete with fast pitching, stolen bases, and plenty of injuries, especially skin abrasions from sliding into bases in short skirts. Although the women exhibited exceptional athletic skills, they were outfitted in tunic-like skirts cut above the knee as a reminder to spectators that these were, indeed, female ballplayers. Makeup was required and hair could not be cut in a short bob. The first crop of players even had to attend a Helena Rubinstein preseason charm school where they were instructed in ladylike behavior. The league dissolved in 1954, victim of the same economic and social forces that killed town ball and many lower-division minor leagues.[25]

Television played a major factor in cutting attendance and so contributed to the demise of the league; it is possible that the league could have found a niche as a new venue for sports broadcasting. That, however, did not happen. The league also was victimized by postwar expectations that women should revert to traditional roles. Thus the idea that women played a hard-nosed form of baseball conflicted with popular convention. As historian Susan Cahn writes, "By continuing to see athletic ability as masculine skill rather than incorporating athleticism within the range of feminine qualities, the league's ideology posed no challenge to the fundamental precepts of gender in American society."[26]

The brief foray of women into a sports realm long believed to be for men only was a small step in a long journey. Compared to the late nineteenth century, much progress had been made, but in fact, as the second half of the twentieth century began, little opportunity existed for the great majority of girls to participate in organized competitive sports. That would change in the decades to come, but the journey remained a long and often tortuous one.

7

"An Evil To Be Endured": Sports on Campus, 1920–1950

From the time he assumed the presidency of the University of Chicago in 1929 at the age of 28, Robert Maynard Hutchins was skeptical about the value of athletic programs as part of the American system of higher education. After a decade-long dialogue over the merits of this elite private institution fielding a football team in the Western Conference (Big Ten), Hutchins convinced his board of trustees to drop the sport. He made his decision at a propitious time, following humiliating 61–0 defeats administered by Ohio State and Harvard, and an 85–0 pasting by Michigan. These lopsided losses contributed to the school's 15th consecutive losing season.

As expected, Hutchins was widely criticized by many alumni, football fans, and sports journalists, but he also received widespread praise. Despite offering accolades for placing educational values above athletics, no other major football institution followed his lead. Hutchins explained that his presidential peers "could not stand the pressure" that fans, coaches, boosters, alumni, legislators, and the sports media created on behalf of the game.[1] Hutchins believed that "education was primarily concerned with the training of the mind, and athletics and social life, though they may contribute to it, are not the heart of it and cannot be permitted to interfere with it." He once quipped, "A college racing stable makes as much sense as college football. The jockey could carry the college colors; the students could cheer; the alumni could bet; and the horse wouldn't have to pass a history test."[2] Hutchins took heart when University of Missouri professor W. E. Gwatkin wrote him a letter of congratulations and pointed out that most university presidents had to tolerate football "as an evil to be endured for the sake of a rather vaguely defined greater good."[3]

Sports in American Life: A History, Second Edition. Richard O. Davies.
© 2012 John Wiley & Sons, Inc. Published 2012 by John Wiley & Sons, Inc.

The Essential Myth of Big-Time College Athletics

As they built their intercollegiate empires, coaches and athletic administrators embraced the English model of amateurism, while university presidents preached the gospel that athletics helped mold good character and moral habits. Intercollegiate sports were promoted as an integral part of the academic mission. Both rationales were at best wishful thinking, at worst hypocritical. Although the amateur ideal was widely presumed to be the basis for American intercollegiate sports, in fact those schools that played "big-time" football or basketball opted for a professional sports model that placed the highest priority upon winning.

When campus administrators took control of athletics between 1890 and 1910, they insisted that athletics had to be funded outside the regular institutional budget. Professional coaches replaced elected student "captains." "Business managers" – the precursor to today's entrepreneurial athletic directors – were appointed to oversee the athletic programs. The arrival on campus of the salaried coach and the athletic director ended any pretext that the college programs were to be run on the pristine English amateur model.

Instead, the working model was that of American capitalism. The principles that underpinned the rise of intercollegiate sports were the same that guided the American system of capitalism: competition and profits. The British concept of amateurism had grown out of a stratified society in which the elite were born to their status and could exclude themselves from significant social interaction with lesser groups. Their social stature was assured by birth, and so the English elite did not have to prove themselves. In egalitarian America, where there was no royalty, where society selected its leaders based upon performance and merit, and where freedom of opportunity and competition were exalted, the amateur model made little connection. Only in a society where a hereditary upper class existed could the English amateur system work. But it served the purposes of American college coaches and athletic directors extraordinarily well.[4]

Thus in the competitive economic environment of the United States, intercollegiate sports reflected the nation's basic capitalistic creed. Rivalries were established between similar institutions, usually through conference affiliation; tickets were sold; boosters were solicited for donations; athletes were granted tuition and fee waivers (in effect "paid") in return for their athletic performance; special facilities were provided for the exclusive use of athletes; tutors were hired to help athletes meet eligibility standards; extensive recruiting programs sought out skilled athletes; and professional head coaches ran the enterprise. Despite all of these examples of professionalism, colleges and universities continued to insist that they were engaged in amateurism. The underlying dilemma, as sports historian Ronald A. Smith has aptly noted, was that: "If a college had truly amateur sport, it would lose contests and thus prestige. If a college acknowledged outright professional sport it would lose respectability … Be amateur and lose athletically to those who were less amateur; be outright professional and lose social esteem."[5]

These policies were established without much, if any, debate or consideration of long-term implications. There was no comparable model that university presidents could study, and there was no national coordinating organization to provide guidelines. Although the National Collegiate Athletic Association (NCAA) maintained a national office, its scope of authority was limited. Until the mid 1950s its responsibilities were limited to writing rules for the playing of games and providing a national forum for discussion of topics of mutual interest among member institutions. Even athletic conferences – just coming into their own in the 1920s – lacked adequate jurisdiction over their members in matters of recruiting, eligibility standards, and financial aid for athletes. Supervision and regulation of athletic programs was the responsibility of individual institutions. In this *laissez-faire* environment, independent athletic departments naturally distanced themselves as far as possible from the academic side of the institutions they represented. By 1920, faculties had largely given up any hope of abolishing big-time football, and had only dim hopes of effectively regulating their campus program. University presidents, who came to their responsibilities from a traditional academic background, were caught up in the assumption that a winning team was essential for institutional wellbeing. Eight decades later, as the twenty-first century dawned, critics of big-time college athletics would continue to lament the same lack of "institutional control" by central administrations over intercollegiate athletic programs.

Using the arcane process of academic accreditation as a guideline, wherein regional accrediting organizations interact with institutions on the basis of a common set of ethical standards and self-governance, the underlying assumption of college athletics was that each campus would be guided solely by high standards of ethical behavior and academic integrity, and would operate internally to achieve those objectives. As per the amateur code, the college athlete was presumed to be a student engaged in a serious process of intellectual achievement. The games he played were believed to provide an important activity according to the Greek ideal of the fusion of body and mind.[6]

The hypocrisy of this system, however, was exposed on every campus where major college football programs existed. Financial incentives to lure athletes to campus – a major deviation from the amateur ideal – were crucial to the building of a successful program. Few big-time college athletes were willing to play simply for the joy of competition. A true amateur did not require professional coaching, but on the campuses the coach not only held a prestigious position, but also commanded a salary far beyond what was paid senior professors. Successful coaches expected ever-larger salary and benefit packages, and if these were not forthcoming, they moved to a school desperate for a winning team. Unlike college faculty members, who often spent an entire career on one campus, football coaches came and went with regularity.

Another important part of the amateur myth was that the athlete was a student first and an athlete second, devoting time to his sport only after his academic work was completed. Faculty oversight committees required that athletes had to be in good academic standing to represent their institution. In fact, however, faced with the expectation of producing winning teams, coaches were forced to recruit the best athletes they could find with only secondary attention paid to their academic interests or abilities. Although the "tramp" athlete of the prewar era – the player who moved from campus to campus each year to play football and disappeared when the season ended – was no longer a problem, academic dishonesty remained an issue. Fabricated admissions documents, the funneling of players into special classes in which a professor was known to look kindly upon athletes, ghostwritten term papers, and other fraudulent schemes were not uncommon. Recruiting and academic scandals were frequent. In 1929, a special study funded by the Carnegie Foundation revealed that serious academic integrity issues existed in at least three-fourths of the 130 institutions it had examined.

During the early years of the twentieth century, several faculties attempted to abolish football – most notably the University of Wisconsin under the leadership of prominent history professor Frederick Jackson Turner (on one notable evening in 1906, an angry mob of students surrounded his house in response to his effort to shut down Badger football). Faculty efforts to curb football fizzled because the game had too many important friends. Off campus, boosters and alumni were vociferous in their support, and on campus students supported football because a wide range of campus social activities were connected to the game. The team fueled a campus-wide unity and a sense of identity, frequently identified as "school spirit." When Lawrence Lowell became president of Harvard in 1909, replacing anti-football crusader Charles W. Eliot, he conceded that football and other sports had their rightful place on campus because "such contests offer to students the one common interest, the only striking occasion for a display of college solidarity." University of Wisconsin faculty member J. F. A. Pyre wrote in 1920 that sports provided "a tradition that fuses together all the forces of an institution in enthusiastic social consent." He continued:

> It is a mistake to suppose that the extravagant enthusiasm lavished upon athletes by students and the alumni implies a proportionate over-estimate of their intrinsic worth. It is a mistake that arises from a puritanical failure to appreciate the significance of a ritual. That "esprit de corps" amongst the undergraduates and graduates of a school that we call "school spirit" requires a rallying point or occasion for demonstration. Athletic contests and rivalries are convenient and pleasurable occasions for its manifestations.[7]

As Professor Pyre observed, college athletics – and football in particular – had become the one special conduit whereby strong connections could be made between the campus and the general public.

Football: Driving the Bus

Early in the twenty-first century, a new cliché entered the lexicon of sportswriters and athletic directors. Football, they said, "drives the bus." The bus in question was the large sports enterprise that most major universities felt compelled to offer, and income derived from football produced the bulk of the revenue that made it all possible. By the 1920s, football had already assumed the role of propelling the athletic department financial bus. During that decade, attendance more than doubled, and to accommodate the growing number of spectators eager to pay good money for a ticket, universities moved boldly to construct large stadiums in which teams could be showcased to large crowds of ticket-buying spectators. Seizing upon the patriotic fervor left over from the war, institutions encouraged wealthy alumni and state legislatures to cough up large sums to build "memorials" in the form of football stadiums to honor the 63,000 Americans who had lost their lives in the trenches of France. What they could not generate from legislative appropriations or private donations, they covered with the sale of revenue bonds. Yale had shown the way when the gigantic Yale Bowl was completed in 1914. By 1930, seven additional stadiums with seating capacity above 70,000 had made their appearance on campuses, and nearly all institutions with serious football aspirations boasted of stadiums with seating for 30,000 or more. In 1921, Ohio State opened its enormous horse-shaped stadium that seated 63,000, and a few years later its archrival Michigan countered with a 72,000-seat showplace for coach Fielding Yost's powerful teams. (Both stadiums have since been expanded to over 100,000 seats.) Other institutions followed suit. In 1926, an American Association of University Professors committee condemned the stadium mania to no effect: "The sheer physical size of the stadium dwarfs the significance of the library, laboratory, and lecture hall."[8]

A tour of campuses today reveals the centrality of football nearly a century ago; almost all the stadiums constructed in the 1920s remain in use (expanded and modernized). They stand near the center of the campus, massive monuments of brick and concrete to the "Golden Age" of college football. In 1924, coach Amos Alonzo Stagg convinced the University of Chicago board of trustees to permit the doubling of the Stagg Stadium seating to 60,000, obviously envisioning days of pigskin glory to come. Ironically, 1924 would be the year of Chicago's last winning season. A planned second deck (to take the capacity to 80,000) was never added, and after the university dropped football in 1939, the locker rooms underneath the stadium were the secret location of the nation's first nuclear pile. It was there in 1942 that the first self-sustaining nuclear reaction occurred, a decisive step toward the making of the atomic bomb that ended the Second World War.[9]

Football's Golden Age: The Twenties

The excitement that teams provided during the 1920s seemed to justify the construction of these huge facilities. Major changes in the rules produced a more exciting game than Walter Camp ever envisioned. Most teams now operated out of single-wing formations designed to produce exciting long gains. These formations featured a direct snap of the ball to a fleet-footed halfback who usually ran or passed the ball. The formations also included the use of deceptive "spinner" plays in which the ball carrier would turn (or "spin," sometimes a full 360 degrees) and either hand off the ball to another back or conceal it from defenders and run himself. The quarterback seldom touched the ball but was used as a lead blocker. The single wing required intricate timing, precise blocking, and careful ball handling, which made possible tricky misdirection plays, forward passes, sneaky reverses, open-field laterals, and exciting end sweeps. Coaches adopted the wide-open style of play in response to spectator demand for an exciting brand of football.

The most spectacular player of this era was unquestionably Harold "Red" Grange, a whirling dervish of a running back at the University of Illinois. During his sophomore year he captured national attention when he scored three touchdowns and gained over 200 yards in his initial game against the University of Nebraska. He subsequently scored the winning touchdowns in close games against Ohio State, Wisconsin, and Chicago as he led the Fighting Illini to an undefeated season and the conference co-championship. He was named an All-American.[10]

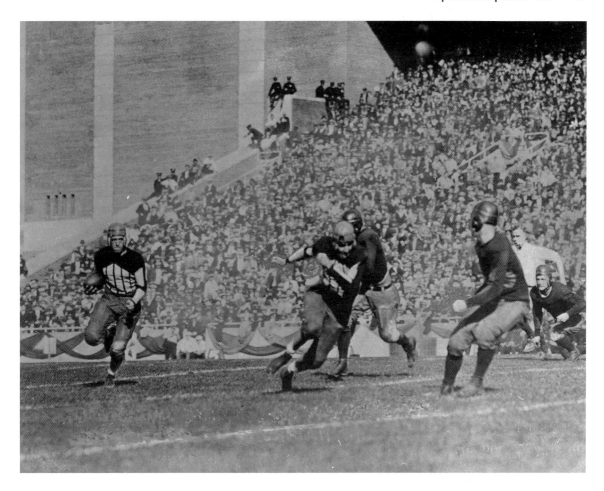

Fans were enthralled by Grange's ability to elude tacklers for long gains. His amazing display of speed and balance introduced the term "broken field runner" into the football lexicon. One sportswriter was compelled to note that he "picks his way through the line with infinite care," and another noted after one spectacular performance, "They knew he was coming; they saw him start; he made no secret of his direction; he was in their midst, and he was gone." One such performance came on October 18, 1924, when Grange helped inaugurate the 67,000-seat Memorial Stadium, dedicated to Illinois students who had not returned from France. The opponent was Michigan, which came into the game with a three-year unbeaten record and with its venerable coach, Fielding "Hurry Up" Yost, boldly proclaiming that his team would "stop Grange cold." Unfortunately for the Wolverines, Red Grange had what is now called "a career day." He returned the opening kickoff 95 yards for a touchdown, and before the first quarter had ended he had scored on runs from scrimmage of 67, 56, and 44 yards. After sitting out the second quarter, he ran for a fifth touchdown in the second half and passed for yet another. He amassed 402 yards rushing and

Figure 7.1 Red Grange runs around Michigan tacklers in 1924. This game was the first played in the new 67,000-seat Memorial Stadium on the Illinois campus. Journalist Grantland Rice watched Grange score five touchdowns that day and dubbed him the "Galloping Ghost," helping make him one of the most famous sports figures of the 1920s. *Image © Bettmann/ Corbis*

another 60 passing in a sparking individual performance. Sportswriter Grantland Rice proclaimed him "The Galloping Ghost." Even this performance, however, did not satisfy skeptics in the East, where doubts still lingered about the quality of "Western" football. In Philadelphia, early in his senior season of 1925, Grange responded by rushing for 369 yards and three touchdowns while leading his team to a decisive 24–2 walloping of the pride of the East, a University of Pennsylvania team that had enjoyed an undefeated season in 1924.[11]

American sports fans had a new star. They saw in Grange the traditional qualities long esteemed by Americans: a strong work ethic, abstention from tobacco and drink, a determination to overcome financial disadvantages, and an "aw shucks" response to praise of his athletic accomplishments. Although few football fans had the opportunity to see Grange confound tacklers in person, millions thrilled to his darting runs on the weekly newsreels being shown in motion-picture theaters. The primitive film technology of the day – producing herky-jerky images that flickered on the screen – made Grange's runs seem even faster and more daring than they were in real life. Few fans doubted the verdict handed down in 1925 by Grantland Rice:

> A streak of fire, a breath of flame
> Eluding all who reach and clutch;
> A gray ghost thrown into the game
> That rival hands may never touch;
> A rubber bounding, blasting soul
> Whose destination is the goal.[12]

Public adulation turned to disappointment, however, when Grange turned professional immediately after his final college game, well before graduation. After leading Illinois to a hard-fought 14–9 victory over Ohio State at Columbus before a record 85,000 fans, he announced that he had already agreed to a lucrative contract with the professional Chicago Bears. Advised by a shrewd agent, C. C. ("Cash and Carry") Pyle, Grange had agreed to drop out of college and embark immediately upon a nationwide barnstorming tour from which he would receive half of the gate receipts. At a time when most sports purists considered professional football a "dirty little business run by rogues and bargain-basement entrepreneurs," Grange had broken with the myth of amateur college sports. A college degree apparently meant little to this young All-American. His comments to the press did not help: "I'm out to get the money and I don't care who knows it." When critics denounced Pyle as "a notorious money-hungry promoter" who had misled the nation's collegiate hero, Grange retorted that his agent had merely followed his instructions and "was one of the finest people he had ever known."[13]

Coach George Halas of the Chicago Bears took his new star player and team on a midwinter barnstorming trip across the United States that attracted record attendance, earning Grange an estimated quarter of a million dollars. His professional career continued until 1935, but a serious knee injury slowed his running ability. A spectacular catch of a touchdown pass while lying flat on his back in the 1932 NFL championship game against the Portsmouth (Ohio) Spartans added to his storied legend, and in 1933 he made a last-minute open-field tackle to preserve another championship for the Bears. Red Grange moved on to a lucrative post-playing career as a businessman and radio and television football commentator. His years of glory, however, were those at Illinois when he demonstrated the excitement that a college football star could generate. More than any other individual, Red Grange established the importance of big-time college football in American popular culture.

Grange might have exemplified the role of campus football hero, but the game had become the province of the professional coach. Along with several assistant coaches, they established networks among alumni and boosters to provide tips on talented high school players. Winning coaches were commonly viewed as brilliant strategists who devised secret plays to confuse the opposition, and they encouraged such perceptions. Coaches expected their charges to carry out their carefully designed plays and demanded that individual players submit to team discipline. Just as America's corporations were attacking their competitors with finely tuned strategies and well-oiled operations, so too were football teams reflecting the same commitment. It was no surprise that football became a special passion of many male business executives.

One point of contention among faculty was the salaries paid to the head coach, which were substantially higher than those of the best-paid professors. Unlike tenured faculty, however, the coach's employment status was tenuous, subject to won–lost records and the whims of boosters and campus presidents. For those who produced winning teams year after year, however, the rewards could be considerable. The success of coaches such as Yost at Michigan, Stagg at Chicago, Glenn "Pop" Warner at Pittsburgh and Stanford, Dana X. Bible at Texas, John Heisman at Georgia Tech, and Bob Zuppke at Illinois, were the stuff of campus lore. The coach who made the greatest contribution to the development of the game was Warner, who began his coaching career at Iowa State Agricultural College in 1894 after a successful playing career at Cornell. He went on to Georgia in 1896 and turned a humdrum team into an undefeated team in two seasons. After producing powerful teams at Carlisle Indian School between 1898 and 1914 (where he tutored Jim Thorpe), Warner schooled the Pittsburgh Panthers who won 33 straight games and laid claim to three national championships. He moved to Stanford in 1924 and led the Indians to three Rose Bowl victories. Warner was considered the most creative coach of the period, introducing several innovative offensive formations and plays, as well as being given credit for helping design shoulder pads and helmets. To assist spectators in identifying individual players, he placed numbers on the backs of jerseys.

Knute Rockne and the Making of Notre Dame Football

Pop Warner's name would become a permanent part of football lore when a youth program was created in 1929 that still carries his name, but in the realm of public relations Notre Dame coach Knute Rockne upstaged him. Rockne's 13 years at the helm of the Fighting Irish created the fabled football tradition at the private university located 75 miles east of Chicago. He possessed an engaging public personality that featured a flair for the dramatic, a quick wit, and a penchant for innovation (choreographed calisthenics, the famed Notre Dame shift, and box backfield formation). At Notre Dame, he almost single-handedly devised what Murray Sperber has called "the unique formula" that enabled Notre Dame to reign supreme atop big-time college football for over three-quarters of a century.[14] Even on those infrequent occasions when the Irish have endured losing seasons, football fans everywhere have remained in awe of the mystique that encompasses Notre Dame football. The formula that Rockne produced during the 1920s could never be duplicated elsewhere. Rockne grew a national fan base that included not only former students but also the so-called "subway alumni" – dedicated fans who had neither attended the university nor even set foot on its campus. Because the institution shrewdly permitted radio stations free access to its game broadcasts, millions of fans across the country became hooked on Notre Dame football during the 1920s.

At the heart of Rockne's fame was the fact that he lived the American Dream, beginning with his arrival in the United States at age five from Norway. At age 22, having saved some money from a job in the post office, he decided to enroll at the small university located in South Bend, Indiana. Founded in 1844 by a small French religious order, the Congregation of the Holy Cross, the college had a liberal arts curriculum that attracted a few hundred students who were largely of Catholic immigrant stock. When Rockne arrived in 1910, Notre Dame had a modest academic reputation and was better known for the quality of its baseball teams than for its football. Rockne earned a degree with a major in chemistry, and played end on the football team while excelling as a middle-distance runner in track.

One particular game began the Rockne mystique. During the summer before his senior year in 1913, while working at the Lake Erie resort at Cedar Point in Ohio, he and quarterback Gus Dorais practiced the forward pass on the resort's vast expanse of sandy beach. That October, the Irish pulled off a 35–13 upset win over baffled Army defenders who had seldom before seen a forward pass. Dorais rifled a first-half 40 yard pass to Rockne, who scampered into the end zone untouched, and by day's end, Dorais had completed 13 of 17 passes for more than 200 yards. The next day the *New York Times* headlined the game story with "Notre Dame Open Play Amazes Army!" The lead sentence told it all: "Football men marveled at this startling display of open football, as the Westerners flashed the most sensational football ever seen in the East." It should have come as no surprise to the Cadets, because Notre Dame had utilized the forward pass ever since head coach Jesse Harper arrived the previous season. Several other teams had experimented with the forward pass after it was legalized in 1906; the first forward passes attempted that year were apparently by Marietta College and St Louis University. By 1913, the forward pass was no secret, as was later implied by Rockne myth-makers.[15]

After graduation, Rockne assumed an assistant coaching position at Notre Dame, where he also taught freshman chemistry laboratories. In 1916, he got his first taste of being a head coach when Harper came down with a heavy chest cold. Rockne rose to the occasion in the locker room when he fabricated a story that the opposing Wabash College team – certainly no powerhouse – had been strengthened by several mercenaries and harbored anti-Catholic sentiments. He concluded this, the first of his famous pre-game histrionics, by shouting an apt metaphor befitting a religious institution: "Now get out there and crucify them!"[16] And indeed they did, to the tune of 60–0. In 1918, Rockne accepted the position of head coach and quickly implemented his system, which emphasized guile, speed, and agility over sheer brawn. He had the pick of the best Catholic players throughout the Midwest, who naturally gravitated to what was rapidly becoming a formidable football power. By the mid 1920s, building upon his team's success, he operated a recruiting system that utilized an informal national network of Catholic churches and organizations as well as the efforts of members of the subway alumni.

Rockne shrewdly promoted Rockne. He found himself much in demand as an after-dinner speaker, always fusing his commitment to a winning football program with his university president's dream of making Notre Dame "the Yale of the West." By playing a national schedule – creating traditional rivalries with the Army and Navy in the East and Southern California in the West – he built not only Notre Dame's football reputation but also its national fan base. During Rockne's first three years, his star player was George Gipp, whose derring-do on the field pleased the fans but whose behavior off it dismayed faculty and administrators. After he led Notre Dame to a 9–0 record in 1919, the All-American team captain was expelled due to his lack of commitment to his studies. Dismayed Irish fans learned that the mercenary Gipp was about to depart to play either for Michigan, where "Hurry Up" Yost was eagerly awaiting his arrival, or West Point, where recruitment of football "tramps" was widely recognized. Ultimately, Notre Dame president Father James Burns reinstated Gipp in time for his senior season in response to plaintive appeals from the business community of South Bend, which had become convinced that Notre Dame football was essential to the health of the local economy.[17]

Gipp rewarded his supporters as he led the Irish to an undefeated season in 1920. He played little in the final two games, however, because he had contracted a respiratory infection that would kill him shortly before Christmas. The 1920 season firmly established Notre Dame as a football giant, and its fans reveled in a national championship. That year the Irish had played before 90,000 fans, despite the limited capacity of Carter Field (replaced in 1930 with the stadium that lies in the center of campus today).

Year after year, Rockne's teams rolled to victory. His 1924 squad trampled its opposition by a combined score of 258–44. Among the most significant victories was a hard-fought 13–7 win at the Polo Grounds in New York City over West Point. This victory on a dark and dreary November day set the stage for one of the most memorable moments in Notre Dame football history. Grantland Rice was driven to hyperbolic heights when he began his game report with the most famous passage ever written by a sports journalist:

> Outlined against a blue-gray October sky, the Four Horsemen rode again. In dramatic lore, they are known as Famine, Pestilence, Destruction, and Death. These are only aliases. Their real names are Stuhldreher, Miller, Crowley, and Layden. They formed the crest of the South Bend cyclone before which another fighting Army team was swept over the precipice at the Polo Grounds this afternoon as 50,000 spectators peered down upon the bewildering panorama spread out upon the green plain below.[18]

These few words etched forever in the memories of football fans everywhere the legend of Notre Dame football. In reality, the exploits of the "Four Horsemen" were nothing spectacular – they were good but hardly great athletes – and their size (they averaged 160 pounds each) was relatively small even for this period of college football. There have been many backfields at South Bend more talented than the 1924–5 quartet, but Grantland Rice

Figure 7.2   Journalist Grantland Rice called the Notre Dame backfield the "Four Horsemen" after he watched them lead the Fighting Irish to victory over a strong Army team in 1924. The four men – (from left to right) Don Miller, Elmer Layden, Jim Crowley, and Harry Stuhldreher – posed for this iconic photograph the week after their dramatic victory in the Polo Grounds in New York City. *Image © Bettmann/Corbis*

placed the Four Horsemen in a special identity that Professor Sperber says "floats through American sports history, assuming a mystified reality."[19]

Sports journalists became enamored with Notre Dame because of its success on the field, but also because of the accessibility of the affable head coach, who was always ready with a humorous quip or a compelling story to fill the next day's column. The most memorable legend revolved around the 1928 half-time pep talk that Rockne gave to his team, tied 0–0 with an undefeated Army team. Rockne reportedly recalled the last words of George Gipp, who died of influenza in December 1920. Lying on his deathbed, as Rockne recalled, "He turned to me. 'I've got to go, Rock. It's all right. I'm not afraid. Some time, Rock, when the team's up against it; when things are going wrong and the breaks are beating the boys – tell them to go in there with all they've got and win just one for the Gipper. I don't know where I'll be then, Rock. But I'll know about it, and I'll be happy.'"

There is no evidence that Gipp ever said anything approaching what Rockne relayed to his team in the locker room eight years later. One of his players,

Jim Crowley, kept a long list of fabrications and half-truths that the dramatic Rockne presented to his teams in order to stimulate their enthusiasm for the task at hand. "They were all lies, blatant lies," Crowley later said. "The Jesuits call it mental reservation, but he had it in abundance." Whatever, following the Gipper half-time oration, the Irish stopped the Cadets on the 1 foot line as the game expired, preserving a 12–6 upset victory and adding to the Notre Dame legend. Two weeks after the game, a ghostwritten article about the pre-game oration appeared in *Collier's Magazine*, and it was reprinted in Rockne's posthumous autobiography in 1931. In 1940, this story of dubious origins took on even greater mythological proportions when actor Ronald Reagan played the role of Gipp in a popular motion picture that produced many a tear among sellout audiences during the deathbed scene. Upon such fiction was the reality of Notre Dame football constructed.[20]

Even Knute Rockne's sudden death at age 43 in an airplane crash in 1931 added to the mythology of Notre Dame football. Although it was later said he was on a trip to "help his boys" when the commercial airplane crashed in a

Figure 7.3 Seventy-three thousand fans jam Memorial Stadium at the University of California in Berkeley for the Big Game against Stanford in 1928. Clearly visible are the student card sections located along the 50 yard line. On cue, participating students would flash spirited messages and images to the other side. This massive stadium was one of many built during the 1920s as college football became an important component of American college life. *Image © Waters & Hainlin/Corbis*

snowstorm in western Kansas, in fact Rockne was en route to the West Coast to make lucrative personal appearances for a sporting goods chain and to finalize a $75,000 motion-picture contract deal with Universal Pictures, which planned to make a movie of his life. Rockne was the first American celebrity to die in a commercial airplane crash, and news of his death stunned a Depression-mired nation. The ensuing mourning was truly a national event, and his funeral in the Notre Dame chapel added to the football legacy as the university choir ended the service by singing the fight song that had become familiar to millions of Americans, the "Notre Dame Victory March." Rockne's won–lost record of 105–12–5 would never be equaled. That record, coupled with his flair for public relations, enabled him to escape the criticisms that would have damaged mere mortals. He was reputed to have been unwilling to discipline outstanding players for their drinking, gambling, and carousing. He demonstrated only casual interest in academics. The administration fretted over his frequent flirtations with head coaching positions at other institutions as a ploy to generate a salary increase. He also aggressively used his position to earn large sums from speaking engagements and product endorsements that enhanced his high salary.

More than three-quarters of a century after his death, Rockne is still recognized as one of the most successful coaches of all time. It was he, more than anyone else, who established the template for future generations of big-time college coaches. By his example, as John Thelin concludes, the many sides of Knute Rockne "demonstrated that the big-time college football coach had drifted from the company of professors … The activities of recruiting, promoting, and public speaking, along with the lures of endorsements, indicated that by the 1930s the role of the big-time college coach had evolved very differently from that of university faculty."[21]

The Second Challenge to Big-Time Football

Not even the vast public enthusiasm for football and the leadership of public luminaries such as Rockne could stanch the criticisms that the enterprise regularly generated. The game had escaped virtually unscathed from the crisis of 1905, but again in 1929 it encountered criticism and cries for substantive reform. Even during the glory days of the 1920s, many university faculty and administrators remained skeptical about the game's impact on academic quality and institutional integrity, yet they were overwhelmed by public enthusiasm for the game. With abolition no longer a realistic option, focus shifted to enhancing institutional controls. In 1926, the Carnegie Foundation funded an extensive study that culminated in the publication in 1929 of a scorching indictment of big-time college football. The commission's findings were succinctly summarized in one blunt sentence: "Apparently the ethical bearing of intercollegiate football contests and their scholastic aspects are of secondary importance to the winning of victories and financial success."[22]

The chief executive of the Carnegie Foundation, the former president of the Massachusetts Institute of Technology, Dr Henry Pritchett, vigorously pursued this investigation. Pritchett was no anti-football fanatic, but he perceived the existence of several abuses, including the amount of time and effort demanded of college football players that precluded "any serious intellectual effort" on their part. Although his criticisms were similar to those made earlier by Harvard president Charles Eliot, Pritchett did not present them in the context of a morality play. Instead, reflecting his engineering profession, he expressed concern about educational efficiency and academic quality.

Although the Foundation had earlier sponsored a small study of football at a select number of Southern institutions and another of sports at British universities, the board was reluctant to support the large-scale study Pritchett desired. That reluctance, however, melted before a series of events in 1925, among them the revelation of Red Grange's abandonment of his education for the professional game the very same day that he played his final college contest. Shortly before the 1925 season began, a syndicated article appeared in many newspapers across the country, written by an anonymous "graduate manager" of football who claimed to be working at a big-time Eastern school. His story carried too many plausible accusations for it to be dismissed outright, although football's defenders made a determined effort to undercut its impact. The author told of a large well-funded alumni-booster organization that assisted the football program, beginning with paying a large network of scouts to identify potential recruits and bring them to campus for a lavish visit. Once the recruits were enrolled, the graduate manager oversaw their registration, provided tutors, hired handlers to make certain they attended classes, encouraged faculty who were friendly to football to permit their enrollment in easy classes, and in particular, looked out after their financial wellbeing. In a day before the introduction of "athletic scholarships," the manager made certain that tuition and living expenses were taken care of, often by the creation of fictional campus jobs that required the player only to show up to receive a paycheck. The author even discussed a program to hide top recruits at remote summer camps as counselors, so that rival institutions could not entice them to their campus at the last minute.[23]

While football critics were mulling over the revelations of this insider exposé, they also focused on the replication of William Rainey Harper's strategy of using football to gain instant national recognition for the University of Chicago. Ironically, the best new example was Northwestern University, located just a few miles north of downtown Chicago. President Walter Scott, a former Northwestern football player himself, launched an effort to make his institution a national power in football. He funded a successful team, which he then used to attract big donors to support his dream of building an elite academic institution. Scott used private contributions not only to build the 47,000-seat Dyche Stadium but also to construct many academic buildings. He created endowed faculty chairs and established an impressive array of professional colleges on Chicago's affluent North Side. In 1925, the "Fighting Methodists" tied for the Western Conference (Big Ten) title, which was capped by an improbable 3–2 victory over Michigan in a game played before 100,000 spectators at Soldier Field. Suddenly the University of Chicago, which had long dominated the football scene in the Windy City, had a powerful local competitor both academically and athletically. Chicago coach Amos Alonzo Stagg took particular umbrage over a new football endowment at Northwestern that would fund 50 part-time scouts to procure the top talent available. Without a hint of the irony his words conveyed, Stagg wrote a letter to Fielding Yost of Michigan: "I am satisfied that Northwestern at the present is loaded with athletes who have been induced to go there by the offer of free tuition and in certain cases something additional."[24]

Although the scope of the project was intended to survey all of collegiate athletics, football naturally emerged as its central focus. During 1926–9, social scientist Howard Savage led a team of researchers in an intensive study of the athletic programs of 130 colleges and universities. They did not rely simply on documents submitted by the institutions, but visited each of the campuses. Although the final report, issued during the midst of the 1929 football season, encompassed 12 chapters and 347 pages, the chapters on recruiting and financial aid to athletes received the most attention. Writing more than 20 years later, Savage took satisfaction in his accomplishment, calling it "encyclopedic in scope" and "unprejudiced in method." He noted that "its chief faults were its length and its detail and yet without sufficient preponderance of evidence it would have failed of its purpose altogether."[25]

The report documented the complex system that college football had become. In many respects, the report illustrated that the game had merely evolved and expanded from that of the 1890s. What the Carnegie researchers discovered was that even at institutions that played football at a modest level, a sophisticated system of recruitment and financial subsidy was in place. Only a handful of schools were reported as operating completely clean programs – Tufts, Wooster, MIT, Reed – which only served to emphasize the extent of deception that occurred at such big-time football schools that were included in the study: Wisconsin, Northwestern, Illinois, and the Army. Even colleges that never dreamed of national recognition were singled out for improper practices, including Lafayette, Rutgers, Lehigh, Grove City, Lebanon Valley, and Carnegie Institute of Technology.

Perhaps the most sensational revelation was that most institutions had quietly, with substantial subterfuge, created a new form of assistance that was considered at the time highly unethical – the athletic scholarship. Not that it was so identified by the institutions. Instead students were provided funding that covered their expenses from programs nebulously labeled as "student leadership" or "campus activities." Until this point, colleges had maintained that athletes could receive scholarships only on a competitive academic basis. Additionally, it was learned that many athletes also received "loans" from alumni and boosters, with the implicit understanding that they need not be repaid. Savage reported that many schools set aside on-campus jobs for athletes that were paid at a higher rate than for non-athletes. Many of these "jobs" were make-work positions requiring little or no actual work. The report also uncovered several secret accounts, usually controlled by the head coach or athletic director, which were used to pay players directly.

The vociferous denials and protests from the coaches and presidents of institutions identified with the practices the report described served to confirm its accuracy. Interestingly, the report identified four prestigious private Eastern institutions – Pennsylvania, Columbia, Brown, and Dartmouth – as conducting recruiting and under-the-table financial assistance in a manner no different from the most egregious of the practices it found at such public institutions as Michigan, Wisconsin, and Washington State. The report rightfully identified the professional coach as one glaring manifestation of the problem, but it also focused attention on the failure of campus presidents to insist on a clean program. Many coaches claimed that the investigators had deceived them. Presidents went on record denying they knew of the alleged practices, while the dissembling of others made it clear that they did not *want* to know the facts. The report left the distinct impression that most campus presidents were unable or unwilling to challenge wealthy alumni, boosters with open checkbooks, college trustees, and powerful politicians who placed a high priority upon a winning football team. The collective behavior of the presidents seemed to confirm one of the conclusions of the Carnegie study: that the academic reputation of an institution had become secondary to the winning of football games.

Not surprisingly, however, following a brief flurry of media accounts and public discussion, the coaches went about their work with business as usual, knowing full well that if they did not produce a winning team their president would not hesitate to terminate their employment. In a telling commentary, Knute Rockne told a Buffalo audience in 1930 that the Carnegie Commission failed to understand the crux of the matter: he said the problem with college football was that it was not commercial enough.[26] In the years that followed, despite the economic crisis, college football continued to grow in popularity, while the Carnegie report collected dust on library shelves.

Hoop Dreams

During the 1930s, men's college basketball enjoyed substantial growth in popularity. Most teams played their games in cramped campus gymnasiums designed primarily for physical education classes. The game was played conservatively, with an emphasis on zone defenses and deliberate offenses, and with most field goal attempts being of the two-handed variety; most coaches demanded that free throws be released underhanded. When a basket was scored the teams returned to center court for a jump ball (a rule that was changed in 1937). Scoring was limited, with games ending in the 20s being commonplace.

The decision of Madison Square Garden officials in New York City to feature college games led to increased coverage by local newspapers and contributed to interest across the country. Impressed by the enthusiastic standing-room-only crowds he encountered at games held in small on-campus gymnasiums, a young reporter for the *New York World-Telegram* proposed to officials that he promote college games at Madison Square Garden. His Saturday night promotions often featured two games. Even Ned Irish was surprised when more than 16,000 fans turned out on the evening of December 29, 1934 to witness New York University defeat Notre Dame and Westminster College of Pennsylvania upset St Johns. Irish soon thereafter became the full-time director of basketball for the Garden.

Coaches and athletic directors eagerly solicited invitations to come to the Big Apple, seeking both the national spotlight and a hefty payday. In 1938, Irish invited 16 teams to compete in a new tournament that he called the National Invitation Tournament (Temple defeated Colorado 60–36 in the final), and it would be the premier college basketball event for more than a decade. The following year, the NCAA responded by creating its own tournament, but it did not surpass the NIT as the premier postseason tournament until the 1950s.

It was during one of Irish's intersectional games in December 1936 that basketball would be forever changed. The game featured nationally ranked Long Island University, coached by the famed Clair Bee. The Blackbirds came into the game with a 43-game winning streak. Their opponent was Pacific Coast Conference defending champion Stanford. In this game,

6 foot 3 inch Stanford forward Angelo "Hank" Luisetti stunned basketball-savvy New Yorkers with a revolutionary one-handed jump shot, launched 15 feet from the basket. Traditionalists, familiar only with shots being launched two-handed with the feet firmly planted, gasped in shock. Luisetti scored 15 points against befuddled Blackbird defenders to spark an upset victory. They had never before encountered his athletic maneuver. Even the thousands of disappointed LIU fans rose in a standing ovation when he left the floor. Players everywhere, to the exasperation of their hidebound coaches, began to experiment with variations of the Luisetti one-hander. The two-handed set shot was soon relegated to the history books, and the same fate befell the once-ubiquitous underhand free throw. Innovative coaches began to experiment with a much more rapid-paced game, including full-court pressing defenses and fast-break offenses.

The Second World War proved to be a boon for college basketball. Colleges were forced to cut back or eliminate football due to the loss of players to the military and restrictions on travel by large groups. Basketball, however, was not similarly affected. It was relatively easy to obtain travel permission for small basketball squads, and the military had a height restriction on recruits that worked to basketball's distinct advantage. Based on the standard size of military beds and uniforms, men who stood over 6 feet 6 inches were automatically exempt from military duty. Thus some of the best players remained in colleges, including the top basketball player of the first half of the century, the high-scoring 6 foot 10 inch De Paul center George Mikan. College basketball actually thrived during the war years by filling a void left when most football schedules were either canceled or sharply curtailed.[27]

Due to Ned Irish's promotions, college basketball became closely identified with New York City. Irish added stops in Buffalo and Philadelphia to his promotions and offered teams a three-game swing through the East. After the war, he was promoting about 25 events a season and attracting more than a quarter-million spectators. Irish drew large crowds by featuring local teams, such as New York University, City College of New York, Long Island University, Manhattan College, and Brooklyn College. Many urban Catholic universities that had moved away from football because of its high costs were not far behind in developing their own programs: De Paul and Loyola in Chicago, St Louis University and Xavier in Cincinnati, Villanova and La Salle in Philadelphia, Duquesne in Pittsburgh, St Bonaventure, Niagara, and Canisius near Buffalo, and Fordham, St Johns, and Seton Hall in the New York City area were among the top-notch college basketball programs of this era. New York reigned as the basketball capital of America, and area teams often rested atop the national rankings.[28]

In the Midwest, where the high school game had become a way of life in small farming communities, three public universities rose to prominence due to the presence of charismatic coaches who dedicated themselves to a lengthy career at one institution. One of the first coaches to gain national visibility was Forrest "Phog" Allen of Kansas University. He had the unique opportunity of replacing the "father of basketball" as the Jayhawks' coach when Dr James Naismith stepped down from coaching in 1907. Allen had played for Naismith and left two seasons later, but then returned in 1920 to coach the Jayhawks until his retirement in 1956. Possessed of a booming "foghorn" voice, which led a Kansas City journalist to coin the nickname "Phog," Allen turned out teams year after year that dominated the opposition. He prided himself on his ability to mold Kansas farm boys into powerful teams. He compiled a career won–lost record of 591–219. One of the few exceptions he made to his philosophy of recruiting players primarily from Kansas and nearby farm states was when he lured the high school phenomenon, 7 foot 2 inch Wilt Chamberlain, from Philadelphia to Lawrence in 1955.

One of Allen's perennial competitors was Hank Iba, who began coaching at Oklahoma A&M in 1934. Known for a deliberate style of play that featured a weaving "swinging gate" offense and a tenacious man-to-man defense, Iba won back-to-back NCAA championships in 1945–6 using the shot-blocking talents of 7 foot center Bob "Foothills" Kurland. Although his slowdown strategy largely went out of style by the 1950s, Iba remained at Oklahoma State until 1970, when he retired with a 767–338 career record.

Basketball fans appreciated the up-tempo teams produced at the University of Kentucky by one of Allen's former players. Adolph Rupp went to Kentucky in 1930 and immediately turned the state into a hotbed for college basketball. More than 80 percent of his players came from within the state. During his 42 years at Kentucky, the "Baron of the Bluegrass" captured 27 Southeastern Conference championships and four NCAA titles en route to winning 875 games. Rupp's teams dominated the Southeastern Conference at a time when many of its football-happy members did not take basketball seriously. Nonetheless, his teams became nationally famous for their use of a high-powered offense that featured tenacious defenses and a blistering fast break.

These teams from the nation's midsection, however, were dwarfed by those located near New York City. Clair Bee not only won several national titles and produced incredible won–lost records at Long Island University, but also established himself as the intellectual leader of the game by writing 21 books on coaching methods. He attracted large crowds to his popular coaching clinics. He also published for the teenage market 23 novels that featured a clean-living, multisport athlete named Chip Hilton who managed to overcome various adversities to help his teams win championships fair and square against unsportsmanlike opponents. Bee had to share the New York spotlight with Nat Holman, an egocentric former professional star and long-time college coach who fawning sportswriters referred to as "Mr Basketball." Holman had learned the game on the streets of New York City and in the 1920s was the much-proclaimed star scorer and passing wizard of the pioneering professional team, the New York Original Celtics. In addition to playing professionally, Holman began coaching the Beavers of City College of New York (CCNY) in 1919, where he taught a tough street-smart style dubbed "the city game." He introduced the concept of the pivot player and created the switching man-to-man defense; throughout the 1930s and the 1940s, his teams battled Long Island University for local bragging rights while also contending for national honors. In 1950 Holman reached the height of his profession when his team won both the NCAA and the National Invitation tournaments.[29]

Hoop Nightmares

The careers of several of these renowned coaches intersected in the early 1950s during the revelations of a massive gambling scandal that threatened to destroy, or at least greatly slow, the growth of major college basketball. On January 18, 1951, the *New York Journal American* broke a front-page story that District Attorney Frank Hogan was about to indict several top college basketball players for "controlling" the outcome of games by "shaving points." Within two months, Hogan's investigation had revealed evidence that some 49 games had been tampered with by gamblers who gave bribes to 32 college players from seven different universities. Insiders believed that far more games and athletes were actually involved and that the investigation was terminated prematurely under intense political pressure. What came to light, however, was that the attraction of major college basketball in the urban areas, and New York City in particular, was not simply the high quality of play; many of the spectators at Madison Square Garden came to watch teams upon which they had placed bets. Although the scandal was centered in New York, its tentacles reached into the nation's heartland as players were implicated at Toledo, Bradley, and most shocking of all, Adolph Rupp's vaunted Kentucky Wildcats.

The scandal broke in 1951, but it had been building for more than a decade. As early as 1945, Phog Allen had received headlines when he warned of the influence of gamblers. But his warnings were ignored, and even made light of by his fellow coaches. Betting on college football had become established during the 1920s. In the large cities of the Northeast and Midwest, illegal bookies set odds and took bets on college football and professional baseball that were popularly marketed to guileless clients on "pool" cards requiring a bettor to pick several winning teams in order to win. New York City's gambling chieftains naturally took note of the Madison Square Garden games promoted by Ned Irish and developed a flourishing trade during the 1930s. Basketball historian Charley Rosen insists that well before the Second World War gamblers fixed games. The attractiveness of basketball to corrupt gamblers was greatly intensified during the war years when Chicago bookmaker Charles McNeil introduced a new approach to betting on team sports – the "points spread" – in which the favorite team had to win by more than the number of points set by the bookmaker. By 1950, the points spread system had been widely adopted for betting on football and basketball. As one bookie told journalist Rosen, by replacing the awkward odds system, the points spread had generated much more "action" on games by making it possible for him to attract bets on even the most one-sided games. This appreciative bookie considered the new betting format "the greatest discovery since the zipper."[30]

While the points spread made business more lucrative for the bookmaker, it created new headaches for coaches and athletic administrators. Under the odds system, unscrupulous gamblers had to bribe players to lose a contest; now they merely had to get them to win a game by less than the points spread. It was now possible to convince a college basketball player that he could earn several hundred or even a few thousand dollars by making a few misplays so as to keep the final score differential below the spread while still helping his team win the game. In February 1951, Hogan announced the arrest of three of Nat Holman's top CCNY players and the *Sporting News* "College Player of the Year," LIU All-American center Sherman White for "shaving points." Hogan's investigation shocked the nation, especially when he subsequently indicted three players from the 1948 and 1949 national champion University of Kentucky Wildcats team. When news of the scandal first broke, the imperious Kentucky coach, Adolph "Baron" Rupp, arrogantly told the press, "Gamblers couldn't touch my boys with a ten foot pole." A few weeks later, he was stunned when two All-Americans, guard Ralph Beard and center Alex Groza, along with forward Dale

Barnstable, admitted taking bribes from gamblers throughout their college careers. Beard and Groza, who had led the 1948 United States Olympic team to a gold medal, even confessed to throwing a game in the 1949 National Invitation Tournament. At the time of their indictments, they were playing professionally for the Indianapolis Olympians in the National Basketball Association, from which they were summarily banned.[31]

Most of the players involved agreed to plea bargains or were convicted in federal court on charges of bribery, conspiracy, and illegal gambling. One of the several CCNY players involved, Norm Mager, recalled his participation more than 40 years after the fact: "We were just dumb, naive kids, 19, 20 years old. We didn't know of any law that said you shouldn't shave points – we weren't throwing games, after all. And we thought, hell, the money looked pretty good. Even if it wasn't a lot, it seemed a lot to us, since we had almost nothing."[32] Although a few players served short jail sentences, most received suspended sentences while a few took an option to serve in the military in lieu of a prison sentence. The major perpetrator of the fixes, however, New York City gambler Salvatore Sollazzo, ended up doing 12 years of hard time in maximum security Sing Sing state prison. His associate, former LIU star Eddie Gard, served three years.

Apologists for college sports argued that the scandal involved only a small number of athletes and that the system itself was sound. However, the judge who presided at several of the trials saw much more than moral failure of a few athletes. In a scorching commentary, Judge Saul S. Streit laid the blame for the scandals at the feet of the culture of big-time college athletics, which he charged was infused with "a moral debasement." Streit called for fundamental reform of "this evil system of commercialism and overemphasis." The critics of college sports seemed to get a second wind from the scandals. Some asked a simple question: if colleges could pay players to *make* baskets, why should players not take payments to *miss* them? Even the humbled Clair Bee understood: "Something must be done before all sports are discredited," he wrote in a national magazine. Echoing the words of the Carnegie Commission in 1929 and anticipating the criticism of future critics, he concluded, "Nothing will be accomplished until college presidents take aggressive action in cracking down on irregularities in their athletic departments."[33]

Thus the irony: while football had dominated college sports from the inception of intercollegiate athletic programs and had been a continuing target of criticism, a less prominent sport illuminated the corruption that infected big-time intercollegiate athletics. Just as the headlines began to fade on the basketball point-shaving scandal during the summer of 1951, football once again dominated the news when a widespread academic cheating scandal was uncovered in a leading football program. Shortly before the opening of fall practice, West Point, poised to make a run at a national championship under head coach Earl "Red" Blaik, dismissed 90 cadets for violating the Academy's strict honor code by cheating on tests. Nearly half of the disgraced cadets were members of the vaunted Black Knights football squad. President Harry S. Truman ordered a thorough investigation, and several congressmen demanded the abolition of sports programs at the two military service academies. Newspaper columnists and editorial writers pointed toward the obsession with victory that had long infected college athletics. Could it be, they collectively asked, that contrary to popular myth, sports did not build good character but instead encouraged negative, even illegal behavior?

8

Sports in an Age of Ballyhoo, Depression, and War, 1920–1945

The two decades that fell between two world wars constituted a pivotal period in American history. The "Roaring Twenties" saw the emergence of a celebrity culture in which mass marketing, the expansion of specialized professions, and the introduction of myriad new products and services helped produce a significant rise in disposable income among an expanding middle class. By 1927, two national radio networks, NBC and CBS, were broadcasting the same profitable combination of drama, comedy, news, music, and sports coast to coast. The American people embraced this new age of mass production and mass consumption because a rapidly expanding economy lifted many boats, putting disposable income into far more hands than ever before. Chain stores, such as A&P grocery stores, Rexall Drugs, J. C. Penney, and Sears Roebuck, invaded towns large and small, bringing lower prices and greater consumer options, at the same time undercutting local merchants. The urban department store, offering everything from cosmetics and clothing to refrigerators and wristwatches, became the Mecca of a nation of dedicated consumers. The new automobile age, with nearly 30 million vehicles prowling the streets and highways of America by 1930, provided a new sense of independence and freedom. The 1920s ended not with a loud roar but with an ominous thud. The crash of the stock market in October 1929 was prelude to the Great Depression, rattling the foundations of America's basic economic and political institutions. By 1932, the stock market had lost over 80 percent of its value, giving back all of the gains since 1910. When Franklin D. Roosevelt assumed the presidency on March 4, 1933, about one-quarter of the American workforce was unemployed. Soup lines and apple peddlers became a familiar scene on city streets, as did the mortgage foreclosures in the countryside as family farms were devastated by plummeting prices and demand. No area of American life remained untouched, and historians consider it to have been one of the greatest challenges confronted during the 200 years of life under the Constitution.

Sports in American Life: A History, Second Edition. Richard O. Davies.
© 2012 John Wiley & Sons, Inc. Published 2012 by John Wiley & Sons, Inc.

The economic disaster would not end until a military buildup was instituted in 1940 to prepare for the possibility of war with Nazi Germany and Imperial Japan. American sports became an integral part of the glitz and glitter of the 1920s, and the sports world likewise suffered from the economic disaster of the 1930s. The so-called Golden Age of American sports of the 1920s gave way to a dour and disconsolate era for sports enthusiasts that reflected the tough times of the 1930s. The Great Depression seemed to cut even leading sports figures down to size. Popular writer John Tunis noted that "as business fell away, American [athletic] prowess also suffered. After 1930 our stream of super-champions ran dry, replaced by a turgid brook. The champions were now just ordinary mortals, good players but nothing more."[1]

Gee-Whiz: Sports Journalism during the 1920s

In 1931, journalist Paul Gallico assessed the previous decade of sports reporting:

> Never before had there been a period when, from the ranks of every sport, arose some glamorous, unbeatable figure who shattered record after record, spread-eagled his field and drew into the box office an apparently unending stream of gold and silver. We have lived through a decade of deathless heroes.[2]

Gallico was describing the "Gee-Whiz" school of sports journalism that blossomed during the 1920s, which tended to romanticize athletes and their performances by focusing upon the positive while giving scant attention to the negative.

The leading sports journalist was Grantland Rice, a pleasant Southerner possessed of a florid vocabulary and a passion for sports. He preferred to write about heroic effort and stunning victories rather than underachievement and defeats. He would have been very uncomfortable in the world of investigative reporting that came to characterize sports reporting by the late twentieth century. He considered the personal failings of athletes out-of-bounds; even their setbacks and failures on the field of play were treated with understanding. Rice summarized the approach of himself and his many imitators: "I give the other guy a break. That's because I've been an athlete and made mistakes too. In a 2–0 baseball game, for instance, I tend to give the pitcher credit for a good game, instead of belaboring the other team for poor hitting."[3] Under the protective wing of Grantland Rice and his many emulators, Babe Ruth's off-the-field excesses were chalked up to "youthful exuberance," and the pathological behavior of Ty Cobb somehow was transformed into the rosy image of the "Georgia Peach."

During the 1920s, the sports "star" became a popular symbol of the new consumer culture. Historian Lynn Dumenil has observed that sport stars "embodied the new culture" and reassured a nervous people caught up in a time of rapid change because they

> seemed to reaffirm older ideas about success. They represented a path to attainment outside the bureaucracy and regimentation of the corporation, and they held out the reassuring prospect that success was linked not just to hard work and individual discipline but also to the clear-cut rules of the individual sport and sportsmanship.

The media-created sports stars endorsed consumer products and were celebrated in pulp magazines and newspaper headlines. Dumenil writes that there emerged "an ethos of leisure and spending … that placed private, individual commodity-based self-realization at the center" of American life. "That world came tumbling down with the collapse of the economy during the 1930s, giving way to the new outlook of pessimism and doubt that cut the once superheroes down to human size." Dumenil quotes Paul Gallico, who looked back upon his own work during the hyperbolic 1920s from the mid 1930s: "I was spinning a daily tale in the most florid and exciting prose that I could muster, part of the great ballyhoo, member of the great gullibles, swallower of my own bait."[4]

Rice was a caring individual who viewed sports as a metaphor for life itself; the strong moral sense he brought to his craft often surfaced in his writings. He believed that the contests he reported were important as much for the struggle as for the outcome. Rice often inserted his own verse into his columns and game reports, including the famous words written early in his career in 1908 when he was a reporter for the *Nashville Tennessean*:

> For when the Great Scorer comes
> To write against your name,
> He marks not that you won or lost –
> But how you played the Game.[5]

Born and raised in Tennessee, Rice graduated from Vanderbilt in 1901. Discouraged by his parents from pursuing a professional baseball career because of the game's besmirched image, he gravitated to the emerging field of sports journalism. He secured a position with the *New York Herald Tribune* in 1912 and by the 1920s had become the nation's most widely read sportswriter. His daily column was syndicated in more than 100 newspapers. When Walter Camp died in 1925, he assumed the task of picking the All-American football team, and he produced Spotlight Films, a monthly 10 minute motion-picture newsreel on major sporting events. A generalist who covered all sports, Rice played an important role in making tennis and golf popular spectator sports, all the while writing extensively on the mainstream sports of college football and professional baseball. At the time of his death in 1951, it was estimated that he had published 67 million words.

Rice set the standard for hyperbolic writing, such as when he described Babe Ruth's three-home-run effort in a 1926 World Series game:

After the manner of a human avalanche hurtling on its downward way from the blue Missouri heavens, the giant form of Babe Ruth fell upon the beleaguered city of St Louis today and flattened it into a pulp of anguish. If another mighty planet had slipped its ancient moorings to come crashing through unlimited space against the rim of the earth it could not have left one sector in its path more dismantled or forlorn … An enraged bull in a china shop of fragile bric-a-brac would be a mere kitten playing with yarn compared to the astonishing infant who lashed the ball over the stands into Grand Avenue twice and then hammered another home run into the center field seats 430 feet away … It is just a picture of a large portly form taking a wild cut at the ball and then loafing along the open highway with a stunned and startled crowd wondering who let old Doc Thor or the bolt-heaving Jupiter into the show. It was smash-smash-smash and then a steady, even unhurried trot from the plate back to the plate with the ball bounding on its way down St Louis thoroughfares through brokenhearted crowds.[6]

When radio stations began experimenting with live broadcasts of sporting events, Rice decided to give the new medium a try. During the 1922 World Series, he was seated next to the Yankee dugout before a microphone. Station WJZ had a signal that reached 300 miles from New York City, reaching an estimated 1½ million baseball fans. Rice, however, was not comfortable behind the microphone and permitted long periods of silence to fill the airways. One listener said, "I would hear the crowd let out a terrific roar and it would seem ages before I knew whether it was a single or a three-bagger that had been made or whether the side had been retired." Surprisingly, for a man for whom words flowed naturally from his fingertips to his typewriter keys, Rice was too often left speechless before the microphone. "I didn't know what to say," he confessed. But he persevered and the following year signed on to broadcast the series for another New York station, WEAF. Once again Rice discovered that the words simply did not flow into the microphone as when he was hunched over a typewriter. He abruptly quit in the fourth inning of the third game and turned the microphone over to Graham McNamee, an aspiring opera singer who was making a living as a radio station announcer.[7]

McNamee took advantage of this opportunity, and within a few years became the nation's leading sports broadcaster. His experience as an amateur boxer and youthful baseball and football player helped him to convey the drama of sporting events. In one of his first major broadcasts, he was able to describe the many blows and defensive tactics displayed in the 1923 Johnny Wilson–Harry Greb middleweight championship fight. Possessed of a staccato voice, McNamee described boxing matches, college football games, and the World Series to large NBC audiences. He had the distinction of broadcasting the first game carried coast-to-coast: the 1927 Rose Bowl game between Stanford and Alabama. According to one critic, McNamee had the ability "to take a new medium of expression and through it transmit himself – to give out vividly a sense of movement and of feeling." Rival network CBS developed its own broadcast star, Ted Husing, whose rich detail and comprehensive commentary seemed to put the listener inside the stadium. He was CBS's major sportscaster until after the Second World War. One commentator said that Husing may have been even more capable than McNamee, because he "has given more complete information, more accurate and prompt news of the changing position of the ball and acute observations as to place, possibilities and potentialities of the teams and individual players on the field before him."[8]

Radio brought to millions of Americans the exciting flavor of big games being held at distant locations. Along with the sports segments included in weekly newsreels shown at movie theaters, radio contributed greatly to the "Golden Age" of American sports.

Heroes for a Heroic Age

One of Grantland Rice's important contributions to the transformation of sports into mass spectacle was the attention he devoted to sports of limited mass appeal. Golf had arrived in America by the 1890s but play was largely restricted to private country clubs. Not surprisingly, the game was widely perceived to be one reserved for the elite. Until the 1920s, even most important tournaments received relatively little media attention. Tournament sponsors could offer only small prize monies for the professionals; many of the best golfers were amateurs. Such was the case in 1913, when the 20-year-old son of a Boston gardener and handyman, amateur Francis Ouimet, shocked the two dominant English professionals of the time, Harry Vardon and Ted Ray, in the US Open. The tournament was held in suburban Boston at the Country Club in Brookline, where Ouimet had once worked as a caddy. Playing in a three-way 18-hole playoff, Ouimet out-dueled the Englishmen, winning the championship by five strokes. Unlike the sparse crowds that had watched previous major American tournaments, an unprecedented crowd estimated to be over 3,000 trampled over the course following the three competitors.[9]

Ouimet's stunning victory swept golf onto the front pages of American newspapers. A working-class American had toppled the giants of the world of golf. Although Ouimet continued to play competitively for the next three decades, he never won another major tournament, but he had awakened the American people to the exciting possibilities of golf. Middle-class American men and women began to take up the game in the 1920s as public courses opened in most cities. By 1925, an estimated 2½ million Americans played the game. Many businessmen, confined to office or store, found relief from job pressures playing in the open air on well-groomed courses that blended grass, sand, water, and trees into bucolic vistas. Businessmen discovered that the golf course was a perfect location for cutting deals and building relationships with clients. During the dry years of Prohibition, members realized the most hospitable place on the grounds was the "19th hole," which featured a well-stocked bar located within the secure confines of a private club.

After the First World War, Ouimet gave way to a new generation of golfers. One of those men was Walter Hagen. Born into a middle-class family in Rochester, New York in 1892, Hagen became a golf professional at the Country Club of Rochester. This meant that he was expected to earn his living overseeing the entire day-to-day operations – supervising groundskeepers, giving lessons, assigning caddies, and managing the pro shop, club restaurant, and bar. In 1914, Hagen won the US Open, and more victories followed. His flamboyant, if not arrogant, personality and sharp golfing skills led to the media-inspired nickname "Sir Walter."[10] Hagen made golf history in 1922 when he became the first American to win the British Open, and for several years he reigned as the world's greatest golfer, winning two more British Opens (1928 and 1929) and four consecutive Professional Golf Association (PGA) tournaments (1924–7).

The flamboyant Hagen attracted widespread public acclaim and helped to democratize the game of golf. Newspaper writers loved him for his celebrity and fans flocked to his exhibitions, where he bantered with members of the gallery and joined them at the bar afterwards. But the charismatic Hagen had to share the spotlight with another public favorite, the unassuming Bobby Jones, son of a prominent Atlanta family. Both men, in their own way, contributed to golf's growing popularity. Jones not only rose to the top of the golfing world but also graduated from college and law school, passed the Georgia Bar, and launched a successful career as a practicing attorney. At a time when many Americans still believed that the true sportsman was an amateur who played for the joy of competition rather than hard cash, Jones became a public favorite because he refused to turn professional.[11]

In 1923, after gaining considerable attention as a teenage prodigy, Jones won the US Open in dramatic fashion in an 18-hole playoff with Bobby Cruickshank. On the final hole, he boldly ripped a two-iron out of the rough 190 yards over a water hazard onto the green. His ball rolled within a few feet of the hole and he sank his putt for a one-stroke victory. Grantland Rice exulted:

> The red badge of courage always belongs upon the breast of the fighter who can break and then come back with a stouter heart than he ever had before. This crimson decoration of valor came to Robert Tyre Jones, of Atlanta, 21-year-old amateur, when he rode at last yesterday to the crest of the open golf championship of the United States on one of the greatest iron shots ever played in the game that goes back through 500 years of competitive history.[12]

Over the next seven years, Jones – who handled the wooden-shafted clubs of his day with both finesse and power – won 12 more major tournaments at a time when amateurs could enter only a handful each year. In 1930, even Grantland Rice had trouble finding the words to describe Bobby Jones's domination of the world of golf. That year Jones won golf's four most prestigious tournaments, the equivalent of today's Grand Slam – the US Open, the US Amateur, the British Open, and the British Amateur – bringing his total major tournament victories to 13. His classic swing, fearless approach to the game, and quiet personality helped make golf a public spectacle. Unprecedented large crowds followed his every tournament round, and his name became a household word. When he came onto the scene, there were fewer than 500 courses affiliated with the United States Golf Association, but by 1930 there were 1,154 private clubs, and the flurry of construction of public courses meant that there was a total of nearly 6,000 golf courses in the country. After winning the Grand Slam in 1930, Jones abruptly announced his retirement from competitive golf at the age of 28. Rice conceded that Jones had at least 20 good years left in him, but with no new "worlds to conquer" any future victories would be "nothing but anticlimax."[13]

The game of tennis had more difficulty in overcoming its elitist image, but during the 1920s Bill Tilden and Helen Wills attracted considerable attention in the mainstream media. Playing at a time when standard equipment was a small wooden racquet that would be dwarfed by the oversized weapons of today, "Big Bill" Tilden mastered every stroke. Famous for his come-from-behind victories, Tilden's court behavior often pushed the outer limits of what was supposed to be a "game of gentlemen and ladies." A writer for the *New Yorker* described tennis's big star on the court:

> He will turn and glare at any lineman who dares give a decision against his judgment; before the thousands in the stands he will demand the removal of the offender; he will request "lets" at crucial moments, object when new balls are thrown out. When he miss-hit a shot he would stand with his hands on his hips and exclaim, "Oh, Peaches!"

Writing in 1953 upon Tilden's death, veteran sportswriter Al Laney recalled that Tilden was "arrogant, quarrelsome, unreasonable; very hard to get along with." All in all, Tilden's tantrums made him a favorite of the press, in particular Grantland Rice.[14]

Possessed of a slender body, Tilden appeared much taller than his 6 foot 1 inch frame, which led to his nickname "Big Bill." Biographer Frank Deford contends that "no man ever bestrode his sport as Tilden."[15] Indeed, after becoming the first American man to win the singles title at Wimbledon in 1920 (a feat he repeated the following year), Tilden proceeded to win the US Open championship in six consecutive years (1920–5), while also leading the American Davis Cup team to the title for seven consecutive years. At a time when the tennis establishment would only recognize amateur players, Tilden played technically as an amateur although, like other top players, demanded substantial payments to "cover expenses." In 1928, the United States Lawn Tennis Association declared him ineligible because he was being paid $25,000 a year by a newspaper syndicate to write about tennis; the association contended that his tennis articles made him a professional. This shocking decision came on the eve of the Davis Cup matches with France, and the controversy for a time knocked the Herbert Hoover–Al Smith presidential race off the front pages. Reinstated at the last possible moment, he led the United States to victory with a dramatic five-set victory over French star René Lacoste. Angered by the USLTA's ruling, and in need of money, Tilden announced the next year that he was turning professional, which meant that he played exhibition matches for pay for several years because the professional circuit was in its formative stages. His financial circumstances declining, he relocated to Los Angeles where he taught tennis lessons, struggled with little success as a novelist and playwright, and failed to establish himself as a stage and motion-picture actor. Never discreet about his homosexuality, Tilden was arrested in 1946 and convicted of "contributing to the delinquency of a minor," and spent a year in prison. In 1949 he was once again arrested on the same charge and incarcerated. He died of a heart attack in 1953, alone and near penniless in a shabby Hollywood apartment.

Boxing Gains Respectability

The 1920s gave rise to the professional sports promoter. The prototype for this important role was the flamboyant George "Tex" Rickard, who concentrated his considerable abilities upon the long-derided sport of boxing. His creative flair for the dramatic enabled him to help move boxing from the shadows of public skepticism and dubious legal status to mainstream legitimacy. During the 1920s, he promoted five championship fights that grossed over $1 million at the gate and drew crowds that reached the unprecedented figure of 100,000.[16]

Rickard arrived on the scene at the right time. Boxing had been used by the Army to help prepare soldiers for combat in the Great War, and changing public attitudes led to the legalization of the sport in many states, including New York in 1920. With intensive newspaper coverage, it became fashionable for politicians, business executives, and social leaders to be seen at championship fights in the company of their lady friends. During the 1920s, boxing became an integral part of the era of sports ballyhoo, and Tex Rickard was just the person to exploit it. Born in 1871 to itinerant Texas parents, Rickard worked for a few years as a cowpuncher, and at age 19 became a town marshal. In 1895, he migrated to the Klondike in quest of gold, but he soon discovered that it was more profitable and less arduous to mine the miners than to dig for gold himself. He operated saloons in Dawson City and Nome where he installed gambling tables and promoted boxing matches to attract customers. He lost his fortune in search of diamonds in South Africa, but showed up in Goldfield, Nevada, in 1906 in the midst of a gold mining boom. There he established another saloon and became famous when he promoted a world championship fight between middleweights Joe Gans and "Battling" Nelson, putting the $30,000 purse on display in the window of his saloon in the form of stacks of $20 gold pieces. In 1910, he promoted the "fight of the century" in Reno, where Jack Johnson defeated the "Great White Hope" Jim Jeffries.

After losing his fortune running a cattle ranch in Paraguay, Rickard returned to the United States and in 1916 resumed promoting boxing matches. Aware that his future rested with boxing, Rickard went in search of a "killer" boxer who would become his next meal ticket. He found him in Jack Dempsey, who had been earning a few bucks taking on all comers in Nevada saloons. Cursed with spindly legs and an unimposing physique, complete with a high-pitched effeminate voice, Dempsey was also saddled with an unspectacular record. Rickard was undaunted. He dubbed Dempsey the "Manassa Mauler" (after Dempsey's small Colorado hometown) and arranged for a match in Toledo with the aging "Pottawatomie Giant," the 6 foot 6 inch, 245 pound reigning champion Jess Willard, whose career was in sharp decline. Rickard placed Dempsey under the tutelage of skilled trainer Jake Kearns, and on July 4, 1919, he knocked Willard down five times in the first round and finished him off in the fourth round. Standing barely 6 feet tall and weighing only 187 pounds, Dempsey was now, the press gleefully reported, "Jack the Giant-Killer." Rickard moved to New York City and Madison Square Garden, where he signed a deal to promote boxing and other attractions.[17]

In the immediate postwar era the flames of patriotism still burned brightly, and Rickard had himself a powerful gimmick with which to promote Dempsey's fights. The new champion was considered a "slacker," the term applied to men who found a way to avoid military service in France. Dempsey was tried in federal court in 1920 for his failure to serve, but won acquittal on the grounds that his wife and mother required his financial support. Rickard thereupon matched Dempsey against a decorated French soldier, Georges Carpentier. After scheduling the bout for Madison Square Garden, Rickard had to move it across the river to Jersey City when public criticism of Dempsey mounted. Billing the fight as one between a war hero and a draft dodger, Rickard also informed the press that Carpentier was an upper-class dandy who used French perfume and preferred dancing to fighting. Conversely, Rickard portrayed Dempsey as a working-class Irish "mauler" and "abysmal brute" whose pummeling of Willard was only a sign of things to come. Eighty thousand fans paid good money to see the bout, including many of New York's rich and famous. Rickard raked in over $1.6 million at the gate, and Dempsey lived up to his reputation, knocking out his outclassed and over-hyped opponent in the fourth round.

Dempsey grew in popularity as memories of his war record waned. He seldom defended his crown, and when he did it was against weak opponents. In 1923, Rickard matched Dempsey with Luis Firpo of Argentina, whom Rickard dubbed the "Wild Bull of the Pampas." Actually, Firpo had last worked as dishwasher and possessed only marginal pugilistic skills; he came into the fight having won a few contests over opponents that Rickard had lined up to create an aura of respectability. Rickard again played the nationalism card, noting that this was an epic battle between North America and Latin America. Writer Bruce Blevins bluntly wrote, "We are here to see the Nordic race defend itself against the Latin."

Once again, this time at the Polo Grounds, Rickard generated another million-dollar gate. The fans got their money's worth. Dempsey knocked the hapless Firpo to the canvas seven times in the first round, but as the round neared its end, Firpo somehow arose from the canvas and unleashed a wild swing that caught Dempsey flush on the jaw, knocking him completely out of the ring. The dazed champion got back into the ring only with the help of ringside reporters and an obliging Western Union telegrapher. Dempsey managed to hold on until the bell, but 88,000 fans had just witnessed one of the most sensational rounds in boxing history. Firpo's lucky punch only served to enrage Dempsey, who finished him off with two more knockdowns in the second round. Firpo had been decked nine times in less than 5 minutes. An editorial writer for the *Brooklyn Eagle*, satisfied with the outcome, read a great deal into a mere prizefight: "One shudders to think what might have happened to the Monroe Doctrine if Firpo had won. Today it is safe to say that South America has more respect for us than ever before."[18]

Despite his growing popularity, Dempsey did not defend his crown for another three years. He enjoyed his role as a celebrity and earned large sums from public appearances, motion-picture roles, and product endorsements. Rickard was busy making money with various Madison Square Garden promotions and was content to wait until the right opponent came along. For certain, he did not want Dempsey to fight the logical contender, Harry Wills, an African American from New Orleans. Despite demands from leading New York politicians for a title defense against "the Brown Panther," Rickard refused to book the fight. Critics charged that Rickard harbored racist sentiments, but historian Randy Roberts concludes that Rickard, who had promoted the controversial Jeffries–Johnson fight in 1910, simply did not want to upset what he considered a "delicate balance of race relations in the United States."[19]

Finally, in 1926, Dempsey agreed to defend against the light-heavyweight champion Gene Tunney. The New York City native had learned to box as a teenager and was fascinated with the "scientific" aspects of the sport, excelling in dodging punches. He became a Marine Corps champion during the war and afterward won a series of light-heavyweight bouts, defeating "Battling" Levinsky for the title in 1922. The following year, he lost to Harry Greb in a bout that saw him battered for 14 rounds, absorbing a beating so savage that he was hospitalized for several days. Undaunted, Tunney decided that his beating was the result of bad strategy, changed his tactics, and regained the crown. Tunney had reportedly read the major works of Shakespeare, and after he turned professional in 1919 carried books with him everywhere he went. His love of reading was probably exaggerated, but he used his reputed erudition to irritate boxing writers and hype ticket sales. Rickard thereupon dubbed Tunney a "sissy" and a "snob."

Although few experts gave Tunney much of a chance, he was a quality opponent. Other than Wills, he was the logical challenger. Although memories of the war had dimmed, Rickard nonetheless had himself a match between a slacker and a marine who had served in France. A throng of 120,000 fans turned out in Philadelphia expecting to watch Dempsey knock another challenger senseless. As the bout unfolded, however, the impact of Dempsey's three-year layoff became apparent. He was unable to develop a rhythm against his clever opponent and appeared in less than tip-top shape. Conversely, Tunney demonstrated impressive boxing skills as he forced the champion to miss frequently while peppering him with jabs and counterpunches. At the end of the bout, Dempsey's face had been cut in several places and both eyes were swollen. The judges did not award Dempsey a single round, and Rickard moved swiftly to set up a lucrative rematch.[20]

That battle occurred at Soldier Field in Chicago on the evening of September 2, 1927. It is one of the most memorable boxing matches ever staged. Tunney, who upon occasion lectured reporters on their bad manners, irritated them once more when he announced upon his arrival in Chicago, "I'm here to train for a boxing contest. I don't like fighting. Never did." Little wonder *The New York Times* had written that Tunney had "an unconcealed dislike for the sport."[21] An immense crowd estimated at 145,000 filled the football stadium. Rickard kept the attendance figures secret, but the gate was reported to be an astounding $2.6 million, and an estimated 50 million Americans listened to the dramatic description provided by Graham McNamee. The fight began much like the first one had ended, with Tunney controlling the pace and easily sidestepping Dempsey's wild swings while connecting with his stinging counterpunches. But then in the seventh round, a series of events occurred that created the most controversial moment in boxing history. Dempsey managed to connect with a powerful barrage of blows to the head and Tunney dropped to the canvas. An apparent knockout had occurred. The referee motioned to Dempsey to move to a neutral corner as specified in the rules of the Illinois Boxing Commission. But Dempsey ignored him and remained in mid-ring, leering down at his stunned opponent as he once did in Nevada saloons. An estimated 7 seconds passed before he finally moved to a corner. Only then did the referee begin his count. When he reached the count of nine, a wobbly Tunney rose to his feet and managed to survive the round. He then regained his senses and returned to his normal boxing style for the remaining three rounds, frustrating the wildly swinging ex-champion.

When the judges awarded Tunney a unanimous decision, outrage erupted at ringside and across the country. Dempsey, on the one hand, was now the sympathetic victim of a referee's insistence upon enforcing a rules technicality; Dempsey, the one-time slacker, was now transformed into the people's champ. Tunney, on the other hand, because of the "long count," was considered an accidental champion.

After defeating Tom Heeney in 1928, Tunney retired, becoming the first heavyweight champion to vacate the title. Tunney's intellectual qualities proved to be real as he went on to a long and successful career as a business executive and writer, and served as a commander in the US Navy during the Second World War.

With Tunney's retirement and Dempsey no longer active, Rickard lacked a credible fighter to promote. That problem became moot on January 6, 1929, when the master of ballyhoo died suddenly in a Miami hospital, the victim of an infection from a ruptured appendix. Tex Rickard died with Jack Dempsey holding him in his arms. Boxing's heyday came to an unexpected end. During the Age of Ballyhoo of the 1920s, there had been five million-dollar fights – all promoted by the one-time cowboy from Texas. There would be only four million-dollar fights in the next 30 years. More than 20,000 admirers filed past Tex Rickard's casket as it rested on the floor of Madison Square Garden. The man who, Will Rogers said, had a "Midas Touch" departed the sports scene as the sizzling twenties were winding down and the bleak years of depression lay just around the corner.

Baseball's Long Slump

Like other American institutions, baseball took its licks during the Great Depression.[22] The game remained popular with the American people, and fans everywhere continued to follow the fortunes of their favorite teams by listening to radio broadcasts and reading game accounts in the newspapers. But far fewer fans could afford the 50-cent general admission price or the top $1.75 ticket for field-level box seats. Attendance fell precipitously as the Depression held America in its tenacious grip. In 1930, major-league attendance reached an all-time high of 10.1 million, but by 1933, the bottom year of the Depression, it had fallen 41 percent to below 6 million. Minor-league attendance fell at about the same rate of 45 percent; five of 19 minor leagues folded during the 1932 season alone. The worst year for baseball, as well as for the national economy, was 1933; the St Louis Browns drew only 80,000 for the entire season, and the Cincinnati Reds, Philadelphia Phillies, and Chicago White Sox, along with the Browns, were all rumored to be on the verge of financial collapse. In 1932, the 16 major-league teams lost $1.2 million, and another $1.6 million the following year despite cost-saving measures, including slashing salaries by about 50 percent. In 1934, Babe Ruth earned only $35,000, a sharp reduction from his $80,000 salary of the previous four seasons. The roster size of major-league teams was reduced from 25 to 23 players, and the number of umpires was reduced to 10 in each league, which meant that many games were umpired by two-man crews rather than the usual three.

Although fans stayed at home, the product on the field was better than ever. Most of the stars of the 1920s had fallen into the twilight of their careers, but a new generation of exciting players replaced them. In the National League, the shrewd management of Branch Rickey produced aggressive teams in St Louis that won two pennants in the late 1920s, two during the 1930s, and four more during the 1940s. Rickey's intensive scouting program and his elaborate farm system – which reached 30 affiliated teams in 1938 while controlling 750 player contracts – produced a bountiful crop of talented players, many of them poor farm boys from the South. In 1931, the Cardinals upset the favored Philadelphia Athletics in a seven-game World Series, but only 20,000 St Louis fans turned out to watch the Cardinals win the deciding seventh game.

The 1934 Cardinals included an intriguing group of characters who were dubbed the "Gas House Gang." Damon Runyan called them "a warrior club, with warrior spirit."[23] Led by their fiery player-manager, second baseman Frankie Frisch, they played in dirty uniforms, ran the bases with abandon, and partied long into the night. Popular third baseman Pepper Martin epitomized the team. Not blessed with great talent, he went all-out on every play that featured his aggressive base running and belly flop slide. Possessed of a modest physique and limited natural skills, Martin came to symbolize the "forgotten man" of the Great Depression who had to scratch and fight to survive. The native of Osage, Oklahoma had spent seven years in the minor leagues and finally made the Cardinals roster by dint of sheer determination. At shortstop, the Cardinals had the light-hitting but feisty Leo Durocher, a throwback to John McGraw, and in left field the power-hitting Joe "Ducky" Medwick, who led the team with 18 home runs while batting .319. Fans loved the barrel-chested Medwick because he would swing lustily at any pitch that came anywhere close to the plate. The heart of this zany team was the extraordinarily talented and free-spirited pitcher, Jerome "Dizzy" Dean. The son of Arkansas sharecroppers, Dean was irreverent and brash ("It ain't braggin' if you back it up"), possessed of a live fastball, a nasty curve ball, and a tantalizing change-up, all of which he served up with pinpoint control. Although he was the Cardinals' leading pitcher in 1932 with 18 wins, total innings pitched (286), and strikeouts (191), he nonetheless had his salary frozen the next year at $3,000 as the Cardinals retrenched. "This here depression ain't my fault," he plaintively argued.[24] In 1934, Dean reached his prime, winning 30 games while losing just seven. Joining Dizzy Dean on the Cardinals pitching staff was his younger brother Paul, a phlegmatic 21-year-old who won 18 games without the fanfare that surrounded his brother. Sportswriters pinned the inappropriate nickname of "Daffy" on this quiet young man.

Despite their entertaining antics and a close pennant race, only 335,000 fans turned out in depression-riddled St Louis to see the Cardinals play 77 home games. The 1934 World Series against the Detroit Tigers turned into an apt metaphor for the Great Depression. Detroit's industrial plants were operating on a limited basis and St Louis had been devastated by a sharp drop-off in riverboat traffic and the collapse of the Midwestern farm economy. Dizzy Dean was in his element as the center of attention. The Cardinals won the first game 8–3, although Dean told the press, "I didn't have nary a thing on the ball … It was a lousy, tick-flea-and-chigger-bite ball game." In the fourth game, Dean produced the winning run when, as a pinch runner, he failed to slide into second base during a double-play attempt and the second baseman's throw smacked him flush in the forehead, knocking him senseless. As Dean collapsed in a heap, the ball bounced into left center field, permitting Leo Durocher to score the winning run. When he regained consciousness in the clubhouse, Dean announced that he was ready to pitch the next day: "You can't hurt no Dean by hittin' him on the head." A Detroit newspaper happily headlined: "X-Rays of Dean's Head Show Nothing."[25] Dizzy lost that game, but in game 7 at Detroit's Navin Field he pitched the Cardinals to a lopsided 11–0 victory. In the sixth inning of that final game, Ducky Medwick knocked in the Cardinals' seventh run with a triple, and in typical Gas House Gang style, flung himself into third baseman Marvin Owen with a hard slide. A shoving match ensued, and when Medwick trotted out to his left-field position he was greeted by hostile Tigers fans with a barrage of beer bottles, vegetables, and anything else that they could heave over the fence. With the Cardinals far ahead, Commissioner Landis ordered Medwick to the clubhouse. Despite his productive 17-year career, Medwick is largely remembered as the only player ever removed from a World Series game by order of the Commissioner of Baseball.

The New York Yankees extended their domination of baseball. Beginning in 1932 and concluding in 1943 under manager Joe McCarthy, they won eight pennants and seven World Series titles. Babe Ruth retired in 1935, but the Yankees replaced him the following year with a graceful center fielder with a picture-perfect swing. Just 21 years of age, Joe DiMaggio became an immediate star. Dubbed the "Yankee Clipper" (recalling the sleek sailing ships of the early nineteenth century) DiMaggio gracefully roamed the vast spaces of center field in Yankee Stadium. During his 13 seasons between 1936 and 1951 (he sat out three seasons for military duty), he was an impressive clutch hitter who hit not only for power but for high average. DiMaggio led his team to 10 pennants and nine World Series championships (as compared to the figures of seven and four during Babe Ruth's 15-year tenure at Yankee Stadium). The Yankees won their four consecutive World Series in 1936–9 with an astonishing 16–3 record in games while winning the pennants by an average margin of 15 games.

The Yankees were overpowering. After they beat the Cincinnati Reds 4–0 in the 1939 World Series, the frazzled National League president John Heydler lamented, "Is this thing never going to change? No club can be as good as the Yankees have shown themselves to be in the recent Series against our teams."[26] But they were, and the Yankee juggernaut continued its dominance for the next quarter-century, winning 18 pennants and 12 World Series between 1940 and 1964.

Despite hard times, baseball moved forward during the 1930s with three important innovations. The first of these was the establishment of the annual All-Star Game. Proposed by Chicago baseball writer Arch Ward, the game was played on July 6, 1933, in Comiskey Park, and 49,000 fans showed up. It was appropriate that the managers were Connie Mack, now 70 years of age, and John McGraw, whose health was rapidly deteriorating. It was also appropriate that Babe Ruth, now 38, hit the first All-Star Game home run, a two-run blast into the upper deck in right field, and made a spectacular catch while running into the right-field wall. While the game was conceived as a one-time event to coincide with the World's Fair being held in Chicago, it proved so popular that baseball officials thereafter set aside a three-day mid-season break in which to hold the game. It became an important event of the baseball season.

By the end of the 1930s, all major-league teams had made their peace with the radio and signed contracts for most, if not all, games to be aired. Many owners feared that live broadcasts would cut into ticket sales and only reluctantly agreed to permit live broadcasts in return for much-needed permission rights fees. Showing the way were the Chicago Cubs and the St Louis Cardinals who shrewdly used radio to expand their fan base. By the early 1930s, the Cubs had established a radio network that reached far into the upper Midwest, while the Cardinals created millions of new fans in the mid-South and Southwest. When the worst of the Depression had passed, baseball's leaders recognized that radio had created many new fans, which translated into increased ticket sales. In 1934, Commissioner Kenesaw Landis signed a four-year, $400,000 contract with Ford Motor Company to broadcast the World Series. By 1936, all teams but the three located in New York City had some arrangement for radio broadcasts.

In most instances, home games were broadcast live from the ballpark, but economic constraints kept the broadcasters at home when the team hit the road. Announcers sat in a studio and "recreated" the game based upon minimal information sped to them from a distant ballpark over Western Union telegraph lines. One of the popular broadcasters of this era was Ronald "Dutch" Reagan, who recreated Chicago Cubs games in the mid 1930s for Des Moines station WHO from notes passed to him from a studio telegraph operator. One of the problems he and other announcers faced was what to say when the telegraph lines went down, as they frequently did. Speaking to a Baseball Hall of Fame luncheon in the White House in 1981, President Reagan recalled one such episode with Cubs shortstop Billy Jurges at the plate:

> When the slip came through, it said, "The wire's gone dead." Well, I had the ball on the way to the plate. And I figured real quick, I could say we'll tell them what happened and play transcribed music, but in those days there were at least seven or eight other fellows that were doing

the same game. I didn't want to lose the audience … so I had Billy foul one off … and I had him foul one back at third base and described the fight between two kids who were trying to get the ball. Then I had him foul one that just missed being a home run, about a foot and a half. And I did set a world record for successive fouls, or for someone standing there, except that no one keeps records of that kind. I was beginning to sweat when Curley [WHO's station telegraph operator] sat up straight and started typing … and the slip came through the window and I could hardly talk for laughing because it said, "Jurges popped out on the first ball pitched."[27]

In 1935, Cincinnati Reds business manager Larry MacPhail installed a young Southerner, Walter "Red" Barber, in the WLW studio to recreate all of the Reds' road games, but leery of giving away the product, permitted him to broadcast just 13 home games from Crosley Field. He charged two local stations $2,000 each for the rights. In 1939, MacPhail moved on to Brooklyn as general manager and informed the Giants and Yankees that the Dodgers were withdrawing from their agreement not to broadcast games. He negotiated a hefty $77,000 contract with station WOR to broadcast the Dodgers' games, a sum that paid 40 percent of the Dodgers' salaries. MacPhail brought Red Barber and his soft Southern accent to Brooklyn, where he remained the Dodgers' lead broadcaster until 1954, when he moved across town to join the Yankees' broadcast team. The Yankees and Giants signed their own radio contracts; by 1939 all 16 major-league teams had radio affiliations. Fourteen teams – excluding only the two in Boston – had the sponsorship of General Mills, which saw the advantage of promoting its Wheaties cereal as "the breakfast of champions" to baseball fans. Many breweries also joined in sponsorship in quest of a predominantly male listening audience.

Just as baseball's leaders had been cautious about the All-Star Game and radio broadcasts, so too did they approach gingerly the prospect of illuminating their fields for night games. The technology had been around since the 1920s, when many communities installed outdoor lighting for public recreational activities. In 1930, several minor-league teams began night play and realized a significant bump in attendance. When Larry MacPhail became the general manager of the hard-pressed Cincinnati Reds in 1934, he proposed installing lights at Crosley Field. Owner Powel Crosley met staunch resistance from his fellow owners, who only reluctantly agreed to permit a few games in 1935 as an experiment. New York Giants owner Horace Stoneham abstained, reasoning that fast balls would be too difficult for batters to see: "With pitchers like Dizzy Dean, Roy Parmelee and Van Lingle Mungo throwing at night we may have serious injuries to batsmen. Besides, baseball is strictly a daytime game."[28] At 9 p.m. on the evening of May 24, 1935, President Franklin Roosevelt flipped a symbolic switch in the White House and the bright lights came on in Cincinnati, where the lowly Reds met the equally lackluster Phillies. That season, the Reds averaged 18,700 fans for their seven night games, as compared to 4,300 for day games. By the 1941 season, only the Boston Braves and the Chicago Cubs did not have lights. Cubs owner Phil Wrigley had purchased $185,000 worth of equipment to light the field for the 1942 season, but when the United States entered the Second World War, he donated the electrical system to the military. After the war, the Cubs took special delight in being the only team that played an all-day home schedule. Lights would not shine over Wrigley Field until 1988, 11 years after the chewing gum magnate's death.

The 1941 season was conducted with the winds of war increasing in intensity, but the American people found relief from depressing world news by following the hitting streak that "Joltin' Joe" DiMaggio began on May 15 when he hit a single off Edgar Smith of the White Sox. For the next 55 games, DiMaggio made at least one hit, while batting .408, hitting 15 home runs, driving in 55 runs, and striking out just seven times. As his hitting streak grew, the American people followed the sports news as suspense mounted. On several occasions, DiMaggio got a hit in his last time at-bat, and there were a few scorer's decisions that went in his favor. After he passed the modern record of 42 games held by George Sisler and the "old-timers" record of 45 set in 1897 by Wee Willie Keeler, the American people embraced Joe DiMaggio as one of their new heroes. The streak finally came to an end in Cleveland on July 17 with 67,000 fans looking on. Slick-fielding third baseman Ken Keltner made two improbable backhand snags of hard-hit ground balls near the third-base foul line and followed them up with accurate throws to first base to end the string. Keltner and his wife were escorted out of Municipal Stadium by the police. "Joe had a lot of Italian friends in Cleveland," Keltner recalled, "and the club wanted to make sure I got to my car OK."[29] The next day, DiMaggio started another streak that extended for 16 games.

Throughout his career, DiMaggio benefited from coverage by the influential corps of New York City journalists who created an almost mythical image of "Joltin' Joe." Up in Boston, however, a player of comparable stature became the superstar that Boston's writers loved to hate. Ted Williams did not tolerate aggressive journalists well, with the result that his every misstep was magnified and his accomplishments were marginalized by his tough critics. Many Boston fans joined in the fun of hurling insults at Williams, who responded by refusing to sign autographs and refusing to tip his cap when he hit one of his 361 home runs. He and writers frequently traded angry insults. Williams and DiMaggio engaged in a personal duel that often eclipsed the several pennant races in which the Yankees and Red Sox were engaged. Unlike DiMaggio, who prided himself upon being a complete player, Williams homed in on his goal of being recognized as the greatest hitter of all time. His fielding was uninspired and his refusal to bunt, even when faced with the famous "Williams shift" that left much of the left side of the infield unguarded, became part of his complex legend. But in 17 seasons (he lost five seasons serving as a fighter pilot in World War II and the Korean War) he batted .341 and hit 521 home runs. Known for his uncanny eyesight that enabled him to lay off pitches outside the strike zone, Williams was the last player to bat over .400, but he did so during the same magical 1941 season in which DiMaggio batted safely in 56 consecutive games. Consequently, DiMaggio won the Most Valuable Player award rather than his Boston rival. In a fitting capstone to his career, in his last game at Fenway Park, Williams hit a home run, and true to form did not respond to the cheers from the stands with the customary tip of the cap.[30]

Once the worst of the Depression had passed, fans returned to the ballpark. Beginning in 1935, attendance slowly began to increase, and in 1941 it finally exceeded the record of 1929 with 10.5 million tickets sold. Although the Cardinals and Yankees were the dominant teams, other teams were also blessed with outstanding talent and exciting players who lured the fans back to the ballparks. Among these players was the hard-hitting left fielder of the Detroit Tigers, Hank Greenberg, who attracted more than his share of attention because he was Jewish. Anti-Semitism was alive and well in the United States during the 1930s, and one of its hotbeds was Detroit. The Ku Klux Klan had been active in this industrial city during the 1920s, and during the 1930s Father Charles Coughlin presented weekly radio broadcasts from his suburban Royal Oak parish church to millions of avid listeners on a national network, asserting that international Jewish conspirators and their banking allies had caused the Great Depression. As the 1930s unfolded, Coughlin's tirades became increasingly rabid and supportive of Adolf Hitler. Greenberg later recalled, "Being Jewish did carry with it a special responsibility. If I had a bad day, every son of a bitch was calling me names so that I had to make good. I just had to show them that a Jew could play ball." Not only did Greenberg hear it from fans but also from the opposing dugout where, as he recalled, he was routinely called "a Jew bastard and a kike and a sheenie."[31]

Seabiscuit: Sports Star for the Depression Era

Despite the many top-notch athletes who performed during the Great Depression, it is intriguing to note that arguably the most popular sports figure of this era was a horse. During the latter years of the 1930s, an undersized, knobby-kneed thoroughbred by the name of Seabiscuit captured the affection of the American people by overcoming many obstacles to win several memorable races. The improbable saga of the "people's race horse" has been eloquently captured by author Laura Hillenbrand and is the subject of a popular motion picture released in 2003.[32]

If attendance can be considered a determining factor, thoroughbred racing was one of the most popular sports in America in the two decades between the wars. Attendance at racetracks during this period fluctuated between 3 and 6 million, rivaling baseball. The primary attraction, of course, was the possibility of hitting a big payday on a two-dollar bet. The reputation of horse racing had fluctuated over the years, remaining popular in the South but often becoming the target of anti-gambling crusaders elsewhere. Under relentless anti-gambling pressures, except for some notable tracks such as Churchill Downs in Louisville and Pimlico Race Course in Baltimore, most race tracks had closed by the late nineteenth century. During the heyday of the progressive reform movement during the early twentieth century, matters got worse when legislatures in such prominent racing states as California, Illinois, and New York passed anti-gambling laws. After the First World War, however, legislators took a careful look at a new betting system recently imported from France, the pari-mutuel system, which assured the authorizing government a guaranteed percentage of each and every dollar bet on every race (approximately 15 to 18 percent). Legislatures recognized pari-mutuel as a means of increasing state revenues without having to pass new taxes. Racetracks essentially became partners with state governments, which greatly alleviated the persistent fear of fixed races.

Leading the way was Churchill Downs in Louisville, located near the heart of thoroughbred horse country. Local businessman and marketing expert Matt Winn saved the hard-pressed racetrack from closing down when he took over management in 1902 and created a special aura surrounding the Kentucky Derby. In 1911, he introduced pari-mutuel betting that increased confidence that the races were not being manipulated by trackside bookmakers. During the 1920s, legislators in several states took notice of the Kentucky success story and voted to legalize pari-mutuel betting. State racing boards operated the system, which meant

Figure 8.1   Seabiscuit drives between two horses to take the lead in the home stretch of his last race, the 1940 Santa Anita Handicap. Jockey Red Pollard is aboard the popular horse, making a brave comeback from near-fatal injuries suffered two years earlier when he was thrown and dragged several hundred yards by a young thoroughbred during what was supposed to be a routine workout. *Image © Bettmann/Corbis*

that private bookmakers were banished from the tracks. State racing boards added to public confidence by appointing stewards to oversee track operations. By 1940, more than a dozen states had embraced state-sanctioned trackside pari-mutuel betting, including Maryland, Illinois, Florida, Louisiana, California, and New York.

Horse racing consequently enjoyed a major resurgence during the 1920s and its popularity remained high throughout the Great Depression. The Triple Crown – so named for three-year-old horses that captured the Kentucky Derby, the Preakness Stakes, and the Belmont Stakes – became a powerful narrative when Gallant Fox won all three races in 1930. Fans thrilled to Triple Crowns won by Omaha (1935), War Admiral (1937), and Whirlaway (1941).

It was in this context that the improbable story of Seabiscuit, "the little horse that could," became a major sports story of the Depression years. In 1935, the two-year-old performed so poorly that his famous trainer,

"Sunny Jim" Fitzsimmons, did not enter him in any of the Triple Crown races the following year. Despite his rich heritage – he was descended from the incomparable Man o' War and his sire was the handsomely sculpted Hard Tack – Seabiscuit was undersized and built on stubby legs that would not fully straighten, forcing him to run in a manner that many compared to a waddling duck. His appearance, Hillenbrand writes, gave no indication of his special lineage and "had all the properties of a cinder block."[33]

In 1936, Seabiscuit was sold for a mere $7,500 to San Francisco automobile dealer Charles Howard, who had no prior experience in the unique culture of horse racing. He hired an unknown trainer, Tom Smith, whose career up to this point had been unspectacular despite his instinctive ability to get the best out of cantankerous horses. Smith hired Red Pollard, an unproven jockey with little big-time racing experience. Under Tom Smith's gentle prodding, Seabiscuit began to show promise, and soon he was winning races at California tracks. Racing fans began to take notice of this undersized thoroughbred with the ungainly stride but powerful finish. Seabiscuit's popularity spread as racing fans recognized that the improbable team of Howard, Smith, Pollard, and an undersized horse no one wanted was a fitting metaphor for their own struggles during the Great Depression. In November 1938, this small horse with a big heart was transported to the East Coast to challenge the 1937 Triple Crown winner in a match race. War Admiral – also descended from Man o' War – exuded the perfect image of a thoroughbred: tall, sleek, glistening, perfectly proportioned, and high-spirited. Most of the experts were hidebound Easterners, and few gave the upstart from California with the funny gait any chance; each of the *Racing Form* handicapping experts picked War Admiral, as did 95 percent of sportswriters.

The race took place on War Admiral's own turf at Pimlico Race Course in Maryland. Millions of Americans listened to radio announcer Clem McCarthy make the call. In what everyone conceded was an enormous upset victory, Seabiscuit won by four lengths going away, despite having a substitute jockey due to the multiple broken bones and life-threatening internal injuries suffered by Red Pollard when he was thrown from a horse during a workout. Like so many Americans who had braved the Great Depression with courage and determination, Seabiscuit and his handlers had overcome great obstacles. In 1938, the small horse with the big heart received more news coverage than President Franklin Roosevelt.

In 1940, Seabiscuit went to the starting gate for the last time in the $100,000 Santa Anita Handicap. Red Pollard was aboard although a badly shattered leg had not fully healed. In a thrilling 12-horse race, Pollard expertly guided Seabiscuit from behind, bursting through a narrow opening in a cluster of horses bunched at the head of the home stretch to win a stunning victory before 85,000 spectators. It would be Seabiscuit's last race. As he was applauded and cheered on the way to the winner's circle, Seabiscuit pranced and preened for the crowd. Pollard later recalled, "Don't think he didn't know he was the hero."[34]

Baseball during the War Years

When the United States entered the Second World War following the attack on Pearl Harbor on December 7, 1941, the leaders of baseball recalled the difficult time they had encountered in 1917–18. Commissioner Landis seemed inclined to shut down for the duration.

However, concerns that seasons would be canceled were soon set aside when President Franklin D. Roosevelt urged organized baseball to stay on the field: "I honestly feel that it would be best for the country to keep baseball going. There will be fewer people unemployed and everybody will work longer hours and harder than ever before. And that means they ought to have a chance for recreation and for taking their minds off their work more than before."[35]

Thus the game continued, with full 154-game seasons being played; only the 1945 All-Star Game was canceled when sportswriters concluded that there were too few players who met the definition of "all-star." Within days after Pearl Harbor, many ballplayers enlisted for military duty. By 1943, nearly 1,000 major- and minor-league players had entered the military. Management had to find substitute players, and Cubs owner Phil Wrigley launched the professional All-American Girls Baseball League that put solid teams on the field, attracting substantial attendance and favorable media coverage.

While women's ball provided an alternative for fans in the mid-sized Midwestern cities, major-league baseball had to make do with men that the military did not want. Teams found many older players in the minor leagues, and several retired ballplayers returned to the game. Some very young players were also hustled onto the field. The 1944 Brooklyn Dodgers played 16-year-old Tommy Brown in 46 games, and Cincinnati manager Bill McKechnie inserted a 15-year-old left-handed pitcher from nearby Hamilton, Ohio, into a hopelessly lost game against St Louis; although Joe Nuxhall would eventually enjoy a lengthy career as a pitcher for the Reds (and 35 more years as a Reds broadcaster), his brief appearance was beset by wildness as he gave up five walks and two hits while retiring only two batters. The St Louis Browns even played a one-armed outfielder, Pete Gray, although his signing was not the cheap publicity stunt many people made it out to be. Gray had commendable skills and previously had been selected as the Most Valuable Player in the Southern League. He hit .218 in 72 games for the Browns in 1945 before being released.

Some leading players – including Cleveland shortstop Lou Boudreau and Detroit left-handed pitcher Hal Newhouser – played throughout the war with medical deferments, but most of the younger players ended up in the military. First baseman Stan Musial received a family hardship deferment, did not leave for the Army until 1944, and helped the Cardinals win three wartime pennants and two World Series titles. Boston Red Sox hitting star Ted Williams signed on as a Marines pilot before the 1943 season, and his great American League rival, Joe DiMaggio, volunteered for the Army Air Corps, although he could have received another deferment. Few players actually saw action in battle; many ended up playing baseball for military teams to entertain troops. Cleveland pitcher Bob Feller joined the Navy and saw action against the enemy in both the Atlantic and the Pacific theaters. Only two men who had played in the major leagues died in combat: Harry O'Neill, who caught for one inning in 1939 with the Phillies, was killed in the bloodbath of Iwo Jima; and Elmer Gedeon, who had played in five games for the Washington Senators, died when his aircraft was shot down in Europe. Perhaps the most important development for organized baseball during the war years was that Commissioner Kenesaw Landis died in 1944 and was replaced by former Kentucky governor Albert "Happy" Chandler.

9

America's Great Dilemma

As the Second World War entered its final stages, Swedish social scientist Gunnar Myrdal published a major study of race relations in the United States. In the aptly entitled *An American Dilemma*, Myrdal argued that a pervasive system of racial segregation denied basic rights to 10 percent of the American people, and that its existence constituted an issue that had to be addressed in postwar America. Myrdal noted the supreme irony that the United States was fighting a war in defense of freedom and democracy against Adolf Hitler's totalitarian regime based upon a doctrine of racial supremacy. That the United States was a society in which racial segregation and discrimination were pervasive was simply too great an issue to ignore. Quoting Thomas Jefferson's opening words in the Declaration of Independence with powerful effect – "We hold these truths to be self-evident: That all men are created equal; that they are endowed by their Creator with certain inalienable rights; that among these are life, liberty, and the pursuit of happiness" – Myrdal drove home his message. As the subsequent 1,100 pages of Myrdal's detailed narrative made clear, African Americans were not free to participate in the American Dream. The American people did indeed have a major dilemma to confront in the postwar years.[1]

Although the end of slavery in 1865 gave African Americans their freedom, it soon became clear that they faced a new set of obstacles. By 1900, their right to vote had been stripped away in many parts of the South, and all across the United States discrimination in education, housing, employment, and social settings prevailed. In the extreme, more than 1,000 lynchings had occurred across the South and the border states by 1910. In 1896, the US Supreme Court gave constitutional sanction to the era of Jim Crow in the case of *Plessy* vs *Ferguson*, creating the "separate but equal" doctrine.

This culture of pervasive racism included sports. Just as black schools, churches, hospitals, insurance companies, and businesses were established, opportunities for black athletes existed within a segregated sports world that mirrored the sports scene in white society.

Sports in American Life: A History, Second Edition. Richard O. Davies.
© 2012 John Wiley & Sons, Inc. Published 2012 by John Wiley & Sons, Inc.

Black communities embraced baseball just as enthusiastically as white America. A notable early example was the Philadelphia Pythians club, established in 1866. Although forced to play many of their games against other black teams, they also played white teams from cities as far distant as Chicago. Thus upon occasion, the color ban for crackerjack teams like the Pythians would be relaxed when "exhibition" games against white teams were held.

Between 1880 and 1930, throughout the United States, amateur "town ball" flourished in communities large and small. The number of black teams that existed is unknown, but it was large. At the top of the heap of town ball were semiprofessional teams. The pay was low but the talent substantial and the quality of play frequently sparkling. The best black teams often traveled far and wide in quest of good competition and paying customers on the informal barnstorming circuit. Outstanding players such as pitcher Rube Foster and the hard-hitting infielder Sol White, whose 25-year playing career also included a few brief interludes as a member of white semiprofessional teams, became famous within black communities. These semiprofessional teams provide a vivid example of the effort of black businessmen – their primary backers – to counter the oppression of segregation.[2]

Although a small number of blacks were able to compete successfully in the white sports world – jockey Isaac Murphy of Lexington and bicycle racer Marshall Taylor being among the most notable – in almost all instances the color line was sharply drawn and rigorously enforced. This is what makes the achievement of prizefighter Jack Johnson such a compelling story. When he was able to capture the heavyweight championship of the world in 1908 against champion Tommy Burns in Australia, the result was a crisis of immense importance that engulfed American sports fans.

The "Fight of the Century"

Ever since the heavyweight championship became formalized by the promotions of Richard Kyle Fox, black heavyweights were denied opportunities to challenge white champions. Early in his reign, the popular champion John L. Sullivan announced he would take on all challengers if the money was right, but when confronted with the possibility of such formidable opponents as George Godfrey and Peter Jackson, he modified that pronouncement: "In this challenge I include all fighters – first come, first served – who are white. I will not fight a negro. I never have and never shall." Such a rationale was confirmed by a *New York Times* editorial that suggested a victory by a black challenger would permit "ignorant brothers [to] misinterpret his victory as justifying claims to much more than physical equality with their white neighbors."[3]

It was therefore fitting that when Jack Johnson successfully defended his heavyweight championship in 1910, Sullivan was in the audience. Born in Galveston, Texas, in 1878, Johnson survived a rough childhood and dropped out of school after the sixth grade. As a teenager, he fought in the Texas bare-knuckle circuit and moved on to the national level. By 1903, he had defeated the best black heavyweights and held the unofficial title of "Negro Heavyweight Champion." However, he was repeatedly rebuffed by leading white heavyweights when he attempted to arrange a challenge. Champions Jim Corbett, Bob Fitzsimmons, Jim Jeffries, and Marvin Hart ignored his existence, just as they refused to fight such quality fighters as Sam Langford, Sam McVey, and Joe Jeanette.[4]

Prevailing views of African American fighters competing with whites in lower weight divisions, however, were mixed. A popular lightweight, the "Old Master" from Baltimore, Joe Gans, had won the championship from defending champion Frank Erne in 1902. There were no serious racial repercussions, and during the succeeding eight years he won and lost the title several times. When Gans died in 1914 of tuberculosis, his death was widely mourned by all boxing fans. But racial fears ran deep, as revealed when a reporter for the *New Orleans Times-Democrat* commented upon a bout in which lightweight George "Little Chocolate" Dixon administered a fearful beating to a white opponent: "The sight was repugnant to some of the men from the South … the idea of sitting quietly by and seeing a colored boy pommel a white lad grates on Southerners." The writer concluded that it was "a mistake to bring the races together on any terms of equality, even in the ring."[5]

Jack Johnson got his opportunity when reigning heavyweight champion, Tommy Burns of Canada, agreed to a match at Rushcutters Bay near Sydney, Australia. Burns needed a payday and Johnson was delighted to oblige. The cocky but undersized Burns (he weighed only 175 pounds) believed that his Anglo-Saxon heritage would enable him to defeat his much larger challenger, who stood 6 feet 2 inches and weighed a trim 190 pounds. Johnson, however, pounded the overmatched Burns at will until officials stopped the action in the 13th round. Johnson's victory set off a racial crisis for millions of white Americans who could not accept the fact that an African American now wore boxing's most prestigious crown.[6]

Johnson's persistent flaunting of prevailing racial customs greatly exacerbated the situation. He appeared in public wearing stylish clothing and expensive jewelry, drove high-powered luxury automobiles, and enjoyed the company of attractive white women. During his lifetime, Johnson was married to three different white women. By flaunting one of the most sensitive taboos of the racial code, the independent and self-assured Johnson understood that he was inviting trouble.[7]

With Johnson the undisputed champion, a desperate search for a "Great White Hope" commenced in the United States. Much to the chagrin of white supremacists, the thin pool of talent failed to produce a challenger who inspired confidence. Ultimately the quest focused upon James Jeffries, who had enjoyed a successful six-year tenure as heavyweight champion, defending his title nine times without a loss after wresting the title away from Bob Fitzsimmons in 1899. With no viable challenger in the offing, Jeffries retired in 1905 to his alfalfa farm near Los Angeles. His reputation rivaled that of John L. Sullivan. He was a powerful left-handed slugger whose size and strength were his greatest assets; he was willing to absorb heavy punishment in order to wear down his opponents before unleashing his own powerful blows. He broke three of his challengers' ribs. Boxing experts yet today consider him among the greats of all heavyweight champions. The popular novelist and ardent spokesman for white supremacy, Jack London, perhaps best expressed the thinking of millions when he urged Jeffries to abandon retirement to reclaim the championship for the white race: "Jeff, it's up to you," he implored. "The white race must be rescued."[8]

After nearly six years of retirement, Jeffries was not ready to fight any professional boxer, let alone the superbly talented Johnson. Jeffries had ballooned to 300 pounds from his fighting weight of 225. Eventually he relented to the pressure, persuaded by a guarantee of over $150,000 in fees and movie rights. At times, Jeffries professed indifference to the overriding racial overtones, saying only, "It's money I'm after, man," but on other occasions he said he was motivated by the desire to regain the title for the white race. Promoter Tex Rickard originally announced that the fight would be held in San Francisco, but anti-prizefighting groups forced him to seek another site. After considering several options, in mid June he settled on the small city of Reno, Nevada. Home to 17,000 residents, nearly all white, Reno was located on the main line of the Union Pacific Railroad. Rickard was encouraged by the strong support of local businessmen and assurances from Governor Denver Dickerson that state and local officials would be welcoming. Rickard announced that the bout would be held on July 4, 1910.

Nevadans recognized an economic bonanza when they saw one. A wooden stadium to accommodate 22,000 spectators was hastily erected just east of town, and for a few weeks the high desert town became the center of national attention. Both fighters set up training camps at Reno resorts, normally the temporary residences of wealthy women establishing a six-month residency requirement before appearing in a Reno divorce court.

Pre-fight press coverage revolved almost exclusively around the matter of race. To read the media coverage of 100 years ago is to be stunned by the crude racial slurs that were commonplace at that time. Some Southern white editors grimly predicted a race war if the "Big Bear" from California failed to defeat Johnson, and white ministers were reported to have prayed from their pulpits for a Jeffries victory. So-called boxing "experts" weighed in with all types of assessments, many of them building upon popular racial stereotypes that alleged that African Americans lacked the intelligence and courage to win such an important contest. Novelist Rex Beach typically wrote that Jeffries would win because of "breeding and education." Betting odds on the fight anticipated a Jeffries victory. In the days immediately before the fight, many thousands of fight fans (including a large assortment of gamblers, pickpockets, prostitutes, and scam artists) descended upon Reno, where businessmen eagerly awaited the anticipated economic bonanza.

After an enormous buildup, the fight proved anti-climatic. After Johnson entered the outdoor ring under a blazing sun and "surveyed the sea of white faces," as he later wrote of his experience, "I felt the auspiciousness of the occasion. I realized that my victory in this event meant more than on any previous occasion. It wasn't just the championship that was at stake – it was my own honor, and in a degree the honor of my race."[9]

An estimated 22,000 spectators packed the stadium. They saw Johnson cruise to an easy victory over a former champion long past his prime. Much too fast for his opponent, Johnson punished him with lightning-quick jabs and powerful counterpunches, all the while taunting him for his ponderous efforts. During the middle rounds Johnson seemed merely to toy with his plodding adversary, but in round 15 he hit the already dazed Jeffries with a series of powerful combinations and the former champion slumped to the canvas for the first time in his career. He bravely fought on, but after the third knockdown his corner conceded and Rickard stopped the fight at the count of seven, just before a knockout would have been registered.

An eerie silence descended over the arena. Disappointed Jeffries backers shuffled out of the stadium and headed downtown to drown their sorrows at Reno's 60 taverns. Across the nation a series of violent incidents occurred when white gangs took out their disappointment on innocent African Americans. Random knifings and beatings reminded everyone that the status of African Americans had not changed. In fact, the racial emotions unleashed by this prizefight constituted a major setback to any hopes for racial reconciliation.

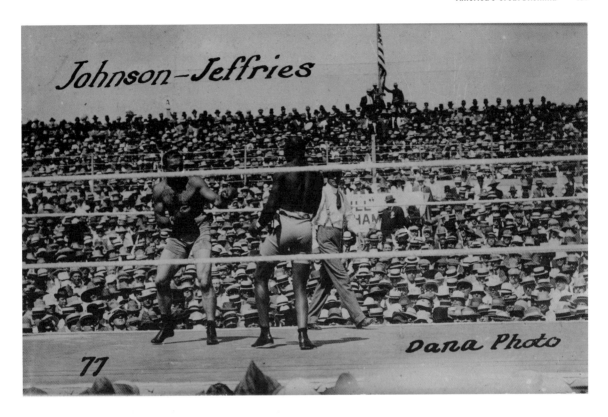

The fight exposed raw visceral racial attitudes that were not easily forgotten. The fight had opened a large chasm in American society. As Thomas Hietala observes, when Tex Rickard raised his hand in victory, Johnson "stood proudly at the summit, and symbolically, millions of African Americans stood beside him. For Johnson and his people, the championship seemed a partial but promising fulfillment of their collective hopes and dreams, a portent of a future brighter than their troubled past and present."[10]

By beating the Great White Hope, Johnson also set in motion a series of events that would overwhelm him. He was hit by a powerful racially inspired backlash led by the United States government. In 1913, he was convicted of violating the Mann Act, a vaguely written federal law passed by Congress in 1910 intended to curb interstate prostitution. The Department of Justice used Johnson's frequent interstate train trips with willing white women to make its tenuous case. Johnson thereupon fled the country and defended his crown in Europe several times. With his skills having diminished over the years, Johnson lost to Jess Willard in Havana in a 26th-round knockout in 1915. In 1920, Johnson returned to the United States, surrendered to authorities, and served one year in the federal prison at Leavenworth, Kansas. Upon his release, he fought a few inconsequential bouts for much needed paydays, traveled the vaudeville and carnival circuit, and died in 1946 in a car accident in North Carolina.

Figure 9.1 Defending champion Jack Johnson and challenger Jim Jeffries square off in the first of many "fights of the century." This one was held outdoors on July 4, 1910 in Reno, the only location where promoter Ted Rickard could be assured of cooperation from local authorities. This fight attracted enormous attention throughout the western world because of strong racial overtones. Heavy media coverage of the fight helped the sport gain wider public acceptance. *Special Collections, University of Nevada–Reno Library*

Separate and Unequal: The Negro Leagues

W. E. B. Du Bois once observed that for African Americans, "One ever feels his twoness – an American, a Negro, two souls, two thoughts, two unreconciled strivings; two warring ideals in one dark body, whose dogged strength alone keeps it from being torn asunder." As Jules Tygiel points out, this comment aptly summarizes the history of what has been termed the "Negro Leagues."[11] The unwritten "gentlemen's agreement" to exclude blacks from organized baseball which took effect in 1885 meant that African Americans had to play professionally in leagues of their own.[12]

The first sustained effort to organize an African American league was made in 1920 by Andrew "Rube" Foster, an exceptional pitcher in his own right (he won 54 games for the Cuban X-Giants in 1904), now owner and player-manager of the Chicago American Giants. In 1920, Foster organized the eight-team Negro National League (NNL) and dreamed of building it to the point where it would be considered a third major league. Much was made of the fact that his own team traveled first class in a private Pullman train car, prompting the *Chicago Defender* to comment that Rube Foster was "the most successful Colored man in baseball, the only one that has made it a business."[13] But the NNL lacked franchises in New York and Philadelphia, and two teams, the Kansas City Monarchs and Foster's own Chicago Americans, dominated play to the point of discouraging fan interest. Foster wanted to demonstrate that African Americans could develop and operate a stable, viable league without financial backing from whites; only J. L. Wilkinson, owner of the Monarchs, was white. The league became well known for its aggressive base running and sharp defensive play, but it suffered from chronic instability produced by dependence upon a fan base comprising primarily low-income Americans. White fans seldom turned out for a game unless it was an exhibition match against a white team. Foster repeatedly told his fellow owners that the league could survive only if everyone cooperated, but he apparently had difficulty following his own advice, and under criticism for his dictatorial ways, was forced to resign in 1925. In 1926, he suffered a mental breakdown and was institutionalized, and he died in 1930. His league limped along briefly after his departure, but it folded under the duress of the Great Depression in 1931. In 1981, Rube Foster was admitted to the National Baseball Hall of Fame in Cooperstown.[14]

The NNL, however, had inspired an upsurge of interest in baseball among urban African Americans during the 1920s. One center of activity was Pittsburgh, where two teams excelled, the Pittsburgh Crawfords and the Homestead Grays. In 1933, Gus Greenlee, the owner of the Crawfords, created a new Negro National League and operated it for several years by bringing together teams from Eastern cities. Anyone who was anyone in Pittsburgh was acquainted with Greenlee, widely known as "Mr Big." He had his hand in many enterprises, some legitimate, others that skirted the fringes of the law. He operated nightclubs, restaurants, and bars, was prominent in the local bootlegging trade, ran a protection racket, and supervised a stable of boxers. A millionaire many times over, he traveled about town in a chauffeured Lincoln, and was known for his generous support of local charities. He also had his hand in the lucrative Pittsburgh numbers racket, which reportedly funneled upwards of $20,000 a week into his pocket. A major player in local Republican Party politics, Greenlee called the shots in the predominantly black Third

Ward. Greenlee spent $100,000 to build a new baseball field in 1932 for his team. The Crawfords were one of a very few Negro League teams to have their own ballpark; most teams lacked the resources available to Greenlee and were forced to rent from white professional clubs.[15]

Although the Crawfords contended for honors with NNL teams now located in Newark, Philadelphia, New York, and Baltimore–Washington, their major competition was the crosstown Homestead Grays, owned and managed by Cumberland "Cum" Posey, Jr. Greenlee, according to one of his veteran players, "looked like the racketeer he was," as he appeared in public wearing expensive suits with a cigarette dangling from his lips. Conversely, Posey was the picture of middle-class decorum, a businessman and civic leader who served on the local school board. He studied chemistry at Penn State and pharmacy at the University of Pittsburgh. Posey's greatest achievement, however, was building the Grays into a nationally recognized baseball club. He contributed to the Pittsburgh sports scene by writing a column in the *Pittsburgh Courier*. Joining the Grays in 1911 as an outfielder, within a few years he controlled the team's baseball and financial operations. By 1920, he was attracting top players from the Pittsburgh area and beyond. The Grays frequently played at Forbes Field when the Pirates were out of town. By the early 1920s, the team was taking on all comers and was recognized as a national barnstorming team.[16]

In the 1930s and the 1940s, the two Pittsburgh teams competed fiercely for local bragging rights. The Grays featured some of the greatest African American players of the 1930s; five members were ultimately voted into the Hall of Fame. Their speedy center fielder, James "Cool Papa" Bell, was a sparkling leadoff batter and base runner. The Grays also featured catcher Josh Gibson, whose prodigious home runs were compared to those of Babe Ruth. At first base was Buck Leonard, known for his smooth swing and graceful play at first base. Between 1937 and 1945, Gibson and Leonard, often called the Babe Ruth and Lou Gehrig of the Negro leagues, led the Homestead Grays to nine consecutive NNL championships. During the hard-pressed Depression years, top players earned about $125 a month during the five-month season, scarcely adequate pay to support their families. This meant they spent the winters playing in the Caribbean or Mexico, or barnstorming through the segregated South, often playing top local white teams. Their pay increased substantially with the economic boom spurred by the Second World War. In 1948, Leonard pocketed $10,000. Gibson's career ended tragically in 1947 when he died at the age of 35 from a stroke.

While Gibson and Leonard powered Cum Posey's Grays, Greenlee's Crawfords countered with the incomparable pitcher, Leroy "Satchel" Paige. Greenlee and Paige, both headstrong men, often argued over money, prompting Paige to depart more than once for a better offer. Paige's petulance often proved distracting, but he was worth the bother. Arguably one of the greatest pitchers of all time, he was blessed with a blazing fastball, a mystifying curve, and several junk pitches to which he gave humorous names ("dipsy-doodle," "bee ball," "hurry-up," "hesitation pitch," "jump ball," "trouble ball"). Born in 1906 in Mobile, Alabama, he acquired his nickname "Satchel" working as a youthful baggage handler at the city's railroad station. Tall and spindly, Paige began pitching for a Mobile semiprofessional team in 1924. The best guess is that he played for eight different Negro league teams before he joined the Cleveland Indians in the American League in 1948 as a 42-year-old rookie. By his own estimate, Paige pitched 300 shutouts and 55 no-hitters, and won 2,000 games of the 2,600 or so in which he participated.[17]

Figure 9.2   Josh Gibson shows his powerful swing in a game played in Pittsburgh. Hall of Fame pitcher Walter Johnson said of Gibson that he was a catcher "any big league club would love. He hits the ball a mile, and he catches so easy he might as well be in a rocking chair. Throws like a rifle. Too bad this Gibson is a colored fellow." Many knowledgeable baseball observers contend he would have been one of the greatest catchers in the history of the major leagues – if he had been permitted to play. *National Baseball Hall of Fame Library, Cooperstown, NY, USA (Public Domain)*

Satchel Paige was undoubtedly the biggest attraction of the Negro leagues. Some historians think he was the second most popular baseball player of his era, after Babe Ruth. His appeal went far beyond his pitching skills, because he was a natural showman, often engaging in various on-the-field charades that delighted fans. Once, during warmups, he placed a burning candle on home plate and proceeded to put out the flame by whizzing a fastball just past the candle. He delighted crowds by fooling batters with his trick pitches. While playing against local teams during a barnstorming tour, he would intentionally walk the bases loaded, order his infielders and outfielders to sit down, and proceed to strike out the next three batters. After the 1932 season, Paige and Dizzy Dean put together two teams – one black, one white – and barnstormed across the South and Southwest. Baseball executive Bill Veeck, Jr, recalled a 13-inning game in Los Angeles in 1934 in which Paige's "All-Stars" defeated Dean's "All-Stars" 1–0 as the greatest baseball game he ever watched. "Dean was superlative, holding the Paige Stars to one run and fanning 15," he later recalled. "But Paige shut out the Dean Stars and fanned 17."

This experiment in racially integrated baseball angered Commissioner Kenesaw Landis, who called the games "demeaning," but his efforts to squelch the postseason games proved ineffective. These interracial games drew large and appreciative crowds. The winter circuit proved so financially successful that it continued into the late 1940s. When Dean's arm failed him, future Hall of Fame pitcher Bob Feller replaced him on the winter junket trail.[18]

The Negro leagues helped create an awareness of black baseball talent which contributed to the rising chorus of demands that organized baseball end its racial ban, but more immediately it filled an important void in the lives of African Americans. The leagues created a sense of racial pride and were a major focus of black newspapers. They provided an important sense of community during the trying years of the Great Depression. Financial instability, however, meant that between 1933 and 1948 the Negro National League had 18 different franchises, many lasting for just one or two seasons (including such long-forgotten teams as the Detroit Stars, the Baltimore Black Sox, and the Bacharach Giants of Atlantic City). In 1938, the Negro American League (NAL) began play, and featured Midwestern and Southern teams. Both leagues were torn internally by conflict and turmoil produced by financial uncertainty and frequent changes in ownership.

The surging economy of the Second World War produced a boost in attendance. With regular paychecks, fans flocked to the ballparks in historic numbers. Salaries went up and league finances stabilized. In 1942, a meaningful Negro League World Series was held for the first time since 1927. The Kansas City Monarchs (bolstered by the pitching of Satchel Paige) defeated the Homestead Grays in an epic confrontation. The next two seasons, the Grays prevailed over the Birmingham Black Barons.

By this time, however, pressures on major-league baseball to drop its color ban were intensifying. Publication of Gunnar Myrdal's damning indictment of American race relations spearheaded a host of publications that raised important public questions, and black leaders focused attention upon the fact that the United States was fighting the racist Nazi regime with a segregated military. Several leading journalists, including influential black writers Wendell Smith of the *Pittsburgh Courier*, Frank Young of the *Chicago Defender*, and Sam Lacy of the *Baltimore Afro-American*, had for years campaigned vigorously for the integration of organized baseball. They pointed to the high caliber of play in the Negro leagues, and the ability of black players to compete on an equal basis with white major leaguers on the winter barnstorming circuit. Their message was often echoed by prominent white sports writers, especially in New York City, but these arguments carried no weight with the one man who counted, Commissioner Kenesaw Landis. Opposition to ending organized baseball's ban on African American players, however, lost public support as the war was winding down, and when Landis died in 1944 he was succeeded by the former governor of Kentucky, Albert "Happy" Chandler, whose racial views were more enlightened.

Negro league baseball enjoyed its most successful times during the later years of the Second World War. The East–West All-Star Game of 1944 played in Chicago's Comiskey

Park drew 46,000 fans. Both Negro leagues went into sharp decline when organized baseball finally admitted black players. By 1950, 150 players had departed, and African American fans preferred watching black players in an interracial setting. The NNL folded in 1948, and a handful of teams from the NAL limped on for a few years before disappearing. With the political winds filled with talk of racial integration, by 1950 black baseball "offered little of value to African Americans," historian Neil Lanctot concludes. Sportswriter Harold Winston observed at the time, "With the various fights for integration going on, the aspect of an all-Negro anything is meeting with increasing opposition from the Negro people," and as NAL president J. B. Martin said, "Why maintain a Jim Crow baseball circuit?"[19]

Out of the Cotton Fields of Alabama: Jesse and Joe

Against the backdrop of the ominous rise of Nazi Germany during the 1930s, two athletes became the focus of intense international scrutiny. Jesse Owens and Joe Louis were the first black athletes to gain national media attention since Jack Johnson, but the manner in which they were perceived indicated that racial attitudes had changed very little. Despite their accomplishments, white America viewed them within a narrow context indicating that racism was alive and well in America.

Owens stunned the sports world with an extraordinary performance at the 1936 Berlin Olympics. Within the space of a few days, he won four gold medals in track and field, setting new Olympic records in the long jump at 26 feet 5.25 inches and a time of 20.7 seconds in the 200 meter dash. He tied the world record of 10.3 seconds in the 100 meter dash and won his fourth gold medal as a member of the 400 meter relay team. He received enormous coverage in the press because he had publicly embarrassed the Nazi leadership. Adolf Hitler initially presented medals to various track and field champions, but when African American Cornelius Johnson won the high jump, he abruptly left the stadium. He likewise was not present on the four occasions when Owens stood atop the victory stand, a fact that the American media reported in full.[20]

American journalists emphasized that Owens's life was the epitome of the American dream, relating the story of his birth as one of 10 children to an impoverished Alabama sharecropping family. Joining the ranks of African Americans migrating from the rural South to the urban North, his family relocated to Cleveland when Jesse was nine. In 1930, Owens led East Technical High School to a state track championship, and in a national meet he individually scored enough points to bring the American high school track and field team championship to Cleveland. He continued his spectacular career at Ohio State University, where he refined his picturesque sprinting technique. His stride was so graceful that grainy motion pictures of his running form are still used by track coaches; he appeared to glide down the track, his feet seemingly not touching the ground. At the 1935 Big Ten track and field championship meet, in a single afternoon, Owens broke five American records (220 yard dash, long jump, 220 yard high hurdles, 200 meter dash and 200 meter low hurdles) and tied another record in the 100 yard dash with the time of 9.4 seconds.

Following his sensational 1936 Olympics performance, Owens found that fame was fleeting. He did whatever he could to earn a living for his wife and young daughters,

appearing briefly on the fading vaudeville circuit as a song and dance man. He even stooped to such humiliating public exhibitions as racing against a horse and an automobile (he lost to both). His dry-cleaning business in Cleveland went bust in 1940, and he barely avoided prison on income tax evasion charges. After the war, he found a niche as a public speaker and founded a public relations firm, using his athletic fame to attract clients. In 1953, he received a political appointment as head of the Illinois State Athletic Commission, whose major responsibility was overseeing professional boxing in Chicago. During the 1960s, he became a spokesman for conservative political causes, received considerable grief from black organizations for his criticism of civil rights demonstrators, and in 1964 endorsed Barry Goldwater's presidential bid. His conservative stance provided access to American corporations, and he flourished as a motivational speaker at sales meetings. When a boycott of the 1968 Olympics by African American athletes loomed, Owens spoke out vigorously in opposition, further separating himself from the civil rights movement. During his later years, Owens lived in Arizona, where he died of lung cancer in 1980 at

Figure 9.3 Sprinter Jesse Owens explodes out of his starting position in classic fashion. After winning four gold medals in Berlin in 1936, Owens struggled through many difficult years before establishing himself as a public relations executive and motivational speaker. His refusal to support civil rights activists of the 1960s and his opposition to a boycott of 1968 Olympics by black American athletes led to widespread criticism during his later years. *Image © Bettmann/Corbis*

the age of 67, the apparent victim of the pack-a-day cigarette habit he had picked up shortly after his return from Berlin in 1936.

While Owens became a national hero for a brief time because of his track and field exploits, which the American press translated into a "humiliating public relations defeat" for Adolf Hitler, another son of an Alabama sharecropping family became the first black sports figure to enjoy sustained popularity among a broad spectrum of white Americans. Well before he won the world heavyweight championship, Joe Louis had become a widely recognized public figure. His early successes in the ring during the mid 1930s pointed toward the likelihood of his capturing the heavyweight championship. Taking note of the heavy media attention Louis was receiving, sports columnist Damon Runyon commented, "It is our guess that more has been written about Louis in the past two years than any living man over a similar period of time, with the exception of [Charles] Lindbergh."[21]

Louis won the heavyweight championship in 1937 and held it for 13 years. Journalists routinely identified his skin pigmentation as a defining trait, revealing just how unusual it was for someone of his race to reach national prominence at the time. They did not simply refer to him by the conventional word of the time, "Negro," but instead had a field day creating race-laden alliterations such as "the tan tornado," "the sepia slugger," "the dark destroyer," and of course the one that stuck, "the brown bomber." He was embraced by African Americans as their hero when they had very few to cheer. After his victories, it was party time in black neighborhoods, especially when Louis knocked out German heavyweight Max Schmeling in 1938 in the pivotal bout of his career.[22]

The perception of Louis held by whites subtly changed over the years. Initially he was viewed through the prism of well-established racial stereotypes, and reporters often quoted him in "darkie dialect," implying that he lacked intelligence and motivation. That he was often called a "jungle killer," even in highly complimentary articles, was testimony to the popularity of racial stereotypes. That image changed when Louis lost to Schmeling in 1936, indicating to the public that he had vulnerabilities like other human beings. When he met Schmeling again in 1938, he carried with him the hopes and prayers of white America, which then embraced him enthusiastically as the self-made American who had knocked out Adolf Hitler's favorite prizefighter. That Louis was the anti-Jack Johnson – never seen escorting white women, deferential to the press and the public, married to a clean-cut black woman, modest to the point of deference after a knockout, never caught up in illegal or immoral situations – reassured white America. During the Second World War, Louis became enormously popular when he enlisted in the Army and was portrayed as a symbol of national unity and sacrifice. After the war, most of the racial references regarding Louis largely disappeared, save for "brown bomber." Editorials and columns praised Louis's public service record and his humanity. The word "dignity" appeared often.

Louis moved to Detroit from rural Alabama with his mother in 1926. She worked at odd jobs and kept tight control over her son, even insisting he take violin lessons. Joe used the 50 cents she gave him for music lessons to pay instead for boxing lessons at a local gym. With his mother's reluctant endorsement, he entered Detroit's Golden Gloves amateur competition in 1932 and soon thereafter became the talk of the local boxing community as he compiled a 50–4 amateur record, 43 of the wins coming by knockout. Early in his boxing career, Louis came under the protective wing of John Roxborough, whose far-flung economic interests included both legal and illegal activities. He provided modest funds and equipment and asked for nothing in return. Louis studiously developed his skills, and in 1934 turned professional and moved to Chicago where he came under the guidance of two men experienced in the fight game, manager Julian Black and trainer Jack Blackburn. They oversaw his professional development. Louis won his first professional bout on July 4, 1934, taking home a purse of $52. Starting his career at a time when most boxers were white, he learned early that white prejudice dominated the sport. Julian Black spoke from experience when he lectured Louis that white judges and referees would judge him: "You can't get nowhere trying to outpoint fellows in the ring. It's mighty hard for a colored boy to win decisions. The dice is loaded against you. You gotta knock 'em out and keep knocking 'em out to get anywheres. Let your fist be your referee."[23]

Both Roxborough and Black recalled how Jack Johnson had contributed to his own demise by flouting the established racial code. Roxborough cautioned Louis:

> To be a champion you've got to be gentleman first. Your toughest fight might not be in the ring but out in public. We never, never say anything bad about an opponent. Before a fight say how great you think he is; after a fight you say how great you think he was. And, for God's sake, after you beat a white opponent, don't smile.[24]

Louis was instructed not to stand leering over opponents after they hit the canvas, and he was careful never to be seen publicly in the company of a white woman. He always treated journalists deferentially, and purposely showed little emotion whenever before a camera. None of the arrogance that Jack Johnson had routinely exhibited was permitted to surface. To white America, Louis was considered "a credit to his race," as one of his biographies was entitled. To African Americans, he was their top sports hero who handily defeated all comers, nearly all of whom were white.[25]

In 1935, Louis made his debut in New York City, knocking out a former champion, the gigantic 6 foot 6 inch, 260 pound Primo Carnera, in the sixth round at Yankee Stadium. His next big fight came on June 19, 1936, against another former champion, Max Schmeling, pride of the German Reich. The fight was held in New York City at the time Adolf Hitler was consolidating his power in Germany and preparing to host the Olympics. Louis did not train rigorously for this fight, and in round 12 Schmeling tagged him with a series of right-hand blows, knocking him out. The Nazi propaganda machine quickly pronounced the result evidence that the Aryan was the "Master Race." Louis was humiliated and upset that millions of his African American fans were severely disappointed.

In 1937, Louis trained hard and won the world heavyweight title on June 22 by knocking out James Braddock. Although he himself had been decked, Louis dominated the fight and at age 23 became the youngest man to win boxing's most important title. He would hold the title before retiring in 1949. Although he was now world champion, the defeat to Schmeling still rankled, and he told the press, "I will not consider myself champion until I defeat him." The pre-fight hype was intense. The Hitler propaganda machine cranked out its usual drivel and the Führer anticipated another public relations coup. Before the fight, President Franklin Roosevelt invited Louis to the White House. One of the photos that made the front pages showed the president admiring the champ's powerful biceps. "Joe, we need muscles like yours to beat Germany," he said, apparently anticipating the eventuality of war with the Nazi regime.[26]

This time a well-prepared Louis wasted no time extracting his revenge, nailing Schmeling with two vicious left hooks as the first round began and following up with a crushing right hand to the jaw as Schmeling's legs wobbled. Louis pressed his advantage and landed a right hand that referee Art Donovan said was powerful enough to "have dented concrete," then administered two shots to the body. Schmeling was down and out. At that precise moment, the live radio broadcast in Germany was cut off the air, and Joseph Goebbels's public information department declared the result "a disappointment but not a national disaster." In the United States, journalists took due note of German comments about "Aryan supremacy" that had followed the first Louis–Schmeling battle.

Louis continued to make the right moves that enabled white Americans to feel comfortable with a black heavyweight champion. Within a month after Pearl Harbor, he enlisted in the US Army, but before he departed for basic training, Louis fought Abe Simon and turned that purse over to the Army Relief Fund. Louis became a poster boy for the War Department, and photographs were frequently released showing him performing various soldierly tasks. However, Louis's major responsibility as a commissioned officer was to deal with public relations, primarily fighting exhibition bouts to entertain troops.

Louis defended his title 20 times between his defeat of James Braddock and entering the military in the spring of 1942, often against challengers of questionable ability. This series of bouts was dubbed the "palooka of the month" campaign by some writers, but on June 18, 1941, Louis struggled to keep his title against the popular "Pittsburgh Kid," Billy Conn. Much quicker than Louis's typical opponents, Conn was winning the fight on points in the 13th round when he got reckless and went for a knockout; Louis saw an opening and floored his opponent with his powerful right hand. The public was anxious for a rematch, which occurred after the war in June 1946 when Louis prevailed with an eighth-round knockout. The champ was now well into his 30s, and cautious manager Mike Jacobs picked Louis's opponents carefully and spaced out his fights. Louis defeated Jersey Joe Walcott twice in close matches before retiring in 1949.

His finances, however, were a shambles. Facing life after boxing, Louis had serious income tax problems, the result of not having paid adequate attention to the disposition of his $5 million in prize money. Louis attempted a comeback but lost to champion Ezzard Charles in 1950 by a decision. The following year he was ingloriously knocked through the ropes by an up-and-coming Rocky Marciano. The purses he won in these two depressing bouts did not solve his financial woes, and Louis ended up a forlorn figure, trying to make a living as a professional wrestler and boxing referee. He eventually worked as a casino greeter at Caesars Palace in Las Vegas before dying from a heart attack in 1981. The night before he died, Louis was given a sustained standing ovation before a championship fight between Larry Holmes and Trevor Berbick. Thomas Sowell wrote upon his death:

> What made Louis a unique figure was not simply his great talent as an athlete. He appeared at a time in America when blacks were not only at a low economic ebb – but were the butt of ridicule. In this kind of world Joe Louis became the most famous black man in America. What he did as a man could reinforce or counteract stereo-types that hurt and held back millions of

people of his race. How he fared in the ring mattered more to black Americans than the fate of any other athlete in any other sport, before or since. He was all we had … Joe Louis was a continuing lesson to white Americans that to be black did not mean to be a clown or a lout, regardless of what the image-makers said. It was a lesson that helped open doors that had been closed for too long.[27]

All America was pleased to know that Louis was to be buried with full military honors in Arlington Cemetery, a long way from the cotton patches of Alabama where his life had begun. His funeral expenses were paid in part by a prosperous German businessman, Coca-Cola executive Max Schmeling.

Jackie

Baseball executive Branch Rickey stunned the baseball world on October 23, 1945, when he announced that he had signed Jack Roosevelt Robinson to a Brooklyn Dodgers' minor-league contract. When the 26-year-old Robinson appeared the following April in a Montreal Royals uniform, a new era had arrived. Rickey's bold action capped a growing movement to challenge the unwritten "gentlemen's agreement" that had kept African Americans out of organized baseball since 1885. The black press, led by the *Chicago Defender* and the *Baltimore Afro-American*, was outspoken in its demand for change. Prominent black sports journalists, such as Wendell Smith and Sam Lacy, repeatedly argued that the top players in the Negro Leagues would elevate the quality of play in organized baseball. Such leading white journalists as syndicated New York columnists Ed Sullivan and Damon Runyon joined them in their crusade. Additionally, such influential writers as Jimmy Powers of the *New York Daily News*, Shirley Povich of the *Washington Post*, Westbrook Pegler of the *Chicago Tribune*, and Dave Egan of the *Boston Record* weighed in on the issue. Despite this pressure, Commissioner Kenesaw Landis adamantly opposed lifting the ban, issuing instead a disingenuous statement: "Each club is entirely free to employ Negro players." He privately hoped that the owners would maintain the racial status quo.[28]

As the Second World War neared its conclusion, pressure against the long-standing "gentlemen's agreement" mounted. Gunnar Myrdal's *An American Dilemma* had moved public opinion, especially among the educated classes, toward a recognition that the United States could not maintain its traditional racial patterns. Rickey was very much aware of shifting public opinion. In early 1945, baseball's new commissioner, Albert "Happy" Chandler, created a Committee on Baseball Integration, but because of the hostile reaction by the New York Yankees owner and general manager, Larry MacPhail, the group never met. New York mayor Fiorello LaGuardia appointed a committee to explore the issue, which put special pressure upon the three major-league teams located in the nation's largest city. In the spring of 1945, New York sportswriter Joe Bostic brought two African American players to the gates of the Dodgers spring training camp and demanded they be given a tryout, but to no avail; the resulting headlines, however, drove home his message. That same spring, the Boston Red Sox gave highly publicized tryouts to Jackie Robinson, Marvin Williams, and Sam Jethroe at Fenway Park because of political pressure from councilman

Isadore Muchnik. "I'm telling you," he later recalled, "you never saw anyone hit The Wall the way Robinson did that day. Bang, Bang, Bang: he rattled it!" Afterward, Red Sox chief scout Hugh Duffy candidly admitted that the tryout had been only for show when he ruefully said of Robinson, "What a ballplayer! Too bad he's the wrong color."[29]

While all of this public posturing was taking pace, Rickey stealthily moved forward with his plan to put an African American in a Brooklyn uniform. He had left St Louis to assume control of the Dodgers in 1942, and was determined to lay the foundation of a competitive team. Rickey's decision to sign Robinson grew out of a multiplicity of motives. Rickey's social consciousness, inculcated in him as a youth by his pious Methodist parents, clearly had been elevated by the growing pressure for reform. But he also wanted to tap a new pool of major-league talent to help make the Dodgers a perennial pennant contender.[30]

At this time, Robinson was well established as a star infielder with the Kansas City Monarchs after receiving a medical discharge from the Army. When he was summoned to Rickey's office on August 15, 1945, he assumed he was going to be offered a contract with a new African American team Rickey had announced he was forming, the Brooklyn Brown Dodgers. Rickey had cleverly covered his tracks. He had no intention of actually putting a Brown Dodgers team on the field, but the concept gave his scouts cover as they searched for the right candidate for what Jules Tygiel has called "Baseball's Great Experiment." Rickey wanted not only a player with undisputed major-league talent but also someone who had the personal traits to inspire support from the African American community, overcome well-known prejudices held by some Dodgers players, and act as a role model, a family man and citizen who would appeal to white fans.[31]

Robinson met Rickey's criteria. He had lettered in four sports at UCLA and would have graduated had he not departed for military duty in 1942. He had been a consensus All-American halfback and had led the Bruins basketball team in scoring. During the spring, he played baseball and ran track, sometimes on the same day. During his secret meeting with Rickey, Robinson was subjected to a combination 3 hour lecture and grilling by a seasoned baseball man who loved to quote the Bible and Shakespeare. Rickey warned Robinson that he would be the target of relentless scrutiny and verbal attacks and would face intimidating bean ball pitches and hostile base runners with flashing spikes. Rickey told him that he would have to have "enough guts not to fight back" when the inevitable physical or verbal assaults came. If he could not maintain his composure, he would not succeed. In his emotional commentary Rickey emphasized that "turning the other cheek" would be necessary. Above all, Robinson would have to produce on the field. "You've got to do this job with base hits, stolen bases, and fielding ground balls, Jackie."[32]

Rickey's announcement of the signing two months later stunned baseball's establishment. Rickey's long-time rival, Yankees owner and general manager Larry MacPhail, predicted that if large numbers of African Americans came to see Robinson play, they would drive away white fans and produce a severe drop in ticket sales. He announced bluntly, "I have no hesitancy in saying that the Yankees have no intention of signing Negro players," and issued an internal memorandum to other team owners that criticized Rickey for "exerting tremendous pressures on the whole structure of Professional Baseball."[33]

After an exceptional minor-league season in 1946 with Montreal, Robinson was elevated to the parent team. For a time in spring training, a handful of veteran Dodgers with

Southern roots, led by star center fielder Dixie Walker, talked variously about requesting trades, a boycott, or a strike. The rumored protests failed to materialize, in part because of the support Robinson received from Kentucky native, shortstop Pee Wee Reese, and adamant stands taken by manager Leo Durocher and Rickey. Nonetheless, it was a tense locker room into which the rookie walked.

Robinson had to adapt to the new position of first baseman, but Brooklyn fans were enthusiastic in their support. His first major test came early in the season at Philadelphia, where manager Ben Chapman, a native of the Deep South, fueled a racially charged verbal barrage from the Phillies' dugout. The abuse continued throughout the game, and as Robinson recalled, it was one of the most difficult days of his life. "I felt tortured and I tried just to play ball and ignore the insults," he later wrote in his autobiography,

> It was really getting to me. I was, after all, a human being … For one wild and rage-crazed minute I thought, "To hell with Mr. Rickey's noble experiment." … To hell with the image of the patient black freak I was supposed to create. I could throw down my bat, stride over to that Phillies dugout, grab one of those white sons of bitches and smash his teeth in with my despised black fist. Then I could walk away from it all.[34]

Of course he did not do so, but he scored the only run of the game, an effective response. The Dodgers went on to sweep the Phillies in three games, and the heavy cloud of fear and doubt that he felt began to lift. Later, Robinson calmly told a *Pittsburgh Courier* reporter, "The things the Phillies shouted at me from their bench have been shouted at me from other benches and I am not worried about it. They sound just the same in the big league as they did in the minor league." Robinson was lifted by the fact that the Phillies' dreadful conduct galvanized his own team behind him, Southerners included. Dixie Walker admonished his fellow Alabaman Ben Chapman, and Dodgers second baseman Eddie Stanky was reported to have shouted across the field, "Listen, you yellow-bellied cowards, why don't you yell at somebody who can answer back?" Branch Rickey had, of course, helped prepare Jackie for the ordeal, and he later said, "Chapman did more than anybody to unite the Dodgers. When he poured out that string of unconscionable abuse, he solidified and unified thirty men … Chapman made Jackie a real member of the Dodgers."[35]

The pressure nonetheless continued throughout the season. On the road, Robinson had to stay in private homes in several cities because some hotels used by the Dodgers would not accept him. He was dismayed by the thousands of hate letters he received, many of them containing death threats, but these were more than offset by a tidal wave of letters and telegrams of encouragement. On the field, he was the target of many high and fast pitches; by July he had already set a league record for the number of times hit by pitches. Pitchers, of course, attempted to intimidate all rookies with inside pitches, but they discovered that if they hit Jackie, he would promptly make them pay by stealing second base. The tight inside pitches became less frequent as the season passed.

By the end of the 1947 season, Robinson had more than justified the trust displayed by Branch Rickey in selecting him from among several candidates for this historic role. He batted .297, scored 125 runs, and stole 29 bases, while fielding his position skillfully. He had helped his team win the pennant that preceded an epic seven-game World Series battle with the Yankees.

Figure 9.4 Jackie Robinson steals home with his usual flourish against Philadelphia on July 2, 1950. Star first baseman Gil Hodges backs away from the plate, while catcher Andy Seminick is late in applying the tag. The Phillies later won the pennant on the last day of the season, when Dick Sisler hit a home run in the 10th inning to beat star pitcher Don Newcombe and the Dodgers. *Image © Bettmann/Corbis*

He was named "Rookie of the Year" by the venerable *Sporting News*, edited by J. G. Taylor Spink, who had long been an outspoken opponent of the integration of organized baseball. As the Dodgers closed in on the pennant in late September, *Time* magazine put Robinson's picture on its cover. He had, by his quiet courage and resolute play, captured the hearts of a people who liked to root for the underdog. He was truly a historic figure, using the nation's most popular game as a means of breaking down racial stereotypes and taboos. As such, he did much to prepare the nation for the civil rights movement that would soon take wing.

Robinson did not join the Dodgers until he was nearly 28 years of age, but he enjoyed success until he retired after the 1956 season. With Eddie Stanky traded after the 1947 season, Robinson moved to his natural position of second base and fielded at a Gold Glove level. He helped propel the Dodgers to five more National League pennants, and in 1949 was named the league's Most Valuable Player after a season in which he batted .342, stole 37 bases, and batted in 124 runs as the Dodgers beat out the Cardinals on the last day of the season.

Robinson was a perennial member of the All-Star team, and recognized as a leader both on and off the field. In the 1952 World Series, he helped rally the Dodgers to tie the series at three games apiece, but they lost to the Yankees in game 7. The following year, they were again frustrated by the Yankees, but in 1955, the Dodgers finally broke through to take the World Series in seven games over the Yankees. Showing his years, Robinson missed 40 games that season due to injuries while his batting average fell to .259. Feeling the effects of the onset of diabetes and with his skills now rapidly eroding, and with a trade to the cross-town Giants in the works, he retired after the 1956 season. In 1962, Jackie Robinson was the first African American elected to the Baseball Hall of Fame, winning admission the first time that he was eligible for consideration.

Following his retirement, Robinson entered several business relationships and spoke out vigorously on civil rights issues. However, by the mid 1960s his health had visibly declined from diabetes. By 1970, he could barely walk and had lost the sight of one eye and most in the other. Losing weight but unable to control either his high blood pressure or his cholesterol levels, he suffered a series of strokes and a heart attack, and on October 24, 1972, at the age of 53, the brave and outspoken man who had broken the color line of baseball was gone, much too early. In 1997, baseball commissioner Bud Selig announced on the 50th anniversary of Robinson's first season with the Dodgers that his number 42 would be retired by all baseball teams.

In the Shadow of Jackie Robinson

When Jackie Robinson trotted out to take his position at first base on April 15, 1947, America changed forever. His appearance on a major-league diamond brought the issue of racial justice into sharp focus. On July 5, 1947, team president Bill Veeck signed center fielder Larry Doby to a Cleveland Indians contract, and by season's end five African Americans had appeared in major-league games. The following year, Veeck signed Satchel Paige, making him a highly publicized 42-year-old "rookie" who pitched well enough to be named to the American League All-Star roster and contributed to the Indians World Series championship with a 6–1 season record along with a 2.48 earned run average in 72 innings of pitching.

Several clubs, however, were reluctant to follow the example set by Rickey and Veeck. For more than a decade, the Yankees did not aggressively pursue African American prospects. In late 1945, the Yankees lured one of the nation's best scouts, Tom Greenwade, away from the Dodgers but Greenwade was instructed by club president Larry MacPhail not to sign African Americans. Greenwade, who had been heavily involved in Branch Rickey's secret search, was forced to pass on several top African American players he had identified as having major-league potential, including future Hall of Fame shortstop Ernie Banks. Greenwade probably knew the pool of available black talent better than anyone else, and he would later speculate that the tailspin the Yankees experienced in the late 1960s was a direct result of the team's refusal to sign African American players.[36] Several good prospects, including future All-Star first baseman Vic Power, were traded away. It was not until 1955 that the Yankees inserted an African American into the starting lineup, recognizing that Elston Howard was simply too talented to trade away.

The National League moved much more rapidly than the American League in signing African Americans. As David Halberstam explains, what blacks brought to the game more than anything else was speed. On the base paths and in the field especially, their impact was immediately recognized. With the Dodgers signing several outstanding blacks, other teams followed suit, if for no other reason than to keep pace. As a result, during the 1950s the National League moved well ahead of the American League in talent. Among those teams that enjoyed considerable success as a result were the St Louis Cardinals, the New York/San Francisco Giants, and the Cincinnati Reds. It was no mere coincidence that between 1960 and 1980 the American League would win only two All-Star games. The last major-league team to put an African American into their lineup was the Boston Red Sox, when Pumpsie Green joined its infield in 1959. By this time, 15 percent of the 400 major-league players were African American.[37]

Within three years after Jackie Robinson set foot on Ebbets Field, the Negro leagues had collapsed. The Negro National League folded after the 1948 season and the Negro American League ended all pretense of being a viable enterprise in 1950. The iconic Homestead Grays were no more, and the once-powerful Kansas City Monarchs played exhibition games for a few years in obscure towns before disbanding. "The big league doors suddenly opened one day and when Negro players walked in, Negro baseball walked out," Wendell Smith jubilantly wrote in the *Louisville Courier*; and fellow black journalist Frank "Fay" Young informed his Cleveland readers, "Far from being sorry … [African Americans] are glad."[38]

Change also occurred in other professional sports. In 1933, the fledgling National Football League, after having permitted blacks to play since the league's inception, moved to an all-white policy at the behest of the Boston (soon to be Washington) Redskins' owner George Preston Marshall. In 1946, however, a rival professional league, the All-American Football Conference, began play and the Cleveland Browns featured two black players destined for the Hall of Fame: fullback Marion Motley and defensive lineman Bill Willis. At the same time, the Los Angeles Rams of the National Football League signed Woody Strode and Kenny Washington who had played football at UCLA with Jackie Robinson.

Although their appearance in professional football occurred one year before Robinson joined the Dodgers, they attracted little media attention. With professional football still a relatively modest operation, these four players were able to go about their business without the attention that engulfed Jackie Robinson. In 1946, the Rochester Royals of the even more obscure Basketball Association of America, a forerunner to the National Basketball Association, added the first black to its roster without much fanfare. But in 1950, when the New York Knicks of the new National Basketball Association managed to lure Nat "Sweetwater" Clifton away from the Harlem Globetrotters, the media presented it as a major news story. That same year, the Washington Capitols signed West Virginia University star Earl Lloyd and the Boston Celtics drafted Duquesne University's All-American Charles Cooper.

Ever since its inception during the 1920s, professional basketball had limped through its seasons in relative obscurity. Salaries were low, and "major-league" franchises were located in such small venues as Syracuse, Moline, Sheboygan, Fort Wayne, and Rochester. Games were played in aging civic auditoriums and high school gymnasiums before small crowds. The arrival of black players in the 1950s, however, moved the NBA into the mainstream of professional sports. In 1956, the Boston Celtics signed 6 foot 10 inch Bill Russell, one of the all-time defensive and rebounding greats, and the Philadelphia Warriors countered in 1959 with 7 foot 2 inch scoring and rebounding dynamo Wilt Chamberlain. Their titanic battles captivated basketball fans, and attendance soared. Backcourt stars such as Lenny Wilkens and Oscar Robertson entered the league in the early 1960s, bringing an abrupt halt to the practice of permitting only whites to run the offense from the point guard position. By 1970, fully 50 percent of the NBA roster positions were filled by African Americans and the game continued to grow in popularity. The fears of some owners that this trend would alienate white fans proved unfounded.

Gentlepeople and Sanctimonious Hypocrites

Right from the start, tennis in the United States became the special province of the urban elite. The languid style of play, a conservative dress code that mandated all-white clothing, emphasis on good manners and court decorum, and a private club setting all contributed to an image of snobbish elitism. Mimicking the pattern set by private golf clubs, the United States Lawn Tennis Association (USLTA) did not accept African American members. Excluded from sanctioned tournaments, top black players could not qualify for the US Open tournament held at Forest Hills, New York. That barrier came crashing down in 1950, largely as a result of a blistering article in *American Lawn Tennis* magazine written by former US Tennis Women's Open champion Alice Marble. She denounced the USLTA and its all-white membership for its "bigotry" in excluding African Americans from tournaments. In particular, she had in mind Althea Gibson, the perennial women's champion of the American Tennis Association (ATA), a struggling black tennis organization. "If tennis is a game for ladies and gentlemen," Marble wrote, "it's also time we acted a little more like gentlepeople and less like sanctimonious hypocrites."[39]

Later that year a chastened USLTA invited Gibson to enter its premier annual tournament held at exclusive Forest Hills. In her second match, Gibson found herself on center court before several thousand curious spectators. Across the net stood Wimbledon champion Louise Brough, who breezed through the first set 6–1, as Gibson seemed in a daze. Obviously nervous – a reporter wrote she looked "scared to death" – Gibson gained control of her emotions and unleashed thundering groundstrokes and pinpoint volleys to take the second set 6–3. Reporters in the bar got word of an enormous upset in the works and hustled to the stadium to watch Gibson take a 7–6 lead in the final set (rules at the time required a two-game victory margin) when a thunderstorm forced postponement. Gibson had all night to think about a potential upset victory, and the next day, just four points from victory, once again surrendered to nerves. "The delay was the worst thing that could have happened to me," she recalled after she lost the match 6–1, 3–6, 9–7.

That Althea Gibson was even playing tennis at Forest Hills was a personal triumph. She grew up in poverty-stricken Harlem during the Great Depression, and spent her time dodging truant officers while playing tennis on public courts. In 1946, two physicians who had a strong interest in tennis observed her play and took her under their wings and into their homes. They provided private tennis instruction and got her on an academic path that led to a belated high school diploma and a scholarship at Florida A&M.

Figure 9.5   Althea Gibson shows her crisp backhand form in this match at Wimbledon in the 1957 finals against fellow American Darlene Hard. In 1957 she became the first African American woman to be selected as the Associated Press's Female Athlete of the Year. *Image © Bettmann/ Corbis*

In 1951, she became the first African American to be invited to play at Wimbledon but lost in the early rounds. Her game continued to improve and she joined a world tennis tour in 1956 that concluded at the French Open in Paris. The unseeded Gibson shocked the tennis world by winning the French singles title, and the following year won on the grass at Wimbledon, defeating Darlene Hard in straight sets. At the concluding Wimbledon Ball, she was introduced to Queen Elizabeth. "Shaking hands with the Queen of England was a long way from being forced to sit in the colored section of the bus going into downtown Wilmington, North Carolina," she later recalled.[40] Gibson received a tickertape parade upon returning to New York, and a month later reached the finals of the US Open before losing a close match to Shirley Fry. However, the following year she reeled off wins at Wimbledon and Forest Hills, feats she would repeat in 1958. Althea Gibson had reached the pinnacle of the world of tennis.

Following the US Open in 1958, Gibson turned professional in order to earn a paycheck of $100,000 playing tennis exhibitions on basketball hardwoods before Harlem Globetrotters games. Because the women's professional tennis tour had yet to be formed, her tournament days were over. Attempting to find a new competitive outlet, Gibson turned to golf, earned her professional card, but did not do well on the tour. Nonetheless, she was once again a pioneer, becoming the first African American to earn her LPGA tour card. She died in 2003 after suffering a series of strokes, but late in life was able to appreciate the accomplishments of such black women tennis stars as Zina Garrison and Venus and Serena Williams. Unlike those women, she never earned the large purses and product endorsements that had become commonplace.

Virginia native Arthur Ashe was born 15 years later than Althea Gibson, and by the time he became a nationally ranked men's player in the 1960s, the civil rights movement had produced some significant advances. As a youth, Ashe had encountered plenty of discrimination in his hometown of Richmond, Virginia, where he attended segregated schools and was denied access to public tennis courts and juniors tournaments. After graduating from UCLA, Ashe became the first African American man to win the US Amateur (1968), the US Open (1968), and Wimbledon (1975).[41] Standing a slender 6 feet 1 inch and weighing only 155 pounds, Ashe did not look the part of a world-class athlete. The fact that he had to wear eyeglasses did not enhance his physical appearance, but once he took the court he was a sight to behold. He possessed a complete tennis game, starting with a powerful serve that was complemented by a booming overhead and an ability to hit crisp volleys at sharp angles. Ashe also was a master of finesse shots, utilizing lobs to the baseline, low-spinning chip shots, and tantalizing drop shots to frustrate opponents.

In 1968, Ashe scaled the heights of the tennis world, reaching the semifinals at Wimbledon and winning the US Amateur and Open tournaments. In the Open final against Tom Okker, his serve was whistling into the service area at 115 mph. He hit 26 service aces, prompting his befuddled opponent from the Netherlands to ask, "What's the use? I can't see it anyway."[42] His powerful serving was an amazing feat because the small wooden racquet was still standard equipment. Oversized metal and composition racquets, which would later produce serves in the 140 mph range, would not make their appearance until the end of Ashe's competitive days.

Although he held strong personal views about racial justice, Ashe kept his thoughts to himself for many years. But in 1970, having turned professional, he found an appropriate means of combining his highly visible tennis stature with social justice, when as the world's number-one-ranked male player he applied for a visa and entrance into the South African Open tennis tournament, then a prestigious world-class tournament. He correctly predicted that he would be denied on both counts, and called a press conference to protest the rigid apartheid policies of the white government of South Africa. His white peers did not honor his call for a boycott of the tournament, but he had made his point. In 1973, however, both the visa and admission to the tournament were forthcoming. Increasingly involved in racial issues, Ashe came under some criticism that he was not devoting himself sufficiently to his tennis game, but he quieted those critics when he defeated fellow American Jimmy Connors in the singles finals at Wimbledon in 1975 – yet another first for this modest man from Virginia.

As Ashe began to contemplate his post-tennis future, he suffered the first of three heart attacks. In 1979, he underwent open-heart surgery to open clogged arteries, and he was forced to retire from competitive tennis. He turned to writing tennis columns, and served as captain of the American Davis Cup team. But in 1983 he had to undergo another heart operation, during which he received several blood transfusions. Five years later he was diagnosed as HIV-positive, undoubtedly having received tainted blood during his second surgery. He subsequently died from AIDS at age 49 in 1993. After his death, the new stadium at Flushing Meadows, home to the US Open, was named in his honor, but he undoubtedly would have taken greater personal satisfaction when in 1996 the city of Richmond, where he had once been denied access to public tennis facilities, erected a large statue of him – a tennis racquet in one hand, books in the other – on the city's Monument Row that honored other famous local residents, primarily Confederate generals.

The Baron and the Bear

The pace of racial integration in American sports intensified during the 1950s and 1960s. Sweeping social change produced high emotions and, not infrequently, shocking incidents. Such was the case when Drake University's football team traveled to Stillwater, Oklahoma, to play a Missouri Valley Conference game against Oklahoma A&M. The Drake Bulldogs were an upstart college football team that year, featuring flashy senior tailback Johnny Bright, an African American who was considered a Heisman Trophy candidate. As both a runner and a passer, he led the nation in total offense. The personable young man was a top high school player in Indiana, but was not recruited by Notre Dame or Purdue, apparently because of his race.

On the first play from scrimmage against the Aggies, Bright casually trailed a run by a teammate, and as the whistle blew he was blindsided by defensive tackle Wilbanks Smith, who slugged him in the jaw. Two *Des Moines Register* photographers captured the vicious blow on film, and their sequential photographs indicated that Smith had delivered a deliberate cheap shot. In that moment, Bright's Heisman hopes were shattered along with his jaw. *Life* magazine published the photographs, and sports fans expressed outrage.[43] The question immediately arose: was Smith attempting to knock Bright out of the game because he was a threat, or because he was black? Or both? The talented tailback had to have a tooth pulled so that he could take liquid nourishment through a wired jaw. He returned late in the season but, having missed several games, finished fifth in the Heisman voting.

The Johnny Bright incident highlighted the precarious state of race relations in college athletics. When the Missouri Valley Conference refused to take corrective action, Drake withdrew from the Conference. Drafted in the first round by the Philadelphia Eagles, Bright opted not to become that team's first black player and instead played for Edmonton in the Canadian Football League where he won all-star honors.

In the South, the intersection of racial politics and sports roiled the waters of big-time college football. Political leaders expected public universities to maintain all-white teams and to play games only against white opponents. During the 1920s, this posed little problem because college teams everywhere seldom had a single black player. In 1934, seeking to enhance its national football reputation, Georgia Tech scheduled a game at the University of Michigan. When it was learned that the Wolverines had one starting black player, end Willis Ward, political leaders in Georgia demanded that he be withheld from the game or the Bulldogs would not take the field. Ward was, in fact, the first black to play football at Michigan since 1892. Georgia officials were adamant that they not break the long-standing unwritten commitment to restrict sports opponents to all-white teams, and Michigan officials agreed. Michigan students launched a protest, and ultimately a compromise was achieved that did little to enhance the stature of the University of Michigan. Administrators agreed to keep Ward on the bench if Georgia Tech pulled its star end, All-American Hoot Gibson. Michigan won the game with the two ends sitting out of the contest, but the fallout from this episode led Southern teams to avoid scheduling Northern teams. This informal boycott lasted until the 1970s.[44]

The issue of black opponents resurfaced at Georgia Tech 21 years later. After the nationally ranked "Ramblin' Wreck" accepted a bid to the 1956 Sugar Bowl to meet the University of Pittsburgh, it was learned that Pitt's starting fullback was black. Georgia governor Marvin Griffin demanded that Tech withdraw from the bowl game. Griffin had become a leader of the "massive resistance" movement against the US Supreme Court's order to desegregate public schools, and he apparently felt compelled to take an adamant stand:

> We cannot make the slightest concession to the enemy in this dark and lamentable hour of struggle. There is no more difference in compromising the integrity of race on the playing field than in doing so in the classroom. One break in the dike and the relentless seas will rush in and destroy us.[45]

A flood of protests from whites within his own state arose when several thousand students marched on the State Capitol and governor's mansion. Griffin called out law enforcement to control the protesters. Frustrated, the students strung up an effigy of Griffin and stalled downtown traffic. The *Atlanta Constitution* published an editorial condemning Griffin's position, and even one staunchly segregationist Georgia newspaper said that the team should play to bring "fame and glory and prestige to the State of Georgia." These demonstrations occurred at the same time that newspapers featured news of the stunning bus boycott in Montgomery, Alabama. An emotional Board of Regents meeting produced a decision to defy the governor. In the football-happy South, an important bowl game had edged out the imperatives of racial segregation; national football rankings were at stake. After the flurry of public controversy, the game itself was anti-climatic. Georgia won a tight 7–0 contest, and Pitt fullback Bobby Grier led all rushers that day as he broke the color line in one of the nation's prominent bowl games. Unable to book rooms at any local segregated hotel, the Panthers team secured housing on a nearby military base. The following year a bill died in the Georgia legislature that would have prohibited public university teams from playing any contest that included African Americans.

Within a few years the issue had been swept away as racial integration occurred slowly, but surely, in all-white Southern universities. If those schools wanted to earn national sports honors, their policy of playing only all-white teams was no longer viable. Similar issues occurred in the Atlantic Coast Conference and the Southwestern Conference with the same results, but only after stubborn resistance was put up by diehard segregationists. Sports played a central role in the long and complex civil rights movement, a fact that has largely been overlooked by historians of the era.[46]

When the National Football League began blanketing the nation with television coverage during the late 1950s, casual sports fans across Northern and Western states learned the names of heretofore relatively obscure Southern colleges. Increasing numbers of NFL players from the South had not attended such well-known schools as Tennessee or Louisiana State, but came from small black colleges such as Jackson State, Grambling, Southern, Texas Southern, Alcorn A&M, South Carolina State, and Prairie View A&M. These players had been systematically ignored during the college recruiting season by coaches from major conferences. Coaches at Northern universities increasingly tapped into this rich lode of talent, aggressively extending their recruiting into the South. A sizeable migration of black athletic talent to schools north of the Mason–Dixon Line commenced during the early 1960s. This trend was highlighted when the University of Minnesota won the Big Ten championship and played in the Rose Bowl on New Year's Day 1961, led by consensus All-American quarterback Sandy Stephens. A standout athlete from South Carolina, Stephens was the first black to play in this leadership position at a major college university in modern times. In 1966, Michigan State tied for the national championship on the strength of several such players, including one of the best defensive linemen who ever played the game, Beaumont native Bubba Smith, who would have preferred to play in his native Texas.

During the early 1960s, the civil rights movement focused upon public universities. Governor George Wallace stood defiantly in the doorway of the admissions office at the University of Alabama in 1963 in a futile attempt to prevent the enrollment of a black student ordered enrolled by a federal court. The previous September, rioting and deaths resulted on the campus of the University of Mississippi in protest of the court-ordered enrollment of James Meredith. With memories of the bucolic Oxford, Mississippi, campus blanketed by smoke and tear gas still fresh in their minds, in March 1963 Mississippi residents found themselves facing another race-inspired issue at the other major state university. The Mississippi State University Bulldogs had won the Southeastern Conference title, but Governor Ross Barnett sought to prevent the team from participating in the NCAA basketball tournament because it would be matched against Northern teams with black players. With a sixth-place national ranking in the final Associated Press poll, university officials wanted to play, and after much public discussion and in open defiance of the fuming governor, the State Board of Education voted to permit the team to travel to Michigan for its first tournament game against Loyola University of Chicago, which had four black starters. The pre-game handshakes became a media event, but the game won by Loyola produced no incidents. Shortly thereafter, Southern universities quietly adopted a new policy stating they would no longer avoid playing teams with African American members. Loyola, as it turned out, ended up winning the national championship.[47]

It was not long after this episode that Southeastern Conference teams began to recruit blacks; coaches and knowledgeable fans understood that if they wanted to compete for national honors they had to recruit the best athletes. To permit a covey of future All-Americans to go north to score touchdowns now seemed a monumental mistake. Teams in the Deep South began to take on a multiracial hue, and by the 1970s whatever informal racial quotas might have existed had largely disappeared. The flood of black talent out of the South to Northern colleges had slowed to a trickle. One ironic result of this change in policy was that traditional black colleges saw their pool of top athletic talent evaporate. Just as the integration of organized baseball inevitably meant the loss of baseball talent by the Negro leagues, so too did the integration of higher education reduce the athletic talent level at black colleges.

The changes occurring during the 1960s in college athletics as a result of the civil rights movement were never more vividly highlighted than at the championship game of the 1966 NCAA men's basketball tournament. Following the 1951 gambling scandals, the National Invitation Tournament held in Madison Square Garden lost most of its luster, and the NCAA-sponsored tournament gained in prestige. It came of age in 1957 as a significant national sporting event when North Carolina defeated a Wilt Chamberlain-led Kansas team 54–53 in three overtime periods. Fears of gambler influence in major cities prompted the NCAA to play tournament games on college campuses. Thus in 1966 the Final Four teams – Duke, Utah, Texas Western College, and Kentucky – assembled on a March weekend on the campus of the University of Maryland to determine the national champion.

Most experts expected the Wildcats of Kentucky to leave Cole Field House with their fifth national championship. Coaching the team was the legendary "Baron of the Bluegrass," Adolph F. Rupp. His teams had won 747 games during his 36-year tenure, racking up 22 Southeastern Conference championships, the 1946 NIT championship, and four NCAA championships. At one point during Rupp's reign they had won 129 consecutive home games. This was an especially intriguing team because it lacked a dominant center. Led by 6 foot 5 inch forward Pat Riley, this scrappy team was fondly dubbed "Rupp's Runts" by Kentucky's enthusiastic fans. The Wildcats came into the tournament ranked first in the nation and Rupp had just added yet another "Coach of the Year" honor to his collection.

Rupp's reputation had been built playing in the segregated Southeastern Conference. Predominantly a football conference, the great majority of its member institutions viewed basketball as little more than something to pass the winter months until spring football practice rolled around. Not so in Kentucky, a state that had a strong high school basketball tradition. The University of Kentucky was the northernmost member of the Southeastern Conference, so Rupp upon occasion slipped across the Ohio River to pick up a few prize recruits from the neighboring basketball-rich states of Ohio, Indiana, and Illinois to supplement his annual harvest of top in-state players. None of his recruits, however, came from the African American neighborhoods of Louisville, Cincinnati, Cleveland, Indianapolis, or Lexington. His Wildcats had always been white, and the imperious Baron gave no indication that this policy was about to change.

Rupp's defenders have since attempted to soften the impact of his racial views, but it seems they were largely reflective of his era. He apparently believed that black players, while perhaps possessed of great natural skills, lacked the essential traits he desired: discipline and intelligence to run complex offensive and defensive schemes. Upon occasion he employed crude racial stereotypes, which were commonly held and expressed by whites during his time. In one inadvertent slip of the tongue regarding the quickness of many black players, he told a radio interviewer, "The lions and tigers caught all the slow ones."[48]

In any case, Rupp knew that as long as the SEC remained segregated the Wildcats would continue to dominate the conference. Instinctively conservative, set in his ways, and a dominant force in a former slave state, the Baron of the Bluegrass was not about to be a spokesman on behalf of racial integration. He was arguably the most popular and powerful person in the state. Even when serious gambling scandals hit his program in 1951, Rupp was able to survive despite a one-year suspension of the program. His Wildcats represented a state that had long endured a backward "hillbilly" image, but on game nights, radios across the state were tuned to the Wildcat Radio Network where the soothing inflections of popular announcer Cawood Ledford, a native of mining-town Harlan, filled the airwaves with descriptions of the action. Wildcat basketball was an important Kentucky institution, and Adolph Rupp was its beloved leader.

The scene was set for the 1966 NCAA championship game when Kentucky slipped by Duke and the virtually unknown Texas Western College Miners upset Utah in the semifinal games. Texas Western – soon to be renamed the University of Texas at El Paso – lacked the basketball tradition of its opponent. It had a young head coach in his fourth year, the gruff Don Haskins, who carried the appropriate nickname of "The Bear." Haskins had graduated from Oklahoma A&M in 1953, where he learned the intricacies of the game from Hank Iba, who coached a style of play that emphasized methodical offenses, high-percentage shots, and tenacious man-to-man defense. The one thing that Iba's teams did not do was play without purpose or control; thus the Aggies seldom ran a fast break. This was precisely the style of play that Haskins taught his Texas Western team. Haskins assembled a talented squad by recruiting in predominantly black neighborhoods in Houston, Chicago, Detroit, and New York City. El Paso was considered a Western and not a Southern school, so it was exempt from the segregationist policies still in place in most Texas public universities.

It was thus a classic confrontation when the two teams took the floor in Cole Field House before 14,000 spectators. Not only were the five starters for Texas Western black, but so were its two primary substitutes. The Miners scored first and never trailed as they played their disciplined offense and sticky man-to-man defense. The final score was relatively close, 72–65, but Texas Western had won decisively. Rupp and his squad were so stunned by their loss that they departed Cole Field House leaving behind the second-place trophy. The national media did not call attention to the racial implications of the game, most likely because writers did not know how to broach the subject. Neither the *New York Times* nor *Sports Illustrated* mentioned the racial composition of the teams, but this game would later come to be viewed as a major milestone in race relations in the United States.[49]

A few weeks later, Vanderbilt University announced the signing of a black basketball recruit, and the racial barriers in the SEC began to crumble. It did not take long for other Southern coaches – eager to win, anxious to keep up with their peers – to join in the hunt for black talent. In 1969, Adolph Rupp signed his first (and only) black player, 7 foot 1 inch center Tom Payne out of Louisville. Rupp retired two years later, but his legend lives on as the Wildcats now play before sellout crowds in cavernous 24,000-seat Adolph Rupp Arena in downtown Lexington. In 1998, the Wildcats won the school's seventh NCAA champion-ship, coached by Orlando "Tubby" Smith, an African American.

10

Television Changes the Image of American Sports

The game was played in Yankee Stadium on December 28, 1958. The favored New York Giants met the Baltimore Colts for the championship of the National Football League in what has often been called "the greatest game ever played." The game stands as a turning point in the history of American sports because it firmly established the NFL as a major professional league and revealed the vast potential that professional football offered for commercial exploitation by television.

Yankee Stadium bulged with 64,185 spectators on a cold, overcast day. The national television audience was estimated at 35 million. At half-time, the underdog Colts held a surprising 14–3 advantage, but in the second half the Giants took the lead 17–14 in the fourth quarter on a 15 yard pass from Charlie Conerly to Frank Gifford. Then the drama began. Taking possession on their own 38 yard line with just 2 minutes remaining, the Colts marched down the field on passes from quarterback Johnny Unitas to Raymond Berry and Lenny Moore. With just 7 seconds remaining, Steve Myhra kicked a 13 yard line field goal to tie the game.

For the first time, an NFL championship would be decided in sudden-death overtime. Most of the players were unaware of the new rule that Commissioner Bert Bell had convinced balky owners to approve. They were exhausted and not overly enthused about playing an extra period. Some had already calculated that they would each receive $3,700 if the prize money were divided equally rather than into winners' shares and lesser ones for the losing team. Bone tired, several players on both sides were ready to call it a day and accept the title "co-champions." Upon learning that the first playoff in NFL history would begin in 3 minutes, however, the capacity crowd rose to its feet and cheered enthusiastically.

The Giants won the coin toss and elected to receive the kickoff, but the offense sputtered and after a punt the Colts took possession on their own 20 yard line. The subsequent 13-play drive against the exhausted Giants defense became an instant legend. Unitas deftly guided

Sports in American Life: A History, Second Edition. Richard O. Davies.
© 2012 John Wiley & Sons, Inc. Published 2012 by John Wiley & Sons, Inc.

the Colts downfield, mixing running plays by fullback Alan Ameche and halfback Moore with passes to Berry and tight end Jim Mutscheller. When the Colts made a first down on the Giants' 8 yard line, however, consternation broke out in the NBC-TV control booth and in homes all across the land. The picture had gone blank! Someone in the crowd behind a goalpost had kicked the plug connecting the cameras to the control booth. Quick-thinking NBC executives responded with ingenuity: a young man in a floppy topcoat ran onto the field and play was halted as he cavorted downfield pursued by police. NBC statistician and business manager Stan Rotkiewicz managed to avoid being caught long enough for the plug to be reattached. Viewers across the country were able to watch the game's stirring conclusion!

Colts coach Weeb Ewbank confounded most observers when he opted not to attempt a short field goal (he considered Myhra unreliable). His strategy was rewarded on third down when Ameche crashed off tackle from the 2 yard line and into the end zone. The scoreboard read 23–17 as thousands of Baltimore fans rushed the field and ripped down the goalposts. Looking down from his box, NFL commissioner Bert Bell, a 30-year veteran of the NFL, shouted to anyone within hearing range, "This is the greatest day in the history of professional football!"[1]

That season the average NFL player earned in the neighborhood of $10,000. One writer commented that prior to the game, professional football players were "working men, tradesmen, glamorous only when compared to miners and factory workers," but in the wake of the overtime game, they became "legends, genuine folk heroes." Even seasoned sportswriters covering the game were caught up in its emotions. *Sports Illustrated* senior football writer Tex Maule proclaimed it the "greatest game ever played," and Arthur Daley of the *New York Times* called it "a wildly exciting and utterly mad affair." He continued, "The enthusiasm shows how completely pro football has arrived. Giants fans were as vociferous as their leather-lunged Baltimore counterparts." On that afternoon, professional football and television sports simultaneously came of age.[2]

The Formative Years of Sports Television

The first televised images were transmitted in England in 1926, and in 1936 an estimated 150,000 Germans witnessed the Summer Olympic Games in large halls in Berlin, Potsdam, and Leipzig. The following year, BBC telecast the Wimbledon men's finals between Don Budge and Frank Parker to some 3,000 British homes. Television in Germany and Britain moved forward more rapidly than in the United States because of government control of broadcasting. The United States Congress, however, had placed broadcasting in the hands of private commercial interests, and during the Great Depression electronics and broadcasting firms were leery about investing in new technologies in an uncertain market. Television was on display in 1939 at the New York World's Fair, where 45 million visitors glimpsed the future on a small black-and-white screen.[3]

On May 17, 1939, the first American televised sports event took place when experimental station W2XBS set up two large, unwieldy RCA Iconoscope cameras at Columbia University's Baker Field and telecast a Columbia–Princeton baseball game. The cameras had difficulty picking up the small white ball, and viewers could follow the action only because of the narrative provided by veteran radio broadcaster Bill Stern. He worked without a monitor and had no idea what viewers were seeing. What they witnessed, in fact, were fuzzy black-and-white images moving about a small screen. As Stern recalled, he spent a lot of time looking back at the camera to see where it was aimed. "I had no monitor. I had no idea where the damned thing was pointing. I never knew whether the thing could keep up with the play or not." The *New York Times* commented that the players seemed like "white flies" flitting about the screen.

With that inauspicious beginning, a new era of televised sports had begun, blurred images notwithstanding. In autumn 1939, several other sports events in the New York area were telecast: an Eastern grass court tennis championship match, a football game between Fordham University and Waynesburg College, a baseball game at Ebbets Field between the Dodgers and the Reds, a heavyweight fight between Lou Nova and Max Baer, and a professional football game between the Brooklyn Dodgers and the Philadelphia Eagles. With only a few hundred television sets located in the New York City area, commercial sports broadcasting remained a decade away, but its potential had been recognized.[4]

Between innings during the 1939 Dodgers baseball game, viewers got a glimpse of things to come when Dodgers radio broadcaster Red Barber whipped out a box of Wheaties, filled a bowl, sliced up a banana, added milk, took a bite, looked into the camera, and proclaimed, "Now, that's a Breakfast of Champions." That the future of American sports television was to revolve around commercial breaks was never in doubt.[5]

Following the end of the Second World War in 1945, the Federal Communications Commission began issuing hundreds of licenses to local stations. Several electronics firms scrambled to produce receivers for the domestic market. Expensive and cantankerous, the first generation of television sets was a source of both pride and frustration for owners because reception was frequently problematic. By 1950, the technology had improved, and 4 million boxy units with 12 inch screens brought programming into 20 percent of American homes. By 1955, 75 percent of American homes were equipped with at least one receiver, a number that jumped to 90 percent in 1960. Transmission of network signals from coast to coast began in 1951, and 10 years later color images became available.

As the preeminent professional sport, organized baseball had to anticipate the potential impact of the new medium. Club owners adopted a policy that permitted each team to develop its own local markets and keep the revenues generated. By 1960, the impact of that decision was already being felt; teams in large media markets were reaping far greater returns than those in small markets. The New York Yankees, for example, were generating $1 million annually in television revenues, while some competing clubs, such as the Washington Senators, received less than 10 percent of that amount.

In 1953, CBS television launched the "Game of the Week" on Saturday afternoons. There had been network telecasts of the All-Star Game and the World Series for several years, but now regular season games were made available. Fans everywhere could watch such stars as Ted Williams, Stan Musial, and Jackie Robinson from the comfort of their own homes. In 1955, CBS put former St Louis Cardinals pitcher Dizzy Dean behind the microphone. He became an immediate hit with his Arkansas twang, corny humor, and shameless self-promotion. Dean's tortured syntax amused his audiences but was the bane of English teachers ("he slud into third"). When the action on the field dragged, Dean might break into dubious song, bellowing out his favorite country tune, "Wabash Cannonball," or reminisce about his playing days. Dean became more popular as a broadcaster than he had been as an All-Star pitcher and free-spirited leader of the Gas House Gang during the 1930s, giving early indication of a phenomenon that would blossom during the 1960s and flourish thereafter: the sports announcer sharing the center of attention as a "star" in his own right, competing for public adulation with the athletes he was covering.[6]

While televised baseball ratings soared, attendance at the 16 major-league ballparks dropped from 21 million in 1948 to just 14 million in 1953, when it bottomed out and remained flat for the remainder of the decade. Minor-league attendance plummeted 70 percent and the number of teams fell from 488 to just 155. At the same time, semiprofessional and "town ball" disappeared. Given a choice of watching major leaguers on television or the town nine in person, fans abandoned the locals.[7] Commercial television also changed the map of baseball. Major-league baseball had been concentrated in the Northeastern quadrant of the country for a half-century. That began to change in 1953 when the Boston Braves moved to Milwaukee, where they drew a hefty 1.8 million fans and profited from a large media market that stretched north and west as far as the Canadian border and into the Dakotas. The move of the hapless Washington Senators to Minneapolis–St Paul in 1961, however, sliced the Braves' media market in half, and so the team moved again in 1966 to Atlanta, attracted by the profit potential of a seven-state radio and television network. In 1954, the St Louis Browns – after decades of performing miserably on the field and at the gate – relocated to Baltimore, and assumed the historic name of Orioles. In 1958, the Giants and Dodgers opened play in California, lured by the state's burgeoning population and lucrative television markets. The Southwest became part of the major-league map in 1962 when a new expansion club, the Colt-45s, was located in Houston (the team took the name of Astros when it began playing in the Astrodome in 1965). The expansion version of the Washington Senators failed to draw fans and in 1971 it relocated to the Dallas–Fort Worth area and assumed the name of Texas Rangers. When owner-manager Connie Mack retired at age 86 in 1954, the Athletics moved from Philadelphia to Kansas City, and embarked for Oakland in 1968. Although many factors contributed to the relocation of franchises – attendance, urban and regional boosterism, politics, the personalities and quirks of owners – the lure of increased television revenues provided a major motive.[8]

Tale of the Tube: Boxing

In 1950, NBC-TV began to telecast the Friday night fights from Madison Square Garden. NBC radio had broadcast the featured Friday night fight since the 1930s, with Don Dunphy providing a rapid-fire blow-by-blow narration. The Gillette Company had long sponsored these radio broadcasts and readily assumed sponsorship of the televised bouts, proclaiming the wonders of its distinctive "blue blades" with a cartoon parrot chirping, "Look Sharp! Feel Sharp! Be Sharp!" Almost overnight, boxing became the most popular sport on television. Although most viewers had never before seen a live match and were oblivious to the game's "scientific" strategies and nuances, they became instant experts. By 1955, an estimated 8.5 million American homes regularly tuned into the fights.[9]

Professional boxing's roots lay in the hundreds of gyms and fight clubs that offered prospective fighters instruction and apprenticeships. There, in a dank environment reeking of liniment, cigar smoke, and sweat, young boxers learned the fundamentals of the manly art. They came primarily from the lower levels of society – racial and ethnic minorities, recent immigrants, the poor – who had dreams of earning big purses and championships. The most promising were funneled into local amateur Golden Gloves tournaments, and if they showed professional potential, were signed to a contract by a manager who provided professional guidance. Some of the more prominent clubs periodically offered a card of several bouts to give these fledgling fighters experience and exposure. It was a long and grueling process, with only a few survivors eventually emerging to appear in bouts on a civic auditorium card offered by a local promoter. Before the advent of television, it was not unusual for a professional fighter to have been in 40 or 50 bouts before getting a shot at lucrative main events in large cities. Joe Louis, for example, a product of the clubs of Detroit and Chicago, did not enter the ring in quest of the heavyweight championship until his 47th bout. One of the all-time great light-heavyweights, Archie Moore, fought in nearly 200 professional fights before getting a shot at the title. It was not unusual for a young boxer learning the intricacies of the sport to lose one or even several bouts but still rise to national contention. The American fight game, for all of its sleaziness, corruption, ties to organized crime, gambling influence, violence, permanent injuries, and occasional deaths, nonetheless provided opportunities for hopeful would-be champions to earn a big payday. In the process, they provided exciting action on fight cards at local clubs.[10]

The Friday night televised fights were instant hits. Arthur Daley, sports columnist for the *New York Times*, observed in 1954 that "the ring is small enough to always be in focus. The contestants are the absolute minimum of two. It's the ideal arrangement because every seat in front of a video screen is a ringside seat. And the price is perfect – free."[11] Within a year after NBC-TV launched its Friday night series, CBS-TV introduced its own "Wednesday Night Fights," sponsored by a beer company seeking to target an adult male audience. Local stations added to the clutter by putting on their own "studio" bouts. After a few years of too many lackluster fights on too many channels on too many nights, with even championship bouts becoming all-too-routine, the once-enormous television boxing audience began tuning out while network executives pondered plummeting ratings.

Long-standing boxing aficionados were dismayed by what television did to the sport. They protested that television viewers did not appreciate the nuances of the "sweet science" of boxing, such as slipping punches on the ropes, forcing a clinch to regain one's composure, slowly wearing down an opponent, counterpunching, keeping the opponent off balance with sharp jabs, throwing short body punches while in a clinch, even moving backward and side to side to wear down an opponent. These time-tested tactics – learned from long hours spent at local gyms – seemed tedious and boring to the untrained eyes of new fans. The television camera best picked up the looping overhead punch thrown by the slugger rather than the sophisticated in-fighting tactics used by the skilled boxer. When the balletic featherweight champion Willie Pep easily defeated the wild-swinging challenger Ray Famechon in 1950, he did so by sidestepping the flailing Frenchman's errant blows while repeatedly landing crisp counterpunches. It was, John Lardner said, "a classic exhibition of evasive skill and science." The judges voted Pep the fight by a whopping 12 rounds to three, but during the next several days the International Boxing Club and NBC were inundated with complaints that Famechon had been robbed; television viewers had completely missed the fact that Pep had outclassed his futilely flailing challenger. With the advent of television, technique was less appreciated than the sensational knockout punch. One experienced boxing writer noted the change in the sport: "Today's fighter is primarily a slugger. The boxer, the hitter, the combination man is gone. The sponsor does not want him. The sponsor wants a man who'll sell his product, somebody popular, and colorful."[12]

Promoters were pressured by television executives to arrange bouts that had special appeal. In particular, they wanted matches featuring two undefeated fighters in order to attract high viewership ratings. This demand undercut the traditional system whereby young fighters systematically worked their way up the ladder, sometimes absorbing a few defeats during the process. The result was that the endless quest for high ratings pushed promising young boxers too far, too fast.

Such was the unfortunate case of Chuck Davey. The 26-year-old was attractive to television producers because he was goodlooking, was possessed of curly blond hair, held a master's degree from Michigan State, and gave a polished interview. A four-time national NCAA welterweight champion, between 1950 and 1953 he won 39 straight professional fights. The "clean-cut" left-hander became the darling of television audiences because of his fancy footwork and impressive record compiled largely against inferior opponents. Pressure from television executives put Davey into a Chicago Stadium ring in February of 1953 with defending welterweight champion Kid Gavilan of Cuba. It was brutal. Thirty-five million viewers watched the ring-savvy Gavilan systematically savage the outclassed challenger, toying with him until eventually knocking him out in round 10 after administering the former college student a painful lesson in Boxing 101. Davey spent a week in hospital recovering and retired shortly thereafter. His fate was typical, wrote Arthur Daley in the *New York Times*: "There aren't that many good fighters any more. They are brought up before they are ready for that quick buck. They go down as fast as they rise."[13] Almost overnight, Chuck Davey had gone from being a star attraction to a discarded has-been.

One of the unintended consequences of television's exploitation of boxing was the demise of the boxing gyms and clubs that had prepared young fighters for the professional game. With featured bouts being telecast several times a week into the homes and taverns of America, boxing fans abandoned local clubs and their monthly fight cards, thereby undercutting the development of new talent. During the decade, the number of fight clubs fell from 300 to 50, and the small-city boxing circuit, where over the years many top fighters had gotten their start, virtually disappeared. By the end of the decade, the number of professional fighters had been reduced by 50 percent. Television also cut deeply into attendance. In 1948, an average crowd of 12,000 would pay good money to see the Friday night card at Madison Square Garden; 10 years later, the audience averaged about 1,200. The vast Garden floor had become little more than a television studio. In 1951, one-third of the nation's television sets were tuned to the Friday night fights, but by 1959 the number had fallen to just 10 percent. Ratings-conscious television executives naturally looked elsewhere for new features with which to sell advertising.[14]

In 1960, NBC-TV announced that it was dropping Friday night fights. The sport moved into a new era, where it limped along on the fringes of respectability. The fight game now seemed to be more and more reliant on championship confrontations staged in Las Vegas, where hotel-casinos used high-profile boxing matches as a means of attracting "high-roller" gamblers to their green felt tables. But the traditional fight game had essentially ceased to exist, knocked down for the count by television.

Professional Football Comes of Age

It is not surprising that professional football, which today constitutes a multibillion-dollar sports and entertainment enterprise, came into prominence with commercial television. Founded in 1921, the National Football League for years struggled to survive, with franchises located in such small Midwestern cities as Canton, Duluth, Marion, Dayton, Portsmouth, Decatur, Evansville, and Green Bay. By the eve of the Second World War, however, the league had stabilized, with franchises in Philadelphia, Chicago, Washington, DC, New York, Detroit, and Pittsburgh. The league championship game was broadcast nationwide for the first time in 1940, although the anticipated close game between the Chicago Bears and the Washington Redskins ended up with a lopsided score of 73–0 against the hometown 'Skins.

Between 1945 and 1960, the NFL came of age. In 1946, NFL team owners selected Bert Bell as their new commissioner. Reflective of the league's stature, for several years he ran the league out of his home, eventually moving to a small office in a suburban Philadelphia bank building. Bell took over the league at a difficult time, because in 1945 Chicago sportswriter Arch Ward had orchestrated the establishment of a new professional league – the All-American Football Conference (A-AFC). His intent – at least his public statements so indicated – was to create a league equal to the NFL, with the two league champions squaring off in December for the national title.

The A-AFC's president, former Notre Dame Four Horseman Jim Crowley, attempted in vain to find a way to avoid a bidding war for players and to get agreement on a postseason championship game. The A-AFC got off to a good start, signing 44 of the 60 top college players selected for the All-Star Game, and luring away about 100 established NFL players with salaries in the $5,000 to $12,000 range. However, the A-AFC's biggest catch was Paul Brown, a 37-year-old coach who had an 80–8–2 record while winning six state championships at Massillon High School in northeastern Ohio during the 1930s, and had guided Ohio State to its first national championship in 1942. After being turned down by Notre Dame's head coach Frank Leahy, Cleveland owner Arthur "Mickey" McBride hired Brown as his coach, and delighted Cleveland fans voted to name the new team the "Browns." McBride, whose financial interests included a large taxicab company, lured Brown with a stunning salary of $25,000 plus 5 percent ownership of the team.

Brown was an innovative coach who had pioneered in providing playbooks for players to study, the use of game films to evaluate players and to analyze upcoming opponents, and systematic scouting of future opponents. He continued to innovate when he took over the Browns. When unlimited substitution was legalized in 1949, he shuttled two offensive guards in and out after each play to communicate the next play to quarterback Otto Graham. Brown contributed greatly to the enhancement of the coach's control of the game, a trend that continues to the present. He called the offensive plays and set the defense before each play. Brown was one of the first coaches to put assistant coaches in the press box to get an overview of the game, from where they communicated their observations and suggestions via telephone to coaches along the sidelines.

Owner Mickey McBride liked to win and was willing to spend plenty of money to that end. He gave Brown a free hand in running the team. Cleveland became the first professional team to hire full-time assistant coaches who worked year-around, rather than just during the season. When Brown announced that he was hiring five full-time assistants, shock waves reverberated throughout professional football. He also enjoyed a built-in advantage over other teams when it came to stockpiling talent. With the active team rosters limited to just 33 players, he convinced McBride to hire several reserves as cab drivers. Come practice time, a fleet of McBride's taxicabs would be seen parked outside the Browns' practice facility. Brown thus had a group of replacements available in case of injury to a roster member.[15] That legacy lives on today. The NFL permits each team to keep eight players under contract beyond the 45-man regular roster; that supplemental group is known as the "taxi squad."

Brown assembled a talented team that would produce seven members of the Hall of Fame: quarterback Otto Graham, fullback Marion Motley, receiver Dante Lavelli, offensive lineman Frank Gatski, defensive lineman Bill Willis, defensive end Len Ford, and offensive tackle and place kicker Lou "The Toe" Groza. Brown's teams won the A-AFC championship four consecutive years, and the lack of competitive balance clearly hurt attendance. Even Browns fans became complacent, and by 1949 Cleveland's average attendance had fallen from 50,000 per game in 1946 to just 20,000. When the Browns defeated the San Francisco 49ers 21–7 in the fourth and final championship game, only 22,500 fans watched in Cleveland's mammoth 80,000-seat Municipal Stadium.

The NFL was also hurting in attendance, a result of the loss of talent to the rival league. Salaries had also escalated. A merger was the logical solution, and after much wrangling, the NFL agreed to accept three teams from what its leaders considered an inferior league: the Browns, the San Francisco 49ers, and the Baltimore Colts. Enmity on the part of NFL executives lingered, and Bert Bell decided to teach Paul Brown and the A-AFC a lesson. He scheduled Cleveland to open the 1950 season at defending champion Philadelphia, but the Browns dominated the Eagles convincingly, 35–10, as 71,000 Eagles fans looked on in shock. The Browns went on to a 10–2 season, capping it off with dramatic last-minute field goals by Lou Groza to win the divisional playoff with the Giants and the championship game against the Los Angeles Rams.

Throughout the 1950s, the NFL overcame several changes in franchise ownership and became a much more stable operation. The value of a franchise hovered between $500,000 and $1 million during the decade, and unlike baseball, attendance grew steadily, jumping from an average of 25,300 to over 40,000 per game between 1950 and 1960. There were more and better players, and with the introduction of unlimited substitution, they were able to concentrate upon refining specific skills, leading to a more exciting brand of play. Rules changes sought to stimulate scoring, including placing the goalposts on the goal line to encourage more field goal attempts. Specialization became the rule, and only a few players still went "both ways." By 1960, only the Eagles' Hall of Fame center/linebacker Chuck Bednarik did so with regularity.

The NFL's steady growth during the 1950s can be traced to an enlightened television policy that Bert Bell sold to the league's owners. Bell negotiated his first league-wide television contract with the fledgling DuMont network in 1951 that included a provision to black out local games. In 1953, federal district judge Allan K. Grim ruled that the NFL could black out games within a 75 mile radius of the location where the game was being played. Although this did not give the NFL complete control over television, it provided the necessary protection for ticket sales. In 1956, CBS paid over $1 million in rights to televise selected games nationally, while several teams created their own regional networks. When Bell suffered a fatal heart attack on October 11, 1959, while watching the Eagles and Steelers play at Franklin Field in Philadelphia, an important transitional era in the history of the NFL came to an end. Bert Bell had guided the league to a prosperous platform from which it was about to embark on an extended period of expansion, thanks in large part to the groundwork he had established with an enlightened television policy.[16]

Pete and Roone

Bert Bell's death came at a crucial time for the NFL. In 1959, yet another new rival league, the American Football League (AFL), had been created. The premise of this new league was that it could become profitable from a lucrative television contract. By this time, up-and-coming ABC-TV was anxious to get into the football business and was prepared to fork over the princely sum of $2 million for the rights to the initial AFL 1960 season. The league was the brainchild of 27-year-old Texas oilman Lamar Hunt who, angry at being rebuffed by the NFL in his attempt to buy an existing franchise and move it to Dallas, decided to create a new league. He lined up such wealthy investors as Bud Adams in Houston, Bob Howsam in Denver, and Max Winter in Minneapolis to join in his enterprise. By November 1959 he had an eight-team league assembled.

Thus the challenge from the AFL was on the minds of the 12 NFL owners when they convened for their annual meeting in Miami Beach in January 1960. They fired a shot across the bow of the new league by creating two expansion franchises: they launched the Dallas Cowboys and lured Max Winter and the Minnesota Vikings away from the AFL. They also had to elect Bert Bell's successor. The meeting turned contentious when vote after vote failed to give one of the top candidates the necessary two-thirds margin. The politicking lasted for 10 days before, in exasperation if not desperation, they finally named as their new commissioner the young Los Angeles Rams general manager, Pete Rozelle. An exhausted group of owners could only hope for the best.[17]

The 32-year-old Rozelle did not have a compelling football résumé. He had earned a journalism degree from the University of San Francisco and worked for a public relations firm before joining the Rams as a publicist. In 1957, he assumed the position of general manager. Skeptical journalists thought Rozelle looked like a short-timer and caustically labeled him the "Boy Czar."

The skeptics were quickly disabused of their initial impressions. Beneath Rozelle's calm and friendly demeanor lurked a tough-minded negotiator who would brook neither nonsense nor any challenge to his authority (soon after taking office, he had the temerity to discipline the recognized father figure of the NFL, the founding owner and coach of the Chicago Bears, George Halas). Rozelle's first substantive decision gave an indication of what he thought the NFL should be about. He moved the league's headquarters to Park Avenue in downtown Manhattan, close by the offices of the three television networks. He had learned much about dealing with the television industry in Los Angeles, and he correctly perceived that the networks were ready to invest heavily in professional football. From his first days in his new position, Rozelle embarked on an audacious plan to tap into television revenues. But first he had to convince his millionaire capitalist owners of the many blessings to be gleaned from, of all things, socialism.

Just as Bert Bell had preached the gospel of maintaining a league of competitive teams, so too did Rozelle, but he extended that concept to the point of taking away millions of dollars from teams located in large media markets. Rozelle proposed to the owners that the league sell the television rights of all teams in a single package and that each franchise share equally in the income. He persuaded the owners that if this were not done, then big-media-market teams would dominate the league. In the long run, he argued, sharing revenues would generate more income for everyone by enabling all franchises to field competitive teams. His theory came to be known as "league parity." He especially had to win over the barons whose franchises were located in the nation's three largest media markets: Wellington Mara of the Giants, Dan Reeves of the Rams, and George Halas of the Bears. With grudging agreement from these influential owners, Rozelle was off to lobby Congress for special legislation exempting the league from antitrust laws. He was rewarded in September 1961 with the Sports Antitrust Broadcast Act, which permitted leagues to pool their broadcast rights and sell them as a single entity. That ended all talk about a "boy czar." Rozelle served as commissioner until poor health forced him into retirement in 1989.[18]

For the 1962 and 1963 seasons, Rozelle's hands were tied because nine of the teams had already signed agreements with CBS, but nonetheless he was able to secure a record-high league contract that paid $4,650,000 per season, amounting to $330,000 per team. But Rozelle was only warming up. When the rights for 1964 and 1965 came up for renewal, he orchestrated a highly publicized secret bidding process in which he played each network off against the others. Speculation abounded as to which company would fork over the largest pile of money. ABC saw the bidding as an opportunity to gain equal stature with its two larger rivals, while NBC and CBS were determined to protect their elite status. When Rozelle opened the sealed bids in a public ceremony, NBC came in with an unexpectedly high bid of $10.75 million for each of two seasons, and upstart ABC topped that with a figure of $13.2 million. Rozelle then casually opened the final bid. He later recalled, "I figured the CBS bid had to be anticlimactic. So I opened their bid kind of lackadaisically. The number itself was sitting way down toward the bottom of the second page. I looked at it, and … 'Good God,' I thought, 'it's for $14,100,000 a year!'"[19] The new financial reality of professional football's marriage with television was evident to ABC vice president Ed Scherick, who thought, "Good Lord. Here we had gone in with more than *twenty-six million bucks*. And we had been *rejected*! The whole damned *network* had cost only $15 million in 1951!"[20]

ABC's audacious bid, however, indicated that the network intended to become a major player in sports television. Its new vice president, Roone Arledge, brought to his job imagination, energy, and a willingness to take a chance. He joined ABC in 1960 shortly after the network had signed on to broadcast the Saturday college football game of the week, in addition to AFL games. Arledge brought to his position the conviction that if he offered casual viewers entertainment and drama that went beyond the game itself, they would tune in. Within a few years, Arledge had revolutionized the way television covered sporting events: "What we set out to do was to get the audience involved emotionally. If they don't give a damn about the game, they still might enjoy the program."[21]

Arledge instructed his college crews to capture not just the action on the field but the total atmosphere within the stadium. Special microphones were placed on the field to pick up the "thud" of players smacking into each other, cranes provided overhead shots, and zoom cameras caught the action up close. His producers also blended in interviews with coaches, sounds of marching bands, and close-up shots of anguished coaches prowling the sidelines. He tossed in images of attractive coeds in the grandstands, cheerleaders doing their acrobatic routines, and baton twirlers prancing in front of the band. Seeking to maximize the impact of color television, Arledge gave his audiences a sense of the colorful atmosphere within college stadiums, offset by sounds of players colliding with each other. Especially popular was the introduction of slow motion and instant replay that made it possible for viewers to see crucial plays over and over again. Arledge thus presented football not just as a game, but also as a spectacle full of excitement and drama. Ratings soared, and so did Roone Arledge's career.[22]

Arledge also launched his weekend sports anthology "Wide World of Sports." Using the catchy phraseology suggested by announcer Jim McKay, ABC "spanned the globe" to bring viewers "the thrill of victory and the agony of defeat." As McKay later recalled, the program was not "born out of a creative explosion. It was, as the old saying goes, born of necessity." Operating on a limited budget, Arledge found unique and inexpensive ways to fill those time slots. He seldom presented live events, instead utilizing the recent innovation of videotape to condense the action. Thus his producers compressed a 26 mile marathon into a few minutes of viewing time – showing the fresh pack of runners taking off from the starting line, their agonized faces as they slogged up a hill or struggled to keep going when "hitting the wall" at the 20 mile mark, and finally the exhausted leaders attempting to sprint to the finish line after more than 2 hours of grueling effort. As ABC cleverly said, the shows were "shot live on tape." ABC crews combed the globe in search of anything remotely connected with sports that might prove entertaining to American audiences … and inexpensive to show. In its first year "Wide World of Sports" reported on rodeos from small towns in the West, track meets in Iowa, tennis in Mexico, soccer from London, auto racing from Le Mans, curling from Canada, hydroplaning from Seattle, mountain climbing in the Alps, and surfing from Maui. Lead announcer McKay, who usually did the voiceover in the New York studio after film crews sent in their footage, revealed a special talent for making even the most inconsequential event seem interesting by emphasizing underlying storylines – colorful personalities, danger to contestants, feuds between competitors, and the exotic location in which the event was held.[23]

Although initially "Wide World" tended to cover legitimate, if obscure, sports over the years, the program tended to stretch things a little – and then some. The program's potpourri eventually included jai-alai, badminton, wrist-wrestling, log-rolling, cat shows, dog shows, horse shows, truck pulls, horse polo, water polo, water skiing, figure skating, bobsledding, chess, ski races, bicycle races, motorcycle races, stock car races, marathon races, and dog sled races – and the list goes on and on. At times, the show went over the top with automobile demolition derbies, a climbing race up the Eiffel Tower, cliff divers plummeting several hundred feet into the Pacific Ocean at Acapulco, and high-wire walks without a safety net. The most extreme moment came on New Year's Day in 1968, when daredevil Evel Knievel attempted to jump the bubbling water fountain in front of Caesars Palace in Las Vegas on a motorcycle. He landed in a heap, suffering a broken spine and a crushed pelvis, but appeared on "Wide World" 15 more times doing weird and dangerous things – always to high ratings … and that was sufficient justification.[24]

When Arledge arrived at ABC, he plunged immediately into the bitter squabble between the NFL and the newly created American Football League. In its first year, the upstart league suffered low attendance, its eight teams losing an estimated $3 million despite the ABC contract. Contrary to broadcasts of college games where pictures of fans in the grandstands were common fare, ABC's cameramen were instructed to follow AFL games without showing the embarrassing expanse of empty seats. In 1963, multimillionaire David "Sonny" Werblin purchased the New York Titans for $1 million. He hired Weeb Ewbank to lead the renamed New York Jets, moved home games to recently opened Shea Stadium, and stunned the sports world when he signed University of Alabama quarterback Joe Namath to a $420,000 three-year contract in 1965. With Namath tossing passes and enjoying his life as a Broadway celebrity, Jets attendance jumped from 22,000 per game to over 40,000. The AFL had gained instant credibility, but the Namath contract set off a bidding war that escalated players' salaries.

In 1964, the AFL signed a five-year $42 million contract with NBC, more than five times what it received from ABC. Its survival was now assured. With the AFL not going away, Pete Rozelle engaged in a series of secret meetings with AFL leaders that produced a merger agreement. Rozelle would become the commissioner of a greatly expanded National Football League, and a single draft would eliminate the bidding for players. Not only did the NFL agree to merge with all 10 AFL franchises, but Rozelle also agreed to put an expansion franchise in New Orleans as a condition of gaining the critical support of Senator Russell Long and Congressman Hale Boggs of Louisiana for passage of an antitrust legislative exemption for the merger. That legislation quietly sailed through Congress as a rider to an appropriations bill, and three weeks later the establishment of the New Orleans Saints was announced to an unsuspecting world.[25]

Super Sunday and Monday Night

With Rozelle's greatly expanded 26-team empire now tucked under one tent, it was only natural that a final championship playoff game be held between the American and National Football Leagues (changed to "conferences" in 1970). Although the owners wanted to call it the World Championship Game, Rozelle opted for the more regal title of "Super Bowl." In 1971, with the fifth Super Bowl approaching, Rozelle gave the upcoming Dallas–Baltimore game a classic touch by designating it with a distinctive Roman numeral: Super Bowl V. What was retroactively dubbed Super Bowl I was played in spacious 100,000-seat Los Angeles Coliseum on January 15, 1967; just 35,000 fans paid the top ticket price of $12 to watch coach Vince Lombardi's Green Bay Packers trample the Kansas City Chiefs 35–10. The first game was telecast by both NBC and CBS, which sold advertising at $35,000 per 30 seconds; thereafter, the two networks alternated through 1984 as part of the ongoing contract with the league, at which point ABC joined in the fun.

The Super Bowl became the most watched event on the American sports calendar, eclipsing the World Series, Kentucky Derby, Indianapolis 500 race, and New Year's Day college bowl games. It was Super Bowl III that thrust the game into the forefront of American sports. Las Vegas bookmakers made the Baltimore Colts of the older league a prohibitive 17-point favorite over the upstart New York Jets, led by quarterback "Broadway Joe" Namath, who had become a much-publicized New York bachelor. A few days before the January 12, 1969 game, Namath brashly "guaranteed" a Jets victory. Much to the surprise of football experts, he delivered in dramatic fashion by engineering a 16–7 victory. He completed 17 passes for 208 yards, and directed a powerful running game featuring backs Emerson Boozer and Matt Snell while the Jets' defense stifled the Colts' offense. Even Pete Rozelle, the master of public relations, could not have written a better script.

Thereafter, the Super Bowl became a major event, complete with overblown media coverage that generated a commercial frenzy. Super Bowl Sunday was not merely another day to watch a football game on television, but became an informal national holiday. Each year, it seemed to grow ever more extravagant, ever more outrageous. Several thousand media personnel assembled at the game site a week before kickoff to fill the airwaves and newsprint with an avalanche of mostly trivial stories. Fortune 500 companies held lavish parties for important guests in which they strived to outdo the others with their excess. Ticket prices accelerated each year, reaching a face value of $500 in 2004. But scalpers could usually sell tickets for upwards of four times their face value. Six months before Super Bowl XLV was held in Dallas in 2011, brokers offered a price range for tickets that began at $1,500 for a seat high above the end zones and climbed to above $7,500 for a prime location. Each year the game generated wagers – legal and otherwise – that were estimated to total several billion dollars. Across the country private parties were planned – newspapers even printed suggestions for Super Bowl buffet menus for struggling hosts – and vast amounts of alcohol and food were consumed.[26]

Major corporations eagerly lined up to buy advertising. By 1980, the cost of commercials had reached $250,000 per 30 seconds. In 2005, the half-minute rate had spiraled to the astronomical level of $2.5 million, and in 2011, despite a severe recession that was in its third year of wreaking economic havoc, advertisers paid $2.8 million for 30 second access to the nation's largest television audience. Agencies that designed advertisements – largely for beer, technology, automobile, and soft drink companies – were caught up in an informal contest for the most creative advertisements, which became part of the post-game media dissection. The importance of the Super Bowl to the television industry was driven home when Pete Rozelle admitted ABC to the network rotation for the 1985 game in return for an $18 million "admission fee."

It was inevitable that two creative men such as Pete Rozelle and Roone Arledge would find a way to combine their talents. For several years, Rozelle had chafed under the limitations that confined NFL games to Sunday afternoons. He dreamed of putting his product on prime time, but both CBS and NBC continued to view sports with indifference.

All three networks viewed Saturday nights as sacrosanct for their top-rated programs, and Fridays were considered unavailable because that evening was traditionally reserved for high school football. Except for the tradition of the Detroit Lions' Thanksgiving Day game, midweek seemed inappropriate.

What about Monday night? Rozelle was rebuffed by CBS for fear of losing women viewers who flocked to the network's popular Monday prime-time feature movie. NBC expressed interest but backed off when Johnny Carson balked at pushing his highly rated "Tonight Show" back from its regular 11:30 p.m. time slot. That left ABC, which after some hesitation and much trepidation, decided to take the risk. Skeptics predicted a ratings disaster – football was, after all, a weekend event – but when "Monday Night Football" (MNF) made its appearance in September of 1970, the all-important Nielsen ratings went through the roof. Under Roone Arledge's magic touch, "Monday Night Football" became a national institution and one of the most profitable and longest-running programs in the history of television.[27]

Part of the magic was that Arledge pulled out all the stops by utilizing modern television gadgetry. Instant replays, isolation shots of individual players, fancy graphics, and other special effects dazzled viewers. Cameras honed in on outrageously costumed fans (dressed like dogs in Cleveland, hogs in Washington), and homemade signs were draped around the stadium carrying clever messages that often incorporated the letters ABC.

But the real show was in the broadcast booth. Instead of the traditional two-man broadcasting team, Arledge decided to put three men in the booth, including two "color" commentators who brought contrasting styles and personalities. One was Don Meredith, a former quarterback for the Dallas Cowboys. Possessed of a healthy skepticism about the essential importance of the game in which he had been a star, Meredith offered up many an irreverent comment. On those occasions when he arrived in the broadcast booth well fortified from a visit to the hotel bar, he might even break into an off-key country-western song. Meredith left the show in 1974 but returned for another seven years in 1977. Arledge defied many skeptics by placing alongside Meredith the outspoken and contentious Howard Cosell. After graduating from law school in 1940 and completing military service, Cosell practiced law for several years in New York City, building a practice that included several professional athletes as clients. He began dabbling in sports radio, eventually closing his law office in 1956 when he joined ABC as radio sports commentator. By 1960, he had emerged as a skilled boxing commentator for ABC's televised fights, but excelled covering other sports as well.[28]

Cosell became famous for his lucid, erudite, and penetrating commentaries, which he did extemporaneously, thanks to his amazing facility for accurately recalling sports trivia. He had long been critical of fawning sports announcers who seldom had anything negative to report about any sports figure. Possessed of a massive ego, Cosell did not hesitate to make critical comments about a particular player's weaknesses or a coach's limitations as if he were expounding upon newfound truths soon to be etched in stone. His Brooklyn accent and palpable arrogance grated upon Middle America. Well before his arrival on MNF, he had established his reputation for "telling it like it is" – that is, providing blunt commentary that set him apart from other mainline sports announcers. In the initial Monday night game, Cosell sparked a flurry of angry demands that he be removed from the broadcasting

team when he criticized Joe Namath for forcing a pass into heavy coverage which led to an untimely interception. The same fan response occurred when Cosell said that star Cleveland running back Leroy Kelly was "not having a compelling game." Fans were not used to such mildly critical appraisals of their favorite star players.

Meredith and Cosell began their stint on MNF by joking with each other, but soon were engaged in a game of one-upmanship. As the years rolled by their banter increasingly became more pointed, and often was more entertaining than the game on the field. Their relationship, rocky from the start and fired by personality differences and competition, reached an adversarial level the first season on one cold November night in Philadelphia when Cosell, possibly suffering from the flu but definitely feeling the effects of a few martinis, was condescendingly critical of Meredith's game analysis and then unceremoniously threw up on Meredith's fancy cowboy boots. The third man in the booth, Keith Jackson, had the responsibility of providing play-by-play description, but his combative partners overshadowed him. After one season, Jackson returned to his first love of college football and was replaced by former New York Giants star halfback Frank Gifford. This trio made Monday nights an exciting time, drawing high ratings by enticing millions of viewers to the show even if they cared little for football. Both Cosell and Meredith had left MNF by the mid

Figure 10.1 The "Monday Night" ABC team appears on camera before a game in 1971. Howard Cosell is where he felt most comfortable – front and center dominating the microphone – while Don Meredith smiles laconically at one of Cosell's loquacious observations and a diffident Frank Gifford ponders how he got himself joined with such a contentious pair. The increasingly barbed comments between Cosell and Meredith paralleled the rising ratings enjoyed by ABC television. *Bettman Archive/Corbis*

1980s, and other announcers came and went over the years. Try as it might, ABC and ESPN, after it took over the program in 2006, could never replicate the special magic generated by the Howard and Dandy Don show.

ESPN: All Sports, All the Time

Chet Simmons knew sports broadcasting. In the late winter of 1979, he stood astride the world of televised sports as president of NBC Sports. As a young television executive in the 1960s, Simmons had helped launch the "Wide World of Sports" at ABC, and more recently had made NBC the first among equals in the small, clubby world of network sports. When asked his response to an announcement about the creation of a cable network dedicated exclusively to sports, Simmons confidently predicted, "Cable sports networks won't work. There are not enough people watching cable. I think this sports network is doomed, to be honest."[29]

Like Simmons, most established network executives viewed the idea as ill advised, if not simply goofy. How many viewers wanted to watch sports at three o'clock in the morning? Would oversaturation of the market drive down ratings? Where would the network get enough content to fill 168 hours of programming each week? With only 13 million homes connected to cable – just 18 percent of the total television market – how could it hope to attract serious advertising dollars? Would independent cable companies be willing to pay for the rights? With American sports fans conditioned by 30 years of receiving their sports for free over the three major networks, how could viewers be expected to pay?

Three months later, Chet Simmons changed his mind and signed on as the new president of the Entertainment and Sports Programming Network. Simmons knew that Cable News Network (CNN) had demonstrated that it could attract viewers. Why not one that catered exclusively to sports? His decision stunned the communications industry. It would be only the first of many surprises that ESPN would provide over the next three decades.[30]

The idea that a 24 hour sports cable network could succeed was the brainchild of sports publicist Bill Rasmussen. He obtained $10 million of start-up money from Getty Oil executive Stuart Evey and located his company in the small city of Bristol, Connecticut, when the city offered him a good deal on a large plot of land.

On September 7, 1979, ESPN hit the airwaves with a brief promotional announcement followed by a slow-pitch softball game, bouncing its signal to 650 affiliates across the United States and their 2 million subscribers via satellite. Initial reaction by subscribers was positive, but Wall Street and Madison Avenue remained skeptical. Investment analysts said the viewing public would soon lose interest, taking note that the three major networks broadcast 18 hours of sports a week between them. Who could possibly want more than that? *Sports Illustrated*, more closely attuned to the American people's insatiable appetite for sports, presciently suggested that the new station "may become the biggest thing in TV sports since "Monday Night Football" and nighttime World Series games."[31]

Initially, the fledging network relied heavily upon taped reruns and a wide range of inconsequential contests it could broadcast at little cost. Viewers were fed a menu of diverse events: college lacrosse, Australian football, marathon races, college baseball, wind surfing, water skiing, European professional soccer, volleyball, swimming and diving meets, fencing, plus an inordinate number of events never before seen on television: karate, mud-wrestling, tractor pulls, demolition derbies, bicycle races, checkers and chess, and semiprofessional women's softball. In its first year ESPN featured 65 different events.

On September 7, 2010, ESPN celebrated its 25th anniversary.[32] Its Bristol headquarters had grown to a massive complex of seven large interconnected buildings and its employees numbered over 2,500. The company had gone through several corporate owners, including Getty Oil, Capital Cities, and Walt Disney. It had become an enormously profitable enterprise, earning an estimated $100 million a year. When Disney purchased Capital Cities, a holding company that included ESPN and ABC, Disney chairman Michael Eisner said that the cable company was "the crown jewel" in the mega acquisition. Its number of subscribers approached 80 million and the small town of Bristol had improbably become the *de facto* capital of the burgeoning world of American sports.[33]

ESPN succeeded because it was able to fill the niches that the three networks left open – or fumbled away. In 1981, the National Hockey League was the first major professional league to sign on, and that same year ESPN thrilled college basketball fans with its coverage of the early rounds of the NCAA tournament, delighting viewers by switching from one game to another to show upsets in the making or exciting overtime games. It began telecasting NASCAR races in 1981 and increased its coverage with the growing popularity of the sport, which it in turn helped generate. It added Sunday night NFL games in 1987 and major-league baseball in 1990. After the NCAA lost its monopolistic control of college football in 1983, college football and basketball games became a major staple, and not just on Saturday afternoons and evenings; "mid-major" conferences found that they could get heretofore unavailable national exposure by agreeing to play games midweek. ESPN also became the normal venue for weekly boxing. The problems of oversaturation and of lack of material were long forgotten, although a healthy dose of reruns continued to fill the long late night and early morning hours.[34] ESPN was satisfying the American public's obsession with sports, and in turn creating even greater demand.

The network attracted high-quality writers, producers, and on-camera personalities. Talented individuals carved out niches in sports reporting heretofore unknown: Mel Kiper, Jr, established himself as the expert on the springtime NFL college draft, Dick Vitale became a popular hyperventilating basketball commentator, and Roy Firestone created a special niche with his sensitive in-depth interviews with sports figures. Platoons of retired players and former coaches were given positions as analysts, and management continually combed the nation for promising new talent. During the early 1990s, the "tag team" pair of Dan Patrick and Keith Olbermann took "SportsCenter," the centerpiece of the daily schedule, to new heights of popularity with their pungent writing, candid analysis, and irreverent, spontaneous humor. "SportsCenter" became one of the nation's most watched nightly news shows, the unquestioned best television source for national sports coverage.[35] In 1992, the company launched its 24 hour radio network and soon had more than 300 affiliates across the nation.

ESPN's search for top talent included minorities and women. Greg Gumbel joined the network in 1981 and many African Americans followed. The first woman to anchor

"SportsCenter" was Gayle Gardner, whose sharp writing and on-camera skills made her an instant hit in 1981. Soon thereafter other talented women arrived as anchors, reporters, and behind-the-scenes writers, producers, and front office personnel – their professional work giving the lie to the assumption that women could not understand and interpret sports at a high professional level.

During the 1990s, with the assurance of financial stability provided by an ever-increasing profit stream, ESPN vigorously launched new ventures. The result was that the lines between straight news reporting and the promotion of its own investments in upcoming programs became increasingly blurred. The cable network grew so rapidly and attempted to do so many things simultaneously that at times its focus seemed muddled and unfocused. On the one hand, ESPN promoted itself as the major source for high-quality sports journalism, reporting on and analyzing mainstream American sports – with heavy emphasis upon football, basketball, and baseball – by deploying an impressive array of reporters and analysts. Its in-depth analysis of sporting events often seemed to surpass the professional quality and depth of the mainstream media's treatment of national politics and business.

At the same time, however, ESPN also promoted its own commercial interests by stimulating interest in events of its own making or by generating interest in activities that previously had gone largely unnoticed by the average sports fan. In 1993, the network inaugurated the ESPY awards, the name given a tortured acronym: the Excellence in Sports Performance Yearly award. In 1995, the Extreme Games were created to tap into the market of younger Americans who were taking to skateboards, off-road bicycles, and snowboards. Soon dubbed the X-Games, these new events filled hours of television time and attracted new sources of advertising. The summer X-Games featured high-flying competitions of skateboarders and bikers, and the winter games brought the excitement of snowboarding bravado in the halfpipe to the television viewer. To fill the long summer months, the Outdoor Games were created and included contests of wood sawing, tree climbing, log rolling, fly fishing, trap shooting, and hunting dogs racing over and under barriers. Even poker tournaments became a "sport" deemed worth covering.

Various efforts by rival networks to supplant ESPN – Rupert Murdoch's initiative in 1999 to connect nine regional sports networks into a national competing network, in particular – could not dislodge ESPN's stranglehold on the market. ESPN demonstrated an ability to continue to innovate and reinvent itself. It also preempted the intentions of its potential rivals by launching ESPN-2 in 1993. Originally intended to appeal to younger sports fans, with hard-hitting commentary and emphasis upon such offbeat sports as women's beach volleyball, skateboarding, outdoor fishing and hunting, along with other alternative sports, ESPN-2 tended to morph over the years into a pale imitation of the parent company, with its programming featuring such events as "mid-major" football games during the middle of the work week, and a flood of college basketball games not deemed worthy to run on the primary network. Even some high school football games were included in the programming. College sports coverage was expanded in 2005 with the launching of ESPN-U, and in an effort to reach Hispanic viewers in the United States and Latin America, ESPN Deportes La Revista was launched in time for the 2006 World Cup. In 1996, the company moved into print journalism, launching *ESPN: The Magazine*. Edited in a flashy manner to appeal to the age demographic of 18–34, it proved an immediate success. Circulation reached 2.1 million in 2010. Sports fans were also lured to enormous glitzy ESPN sports bars and restaurants in Los Angeles, Washington, DC, New York, and other cities, where they could watch all of the ESPN cable networks simultaneously on large screens while munching on burgers and chicken wings and sipping a boutique draft beer.

What insiders now called Planet ESPN had become the cash cow for the Disney Corporation, producing an estimated 25 percent of Disney's annual profits. In 2004, one Wall Street analyst estimated that ESPN was generating in excess of $500 million in profits on revenue of $1.5 billion. The venerable Wall Street firm of Sanford C. Bernstein estimated the company's market value at $15.5 billion.[36]

11

College Sports in the Modern Era

Writing in 1929, Henry Pritchett of the Carnegie Foundation summarized the dilemma confronting college athletics:

> It takes no tabulation of statistics to prove that the young athlete who gives himself for months, body and soul, to training under a professional coach for a grueling contest, staged to focus the attention of thousands of people, and upon which many thousands of dollars will be staked, will find no time or energy for any serious intellectual effort.[1]

As the Carnegie Report made clear, big-time programs had already crossed the line from amateurism to a quasi-professional model. In one way or another, institutions found ways to pay their athletes and academic objectives were often a mirage. Journalist John Tunis aptly summarized the issue: "If the presidents really desired to clean up the athletic situation, they could do so and they would find an amazing number of alumni behind them. But alas, in that event no money would be made." Tunis opined that the presidents "will probably do nothing" about the matter, but concluded that such reluctance served the purpose of exposing "the intellectual dishonesty of the American college."[2] With stadiums to fill and coaches to pay, big-time college football in 1929 was already well along the road to becoming, as Murray Sperber would later describe the multibillion-dollar commercial enterprise, "College Sports, Inc."[3]

As the decades went by, the issues that the Carnegie Commission had identified were magnified many times. Walter Byers served as executive director of the NCAA from 1951 until 1987. One would assume that this executive would be among the staunchest defenders of the system he helped create. But after his retirement, Byers published a surprising *mea culpa*, confessing his sins and turning upon the organization with considerable vengeance. Ascribing the treatment of "student-athletes" by the collegiate athletic system to a

Sports in American Life: A History, Second Edition. Richard O. Davies.
© 2012 John Wiley & Sons, Inc. Published 2012 by John Wiley & Sons, Inc.

"neo-plantation" mentality, Byers complained that the policies of the NCAA were "biased against human nature and simple fairness."[4]

On the eve of the Second World War, intercollegiate athletics remained firmly under the control of individual schools and, in some instances, conferences. The guiding principle was "home rule." This meant that each institution was responsible for supervising itself in the matters of recruitment, academic eligibility, and financial aid. The NCAA had no significant enforcement powers and was little more than a national clearinghouse that established game rules. In 1940, its largest source of income was a $10,000 profit made on a modest eight-team national basketball tournament. Its second source of income was the annual dues of $25 paid by each institutional member, which numbered about 250.

During the 1930s, big-time football found itself on the defensive. The echoes of the Carnegie Report resonated, and several motion pictures presented football in an unfavorable light. Influential journalists – including John Tunis, Sol Metzger, Francis Wallace, and Paul Gallico – published critical articles in popular magazines. For example, Gallico wrote in 1939 that college football was "one of the last strongholds of genuine old-fashioned hypocrisy … the leader in the field of double-dealing, deception, sham, cant, humbug, and organized hypocrisy."[5]

The Sanity Code Is Scuttled

Between 1939 and 1948, NCAA membership conducted an ongoing discussion about the role of intercollegiate athletics and the policies under which it should exist. As a result, in 1948, the Sanity Code was adopted. Under the Code, the NCAA recognized the right of member institutions to provide full tuition (but no living expenses) to athletes, but *only if* they met the same academic standards required of other students and *only if* financial need existed. Athletes could hold legitimate jobs, on or off campus, to pay for living expenses. The NCAA created a small enforcement committee with the power to investigate violations and impose sanctions, including expulsion.[6]

Within a year the NCAA found itself in crisis. Many institutions complained long and loud about the Code, contending that their football programs would be devastated. Southern schools were especially vocal, arguing that many athletes came from impoverished backgrounds, did not qualify for academic scholarships, and could not attend college without athletic grants. Several institutions defied the new policy by openly granting what amounted to scholarships for athletic ability. NCAA officials responded by announcing that seven schools were in violation of the Sanity Code and recommended expulsion. Most were members of the Southern Conference: Virginia, Virginia Military Institute, Virginia Polytechnic Institute, the University of Maryland, and the Citadel. In addition, Boston College and Villanova were placed on the list of the "Sinful Seven." Faced with the possibility of the breakup of the association, the NCAA governing body ingloriously retreated. At its national convention in 1950, a motion to expel the seven institutions failed to receive a two-thirds majority, although more than one-half of the members voted in favor. The Sanity Code was effectively scuttled.

In 1952, the NCAA annual convention changed course and voted to permit scholarships based solely on athletic ability, deleting academic achievement or financial need as a requirement for granting an athlete financial aid. Under its first full-time executive director, former Big Ten associate commissioner Walter Byers, the NCAA adopted an "Official Interpretation" that allowed each institution to provide an athlete with educational expenses covering tuition and fees, books, room and board, and $15 a month for incidental living expenses. Byers instructed all members that they should refer to the individuals receiving the so-called "full-ride" athletic scholarship as "student-athletes."[7]

Creation of a Cartel

Under Byers's leadership, the NCAA was transformed from a weak, coordinating body with limited powers into a powerful economic cartel. This transformation began, not surprisingly, during a time of crisis. Just as the shock of the basketball points-shaving scandals of 1951 were receding from the headlines, a series of academic fraud cases took their place in the same year, beginning with the expulsion of nearly half the high-ranked West Point football team for academic cheating. It was subsequently revealed that officials at William and Mary College, which had aspirations of becoming a major football power, had engaged in massive fraud that included forged high school transcripts, coaches giving grades of "A" to players for physical education courses they did not attend, and payment for non-existent campus jobs. In 1953, Michigan State, recently admitted to the Big Ten, was hit by revelations that it made an estimated $50,000 of illegal payments to football players. On the West Coast, the Pacific Coast Conference simultaneously placed four of its eight members – California, UCLA, Southern California, and Washington – on probation for recruiting violations; each institution was using booster donations to pay football players. This flurry of negative publicity fueled a call for the NCAA to create a full-time rules enforcement division.[8]

The NCAA had demonstrated its power to discipline a member institution in 1952. Byers and his executive committee worked behind the scenes with the Southeastern Conference to force the University of Kentucky to cancel its 1952–3 basketball season because of player involvement with gamblers. Byers said that the punishment dealt to Kentucky "gave a new and needed legitimacy to the NCAA's fledgling effort to police big-time college sports." Big Ten Commissioner Wayne Duke concurred: "The Kentucky action just indelibly stamped on the public that the NCAA meant business. It was first thing out of the box … and it gave the NCAA clout."[9]

At the same time, the NCAA assumed control of the televising of *all* college football games. According to historian Ronald A. Smith, the NCAA's bold move put it "on its way toward national control."[10] The plan was to permit the national telecast of one game per week, with a set of regional games being offered about once a month. The University of Pennsylvania, with a three-year $850,000 contract in hand with the DuMont Network, was not about to give up its television income without a fight, assuming that its position would be supported in federal court. The NCAA responded by declaring Penn a member "not in good standing" and threatened expulsion; University President Harold Stassen considered a lawsuit alleging violations of antitrust laws, but when President Theodore Hesburgh of Notre Dame decided against a similar action, Stassen acquiesced. Within a short time the

Quakers fell from their lofty perch as a national power and became a member of the newly created Ivy League that had spurned any pretensions about playing big-time football.

The NCAA received $1.25 million in 1955 from its television contract. That figure rose to $3 million in 1960. The NCAA's enforcement division learned that a threat to exclude an institution from appearances on television was a powerful club by which to keep wayward institutions in line. The new leadership of the NCAA now wielded real authority. It was well on the way to becoming a powerful cartel operating a rapidly growing economic juggernaut.

Emphasis and De-Emphasis

Although much of public scrutiny was directed at major college basketball and football, in fact the NCAA was becoming a diverse organization that embraced a wide variety of missions. The great majority of the members of the NCAA were small institutions that fielded a variety of teams with no pretensions of athletic grandeur. In 1973, the NCAA created a three-tiered grouping of schools. Division III contained several hundred small colleges that offered no athletic scholarships, Division II schools offered a restricted number of athletic grants-in-aid, and only Division I schools – the so-called big-time programs – were permitted to provide "full-ride" grants-in-aid. In 1978 a category for football only was created within Division I, with the designation of a Division I-AA that permitted schools to fund a maximum of 65 scholarships and compete in a 16-team playoff to determine the national championship.

The primary focus of intercollegiate athletics was on big-time football. The cost of operating a Division I football program was very high, and as a consequence, by 1960 more than 60 institutions had either dropped the sport altogether or opted to slash budgets and play a modest schedule. The flurry of canceled programs by such once-prominent football institutions as Carnegie Tech, Washington University, and Western Reserve was reason for concern among football enthusiasts. A large number of private urban Catholic universities were among those leading this movement. The University of San Francisco stunned the football world when it dropped the sport on the heels of an undefeated, untied, 10th-ranked season in 1951. The winning season had also produced a huge deficit. The most prominent university to drop football during this period was Georgetown University, which in the late 1930s had won 43 consecutive games. Its president cited football's lack of educational value in an article in the *Saturday Evening Post*, commenting that the sport provided nothing beneficial for the academic mission of the university. Other Catholic institutions followed suit, among them St Bonaventure, Duquesne, Villanova, Fordham, Detroit, Xavier (of Cincinnati), and Marquette.

The most significant change in football occurred ironically on the campuses where the sport had originated. One-time football giants Yale, Princeton, and Harvard decided to end any pretensions of competing for national football honors. These private institutions had long resisted granting control over their campus programs to an athletic conference. In 1945, eight elite Eastern institutions signed the first Ivy Group Accord, which emphasized unsubsidized football and the maintenance of high academic standards for athletes.

Between 1952 and 1956, the Ivy Group formalized itself into the Ivy League and adopted policies aimed directly at eliminating the excesses of big-time football. The League's membership included Princeton, Columbia, Yale, Dartmouth, Harvard, Brown, Cornell, and Pennsylvania. For starters, the new league banned spring practice. Off-campus recruiting was sharply curtailed and the practice of boosters paying for an athlete's college expenses was eliminated. Special admission policies for athletes were abolished. So too were postseason bowl game appearances, training tables, financial subsidies to athletes (although they could compete for academic scholarships), athletic slush funds, cushy on-campus jobs, and clinics for high school coaches (another recruiting subterfuge). Beyond doubt, the Ivy League schools took the position that they no longer had any interest in seeking national football fame. The storied days of national championships were history.

Although many alumni protested, the eight Ivy League schools had made the critical determination that national football honors were not worth the costs. Athletic programs were now intended to be "independent of won–loss or competitive record" by "approaching athletics as a key part of the student's regular undergraduate experience." Ivy League football teams compete at the Championship Subdivision level (but do not participate in the national playoffs) while the other teams compete in Division I-A. Upon occasion, its basketball champions have won NCAA tournament games, with Princeton in 1965 and Pennsylvania in 1979 reaching the Final Four. The Ivy League has remained an eight-school operation, and today supports competition in more than 30 separate sports for men and women, with many teams excelling and winning national championships in lacrosse, rowing, swimming, tennis, squash, and handball. The Ivy League also prides itself on its "rigorous academic standards" that have routinely produced the highest graduation rates of any athletic conference in the country. As other Division I-A programs opted for a professional model designed to enhance commercial opportunities, the Ivy League became a lonely beacon adhering to values that college administrators and coaches had long talked about but never quite got around to supporting.

Woody and the Bear

When the Sanity Code was eliminated and financial aid for athletic performance given explicit approval, those schools pursuing big-time football established a commercial model for intercollegiate athletics. Over the years, the big-time football schools exerted their power to move the major conferences farther and farther away from the amateur ideal, leaving the Ivy League increasingly isolated as an anomaly, a curious island of integrity in a rising sea of rampant commercialism. With football producing the bulk of sports revenue, head football coaches were able to build their power and influence by courting influential boosters, often running effective power plays during campus budget discussions. Between 1955 and 1965, restrictions on substitutions were removed and an era of free substitution was created. Players no longer played "both ways" but instead focused on refining their skills for either an offensive or a defensive position. Free substitution also led to the creation of "specialists" such as punter, place kicker, and kickoff and punt returner. Where squads once consisted of 50 players, coaches now assembled squads twice as large. Free substitution produced a much more exciting type of game, but it required large increases in football budgets. Coaches signed 30 to 40 new players to grants-in-aid each recruiting season, and the size of travel squads increased from 35 to more than 60.

Time and again, the NCAA acceded to the demands of coaches. In 1972, the NCAA membership voted to permit freshmen to play, a major policy change that most academics deplored because they believed it essential for freshmen to have an opportunity to adjust to college life without having to compete in games. At the same time, the "red shirt" policy was approved whereby an athlete could complete his four years of eligibility over a five-year period. This meant that most football coaches held freshmen out of competition but required them to practice regularly while their bodies added bulk and muscle and they became acclimated to campus life. In 1973, the NCAA annual convention made a major policy change that greatly enhanced the power of the coach when it voted to reduce grants-in-aid from a four-year commitment to just one year. This meant that an athlete who was not playing at an acceptable level could be dropped from scholarship. This change was the result of coaches and administrators wanting to be able to place greater demands upon athletes, but as Michael Oriard observes, the policy was also intended to control behavior following an era in which some athletes had engaged in controversial protests against discriminatory campus racial polices and the war in Vietnam. That same year, the NCAA lowered eligibility requirements for a grant-in-aid to the point that nearly any high school graduate could meet minimum standards.[11]

Well-paid coaches were expected to produce winning teams and annual trips to postseason bowl games. They responded by generating what became known as the "arms race," a never-ending quest for higher recruiting and operating budgets, larger coaching and support staffs, construction of new training facilities and athletic dormitories, and increased salaries and related "perks." The argument for these enhancements, strongly endorsed by powerful political friends and influential boosters, was that football paid the cost of "non-revenue" sports, and they were necessary to keep pace with opponents who were also engaged in program enhancement. In reality, most football programs actually lost money each year and required subsidies from other university sources. Economists who have attempted to make sense of athletic budgets confess that there is no way to determine actual bottom lines. Economist Andrew Zimbalist has examined the issue extensively and concludes that only a very few major athletic departments break even. To balance their budgets, in cooperation with compliant university administrators, athletic directors shift costs to other university budget lines, tap into campus maintenance budgets to maintain facilities, and offload salaries to instructional and administrative budgets. Long-time critic Murray Sperber has gone so far as to argue that the deficits created by athletic programs have negatively impacted academic programs because of stealth transfers of funds from instructional budgets to cover athletic department deficits. Multimillion-dollar athletic programs, he points out, have been able to shield themselves from the Internal Revenue Service by claiming to be part of a non-profit university.[12]

Establishing the template for the major football program as a commercial enterprise were two men who dominated the game from the 1950s until the late 1970s, Wayne Woodrow "Woody" Hayes and Paul "Bear" Bryant. Their programs set the standard that competing schools tried to replicate. The two men became the most popular men in their respective states, buoyed by winning seasons, conference championships, frequent bowl appearances, and multiple national titles.

The 43-year college coaching career of Woody Hayes spanned a time of rapid growth and change in college football. A 1935 graduate of Denison University, Hayes first coached in Ohio high schools, taught social studies, and served in the US Navy during the Second World War. When he returned from the South Pacific in 1946, Hayes assumed the head coaching position at his alma mater, and then moved on to Miami University in Oxford, Ohio in 1949. After producing a 10–1 record and a Salad Bowl upset win over Arizona State in 1950, Hayes was selected as head coach at Ohio State to replace Wes Fesler, who had compiled three consecutive winning seasons, a Big Ten championship, and a Rose Bowl victory, but had committed the unforgivable sin of losing four consecutive times to archrival Michigan.[13]

Hayes was possessed of a fiery temper and was committed to a philosophy of football that emphasized dedication to a simple playbook based upon physical domination of the opponent. He had a knack for recruiting, and enjoyed the advantage of coaching the only big-time college team in talent-rich Ohio, where some 40,000 high school boys played each fall on 800 teams. A steady stream of skilled players onto the Columbus campus enabled him to field a nationally ranked team every season after his initial 4–3–1 debut. In 1954, the Buckeyes went undefeated and stomped Southern California in the Rose Bowl, producing Ohio State's second national championship. He won another national title in 1957 and had become the most popular man in the state. His teams became famous for his "three yards and a cloud of dust" offense, in which powerful running backs ran off-tackle behind massive offensive linemen. He became well known for his disdain for the forward pass, stating that "three things can happen when you pass, and two of them are bad" – an incomplete pass or an interception.

Conservative and outspoken in his politics as well as his coaching, Hayes became a confidant of Republican governors and senators. Buckeye fans admired his knowledge of military history, appreciated his inability to accept defeat graciously, and rationalized his temperamental outbursts during game. On autumn Saturday afternoons his teams played before 90,000 scarlet-clad fans in the famed "horseshoe" Ohio Stadium while millions listened in on a statewide radio network. Hayes became the epitome of the controlling coach. He prowled the sidelines in a state of near-constant fury during games, often smashing equipment, turning his rage equally on referees and his own players. His practices became legendary for their ferocity and he drove his coaching staff to work long hours. Feeding the Buckeye football juggernaut was a statewide network of boosters and alumni that gave him entrée to the elite high school players in the state.

For more than a century, the Ohio State–University of Michigan rivalry has been one of the most intense in all of college football. Representing neighboring Midwestern states, the two universities first played in 1897. When Ohio State joined the Western Conference (later renamed the Big Ten) in 1912, the rivalry intensified. Coaches at both schools ultimately kept or lost their jobs based on their record against their rival. Although Hayes lost his first Michigan game, he proceeded to win 11 of the next 15 games, earning the affection of Buckeye fans.

The rivalry grew white-hot in 1969 when Glenn "Bo" Schembechler stunned Hayes by accepting the Wolverines' head coaching position. Hayes viewed it as a personal betrayal by

one of his top students. Often called "Little Woody," Schembechler had played tackle for Hayes at Miami of Ohio, and served as Hayes's offensive-line coach from 1959 through 1963, at which time he returned to Miami as head coach. Schembechler was Hayes's equal when it came to emphasizing fundamental football strategies based upon hard-hitting blocking and tackling. He also exhibited the same inner drive as Hayes, but his sense of humor and humane outlook on life enabled him to become highly respected on the politically diverse and often rebellious Michigan campus. Hayes and Schembechler turned the rivalry into a personal no-holds-barred street fight that captivated the attention of the people of both states and became recognized as one of the most compelling college football rivalries of all time. The stakes were raised even higher when Schembechler invaded Ohio during recruiting season to pick off some of Ohio's top prospects. Hayes, however, disdained recruiting players from "that state up north" (he was famously known for refusing to utter the word "Michigan"). Nearly one-third of Schembechler's squads comprised Ohio high school graduates, adding additional spice to the November game. During the 10 years that these two men competed against each other, the Big Ten Conference became known as the "Big Two and the Little Eight," because either Michigan or Ohio State won the conference championship each year.[14]

Figure 11.1 Bo Schembechler (left) played for Woody Hayes (right) at Miami of Ohio before serving a coaching apprenticeship with him at Ohio State. They exchange greetings before their first confrontation as head coaches at rival schools in 1969. Michigan upset the top-ranked Buckeyes, a team Hayes later said was the best of his 28-year career at Ohio State. These friendly rivals set the standard for big-time college football during the 1960s and 1970s. *AP/Press Association Images*

Hayes's frequent, well-publicized public eruptions on the sidelines were an embarrassment to the university – breaking yardstick markers, pushing cameras into the face of photographers, angrily confronting officials at midfield – but university administrators took no action. Winning, the old saying goes, covers a multitude of sins. It was thus fitting that Hayes's famous temper led to a premature end to his coaching career. Near the end of a close game in the 1978 Gator Bowl against Clemson, with the Buckeyes marching to take the lead, Tigers linebacker Charlie Bauman picked off an errant Ohio State pass in front of the Ohio bench, ensuring Clemson's victory. As Bauman ran out of bounds, Hayes slugged him in the face, an instinctive act that television cameras picked up and showed repeatedly on instant replay. Such an egregious act could not go unpunished, even if committed by the legendary Woody Hayes. The next day, he was fired, bringing an abrupt end to his 28-year career at Ohio State. His well-oiled football machine had produced a record of 205–61–10, including 13 Big Ten and five national championships.

If Woody Hayes was idolized in Ohio, his many peccadilloes notwithstanding, Paul "Bear" Bryant was immortalized in Alabama. More than two decades after he retired, head coaches of the Crimson Tide were still compared to the Bear – and found wanting. Born the 11th of 12 children to a poor sharecropping family in Arkansas, at the age of 13 young Paul gained his nickname when he accepted a challenge to wrestle a live bear at a carnival for one dollar. Bryant escaped from rural poverty in the midst of the Great Depression when he accepted a football scholarship to attend the University of Alabama. He played end opposite one of the greatest pass receivers ever to play the game, Don Hutson. In 1945, Bryant became head coach at Maryland, but left for the University of Kentucky the following season after losing a disagreement over his stringent team discipline policies with the university president. His UK teams compiled a 60–23–5 record at a school that had never enjoyed much gridiron success. Bryant, however, realized that basketball would remain king in Bluegrass Country, and moved on to Texas A&M. Before the first season in 1954, he famously took his squad to remote Junction, Texas, where he conducted a "brutal boot camp" for 10 days in searing heat to establish himself as the man in charge. Sixty players quit the team before it returned to College Station, and the depleted Aggies won but one game that season. But Bryant had put his personal stamp on the program and top recruits flooded to College Station. In 1956, the Aggies won the Southwest Conference championship with a 9–1 record.[15]

In 1957, Bryant returned to his alma mater to resuscitate a Crimson Tide program that had fallen on hard times. His initial salary as coach and athletic director was an astronomical $57,000. Alabama might have been a financially hard-pressed university with bottom-tier faculty salaries, but finding booster support to secure the services of a winning football coach was no problem. Bryant's teams more than satisfied his financial backers. His first team won five games, one more victory than had been won in the three previous seasons, and in 1959, his team went 7–2–2 and ranked 10th in the nation. That team went to a bowl game, beginning a 24-year string of consecutive postseason appearances. His first winning season at Alabama was only the prelude to a record-setting run. Under Bryant, his teams won six national championships between 1961 and 1979. Utilizing the support of a large and generous group of alumni, Bryant had the resources to build state-of-the-art facilities that helped him out-recruit other Southeastern Conference schools, in-state rival Auburn in particular. His squads included 125 players on grants-in-aid and many other "walk-on" hopefuls. His enormous coaching staff included 17 full-time assistants, supplemented by a cadre of graduate assistants and other support personnel.

In 1963, his career was threatened when the *Saturday Evening Post* published an article alleging that he had conspired with the athletic director at the University of Georgia to obtain information about the Bulldogs team prior to the season-opening game. According to the convoluted story, Georgia athletic director Wally Butts had been removed from his head football coaching position against his will, and in retaliation sought to sabotage the coach who had replaced him. The alleged scheme that the *Post* reported said Butts, deeply in debt and facing a forced retirement, sought to assure that the Crimson Tide would cover the points spread of 17 in order to make a killing on a bet with a Chicago bookie. The evidence hinged upon allegations made by an Atlanta insurance agent who claimed that while making a long-distance telephone call he was somehow accidentally patched into a conversation between Butts and Bryant in which he listened for 15 minutes while they discussed the Bulldogs' game plan and secret plays. Both Butts and Bryant angrily denied these sensational allegations and sued the magazine. The allegations were not proven in an Atlanta federal courtroom and the *Post* was ordered to pay Butts over $3 million in damages, later reduced to $460,000. Bryant was a star witness against the magazine. Shortly thereafter Bryant and the *Post* settled out of court for $300,000. Afterward, some skeptics nonetheless maintained that the *Post* was onto something sinister, but the preponderance of evidence presented at trial indicated that the *Post*'s editors had breached the ethics of journalism.[16]

Although this bizarre episode for a time threatened Bryant's career, it was soon forgotten as the Bear continued his winning ways. Bryant had long quietly chafed under the "white-only" gentlemen's agreement that precluded the recruitment of black players. His defenders say that because Bryant was coaching in a state university when segregationist George C. Wallace was governor, he had to bide his time. When desegregation began at Southeastern Conference schools, however, he aggressively recruited African American players. By 1973, his squad numbered 40 percent African American players. When Bryant retired after the 1982 season, he had won six national championships and 13 Southeastern Conference titles, and amassed a career record of 323–85–17 that broke Amos Alonzo Stagg's all-time winning record. He had been named national Coach of the Year three times by Associated Press. After his death in 1983, the AP's Coach of the Year award was named in his honor. The bizarre story of the alleged conspiracy to obtain a rival team's secrets had long since been forgotten, and Bryant's harsh treatment of his Texas A&M players in 1954 became the subject of a popular movie in 2002 that does not back away from revealing the brutal practices in 100 degree temperatures that reduced a squad of 100 to just 35 players.

Criticism of Major College Sports

In 1990, Murray Sperber published *College Sports, Inc.*, a book that the NCAA and big-time college sports departments wished had never been written. Marshaling a vast array of data to support his view that the NCAA had become a powerful, multibillion-dollar cartel, and that athletic departments had become essentially for-profit economic enterprises, the

Indiana University professor painted a picture of overpaid coaches and athletic directors, of exploited athletes who spent little time in the library or classroom, of timid college presidents reluctant to challenge boosters, donors, and trustees. In particular, he contended that even the most successful athletic programs were "awash in a sea of red ink" and routinely found ways to subvert money from instructional budgets to bail out excessive spending by athletic departments. A decade later, Sperber returned to the attack in *Beer and Circus*, in which he accused senior campus administrators of abandoning their responsibilities by refusing to corral profligate athletic programs.[17] Sperber's critique never connected with the general public or sports fans whose only interests were entertainment and rooting for their favorite teams. Throughout Sperber's informed and revealing books, the words "corruption," "fraud," and "hypocrisy" resonate. During the Watergate scandal of the early 1970s, Indiana University basketball coach Bob Knight commented, "When they get to the bottom of Watergate, they'll find a basketball coach." He spoke with a self-serving ironic bite, of course, but gave expression to the fact that his profession had more than its share of serious ethical lapses. During the half-century that the NCAA has maintained its enforcement division, at any time programs at about 20 percent of Division I institutions were either on probation or under investigation. Over the years, a high percentage of the most prominent big-time colleges were exposed for major violations, many of them so flagrant as to defy the imagination. The reason for this was quite simple: it takes outstanding (so-called "blue-chip") athletes to win championships. In addressing the issue of the importance of recruiting, back in 1951 the head football coach at Wake Forest, Douglas "Peahead" Walker, laconically noted, "You don't go bear hunting with a switch." The successful football coach at Iowa, Forest Evashevski, told a reporter in 1957 that the only objective in college football was "to go out and win." He confessed, "At most colleges the pressure is on the coach from the president on down. The coach enters into a tacit understanding with the president that he will recruit good ball players by any means short of larceny. And if the coach doesn't come through with good recruiting, out he goes."[18]

According to many critics, the greatest fraud in the entire college sports enterprise has been the lip service given to "academics." Such commitment is *de rigueur* during the interview process when a new coach is hired and during the after-dinner speeches coaches deliver to alumni and boosters. But coaches know that the graduation rates of their players are of minor consideration in the grand scheme of things. Players have long been counseled into "snap" courses to maintain eligibility and are required to put in long hours at practice that leave them too exhausted to do serious study. Expanded schedules and postseason games mean they miss more classes than ever. A coach's priority has to be on winning, and winning consistently. Coaches know that athletic directors have always been ready to change coaches if the number of losses mounts, and ticket sales fall, and postseason game appearances do not bring in additional revenue. As the years went by, and the revenue driven by television contracts, ticket sales, booster donations, and postseason bowl or tournament invitations got ever larger, the pressures upon big-time coaches to produce winning teams got ever greater.

The recruitment of athletes has always been a major source of unethical practices. Many coaches have said in unguarded moments that they find the system degrading and humiliating. But successful recruiting is essential to a winning program. The history of college

Figure 11.2 Between 1964 and 1975 UCLA won 10 NCAA championships under the coaching of John Wooden. One of the many outstanding players who helped set this record was 7' 2" center Lew Alcindor, shown dunking against Georgia Tech in 1967. Before his senior year, Alcindor announced his Muslim faith and changed his name to Kareem Abdul-Jabbar. He later played 19 seasons in the NBA with the Milwaukee Bucks and Los Angeles Lakers, setting scoring and rebounding records while earning six Most Valuable Player awards. *Image © Bettmann/Corbis*

recruiting is filled with stories that make a mockery of the dedication to educational objectives and concern for the "student-athlete." Over the years, a once-slender NCAA manual on rules enforcement grew to more than 500 pages as the organization struggled to keep pace with the innovative ways recruiters found around the rules. Many a faculty representative to the NCAA, charged with overseeing rules compliance on each member campus, has complained that the rules became so complex that some violations, however "minor" they might be, are almost inevitable. Coaches have long complained that enforcement is highly selective and that the established winning programs are given a free pass, a charge that NCAA executives have denied emphatically.[19] Because the NCAA is a private entity, its enforcement officials lack the power to subpoena witnesses and must rely on individuals voluntarily testifying. Many investigations have fizzled due to a lack of willing witnesses. Even when it was able to prove violations, the punishment meted out seems not to have had its intended deterrent effect. Coaches caught with major recruiting violations often moved on to other colleges or to the professional ranks and escaped punishment, leaving their former employer to bear the burden of NCAA sanctions. Typical punishments the NCAA imposed on a wayward program proved insufficient to stop cheating: reducing the number of scholarships, banning postseason games, limiting recruiting, forfeiting opportunities to appear on television. But as revelations of one scandal after another were announced, it seemed that risking an NCAA investigation was the price for doing business.

By 1985, the frustration – if not desperation – of NCAA officials with their inability to curb rules transgressions led the organization to hold an "integrity convention." That convention authorized a get-tough policy that included the power to close down a program if it repeatedly engaged in improper conduct. The new penalty called for the suspension of a program for two years if a college administration did not exert proper "institutional control" over its athletic program and if a consistent pattern of repeat offenses was demonstrated.

It did not take long for the death penalty to be invoked. NCAA investigators uncovered a massive scam at perennial national football powerhouse Southern Methodist University. Coaches had enticed recruits with cash and other gifts, and once they arrived on campus they were put on an illicit "payroll." These illegal payments were funded by wealthy alumni and boosters. The annual amount of the "payroll" had grown to an estimated $400,000 a year when the NCAA concluded its investigation in 1987. Not that the university had not been warned: its football program had been hit with probation in 1958, 1965, 1974, 1976, 1981, and 1985. It was also reported that boosters provided free apartments and automobiles. The crucial witness was a Pennsylvania high school recruit who was given $5,000 in return for his signature on a national letter of intent. Incredibly, the monthly payroll payments continued even after the institution was informed that an official NCAA investigation was under way. These payments were authorized by the chairman of SMU's board of trustees, William Clements. Apparently, Clements and other officials believed that, should they halt the illicit payments, angry players would tell all to NCAA investigators. That Clements had served Presidents Nixon and Ford as a deputy Secretary of Defense and had served as Governor of Texas (and was in the midst of launching another campaign for that office) underscores the extent to which prominent citizens might go in order to enjoy bragging rights from a winning football team.[20]

This church-affiliated university suffered greatly for the sins of its athletic program and boosters. SMU's governing board, including Governor Clements, was fired by the Council of Bishops. President L. Donald Shields resigned, citing health reasons, as did the recently hired football coach Bobby Collins and athletic director Bob Hitch, who had inherited the mess but was believed to have attempted to cover it up. The football program never regained its former stature, and the undefeated season of 1982 would be its last. Coach Ron Meyer, during whose tenure the payments had begun (although he adamantly says he was unaware of their existence), had departed in 1981 for the head coaching position of the New England Patriots and was unscathed by the scandal. After the program was reinstated, the Mustangs suffered through long losing seasons and did not return to a bowl game until a 7–5 record in the 2009 season produced an invitation to the Hawaii Bowl. The impact of the death penalty upon this once-dominant football power was so severe that it was compared to a "nuclear option" and never imposed again by the NCAA, although many observers believed that other out-of-control programs were richly deserving of the same punishment that was dropped on SMU.

The enforcement mechanism of the NCAA is predicated upon the anticipated cooperation of member institutions. It is based upon an informal set of policies and procedures that expects institutional leaders to cooperate once an investigation is begun and to accept the punishment that might be imposed. It is important to understand that when conducting investigations into allegations of misconduct, the NCAA does not have subpoena power and cannot compel individuals to testify. This raises an intriguing question: what happens when a member institution decides *not* to cooperate with the NCAA enforcement officers? What happens when a coach refuses to accept the dictates of the NCAA enforcement division? Or what is the outcome when he is supported in that defiant stance by the university president, the athletic director, boosters, and trustees, indeed by the entire power structure of a state? Can he thumb his nose at the enforcement officers and the NCAA and not pay the consequences? The long-running feud that lasted for almost three decades between the NCAA hierarchy and the very successful basketball coach Jerry Tarkanian is therefore most instructive.

Ever since he gained national attention at Long Beach State in the late 1960s, after compiling an enviable won–lost record at two California junior colleges, Tarkanian and the NCAA were on a collision course. Tarkanian followed a simple formula throughout his 40-year coaching career that saw him win 990 games (including his junior college teams) and have an unequaled winning record of 83 percent. He recruited top talent overlooked by other programs and molded them into championship teams. Tarkanian loved to play the role of "Father Flanagan," giving young men who faced social and economic obstacles an opportunity to escape their past. His willingness to take a chance on players passed over by other schools – high academic risks, unpolished but promising athletes – enhanced his reputation. Between 1968 and 1973, he turned a mediocre Long Beach State program into one that enjoyed national rankings and appearances in the 16-team NCAA tournament. He compiled a 122–20 record, and in the process attracted the attention of the NCAA, leading to 23 violation charges and two years of probation for Long Beach.[21]

By the time the penalties were handed down, however, Tarkanian had already departed for Nevada's recently opened state university in Las Vegas. Within a week after his appointment was announced, the NCAA announced that it was reopening a dormant investigation of the UNLV basketball program. To Tarkanian, this move was clear evidence that he had been singled out by executive director Walter Byers and director of enforcement David Berst. He believed that a comment he made in a Long Beach newspaper in 1973 had precipitated the investigations. In that article, he charged the NCAA with something that many coaches believed but wisely elected not to say publicly: the organization followed selective enforcement policies that protected the prestigious programs while punishing those which sought to reach a higher level. "It's a crime that Western Kentucky is placed on probation," he said. "The University of Kentucky basketball program breaks more rules in a day than Western Kentucky does in a year. The NCAA just doesn't want to take on the big boys."

UNLV officials readily admitted they were using basketball to achieve national visibility. Tarkanian delivered on his promises and turned the UNLV basketball team into a popular Las Vegas extravaganza. The "Runnin' Rebels" provided an exciting high-scoring machine that reached the Final Four of the NCAA tournament in 1976. That same spring, however, the NCAA levied new allegations about improprieties in the UNLV basketball program committed since Tarkanian's arrival. Instead of meekly accepting the informal justice system of the NCAA, however, UNLV and Tarkanian counterattacked, denying all charges. UNLV vice president Brock Dixon conducted an investigation and concluded that the evidence presented by David Berst was "clearly in doubt" and that it demonstrated a "standard of proof and due process" that was "inferior to what we might expect." Dixon told the press, "In almost every factual situation delineated by the NCAA, the university's own investigation has been able to find a substantial body of conflicting evidence."

Tarkanian complained that he was being judged by the same persons who brought the indictment and that the informal disciplinary procedures of the NCAA prevented him from confronting his accusers, thus denying him the right of due process. For the first time in its history, the NCAA's enforcement mechanism – essential to its control of college athletics – was being openly challenged. Economists who have studied the behavior of economic cartels have frequently noted that they do not tolerate contrarian behavior, and this was the case in 1977 when the NCAA hit UNLV with a ruling stipulating that Tarkanian be suspended for two years without pay. This was indeed an unprecedented penalty. Subsequent developments indicate that Tarkanian had plenty of reason to suspect that he was being singled out.

Tarkanian – carrying a nickname that could be interpreted many ways, "Tark the Shark" – responded just as he would as a coach when an opponent threatened to upset the Rebels. He went on attack with the legal and political equivalent of a full-court press, suing the NCAA, launching a media backlash through his journalist friends in Las Vegas, denouncing the NCAA for attacking him with "lies, distortions, and half truths" in a "Star Chamber" environment. He rallied support from the casino monarchs of Las Vegas and powerful Nevada politicians. The Nevada Board of Regents and the UNLV administration joined in his defense. A flurry of lawsuits and legal motions were filed in Nevada courts that stopped the suspension in its tracks, and the litigation that ensued extended for nearly 20 years. To say that the hierarchy of the NCAA was perturbed by his response is an understatement. It was stunned by the enraged response coming from Nevada.

In the meantime, Tarkanian's Runnin' Rebels were dominating the Big West Conference, enjoying high national rankings and – much to the dismay of Berst and Byers – appearing every year in the NCAA postseason tournament, making it to the Final Four in 1987, and winning the championship in 1991 with an unprecedented 30-point blowout victory over Duke in the championship game. The following year, the Rebels went undefeated

throughout the regular season, but lost to Duke in an upset in the semifinals of the Final Four. Much to the consternation of NCAA executives, Tarkanian never served his two-year suspension.

Just as Tarkanian's teams crested atop college basketball, his empire began to crumble. He received strong criticism, even in Las Vegas, when it was revealed that he had gone into a California medium-security prison to sign one recruit to a letter of intent, and when one of his prize junior college recruits, Lloyd Daniels, whose academic record was suspect, was nabbed by an undercover police team for purchasing drugs. In June 1991, the *Las Vegas Review-Journal* published front-page pictures of three members of the national championship team sitting in a hot tub drinking beer at the posh Las Vegas home of a notorious sports gambler. Richard "The Fixer" Perry had been convicted of fixing harness races in Massachusetts and bribing Boston College basketball players to shave points.

By this time, Tarkanian had become engaged in a power struggle with UNLV president Robert Maxson, who feared that the renegade image of the Runnin' Rebels was undercutting his efforts to upgrade the academic reputation of UNLV. Tarkanian's popularity within the Las Vegas community began to slide. When he resigned under pressure shortly thereafter, the community was bitterly divided. Maxson himself found it necessary to resign in the wake of the angry

Figure 11.3   Bob Knight coached basketball at Indiana from 1971 to 2000, winning eleven Big Ten and three NCAA championships. Knight was widely praised for his teams' disciplined play and academic success, but his strong personality and unpredictable and controversial tactics stimulated widespread criticism. Known as "The General" for his demanding coaching style, Knight is seen here berating a player during a game in 1987. He finished his turbulent career at Texas Tech and retired in 2008 with 902 victories, a career record for any college coach.
Image © Bettmann/Corbis

reaction of Rebel boosters, but ironically soon thereafter accepted the presidency of Long Beach State where Tarkanian had once coached.

Tarkanian moved on to a brief 20-game coaching career in the NBA with the Dallas Mavericks and then returned to his alma mater, Fresno State. Between 1995 and 2002, he continued his winning ways, but some players were caught up in various scrapes with law enforcement that further clouded his reputation. Charges that gamblers influenced the outcome of some Bulldogs games were leveled at the program, but never proven. In 1998, Tarkanian won perhaps the greatest victory in his coaching career when the NCAA decided to settle without admission of guilt a lawsuit that Tarkanian had brought against the organization. The settlement payment of $2.5 million was the first in the NCAA's history and was viewed by many observers as evidence that Tarkanian had been unfairly persecuted. "They've never paid money to anybody [before]," he told the press, "I feel vindicated. They beat the hell out of me for twenty-five years."[22]

Nonetheless, the rebellious image of "Tark the Shark" continued to cloud Tarkanian's image even after he had retired. Perhaps that explains why he was never elected into the Basketball Hall of Fame, despite his lofty won–lost record and many championships that spanned four decades of college coaching.

Revenue vs Reform: An Unresolved Contradiction

Leaders of big-time college sports have wrestled with an unresolved contradiction ever since football became a national phenomenon in the 1890s: is the purpose of intercollegiate sports to provide an educational experience or is it a commercial venture? Coaches and athletic administrators, echoed by college presidents, boards of trustees, and the hierarchy of the NCAA, have insisted that they are engaged in an educational exercise. But in fact, these individuals have often made major policy decisions with the sole intent of increasing revenue. Caught in the middle have been the "student-athletes" who have generated millions of dollars of revenue with their efforts on field and court but have received only educational benefits in return.

The professional/commercial model of intercollegiate athletes was evident as early as the 1890s when college administrators turned football from an extracurricular activity into a money-making enterprise: creating athletic departments, hiring professional coaches, recruiting skilled athletes, and constructing large stadiums. By the end of the 1920s the commercial model was fully established. However, administrators continued to embrace the concept of amateurism, refusing to pay athletes while simultaneously selling tickets to their performances. They even stoutly maintained that financial aid given to athletes was not in fact payment for their athletic skills. A long-simmering conflict during the 1930s and 1940s was waged between Southern schools that wanted to provide athletes with financial aid based solely upon their athletic abilities, and institutions throughout the rest of the nation that insisted such a practice would undercut the amateur model. That debate ended when the NCAA authorized the awarding of financial aid solely on the basis of athletic ability. College athletics had indeed become a commercial enterprise. The NCAA insisted, however, that the scholarships be four-year grants designed to enable "student-athletes" to receive an education; such a scholarship recipient could, in fact, quit the team and the institution was required to honor the scholarship for the full four years. This requirement created a façade of academic integrity behind which the NCAA operated, although its policy on minimum academic eligibility was set at an embarrassingly low C–/D+ predictability for a freshman to receive financial aid.

Even that thin veneer of respectability disappeared in 1973 when the eligibility for a freshman athlete was changed to require only a C– high school average no matter what courses had been taken. Without fanfare, the NCAA also ended the four-year scholarship commitment and replaced it with a one-year grant renewable at the discretion of the athletic department. Some coaches apparently wanted this change in order to control the off-field behavior of athletes who had participated in civil rights and political protests, but others simply wanted the right to run off underperforming athletes. The fiction that financial aid to athletes was strictly to support academics had ended. Michael Oriard concludes that the new policies had "redefined student-athletes as athlete-students."[23] During the 1980s, critics bombarded university leaders over the poor academic performance of male athletes, football and basketball squads in particular. Thus in 1986, the NCAA approved minimal standards for freshmen eligibility with passage of Proposition 48, but the standards agreed upon were so low that they were ridiculed by knowledgeable observers. Nonetheless, Proposition 48 was criticized by many coaches and athletic administrators determined on protecting the status quo for discriminating against minorities.

Much of college athletics' contemporary problems can be traced to the huge amounts of money available from the sale of television rights for football and basketball. This began innocently enough in the early 1950s when the NCAA secured control of football television revenues. As the revenue stream increased with the passing of the years, the great majority of NCAA member institutions were pleased with the arrangement because they received a large percentage of monies. In 1968, the NCAA signed its first national contract for televising the national basketball tournament – a $2 million deal with NBC. The popularity of this event grew steadily during the 1970s, climaxing with the 1979 championship game between Michigan State and Indiana State, which featured two of the most exciting players of the century, Earvin "Magic" Johnson and Larry Bird. The tournament, now labeled "March Madness," filled a void in the annual sports calendar, setting off a nationwide gambling frenzy based on "bracket" predictions and pools conducted in offices and sports bars. In 1985, the NCAA expanded the field from 32 to 64 teams (and to 68 in 2011), doubling the number of games to be televised. The men's basketball tournament became a cash cow for the NCAA, funding over 80 percent of its total operations. In 1989, CBS signed a seven-year $1 billion contract for the broadcast rights, and in 2002 the network agreed to an 11-year $6.2 billion deal.

The basketball windfall came at a propitious time because in 1984 the NCAA lost control of its football television monopoly. When the NCAA established its absolute control in the early 1950s, Notre Dame had reluctantly gone along with the plan. But Notre Dame's president, Father Theodore Hesburgh, believed that the program was "socialistic" and denied the Fighting Irish millions of dollars of additional revenue each season. In 1976, Hesburgh and like-minded university presidents formed the College Football Association (CFA) with the objective of wresting control of television revenues from the NCAA.[24]

Those efforts were rewarded when a lawsuit filed in federal court by the universities of Oklahoma and Georgia and supported by the CFA resulted in a ruling that the NCAA was in direct violation of antitrust laws by its "presumptuous seizure" and "commandeering" of television rights. Judge Juan Burciaga ruled that the NCAA's television policy and controls on member institutions were "unreasonable, naked restraints on competition" that were motivated by "rank greed" and "a lust for power." Judge Burciaga's sharply worded decision made it clear that the NCAA was not the educational association it claimed to be, but rather a commercial entity operating in the manner of a powerful cartel by fixing prices, restricting access, and restraining the free flow of commerce.[25] In 1984, the US Supreme Court upheld the decision by a 7–2 vote. The irony that an "amateur" sport had been ruled in violation of antitrust laws was lost on most sports fans. The NCAA, however, had suffered a major setback and the television networks were soon awash with college football games. Thus the NCAA turned toward basketball television rights as its primary source of income.

Unlike all other sports sponsored by the NCAA, only its top football echelon of some 120 institutions (now called the Football Bowl Championship Division) did not have a national championship playoff system. It was the only sport that had its "national champion" determined by the vote of coaches and/or journalists in two separate polls. This sometimes created confusion, with two different teams being elected the national champion at season's end. On the surface, resistance to a playoff seemed strange, especially when it was estimated that the television rights for a playoff would generate $100 million a year. The response given by university presidents for their refusal to create a playoff system was that it would adversely affect the academic welfare of student-athletes. That of course was nonsense, because the presidents had often supported policies that adversely affected the academic welfare of athletes. Advocates of a playoff pointedly observed that the NCAA sponsored 16-team playoffs for schools playing football at the Football Championship Subdivision (formerly I-AA) and Divisions II and III.

In reality, big-time football schools opposed a playoff for several reasons. Because most bowl games are held in warm-climate locations, over the years Southern and Southwestern schools benefited handsomely from the informal invitation process; close relationships developed between athletic directors, coaches, and bowl directors, and a playoff system would negatively impact many bowl games. Several bowls also were steeped in football tradition. The Big Ten and Pac-Ten had enjoyed their Rose Bowl rivalry since 1947 and were reluctant to abandon that tradition. Bowl executives, their own livelihoods on the line, became ardent lobbyists against a playoff system whenever the idea reached the NCAA Presidents' Council. The great majority of head coaches, already under enormous pressures to produce winning teams, did not want the additional stress of a playoff system wherein all but one coach would end the season with a loss. It would be much better to have an opportunity to win one of a myriad of bowl games. The national media, however, reflecting strong football fan sentiment, demanded that a national playoff system be established. This pressure eventually led in 1998 to the creation of the Bowl Championship Series (BCS) that sponsored four (later increased to five) bowl games. The BCS was organized outside the NCAA and was controlled by the commissioners of the six most prestigious football conferences – Big East, Big Ten, Atlantic Coast, Southeastern, Pac-Ten, and Big 12. Each conference champion was guaranteed a spot in one of the four BCS New Year's Day games.

Independent Notre Dame was assured a slot if the Irish were ranked among the top eight teams. The BCS negotiated network contracts that paid each participating team approximately $17 million (to be shared with other conference members); some 25 lesser bowls were also held that paid participating teams between $750,000 and $2.0 million. For several years, one of the four major bowls was designated to host the National Championship Game on a rotating basis with the two participants selected by a complicated computer-generated formula that included won–lost records, "strength of schedule," final national poll rankings, so-called "quality wins," and "power rankings." The six conference champions had to be included in the four games, and teams finishing second in their conference could also be selected. The BCS format held out the possibility that one non-BCS program could be selected from the five other Division I-A conferences – Mountain West, Mid-America, Sun Belt, USA, and Western Athletic – if they were ranked within the top 12 teams in the nation. Not surprisingly, in the first six years of operation no such selection occurred. Finally, after the 2004 season, the undefeated University of Utah from the Mountain West Conference was named to play in the Fiesta Bowl and easily defeated the University of Pittsburgh.

Much to the chagrin of the BCS leadership, the one game that most football fans identify today as the "greatest ever played" was the 2007 Fiesta Bowl, when undefeated but lightly regarded Boise State of the Western Athletic Conference upset heavily favored Oklahoma in a dramatic overtime game that saw a first-year head coach and his team outsmart and outplay the Sooners. After falling behind late in the game, the Broncos tied the game in the final seconds on a sensational "hook and ladder" play, and won in overtime thanks to another superbly executed gimmick play that caught the Sooners flatfooted.

The BCS system created a two-tiered pecking order within the ranks of the Football Bowl Subdivision that enabled 55 of the 120 I-A schools to control 70 percent of the lucrative postseason bowl revenues. The computer-generated ratings designed to select the top two teams for the national championship proved to be a source of great controversy when the computer spit out its final numbers. The two teams selected sometimes conflicted with national polls, thereby angering those whose teams were overlooked. Although the selections were determined by a previously adopted statistical model, the results revealed serious oversights on the part of the human beings who created the formula. Each year, the formula was revised to respond to the most recent glitches and criticisms, indicating that the entire concept had inherent flaws. As the BCS encountered continued criticism from many quarters, demands for some form of national playoff system for Division I-A (to being sponsored by the NCAA) were heard each year – demands BCS school presidents were determined to rebuff.

College Sports as Big Business

In 1989, the Knight Foundation funded an extensive examination of the state of big-time college athletics. The findings were reminiscent of those of the Carnegie Commission in 1929. So too were their impact on changing the culture of major college athletics: negligible. The commission's concerns were aptly expressed by *Time* magazine at the time of its creation: college sports constitutes "an obsession with winning and moneymaking that is pervading the noblest ideals of both sports and education in America." The Commission's report, issued in 1991, was replete with indignation and frustration over the debasement of higher education by athletic departments.[26] More than 50 percent of the Division I programs had been sanctioned or put on probation during the 1980s, and Southern Methodist had its football program shut down for two seasons. The news media produced a continuous barrage of negative publicity about tutors taking examinations and writing papers for athletes, avoidance of standardized admissions requirements, criminal acts committed by male athletes – often against women – illegal payments to players, unethical and even bizarre behavior by coaches, and embarrassingly low graduation rates (especially among football and men's basketball squads). A random survey of former and current professional football players indicated that one-third of them had received illicit payments while in college. Most significantly, they saw nothing wrong with that fact.

The commission identified the monies generated by television broadcasting contracts as the primary reason these relationships "moved colleges and universities into the entertainment business in a much bigger way" that attracted a primary viewing audience not associated with the campus or its alumni – "people who valued winning more than they did the universities' underlying purposes." Thus "the thrill of victory, sports as spectacle, sports for gambling – these were their lodestones." The solution rested not with the NCAA because it was a willing partner in maintaining the status quo, but with campus presidents who were "directed toward academic integrity, financial integrity, and independent certification."

A cursory examination of the names of the members of the Knight Commission, however, indicated that several of these reformers had been major players on their campuses in helping to create or at least to permit the existence of the problems they now decried. Their recommendations sought to shift some control of sports programs away but did not recommend reducing the size of the programs or returning to pure amateurism. Although written in compelling language, the report's recommendations, if fully implemented, would have done little to change the underlying assumptions or *modus operandi* of intercollegiate athletics. On the issue that critics of college athletics have frequently raised, that the athletes did not share in the vast pool of revenues they helped generate, the Knight Commission was strangely mute. Because of a lack of consensus among participants, the Commission also remained silent on the obvious issue of whether or not freshmen should be permitted to participate in games. As one critical book by several prominent economists concluded, "Until this is done, the rest of the so-called reform movement can be seen for what it is: a bunch of people shedding crocodile tears for the young men and women on the playing field."[27]

At the time the Knight Commission issued its initial report, Bo Schembechler, athletic director at the University of Michigan, derisively dismissed the report with the comment that while the recommendations would attract a great deal of initial attention, "by the turn of the century, things will return to their normal state. The hubbub will pass, as will the so-called reformers." His cynical comment was, of course, absolutely correct. When the Commission reassembled on its 10th anniversary in 2001 to assess its impact, it had to conclude that nothing had changed for the good, and that "the problems of big-time college sports have grown rather than diminished." Academic dishonesty had produced several new high-profile scandals. The amount of money being spent on athletics programs had greatly accelerated as institutions increased stadium seating capacities, added more seats and luxury boxes for big donors, built enormous basketball arenas and indoor football practice facilities, and sought to attract recruits with ever more lavish locker rooms, study areas, weight-training rooms, and athletic "halls of fame" that proclaimed the glories of past athletic triumphs – a sure stop during every recruit's visit to campus.[28]

Perhaps most egregious was the fact that salaries for high-profile coaches had continued to escalate. Some critics had always viewed comparatively high pay for college coaches relative to campus deans and senior faculty as a problem. In 1986, the average salary was reported in the neighborhood of $150,000, but in the ensuing years one prominent head coach's large raise would cause a massive ripple effect at other institutions who felt compelled to match that figure to keep their own coach from moving. In 1995, Bobby Bowden, riding the crest of a 1993 national championship and a string of winning seasons, received a $1 million contract from Florida State. That amount was soon doubled by rival University of Florida to reward Steve Spurrier for his winning ways and a 1996 national championship. By 2005, coaches in the Football Bowl Division were averaging $1.0 million and some premier coaches, such as Bob Stoops of Oklahoma, Joe Paterno of Penn State, Urban Meyer of Florida, and Pete Carroll of Southern California were reported to be making in excess of $3 million. The case of Nick Saban is instructive. He was hired away from Michigan State by Louisiana State in 1999 for a salary estimated to be about $1.3 million, more then doubling his income. After five successful seasons he left a $2.0 million salary for the head job of the professional Miami Dolphins for $5.0 million a year. After two losing seasons (15–17) and repeated assurances he was not moving, he accepted the head coaching position at Alabama for an estimated $3.5 million. By his third season in Tuscaloosa, he had reversed the Crimson Tide's fortunes, defeated defending national champion Florida in the SEC championship game, and trounced Texas in the National Championship game to cap a 14–0 season. He signed a new contract extending through 2017, with his 2010 salary estimated to be hovering near the $4.5 million figure. In appreciation for his winning ways, a larger-than-life statue of Saban was put in place beside that of Bear Bryant outside the 95,000-seat stadium.

Such astronomical salaries for head coaches naturally attracted criticism for a distortion of the purpose of a university, but presidents and athletic directors defended these Fortune 500 CEO-level compensation packages as being "market driven" and reassured critics that the money came from funds other than those provided by taxpayers. The message was clear from the job-hopping saga of Nick Saban: pay for coaches who produced winning teams and generated millions of dollars in revenue from ticket sales, booster donations, television fees, and bowl appearances was money well spent. Beyond the eye-popping salaries for the head coach were the large increases also paid to top assistant coaches. Other costs also escalated. Support staffs grew ever larger. The so-called "arms race" waged between rival programs meant that the "need" for additional staff and facilities was never-ending. When one program added a new locker room or weight-training room, rival coaches expected the same for their own program. Thus locker rooms became ever more lush, and indoor football practice facilities became near-essential items, all of which had the primary goal of impressing recruits and their parents. In the 1980s, athletic dormitories with amenities not available in regular student housing were constructed on several campuses, but excessive criminal behavior in those hallowed halls, coupled with criticisms by faculty and deans of student affairs that these residential facilities segregated athletes from the larger campus community, led to their abandonment. A few inquisitive economists and journalists ruefully reported that no matter how great the increase in revenues into athletic department coffers, nearly all departments still could not do better than break even. Like a hamster on a treadmill, the faster the athletic department ran after money, the faster it had to go to keep up with its rivals.

The Knight Commission glumly concluded in 1991 that it had found vast "evidence of the widening chasm between higher education's ideals and big-time college sports." The problem was "money-madness," but levels of income and expenditure continued to grow in the next two decades. Even a serious recession that began in 2008 and showed no sign of abating two years later did not put a curb on big-time spending for big-time athletic programs. The Knight Commission had already conceded that the NCAA was incapable of living up to its written role statement of maintaining intercollegiate athletics as "an integral part of the educational program, and the athlete as an integral part of the student body, and to return a clear line of demarcation between intercollegiate athletics and professional sports." The Commission had to concede that the NCAA's "dual mission of keeping sports clean while generating millions of dollars in broadcasting revenue for member institutions creates a near-irreconcilable conflict."[29] In light of subsequent developments, the message of the Knight Commission seems to have been no more than yet another well-intentioned critique that had no influence in deterring the ever-increasing importance of big-time sports on the American college campus.

12

Play for Pay

Prior to the introduction of commercial television, only professional baseball enjoyed widespread popularity. Television helped undercut "America's Pastime" to the point where its popularity fell behind professional football and was even challenged by NASCAR as the nation's primary spectator sport. Professional basketball enjoyed a surge of popularity during the 1980s and the 1990s, and even for a time hockey and soccer enthusiasts thought that with nationwide expansion their sports would become another spectator sport with broad appeal.

The story of professional sports is much more than the games played, because they became enmeshed in a continuum of labor disputes and aggravating strikes, the movement of franchises from city to city by owners seeking sweeter financial deals, and endless jousting with television networks for extended coverage and higher audience ratings. Although the sports fans focused on game scores and championships won and lost, businessmen operated those teams and depended upon inordinately skilled athletes who were supremely interested in the size of their paychecks and job security, just like employees everywhere.

A Tale of Two (Football) Cities

Cleveland is a football town. Its population is descended from immigrants who came to work in its bustling mills, foundries, factories, and refineries during the two great human migrations that transformed the United States. Between 1865 and 1914, 25 million persons left their homes in Eastern and Southern Europe for America, and between the 1890s and the 1960s, an estimated 15 million rural Southerners left small towns and farms for the urban North and West. From the moment the Cleveland Browns played their first games in the new All-American Football Conference in 1946, residents of the city and the

Sports in American Life: A History, Second Edition. Richard O. Davies.
© 2012 John Wiley & Sons, Inc. Published 2012 by John Wiley & Sons, Inc.

surrounding region enthusiastically supported the team. On autumn Sundays, 70,000 fans flocked to aging and decrepit Municipal Stadium – the much criticized "Mistake by the Lake" – to cheer for their team. More popular than the baseball Indians, the orange, brown, and white clad Browns epitomized this hard-nosed industrial city and its ethnically and racially diverse population.

After an extended championship-filled run under coach Paul Brown, young owner Art Modell fired him in 1963, and the fortunes of the team fell into decline soon thereafter, mirroring the sagging economy of this prototypical Rust Belt city. The Browns won their last NFL championship in 1964 on the strength of the running of Jim Brown and the talented squad Paul Brown left behind. Soon thereafter, Cleveland had entered into a devastating economic decline and become the butt of comedians' jokes about a Cuyahoga River so polluted with industrial waste that it actually caught on fire in 1969 (the evening news showed the improbable picture of city firemen squirting water on a river to put out ugly toxic flames).[1]

From the perspective of 2001, Cleveland native Joe Posnanski recalled:

> The old Browns were the heartbeat of old Cleveland. Lives were built around those Browns. All week long, they were the pulse that kept the town going. Monday you reviewed the game, Tuesday you argued who should be quarterback, Wednesday you wondered why they were not getting sacks, Thursday you called into the radio station to be the ninth caller and win those tickets, Friday you were in love … And the games on Sunday were like nothing else. It was always 25 degrees colder inside old Cleveland Stadium and … you screamed against the wind. Cleveland Browns football was everything. Everything.[2]

Even the futility of mediocre Browns teams (as well as the baseball Indians), and watching the rival Pittsburgh Steelers enjoy an extended championship run during the 1970s, did not deter the Browns' faithful. During the 1980s, on three separate agonizing occasions, the Browns were thwarted in playoff games just short of the Super Bowl: in 1980, Oakland intercepted a Brian Sipe pass deep in Raider territory; in 1987 Denver Broncos quarterback John Elway engineered a last-minute 98 yard drive to tie the game and set up a Denver overtime victory; and the following year Browns running back Ernie Byner was heading for the tying touchdown when a tackler stripped him of the ball at the 2 yard line. After those disasters, Browns fans had good reason to believe their team was suffering from a diabolical curse. "In Cleveland, in those days," Posnanski recalls, "there was desperation. When the Browns won, you felt alive. When they lost, you were left with snow piled halfway up your window and potholes the size of Olympic swimming pools and a million gray days and a million Cleveland jokes."[3]

This special connection between team and town ended abruptly on November 6, 1995. On that day, Modell announced he was moving the Browns to Baltimore, citing a lucrative offer from city and state officials that included $65 million in up-front money to cover transition costs, the construction of a 70,000-seat stadium that his team would use rent-free, and substantial supplemental income from luxury box rental, seat licenses, parking, concessions, and stadium advertising. Modell was peeved at Cleveland's politicians: a new baseball park had been built for the Indians and a new arena for the basketball Cavaliers, while his demands for a modern stadium had been ignored.[4]

Incredulity and shock swept through northern Ohio, and it produced a tsunami of angry recriminations. In 1961, the 34-year-old Modell convinced a Cleveland bank to loan him $4 million to buy the Browns. Over the years, he was viewed as a popular community leader, but that ended abruptly with his shocking announcement. Radio talk show lines lit up as fans excoriated the pariah. Angry messages, including a few death threats, were furiously dispatched. Newspaper editorials denounced Modell's greed and perfidy. Politicians from city council to the US Senate gave fiery speeches and city officials hustled a team of lawyers into court in a futile effort to stop the move. Resolutions came streaming out of city government, clergy preached sermons about the sacred value of community and personal trust, and conversations at local watering holes were animated. What Modell failed to appreciate, Posnanski lamented, was that, "The Cleveland Browns weren't a football team. They were religion and family and history and the only pride of a city that had taken too many punches."[5]

The NFL agreed to put a new expansion team in Cleveland by 1999, and Modell permitted the expansion franchise to retain team colors, name, and 50 years of records. A public contest in Baltimore renamed his franchise the Ravens in recognition of the city's brooding writer, Edgar Allan Poe. While Cleveland fans felt terribly violated, giddy Baltimore was repaid for the loss they had suffered when their Colts – the storied franchise that in 1958 had ridden the powerful right arm of legendary Johnny Unitas to the NFL championship in the "greatest game ever played" – had literally left town in the middle of the night in 1984. For several years, Colts' irascible owner Robert Irsay had been demanding that Maryland taxpayers build his team a new stadium, but when a grouchy Maryland legislature passed a bill that permitted the state to use its power of eminent domain to wrest control of the team away from the owner, Irsay decided to take the best offer. It came from Mayor Thomas Hudnut of Indianapolis, who was seeking a tenant for the new 65,000-seat Hoosier Dome. Irsay accepted his offer after learning of impending legal action by the Maryland attorney general that would have tied his team up in court for years. In the dead of night, to avoid a possible court injunction the next day, workers frantically loaded office files and equipment, film and projectors, team uniforms, even weight-training equipment, onto a fleet of 12 moving vans. Not until the last van had crossed state lines did Mayor Hudnut announce that the Baltimore Colts were now the Indianapolis Colts. In response to irate Maryland fans, Irsay snapped, "This is my team. I own it, and I'll do whatever I want with it."[6]

It was more than a decade before Baltimore again became the host city of an NFL team. In 1995, a journalist reported that 37 of the existing 113 professional teams "came from somewhere else." Noting that over the course of 33 years Art Modell had become a symbol of stability in the NFL, and had openly opposed awarding an expansion franchise to Baltimore just two years previously, another journalist concluded, "What makes the Modell move so galling [is that] Modell is so mainstream in the league … the thinking goes that if Modell goes, anybody will go."[7] Modell became the toast of the town in Baltimore, but he wisely never returned to Cleveland. But life goes on, and the new Browns, owned by locals who (of course) pledged never to move the team, began play in 1999 in a magnificent new stadium, courtesy of Cuyahoga County taxpayers. It was just as big and spiffy as the stadium that lured Art Modell to the shores of Chesapeake Bay.

Urban Relocation, Redevelopment, and Promotion

The triangular Baltimore–Indianapolis–Cleveland shuffle was but one of a long continuum of franchise relocations. Most of these moves were predicated upon the owners of a profess-ional franchise demanding taxpayers to foot the bill for a venue where the team could perform. The year after Art Modell took the money and ran, the Houston Oilers announced that the failure of their city to build a new stadium (to replace the 30-year-old Astrodome) had forced its move to Nashville, whose city leaders had promised a modern stadium. Today, the St Louis Rams play in a publicly financed domed stadium built along the banks of the Mississippi River. The Rams arrived in the Gateway City in 1994, having relocated from Anaheim, the sprawling suburb best known as the home of Disneyland. They had moved there a decade earlier from the 100,000-seat Coliseum in downtown Los Angeles. Southern California lost not only the Rams to St Louis (which had previously lost its football Cardinals to Phoenix in 1988), but also the Los Angeles Raiders, who decamped for Oakland, a city from which they had originally moved in 1982 in search of larger crowds and tantalizing but not-forthcoming pay-per-view cable revenues. The departure of the Rams and the Raiders left the nation's second largest metropolis without professional football, a void that the owner of the Seattle Seahawks Kenneth Behring eagerly sought to fill. That move was stopped by a flurry of lawsuits, threats of political retaliation, and ultimately a new owner who promised to keep the team in the Pacific Northwest, retired multibillionaire Microsoft executive Paul Allen. He extracted from the Washington State Legislature a special tax to pay for the 67,000-seat Seahawk Stadium to replace the dim and dank King Dome, which was unceremoniously imploded to make way for the new football stadium and a large parking lot. Nearby stood the recently constructed Safeco Field with its retractable roof, built by taxpayers in 1999 for $517 million to keep the baseball Mariners in town. In 2008, however, Seattle's leaders balked when the new owner of the NBA franchise, the Seattle Supersonics, demanded a $500 million arena be built at taxpayers' expense to replace the recently remodeled Key Arena that seated only 17,000. After the usual legal wrangling, the team relocated to Oklahoma City and took the name of Thunder. Whether or not Seattle has begun a new trend by rejecting relocation threats by professional team owners remains to be seen.

The growth in the number of major-league professional franchises in the past 60 years has reflected the doubling of the American population, from 150 million in 1950 to 308 million in 2100. In 1950, all major-league franchises were located east of the Mississippi River and north of the Mason–Dixon Line. A half-century later, teams were spread across the continent. In 1950, there were 44 major-league football, baseball, basketball, and hockey franchises in the United States, along with two Canadian hockey teams. By 2010, that number had increased to 113 American and eight Canadian franchises. Rapid population growth in the South and West was reflected in the location of many franchises in those areas. Although hockey originated and thrived in Canada, by 2010 only six of 30 NHL franchises were located in Canada. Such Northern American cities as Detroit, Chicago, New York, and Boston had NHL teams since the 1920s, but recent expansion extended the game deep into the Sunbelt where there was absolutely no hockey tradition: Charlotte, Atlanta, Nashville, Dallas, Phoenix, Anaheim, San Jose, Tampa, and Miami.

Construction of modern-day sports facilities was often tied to efforts to revitalize declining central cities. In 1996, Cincinnati taxpayers voted to build separate stadiums for the football Bengals and the baseball Reds along the Ohio River as the hub of an intensive downtown renewal. Construction of the Super Dome in New Orleans in the mid 1970s provided a major boost to the Crescent City's effort to lure tourists, setting off a boom in hotel construction. Atlanta's construction of a new baseball stadium for the Braves, an indoor football venue for the Falcons, and an arena for hockey and basketball (the Thrashers and Hawks) provided the centerpiece of a grand urban redevelopment effort. Coors Field for the baseball Rockies was erected in a warehouse district of Denver and stimulated a remarkable surge in upscale business and residential development. One of the most oft-cited examples of downtown revitalization is Oriole Park at Camden Yards in Baltimore, completed in 1992 as part of the larger Inner Harbor redevelopment project that transformed an industrial slum into an upscale tourist and business core. To accommodate the Ravens, a 70,000-seat stadium was built adjacent to Oriole Park so that parking facilities could be shared.

While the focus of new stadium and arena construction has often been in declining inner cities – Seattle, Oakland, Cincinnati, Atlanta, Cleveland, Boston, Minneapolis, Columbus, and Denver, to name just a few – other cities decided to locate their new facilities in the suburbs along major freeways to accommodate affluent suburbanites. In 1967, voters approved a $102 million bond to construct the Harry S. Truman Sports Complex 15 miles from downtown Kansas City at the confluence of two major freeways. Unlike the "cookie-cutter" multisport stadiums built in many cities during this era, the complex featured separate stadiums for the baseball Royals and football Chiefs. Enthusiastic voters approved a $102 million bond issue shortly after the Chiefs played in the first Super Bowl, and in hopes of persuading owner Charles O. Finley not to relocate the baseball Athletics. Detroit, suffering from the heavy blows of major race riots in 1967 and a severely deteriorating inner city, saw the football Lions move to suburban Pontiac and the Silver Dome in the mid 1970s. This structure featured an innovative inflated Teflon fabric roof floating over 80,000 seats. In 1988, the basketball Pistons followed the Lions out of inner-city Detroit to the Palace located in suburban Auburn Hills. Early in the twenty-first century, however, the Lions returned downtown to the new domed Ford Field, located near the baseball Tigers' new Comerica Park in the refurbished central city neighborhood of Foxtown.

In nearly every city that professed major-league aspirations, bitter political battles occurred over public financing of facilities. Sweetheart deals awarded to teams as incentives often aroused citizen protests, lawsuits, and ballot initiatives. Seldom, however, did opponents to new athletic facilities succeed. Economist Michael Danielson has concluded, "The purported benefits in terms of jobs, tax revenues, and general economic development are overstated and the costs understated … [E]conomic benefits have become harder to realize." Consequently, sports enthusiasts have attempted to sell the latest new stadium on intangible factors, such as community spirit, civic pride, and "quality of life," rather than on direct economic benefits.[8] Kurt Schmoke, the mayor who pushed hard for the redevelopment of Camden Yards, repeatedly talked about the Orioles "as the glue … to help hold the community together." A city official in St Petersburg, Florida, where an indoor stadium was built in the 1980s in hopes of attracting a major-league baseball team, spoke of the ability of professional teams to bridge the yawning gaps in the urban social fabric: "Sports is one of the few things in life that transcends all strata of the community. It is one of the few things left in society that ties us together, regardless of race, economic standing or gender."[9]

The Economics of Organized Baseball

The central theme of baseball in recent decades has been expansion and an ongoing battle between owners and players over compensation issues. Between 1953 and 1998, 12 new franchises were created and nine relocated. Despite increased attendance and revenues, the game was disrupted several times by embittered labor disagreements between the owners and the Players' Association. Four strikes disrupted regular season play. The longest to date resulted in an unprecedented cancellation of the 1994 World Series, a cataclysmic event that two world wars could not accomplish.

Inept management decisions and shrewd legal maneuvering by Players' Association executive director Marvin Miller led to the end of the restrictive reserve clause during the mid 1970s, setting off a new era dominated by free agency that permitted players to offer their services to the highest bidder after four years under contract. The result was an escalation of salaries that made the pre-free-agency pay scales seem minuscule by comparison. Unlike the NFL and NBA, where reasonable constraints on players' salaries and mechanisms for the sharing of revenues were in place, organized baseball proved unable to establish adequate revenue-sharing mechanisms while efforts to restrain salary escalation proved futile. Disparity in team income from radio and television contracts exacerbated the competitive balance of the two leagues. Vast differences in club revenues meant that in 1999 the New York Yankees were able to spend $77 million more than the Montreal Expos on players; by 2010, the Yankees had a payroll of $206 million (for a roster of 25 players). The next highest team payroll was the Boston Red Sox at $160,000 million, but those two teams were locked in a pennant race with division rival Tampa Bay operating on a mere $72 million payroll.

In 1953, after 50 years of stability, two financially strapped teams whose season's attendance had fallen to below 300,000 moved to greener pastures: the St Louis Browns to Baltimore and the Boston Braves to Milwaukee. In 1954, 86-year-old Connie Mack sold his Philadelphia Athletics to financier Arnold Johnson, who relocated the team to Kansas City. These moves, however, did not reflect the rapidly changing demographics of postwar America, which saw most population growth occurring in the Sunbelt. California became attractive to baseball executives after the introduction of commercial jet fleets in 1957 reduced coast-to-coast travel time to 6 hours. The map of major-league baseball changed dramatically when the New York Giants and the Brooklyn Dodgers announced they were relocating to the West Coast for the 1958 season. Horace Stoneham's announcement that his Giants were San Francisco bound was greeted with disappointment by New Yorkers, but everyone recognized that the antiquated Polo Grounds ballpark no longer constituted a major-league venue. San Francisco mayor George Christopher promised Stoneham the construction of a publicly financed 40,000-seat stadium at Candlestick Point with parking for 12,000 automobiles. This deal would be the beginning of a trend of local governments paying for stadiums to attract (or keep) major-league franchises.

The owner of the Brooklyn Dodgers, however, was viewed as a heinous traitor when he announced that his team was also California bound. Well before the Dodgers beat the Yankees in the 1955 World Series, owner Walter O'Malley was contemplating relocating the Dodgers. His initial destination of choice was a prime vacant lot in Brooklyn. With a capacity of less than 35,000 and located on the edge of a declining neighborhood, aging Ebbets Field had become hopelessly inadequate. It had only 700 parking places, and despite championship-contending teams, attendance had declined every season since 1948. New York politicians did not take O'Malley seriously when he threatened to move if an accessible plot of land sufficient for a 40,000-seat ballpark with 12,000 parking places was not made available. O'Malley did not request that taxpayers foot the bill for a new stadium; he just wanted a plot in Brooklyn on which to build the modern stadium he envisioned. City planner and egocentric power broker Robert Moses, however, stipulated that the city build and operate the ballpark, and his preferred location was the site of the 1939 World's Fair in Flushing Meadows.[10]

Figure 12.1   Willie Mays was one of the most complete baseball players in history. He loved the game so much that during his first few seasons as a New York Giant, he played stickball in the streets with neighborhood kids after finishing his day's work at the Polo Grounds. *National Baseball Hall of Fame Library, Cooperstown, NY, USA (copyright status unknown)*

When negotiations between the Dodgers and Moses reached an impasse, O'Malley turned his attention to Los Angeles where Mayor Norris Poulson promised 307 acres of prime real estate near downtown Los Angeles. In late September 1957, the Los Angeles City Council voted 10–4 to issue a formal invitation to the Dodgers to make their new home in Chavez Ravine – and the Dodgers were bound for Los Angeles. The reaction throughout the five New York boroughs was the verbal equivalent of a firestorm. O'Malley was accused of high treason, of machiavellian manipulation, of greed, even piracy. New York's decision-makers apparently believed no rational person would leave the Big Apple. In 2009 O'Malley was inducted into the Baseball Hall of Fame, an honor that was long denied him by New York-oriented journalists who sought revenge for his "treason." Yet today, more than a half-century later, O'Malley's name is anathema in the city he abandoned.

Despite a dismal seventh-place finish in their initial season, the Dodgers drew 1.8 million fans to a hastily reconfigured diamond squeezed into the Los Angeles Coliseum that was initially designed for football and track meets. Many purists believed the short left-field wall with the high screen made a mockery of the game, but in 1959, the Dodgers thrilled all of southern California by winning the National League pennant in a playoff and beating the Chicago White Sox in the World Series as 90,000 fans looked on. "Who will have the effrontery to tell us now – the several million of us – that the movement to supply the Dodgers with a decent playing yard was against the public interest?" the *Los Angeles Times* editorialized. Taking note of the widely dispersed population in the sprawling metropolis, the *Times* suggested that the cost of bringing major-league baseball to the region was worth every penny:

> Their triumph is that they have created one of those centers of attachment that the metropolitan area of Los Angeles has needed so desperately. The team has made the people for a couple of hundred miles around aware that they have a common interest. A major league baseball team does not a city make, but in our agglomeration of Southern California communities any joint enterprise which excites a wide interest serves as a sort of civic glue.[11]

In 1962, the Dodgers opened the season in spiffy new Dodger Stadium, and attendance for the next three decades hovered annually near the 3 million mark.

The success of the Giants and the Dodgers encouraged 78-year-old Branch Rickey to propose a new league, the Continental. Memories of the costly Federal League challenge were dusted off, and organized baseball soon cut the Continental League off at its knees by launching an aggressive expansion program. The Dodgers and the Giants were replaced in New York by the Mets, and cowboy-movie star Gene Autry was given an American League franchise that he named the California Angels, to be located down the street from Disneyland in Anaheim. Calvin Griffith was permitted to move the perennial lower-division Washington Senators to Minneapolis–St Paul, where he bridged the urban rivalry between the two cities by renaming his team the Twins. To placate fussy congressmen, an expansion American League franchise was placed in the nation's capital that appropriated the name Senators. A new National League team was located in Houston; the team played under the name of the Colt-45s for a few years before adopting the name Astros in recognition of the location of NASA's Johnson Space Center near the city. In 1969, the expansion Royals opened play in Kansas City to replace the Athletics who had departed for Oakland. Missouri's powerful

US Senator Stuart Symington had wielded his considerable political clout to secure the new franchise after owner Charles O. Finley made good on his many threats to move the Athletics because of lack of fan support for his inept teams.

Rosters of expansion teams were built by drafting from a list of castoffs provided by existing teams, and not surprisingly were not immediately competitive. Under 73-year-old legendary manager Casey Stengel (who upon occasion fell asleep during games), the "Amazin' Mets" set a major-league record for the most losses in a season (122) as New York fans made light of the bonehead plays, multiple errors, and flailing swings of inept first baseman "Marvelous Marv" Throneberry. In 1969, the "Miracle Mets" under manager Gil Hodges, the former star Dodgers first baseman, and young pitcher Tom Seaver jumped from a ninth-place finish the previous season to upset the Atlanta Braves in the playoffs and ambush the powerful Baltimore Orioles in the World Series.[12]

When it opened on April 3, 1962, Dodger Stadium set a new standard of excellence for sports venues. It was everything – and more – that Walter O'Malley had wanted for Brooklyn: 52,000 thousand seats with unobstructed views of the field, and 24,000 parking places in a city that set the standard for automobility. It was unfortunate that the many other new stadiums built in the following decade did not emulate Dodger Stadium. In an attempt to placate taxpayers, architects sought to design facilities that would accommodate both football and baseball. The multipurpose stadiums that appeared in San Francisco, Pittsburgh, Cincinnati, New York, Philadelphia, Oakland, St Louis, and Anaheim seemed to be mirror images of each other. When football was played, the field was laid out from home plate to center field, leaving many fans seated far from the field of play; during the baseball season the circular configuration led to vast swaths of foul territory. Built of gray precast concrete, the dull, unremarkable features reminded architectural critics of the best efforts of Soviet planners of the Stalin era. To reduce the cost of maintenance and encourage the holding of rock concerts and other large events, artificial turf was installed that led to a rash of knee injuries for football players and to unusual bounces of the baseball that threatened the integrity of the game. Two major deviations from this dreary pattern at this time were the Houston Astrodome and the Harry S. Truman Complex in Kansas City. The Astrodome was not without its own problems: the original glass ceiling made it difficult to see a fly ball during day games, but its air-conditioned and mosquito-free environment delighted long-suffering Houston fans. In Kansas City, voters approved both the 80,000-seat Arrowhead Stadium for the football Chiefs and the 41,000-capacity Royals Stadium (now Ewing Kauffman Stadium) for baseball. In 2004, Kansas City voters approved a sale of bonds to renovate both stadiums, assuring that both would continue to be considered among the best-designed stadiums in the United States.

By the early twenty-first century, most of the ill-designed "cookie-cutter" stadiums had been leveled by wrecking balls. Several were "imploded" by explosives while thousands of fans cheered their obliteration. Beginning in the early 1990s, they were replaced by ballparks designed for baseball only, which featured a "retro" style that sought to capture the ambience of older, more intimate ballparks that featured red brick exteriors and traditional green seating and fences. They also offered the obligatory modern amenities, such as enormous electronic scoreboards and replay jumbo screens, luxury boxes, and upscale food and beverage service. This new "retro" trend was begun with Orioles Park at Camden Yards in

Baltimore in 1992, which had an ambience reminiscent of the ballparks built early in the twentieth century, complete with a dark green interior and non-symmetrical fencing. Despite its popularity upon opening, Camden Yards had been strongly opposed by local activists and was only approved by nervous city officials when they came to fear that the Orioles would fly the coop just as the Colts had done. Soon new baseball-only stadiums with seating capacities in the 40,000–50,000 seating range appeared in Cleveland, San Francisco, Arlington, Detroit, Atlanta, Denver, Houston, Philadelphia, Seattle, Cincinnati, Pittsburgh, and San Diego.

Baseball traditionalists, however, contended that the three surviving parks of a much earlier era – Fenway Park in Boston, Wrigley Field in Chicago, and Yankee Stadium (having been given a $100 million remodeling in 1976) in the Bronx – remained the architectural crown jewels of baseball. Yankee owner George Steinbrenner, however, was not content with the classic stadium opened in 1923, and during the final years of his life orchestrated a complex deal with city leaders for various indirect subsidies and tax breaks to construct a new and extraordinarily opulent Yankee Stadium at a cost estimated at $1.5 billion. At the same time the Mets constructed their new Citi Field adjacent to dreary Shea Stadium in Flushing Meadows, but at a cost of less than half of the new Yankee Stadium. Unlike the Yankees, but similar to many franchises seeking to maximize revenue streams, they sold the "naming rights" of their new park to one of the nation's largest commercial banks. Though Mayor Michael Bloomberg condemned both as epitomizing "corporate welfare" provided by taxpayers, they opened in 2009.

The construction of Candlestick Park in San Francisco with the arrival of the Giants began a powerful new trend. Team owners and politicians now sang the same chorus: a professional team is a major economic stimulant to a city, attracting tourists, creating jobs, revitalizing depressed neighborhoods, and creating millions of dollars of "free" publicity. They were portrayed as sound investments by local governments that justified the enormous cost to taxpayers. Economists who have studied the impact of new stadiums have concluded that there are at best only limited economic benefits to be derived by cities from construction (and ongoing maintenance and operation) of a modern stadium or arena. Economist Andrew Zimbalist is a leading critic of this line of argument: "The overwhelming conclusion of studies that have tried to estimate the economic benefit of a football or baseball stadium is that there isn't any." Several decades later, when some of these stadiums were torn down to make way for new ones, it was discovered that in some instances political leaders averse to raising taxes had opted not to pay off the principal of the bonds but simply to make annual interest payments. Such politically expedient decisions left their angry successors and taxpayers with the responsibility of paying off debts of many millions of dollars on buildings that no longer existed.[13]

Managers of most of the new sports venues have sought to extract additional monies from advertisers, permitting corporations to place their name on the ballpark with instructions given to broadcasters that they had to specify that the game was being played at such places as Comerica Park in Detroit, Chase Field in Phoenix (originally Bank One Park until bought out by J. P. Morgan Chase in 2005), Safeco Field in Seattle, Cinergy Field in Cincinnati, Petco Park in San Diego, Heinz Field (football) and PNC Park (baseball) in Pittsburgh, Coors Field in Colorado, Citizens Bank Park (baseball) and Lincoln Financial Field (football) in Philadelphia, or Pac Bell Park (renamed SBC Park in 2004 following a corporate realignment, and then ATT Park in 2006) in downtown San Francisco. The selling of the name led not only to frequent name changes as corporate mergers occurred, but sometimes also to embarrassment. When the new $250 million baseball park in Houston opened in 1999, it was named Enron Field after the high-flying Houston energy company, but when Enron went bankrupt in 2002 amidst one of the greatest corporate scandals in American history, where top executives were indicted and convicted of federal crimes, the name was changed to the more prosaic Minute Maid Field, where among other things, fans could participate in a so-called "squeeze play" sponsored by the fruit drink company.

Baseball's Labor Disputes

By the 1970s, major-league baseball players might have been playing in larger ballparks before much larger crowds, but they were not sharing much of the increased revenues. Ever since the Federal League fiasco of 1915, players had tended to defer to management at contract time. An occasional star might hold out for a few extra bucks during spring training, but for the most part players were content to earn on average about twice to three times the annual salary of skilled industrial workers. In 1965, the average major-league salary was $12,000, with salaries of a few superstars hovering around $100,000. In spring 1966, however, that began to change when the Major League Players' Association hired Pittsburgh labor lawyer Marvin Miller as executive director. Within a short period, Miller had won the support of players and the everlasting enmity of the owners. In 1968, hinting at a work stoppage, he got the owners to sign a new "Basic Agreement" that increased the minimum salary from $7,000 to $10,000 and guaranteed players the right to be represented by an agent. In 1969, Miller called for a boycott of spring training games when the owners balked at tying rising television revenues to increased contributions to the players' pension fund, but when the opening of the season was imperiled, the owners agreed. In 1972, a unified union delayed the start of the season for three weeks with a strike over a myriad of contractual issues, including demands for increased playoff shares and pension contributions. Under Miller, the players became united, and Miller exploited bitter divisions among owners as he advanced the financial interests of his clients. In 1973, the Basic Agreement incorporated the right of a player with two or more years of major-league experience to seek independent arbitration of his salary; fears of losing arbitration hearings led management to offer higher salaries and negotiate multi-year deals, all of which tended to increase salaries. By 1975, Miller had renegotiated the minimum players' salary up to $16,000.[14]

Miller might have been able to obtain substantial increases in pay and fringe benefits at the negotiating table, but the owners still had the power of the reserve clause. By 1975, however, by combining skillful legal maneuvering with a healthy dose of pure luck, Miller had killed the reserve clause, and a new era of free agency was at hand. Players' salaries soon soared to seemingly astronomical heights, and then they went much higher. The end to the reserve clause began in 1969 when St Louis Cardinals center fielder Curt Flood refused to accept a trade to Philadelphia and brought suit against organized baseball, challenging the legality of the reserve clause as a "vestige of slavery." In 1972, a split US Supreme Court ruled 5–3 against Flood. In *Flood* vs *Kuhn* the majority said that they were loath to overturn a prior decision (*Federal Baseball Club* vs *National League*, 1922) that exempted organized baseball from antitrust laws. The failure of Congress to act on the issue, the three dissenting justices wrote, "should not prevent us from correcting our own mistakes," and the *Washington Post* correctly editorialized that when it came to the reserve clause, "tradition had once more won out over logic."[15]

The decision proved to be but a temporary victory for the owners, because Miller and the players tightened the screws in future negotiations. Their major break came in 1974, when the cantankerous owner of the Oakland Athletics, Charles O. Finley, failed to contribute to a deferred annuity specified in pitcher Jim "Catfish" Hunter's contract. Arbiter Peter Seitz ruled that Finley's action had voided the contract. He declared Hunter a free agent and ordered Finley to pay the $50,000 in question. Now the talented pitcher had the unique opportunity of discovering his real market value. The result was startling. Hunter had won 161 games over 10 seasons and had earned $100,000 the previous season. He learned that he was actually worth $750,000 a season when the new owner of the New York Yankees, George Steinbrenner, made his startling offer. Steinbrenner was castigated by his fellow owners for undercutting the existing low-salary structure, but he was just beginning a pattern of purchasing top players at high prices to make his Yankees a perennial championship contender.[16]

In 1975, Marvin Miller once again outsmarted the owners and plodding Commissioner Bowie Kuhn. His study of the standard player contract revealed a gaping hole in the reserve clause as it was written. It stated that if a player refused to sign a contract, he could be renewed for one year without his signature, but the reserve clause policy was silent on anything beyond that time. Miller convinced two established pitchers, Andy Messersmith of the Dodgers and Dave McNally of the Montreal Expos, to play that season without a contract. Owners had assumed – erroneously it turned out – that under the reserve clause they could control a player *ad infinitum* without a new contract. Arbiter Peter Seitz ruled on behalf of the players, saying that the standard contract stipulated one year and one year only. Seitz declared the two men free agents, dealing the reserve clause a near-fatal blow. Messersmith signed for $1.7 million a year with the Atlanta Braves, and McNally, suffering from arm problems, retired with the satisfaction of having opened the door to great wealth for those who would follow. A new day had dawned for organized baseball, with the pendulum of power having swung decisively in favor of the players.[17]

For the first time in baseball history, the players held the upper hand in salary negotiations, and their pay rates jumped spectacularly. Miller negotiated an agreement whereby players would be eligible for free agency after four years. By 1980, the average player pay was $144,000, and it reached $891,000 in 1991. When the 2010 season opened, player salaries had skyrocketed to an average of $3.3 million, and established players were making between $5 and $15 million annually. In 2001, the ultimate potential of free agency was realized when the Texas Rangers signed Seattle Mariners shortstop Alex Rodriguez, widely believed to be the best all-around player in baseball at the time, to a 10-year, $252 million contract. The Yankees purchased his contract in 2004 and two years later owner George Steinbrenner signed the 33-year-old superstar to a 10-year, $275 million extension. In 2010, "A-Rod" earned $33 million, and three teammates were also pulling down astronomical salaries (pitcher C. C. Sabathia at $24.3 million, shortstop Derek Jeter at $22.6 million, and first baseman Mark Teixeira at $20.6 million).[18]

Owners repeatedly sought to rein in escalating salaries, but their efforts failed each time. Most notably in 1981, an attempt to abolish the free-agency market led to a mid-season strike that saw the players unified (they forfeited more than $30 million in salaries). When owners' strike insurance ran out, they surrendered, but not before 713 games had been canceled with the loss of an estimated $72 million in ticket sales. In 1985, owners stopped making offers to players eligible for free agency and for three years there were no significant free-agent signings. An appeal to an independent arbitrator by the Players' Association led to a finding that the owners had engaged in a massive collusion scheme, and they were ordered to make payments to former free agents totaling a whopping $280 million.[19] A new round of free-agency signings by the wealthy clubs ensued, and soon salaries for star players had reached $10 million or higher, with even utility players earning well into seven figures.

In the early 1990s, several owners expressed their desire to establish some form of salary restraint (or "salary cap"), as existed in professional basketball and football, but now they faced a unified and strong union headed by Miller's former assistant, attorney Donald Fehr. In 1993, a season in which Toronto defeated the Philadelphia Phillies in an exciting six-game World Series, season attendance figures reached a record 70 million. Although baseball probably had never been in a better overall financial position, the owners were determined to take back much of what the players had gained over the previous two decades. The 1994 season began under a heavy cloud: the Basic Agreement had expired, but talks between the two sides continued with both staking out extreme bargaining positions. Ultimately, the Players' Association decided to strike on August 12, hoping to force concessions before the season entered its final weeks. Acting Commissioner Bud Selig, owner of the Milwaukee Brewers, threatened to cancel the playoffs and the World Series unless an agreement was reached by September 9, apparently believing the ultimatum would force the players to capitulate. However, they did not blink and the season was canceled. For the first time in 89 seasons, there was no World Series.[20] The "Fall Classic" had somehow survived two world wars, but now a dispute among millionaire owners and millionaire players abruptly ended the season.

The strike continued well into spring training in 1995. Finally, the National Labor Relations Board issued a preliminary finding that concluded owners had conspired to abolish free agency and impose a salary cap. The players had won again, and the season began a week late. Angry fans retaliated: attendance fell by 20 million from the 1993 season. Fans put the blame on both owners and players, believing that neither side could be counted on to protect America's Game. The strike broke the game's continuity with the past; records and statistics were forever disrupted, and fans' emotional connection to the game was seriously jarred. Only the most naive persons could look at the game and not see that it was no longer the special "National Pastime" that connected generations; baseball was now just another business.

It was not until the season of 1998 – when Sammy Sosa of the Chicago Cubs and Mark McGwire of the St Louis Cardinals went on a home run hitting binge that saw both surpass Roger Maris's record – that fans returned to the ballparks in pre-strike numbers. The two sluggers enjoyed the competition and engaged in a friendly duel that helped erase the many bad feelings created by the strike. Fans returned to the ballparks and followed the home run derby with excitement. The powerfully built McGwire ultimately hit a record-setting 70 home runs, while Sosa settled for 66.[21] The joy of 1998, however, soon led to cynicism. In 2005, congressional hearings confirmed what many observers had come to believe, that many major-league players had for years been using steroids and human growth drugs. Both stars of the epic slugfest of 1998 were linked to steroid usage. Neither man admitted using such substances, much to the disbelief of congressmen, sports writers, and fans. McGwire made a convoluted evasive statement to a congressional committee in 2005 that greatly damaged his reputation, and in 2010 he finally admitted in public that he had used steroids.

Ever since the explosion in baseball salaries, with some notable exceptions, pennant races have been generally dominated by teams from large media markets. George Steinbrenner of the New York Yankees, who time and again signed leading free agents at high salaries, came in for much abuse from other owners and sports writers. But he was only playing by the rules. Several informed commentators, such as broadcaster Bob Costas, argued that the future of baseball rested upon the possibility of players and owners agreeing on some revenue-sharing mechanism that would enable all 30 teams to be competitive. Although some teams with limited revenue won divisions and competed for slots in the World Series – the Oakland Athletics and the Minnesota Twins fit that narrative – the truth is that few teams whose payrolls were not in the top 25 percent have managed to get to the World Series since the great strike of 1994. As Costas argues, such far-reaching reform would enable fans to view baseball "as a game, rather than a business that has taken over the game."[22]

The Magic of Parity: The National Football League

The leadership of baseball proved unable to emulate the successful policies designed to assure financial parity of all franchises that enabled the National Football League to enjoy economic success in the front office and competitive balance on the field. Ever since the 1960s, most NFL games were sellouts, and television ratings remained high. When Pete Rozelle became commissioner of the NFL in 1960, he preached the doctrine of competitive balance and implemented it effectively with sharing of television fees and gate receipts. This balance is reflected in the fact that between 1967 and 2010, 28 different teams have played in at least one Super Bowl.

That did not mean, however, that certain well-managed and well-financed teams did not enjoy extended periods of success. During the early 1960s, the Green Bay Packers set the standard for excellence under head coach Vince Lombardi, winning the NFL championship in 1961, 1962, and 1965, and then defeating the American Football League champions, Kansas City Chiefs and Oakland Raiders, in the first two Super Bowls. In 1959, he inherited a team that had limped through 11 consecutive seasons without a winning record, but within a few years the small city of Green Bay had become "Titletown USA." Lombardi's success was his ability to evaluate talent and then get the best out of his players by emphasizing precise execution and total effort on every play.[23]

Although the National Football League had enjoyed success since its merger with the upstart American Football League in 1966, the road nonetheless was often rocky. During the 1980s, the league endured two strikes that disrupted regular season play. In 1982, the league played only a nine-game regular season, and in 1987, the owners hired "replacement"

players (players' union officials called them "scabs") for three games before complex economic issues were settled with neither side able to claim a clear victory. Although the two strikes faded into the background, they underscored that, with increased success and rising revenues, the stakes for owners, players, and host cities had risen dramatically.[24]

The financial success of the expanded NFL stimulated two rival leagues, both of which sought to take advantage of television. In 1974, Los Angeles businessman Gary Davidson announced the formation of the World Football League (WFL). It featured teams with such exotic names as the Shreveport Steamer, the Philadelphia Bell, and the Chicago Fire. Although the 12 teams managed to create a few ripples in the waters of professional football, the anticipated big television contract was not forthcoming and the WFL disappeared after two desultory seasons. Ten years later, the United States Football League made its appearance, and with such high-profile owners as financier Donald Trump, it initially seemed to pose a substantial threat to the NFL. The USFL played its first season in the spring and early summer months and attracted an average attendance of over 20,000. However, it decided to move its games to the fall and challenge the NFL in several cities. The NFL naturally fought back, and its retaliatory actions stimulated a $600 million antitrust suit by the new league,

Figure 12.2 Vince Lombardi is shown during the first Super Bowl played in Los Angeles against the Kansas City Chiefs on January 15, 1967, a game his polished Green Bay Packers won 35–10. Three star Packers are seen in this sideline photograph: fullback Jim Taylor (31), halfback Paul Hornung (5), and quarterback Bart Starr (15). Lombardi is widely considered one of the greatest coaches in the history of professional football. *Image © Bettmann/Corbis*

charging the NFL with attempting to prevent its securing a major television contract. The NFL faced possible treble damages of $1.6 billion. After two months of trial, the jury agreed with the USFL and found the NFL guilty, assessing it the magnanimous amount of $1 in damages. When that was tripled, in accordance with the law, the USLF walked away with a check for $3. Shortly thereafter, the new league vaporized. The jury apparently felt that the NFL had conspired to restrict the USFL from access to the networks, but that the new league, by deciding to change its original philosophy of playing its games between spring and fall, had broken faith with fans and had demonstrated bad business judgment.[25]

The USFL's most significant impact was to break the NFL's unwritten agreement with college football not to draft or sign college players until their four years of eligibility had expired. The NFL, which had refused to establish any form of costly minor-league developmental team structure, preferred to let the colleges do that work for them; in return, the league had not drafted college players until they had exhausted their eligibility. However, the USFL recognized that there was no legal basis to deny playing opportunities to underclassmen. In 1983, Donald Trump signed junior running back and Heisman Trophy winner Herschel Walker to a New Jersey Generals' contract off the campus of the University of Georgia for $4 million, a seemingly astronomical salary for professional football at the time. Several other underclassmen were drafted thereafter.

While the two rival leagues caused occasional heartburn at NFL headquarters, issues surfaced within the league that were of greater import. The most significant of these distractions was the work of the brilliant but obstreperous Al Davis of the Oakland Raiders. Ever since the merger of the AFL and the NFL in 1966, Davis had demonstrated his fiery independence, accentuated with his penchant for filing lawsuits. In 1963, he became the head coach of the struggling Oakland Raiders of the American Football League and produced a 10–4 record in his first season, and in 1966, became the commissioner of the AFL. He led the negotiations that led to the merger with the NFL, but when that deal was consummated, he apparently was upset by the "indemnities" that the NFL extracted from AFL teams, as well as by the decision that Pete Rozelle, and not he, would become commissioner of the merged league.[26]

Davis embraced the image of the Raiders as a renegade outfit, often signing players who had previously encountered discipline problems with other teams, as well as some whose encounters with law enforcement and histories of drug use and heavy drinking were legendary. The Raiders lost to Green Bay in the 1968 Super Bowl, but won the 1977 and 1981 Super Bowls. When the Los Angeles Rams began exploring the possibility of leaving their long-time home in the Los Angeles Coliseum in 1979, Davis expressed interest in moving the Raiders to southern California. He knew, of course, that NFL polices required approval by the other team owners, but he forged ahead and dared the league to stop him. When he signed the first legal papers with Los Angeles officials, lawsuits flew quickly and furiously. In 1982, a federal court in Los Angeles ruled that Davis was correct in charging the NFL with antitrust violations in denying the Raiders' right to move to Los Angeles, and in April 1983, a second jury not only upheld the original verdict but assessed the NFL $35 million in damages. It was the biggest setback in Rozelle's 29 years at the NFL helm.[27]

The Raiders never caught on with fans in Los Angeles, and when various new stadium proposals fizzled and an extensive remodeling of the Coliseum was rebuffed, Davis cut a sweetheart deal with the Alameda County Commissioners and moved the Raiders back to Oakland in 1995. Shortly thereafter, when ticket sales did not produce sellouts in a remodeled Oakland Coliseum (seating expansion being part of the deal to lure the Raiders back to Oakland), Davis promptly sued the county. Finally, following the 2002 season, the renegade team that Davis had long touted as having "Pride and Poise" and "Commitment to Excellence" finally returned to the Super Bowl, only to be soundly trounced 48–21 by the Tampa Bay Buccaneers, now coached by Jon Gruden, a bright and promising young head coach who had left the Raiders just 10 months earlier because of his difficulties in working under the aging and increasingly cranky Raiders managing general partner, Al Davis.

One of Pete Rozelle's lasting legacies was his commitment to the proposition that all teams should have an opportunity for success. Five years after Rozelle retired, new commissioner Paul Tagliabue, an attorney by profession, added to Rozelle's legacy by working with the NFL Players' Association to maintain a highly competitive environment. In the new Collective Bargaining Agreement concluded in 1994, the NFL took a major step to address an imbalance that many critics had come to believe threatened Rozelle's equity policy. The target was the free-spending owner of the San Francisco 49ers, Eddie DeBartolo, whose large budgets provided the players for five Super Bowl titles between 1982 and 1995. It was rumored around the league that the 49ers had better backup players than many of their opponents had starters.

The new Collective Bargaining Agreement established a firm salary cap that limited the total amount that a team could spend on its payroll. The owners recognized that DeBartolo's pursuit of free agents had driven up salaries across the league. The new salary cap was linked to a complicated computer-driven formula based upon anticipated league revenues from television contracts and ticket sales, with 63 percent of the amount reserved for players' compensation. In return for agreeing to such a cap, the players received the right to free agency after four years under contract to a team. The players also received a guaranteed minimum salary. In 1994, when the new agreement went into practice, each team was limited to $35 million for player compensation, a figure that grew with inflation, increased television revenues, and higher ticket prices to $85 million for the 2005 season and jumped to $123 million in 2009. The impact of the salary cap was immediate. All teams were permitted to spend the same amount for player salaries, which meant that the expertise of the front office in drafting college players and signing free agents, and the skill of the coaching staff, could turn a losing team into a winning team very quickly. It also seemed to mean that the likelihood of one team dominating the league for any extended period of time was highly unlikely, although the sustained competitiveness of several well-managed franchises – the Patriots, Colts, Steelers, and Ravens, for example – seemed to defy that generalization.

The Wondrous World of Magic, Larry, and Michael

The National Basketball Association has deep roots in East Coast seaboard cities such as Boston, Philadelphia, and New York. Professional basketball was played during the 1920s and the 1930s in the Eastern League and American Basketball League, but teams and associations came and went with frequency. The New York Original Celtics and the Philadelphia SPHAs (named for the South Philadelphia Hebrew Association) enjoyed a loyal local fan base, often playing games before 4,000 or more. In 1949, the unstable nature of professional basketball began to change when the National Basketball Association (NBA) was formed. The NBA developed slowly with franchises located in such small venues as Syracuse, Rochester, the Tri-Cities, and Fort Wayne. During the 1950s, the Boston Celtics emerged as an exciting team that captured national attention, thanks in large part to the ball handling magic of guard Bob Cousy and the up-tempo style coached by Arnold "Red" Auerbach. The fortunes of the team skyrocketed in 1956 when 6 foot 10 inch center Bill Russell, a defensive and rebounding standout, joined the team after leading the University of San Francisco to two NCAA championships. Russell was one of many stars who combined their talents to win eight consecutive NBA championships. In 1966, Auerbach turned over the coaching duties to Russell – making him the NBA's first African American coach – who guided the Celtics to two of the next three titles as player-coach. Russell's play revolutionized the game, as he turned blocked shots and rebounds into outlet passes to speedy teammates who ran a devastating fast break offense.

When 7 foot 2 inch, 275 pound Wilt Chamberlain joined the Philadelphia Warriors in 1959, the titanic battles between this new high-scoring center and the great defender in Celtic Green became the stuff of hoops legend. "Wilt the Stilt" had speed and agility, and in 1960, he scored 100 points in a game against the New York Knicks. During the 1961–2 season, he averaged 50 points a game, and during his 14 years in the league pulled down 23,928 rebounds, both records. He helped the Philadelphia 76ers win the 1967 NBA championship, and in his final year in the league in 1972 became a defensive specialist to help the Los Angeles Lakers, led by guard Jerry West, win a championship.

During the 1960s and the 1970s the league expanded into the South and West, adding 21 franchises in all. The success of the NBA, and the potential of television revenues, naturally spawned an imitator. In 1967, the American Basketball Association (ABA) made its appearance in 12 cities, featuring a red, white, and blue ball, with shots from beyond 21 feet counting for three points. The league was plagued by franchise failures when the anticipated lucrative television contract failed to materialize, but the ABA managed to survive for nine years. During that time, 31 franchises came and went, and at the end there were only 12 left standing. The ABA had its share of talent, but no player approached the skills of Julius "Dr J" Erving, who entered the league in 1971 with the Virginia Squires and ended up playing for the New York Nets. Known for his soaring drives to the basket and an incredibly soft touch off the glass, Erving went on to star in the NBA with the Philadelphia 76ers. Throughout its nine years, the ABA was colorful and exciting, but it never established a sufficient fan base. In 1976, the NBA agreed to absorb four of the best franchises – the New York Nets, Denver Nuggets, Indiana Pacers, and San Antonio Spurs – while such teams as the Kentucky Colonels, Minnesota Muskies, and Spirits of St Louis disappeared.[28]

The demise of the ABA occurred during a down period for the NBA. With the great stars of the boom years of the 1960s now retired, the league lacked star appeal. That changed in 1980, when Earvin "Magic" Johnson and Larry Bird entered the league. The two had attracted high television ratings when their college teams, Michigan State and Indiana

State, met in the 1979 NCAA championship game. Johnson and Bird continued their intense, if friendly, rivalry for more than a decade with the two premier teams of the NBA. Their popularity turned professional basketball into a major spectator sport with national appeal. In Bird's first season in 1979–80, the Boston Celtics won 61 games, reviving memories of the great Boston teams of the 1960s. Magic Johnson teamed with veteran center Kareem Abdul-Jabbar to transform the Lakers from a lackluster team into NBA champions in 1980. The following season, Bird led Boston on a championship run when he teamed with center Robert Parish and forward Kevin McHale to form one of the most formidable front lines in NBA history.

The personal rivalry between Bird and Johnson reached its peak between 1983 and 1988, with one of their teams capturing the NBA title each year.[29] The style of play between the two was a study in contrasts. The 6 foot 8 inch Johnson was a dynamo of speed and incredible balance and agility, at times leading fast breaks, making no-look sleight-of-hand passes, driving for an acrobatic layup, playing the point guard position to set up his teammates for easy baskets, but upon occasion posting himself near the basket to take advantage of a smaller defender. Bird was markedly slower and less athletic and relied upon his mastery of fundamentals and effort. He became famous for his ability to block out opponents to snare a crucial rebound, to set up a teammate for an easy basket with uncanny passes, and to hit a jump shot at a crucial moment in a close game. By the time Bird retired in 1992, the Celtics had won three NBA titles and finished second twice; Johnson's Lakers had won five championships while losing in the finals four times.

As the magisterial competition between Bird and Johnson began to wane in the late 1980s, league officials feared that the game would fall into another trough of public apathy. That did not occur because of the emergence of Michael Jordan. As a freshman in 1982, Jordan led the University of North Carolina to the NCAA championship when he sank a last minute 15 foot jump shot to defeat favored Georgetown. After earning All-American honors the next two seasons, he declared himself available for the NBA draft after his junior year. In 1984, he was drafted third by the Chicago Bulls.[30]

Biographer David Halberstam contends that although Jordan possessed incredible natural ability, the key to his success was a strong work ethic. During his first NBA season in 1984–5, Jordan averaged 28.2 points a game and was selected for the All-Star team and named Rookie of the Year. He became known for his spectacular, even artistic crowd-pleasing slam-dunks in which he seemed to hang above the basket as if suspended from the ceiling. Opponents recognized that he played defense better than almost anyone in the league. Jordan's shining personality helped make him a media favorite, and this, coupled with his superior athletic talent, prompted the aggressive Nike sports apparel company to make him its surprising choice to endorse a new brand of basketball shoe that featured a pocket of air in the heel. Soon fans everywhere were calling both the player and his shoe "Air Jordan."

Despite Jordan's heroics, the Bulls struggled for several years, but then, in 1989, the Bulls hired Phil Jackson as coach and bolstered the players' roster with forward Scottie Pippen and center Horace Grant. The Bulls lost in a seven-game series against the Detroit Pistons in the Eastern Conference finals, but the following year they won 61 regular season games,

Figure 12.3   Many sports observers believe Chicago Bulls forward Michael Jordan to have been the greatest athlete of the twentieth century. He is shown here dunking the ball in a NBA playoff game against the Detroit Pistons in 1988. Jordan was the first African American athlete to receive substantial endorsement contracts, helping him create a financial empire that compares favorably with the economies of some Third World countries. *Image © Bettmann/Corbis*

deposed the defending champion Pistons in the conference finals, and took out the Los Angeles Lakers in five games to win the NBA championship. Jordan took time out in summer 1992 to spark the "Dream Team" to an easy victory in the Barcelona Olympics, the first time the United States sent professional athletes to compete in the Olympics.

By fall 1993, due to his Nike commercial appearances and exceptional level of play, Jordan had become one of the most famous persons in the world. His ubiquitous red and black number 23 jersey had been observed even on the remote plains of Outer Mongolia. He had become undoubtedly the most recognizable and popular American sports figure. In his commercials, Jordan's sparkling personality connected with his audience as almost no other athlete had done since Babe Ruth. He became a national icon for the American world of commercial entertainment, in a culture obsessed with celebrity and in awe of superior athletic achievement. He did this at a time when African American athletes had previously been given only limited opportunities to cash in on product endorsements. When Jordan retired from playing in 1998, *Fortune* magazine estimated that he had generated $10 billion in revenues. Michael Jordan, Inc. was larger than many Third World countries.[31]

Always Turn Left: NASCAR Takes the Checkered Flag

As the twentieth century wound down, the most rapidly growing sport in the United States was stock car racing. Controlled by the privately owned National Association of Stock Car Automobile Racing (NASCAR), by the 1980s the sport's major races were drawing crowds of 150,000. Although NASCAR first appeared on national television in 1979, by the mid 1990s its annual television revenues had exceeded $1 billion and its total viewing audience was second only to professional football. In 2001, NASCAR signed a six-year $2.8 billion multinetwork contract with Fox, NBC, and Turner Cable, and its ratings continued to rise.

Until the breakthrough decade of the 1990s, NASCAR had a distinctly rural, white, Southern "redneck" flavor. Its fan base was concentrated in former Confederate states, and a down-home culture of barbeque, beer, pickup trucks, and country music prevailed on race day. Confederate flags were much in evidence. NASCAR originated in the 1930s, when unemployed young men sought to make a few dollars during tough economic times delivering moonshine whiskey from mountain stills to urban distributors. These "whiskey trippers" were hounded by tax agents of the federal government and often had to put the pedal to the metal to outrun the "revenuers." The risks to these drivers were great, but the profits irresistible: a typical load of 25 gallon jugs of "white lightning" would bring $250 at a time when jobs were scarce or even non-existent.[32]

The more audacious drivers sought local bragging rights by racing their fellow whiskey trippers down country roads, and testing their skills on dirt tracks cut out of pastures and red clay hillsides. Races often ended in beer-drenched brawls. One historian recalls: "The rules weren't uniform, they weren't fair and the promoters couldn't be trusted. Everybody who'd been in racing longer than a week knew about getting cheated out of a win, swindled out of a purse, or tricked in one way or another."[33]

William France operated an automobile repair shop in Daytona Beach, but on the weekends he raced his 1935 Ford on nearby ocean beaches. In 1938, he began promoting local races and became infatuated with racing cars taken from the show lot stock of local automobile dealers. After the war, "Big Bill" decided that stock car racing had a viable financial future if it was properly organized. He understood that America's fascination with automobiles could be converted into a spectator sport. "We need to have races for the most modern automobiles available. Plain, ordinary working people have to be able to associate with their cars. Standard street stock cars are what we should be running." France envisioned an annual national championship built upon a series of sanctioned races. As Scott Crawford writes, "He had a dream of creating a national organization that would transform a rough, informal, redneck activity into a structured, formal sport."[34]

In 1948, France established NASCAR by bringing together several regional competing circuits and organizations. At the planning meetings that he called and over which he presided, France made certain he would be in complete control. On many occasions Big Bill was accused of being a "dictator." His patented response was, "Well, let's make that a benevolent dictator."[35] His successor, son Bill Jr, would continue that domineering style and operate a national program in which the participant-owners had little, if any, say or control over the operation of a multibillion-dollar entertainment and sporting enterprise. NASCAR was and remains a private family-owned enterprise. The advantages that France offered participants were more than sufficient to prevent an insurrection.

France established his full authority during the first year of operation. At the 1949 "strictly stock" Grand National Championship held in Charlotte, NC – NASCAR's first major race – he disqualified apparent winner Glenn Dunnaway for placing wedges in his Ford's shock absorbers (a trick, incidentally, that whiskey trippers had often used to keep firm control on the sharp curves on hill-country roads). It was later determined that Dunnaway's car had actually been used the previous week to transport moonshine! The owner went to court to get France's decision overturned, but the judge upheld NASCAR's power to set and enforce its rules. Thus France's formula for success was in place: the races would be conducted on a level field with owners and drivers held to rigorous standards. The result was that many races would be decided by a few seconds with less than a car length often separating the frontrunners after several hundred miles circling an oval track. Such exciting finishes, France knew, would bring spectators back for more. He had hit upon an appealing formula.

Not that France was unwilling to change. In the 1950s, he began a process of permitting the substantial modification of cars to the point that they only *looked like* vehicles off the showroom floor. The "stock" vehicles that fans saw were, in fact, hand-built, custom-made engineering marvels modified in every way possible to enhance speed. During the 1960s, France forcefully established the power of his organization to control every tiny part of the vehicles on the track, which looked from afar like nothing more than the neighbor's Chevrolet. By the mid 1960s, speeds approaching 200 mph were recorded.

In 1959, France opened the Daytona International Speedway. The new track was designed to encourage both safety and high speeds, a sure formula for creating excitement. Over the years, the Speedway was transformed into a 480 acre venue of museums, shops, restaurants, vast public parking lots, and an amphitheater that could seat 165,000 fans. It is the site each February of the first of many NASCAR point-system races. (Unlike other sports, NASCAR holds its premier event as the first of the season, not the grand finale.) In 1961, France's control of NASCAR was threatened by an effort by several discontented drivers to join the Teamsters Union, but he managed to halt the effort, at one point threatening to "plow up" his Daytona racetrack if the Teamsters became part of stock car

racing, and he later banned for life those drivers he believed were behind the union movement.[36] In a classic "the end justifies the means" rationale, racing journalist Steve Waid had this to say about the organization of NASCAR in 1996: "It is a dictatorship, pure and simple. Let's make that a benevolent dictatorship. It makes the rules; calls the shots. As a result, everyone might not agree, but everyone does what they are told – and the positive results have become obvious."[37]

As NASCAR gained popularity, the regionalism of the sport became one of its major strengths – and weaknesses. The ties to moonshine running – a game of "cops and corn" as one writer put it – became a nostalgic part of stock car racing lore. In 1965, journalist Tom Wolfe published "The Last American Hero is Junior Johnson. Yes!" in *Esquire* magazine. It was a romanticized story of Robert "Junior" Johnson, a "country boy" who delivered moonshine to city folk from his father's still located in the heart of Wilkes County, North Carolina. At

Figure 12.4 Contemporary NASCAR fans would scarcely recognize the popular sport of stock car racing from this 1953 photograph of a multicar pileup on the then dirt track at the Daytona Speedway. Over the years, the France family financial empire that operated NASCAR built Daytona into an ultra-modern racing venue. *Image © Bettmann/Corbis*

one point the authorities caught Johnson red-handed, and he served 10 months in a federal detention center. Upon his release he focused his attention on stock car driving, winning more than $100,000 on the NASCAR circuit. This felon-turned-racing-star had become, according to Wolfe, "a famous driver, rich, respected, solid, idolized in his home-town and throughout the rural South."[38]

Over the years, the informality and Southern small-town ambience of stock car racing inexorably waned, replaced by images of corporate America with all the bureaucratic organization, computer-driven efficiency, top-down regimentation, and tight regulation that was the norm of modern American corporations. In 1969, under pressure from anti-smoking groups, the federal government banned all cigarette advertising on radio and television. The Phillip Morris Company responded to this challenge by sponsoring the Virginia Slims women's professional tennis tour. Taking a cue from its larger competitor, R. J. Reynolds opted to sponsor the 31-race NASCAR championship series. Thus was born the Winston National Championship Cup, a year-long event in which each driver was awarded points in a complex scoring system based upon the finishing place and lap-by-lap standings. At season's end, the driver with the highest points total was declared the champion. In 2005, NASCAR created The Chase for the Championship, a season-ending series of races featuring a showdown between the top 10 ranked drivers.

The connection between cigarettes and auto racing proved to be profitable for both sides as the Winston Cup became a bigger event with each passing year. As anti-smoking groups fumed, in 1979 the Winston label would be seen on national television when CBS carried the Daytona race live on a February Sunday afternoon. In 1982, the Turner cable network signed a $450,000 contract to broadcast several races, a contract that expanded to $1 million in 1990. However, the promoter of each NASCAR race had the right to negotiate its own television contracts, so viewers were forever channel surfing. In 1999, however, emulating the centralized NFL approach, NASCAR officials negotiated a uniform contract with a combination of three networks for six years totalling a cool $2.8 billion.

Ever since the sport's early days, stock car racing owners had willingly cut sponsorship deals with various manufacturers. Many such contracts called for bonus payments for victories, Winston Cup rankings, and other notable achievements. In the early days, sponsorship was pretty much small-time stuff, but in 1972, leading driver Richard Petty signed the first national sponsorship deal with the STP fuel- and oil-additive company, while rivals David Pearson and Davey Allison signed on with Purolator and Coca-Cola. National television exposure, however, made it desirable for many major corporations to sponsor race teams: these soon included automobile manufacturers, oil companies, automobile-parts manufacturers, tobacco firms, and beer companies.[39]

One of the allures of stock car racing was that fans could identify with a particular automobile maker, and several auto manufacturers readily cooperated with team owners to produce a specially engineered automobile that only looked like the auto on the showroom floor. Fans were also attracted to the different personalities of the drivers, and the sale of personalized merchandise became a major source of revenue. The first major star of NASCAR was Richard Petty, whose father Lee had been a pioneering stock car driver. During the 1960s, the native of Level Cross, North Carolina, won a series of major races and two Grand National Championships. In 1967, he won 27 consecutive races, becoming one of the fans' favorites. His public appearances were designed to create a special persona; they featured his flowing mustache, cowboy hat, and dark shades. In 1971, he was the first driver to surpass $1 million in prize money and won five Winston Cup Championships as well as four Daytona International races. In 1984, Petty won his 200th race – and, as it would turn out, it was his last victory.

As with many top NASCAR drivers, family heritage was important because racing constituted a year-around immersion. Thus Lee Petty's son Richard passed on the opportunities for success to his son Kyle, who in turn prepared his son Adam to follow in the family tradition. Adam began racing go-karts at age 6 and, while still a teenager, qualified for the Winston Cup series. All did not unfold according to family plans, however, because at age 19 Adam was killed at the New Hampshire International Speedway when he smacked into a retaining wall during a practice run on May 12, 2000.

Richard Petty – who enjoyed the nickname of "The King" – dueled with many top drivers who also won more than their share of races – Darrell Waltrip, Cale Yarborough, Bobby Allison, and "The Intimidator," Dale Earnhardt. Like so many who rose to the top of the NASCAR world, Earnhardt came to the sport as part of family tradition. His father had won more than 350 races, and so it was natural that young Dale became a stock car driver. He won his first major race at Bristol, Tennessee in 1979, and the following year captured the Winston Cup. He drove with little apparent concern for his personal safety, was often criticized for bumping rivals out of his path, displayed a reckless determination that contributed to many a smash-up, and in the process received many reprimands and an occasional suspension. By 1994, he had won his seventh Winston Cup and was averaging more than $3 million annually in prize money. Befitting his "Intimidator" image, Earnhardt wore black racing gear and his famed Number 3 Chevrolet was painted the same supposedly ominous color.

Earnhardt became an icon for a new form of individuality and rebelliousness in a sport that was, in fact, now dominated by corporate money and beholden to national television networks. Earnhardt's image was reinforced when he was killed on the fourth and last turn of the final lap of the 2001 Daytona as he typically attempted to fight through several cars to gain the lead; instead, he brushed another car and drove headlong into the concrete restraining wall at 180 mph. His neck was broken and he died almost instantly. As in many other racing families, the beat went on as Dale Jr took his father's place as the Earnhardt crew's top driver, winning several races and pushing himself toward the top of the annual Winston Cup standings. Like father, like son, like grandson. So it goes in the close-knit, family-bound world of NASCAR.

Television and corporate sponsorships dictated that NASCAR move beyond the comfortable Southern cultural cocoon in which it had for so long existed. National television networks quietly removed the Confederate flags that had once dotted the racing grounds. The fact that early in the twenty-first century fewer than 10 percent of NASCAR fans were non-white became an important issue among its image-makers, who now had every intention of making it a national sport. That meant increasing the commitment to racial diversity and diminishing the redneck image. That there had been only one African American ever to race on the NASCAR circuit said much about its racial and cultural origins. Wendell Scott of Virginia raced for 13 years on the NASCAR circuit, but he never obtained the sponsorships necessary to compete in the top rankings. With limited funds, he was forced to do much of his own mechanical work and lacked the support staff of many of his competitors. Journalist Joe Menzer writes that during the 1960s, Scott was often forced to enter race grounds by the back entrance and was denied service at food stands, and his car was seemingly targeted for unnecessary bumps during races. In 1963, at the Jacksonville Speedway, Scott surprised everyone by crossing the finish line well ahead of the pack, beating Buck Baker by two full laps, but the race official somehow neglected to drop the checkered flag and the victory was awarded to the second-place finisher. In fact, track officials were so fearful of having an African American publicly declared the winner that they did so quietly 2 hours after the race had ended when they allegedly discovered their "mistake."[40]

Scott never won another race and retired in 1973 after suffering serious injuries in a crack-up at Talladega. His racing career – including a brief stint as a moonshine runner– became the stuff of racing legend when it served as the basis for the 1977 motion picture *Greased Lightning*, starring actor Richard Pryor. Scott's difficult time on the circuit more than supported Menzer's commentary in his history of stock car racing:

> NASCAR was a white man's sport in a white man's world, and there was little or no sympathy for Scott when his NASCAR effort met with resistance. A handful of drivers accepted him for what he was – a man, like them, with a burning passion for driving race cars and possessing the physical skills to do it at unusually high speeds. However, many hated him because of his skin color and tried to make his life miserable whenever he showed up at a racetrack.[41]

In 2001, the France family gave up direct control of their private business, and long-time executive and close family friend Mike Helton took control. Helton's challenge was to continue the growth of the sport, and his focus was on moving NASCAR into the mainstream of the nation's sports fans. Already major tracks outside the South hosted Winston Cup races in New Hampshire, Delaware, California, Nevada, Arizona, and Michigan, with new facilities being planned outside Chicago and on Long Island. A nagging concern for the image-makers of NASCAR was the 30-year-old sponsorship by the R. J. Reynolds Tobacco Company (now RJR) as the anti-smoking movement continued to gain momentum. In 1998, the cigarette industry's $206 billion settlement with 46 state attorneys general created new problems relative to adhering to their pledge to stop all advertising aimed at individuals under the age of 18. The company asked to be released from its $50 million annual Winston Cup sponsorship in 2003, and the new sponsor seemed to fit well with NASCAR's efforts at broadening its appeal and attracting a diverse national audience. The giant utility Nextel, a major manufacturer and distributor of wireless telephones, fitted the high-tech image that Helton was seeking. A corporate merger with another telecommunications company produced another name change in 2008 to the Sprint Cup.

It was not until the 1970s that NASCAR sped past its more famous big racing brother that featured the high-performance one-passenger open wheel racing vehicles. Although several regional tracks held races, the Memorial Day 500 mile race around the 2 mile oval at Indianapolis concentrated the public's attention. Heavy influence by European companies and drivers, accelerated by several deep organizational feuds, undercut public interest, creating a large void that NASCAR eagerly filled. The Indianapolis 500 still generates fleeting interest but it has been lapped many times by the business acumen that has driven NASCAR to the winner's circle. As early as 1989, CBS reporter Harry Reasoner told a "60 Minutes" audience that "the most successful business in American sports is stock car racing." In 2008, two academic economists echoed that comment in *Fans of the World Unite: A (Capitalist) Manifesto for Sports Consumers* by attributing NASCAR's success to its centralized authority operated on an entrepreneurial model designed to "identify the best locations for racing, establish complex rules designed to produce close racing with cars perceived to be similar to those driven by fans, and determine the appropriate rewards that would attract the best drivers, engineers, and crews." Compared to other major sports organizations, which economists Stefan Szymanski and Stephen Ross characterize as being "dominated by quarreling owners, weak central leadership, and players' unions, all of which encourage mediocrity," NASCAR moved into the twenty-first century at full speed. NASCAR had come a long way from the days of dirt tracks in small Southern towns and the screeching of tires as whiskey trippers sped away from a revenuer's roadblock.

Struggling To Be Major League

The rise of NASCAR was one of the most significant developments in professional sports in the late twentieth century. As stock cars gained in popularity, it became evident that public tastes were subject to many influences, but particularly to television. By the turn of the century, NASCAR had developed a large and loyal fan base, leaving such sports as professional hockey and soccer far behind. Despite the location of teams in Southern and Western states, the indigenous Canadian sport of hockey remained a niche sport with a dedicated but relatively small fan base. It is often said that hockey is one of the greatest of all spectator sports if watched in person, but television producers could not create that excitement for the typical American who had little experience with the game. The speed and agility of the skilled skaters did not translate well onto the television screen, the distinctive swishing sound of the skates as they cut through the ice did not resonate across the airwaves, and the small black puck zooming at high speeds was difficult to follow. Such superstars as Wayne Gretzky of the Los Angeles Kings stimulated media interest, but attention dropped off when they retired, as Gretzky did in 1999. With ticket sales flat and television revenues in jeopardy, hockey faced many difficult challenges as the twenty-first century began. The National Hockey League suffered a disastrous season-ending lockout that cancelled the entire 2004–5 season when owners attempted to impose a salary cap atop a lower pay scale and were defied by a unified players' union. More than 200 players ended up in Europe playing for a fraction of their former salaries. When the NHL resumed play in fall 2005, the owners had their new salary model in place, but the great majority of American sports fans seemed unaware that the NHL had forgone an entire season.

While the NHL struggled to increase its visibility, efforts were made to introduce soccer as a professional sport. Its proponents, however, had to combat the game's lack of resonance within the predominant American sports culture. Its primary fan base rested with the growing urban Hispanic population. Youth soccer programs, however, became popular to the point that politicians fretted about voting patterns among suburban "soccer moms."

Parents supported the game for their children as a healthy outlet, and by the mid 1990s participant numbers had exceeded those of youth baseball and football combined. Soccer was added to most college intercollegiate programs, especially as a new women's sport for purposes of Title IX compliance.

Professional Major League Soccer (MLS) began play in 1996 with most players imported to play alongside the best American players available. The new league was established following the 1994 World Cup tournament held in the United States that set all-time attendance records of 69,000 per match. However, the hoped-for development of soccer into a national craze similar to that which exists throughout much of the world did not occur. MLS opened play with 10 teams but attendance was low and investors lost millions. Fifteen years later MLS had apparently reached a break-even point and had grown to 16 teams. Television coverage, however, was mostly limited to small cable networks serving Spanish-speaking stations. Most teams were forced to play in stadiums designed for baseball or football, although a few new venues were built specifically for the game. A 20,500-seat stadium built by oil magnate Lamar Hunt for the Columbus Crew was the prototype. On September 4, 2010, the AAA baseball Portland Beavers played their last game in a city-owned ballpark after being evicted to make way for a major reconfiguration of an aging facility to house the city's new entry in MLS, the Portland Timbers. That this move indicated soccer was beginning to challenge the American Game for the affection of fans seemed doubtful.

MLS benefited from a growing number of American players, including such standouts as Demarcus Beasley, Landon Donovan, and Tim Howard. The fact that the league permitted the drafting by D. C. United of 14-year-old Fredua "Freddy" Adu in 2004, however, suggested that MLS had to resort to gimmickry to attract spectators. The fascination with Adu stemmed in part because he was a naturalized American citizen who was born in Ghana. He never quite lived up to the publicity, however, playing a backup role for the Red and Black before being traded to Real Salt Lake in 2006. He also played professionally in Europe, but never reached the potential predicted when he prematurely turned professional. In 2007, the Los Angeles Galaxy created a stir by signing the legendary Manchester United superstar David Beckham for a league-record $6.5 million per season. A serious knee injury and two half-seasons spent playing in Europe limited his impact upon American soccer, and the anticipated effect on the popularity of MLS seemed marginal. In 2010 MLS operated 16 teams in two divisions and played before crowds of dedicated soccer fans typically ranging between 10,000 and 15,000 people. Significantly, MLS had yet to receive much attention on ESPN's influential "SportsCenter." Despite the best efforts of promoters, professional soccer seemed destined for the same fate as hockey in a country in which the homegrown American sports of football, baseball, and basketball maintained their vice-like grip on the attention of the American people.

13

Do You Believe in Miracles?

The president's wife, Rosalynn Carter, called it a "national malaise." Others had even less charitable things to say about the mood of the nation as the decade of the 1970s wound down. The decade had seemingly been one of the worst in the nation's history, right behind those of the Civil War and the Great Depression.

It began with the rising tide of protests over the war in Vietnam that saw four students killed and 13 others wounded by the Ohio National Guard on May 5, 1970, on the normally placid campus of Kent State University. In the aftermath, hundreds of campuses erupted in protests and rioting, and classes, even spring commencements, were canceled. In 1973, the Organization of Petroleum Exporting Countries (OPEC) of the Middle East shut off oil shipments to the United States, producing severe shortages at the gasoline pumps and near-panic among automobile-dependent Americans. Late that same year, it was revealed that Vice President Spiro Agnew had been accepting hundreds of thousands of dollars in bribes from road contractors with whom he had done business while a county commissioner in suburban Baltimore and as governor of Maryland. The wave of scandal also engulfed President Richard M. Nixon when revelations of the June 16, 1972, Watergate burglary of the Democratic Party national headquarters incrementally piled up to the point where he had to resign on August 8, 1974. What began as a "third-rate burglary," as Nixon once described it, revealed an administration that had engaged in systematic criminal behavior, including illegal telephone taps, breaking and entering, bribery, and using the FBI and other government agencies to obstruct justice. As the American people grappled with the fact that their president and his top aides had committed felonies and systematically lied about them, they also saw their purchasing power suffer from rapidly rising inflation. The loss of millions of jobs in the industrial sector, including the near-collapse of the once-dominant American automobile industry before the onslaught of foreign vehicles, raised serious

Sports in American Life: A History, Second Edition. Richard O. Davies.
© 2012 John Wiley & Sons, Inc. Published 2012 by John Wiley & Sons, Inc.

questions about the future of the American economy as Presidents Gerald Ford and Jimmy Carter wrestled with a stagnant economy.

As the end of the decade neared, news did not get any better. Another serious oil shortage in 1979 once more produced anxiety and long lines at service stations. In Pennsylvania the Three Mile Island nuclear power-generating station was crippled by a malfunction that for a time threatened a catastrophic meltdown. With annual inflation at 10 percent and interest rates at times reaching 20 percent, the American people began discussing the possibility that the United States had entered an ominous period of decline and decay. In November 1979, a group of angry Iranian students stormed the US embassy in Tehran to protest the Carter administration's decision to protect the Shah of Iran, now living in exile in New York. Fifty-three Americans were taken hostage and held for more than a year. As the news media reported nightly on their plight, Americans felt both angry and helpless. The crisis generated by the Iranian hostages symbolized the sense that America had lost its way. President Carter correctly summarized American opinion when he commented that a "crisis of confidence" had enveloped the nation, striking "at the very heart and soul of our national will."

On February 22, 1980, the fog began to lift as the American people were given an unexpected morale boost. That evening, they watched as a supposedly hopelessly outmanned collection of college hockey players pulled off one of the biggest upsets in American sports history, defeating a veteran Soviet Union team 4–3 in the Olympic Games. Even ABC had no premonition that an American victory was in the offing or it would have shown the game live rather than on a tape-delayed basis. The 1980 Winter Olympic Games were held in Lake Placid, New York, with the rivalries and tensions of the Cold War ever present. Journalists from both sides of the Iron Curtain kept medal counts and wrote of the games as an extension of Cold War power politics. The outcome of individual matches was viewed as an integral part of the ideological conflict between the forces of communism and democratic capitalism. Although the International Olympic Committee (IOC) still maintained the fiction of amateurism, that myth had long since been revealed as a sham. The Soviets were officially considered by the IOC to be "state amateurs," a clever euphemism that accepted they were members of the Soviet military and spent their time working at nothing other than their profession of hockey. The Soviet national team that took to the ice at Lake Placid was widely recognized as one of the best teams in the world, amateur or professional. The previous year, the Soviets had handily defeated a National Hockey League all-star aggregation by 6–0, and had won the World Championship with an easy 5–2 victory over the Canadian national team.

The American team was overmatched, but it nonetheless had plenty of young talent. Coach Herb Brooks, whose University of Wisconsin teams had won three NCAA championships, spent nearly 18 months preparing his team. He put several hundred candidates through psychological tests and grueling workouts before culling them down to a team of 20. He then worked them unmercifully, recognizing that the only way they could compete with the world's best teams was through speed, endurance, conditioning, and disciplined play. His players nearly rebelled as he drove them to physical exhaustion and emotional distress. "He messed with our minds at every opportunity," one player recalled, and team captain Mike Eruzione later commented, "If Herb came into my house today, it would still be uncomfortable."[1] As the Winter Olympics approached, the political fires were stoked when the Soviet Union invaded Afghanistan on Christmas Day, 1979. World tensions mounted, and speculation about an American boycott of the Olympics in protest at the invasion began to circulate. Just one week before the Games opened, in the last pre-Olympic exhibition game, the Soviet team destroyed the United States team at Madison Square Garden by an embarrassing 10–3 score. Things did not look good for the Americans.

In the preliminary round the Americans had to come from behind to tie Sweden, but surprised a strong Czechoslovakia team 7–3 and defeated Norway, Romania, and Germany. Entering the four-team medal round, the Americans were considered no match for the powerful Soviets. Among other things, they had to find a way to get the puck past goalie Vladislav Tretiak, arguably the world's best net man. Late in the first period the score stood 2–1 in favor of the Soviets, but there were signs that this was the Americans' day. American goalie Jim Craig managed to stop a barrage of shots on goal; he turned away 39 during the game. Then, with only seconds remaining in the first period, American forward Dave Christian fired a 25 foot shot that Tretiak easily turned away. However, the Soviet defenders, thinking the period had ended, did not provide cover, and Mark Johnson slapped the puck past a surprised Tretiak. A replay indicated that Johnson had scored with 1 second remaining.

As the second period began, angry Soviet coach Viktor Tikhonov inexplicably benched Tretiak – a horrendous strategic mistake – but the Soviets continued to dominate play; the Americans managed only two shots on goal and were happy that the period ended with them trailing 3–2. In the final period, Brooks's emphasis on speed and conditioning began to pay off. While Tikhonov kept his veteran players on the ice, Brooks substituted frequently. Johnson tied the score off a fumbled puck, and with 10 minutes left in the game, captain Mike Eruzione stole a pass, outskated the defenders, and flipped a shot past the reserve Soviet goalie – a shot that Tretiak could have stopped in his sleep. The Soviets launched a frantic attack, but Craig made several stops and, as the last seconds counted down, excited ABC announcer Al Michaels screamed into the microphone, "You got ten, nine, eight … five seconds left! Do you believe in miracles? Yes!" As the American team celebrated, their ecstatic fans waved American flags and chanted, "USA! USA!"

The next day, newspapers across the United States blared the good news in large headlines and television news programs led with the story. All across the country, flags flew in front of homes and from the aerials of automobiles. An upsurge in nationalistic sentiment swept the nation. The team's victory was right out of American mythology: the overmatched underdog persevering against all odds to pull off an improbable triumph. The gold medal game against Finland seemed anticlimactic. Once again the Americans came from behind to win, 4–2. Pictures of goalie Jim Craig skating exuberantly around the rink draped in an American flag appeared on front pages all across America.

The new decade seemed to bring renewed optimism. As President Reagan took office on January 20, 1981, the hostages were released in Iran, and in the months that followed the economy began to grow. As Reagan's second term wound down, a tenuous détente with the Soviets took hold, leading to a significant reduction in nuclear arms in 1987. Although it is a stretch to credit any of these events to a single hockey game, nonetheless the "Miracle of

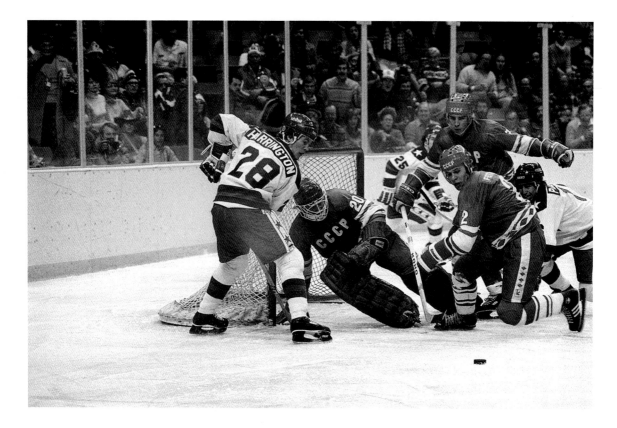

Figure 13.1   Action at the net in the dramatic 1980 Olympics semifinal hockey game between the United States and the Soviet Union. The improbable 4–3 American victory was hailed as the "Miracle on Ice," and historians have considered it an important symbolic moment as the United States began to move beyond the 1970s when many Americans questioned the capability of their country to solve its problems. *Image © Bettmann/Corbis*

Lake Placid" came to be viewed as the time when the "long national ordeal" had finally bottomed out. If nothing else, the hockey triumph proved to be a classic example of how politics and sports had become intricately intertwined.

The Cold War Shapes the Olympics

Two major forces influenced the evolution of the Olympic Games after the Second World War. The Cold War inevitably became an underlying issue as the United States squared off against the Soviet Union and other Soviet bloc nations. The quest for gold medals led inevitably to the erosion of the original amateur conception of the Olympics, and with the IOC anxious to collect millions of dollars for the sale of television rights, the inevitable pressure to make the Games another forum where professional athletes performed and reaped large monetary rewards transformed the Games into a quadrennial capitalistic extravaganza.

The founder of the modern Olympics would have been appalled. Late in the nineteenth century, Frenchman Baron Pierre de Coubertin had conceived of the modern Olympic movement in the pristine image of athletic amateurism.

His world was that of the European aristocracy. Impressed with the English upper class and its casual, almost indifferent approach to athletics, Coubertin conceived of an international competition between gentlemen who would strive to represent themselves and their countries in an atmosphere of good sportsmanship. He believed that the amateur sportsman should play the game purely for the joy of participation: "The most important thing in the Olympic Games is not winning but taking part; the essential thing in life is not conquering but fighting well."[2]

In 1894, Coubertin assembled a group of like-minded men in Paris, and that is when the IOC was formed. Its essential philosophy was that of Coubertin. Every four years strictly amateur male athletes would meet to compete in track and field, gymnastics, and swimming – the number of events would grow over the next century to nearly 200 – in an atmosphere of fair play and international goodwill. To assure that the Games would be free from international politics, each participating nation would have its own privately organized national Olympic committee that was independent from its government. In 1914, Coubertin created the official Olympic flag of five interlocking colored rings on a white background. As he liked to say, at least one of those colors – red, green, black, orange, and blue – was found in every national flag in the world. "The Olympic Games are for the world and all nations must be admitted to them," he said. But he also believed the Games were not designed to intensify nationalist sentiments but instead existed "for the exaltation of the individual athlete." Although Coubertin was emphatic about reviving the ancient Greek Olympics, he conveniently ignored the fact that the Greeks had lavished booty upon their sports heroes, and in fact many of the best ancient athletes were essentially full-time professionals who trained for competitions and expected to reap rewards for their efforts. The modern Olympics were a product of the values of the European elite of the late nineteenth century, not ancient Greece.[3]

Coubertin served as president of the IOC until 1925, and for the most part managed to remain true to his idealistic values. Significantly, he lost the battle to keep women from participating. In 1920, women competed for the first time in swimming and gymnastics, but only in 1928 were they permitted to compete in a few track and field events. Coubertin and like-minded committee members believed that track and field was too strenuous a sport for females, a myth that Babe Didrikson emphatically put to rest in 1932 at Los Angeles. The Games that occurred just before Coubertin's death must have disturbed him immensely. In 1929, at which time the Games scheduled for 1936 were awarded to Germany, the Nazi Party was only a slight blip on the political screen of European politics. Adolf Hitler assumed power in 1933, however, and by 1935 the malevolent goals of his regime had become all too evident. As the Games approached, Jewish leaders in the United States urged a boycott. For a time this seemed possible, but the chairman of the United States Olympic Committee, Chicago millionaire businessman Avery Brundage, maneuvered adroitly to assure that the United States participated. The 1936 Berlin Olympics were awash in the rising tide of German nationalism that Adolf Hitler's regime had unleashed; Berlin set the tone for the Games that occurred after the Second World War.

War caused the cancellation of the 1940 Games scheduled for Tokyo and the 1944 Games, but the IOC was determined to celebrate the end of the war by holding the Games, however limited they might be, in war-ravaged London in 1948. Everywhere spectators and participants went in London, burned-out buildings and piles of rubble provided grim reminders of the horrendous Blitz. Little new construction was attempted as the financially strapped British held the Games in Wembley Stadium and other existing venues. Fifty-nine countries sent delegations, but the Americans dominated by winning a total of 84 medals, 38 of them gold. Most of the media attention in the United States focused upon Bob Mathias, a teenager from Tulare, California who had won the decathlon.[4]

The biggest story of the London Olympics, however, was that the Soviet Union was invited but chose not to send a delegation. The defeated nations of Japan and Germany were not invited. In the three years following the end of the war, the tenuous alliance between the United States, Britain, and the Soviet Union had disintegrated as traditional political and cultural issues resurfaced. As Eastern European nations were pulled into the Soviet orbit, communist governments were established that took directions from Moscow. Former prime minister Winston Churchill had denounced the "Iron Curtain" that now divided Europe in a memorable 1946 speech, and the following year the United States had launched its containment program against the Soviets and their "satellites" with the Truman Doctrine and Marshall Plan. As the London Games began, West Berlin was under a Soviet blockade and the civil war in China was not going well for Chiang Kai-shek's forces in their battle against the communist forces of Mao Zedong.

The Cold War was the controlling factor of the 1952 Olympics, held in Helsinki. President of the IOC, J. Sigfrid Edström of Sweden, had to deal with the difficult political question of whether to permit the Soviets to participate. Although the Olympic ideal of inclusion indicated that the communist countries be invited to compete, IOC leaders also understood that the existence of a Soviet Olympic Committee operating independently of the Kremlin was fantasy. Additionally, it was recognized that Soviet athletes were employees of the state – most were officers in the Red Army – and that they were paid to concentrate upon developing their athletic skills. Members of the IOC understood that the Soviet Union violated two of the Games' most sacred concepts – a free and independent national committee, and unpaid amateur athletes – but they were also dedicated to the concept of inclusion. All things being equal, the IOC decreed that athletes from all countries should be permitted to participate.[5] Consequently, the IOC agreed to invite the Soviets.

The competition at Helsinki in 1952 underscored the realities of the Cold War, which now included a nuclear arms race between the United States and the Soviet Union (which successfully tested its first weapon in 1949) and was seriously exacerbated by the American development of a thermonuclear hydrogen bomb in 1952. The Korean War – the first of many military confrontations that the Cold War would spawn – had settled into a bloody stalemate just north of the 38th parallel. The American people were about to elect former general Dwight D. Eisenhower as their new president, on the presumption that he understood the threat posed by the communist bloc. High-ranking Soviet officials had already made many public comments about the importance of Soviet athletes demonstrating their superiority against the representatives of the soft "bourgeois" capitalist countries. Andrei Zhdanov, a cultural spokesman, made this clear in 1949 when he said, "Each new [athletic] victory is a victory for the Soviet form of society and the socialist sports system; it provides irrefutable proof of the superiority of socialist culture over the decaying culture of the capitalist states."[6] That the Soviets were on a serious mission was reflected by the decision to house their athletes not at the Olympic Village, but free from Western influence at a military base just across the nearby Finnish–Soviet border. Everywhere Soviet athletes went in Helsinki, they were accompanied by chaperones to prevent their contact with other athletes.

The Soviets had prepared well for their entrance into the Olympics. Shortly after the end of the war, a National Scientific Research Institute for Sports Culture was established that operated exercise and instructional sites across the country and brought the most promising athletes to Moscow for advanced training. Soviet leaders were determined to develop competitive international teams as part of the global struggle against Western capitalist nations. Victories on field and court would demonstrate the superiority of the Soviet system over "soft" athletes from the West. At home, those victories in turn would inspire the average Soviet citizen and provide fodder for the Soviet propaganda machine.

Americans readily perceived the political importance of the Games, and a national fund-raising drive to "Support Our Athletes" was launched. The United States Olympic Committee arranged for a special television fundraiser that featured comedian Bob Hope and singer Bing Crosby. During the show, Hope cracked, "I guess Joe Stalin thinks he is going to show up our soft capitalist Americans. We've got to cut him down to size. This is the best thing I've ever undertaken and, brother Bing and I are going to throw our best punches."[7] Consequently, the tension during the Helsinki Games was palpable, as repeat decathlon champion Bob Mathias related:

> There were many more pressures on American athletes because of the Russians than in 1948. They were in a sense the real enemy. You just had to beat 'em. It wasn't like beating some friendly country like Australia. This feeling was strong down through the entire team, even [among] members in sports where the Russians didn't excel.[8]

Journalists from the West and from behind the Iron Curtain created points scales to measure overall team results (based on the number of medals won), each designed to give their side an advantage. The Americans won a total of 76 medals to the Soviets' 71, although the United States captured twice the number of gold medals. For all intents and purposes, it was a standoff.

Perhaps the most significant event at Helsinki occurred when the IOC, after 25 secret ballots were cast, elected wealthy Chicago construction executive Avery Brundage as its new president. Brundage had been a track star as an undergraduate at Illinois and had competed in the decathlon at the 1912 Olympics, coming in sixth behind winner Jim Thorpe. As Olympic president, he strived to maintain the spirit of Baron de Coubertin. Brundage had long been active in the Amateur Athletic Union and was elected the head of the American Olympic Committee after the 1924 Paris Games. He approached his duties with messianic zeal: "Sport is recreation, it is a pastime or a diversion, it is play, it is action for amusement, it is free, spontaneous and joyous – it is the opposite of work."[9] Brundage believed deeply that the Olympics should be free of the scourge of professionalism: "The amateur code, coming to us from antiquity, contributed to and strengthened by the noblest aspirations of great men of each generation, embraces the highest moral laws. No philosophy, no religion,

Figure 13.2 Bob Mathias, a Stanford University student from Tulare, California is shown competing in the discus throw at the 1952 Olympic Games held in Helsinki. Mathias said he and his fellow American athletes felt intense pressure to beat the Soviets due to Cold War tensions. *Image © Bettmann/Corbis*

preaches loftier sentiments." The fundamental distinction between the amateur and the professional, he felt, "was a thing of the spirit" because it "exists in the heart and not in the rule book." Condemning professional sports as "as a branch of the entertainment business," Brundage believed that amateurs, by rejecting materialism in their sporting efforts, play "for the love of the game itself without thought of reward or payment of any kind." Unrelenting in his beliefs, Brundage believed that if an individual became a professional in one sport, he forfeited his amateur status in all sports.[10]

Time and again, Brundage found himself in uncomfortable situations where political realities forced him to parse the truth, to set aside his core beliefs, and to cut deals that revealed him to be, in the eyes of his many critics, a shameless hypocrite. His opposition to an American boycott of Berlin in 1936 led to charges that he was anti-Semitic; his willingness to bend the rules to permit the Soviets to compete at Helsinki raised criticism that he was a communist sympathizer; his efforts to include South Africa produced angry accusations that he was a white supremacist. Just three weeks before the Games were to open, the Soviet Union brutally put down a revolution in Hungary when it sent tanks and troops into Budapest. The death of thousands of heroic Hungarians was front-page news, and now threats of a boycott blended with demands that the Games be canceled. Contending that the Olympics transcended international politics, Brundage ordered the Games to proceed: "Every civilized person recoils in horror at the savage slaughter in Hungary, but that is no reason for destroying the nucleus of international cooperation and good will we have in the Olympic Movement. The Olympic Games are contests between individuals and not between nations."[11]

The Melbourne Games proved to be a decisive triumph for the Soviets. They won 98 medals to 74 for the Americans. Further, their dominance was in those sports that attracted considerable media interest and tested strength and speed, thereby taking on a quasi-military symbolic significance: track and field, boxing, wrestling, and weightlifting. The US men's track team won 15 of 24 events, but the Soviets demonstrated talent that anticipated future Olympic track and field glory. The Soviet women were clearly superior to the Americans in track and field. Because medals won by women counted equally to those won by males in the informal medal count, questions began to be raised in the United States about the dearth of competitive sports programs for females. American Tobacco Company heiress Doris Duke contributed $500,000 to the USOC to begin a training program for women athletes. It would take more than two decades for American women to begin to compete on an equal footing with the Eastern bloc women.

The real surprise of 1956, however, was the stunning success the Soviets had previously enjoyed at the Winter Games in Cortina, Italy. In the first ever Winter Olympics the Soviets entered, their athletes won 16 medals including the gold in hockey. Hockey was adopted by the Soviets as a game in which they could compete successfully at the international level only after the end of the Second World War. The gold medal testified to the effectiveness of its systematic athlete development program. In 1960, at Squaw Valley above Lake Tahoe in the Sierra, the United States hockey team, composed of college students, upset the favored Soviet team, but so little media attention in the United States was devoted to those games that the significance of that surprising gold medal escaped the attention of most Americans.

In 1955, two years after the death of Josef Stalin, American president Dwight D. Eisenhower met at Geneva with Soviet premier Nikolai Bulganin. It was the first of many "summit" conferences during the 45-year Cold War. The two heads of state agreed upon a series of cultural exchanges, including a series of annual track and field meets. The first such event occurred in Moscow in July 1958. Although hardline conservatives in the United States denounced this modest effort at mutual cooperation, the Soviet newspaper *Pravda* proclaimed the meet as "part of the principle of peaceful coexistence." Despite the many political overtones, the meet proved to be a great success. As expected, the American men prevailed, but the Soviet women dominated their American counterparts in most events. The highlight of the event was the decathlon between the world's best: Vasily Kuznetsov and UCLA star Rafer Johnson. The duel saw both men put in peak performances, with Johnson overcoming a nagging leg injury to finish the final event, the metric mile, close on the heels of Kuznetsov to claim victory. As the two men entered the final stretch, a crowd of 75,000 spectators stood and cheered both men, who afterwards embraced in a demonstration of mutual respect and friendship.

The USOC found a stopgap solution to the chasm separating the Americans from the Eastern bloc women in the Tennessee State Tigerbelles track team. Leading the Tigerbelles was one of the most improbable track stars in history, the lithe 5 foot 11 inch Wilma Rudolph. The daughter of an impoverished rural family, Wilma contracted polio at age six and was confined to bed for more than a year. Determined to live a normal life, she underwent therapy, exercised relentlessly, and by the time she was in her teens had overcome her disability to become an outstanding basketball player. While still in high school, she began to train as a sprinter with Ed Temple, a sociology professor at Tennessee State who was also the unpaid women's track coach. Rudolph developed into a world-class sprinter and won a bronze medal – one of the few won by an American woman – at the Melbourne Games at age 16. She continued to improve under Temple's coaching and demonstrated at the Rome Olympics in 1960 that American women could compete with world-class athletes. She became the first American woman to win three gold medals in one Olympics – the 100 and 200 meter sprint races and as anchor on the 400 meter relay team. She set world records in all three events, although her 11.0 seconds in the 100 meters was set aside due to high wind. Proclaimed "the fastest woman in the world," Rudolph returned to Tennessee a genuine sports hero. Governor Buford Ellington was anxious to bask in her fame and lead the local celebration, but upon learning of the celebration plans, Rudolph politely declined, saying that she would not participate in a racially segregated event. Ellington and local politicians relented, and the first truly integrated public event ever held in her hometown of Clarksville took place – a parade and a banquet in honor of a young African American woman who was the best sprinter in the world.[12]

Although Cold War tension became less and less important to the athletes during the 1960s, it remained important to politicians and the media. As the athletes became familiar with each other, friendships blossomed, and even before Olympic events, they wished each other "good luck" and warmly shook hands. Emotional embraces between rivals often occurred after a hard-fought competition. However, other emotional issues now pressed to the fore, especially those related to racial discrimination in America and apartheid in South Africa.

Television Transforms the Olympics

Except for the drama created by the standoff of the Cold War powers during the Games at Helsinki and Melbourne, most Americans paid scant attention to the Olympics. Television coverage in the United States was limited to brief reports shown 24 hours or more after an event took place. The first Olympic Games that Americans saw live were the 1960 Winter

Olympics at Squaw Valley in eastern California. CBS was able to obtain the rights for those Games for just $50,000. From the Olympic village located high above Lake Tahoe in the Sierra, it was possible to show only a limited number of live events to American audiences. The coverage was primitive at best. Anchorman Walter Cronkite reported on the action from a mobile setup placed in the back of a station wagon. That summer, CBS covered the Rome Summer Games – for which it paid only $500,000 – by sending videotape by jet aircraft to studios in New York. Although CBS managed to convey the human drama of the Games – especially in the sparkling performances by Wilma Rudolph – coverage of the two events was spotty, and most Americans paid scant attention. However, ABC's new director of sports, Roone Arledge, was a most interested viewer, and he concluded his company could turn the Olympics into a major prime-time television event. ABC paid $500,000 for the rights to the 1964 Winter Games at Innsbruck, Austria, and Arledge threw himself into planning a major breakthrough in television coverage.[13]

He faced tremendous technical problems, with different events being held at remote mountain locations. However, he and his crews had three years of experience of covering events on-site for "Wide World of Sports," and they tackled the challenges with confidence. Austria was six time zones ahead of New York City, so Arledge's producers air-expressed 4 hour black-and-white videotapes to ABC headquarters in time for them to be edited for prime-time showing the next day. Arledge built large audiences by unashamedly focusing only on the top American athletes. Not only did he feature the performance of Americans, but his cameras and microphones also picked up the high-flying drama of ski jumpers, the speed of bobsled teams, and the beauty and grace of figure skaters. Americans stayed glued to their television sets even though only one American won a gold medal, Terry McDermott in 500 meter speed skating. The highlight of the coverage at Innsbruck was a technical preview of things to come: the use of an orbiting satellite made it possible to show about 15 minutes of the closing ceremony live before the satellite moved out of range. American interest in the Tokyo Summer Games of 1964 was low; the fact that NBC delayed the showing of the opening ceremonies until 1 a.m. (after the "Johnny Carson Tonight Show" had ended) suggested the level of national interest, although the rousing gold medal performances of swimmer Don Schollander, heavyweight boxer Joe Frazier, and sprinter Bob Hayes created a brief stir. In a stunning upset, the lightly regarded Oglala Sioux Billy Mills, who had been raised on a South Dakota reservation, won the grueling 10,000 meter race. He was the first Native American to win a gold medal since Jim Thorpe, and remains the only American ever to capture this event.

With his coverage at Innsbruck a commercial as well as a technological success, Arledge focused upon 1968. ABC won the bids for both Games, but the cost had escalated and the network paid a total of $6.5 million for the rights. Twenty years later, that seemingly enormous sum jumped to $309 million. The sophisticated coverage that ABC provided in 1968 turned the Olympics into a major entertainment event. To cover the Winter Games in the French city of Grenoble, ABC inserted 250 staffers who produced fascinating stories about the personal hardships suffered by participants – a television convention that became popular for many Olympiads to come – and coverage of major events that featured American athletes. The Americans did their part with solid performances, led by the incredible beauty and skill of figure skater Peggy Fleming, who won the only American gold medal of the Games. Arledge demonstrated that television coverage, expertly conceived, could transform a sporting event into a mass spectacle in which millions became involved. The Olympics had become a major event that entertained and captivated.[14]

Arledge sent 450 workers to Mexico City in September of 1968 for the Summer Games. In fact, the ABC "team" was larger than all but three of the Olympic teams sent by participating nations. The politics of race became the lead storyline at Mexico City. After Americans Tommie Smith and John Carlos had finished first and third in the 200 meter dash, Arledge captured them on camera as they stood on the victors' stand, their black-gloved fists raised in a Black Power protest salute. As the flag was raised and the "Star Spangled Banner" played, these two African American athletes lowered their heads away from the flag. ABC captured the moment perfectly, as did many newspaper photographers, and those images produced an instant furor in the United States. Immediately after the incident, ABC's Howard Cosell interviewed the gold medal winner and asked Smith pointedly if he was proud of his American citizenship; Smith's evasive answer only exacerbated the situation. Carlos later commented, "Tommie and I were just telling them that black people and minority people were tired of what was taking place in the US and all over the world … The press and TV blew it all out of proportion." The next day, Avery Brundage and the United States Olympic Committee expelled them from the team and sent them home; Brundage made certain the International Olympic Committee banned them from taking part in future Games.[15]

Well before the Black Power salute episode, those protesting discrimination and racism found in sports a useful way to publicize their issues. Leading this movement was Harry Edwards, a former basketball and track athlete at San Jose State. Late in 1967, he began a campaign among premier black track and field stars to boycott the Mexico City Games as a means of protesting racial conditions in the United States. As Edwards toured the country, he met with mixed reactions. While many black athletes were sympathetic to his underlying message, they also understood that they would more than likely have no other opportunity to take part in an Olympics; they did not want to waste years of training and preparation for a protest that did not seem to relate directly to issues within the United States. Besides, the star of the 1936 Olympics, sprinter and long jumper Jesse Owens, also toured the country at the behest of the USOC, spreading the message that there was nothing to be gained by a boycott and much to be lost. The highly publicized boycott effort fizzled but the emotions generated were reflected in the fallout from the Smith–Carlos protest.

When Smith and Carlos held their clenched fists with black gloves high and lowered their eyes, they created a firestorm of protest across white America. Brundage dismissed the two men as "warped mentalities and cracked personalities," comments that engendered charges by Harry Edwards that Brundage was racist. Brundage's narrow view of the situation was that the Olympics stood for equality and international brotherhood, and that by suggesting otherwise Smith and Carlos were using the Games to advance a cause that lay beyond the intended scope of the Olympics. When the Mexican Olympic organizing committee later included the protest in its official film of the games, Brundage was aggrieved: "The nasty demonstration against the United States flag by negroes … had nothing to do with sport, [and] it was a shameful abuse of hospitality and it has no more place in the record of the games."[16]

Figure 13.3   American sprinters Tommie Smith and John Carlos raised their gloved fists in a Black Power salute at Mexico City in 1968 as the American flag was being raised and the "Star Spangled Banner" played. They were suspended from the American team and sent home. In 2005, their alma mater, San Jose State, dedicated a permanent statue on the campus that cast Smith and Carlos in bronze just as they were captured in this famous photograph. *Image © Bettmann/Corbis*

The stark image of the Black Power salute thereafter became the most recognized symbol of the Mexico City Games. It overshadowed stunning athletic achievements, including world records set by Americans Lee Evans and Bob Beamon in the 400 meters and the long jump. Beamon's feat was one of the most amazing in all of Olympic history. Between 1935 and 1965, the world record for the long jump had increased incrementally by just 8 inches, with the current record being set by American Ralph Boston in 1965 at 27 feet 4¾ inches. In just a few seconds, that record was obliterated by New York City native Bob Beamon, when he took off and seemingly flew through the thin Mexico City air, actually landing beyond the reach of the electronic measuring instrument. He had exceeded Boston's record by almost 2 feet with a leap of 29 feet 2½ inches – a record that would not be broken until 1991 (and then by 2 inches). Although Beamon's wondrous jump received its deserved share of publicity, the gold medal victory by boxer George Foreman was given greater attention in the American media when he joyfully danced around the ring waving an American flag after winning the championship. This black man's patriotic display seemed to mute the sting produced by Smith and Carlos, although Foreman later said that his star-spangled victory dance had nothing to do with the sprinters and that he regretted his display was interpreted by the American media as a rebuke of his friends.

ABC got much more than it had bargained for when it signed on to broadcast the Mexico City Olympics. International politics, apartheid, the bubbling over of American racial tensions, a massacre of protesting students – all contributed to an unfolding drama which television helped create.

The Games Must Go On

The experience that ABC gained in Mexico City proved useful when the Munich Games unfolded in 1972. The IOC had awarded the Games to Munich as a symbolic recognition of welcoming Germany back into the fold of civilized nations. The Games were intended to be, among other things, a means of extirpating memories of Nazism. The local committee had constructed a sparkling new 700 acre Olympic venue, with modern athletic facilities built around a massive translucent canopy covering the 80,000-seat stadium. A plush Olympic Village was erected, featuring luxury apartments complete with swimming pools and other upscale amenities. The carefully manicured grounds featured a multitude of bright flowers and several hundred recently planted trees. New hotels and restaurants had sprung up around town, with new expressways and a subway connecting them to the Olympic venues. German efficiency was once again on display, although without the heavy-handed propaganda of the 1936 Berlin Games.[17] Anticipating major economic benefits, Munich mayor Hans Jochen Vogel proudly said, "Obtaining the Olympics has brought advantages of immediate benefit for the future. It has accelerated achievements which otherwise would have taken at least twice the time to be gained."[18] Clearly, the Munich Olympics were seen by the local planners as attracting money – lots of it – to local coffers. But from the point of view of the IOC, it was putting a stamp of approval upon post-Nazi Germany, assisting the German people to move beyond their recent tragic history.

In his comments at the official opening of the Games, German Chancellor Willy Brandt proclaimed them to be the "Olympics of Joy." Spectators and participants alike seemed to share in the spirit of spiritual uplift as the heavy cloud of Hitler's regime faded. The skies were crystal blue, the sunshine sparkled brightly, and even the smiling security forces wore colorful pastel uniforms. ABC got caught up in the spirit of the Games by focusing attention upon a young Russian woman gymnast, Olga Korbut, whose sprightly personality and fierce determination made a good storyline. That ABC was featuring the appealing human qualities of a Soviet athlete was a reflection of the goodwill that the Games were generating. When Korbut fell from the uneven bars late in the gymnastic competition, the images of her tearful eyes produced an outpouring of empathy across the United States.

About 5:00 a.m. on September 5, however, the feel-good atmosphere dissolved when eight members of the Palestinian Black September terrorist organization forced their way into the Olympic Village apartments occupied by Israeli athletes, coaches, and officials. Wrestling coach Moshe Weinberg attempted to block the door but was gunned down by automatic rifle fire. Two other Israelis died in the first moments of the attack. Most of the delegation managed to escape in the confusion, but nine members were taken hostage, and a 24 hour standoff ensued. In an incredibly bitter irony, with the infamous Nazi death camp of Dachau standing only 9 miles away, once again Jews were dying in Germany at the hands of hate-filled individuals. The terrorists, wearing black head masks that gave off the grim visage of hangmen, presented a list of demands that included releasing some 234 prisoners incarcerated in Israel and a number of terrorists held in other countries, including the notorious German terrorists Andreas Baader and Ulrike Meinhof, and providing safe passage by air for the terrorists and their prisoners to an unnamed Middle Eastern country. They threatened to execute two hostages each hour but postponed their deadline several times. To emphasize their demands, they unceremoniously tossed the body of Weinberg onto the street. Israel's prime minister Golda Meir reiterated her nation's policy of not negotiating with terrorists and deferred to German authorities to handle the crisis.[19]

ABC correspondent Peter Jennings somehow managed to gain access to a hidden balcony of a nearby building from which he provided detailed descriptions of the tragic events. ABC's cameras showed grotesque pictures of one hooded terrorist holding high an automatic rifle. On orders from Avery Brundage, however, a limited schedule of Olympic events went forward as hostage negotiations continued. His decision met with widespread criticism in the Western world. Red Smith of the *New York Times* wrote, "Walled off in their dream world, appallingly unaware of the realities of life and death, the aging playground directors who conduct this quadrennial muscle dance ruled that a little blood must not be permitted to interrupt play."[20]

At 9 p.m., after a tension-filled third day, helicopters landed near the compound and the hostages, the terrorists, and three German security personnel were flown to nearby Fürstenfeldbruck airport where a Lufthansa 727 jet awaited. German officials had no intention of permitting the aircraft to take off. It was later revealed that Chancellor Brandt had wanted the inevitable shootout to occur away from the Olympic Village as several sharpshooters waited at the airport. As two of the Palestinians walked out of a helicopter toward the airplane, the sharpshooters fired, killing them instantly. Several Israelis were immediately shot and killed by their terrorist guards, and the others died when a hand grenade was tossed into their helicopter. ABC anchor Jim McKay, who had provided a coherent narrative throughout the long ordeal, tearfully said, "They're gone. My father once told me, that our greatest hopes and our worst fears are rarely realized. Tonight, our worst fears have been realized."[21]

The next day, Brundage postponed the competition so that a memorial service could be held, but many in the audience expressed their displeasure. They had come expecting to watch track and field events, not a memorial service. Even in the midst of this tragedy, politics intruded. Around the stadium where the service was held, the flags of most participating countries flew at half-mast. However, Arab delegations insisted that their flags fly atop the poles in the normal manner. The Soviets ignored the memorial; as the service proceeded within the stadium, just outside the Soviet soccer team practiced for an upcoming match. The final speaker at the memorial service was the 84-year-old Avery Brundage, his entire life's mission of promoting the Olympics as a means of increasing international understanding having essentially been shattered by the events of the previous day. He revealed his adherence to a romanticized Olympic ideal when he interpreted the terrorist attack as one upon his beloved Olympic Games, not upon the dead Israelis. "Every civilized person recoils in horror at the barbarous criminal intrusion of terrorists into peaceful Olympic precincts. Sadly, in this imperfect world, the greater and the more important the Olympic Games become, the more they are open to commercial, political and now criminal pressure."[22]

Then Brundage made one of the most insensitive statements of his career: "I am sure that the public will agree that we cannot allow a handful of terrorists to destroy this nucleus of international cooperation and good will ... The Games must go on."

The "Munich Massacre" ended whatever idealism any thoughtful person still held about the Olympics. That the Games would become enmeshed in the realities of international politics was inevitable, but for the most part the actual athletic competition at Munich had been free from acrimony. Unfortunately for such American athletes as swimmer Mark Spitz, who won seven gold medals and with each victory set a new world record, and Frank Shorter, who was the first American to win the marathon since 1908, the hostage situation overshadowed their triumphs.

The 1972 Games would also be remembered as the time the United States lost its first Olympic basketball game – ingloriously to the Soviet Union in the gold medal game – in a close match that ended in near-chaos as two referees demonstrated either anti-American bias or gross incompetence, perhaps both. With the United States leading 50–49 and 3 seconds remaining in the game, a Soviet pass from beneath the American basket was knocked out of bounds at midcourt; under unprecedented instructions from the head of the International Basketball Federation (not one of the floor referees), the game officials reset the clock at 3 seconds, thereby giving the Soviets another opportunity. The in-bounds pass went to a Soviet player near the free throw line who had contact with two American defenders before scoring a layup. All of this supposedly happened in 3 seconds. According to international basketball experts, five major officiating errors occurred during these waning moments. Both the scorekeeper and a referee from Italy refused to sign the scorebook in protest, but an appeals panel then voted to uphold the 51–50 USSR victory; the panel included jurors from Cuba, Poland, and Hungary who outvoted non-communist bloc jurors. The US team members felt so strongly about the bizarre circumstances that they refused to accept their silver medals.[23]

American athletes did not fare well in the medal count with the Soviet Union and other Eastern bloc countries at either Munich or the 1976 Montreal Games. The Soviet Union clearly swept the medal competition, and at Montreal, East Germany won 90 medals to the 94 won by the Americans. For decades, the American Olympic effort had been a subject of concern, especially by the National Collegiate Athletic Association which felt it lacked sufficient clout in decision-making. In 1975, President Gerald Ford appointed a blue-ribbon committee of private citizens to review the situation, and the President's Commission on Olympic Sports submitted its final report in late 1977. The following year, Congress passed the Amateur Sports Act that granted much more power to a reconstituted USOC that greatly reduced the influence of the Amateur Athletic Union. The USOC raised private funds to develop a national training center in Colorado Springs, and rules governing the financial support of amateur athletes were relaxed. The USOC now operated intensive training programs to produce future American Olympic athletes. However, athletes still had to receive their monies indirectly, with appearance fees and generous travel allowances being channeled through the USOC or other designated individual sports federations.

To Boycott or Not To Boycott

When the IOC announced that the 1980 Games would be held in Moscow, many leading American conservatives, such as columnists William F. Buckley and George Will and Republican presidential contender Ronald Reagan, expressed dismay, urging an American boycott. Although many believed that the IOC had acted in good faith by deciding to hold the Games in a country other than a Western democracy, conservative critics felt otherwise and demanded that the American athletes stay home. Given President Jimmy Carter's idealist approach to international affairs, however, such a prospect seemed highly unlikely. That changed when the Soviet Union invaded neighboring Afghanistan on Christmas Day, 1979. Carter futilely demanded Soviets withdraw from the country. With his re-election campaign about to begin, he felt pressure to improve his low public approval ratings. The recent taking of 53 American hostages in Tehran had become a major unsolved problem that reflected negatively upon Carter's ability to handle an international crisis. The hostage dilemma, coupled with gasoline shortages brought on by another OPEC embargo and double-digit inflation, had undermined his support at home to the point that liberal Democratic senator Ted Kennedy announced he would challenge Carter in the primaries. Carter believed he had to project an image of firm resolve in order to fend off the Kennedy challenge in the spring primaries and win re-election. The Moscow Olympics presented that opportunity.

   Carter used his presidential influence to persuade the United States Olympic Committee to announce that it would not send a team to Moscow and convinced NBC to withdraw from its contract to televise the Games. American athletes were angered by the decision, and public opinion polls revealed that a majority of Americans opposed a boycott. Eventually, 65 countries joined in the boycott, including West Germany, Japan, the People's Republic of China, and Canada. Nonetheless, Carter's objective of forcing the Soviets and/or the IOC to cancel the Games failed. Significantly, France and Great Britain sent their teams and ultimately some 80 countries took part. Several world records fell as the East German and Soviet athletes dominated the Games.

President Carter's foray into the thicket of Olympic politics proved to be counterproductive, ultimately serving only to alienate leading American athletes and millions of sports fans. It also triggered a Soviet boycott of the upcoming Los Angeles Games in 1984. One Soviet official told American businessman Peter Ueberroth, designated to organize the Los Angeles Olympics, "You sometimes call us the bear, the big bear. This time you can call us the elephant because we don't forget."[24] For three years the Soviets had indicated that they would send their team, but the death of Premier Yuri Andropov, who had worked to reduce tensions with the United States, placed hardliner Konstantin Chernenko in charge. He had been a close associate of Brezhnev, who had taken the American snub in 1980 as a personal affront, and so on May 8, 1984, with the Games scheduled to begin in less than three months, the Soviets cited "security problems" in Los Angeles and withdrew. It clearly was payback time.

The withdrawal of 14 Eastern bloc countries meant that not only were many of the world's leading track and field performers absent, but missing too were wrestlers, weightlifters, boxers, gymnasts, and swimmers. Nonetheless, teams from 140 counties participated. With more than 200 hours of coverage, ABC managed to show nearly every American's performance if it generated a medal, while athletes from other countries were given scant coverage. Despite the lack of a Soviet foil for the nationalist theme that pervaded ABC's coverage, the network managed to attract record viewing audiences. The Olympics had become as much a made-for-television spectacle as a major sports event.

With many of the world's top athletes absent, the Americans won a lopsided number of medals: 83 gold and an additional 93 silver and bronze. In 1976, going head-to-head with the Eastern bloc, the Americans won only 94 medals. Romania ignored the boycott and its athletes won 53 medals. The People's Republic of China also ignored the Soviet-inspired boycott, and made its Olympic debut a good one, with male gymnast Li Ning winning six medals. But it was "USA!" all the time on ABC. With the powerful Soviet team missing, ABC had plenty to crow about. Carl Lewis, a 23-year-old native of New Jersey who had been groomed from early childhood by his parents for track and field excellence, performed spectacularly by equaling the accomplishment of Jesse Owens at the 1936 Olympics, actually winning the same events: the 100 and 200 meter sprints, the long jump, and anchoring the 4×100 meter relay team. Lewis, however, was a difficult sell as a likeable sports star, despite ABC's best efforts. He came across as arrogant and selfish. Despite his spectacular performances he was roundly jeered by American fans when, after wrapping up the long jump with a 28 foot leap on his first jump, he refused to take the next two jumps to save his strength for upcoming events; the American fans wanted to see him go for a world record. Controversy would continue to dog his career, especially when he "named names" of other American athletes whom he alleged used illegal steroids. He appeared in the next three Olympics, and when he formally retired in 1997, he was the possessor of nine gold medals. But his personal popularity never equaled his substantial athletic accomplishments.[25]

Such was not the case of a young lady with a made-for-television smile from Fairmont, West Virginia. Mary Lou Retton came into the Los Angeles games with 14 consecutive gymnastics all-around titles in international competitions, but a few weeks before the Olympics suffered a torn knee cartilage. She persevered in her training, postponed surgery, and thrilled the American television viewers when she scored a perfect 10 in the all-around competition, including a dramatic concluding vault. Her gold medal in the all-around competition was a first for an American woman, and she won four other silver and bronze medals to become the athlete with the most medals at Los Angeles – an amazing feat to be certain, but one that she more than likely would not have achieved if the stable of world-class gymnasts from behind the Iron Curtain had been present. But to the American media, the United States had an answer to the 1972 performance of Olga Korbut, and Retton was credited with stimulating an upsurge in the number of American girls who enlisted for serious gymnastics training.[26]

The real star of the Los Angeles Olympics, however, was the 41-year-old California businessman who presided over the local organizing committee. Peter Ueberroth's challenge was to put on the Los Angeles games without government subsidy. The near-disastrous Montreal Games of 1976 had ended with a $1 billion deficit, and none of the Games since 1936 had turned in a profit. Many skeptics predicted that Ueberroth would fail in his mission, but he proved them wrong with a stunning demonstration of organizational and political skill. His charismatic leadership produced an avalanche of sponsor dollars that not only paid for the staging of the two-week event, but also left the organizing committee with a $222.7 million profit on revenues totaling $718.5 million. When the contract between the IOC and the Los Angeles Olympic Organizing Committee was signed in 1978, one new stipulation included was that the local organizing committee would retain any profits. Because not one cent of profit had been made in the previous 50 years, the IOC did not give this much thought. Thereafter, no such provision would be included; the IOC would make certain it got its cut. Ueberroth put together a paid staff of 1,750 to handle the massive project. Domestic and international television rights brought in $260 million, while 30 sponsorships produced another $130 million from such corporations as Coca-Cola, General Motors, McDonald's, IBM, Levi's, and Anheuser-Busch. Sponsorships were sold for each of the competition venues, and a long list of corporations paid good money to be recognized as an "official" Olympic product. Ueberroth's staff also sold T-shirts, hats, key chains, beach towels, and other souvenir items.[27]

A major factor in the financial success was that Ueberroth and his associates decided that they would avoid the large expense of constructing new facilities. The competition venues were scattered throughout southern California. The Los Angeles Coliseum, constructed for the 1932 Games, received a modest $10 million face-lift and seated 100,000 for the opening and closing ceremonies and track and field events. Dormitories at the University of Southern California were converted into a serviceable Olympic Village. Ticket sales were pushed nationwide by travel agencies, and a heavy public relations campaign encouraged local residents to rent their homes to visitors as a means of preventing overbooking at hotels. Predicted traffic snarls did not clog the freeways and cooler-than-normal temperatures for August prevailed, lowering smog levels below usual.

The Triumph of Professionalism

Ever since that day in 1913 when the United States Olympic Committee stripped decathlon gold medalist Jim Thorpe of his gold medals, the issue of professionalism at the Olympics had been an issue. Under the presidencies of Pierre de Coubertin and Avery Brundage, the IOC had steadfastly adhered to the unrealistic code of amateurism. American athletes found ways to support themselves through a wide variety of subterfuges. That the Eastern bloc of countries sent professional athletes to the Olympics was widely recognized, but Avery Brundage was determined to have Iron Curtain nations participate in order to approximate Coubertin's ideal of representation from five continents and all countries. Thus the American teams tended to comprise college-aged men and women who competed against mature adults who had devoted many years to perfecting their skills. That reality was what made the "miracle" of the American hockey team at Lake Placid truly miraculous.

It was inevitable that the Olympics would become the province of professional athletes. The story of decathlon star Bruce Jenner is illustrative. In 1972, after coming out of obscurity to win a spot on the American team that went to Munich where he finished a disappointing 10th, he devoted himself full-time to training for Montreal. Jenner had told anyone who cared to listen that he intended to become a famous Olympian in order to convert his fame into financial rewards. There were no illusions about patriotism or dedication to the competitive amateur ideal; Jenner clearly viewed sports as his entrée to wealth. Whereas Bob Mathias had won the decathlon in London in 1948 after only a few months of practice, Jenner trained for four years, gambling that the effort would produce a gold medal. His wife supported him working as a flight attendant while he trained. At Montreal, his four-year regimen paid off. He finished first in the 110 meter hurdles, javelin throw, pole vault, and 1,500 meter run, leaving his opponents in the distant dust as he compiled an Olympic record of 8,618 points in the grueling competition. In the process, he defeated former gold medalist Nikolai Avilov of the Soviet Union and a strong competitor from West Germany, Guido Kratschmer.

Jenner's victory raised many questions. When the decathlon competition was over, before leaving the track with his gold medal firmly in hand, he announced his retirement; and as if to make a statement about his love for the sport he had just dominated, he left his vaulting poles lying on the ground as he walked away in search of his reward. True to his plans, he signed several product endorsement contracts, went on the paid lecture circuit, made cameo appearances in motion pictures and television shows, and did television sports commentary. He and his second wife – he divorced the spouse that had supported his training – later launched a company that produced fitness and self-defense tapes and marketed a line of exercise equipment.[28]

Perhaps Jenner's cynicism (or was it realism?) helped make it possible for the new president of the IOC, Juan Samaranch of Spain, to get the rules changed so that professionals could participate in all events in 1992. Samaranch believed their presence would make the Games more attractive to international television audiences, and provide sports fans everywhere an opportunity to see the unquestioned top athletes of the world compete. The 1988 Games in Seoul saw the USOC send its last collection of presumed amateurs, but the 82–76 loss by the men's basketball team – a collection of college players – to an experienced Soviet team ended any pretext that the USOC would continue to send amateur athletes.

The 1992 Barcelona Games were notable for two reasons. The collapse of the Soviet Union in 1991 meant that the once-powerful unified USSR team that included leading athletes from what were now 14 independent countries had disappeared. The quadrennial competition between the capitalists and the communists was now a relic of an earlier era. Consequently, much of the drama of the Summer Games was drained away, and American television coverage focused more than ever upon telling the tales of American athletes who had overcome various obstacles to become Olympians. The mini-biographies were intended to create dramatic human-interest stories to attract viewers who otherwise had little interest in the athletic competition itself. The televised Olympics thus became part soap opera and part athletic competition; the medal count competition was now of considerably less significance, although from time to time the audience was reminded by a television commentator of how many medals the Americans had captured.

The appearance of the American basketball "Dream Team" provided American viewers with a novel attraction at Barcelona. In fact, the entire world fixated upon the much-ballyhooed aggregation led by three of the greatest professionals ever to play in the National Basketball Association – Magic Johnson, Larry Bird, and Michael Jordan. This formidable triumvirate was surrounded by other NBA stars: Charles Barkley, Patrick Ewing, Clyde Drexler, John Stockton, David Robinson, and Karl Malone. The only collegiate player was Christian Laettner of Duke University. Coached by Chuck Daly, whose Detroit Pistons had won two National Basketball Association titles, the Dream Team was criticized in some circles for making a mockery of the Games. Yet at Barcelona, members of teams that lost to the Americans by an average of 44 points a game did not seem to care. They were delighted to be on the same floor as the Americans. Only Lithuania, which previously had provided top talent for unified Soviet teams and had sent several players to the NBA, presented a potential threat to the Americans. But in the semifinal round the Americans jumped to a quick 34–4 lead and coasted to a lopsided 127–76 victory. Croatia was no match in the championship game; the Americans waltzed to victory 117–85.

The presence of a collection of NBA stars in Barcelona signaled that a distinct new era in Olympic history had arrived. Coach Chuck Daly was both magnanimous but prescient in his postgame comments about future Olympic opponents after his team captured the gold:

> They knew they were playing the best in the world. They'll go home and for the rest of their lives be able to tell their friends they played against Michael Jordan, and Magic Johnson and Larry Bird … the more they play against our players, the more confident they're going to get. Finally there will come a day – it's inevitably going to happen – that they will be able to compete with us on even terms. And they'll look back on the Dream Team landmark event in that process.[29]

That inevitable day came much sooner than Daly or any American basketball fan might have realized. For one thing, after 1992, many of the very best NBA players no longer wanted to participate; after playing a long NBA season, they preferred a summer vacation rather than more competitive basketball. The 2000 American team, however, included NBA stars Jason Kidd, Kevin Garnett, Gary Payton and Alonzo Mourning. They discovered that the teams they faced were rapidly catching up. At Sydney, Lithuania came within a whisker of upsetting the Americans in the semifinals before losing 85–83. France trailed by only four points in the final minutes of the gold medal game before falling 85–75. Chuck Daly's day of reckoning had arrived much sooner than he most likely expected.

Athens and Beyond

The return of the Olympics to the historic land of Greece, where it all began in ancient times and which was the site for the first modern Games in 1896, seemed like a good idea at first. But as the Games approached in summer 2004, second-guessing became a new gold medal sport. Would the Greeks be able to afford the cost of constructing the facilities? Would they get the construction done on time? Would the traditional hot summer days put a damper on the ability of athletes to perform? And, with the grim visage of the destruction of the World Trade Center in New York City still uppermost in the minds of many Americans, would the Olympics become the target of a major terrorist attack? Although the Summer Games left the Greek people with a $10 billion deficit, due in part to very low attendance from Western countries as a result of the fear of terrorism, the Games went off without a serious problem. Unlike the 1996 Summer Games in Atlanta, where a bomb killed one woman and injured 111 in Centennial Olympic Plaza, no terrorist attacks occurred.

More than 21,000 media personnel assembled to report the Games, outnumbering the athletes by two to one. A record 202 countries sent teams, but the biggest record was established in providing security from the much-anticipated terrorists. Estimates of the number of security personnel (the actual number was not revealed) who covered the city of Athens like a blanket ranged between 45,000 and 70,000 and the official budget figures set security costs at a whopping $1.2 billion. NBC television paid a record $793 million for the rights to televise the Games in the United States. Although ratings were generally high, especially for the ever-popular gymnastics and track and field events, the focus of the American media was upon the exploits of 19-year-old swimmer Michael Phelps, who entered the Games saddled with predictions that he would eclipse the record seven gold medals of Mark Spitz in 1972. That he failed to do so was perhaps not surprising. He withdrew from one event so that a teammate could capture a gold. Phelps paddled away from Athens with five gold and two bronze medals – not a bad haul for a week's effort.

It was not the dominant Phelps, however, who received the greatest amount of attention from American sports fans. Rather, it was the lackluster (by traditional standards) US basketball team. The predictions of 1992 Dream Team coach Chuck Daly came crashing home. The team was coached by Larry Brown, whose long coaching career included NCAA and NBA championships. His team was filled with young NBA stars, but most NBA veteran players were absent. Puerto Rico – ironically a small island territory of the United States – set the stage for US disappointment with a 92–73 pasting of the Americans in the preliminary rounds, as the rest of the world exulted over only the third American loss in Olympic history.

That stinging defeat proved to be a sign of things to come as the Americans lost two more games in decisive fashion – to eventual gold medalist Argentina, and to Lithuania. Facing well-coached teams composed of veteran players who had mastered the fundamentals of the game, the Americans suffered through a nightmare of an Olympics, ultimately salvaging a modicum of self-respect by defeating Lithuania for the bronze medal, 104–96. America's absolute domination of international basketball had come to an end. Apologists complained that several top veteran NBA players had elected not to play for their country. Others, such as commentator Dick Vitale, noted that the team had had little time to practice together, suggesting that future US squads should be the most recent NBA championship team. American critics pointed out that the best international opponents played a much more fundamentally sound style of basketball that emphasized team strategies rather than the showboating one-on-one style – especially the slam-dunk – that had come to dominate the American college and professional games and had become a popular feature of American television sports reporting. That the American women, playing much more as a team, won their third straight gold medal did nothing to assuage the loss by Larry Brown's squad of individual but undisciplined talents.

The stinging loss produced a resurgent effort prior to the 2008 games in Beijing. Duke's Mike Krzyzewski was named head coach and the "Redeem Team" led by a new group of NBA stars, Kobe Bryant, LeBron James, and Dwyane Wade, waltzed through the preliminary contests and bested Spain 118–97 in the gold medal game. The American media took notice of, but did not sensationalize, the success of host Chinese athletes.

In anticipation of hosting the Games, China had mounted a concerted developmental program that produced 51 gold medals, contrasting favorably to the 36 won by Americans. Although serious economic and political rivals, the United States and China were not engaged in a new version of the Cold War.

14

The Persistent Dilemma of Race

Passage of the Civil Rights Acts of 1964 and 1965 brought to a conclusion the first stage of an ongoing struggle against discrimination and segregation by African Americans. Between 1945 and 1965, American society was consumed by an intensifying drive to overturn the most visible vestiges of discrimination and segregation. Forces on behalf of racial equality utilized many strategies and tactics, highlighted by public demonstrations and marches, forceful pursuit of constitutional issues in the federal courts, and political activism to mobilize public opinion and secure changes in discriminatory laws and practices. The major breakthrough occurred on May 17, 1954, when the United States Supreme Court ruled that the "separate but equal" doctrine established in 1896 was unconstitutional. The Court thus ordered the desegregation of public schools throughout the country. The civil rights movement increased in momentum with the year-long Montgomery bus boycott beginning in December of 1955, the passage of the limited (but symbolically important) Civil Rights Act of 1957, the emotional struggle over the integration of Little Rock Central High School, and confrontations between local law enforcement and civil rights activists at drugstore lunch counters, in bus stations, at voting registration offices, and on college campuses during the early 1960s. The enormous public demonstration on the Washington Mall on August 28, 1963, set the stage for passage of important federal legislation.

The Civil Rights Acts of 1964 and 1965, shepherded through Congress by President Lyndon Johnson, produced a new day in America when a hotel or restaurant owner could no longer deny service to someone because of skin pigmentation, when voting booths were opened to African Americans across the South, and when the Department of Justice could and would challenge segregation polices and laws. Under intense media scrutiny, public Southern universities began admitting African American students. None of these accomplishments came easily; the evening television news and morning newspapers frequently featured reports of angry confrontations between determined civil rights demonstrators

Sports in American Life: A History, Second Edition. Richard O. Davies.
© 2012 John Wiley & Sons, Inc. Published 2012 by John Wiley & Sons, Inc.

and embittered segregationists. Schools and churches were bombed, civil rights leaders threatened, physically attacked, and sometimes killed, and across the South the smell of tear gas had became all too familiar.

The civil rights movement transformed the face and structure of American sports. When the pall of segregation spread across American society in the 1880s, organized baseball readily joined in and excluded African Americans. This unwritten but effective exclusionary policy lasted until Jackie Robinson captured headlines in 1947. Until the 1960s, Southern black colleges offered the only meaningful outlet for black athletes. In the rest of the country, economic and social forces precluded many blacks from participation. To look at the team photos of major college teams from the 1920s well into the 1960s is to see virtually all-white squads.[1]

During the 1950s, racial discrimination remained alive and well in American sports. Increasingly, however, administrators at all-white Southern universities had to confront the dilemma created when their all-white teams ventured outside the region; the chances that they would be matched against teams with African American athletes were increasing with each passing season. Although the preponderance of media attention was upon the desegregation of baseball, the 12 teams comprising the National Football League discovered that they could not consistently win without availing themselves of talented black athletes. By the mid 1950s, fans had come to appreciate that heretofore relatively small and obscure Southern black colleges – such as Grambling, Southern, Jackson State, and Prairie View – were sending many top players to the NFL. The Washington Redskins, owned by George Preston Marshall, resisted this pronounced trend despite a long skein of losing seasons. He finally abandoned his defiant stand when the Kennedy administration threatened to cancel his team's lease to play in the new District of Columbia Stadium unless he dropped his all-white policy. Before the 1962 season, the Redskins traded for wide receiver Bobby Mitchell, who became an instant star. Four other blacks were signed, and the Redskins posted a 5–7–2, the team's best record in five years. Mitchell was voted into the Hall of Fame in 1983.[2]

Although black athletes became increasingly prevalent during the 1960s and 1970s, the ranks of coaches remained lily-white. Black athletes often found that they were now subject to a new set of subtle discriminatory practices. College teams engaged in "position stacking" whereby certain positions (quarterback and middle linebacker in football, point guard in basketball, catcher in baseball), believed to require qualities of leadership and intelligence, were informally declared off-limits to blacks, who were "stacked" into other positions such as wide receiver or defensive back. The concept was known as "centrality" in that it placed several blacks that might have been starters in other positions behind each other, thereby keeping them from occupying positions that required leadership and thinking. Young blacks recruited to play sports at predominantly white campuses discovered that important aspects of campus social life were off-limits to them. Leading that list of grievances was coaches' banning of interracial dating. Blacks also complained that athletic department advisors routinely pressured them into "snap" courses rather than into a challenging curriculum. Eligibility to play on Saturday might be assured, but for black athletes subjected to this form of racial stereotyping and discrimination, graduation became an elusive goal that was frequently out of reach.[3]

"I'm the Greatest"

No single individual better captured the cultural conflicts and contradictions of the 1960s than Muhammad Ali. He made his entrance with a grand flourish just as American foreign policy became increasing focused upon developments in Vietnam and while the civil rights movement was in full force. Tall and willowy, fighting at a trim 210 pounds, Ali used his quickness and ring savvy to frustrate his more powerful but less agile opponents. He possessed the cunning and guile of Gene Tunney, the power of Joe Louis, and the charisma of Jack Dempsey. When he refused induction into the US Army in 1967, the reaction of the boxing establishment was sure and swift. He was summarily stripped of his title and boxing license. Ali's opposition to the Vietnam War made him an ironic public figure: an enormously talented professional fighter who embraced the doctrines of pacifism.[4]

When Cassius Marcellus Clay, Jr burst upon the professional boxing scene following his gold medal victory in the light-heavyweight division at the 1960 Rome Olympics, most sports writers and fans enjoyed his brash behavior, writing it off as merely a new wrinkle on an old theme of hyping fights. In 1961, at age 19, Clay turned professional. Under the tutelage of veteran trainer Angelo Dundee, he developed into a leading heavyweight. His penchant for making audacious pre-fight comments – often drawing upon the rhetorical tradition of simple rhythmic verse that was popular with young urban black males – gave reporters something to write about ("Archie Moore will go down in four," or "At the sound of the bell, Terrell will catch hell," etc., etc.). He first employed this shtick as a professional in 1962 when pitted against a seemingly formidable foe, Sonny Banks. At a pre-fight press conference, he told a laughing, if disbelieving, group of reporters: "The man must fall in the round I call. Banks must fall in four." True to his prediction, Clay knocked out his opponent as predicted. At one point, he correctly predicted the round in which he would dispatch his opponent in seven of eight fights.[5]

With decisive victories over such opponents as former light-heavyweight champion Archie Moore and British heavyweight champion Henry Cooper, Clay found himself at age 22 preparing to take on the formidable heavyweight champion, Sonny Liston. The champion had a long police rap sheet and had served time for armed robbery. Violent and sullen, the fearsome Liston appeared to be much more than the youthful Clay could handle. Liston had won the championship with a stunning first-round knockout of Floyd Patterson in Chicago in 1962, and six months later once again dispatched Patterson with a powerful first-round punch. He seemed invincible. Many boxing experts feared that young Clay, despite having won 19 consecutive professional bouts, was not ready for such a formidable opponent. The California Boxing Commission refused to sanction the fight, taking seriously Rocky Marciano's warning that Liston would likely inflict serious damage to the young challenger. The title fight was eventually scheduled for Miami.

During the pre-fight weigh-in, Clay seemingly went berserk, screaming and shouting at an impassive Liston as he bounded about the room. "I'm going to whup you so baaad," he shouted. "You're a chump, a chump!" Stunned reporters concluded that young Cassius was consumed with fear and had lost his senses. During Clay's training sessions, he and Dundee had invoked a new mantra, "Float like a butterfly, sting like a bee." That is precisely what Clay did, as he out-maneuvered his plodding opponent, who never could get set to throw his best punches. Clay peppered his opponent with stinging left jabs and by the fourth round it was apparent that a new champion was about to be crowned. Liston's face was a bloody pulp, and he seemed incapable of landing a solid punch on his much-quicker opponent. Exhausted, frustrated, and physically beaten, Liston did not respond to the bell for round 7. As Liston slumped in his corner, the new champion bounced around the ring shouting, "I told you! I told you! I'm the greatest!"[6]

The shocking outcome was but a prelude to what proved to be the main event. At a press conference the next day, the new champion informed reporters that he had converted to the relatively unknown, but highly suspect, Black Muslim religion. The charming, dashing Cassius Clay became an instant pariah. The Nation of Islam stood far outside the mainstream of the civil rights movement. An indigenous African American religion with Middle Eastern and African roots, it was primarily known for its embrace of black nationalism, its denunciation of whites as evil, and its repudiation of the goals of racial integration. When it was later learned that Clay's conversion had been facilitated by a convicted felon, the militant Malcolm X, public indignation intensified. "I believe in the religion of Islam," the new champion said, "which means I believe there is no God but Allah, and Elijah Muhammad is his Apostle."[7]

His insistence that the press refer to him as Cassius X exacerbated the situation. A few months later, he changed his name to Muhammad Ali, as suggested by leader Elijah Muhammad (Muhammad meaning "one worthy of praise," and Ali after an ancient general who was related to the prophet Muhammad). Nearly all media outlets, even the *New York Times*, ignored Ali's request and for several years continued to call him by what he now referred to as his "slave name" of Cassius Clay. Former champion Joe Louis publicly chastised him, and Billy Conn, who nearly took the championship away from Louis in 1946, said, "He is a disgrace to the boxing profession. I think that any American who pays to see him fight after what he has said should be ashamed."[8]

The champion, however, was unmoved. Instead, he talked about his religion's emphasis on marital fidelity, premarital chastity, and a lifestyle that shunned the use of alcohol and drugs while emphasizing personal responsibility and lawfulness. However, much of white America only saw the policies of racial exclusion, black pride, and advocacy of the use of force in racial confrontations. When white reporters reminded Ali that whites had called Joe Louis a "credit to his race," the new champion bluntly silenced them: "I don't have to be what you want me to be. I'm free to be who I want."[9] With that powerful declaration of independence, black America exulted while white America recoiled in dismay.

Between that momentous night in Miami in February 1964 and the spring of 1967, Ali successfully defended his championship nine times. In a rematch, he knocked out Liston in the first round. Ali claimed that he had connected with a lightning-fast punch that most spectators at ringside did not see and that cameras did not pick up, but cynics quickly charged that an intimidated Liston took a dive from a "phantom punch." The most memorable of his early title defenses occurred in November 1965, when Ali defeated

Figure 14.1 Shortly after he defeated Sonny Liston in February of 1964 and announced his religious conversion to the Muslim faith, Muhammad Ali was photographed with the outspoken Black Muslim leader Malcolm X, who was viewed with fear and hostility by much of white America. Malcolm's criticism of the message of peace and reconciliation of Martin Luther King, Jr and his comment that "killing is a two-way street" underscored deep divisions in American society and led to widespread denunciations of Ali. *Image © Bob Gomel/Sygma/ Corbis*

former champion Floyd Patterson by a technical knockout. During the pre-fight buildup, Patterson became mainstream white America's great hope in a symbolic battle between "the Crescent and the Cross." Patterson was a conservative Catholic who was appalled by Ali's embrace of the Nation of Islam. In pre-fight comments, the former champion repeatedly referred to his opponent as "Cassius Clay" and at one point drew parallels between the Black Muslims and the Ku Klux Klan: "I have nothing but contempt for the Black Muslims and that for which they stand. The image of a Black Muslim as the world heavyweight champion disgraces the sport and the nation. Cassius Clay must be beaten and the Black Muslim scourge removed from boxing." He repeatedly told reporters he was going to "take back" the heavyweight title "for America," saying at one point that Ali (or Clay) was "disgracing himself and the Negro race."[10]

Such pre-fight braggadocio notwithstanding, Ali easily defeated Patterson, but Patterson's comments had connected with mainstream America. The criticism that Ali's membership in the Nation of Islam engendered proved to be merely a prelude to the public reaction when he refused to accept induction into the United States Army in 1967. Like a growing number of Americans, he did not support the American war aims in Vietnam. As he said in an oft-quoted comment, "I ain't got nothing against those Viet Congs." Various veterans and patriotic organizations – recalling that Joe Louis voluntarily enlisted in the Army shortly after Pearl Harbor – contended that Ali was either a coward or the dupe of a radical religious sect. Ali's position, however, was solidly grounded in the teachings of his faith: "I have searched my conscience, and find that I cannot be true to my belief in my religion in accepting [induction]." Thus on April 28, 1967, in Houston, Texas, when his name was called he refused to take the symbolic step forward to repeat the oath signifying his acceptance of induction in the armed forces. He was thereupon arrested.[11]

Ali's action came at a critical juncture of the war when waves of new troops were being inserted into the conflict. By the end of 1967, more than 650,000 American troops were in South Vietnam. Ali thus confronted the American people with the courage of his convictions. Americans were not prepared for a serious statement of faith from a professional boxer, especially one who was a member of the Nation of Islam. The sports media, with the notable exception of ABC announcer Howard Cosell, were swift to condemn his stand. The New York Boxing Commission, without even the pretense of a hearing, stripped him of his title less than 3 hours after he refused induction, and other state commissions followed in short order. Moving with incredible speed, the Department of Justice indicted him and proceeded to trial in a Houston federal court six weeks later. Judge Joe Ingraham gave the jury precise instructions that virtually assured Ali's conviction, then threw the book at him with the maximum sentence permitted by law: five years in federal prison and a $10,000 fine. The judge ordered Ali's passport be seized so the former champion would be unable to earn money fighting abroad.[12]

Public response to these developments depended upon one's point of view. The predominant view of white America was neatly summarized by Congressman Robert Michel of Illinois, who angrily declared;

> I cannot understand how patriotic Americans can pay for pugilistic exhibitions by an individual who has become the symbol of draft evasion. While thousands of our finest young men are fighting and dying in the jungles of Vietnam, this healthy specimen is profiteering from a series of shabby bouts. Apparently Cassius will fight anyone but the Vietcong.[13]

Urban working-class blacks, however, found in Ali a new hero who was not afraid to challenge the white establishment, as he did in a press conference a few days prior to his appearance before the draft board in Houston:

> Why should they ask me to put on a uniform and go ten thousand miles from home and drop bombs and bullets on brown people in Vietnam while so-called Negro people in Louisville are treated like dogs? If I thought going to war would bring freedom and equality to twenty-two million of my people, they wouldn't have to draft me; I'd join tomorrow … I either have to obey the laws of the land or the laws of Allah … So I'll go to jail.[14]

While lawyers appealed his conviction, Ali worked the college lecture circuit where he talked about his religious beliefs and his refusal to serve in the military. Initially, his anti-war position went counter to public opinion, but by 1970 support for the war had dwindled to nearly 50 percent in opinion polls. Public criticism of the former champion became muted, and many persons now spoke about his courageous stand. The change in public opinion led the New York Boxing Commission to reissue Ali's boxing license, and on June 21, 1971, the United States Supreme Court unanimously overturned his conviction by citing an obscure legal technicality while studiously refusing to rule on the issue of whether his religious beliefs made him a bona fide conscientious objector in the eyes of the law. Ali thereupon resumed his boxing career. He regained his championship in 1974 by defeating champion George Foreman, and successfully defended it 10 times (including his fabled 1975 victory over Joe Frazier in the "Thrilla in Manila") before losing to Leon Spinks in 1979 at the age of 38.[15]

Ali's public persona had originally played a crucial symbolic role in the widening chasm in American society during the 1960s, but during the 1970s he became a symbol of healing and reconciliation. In retirement, he became a popular public figure. His seriously deteriorating physical condition caused by Parkinson's disease, likely brought on by the many blows to the head he had absorbed during his 25 years of amateur and professional boxing, further endeared him to the American people. Despite his shocking physical deterioration, Ali maintained a public presence and enjoyed immense public popularity. Once pilloried as a draft dodger, he was transformed into a beloved American icon.

Boycott, Backlash, and Beyond

Muhammad Ali's problems with the United States government occurred during a time of growing protest against racial discrimination by black athletes. Their tactic of choice was the boycott. In part, the movement was inspired by the spirit of the times, which saw the non-violent strategies of the civil rights movement challenged by militant calls for confrontation. The boycott movement included specific grievances by African American collegiate athletes against coaches, athletic governing boards, and college and university administrations. At the center of this movement stood a young college instructor, Harry Edwards, himself a former basketball and track performer at San Jose State University. In 1967, Edwards assumed a position teaching sociology at San Jose State. Before the start of the fall semester, Edwards and several black athletes approached the university's administration with a list of demands that included the abolition of racial discrimination in all campus organizations and activities, including fraternities and sororities. They also demanded a major overhaul of practices and policies in the athletic department, which they viewed "as racist as any of the other areas of college life." After Edwards met with senior administrators about his concerns, he became frustrated: "They literally laughed in my face – they took my concerns as a joke." He reported that Dean of Students Stanley Benz "made it crystal clear that, where the interest and concerns of the majority whites were concerned, the necessities of black students were inconsequential."[16]

Those experiences prompted Edwards to organize a protest demonstration to force the cancellation of the first football game of the season against the University of Texas at El Paso. The national media jumped on the story: would a student protest lead to the cancellation of a college football game? Governor Ronald Reagan offered to send in the National Guard, but the administration decided to cancel the game to avoid the possibility of violence. UTEP got not only a football victory by forfeiture but also a check for $12,000 under a cancellation clause in the game contract.

Encouraged by the success of his first boycott effort, Edwards turned his attention to the 1968 summer Olympic Games scheduled for Mexico City. He later recalled, "We found out that those black athletes who were being shafted on the campuses were the same athletes the nation depended on as part of its Olympic contingent." As he traveled the country, Edwards learned that athletes on many campuses had similar experiences as he had encountered at San Jose State. For a time, the idea of a boycott gained momentum, getting its share of newspaper space along with urban riots, anti-war demonstrations, and the assassinations of Martin Luther King, Jr and Robert F. Kennedy. Edwards had opened a hornets' nest of latent anger and frustration among black athletes on college campuses across the United States. He organized the Olympic Project for Human Rights to spearhead a boycott, which he saw as one small component of "the broader civil rights movement … We wanted to establish an organic link with the struggle of Dr King, the struggle of Malcolm X, the struggle of SNCC, the struggle of CORE, the struggle of the [Black] Panthers." During a visit to New York City, he said:

We're not just talking about the 1968 Olympics. We're talking about the survival of society. What value is it to a black man to win a medal if he returns to be relegated to the hell of Harlem? And what does society gain by some Negro winning a medal while other Negroes back home are burning down the country? … I think the time has gone when the black man is going to run and jump when the white man says so, and then come back home and run and jump some more to keep from being lynched.[17]

Edwards viewed the Olympic Games as a perfect target because it operated on an international stage where "athletes had become soldiers in a global struggle between East and West." Ultimately, the boycott fizzled. Very few black athletes actually refused to take part in the Mexico City Olympics; the most notable defections were several college basketball players, including Lew Alcindor, Bob Lanier, Elvin Hayes, and Wes Unseld. Most athletes had been in training for several years and were reluctant to miss the competition. Looking back on his organizational efforts for a boycott from the perspective of 30 years later, Edwards felt that it failed because most athletes decided "to put their individual aspirations first." That the US Olympic Committee pulled out all the stops to undercut the boycott – including dispatching such prominent black athletes as Willie Mays and Jesse Owens to talk to potential boycotters – helped persuade some athletes to put aside their grievances and compete.[18]

Nonetheless, the spirit of protest spilled over to American college campuses. Sports pages reported on innumerable confrontations between coaches and their athletes, who expressed grievances ranging across segregated housing, team rules against interracial dating, position "stacking," and even team rules that forbade "Afro" hairdos. Between 1967 and 1972, confrontations embroiled prominent football and basketball programs at such universities as Washington, California, Iowa, Michigan State, Oklahoma, Princeton, Western Michigan, Oklahoma City, Kansas, and Marquette. However, it was the boycott of athletic competitions with Brigham Young University that attracted the most attention.

At issue was the policy of the Church of Jesus Christ of Latter-Day Saints (the Mormon Church) that prohibited African Americans from entering its priesthood. In spring 1968, the UTEP track team refused to compete against BYU, and prior to a home game against BYU on October 18, 1969, all 14 black members of the University of Wyoming football squad sought approval from coach Lloyd Eaton to wear black armbands during the game to protest the church policy. Eaton refused, citing unwritten team rules, and dismissed all 14 from the team when they appeared in his office wearing the armbands. When the university president and the governor of the state of Wyoming sought to mediate the standoff on the eve of the game, the athletes firmly stated that they would never again play for Eaton, accusing him of making racially offensive comments. The governor and university president backed the coach, although news reports pointed out that no rules could be found in team manuals that would have prohibited the armbands. It seemed that the major offense committed by the "Wyoming Fourteen" was challenging the authority of their coach.[19]

The Wyoming incident led to several other protests over scheduled BYU basketball and football games, most notably at the universities of Arizona, Colorado State, New Mexico, and Washington. Stanford University and the University of Washington decided to discontinue playing BYU. Faculty members on the BYU campus plaintively pointed out that the issue of membership of minorities in the Mormon priesthood had originally been raised by members of the church itself; soon thereafter, a small number of black athletes began to appear on Cougar team rosters. The idea of boycott, a red-hot issue that captured front-page headlines for a brief period, had all but disappeared by 1972.[20] In 1978, the First Presidency of the LDS Church announced that a "revelation" had been received that men of African descent could in fact be admitted to the priesthood, and Cougar coaches began recruiting African American athletes.

Breakthrough: A New Era in American Sports

By the mid 1970s, a new era in race relations was at hand. After the tragic killing of four students and the wounding of 13 others by Ohio National Guardsmen at Kent State University on May 5, 1970, a sense of introspection set in. The boycott movement faded away, as compromise and conciliation became more prevalent, and the brutal public protests had receded from the front pages. The anger that had characterized the 1960s began to seep out of public discourse. Quiet returned to the college campuses, and the streets of major cities were no longer the scenes of protests and demonstrations. Racial and ethnic patterns, however, did not remain static, but rather indicated that the rate of change was accelerating. One of the most compelling trends was the growing international composition of the ranks of professional baseball.

The growing popularity of football and basketball in African American communities, however, contributed to the reduced pool of baseball talent from that sector of the American population. This trend became evident by the mid 1970s, eventually falling from a high of 17 percent to just 8.4 percent of major-league players by 2010. Although the numbers of African Americans in major-league baseball declined sharply, the number of black players increased dramatically. This was the result of the influx of large numbers of racially and ethnically diverse blacks from Latin America. The number of Spanish-speaking players exceeded 200 by 2010, making them the largest group of minority players in the history of the game at 27 percent. The majority of these players came from the Dominican Republic, Puerto Rico, and Venezuela, and those numbers would have been even larger had the large pool of baseball talent available in Fidel Castro's Cuba been permitted to play in the United States.

The surge in Hispanics was evidence that America's Game had indeed become international.[21] This phenomenon would have occurred much earlier had the game not been constricted by America's policies of racial segregation. In 1908, the Cincinnati Reds visited Cuba on a postseason junket to play exhibitions with top Cuban teams. They lost more games than they won, and in subsequent years the Chicago Cubs and New York Giants also discovered the Cubans could play the game at a major-league level. The Americans were impressed by the skill of their opposition, and in particular pitcher Jose Mendez, a slender right-hander with very black skin. John McGraw told a reporter that he would happily pay $50,000 to sign the overpowering Mendez if he were white. A Cincinnati baseball writer mused about Mendez playing for the Reds: "What a sensation Mendez would be if it weren't for his color. But alas, that is a handicap he can't outgrow."[22]

The first Latino to break into the majors was a light-skinned native of Columbia, Luis Castro, who played 45 games as an infielder for the Philadelphia Athletics in 1902. A Caucasian Cuban, outfielder Armando Marsans, played in the National, Federal, and American leagues between 1911 and 1918, but the most successful early Latino player was another white Cuban, Adolfo Luque. "Dolf" began his 20-year major-league pitching career with the Boston Braves in 1914, spent several seasons with the Reds and Brooklyn Robins, and made his last appearance on the mound with the New York Giants in 1935. He served as pitching coach with the Giants from 1935 until 1938 and collected two World Series championship rings.

Roberto Clemente was the first great Hispanic player to play in the major leagues. Raised in Puerto Rico by his parents who worked in the sugarcane fields, Clemente learned the game on hardscrabble playing fields as a youngster and played professionally for the Santurce Crabbers before signing a Brooklyn Dodgers minor-league contract at age 18. He played well for the AAA Montreal Royals in 1954 and was acquired by the Pittsburgh Pirates in 1955 in a special rookie draft. After adjusting to living in the United States, overcoming language and cultural dislocations and dealing with noxious racial discrimination, Clemente emerged as a perennial All-Star performer, playing the game with a passion that was on display in every game, every inning. By 1960, when he led the long-time second-division club to a National League title and a classic seven-game World Series triumph, he became a special sports star for appreciative Pirates fans. Biographer David Maraniss describes how Clemente played the game with a special "fire of dignity." His superb fielding, and a rifle arm that nailed many a base runner daring to test his rocket-like throw, thrilled Pirates fans. He rose above racial slights from insensitive sportswriters in rival cities who loved to quote his efforts to use the English language with dripping sarcasm, and became the most popular member of the Pirates.[23]

He had important friends among the Pittsburgh writers, however, and they told their readers of his scintillating play, his high personal standards, and his concern for others. He understood that he was, to use an overused term of a later sports generation, a "role model": "This is something that from the first day, I said to myself, 'I am the minority group. I represent the poor people. I represent the common people of America. So I am going to be treated like a human being.'"[24] One of Clemente's enduring legacies was that he genuinely cared for needy children and devoted great time and effort to supporting work on their behalf, in both Pittsburgh and his native Puerto Rico. On and off the field, this proud man demanded excellence of himself and established a high standard for the Hispanic players who followed in his path.

Clemente earned four Most Valuable Player awards and appeared in 15 All-Star games. He never endured a prolonged batting slump, compiling a lifetime batting average of .317. He hit 240 home runs despite playing in Forbes Field with its distant fences. He helped the Pirates win two pennants and two World Series titles, and knowledgeable Pirates fans appreciated his stellar play in right field as much as his timely hitting. Unfortunately, one key element that explains Clemente's icon status is that he died in a tragic airplane crash on New Year's Eve in 1972. He was aboard the flight destined for Managua, Nicaragua to make certain that relief supplies intended for the victims of a massive earthquake were delivered to those in need. He had learned that tons of emergency supplies sent on three previous missions had been diverted by corrupt government officials to their own benefit. It was later learned the aging DC-7 aircraft that crashed into the ocean shortly after takeoff from Puerto Rico had serious mechanical problems, was piloted by an unqualified flight crew, and was 5,000 pounds overloaded.

He had recorded his 3,000th base hit at the end of the 1972 season. Commissioner Bowie Kuhn waived the normal five-year waiting period and he was voted into the Hall of Fame just 11 weeks after his death, an honor only previously extended to one other man who also had died a tragic and premature death: Lou Gehrig. In the decades that followed, many Hispanic players wore Clemente's number 21 in his honor.

Roberto Clemente mentored the many Hispanic players who came to play baseball in America. He took special interest in Orlando Cepeda, with whom he had developed a friendship in Puerto Rico while playing for the Santurce Crabbers. In 1961, despite playing with a painful bone chip in his elbow, Clemente led the National League in batting with a .351 average, but took greater pleasure that Cepeda, in his fourth season with the Giants, had led the league in home runs and runs batted in. Two players from a small island in the

Caribbean had claimed the top three batting titles for the National League – what natives proudly called the Puerto Rico Triple Crown.[25]

Before game 4 of the 2005 World Series, major-league baseball presented to the fans in Houston the Latin Legends Team, an all-time All-Star team composed of Hispanics who were selected in ballots cast by more than 1.6 million fans. The talent on the team was impressive and underscored the contributions made to the game by Hispanic players: catcher Ivan "Pudge" Rodriguez, first baseman Albert Pujols, second baseman Rod Carew, third baseman Edgar Martinez, outfielders Clemente, Manny Ramirez, and Vladimer Guerrero, starting left- and right-handed pitchers Fernando Valenzuela and Juan Marichal, and relief pitcher Mariano Rivera. Many wondered how other stars, some already in the Hall of Fame, could have been left off this team: first basemen Cepeda and Tony Perez, second baseman Roberto Alamar, shortstop Luis Aparicio, and outfielders Sammy Sosa, Tony Oliva, and Minnie Minoso. The 2005 World Series ended that evening in Minute Maid Park, as the Chicago White Sox swept the series by beating the Astros 1–0. Adding an exclamation mark to the Latin Legends, White Sox manager Ozzie Guillen that night became the first Hispanic manager to win a World Series title.

The process of racial healing was readily evident in other sports, although in many instances change came slowly and was not without resistance. The once lily-white professional golf circuit admitted Lee Elder and Charlie Sifford to the PGA tour in the 1970s; in a symbolically important moment, Elder played in the 1974 Masters tournament at the once ultra-exclusive, all-white National Golf Club in Augusta, where segregation had long been a strict but unwritten policy. In another sport long associated with racial discrimination, Virginia native Arthur Ashe knocked down racial barriers in tennis, enjoying a lengthy run as a top-ranked international player.

Baseball's international appeal was further emphasized with the arrival of top-notch baseball players from Japan in the 1990s. The game had taken root in Japan in the 1870s, brought to the country by missionaries. Baseball grew in popularity and was played in schools, amateur adult leagues, and professionally. The first Japanese player to appear in the United States was left-handed pitcher Masanori Murakama who appeared with the San Francisco Giants in 1962. In 1995, Hideo Nomo was signed by the Los Angeles Dodgers and he became the first Japanese pitcher to throw a no-hitter in the majors. By 2011, a total of 43 Japanese had appeared with American major-league teams, with right fielder Ichiro Suzuki being the most outstanding. He was selected to every American League All-Star team since he first appeared with the Seattle Mariners in 2001. He won two league MVP awards and set a major-league record of 262 hits in one season. He also won the Gold Glove award for fielding in each of his 10 seasons. Known to most fans simply as "Ichiro," he enjoyed a special relationship with the substantial Japanese American population in Seattle. Following the 2010 season, he had already collected over 2,400 base hits and 383 stolen bases and had a lifetime batting average of .331. Had he not spent his first nine years in professional baseball playing in his native Japan for the Orix Blue Wave, Ichiro could have very likely made a run at Pete Rose's career hits record.

Ever since the 1920s, the United States Department of State has sent leading college and professional basketball coaches to teach the game around the world. The result has been that the game became popular on all continents, with various countries mounting major challenges to American teams in international competition. Beginning in the 1980s, foreign players began to appear in the NBA. By the year 2000, 25 foreign countries were represented on the rosters of NBA teams. After the fall of the Iron Curtain in 1991, the influx of players from such countries as Croatia, Russia, Lithuania, and Ukraine came in large numbers, and provided ample evidence of the high quality of basketball being played in Eastern Europe. Athletes from Spain, Italy, Argentina, and Puerto Rico added to the multinational mix of professional basketball. Although such stellar players as Vlade Divac and Peja Stojakovic of Serbia Montenegro and Dirk Nowitzki of Germany were of All-Star caliber, the greatest attention was focused upon the 7 foot 6 inch center Yao Ming of China who found a home as an All-Star performer with the Houston Rockets before being sidelined by recurring serious foot injuries.

Despite the increasing number of minority athletes, management was reluctant to entrust head coaching positions to them. By the 1970s the dearth of minority coaches at the college and professional level became an issue with civil rights advocates. It was not until 1989 that a nationally prominent college football program appointed a black head coach, when Stanford University named Dennis Green. In 1992, Green moved on to the National Football League as head coach of the Minnesota Vikings where he enjoyed a successful 10-year run with a 101–70 record. Green was only the second African American coach in the league's history (the first was former All-Pro lineman Art Shell, who was named head coach of the Oakland Raiders in 1989, the same year he was inducted into the NFL Hall of Fame). In 2010, there were six black head coaches in the NFL, three managers in major-league base-ball, and nine head coaches in the NBA. Three baseball teams had Hispanic managers.

A long-time barrier in professional baseball was breached in 1975 when Frank Robinson was named manager of the Cleveland Indians. The number of black managers remained small for the next quarter-century, although such talented individuals as Robinson, Dusty Baker, Cito Gaston, and Don Baylor were viewed with high respect as managers. Gaston became the first African American manager to win a World Series when the Toronto Blue Jays defeated the Atlanta Braves in 1992. In 2009, Don Wakamatsu became the first American of Asian ancestry to become a major-league manager when appointed by the Seattle Mariners. When he was fired less than two seasons into his managerial tenure, the issue of minority managers had faded to the point that no one raised the issue of racial discrimina-tion in his termination; the Mariners had simply not won enough games and management had become concerned about falling attendance.

The dearth of black head coaches among the 120 major college football programs remained a major point of concern as late as 2010. The appointment of Dennis Green by Stanford did not portend a trend. Although there were eight black coaches in 1997, that number had dwindled to just four in 2009. For years the Black Coaches Association had expressed its frustrations even in getting qualified black candidates interviews for college football openings, and a breakthrough of sorts seemed to occur with the hiring of six additional black coaches before the 2010 season, which brought the total to 13 out of 120 major college head coaches. The academic research and educational efforts of Professor Richard Lapchick, who headed the Institute for Diversity and Ethics in Sports, and advocacy by the Black Coaches Association, were beginning to make a difference.

The number of black head coaches in the National Football League was seven during the 2010 season. Tony Dungy became the first to win a Super Bowl when the Indianapolis Colts defeated the Chicago Bears after the 2006 season; significantly, the Bears were also coached by an African American, Lovie Smith. Following the 2011 season, the Pittsburgh Steelers appeared in the Super Bowl under the direction of one of the league's most highly regarded young coaches. Mike Tomlin, a graduate of William and Mary who had learned the craft of coaching as an assistant under Dungy who then coached the Tampa Bay Buccaneers, had guided the Steelers to a Super Bowl victory in 2009. With the success of such men, the issue of the competency of black coaches in football no longer was an issue. As the employment history indicates, unfortunately, such was not the case just a decade earlier.

College basketball had a substantially better record of providing minority candidates opportunities than other sports. An important pioneer in college basketball was George Raveling. After playing at Villanova during the 1960s, Raveling became the first black assistant coach in the Atlantic Coast Conference in 1970 (at Maryland), and in 1972 he became head coach at Washington State in the Pac-Ten, moving on to Iowa in 1983 and Southern California in 1986. Recognized as a leading spokesman for his profession, Raveling took USC to four consecutive NCAA tournaments and was voted the national College Coach of the Year by his peers in 1992. In 1972, Georgetown University named former Boston Celtics backup center John Thompson to head its then-woeful program; by 1979, Thompson had led the Hoyas to a Big East Conference championship, and in 1982 his team lost in the NCAA finals to North Carolina on freshman Michael Jordan's jump shot. In 1984, Georgetown won the NCAA tournament with a 10-point victory over the University of Houston.

Black basketball head coaches became so commonplace as the twentieth century drew to a close that their selection for major college positions no longer produced perceptible public comment. However, the head coach appointments of Nolan Richardson at Arkansas in 1985 and Rob Evans at Mississippi in 1992 were important breakthroughs. Both coaches enjoyed successful careers. Evans brought respectability to the Ole Miss basketball program, winning the school's first road game against powerhouse Kentucky since 1927, and turning in two consecutive 20-game winning seasons (something the Rebels had not done since 1937–8) before moving on to Arizona State in 1998. In 1990, Richardson guided the Arkansas Razorbacks to a Final Four appearance, and in 1994 his team won the national championship, utilizing a swarming full-court pressing defense and a high-octane fast-break offense that Razorback fans termed "forty minutes of hell."

The racial transformation of American sports during the 1970s and the 1980s was truly revolutionary. By 1980, the typical major college football team was composed of about 50 percent blacks, and college basketball teams had substantially more on average. No one blinked any more when a professional or college basketball team started five African Americans. As noted earlier, major-league baseball teams were 17 percent black by 1980, a figure that dropped to just 8.4 percent by 2010 in a stunning reflection of a long-term trend that saw black youth gravitate away from baseball and toward basketball and football. While black representation on the baseball diamond fell, the percentage of players in professional football and basketball soared. NFL football teams were 40 percent black in 1980, but that number rose to 70 percent by 2000. In that same year, NBA squads were 80 percent black. A large majority of the Most Valuable Players in all three professional sports, year-in and year-out, were predominantly African American.

Arguably the two most popular athletes – of any racial or ethnic background – of the last two decades of the twentieth century were basketball player Michael Jordan and golfer Tiger Woods. Whenever they competed, television ratings soared, and their smiling faces were a constant on television and in newspapers and magazines. Jordan and Woods transcended racial barriers to become two of the most popular figures in American life – not just in sports – and were symbolic of a much different outlook on the part of black athletes. Whereas sports pioneers such as Jackie Robinson, Arthur Ashe, Curt Flood, Muhammad Ali, and Hank Aaron were outspoken in their criticism of racial discrimination in America, a new generation of black athletes emerged during the 1980s that were more likely than not to be indifferent to racial and social issues. They assiduously avoided using their star appeal to advance social causes, including race relations. During the 1990s, Jordan came under criticism from various liberal groups for his endorsement of Nike products. He shrugged off allegations that the high-priced "Air Jordan" basketball shoes carrying his name were made in sweatshops in the Far East that exploited women and child labor. His silence gave the implicit message that Asian working conditions were not his responsibility.[26] Woods also skirted the issue during his long and remunerative relationship with Nike, blithely went about his business of winning golf tournaments, and never became identified with political or social issues. That he lived in a posh gated community near Orlando, complete with a private golf course and other upscale amenities, seemed only natural for this superbly talented and incredibly popular multimillionaire.

Despite deeply engrained racial sentiments in American society, in the sports world of the last quarter-century, performance tended to overwhelm once-dominant racist attitudes. Along with Woods and Jordan, the new generation of prominent black sports stars seemed to care little about those early pioneers who had battled entrenched racism so that their successors could have access to extraordinarily lucrative multimillion-dollar players' contracts and hefty product endorsements. "Today's black athlete is very different," sociologist Harry Edwards noted in 1998 on the 30th anniversary of the boycott movement that he had once spearheaded: "Their identity is different – they live in a rich, largely white world, a world where black individuality is tolerated so long as it is without reference to the black community. If you ask them about the history of the black athlete, many couldn't tell you much. They don't find that history relevant to their world." Edwards lamented a conversation with a leading black NBA star about the pioneering role played by NBA guard Oscar Robertson. The response he received was, "Don't know, don't care, and don't take me there!" Unfortunately, Edwards said, contemporary black athletes "don't care about whose shoulders they stand on. They have no idea about who set the table at which they are feasting. And the worse part about it is not that they are ignorant of this history, but they are militantly ignorant."[27]

Jackie Robinson, his uniform number 42 permanently retired by all major-league teams in 1997 on the 50th anniversary of his first appearance in a Brooklyn Dodgers uniform, was definitely of an earlier and much different era.

Hank Aaron Catches the Babe

In 1961, American sports fans carefully followed New York Yankee outfielders Roger Maris and Mickey Mantle as they zeroed in on Babe Ruth's season record of 60 home runs. When it was recognized that one or both might catch the Babe, Commissioner Ford Frick announced in mid season that, should the record be broken, the new mark would be placed in the record books with "a distinctive mark," indicating that the new record was set in a 162-game season rather than the 154 that Ruth played. The issue of the number of games in the season created the only real controversy as Ruth's record was eclipsed by Maris. His home run total stood at 59 after his 154th game, and on the 162nd and last game of the season he hit the record-breaking number 61. His record was thereupon accompanied by an asterisk to preserve the Ruthian achievement of 1927. A very private individual, Maris did not handle his sudden fame well. He suffered from injuries and personal problems and was traded to St Louis in 1966, and when he retired two years later with a career 275 home runs, no one paid much attention. The only significant public display memorializing his baseball career is located in a corner of a shopping mall in his home town of Fargo, North Dakota.

That was not the case a decade later when Henry ("Hank") Aaron of the Atlanta Braves began to creep close to the Babe's career home run number of 714. Born in Mobile in 1934, Aaron first entered the major leagues in 1954 with the Boston Braves and launched a long Hall of Fame career as an outfielder and power hitter. In May 1970, he banged out his 3,000th base hit, but because he never hit more than 50 home runs in any season, no baseball expert anticipated that when he reached his late 30s this slender, lithe athlete would unleash a sustained home run barrage that put Ruth's career record in jeopardy. Aaron ended the 1970 season with 592 home runs, placing him behind Ruth and Willie Mays for career home runs. In the next three seasons, he smacked 121 round-trippers, and at the end of the 1973 season stood at 713, just one behind the Babe. Over the winter, baseball writers speculated endlessly about the implications of the feat that Aaron would surely accomplish early in the 1974 season.

Many white fans did not take kindly to the possibility that an African American would surpass the Babe. As he approached the magic number of 714, Aaron was flooded with nasty, crude letters, some of them threatening bodily harm. During the 12 months before he broke Ruth's record, according to the US Post Office, Aaron received 930,000 pieces of mail, more than any person in the United States other than Watergate-ensnared Richard M. Nixon. The threats made against Aaron were sufficient to justify an ongoing FBI investigation, and the hiring of personal bodyguards.[28] On opening day in 1974, Aaron tied Babe Ruth with a line drive over the left-field fence at Riverfront Stadium in Cincinnati, and on April 8 before a hometown crowd he hit the record-breaking number 715 off veteran left-hander Al Downing of the Los Angeles Dodgers. Baseball Commissioner Bowie Kuhn was conspicuously absent that historic day, and during the midst of a congratulatory telephone call that Aaron received in the locker room from President Nixon, the line suddenly went dead. Downing had a splendid 16-year career in the major leagues, but was defined by that one fastball pitched to Aaron, and suffered from whispering attacks that he had conspired with Aaron to give him a fat pitch to hit. "I got vilified for years for giving up a home run to a man who hit more home runs than anyone who ever lived," he said. "Does that make any sense to anyone?"[29]

Figure 14.2   Henry Aaron played the game of baseball with a healthy respect for its traditions. He began his professional career with the Indianapolis Clowns of the Negro Leagues, and made his first appearance in a Milwaukee Braves uniform in 1954. He stoically endured threats to his safety as he approached Babe Ruth's record of 714 home runs, and ended his career in 1976 with 755 home runs. That record was broken by Barry Bonds in 2006 amidst the controversy about the use of steroids. *National Baseball Hall of Fame Library, Cooperstown, NY, USA* © *NBL*

Hank Aaron recalls that his emotions were bittersweet. As he later wrote in his autobiography, "It should have been the most enjoyable time of my life, and instead it was hell." The angry letters and death threats had taken their toll. He had discovered that the only tangible way he could respond to his many hate-filled correspondents was to go for the record:

> I kept feeling more and more strongly that I had to break the record not only for myself and for Jackie Robinson and for black people, but also to strike back at the vicious little people who wanted to keep me from doing it. All that hatred left a deep scar on me. I was just a man doing something that God had given me the power to do, and I was living like an outcast in my own country.[30]

Aaron retired from baseball in 1976 with a grand total of 755 home runs. His career number of 2,297 runs batted in is also a record, and he is ranked third in total career hits with 3,771. He was later quoted that he hoped that "some kid, black or white," would exceed his record. "I will be pulling for him." However, when that person turned out to be Barry Bonds of the San Francisco Giants in 2005, a power hitter whose use of anabolic steroids was widely rumored, Aaron discreetly distanced himself from Bonds and his new record. He was on public record many times in his opposition to the use of performance enhancing substances, and Harry Edwards perhaps best summarized the complexity created when Bonds broke Aaron's record: "Henry Aaron, Roger Maris, these are the standard-bearers. Mark McGwire, Barry Bonds, these are the record-holders. For the first time ever, the standard of excellence and the record-holder are totally different people."[31]

Can White Men Jump?

During the early 1970s, as black athletes excelled in mainstream American sports, a red-hot debate broke out that said much about the underlying racial assumptions and prejudices that were widespread throughout mainstream white American society. Speculation about the role of race in explaining sports prowess had long bubbled beneath the surface of American sports, but it came into sharp focus in 1971 when a senior writer for *Sports Illustrated* published a lengthy essay that argued black success resulted from a combination of special physiological and psychological factors attributable directly to race.[32] In this article, Martin Kane took notice of successful black performance that had occurred in recent years, especially in those popular spectator sports where strength, agility, and speed were essential. "Twenty-six years ago there were no blacks on any of the big-league basketball, football or baseball professional teams," Kane noted, but by 1971 nearly 50 percent of the athletes in these sports were African American. He concluded that "the black community in the US is not just contributing more than its share of participants to sport, it is contributing immensely more than its share of stars." Noting that at the 1968 Olympic Games in Mexico City, all eight Olympic records set by the American track and field team were the result of performances by blacks, he quoted a European coach, "If not for the blacks, the US team would finish somewhere behind Ecuador."

Although Kane identified many contributing social, economic, and environmental factors, including access to playing facilities (hence the small number of elite black golfers, swimmers, or tennis players), he nonetheless came down hard on the side of racial characteristics as a determining factor. Kane, in fact, identified three areas for examination: race-linked physiological and physical characteristics, race-linked psychological characteristics, and race-linked historical factors. He cited several physiological studies he believed demonstrated that black athletes had more flexibility, longer legs and arms, narrower hips, less body fat, greater bone density, more tendon, and less muscle, all of which produced individuals with greater speed, power, and dexterity. Additionally, Kane cited "a distinctive ability to relax under pressure," a trait which he attributed to "the suppressed life of the black man in America," which had enabled him to endure and survive the indignities of slavery and segregation. "White kids haven't had to live under an oppressive burden," he said. Thus blacks had an inherited ability to "relax" during times of intense stress, as well as a deep-seated subconscious motivation "to exceed whites athletically" whenever given the opportunity.

Kane emphasized the struggle of those African tribesmen who were able to survive captivity by slave hunters in Africa, the brutal and deadly Middle Passage across the Atlantic Ocean, and the inhumane time of "seasoning" or "breaking-in" that prepared survivors for backbreaking labor in the sugarcane fields of the Caribbean and in the tobacco, rice, and cotton fields of North America. Because of these experiences, he concluded that contemporary blacks were the products of "natural selection" resulting from a "survival of the fittest" process that stretched back to the 1600s. He suggested that black athletic ability was further enhanced by selective breeding by white masters of female slaves with the strongest and biggest males. In a brief acknowledgment of the impact of discriminatory economic and social policies upon African Americans, Kane concluded that "every black child, however he might be discouraged from a career with a Wall Street brokerage firm, knows he has a sporting chance in baseball, football, boxing, basketball or track … He has the examples of Willie Mays and Bill Russell, of Frank Robinson and Lew Alcindor to inspire him."

Kane's explosive article, coming as it did on the heels of the assertions by two well-known scholars, psychologist Arthur Jensen and Nobel prize-winning physicist William Shockley, that lower academic achievement by African Americans was attributable to genetics rather than social and cultural factors, set off a heated public controversy. Among those taking up the challenge was Harry Edwards, now holding a professorship in sociology at the University of California, Berkeley. He responded with a blistering article in *The Black Scholar* and in a much more detailed analysis in his textbook, *Sociology of Sport*. Edwards feared that Kane's argument "opens the door for at least an informal acceptance of the idea that whites are intellectually superior to blacks." He pulled no punches, bluntly attributing racist assumptions to Kane's article. "The argument that blacks are physically superior to whites as athletes or as a people is merely a racist ideology camouflaged to appeal to the ignorant, the unthinking, and the unaware in a period heightened by black identity." Summarizing the widely accepted positions of most scholars, Edwards emphasized, "The simple fact of the matter is that the scientific concept of race has no proven biological or genetic validity. As a cultural delineation, however, it does have a social and political reality."[33]

Edwards argued that Kane's article lumped together folk tales, pseudoscience, and unproven assertions, all premised upon racist assumptions. Drawing on an extensive body of sociological and anthropological research, he noted that even the concept of *race* was not well established: "Typically, there has been little success in any effort to derive consistent patterns of valid relationships between racial categories and meaningful social, intellectual, or physical capabilities."[34] He reported what one scholar had clearly demonstrated:

It is quite obvious that Black athletes differ from each other physically quite as much as Whites do … [W]hat physical characteristics does Kareem Abdul-Jabbar have in common with Elgin Baylor, or Wilt Chamberlain with Al Attles? The point is simply that Wilt Chamberlain and

Kareem Abdul-Jabbar have more in common physically with Mel Counts and Hank Finkel, two seven-foot tall white athletes, than with most of their fellow black athletes.[35]

Edwards emphasized that Kane drew upon only a small subset of black Americans – a few elite black athletes – and not the general population of 20 million individuals, who, he noted, came in all shapes and sizes. It was absurd to generalize about a commonality of musculature or bone structure. He pointed out that the great percentage of African Americans lacked special aptitude for sports, just like their white counterparts. A few black athletes, he said, excelled only in those sports to which they had access and ample opportunity to hone their skills. Thus inner-city basketball courts, city streets, and parks provided opportunities to learn basketball, football, and baseball. At best, black youngsters could excel in games offered by public school systems. Private golf courses, segregated swimming pools, private tennis clubs, and remote ski resorts obviously contributed to the dearth of black success in these sports. Additionally, these sports have other features that limit black access: the importance of expensive private lessons, costly club memberships, and equipment priced far beyond the reach of most African Americans. Racial discrimination, not racially determined physical traits, explained black success in a few sports and lack thereof in others. Kane's polemic, he said, even did the most successful of black athletes no favors by emphasizing natural talent over hard work and dedication. He quoted Bill Russell to the effect that he had become a superior basketball player because of the intensive effort he put into his craft: "Russell once stated that he had to work as hard to achieve his status as the greatest basketball player of the last decade, as the president of General Motors had to work to achieve his position."[36]

Although Edwards's dismantling of Martin Kane's hypothesis tended to satisfy the academic world, his powerful analysis apparently did not reach the average sports fan or even prominent sports figures that should have become better informed. In 1987, the general manager and president of the Los Angeles Dodgers, Al Campanis, appeared on the "Nightline" television show for an interview with ABC's Ted Koppel on the 40th anniversary of Jackie Robinson's first appearance in a Brooklyn Dodgers uniform. At one point, Campanis blithely attributed the relatively low number of black managers in baseball to a lack of mental acuity, asserting that they "may not have some of the necessities to be, let's say, a field manager, or perhaps a general manager." When Koppel provided Campanis an opportunity to rephrase his insensitive comments ("Do you really believe that?" he asked, and after a commercial break, "I'd like to give you one more chance to dig yourself out"), the Dodgers executive instead continued to affirm his initial comments, going on to state that blacks also were not good swimmers because they "don't have buoyancy."[37]

Just nine months after the Campanis debacle, another leading sports figure, the sports handicapping guru and CBS television personality, Jimmy "The Greek" Snyder, stepped onto the same landmine and produced front-page stories across the country. While waiting for a table at a Washington, DC restaurant, he casually responded to a query by a reporter about the reason African American athletes had become so successful. It was, he said, due to selective breeding during slavery: "I'm telling you that the black is the better athlete, and he is bred to be the better athlete, because this goes back all the way to the Civil War … The slave owner would breed his big black to his big woman so that he could have a big black kid, you see. I mean that's where it all started." The result would be, he predicted, complete domination of American sports by genetically advantaged black athletes: "They've got everything, if they take over coaching like everybody wants them to there's not going to be anything left for the whites. I mean all the players are black." Just as the Dodgers terminated Campanis for his remarks, CBS wasted no time in firing "The Greek."[38] Three years later, actors Wesley Snipes and Woody Harrelson turned satire upon the issue in the motion picture *White Men Can't Jump*, a humorous treatment about the quirks and vagaries of black and white athleticism. They portrayed a pair of playground hustlers playing two-on-two basketball for high stakes; when black opponents saw the scrawny white kid (Harrelson) shuffle onto the asphalt, they were prime for picking by he and his black co-conspirator.

In the years that followed the Campanis and Snyder debacles, several journalists and scholars attempted to reprise the race-based interpretation of athletic performance. Although these efforts produced the expected mixed reaction, for most part sports fans and journalists paid little attention. Efforts to attribute the success of a few elite athletes to inherited racial traits were soundly debunked from a wide spectrum of scientific perspectives. The noted sports sociologist Jay Coakley aptly summarizes the underlying issue when he writes, "When it comes to using racial classification in our personal lives, we should recognize that the human race contains many combinations of changing physical similarities and differences and that racial categories are based on social meanings given to those similarities and differences, not biology."[39]

Nonetheless, the heavy representation by outstanding black athletes in such mainstream American sports as football, basketball, boxing, baseball, and track and field did not go unnoticed. The fact that African Americans constitute just 13 percent of the American population but well more than 50 percent of elite teams in mainstream college and professional sports continues to fuel popular perceptions that Martin Kane was not far off the mark, academic verdicts on the subject notwithstanding.[40]

Tiger

The difficulty in attributing achievement in sports specifically to racial traits was exemplified by the unprecedented success initially enjoyed by golfer Eldrick "Tiger" Woods. Proud of his mixed heritage (Native American, African American, Asian, Eurasian), he once suggested that journalists refer to him as "Cablinasian." Rising swiftly to the pinnacle of the world of professional golf – long the province of white men – Woods baffled those who sought to use racial characteristics to explain mastery in sports. That he had a natural aptitude for golf was obvious, but Woods's success clearly resulted from his intense personal drive and the encouragement from an early age by his parents. This dynamic young athlete stunned the sports world when he did the seemingly impossible by winning the prestigious Masters tournament on his first try as a professional at age 21. He won by an extraordinary 12 strokes over an elite field of seasoned professionals and set a tournament record with a score of 270.

Overnight, Woods became the hottest name in golf, and his personal magnetism attracted millions of fans. The magic he inspired when he joined the PGA tour did not fade. When he was in the hunt for another tournament title, television ratings soared. He attracted large and enthusiastic galleries. He boomed his drives over 300 yards, hit his fairway woods and irons with confidence, and under great pressure time and again chipped onto tricky greens with uncanny touch. In tight matches, his putter seemed to be transformed into a magic wand. He was such a bigger-than-life presence that his multiracial heritage was seldom noticed. Nonetheless, black Americans saw in him someone who dominated a traditionally all-white sport, while white Americans found redemption from the long-standing critique that golf was a game that was badly scarred for its history of racial discrimination. As David Owen writes, "When white golfers do think about Woods' racial background, it's often with a sense of relief: his dominance feels like an act of forgiveness, as though in a single spectacular career he could make up for the game's ugly past all by himself."[41]

Woods burst upon the relatively staid world of professional golf like a thunderbolt. His parents had prepared him for his role, budgeting for golf lessons and travel to tournaments, but at the same time providing healthy doses of both encouragement and discipline. His father had him swinging a golf club with authority before he was out of diapers, and at age three he appeared before a national audience on the "Phil Douglas Show" in a putting contest with Bob Hope. When he was five, young Tiger was featured hitting golf balls with surprising distance and accuracy on "That's Incredible." He shot his first hole-in-one when he was six. As a teenager he dominated youth tournaments in southern California, and began competing in national juniors tournaments. In 1991, at the age of 16, he was named the Junior Amateur Player of the Year, and in 1994, he became the youngest player ever to win the US Amateur championship. After scorching the college circuit for two years at Stanford, he turned professional in 1996, at which time Nike announced that it had signed him to a long-term $40 million endorsement contract. It was a sum previously unheard of for a golfer, and he had yet to play in his first professional tournament. Woods's multiracial heritage, journalist Gary Smith predicted at the time, would help eradicate racial prejudice from the rarified white world of American golf. *Sports Illustrated* identified him as the "Chosen One" and named him "Sportsman of the Year" before he won his first Grand Slam tournament.[42]

The acclaim that Woods received from fawning media and an adoring public was reminiscent of the adulation that surrounded the public persona of America's first sports superstar. Like Babe Ruth, Tiger also had his dark side, one that would eventually shatter his public image. Unlike Ruth, whose personal life went unreported by a deferential press, Woods lived in an age when the media protected no one and thrived on exposing the rich and famous to public humiliation for their indiscretions. Woods made a perfect target because his seemingly picture-perfect life – carefully crafted by his many sponsors and personal advisors – collapsed with a swiftness that was stunning. Within days, an image that had been painstakingly constructed for 15 years was shattered beyond repair when reports of marital infidelity were splashed onto the front pages of tabloids and became the focus of the blogosphere.

In the early hours of the morning after Thanksgiving in 2009, the 34-year-old Woods slammed his SUV into a tree and fire hydrant near his luxurious home in an exclusive gated community near Orlando. He was trapped in the vehicle but freed by his wife Elin who smashed out a window with a 3-iron. Early news reports indicated he had been treated for facial injuries at an emergency room, and speculation soon raced across the blogosphere that Woods had fled his home after an angry confrontation with his wife. Some accounts went so far as to suggest that his wounds were inflicted by Elin wielding the 3-iron. The incident quickly spiraled into a sensational story that dominated the 24 hour news cycle for weeks as an army of investigative journalists joined the chase. Confirmed reports revealed a pattern of infidelity that was stunning for its excess. More than a dozen women were identified, several who came forward voluntarily to secure their few minutes of fame.

Battered by the unrelenting series of revelations, Woods and his team of advisors went into seclusion while an army of journalists followed the scent of a wounded Tiger. Amidst reports that several of his sponsors were considering ending lucrative endorsement deals, he issued terse statements apologizing for "transgressions" and "personal failings." He asked forgiveness for having engaged in "disgusting behavior," and announced he was taking an indefinite leave from the tour. At one point he was reported to have entered a residential clinic for treatment for "sex addiction." The master of the world of golf, who was widely considered to be a role model for the way he conducted himself in both his professional and private lives, now became the hapless butt of jokes from late-night television hosts. With incredible rapidity, his carefully crafted image had disappeared into a morass of seamy revelations about his secret life. His marriage collapsed, and a divorce was finalized in August of 2010, the details of a multimillion settlement sealed by a Florida court.

Woods's storybook life came to an abrupt end, but not until he had spent 15 years in the limelight. No golfer – neither Hogan, nor Palmer, nor Nicklaus – had ever enjoyed such public acclaim. Every time his game seemed to slip a bit, he responded with even greater resolve and moved on to another stunning triumph. After winning only one tournament in 1998, he launched an intensive program of weight and aerobics training highly unusual for professional golfers, who perhaps practiced several hours a day but were prone to retire to the 19th hole at day's end rather than hit the weights or run 5 miles. He rebuilt his already powerful swing under the tutelage of coach Butch Harmon, practiced incessantly, and added greater distance and accuracy to his game. In 1999, he won nine tournaments, including the PGA.

His play in 2000 cemented his hold on the American sports fan. At the US Open, played at Pebble Beach, Woods eclipsed the field by an almost incomprehensible 15 strokes. Watching Woods leave the world's best professionals far behind, 1982 Open champion Tom Watson was in awe: "Tiger has raised the bar to a level that only he can jump over."[43] Woods proceeded to win the two remaining majors tournaments, outdistancing the British Open field by eight strokes and defeating Bob May in a three-hole playoff to claim the PGA for a second consecutive year. In spring 2001, Woods made it four majors in a row with a two-stroke victory at the Masters over David Duval. No one in history had such a comparable run. It was easy to overlook the fact that Woods had accomplished this by the age of 25, an age when most professional golfers have just begun to reach their potential. Journalist Frank Deford was prompted to ask, "Has anybody in any sport been this much better than everyone else?"[44] After Woods won his third Masters in 2002, critics, more serious than flippant, began to speculate whether the hidebound traditionalists who run Augusta National should redesign the course to make it "Tiger-proof."[45]

Woods had many a stirring victory (and some narrow defeats), but nothing compared with his play at the 2008 US Open. In mid April, after struggling at the Masters, he underwent a third arthroscopic surgery on his left knee. After two months of therapy, he returned in June for the Open held at one of his favorite southern California courses, Torrey Pines. He played erratically, but late in the third round sank a 100 foot putt for an eagle and chipped in from off the green for a birdie to stay in contention. Throughout the tournament he limped visibly, obviously attempting to keep weight off his left leg. He winced in pain after hitting a shot and used an iron for a makeshift cane as he struggled down the fairways. On the 72nd and final hole on Sunday, he sank a treacherous side-hill 12 foot putt to deprive tour veteran Rocco Mediate of his first major title and force an 18-hole playoff. He had to make birdie on the final hole of the playoff to force a sudden-death playoff, which he won when Mediate made bogey. Only later did Woods reveal that he had been playing with a torn knee ligament that required major reconstructive surgery *and* a double stress fracture in his left leg. Mediate could only say, "This guy does things that are not normal by any stretch of the imagination."[46]

When he returned to the tour in 2009 after eight months recovering from surgery, he won six tournaments including his second FedEx title. He came close to a 15th major title when he led by two strokes going into the final round of the 2009 PGA at Hazeltine, but faltered on the final day and lost by three strokes to Y. E. Yang of South Korea. It was the first time that he had lost a major tournament when he entered the final day in the lead. As he began to prepare for the 2010 tour in the wake of the scandalous breakup of his marriage, Woods had won 71 official PGA tournaments, but he had his sights set on eclipsing the record of 18 major titles held by Jack Nicklaus. Tiger's improbable victory at Torrey Pines in 2008 had given him number 14. He had often said he considered Nicklaus the greatest golfer in history. As a child he had memorized the many accomplishments of Jack Nicklaus, and at the age of 13 had matter-of-factly told his parents that he someday planned to surpass Nicklaus's record.

Until his secret personal life was revealed, most experts had assumed that he would surpass Nicklaus within a relatively short period of time, but many now expressed skepticism about whether or not he would ever catch the Golden Bear. Following a self-imposed absence from the tour in 2010, he returned to Augusta in mid April 2011 for the Masters amidst intensive media scrutiny. He seemed able to focus upon his golf and finished just five strokes behind winner Phil Mickelson, but his play then deteriorated to the point of embarrassment. Not only did he lose his control off the tee and from the fairway, but his putting stroke abandoned him as well. Obviously distracted by his personal problems, his once uncanny ability to focus intently on each shot had disappeared. He finished 13 strokes off the pace at St Andrews in the British Open, a course that was the scene of several of his most memorable rounds. He went into a semi-meltdown in August at the Bridgestone Invitational in Akron, missing fairways off the tee and bungling short iron shots to the greens that he used to nail. He missed short putts and, when the carnage had ended, found himself in 78th place, just two spots from dead last. He finished 18 strokes over par and 30 strokes behind winner Hunter Mahan. It was the most embarrassing moment of his entire golfing career. Pundits took notice of the fact that the Firestone course was tailor-made for his style of play and that he had won the tournament seven times since 2000.

Unlike several of his corporate sponsors, Nike stood by its man. Perhaps the company had too much invested in him to walk away, but Nike executives apparently believed that

Figure 14.3   Tiger Woods led a seemingly near-perfect life for the first 15 years of his professional career until sensational revelations of multiple marital infidelities were revealed in 2009. The following year, he failed to win a single tournament, and his career goal of surpassing the 18 victories in major tournaments set by Jack Nicklaus seemed in doubt. He is shown here at the 2002 US Open at Bethpage on Long Island where he captured his eighth major title with a three-stroke victory over Phil Mickelson. *Image © John A. Angelillo/Corbis*

Woods would regain his swagger and once more set his sights on Jack Nicklaus. At age 35, however, the shadows were beginning to lengthen and his multitude of fans – including television sports executives hoping for a return to the high viewer ratings he had produced – yearned for the day when the Tiger of old would return to the tour. No one, however, expected him to regain the public stature that he long enjoyed, that of one of the world's most admired public figures.

Sister Act: Venus and Serena

They burst upon the exclusive world of professional tennis like a stage-five hurricane, leaving in their wake a checkered record of contentiousness and triumph, ultimately producing awe and astonishment at their skill level and domination of women's tennis. Unlike most tennis professionals, they did not come from financially comfortable families that lavished upon their children expensive tennis lessons, tuition at high-powered year-round tennis schools, and costly travel to play a junior tennis tournament schedule in preparation for moving on to the United States Tennis Association tour. Instead, sisters Venus and Serena Williams learned their tennis from their father on the pocked blacktop public courts in gang-infested Compton, California. Richard Williams, who supported his family as part owner of a security-guard firm, had little interest in tennis until he saw a check for $30,000 presented to a tournament winner. He thereupon taught himself to play the game by reading tennis manuals and watching instructional videos, with the specific intent of producing at least one professional champion from among his five daughters. The two youngest showed the most potential, and before their first grade he began putting them through hours of practice, six days a week. By the time they were 10, both dominated junior tennis tournaments in the Los Angeles area. In 1990, Venus won the 12-and-under southern California title and younger sister Serena the 10-and-under. Part promotions whiz, part huckster, Richard launched a marketing blitz that attracted the attention he wanted: several tennis equipment manufacturers came calling, armed with offers of endorsement contracts. In 1991, Richard moved his family to Florida, where he placed the girls under the guidance of professional instructors, who honed their skills to the point that they were prepared for international junior competition.[47]

At this juncture, with plenty of offers of lucrative endorsements, Richard surprised the tennis world by pulling his daughters out of all junior tournament competition, insisting that they needed to concentrate upon their studies. The intense practice regimen continued. Unlike many parents of tennis prodigies who turned their children professional at an early age, Richard decided to postpone that decision. Although confidently predicting that his "ghetto Cinderella," as he called Venus, would someday dominate women's professional tennis, he had his own time-plan: "I'm sick of looking around tennis and seeing these poor kids making a living for their parents, seeing these parents drive around in their Mercedes and Rolls Royces … That's like the parents turning against the kids and prostituting them."[48]

Perhaps it was not surprising that Richard gave in to the money and permitted Venus to turn professional when she was 14. But he restricted her play to only a few events each year. She won her first professional match in a California tournament in 1994 against the world's 59th-ranked player, but lost in the second round to second-ranked Arantxa Sánchez Vicario. After winning the first set, her game fell apart as she succumbed to a case of tournament jitters. Clearly Venus's lack of extensive junior tournament experience showed in her match against Vicario, and for the next three years she played sporadically. Despite a rocky start in her professional career, the Reebok Company was convinced of her future and signed her to a five-year, $12 million contract in 1995. Richard's improbable dream had paid off. Despite his early protestations about the exploitation of youngsters, he was not hesitant to take the money.

Still, Venus's early years on the tour were difficult. At the end of the 1996 season, she was ranked 212 in the world. Then she broke through in 1997, methodically working her way up the rankings. She entered the US Open unseeded with a ranking of 66 and powered her way to the finals before losing in two sets to number-one-ranked Martina Hingis. Venus stunned the tennis world with her powerful ground strokes, and her serves were timed at 120 miles per hour. She tore around the court smashing overheads, volleying with a vengeance, striking her ground strokes with a ferocity that became the talk of the tennis world. As she moved into the top rankings, her confidence – some said arrogance – grew and she appeared on court in dramatic skin-tight outfits, her hair often bedecked with cornrows and colorful beads. Sportswriters wrote admiringly of her power, physical strength, speed, and endurance – and in a manner that linked racial imagery with masculinity. The *New York Times* observed that Venus had a "wide receiver physique" and her younger sister Serena a "running back physique."[49]

The sudden rise of Venus Williams to prominence was replete with racial overtones. On the positive side, *Sports Illustrated* called her "a brilliant new talent – witty, intelligent, and charismatic – a streetwise child of gang-plagued Compton, Calif., who could be sports' next Tiger Woods." Venus agreed, noting, "Tiger's different from the mainstream, and in tennis I also am. I'm tall. I'm black. Everything's different about me. Just face the facts." That reality was not lost on several of her fellow players. Resentment against Venus and her outspoken father – who was quick to play the race card – surfaced at the 1997 US Open as she mowed down her opponents. During her semifinal match, the 11th-seeded Irina Spîrlea intentionally bumped into Venus during a changeover between games, and afterward said she did it purposely because of Venus's allegedly arrogant "in your face" attitude. Richard, however, charged that the motivation was blatant racism, telling the press that he and Venus had both heard players refer to her as "that nigger." Although Richard denounced Spîrlea's intentional collision as racially inspired, he in turn told the press that the Romanian was "a big, ugly, tall, white turkey." The 17-year-old Venus sought to calm the waters in a press conference, invoking the names of Althea Gibson and Arthur Ashe, as white reporters sought unsuccessfully to elicit from her a controversial racially tinged comment. Following this incident, Venus took her 6–0, 6–4 defeat to top-seeded Martina Hingis in the finals in stride, and *Sports Illustrated* predicted that while she possessed "spectacular gifts" that would "energize" women's tennis, at the same time her aloof demeanor and the antics of her outspoken father/coach would also "provide plenty of freewheeling, and damaging, distractions." Tennis insiders now talked about a sensation-seeking father and a standoffish, seemingly arrogant daughter. Undeterred, Richard retorted, "We couldn't care less what people think of us."[50]

The following February, at the 1998 Australian Open, women's tennis got a glimpse of the future when Venus met her 16-year-old sister Serena in the second round and came away with a 7–6, 6–1 victory. But Serena gave every indication that in the long run she might surpass her sister, a prediction their father had already made. A confident Serena told the press afterward, "What you saw was something for the future." Venus concurred, "Seeing her across the net was a little bit odd, but it's to be expected and in the future it'll be the same." So it was. In 1999, Venus lost a long, exhausting three-set match against top-seeded Hingis at the US Open, then had to watch her younger sister defeat the obviously weary world number one in the finals in two close sets. Serena, at age 17, was the first African American to win a Grand Slam event since Althea Gibson in 1958. Both sisters were now ranked among the top five in the world.[51]

Venus and Serena not only became top-ranked rivals who frequently met in the finals of major tournaments but also, much to the surprise of most observers, remained close friends. Apparently their several years of working long hours on the court under their father's demanding glare had brought them close, something that even face-offs at Grand Slam championship tournament finals could not erode. They often entered doubles tournaments as a team, winning at the 1999 US Open and the 2000 Wimbledon championships, and winning the gold medal at the 2000 Sydney Olympic Games. Both enjoyed their moments in the spotlight of Grand Slam finals. Venus won both Wimbledon and the US Open in 2000 and 2001. For a time, Serena emerged as the more successful of the two – however slightly – as she defeated her sister in five Grand Slam finals: the 2002 French Open, the 2002 US Open, Wimbledon in 2002 and 2003, and the 2003 Australian Open. But then Venus revived her game to win the 2005 Wimbledon, winning a 3 hour marathon three-set match from American Lindsay Davenport. And the money rolled in. Beyond their substantial prize monies, Venus capitalized on her fame with a $40 million renewal of her Reebok contract, while Serena enjoyed a multimillion-dollar deal with Puma.

Financially secure beyond even their father's wildest dreams, both women expressed interest in life beyond the narrow world of women's tennis. Both studied fashion design at the Art Institute of Florida, and Venus opened her own design company. Bright and confident young women, the sisters unobtrusively moved away from the shadow of their domineering father. His controversial comments no longer interested tennis fans. With winning came confidence, and the icy reserve with which the sisters had earlier reacted to their peers on the circuit melted away. They no longer isolated themselves from other top women players, no longer refused to talk to them in the locker room or in public venues, as once was their wont (or their father's orders). At the same time that they reshaped their public images, they also went their own individual ways. Serena, enjoying the limelight, was not afraid of making bold statements, but also refused to engage in false modesty: "When I lose a match it is usually because of how I played." Venus remained her more reserved self and sought outlets outside tennis. "Tennis was my father's dream, not mine. Winning, losing, money, riches, or fame don't make you happy." As she reduced her number of tournament appearances, she found pleasure in her interior design company. Thus the hostility that they had initially encountered on the tennis circuit faded away. What once was seen as "arrogance" was now viewed as "confidence," their "brute strength" had somehow morphed into "sleek power," and the tight-fitting, shocking tennis garb that writers had once denounced as "lapses in good taste" had become "bold and provocative."[52]

Both women continued to play major events. In 2010 Serena won the Australian Open and Wimbledon, bringing her Grand Slam total to 13; her sister won her last Grand Slam event at Wimbledon in 2009, which brought her total to 10 championships. Following the 2010 season, both women were ranked in the top five. The 30-year-old Venus had won 585 tournament matches to her young sister's 474 and held a slight edge in tournament

Figure 14.4   The Williams sisters congratulate each other after Serena beat Venus at the 2009 Wimbledon finals. *Image © Wang Lili/Xinhua Press/Corbis*

championships, 43 to 37. In head-to-head matches, Serena held a slight 13–10 edge, and enjoyed the stature of having won the most money of any woman athlete in history, nearly $23 million.

The celebrity and fortune that the Williams sisters enjoyed became the harbinger of a new era of race relations in American sports. Although early in Venus's and Serena's professional careers writers frequently made mention of their humble origins (such as "two ghetto-raised African Americans"), with the passage of time and their rise to top rankings the significance of their race receded to the distant background as appreciation of their talent and sparkling personalities grew. That they were the first black women to dominate professional tennis since Althea Gibson in the late 1950s was perhaps lost on most sports fans, but the substance of their accomplishment can hardly be overstated. The widow of Arthur Ashe got it right when she commented after the sisters' historic meeting in the finals of the US Open in 2001, the first time that siblings had met in the finals since Maud Watson defeated her sister Louise in three sets at the first Open in 1884: "Tennis has come to a different level now – these girls have raised the bar."[53] Indeed, and they found that other top women players were ready for the challenge.

Their success had helped move American sports forward toward a new era, hopefully an era in which an athlete's race would be of little or no consequence no matter the sport. They also had helped elevate public perception of women as athletes equal in their accomplishments to men (during their reign at the top, women's tennis ratings on television regularly exceeded those of the men). One close observer of their careers, tennis writer Julianne Cicarelli, correctly concludes: "Their ascendency in tennis and in corporate sponsorships has helped to change the way Americans view African American women, women athletes, and women in general. The sisters, young, spirited, intelligent, fun-loving, confident, strong, and beautiful, were seen as role models for women in the new century."[54]

15

Playing Nice No Longer: Women's Sports, 1960–2010

During the Second World War American women were encouraged to assume roles in industry and society that had previously been denied them. When victory was achieved in 1945, an effort to return women to pre-1940 gender roles was launched that was reflected in motion pictures, magazines, and television. That rearguard action, however, was doomed to fail because powerful tides of reform had been unleashed that could not be stopped.

The women's rights movement had its roots in the Seneca Falls Convention in 1848, produced the Nineteenth Amendment to the Constitution in 1920 which granted women the right to vote, and crested during the 1960s in a flurry of social activism. During the 1960s, the movement became a prominent part of a larger assault upon discriminatory practices prevalent in American life that included sustained protests by groups representing African Americans, Hispanics, Native Americans, and gays and lesbians. The publication of *The Feminine Mystique* by Betty Friedan in 1963 had a galvanizing effect upon the women's movement, producing in its wake a sustained drive for gender equity. Long-established gender discrimination practices and policies – in education, the professions, employment, and politics – soon began to fall.

This broad social movement revived interest in women's sports, including competitive sports at the public school and college levels and opportunities to play professionally. By the middle of the Great Depression of the 1930s, with a few notable exceptions, most competitive team sports for women had been scuttled by public school boards and college administrators, often at the behest of female coaches and physical education instructors who believed competitive sports were not in the best interest of young ladies. Until the 1960s, professional opportunities were severely limited, and various efforts to create women's professional teams fizzled. Only in limited and sporadic instances did educational institutions begin to once more offer competitive sports programs. One of the popular mottos of the 1970s was

Sports in American Life: A History, Second Edition. Richard O. Davies.
© 2012 John Wiley & Sons, Inc. Published 2012 by John Wiley & Sons, Inc.

a slogan used to advertise a cigarette specifically targeted by marketers for feminine tastes: "You've come a long way, baby!" When one considers the status of women's sports in earlier times, that marketing slogan seems appropriate.

Deceit and Deception: The NCAA and Gender Equity

When Congress passed the Education Act in 1972, few persons took notice of an amendment – labeled Title IX – offered by Edith Green of Oregon. It simply stated, "No person in the United States shall, on the basis of sex, be excluded from participation in, be denied the benefits of, or be subjected to discrimination under any education program or activity receiving Federal financial assistance." Because attention was focused at this time upon the divisive issue of the busing of students to achieve racial balance in public schools, Congresswoman Green's amendment was approved without opposition. Women's groups, however, were delighted and within a short period of time lawyers for public school districts and colleges were carefully reviewing the provision. Attorneys told administrators and governing boards that the law clearly meant that any school receiving federal funds had to establish athletic programs for females at a level consistent with those for males. If institutions failed to do so, they faced the distinct possibility of losing all federal funding. Public schools moved quickly to comply with the law and in most instances little resistance was forthcoming. Budgets were adjusted, locker rooms built, coaches hired, and schedules arranged, and interscholastic competition was soon under way. At the secondary school level the major conflicts seemed to revolve around access for practices to courts, fields, tracks, and pools. If school administrators or board members wanted to slow down the process of compliance, they ran into the political reality that parents were determined that their daughters have the same opportunities for sports competition as their sons.

Strong parental support for competitive girls' programs reflected a seismic change in thinking regarding the impact of competition and vigorous physical exercise for girls. At the time Title IX was enacted, most public and private schools offered little or no sports programs for junior and senior high school girls. There were exceptions to this rule, of course, such as in Iowa and Texas where girls' basketball had survived the budget cuts of the 1930s, and private prep schools located primarily on the East Coast, where a wide range of sports was offered. Well into the 1960s, prevailing attitudes toward gender roles assumed that young boys played with balls and girls played with dolls, and that by the time girls reached high school their proper place was on the sidelines as cheerleaders or drill squad members. If a young girl exhibited strong interest in sports, she risked being labeled a "tomboy," and if that interest persisted into her teenage years, she was advised to find other activities. Rigorous exercise, it was commonly believed, would make them "muscle-bound" and unladylike.

Given these widely accepted social standards, girls tended to avoid sports and concentrate their energies on activities deemed acceptable. Peer pressure and parental guidance meant that few girls spent time developing their athletic skills, thus confirming widespread beliefs that girls lacked the coordination and strength to compete. It became a vicious cycle. Since girls did not spend time developing athletic skills, did not receive coaching, and only rarely were encouraged by parents to engage in sports, they consequently did not develop athletically. Few fathers ever thought to invite their daughters to shoot baskets or toss a ball as they did their sons. Consequently, on the few occasions when girls were called upon to perform athletically, they usually looked inept, or worse.

Such attitudes and behaviors, however, were now undergoing substantial change. The development of the women's rights movement during the 1960s meant that traditional stereotypes were being seriously challenged. Title IX sparked a compelling new question that confounded male sports administrators seeking to protect the status quo: if, as popular perceptions suggested, competitive sports taught important values and attitudes believed essential to success in the competitive adult world – teamwork, perseverance, dedication, goal-setting, preparation, sportsmanship, the ability to respond positively to setbacks, and high performance under pressure – then why should those experiences be denied girls? If, as was often said, the lessons learned in the locker room led to success in the corporate boardroom, then young women were being given short shrift by the educational system. Psychologist David Auxter placed the issues created by Title IX in such a context:

> We value athletics because they are competitive. That is, they teach that achievement and success are desirable, and that they are worth disciplining oneself for. By keeping girls out of sports, we have denied them this educational experience. Better athletic programs will develop more aggressive females, women with confidence, who value personal achievement and have a strong sense of identity. I think that would be a good thing for us all.[1]

The response by the all-male NCAA to Title IX was complex. Executive Director Walter Byers had often conferred with women athletic administrators and coaches, even making public statements indicating that at some future time the NCAA would become involved in sponsoring women's championships. But in 1965, the annual convention adopted a resolution prepared by its executive committee: "The games committee conducting any NCAA event shall limit participation to eligible male student-athletes." Consequently, in 1971, a group of women interested in developing an intercollegiate sports program established the Association for Intercollegiate Athletics for Women (AIAW). At the outset, this new organization identified itself closely with the anti-competition orientation that had gained widespread acceptance during the 1920s. The founders of the AIAW clearly did not want to build their association after the professional, competitive model of the NCAA. Initially, the AIAW prohibited the granting of athletic scholarships. Coaches could not recruit off campus or pay for a prospect's trip to campus. Compliance would be the responsibility of participating institutions. Essentially, the AIAW was structured to protect athletes from institutional exploitation and to avoid the many ethical problems that plagued men's intercollegiate athletics.[2]

Such naivety, however, did not last for long. Within a few years it became apparent that the leadership of the AIAW was out of touch with the feminist movement. Passage of Title IX produced a serious dilemma within the ranks of women coaches and athletic directors, and inevitably, the AIAW leadership. Could an institution meet the federal standard of equal protection and gender equity if it awarded athletic scholarships to men but not to women? Many women argued that equal opportunity meant that women athletes should receive the same financial aid as was awarded to men, while the leadership of the AIAW countered that it would debase women's programs. Leading the challenge was the women's athletic director at the University of New Mexico, Linda Estes, who argued for equal treatment of women athletes, including full scholarship aid and the opportunity to compete for national championships. As Byers recalls in his memoirs, "Women's athletics leaders discriminated against themselves through the years by refusing to accept competitive athletics as a proper pursuit for teenage women."[3] In 1973, the hierarchy of the AIAW reluctantly agreed to permit athletic grants-in-aid, but with male athletic directors controlling university athletic budgets, the amount of financial aid available to women proved inconsequential.

While women coaches and administrators argued about philosophical issues, the NCAA aggressively sought to subvert Title IX. Susan Cahn reports that during the mid 1970s, athletic administrators were spending about 1 percent of their athletic budgets for women's programs. It is not surprising that the NCAA hierarchy viewed Title IX as a "crisis of unprecedented magnitude."[4] Byers contended that its implementation would mean the "possible doom of intercollegiate sports." In his memoirs, Byers points out that the AIAW began pressuring the Department of Health, Education and Welfare (HEW), which had oversight responsibilities for Title IX, to establish guidelines that stipulated 50 percent of intercollegiate athletics budgets should be reallocated to women's athletics, and that administration should be reassigned to an independent women's athletic department. Their theme, Byers ruefully says, was "equal numbers and equal dollars," a position that he and the NCAA deemed radical beyond belief. The entire scope of college athletic programs, including budgets, was now in play. In particular, the NCAA feared for the future of major college football budgets. Contending that so-called "revenue-producing sports" (i.e., football and men's basketball) should be exempt from Title IX, Byers derisively dismissed the claim that "football and women's field hockey immediately deserved the same per capita expenditures" as "financial lunacy."[5]

The NCAA leadership implemented an opposition strategy that sought to exploit the close connections between coaches and their friends in Congress. Initially, the NCAA endorsed an amendment offered in 1974 by Republican senator John Tower of Texas to exempt intercollegiate athletics from the purview of Title IX. When that failed in committee, leading football schools launched an extensive lobbying effort in Congress to delay the issuance of compliance guidelines. President Gerald Ford, himself a former All-American center at Michigan, received a barrage of letters from across the land from coaches and athletic directors and their friends; he even met with coaches Bear Bryant of Alabama and Barry Switzer of Oklahoma, who urged him (without success) to exempt football from Title IX compliance. An NCAA-hired law firm filed suit in federal court contending that if an athletic program did not receive direct federal aid, then it should be exempt from compliance reviews. The argument was that because athletics were not specifically mentioned in Title IX, HEW had exceeded its rightful authority by applying it to college athletics. The federal district court in Washington, DC, summarily dismissed the case in 1978.

Enforcement of Title IX moved at a glacial pace. The Department of Health, Education and Welfare did not issue its initial set of guidelines until 1975 and gave schools until 1978 to be in compliance. Faced with the reality that the federal government was determined to enforce the guidelines for Title IX, the NCAA moved to destroy the AIAW and take over women's sports programs. It announced that it would begin offering championship tournaments for women at the Division II and III levels in 1981 and for Division I in 1982. Then it offered various financial inducements that prompted many AIAW members to switch to the NCAA. With its financial resources dwindling, the AIAW gambled on a lawsuit against the NCAA, alleging antitrust violations. Legal costs from pursuing the suit depleted the organization's remaining financial reserves. After its case was dismissed in June 1982, the AIAW was doomed.[6]

Among women athletic administrators, New Mexico's Estes and Mary Alice Hill of San Diego State were in the forefront of scuttling the AIAW. Byers praised them for their embrace of the professional-competitive model of the NCAA: "Right or wrong, [they] sought high-level competition, and national exposure for women's college sports. They were committed to the NCAA's philosophy – to the winner belongs the spoils." A different perspective was held by N. Peg Burke, a former president of AIAW: "I think it is interesting that an organization that has been so active in fighting equal opportunity for women now wants to offer championships for them," she said. "This is not the consent of the governed. In certain circumstances involving men and women, lack of consent is classified as rape."[7]

The consolidation of women's and men's athletic programs under the control of the NCAA changed the nature of the battle, but the fight for gender equity had just begun. In most institutions, women administrators were appointed to posts clearly subordinate to the male athletic director, who retained control of budgets. As universities implemented a wide range of women's sports programs, they encountered a severe scarcity of qualified female coaches. The half-century hiatus in which there were few women's intercollegiate programs meant that few experienced female coaches were available. In some instances, women with degrees in physical education were hired, but they lacked competitive playing and coaching experience. Consequently, aspiring male coaches discovered they could become a college head coach – of a women's team. During the 1980s, the percentage of women head coaches actually declined by 50 percent because men were appointed to fill vacancies as women's teams were established.

Struggles within athletic departments erupted over a wide range of issues: access to facilities, recruiting budgets, travel budgets (often men went by air, women by van), coaches' salaries, and the number of scholarships offered. In some instances, even the difference in quality and quantity of game and practice uniforms provided men's and women's teams became an issue. Not until the mid 1980s was the first female athletic director – Judith Sweet of the University of California, San Diego – appointed with control over men's programs. She later became the first elected woman president of the NCAA (1991–3) and became a senior administrator in the NCAA. Few women, however, were appointed to the post of director of athletics of major college programs; the widespread perception was that presidents did not want to place a woman with oversight responsibilities for football. In 2010, the number of women athletic directors at major college programs had reached five: Deborah Yow of Maryland, Sandy Barbour of California, Kathy Beauregard of Western Michigan, Lisa Love of Arizona State, and Cary Groth of Nevada.

While embittered battles over gender equity issues were fought on many campuses in the 1980s and beyond, the struggle also continued at the level of the federal government. With the NCAA now responsible for women's programs, the organization ironically found itself attempting to prevent Title IX from being undercut by social conservatives, a 180-degree reversal from its position in the 1970s. The Reagan administration showed scant enthusiasm, and the pace of compliance reviews slowed markedly during the early 1980s as compared to the time of the Carter administration. In 1984, the United States Supreme Court dropped a bombshell on women's athletics when it agreed with the NCAA's earlier legal position in *Grove City College* vs *Bell*. The High Court ruled that Title IX applied only to programs receiving direct federal financial aid and that unfunded programs, such as intercollegiate athletics, were exempt even if a university received federal assistance for other programs.

For a time it seemed that *Grove City* had derailed women's athletics, but momentum for women's programs had been building for more than a decade and could not be stopped by a mere Supreme Court ruling. The grassroots development of high school and college programs had produced a new perspective among the American public that assured that women's programs would not be scuttled. Budgets for women's programs continued to improve, although the Reagan administration halted more than 800 compliance reviews and related investigations by the Department of Education (established in 1979). Many university presidents, now under intense pressure from female faculty and community leaders, made clear to their athletic departments that long-term plans for achieving compliance with Title IX would continue to be implemented no matter what the courts had ruled. The NCAA hired women for key administrative positions and placed them within that organization's decision-making bureaucracy where they exerted authority. The issue was finally resolved for good in 1988, when, in spite of President Reagan's veto, Congress passed the Civil Rights Restoration Act, which restored the original intent of Title IX. Any gender discrimination in public schools or higher education, including sports programs, was once again in violation of federal law.[8]

By the early years of the twenty-first century, women's sports had come of age as an integral part of American higher education. The pipeline of athletes was surging, as young girls now had many opportunities to perfect their skills prior to entering college. That they had opportunities in sports not available to their mothers and grandmothers probably seemed somehow arcane to them, if not irrelevant. They developed skills in summer camps, played competitive softball, volleyball, and soccer in organizations and leagues affiliated with national associations, or concentrated upon individual sports such as tennis, golf, and swimming. They had a wide range of team and individual sports in junior and senior high school from which to choose. By the time young girls reached junior high school, competent coaching was available. Competition became as intense as had long existed among boys, and arduous practice and physical conditioning were no longer considered unfeminine. For exceptional female athletes, like their male counterparts, a "full-ride" university "athletic scholarship" could be the reward.

Title IX at all levels exerted a revolutionary force on American sports. A young girl in today's society has a wide vista of opportunities that her mother did not enjoy. If long-term trends are any indication, the gap between funding and opportunities for women as compared to men will continue to narrow, but important social and psychological implications remain. The quest for equality of opportunity for women, however, does not simply entail requiring men to make room for the women. It also means that men have to abandon their once-unique masculine identification. As women continue to improve as athletes, they will continue to narrow the gap between men's and women's performance levels, thereby assuming many of the traits once identified as masculine: strength, agility, speed, skill. These traits, as Susan Cahn explains, will "become human qualities and not those of a particular gender." She notes that historically, sports had enabled boys to acquire the qualities needed to assume leadership roles in adult society, and girls were now being given the same opportunities. This will ultimately lead, she suggests, to the reformulation of traditional models of masculinity and femininity, undercutting "the social hierarchies that have historically granted men greater authority in political, economic, religious, family, and athletic matters."[9] If Cahn is correct in her analysis, women's expanding role in sports will ultimately lead to a transformation of gender roles and relationships in America.

Titanic Rivalry: Connecticut and Tennessee Basketball

When it became evident that gender equity in intercollegiate athletics could not be side-tracked, college administrators began to develop programs that would meet the guidelines of federal oversight officials. With an eye toward potential revenues, many major college programs decided to emphasize women's basketball. Among this group was the University of Tennessee. That decision in part stemmed from the rapid ascension of the "Volettes" in the 1970s to national prominence under a young head coach. Patricia Head had been an outstanding player at Tennessee–Martin and had enrolled in the graduate program in physical education at Tennessee in the fall of 1974. Part of her duties as a graduate assistant was to help coach the women's basketball team, but when the head coach resigned shortly before fall practice began, she was appointed as "interim" head coach at age 22 with a salary of $3,000. Thirty-seven years later she was still on the job, had never had a losing season, had won over 1,000 games, and had secured eight national championships. Her annual salary exceeded $1 million.[10]

Her initial team racked up a 16–8 record, sufficient for her to be made the permanent head coach at a salary of $8,900. Her second season produced a 16–11 record. However, in her third year, with her own recruits now assuming major roles, and with her disciplined offense and stifling man-to-man defense coalescing into an established system, the Lady Vols (the sexist "Volettes" moniker was discarded) cruised to a 28–5 record and won two tournament games, but eventually lost in the semifinals of the AIAW Final Four. In 1980, she married Knoxville banker R. B. Summitt.[11]

By the time the NCAA held its first national women's championship tournament in 1982, Pat Summitt had already become established as a leading women's coach. She was named an assistant coach of the 1984 Olympic team, and with increased budget support expanded her recruiting base throughout the South. With top talent flowing into the program, the Lady Vols were nationally ranked each year and made trips to the Final Four almost an annual event. For several seasons a national championship eluded her grasp. In 1985, however, she recruited Bridgette Gordon, a multitalented forward who led the Lady Vols to their first national title in 1987. Tennessee demolished Louisiana Tech in the championship game, 67–44. In 1989, Gordon led the Orange and White to its second national title. "We were good when she came here, but she put us on the national map," Summitt said afterward.[12] Tennessee basketball had become the standard of excellence in a rapidly developing women's sports world.

The Lady Vols, however, eventually found their equal in the University of Connecticut. The Huskies came to national prominence in the 1990s, but once there they established themselves on a par with Summitt's program. Like many institutions seeking to meet minimal Title IX compliance guidelines, UConn established a low-budget women's basketball program in 1974. Administrators expected little and that was precisely what they got. Eleven seasons later, the Huskies could boast of only one winning season, a 16–14 record in 1984–5. The program languished in obscurity at the bottom of the Big East Conference.

That situation changed when Geno Auriemma was appointed head coach before the 1985 season. Although the search committee was intent upon hiring a woman, this brash and self-confident 31-year-old man talked himself into the job. Well versed in the strategic nuances of the game, but best known as a recruiter at the University of Virginia, Auriemma had opted to coach women because his slender basketball résumé was insufficient to get him an opportunity in the college men's game. Auriemma was one of untold numbers of men who seized an opportunity to coach at the college level during the 1980s, taking advantage of the dearth of women in the coaching pipeline.[13]

Within a few years, Auriemma had turned the program into a Big East champion, but in 1991, in what locals considered a near-miracle, the Lady Huskies played their way into the Final Four. Building upon that success, he was able to recruit such blue-chip players as 6 foot 4 inch Rebecca Lobo. In the 1993–4 season, Lobo and a host of talented teammates powered the Huskies to a 30–3 record, but lost a close game to eventual national champion North Carolina in the regional finals.

The following January, the Huskies won the most important game in the history of the program up to that time when they defeated Tennessee on their home floor before a capacity crowd of 8,000. The Huskies then marched into the NCAA tournament in Minneapolis undefeated, but awaiting them in the championship game were the Lady Vols, seeking to avenge that loss. It was arguably the most important game in the history of college women's basketball. Anticipation of a rematch sparked an unprecedented level of national interest. Before a national television audience, Tennessee led at half-time 38–32 and early in the second half increased that lead to nine points, but UConn's control of the backboards enabled the Huskies to take their first lead at 58–55. With barely a minute left and the score tied at 61, Tennessee took time out to set up a play for their leading scorer, Nikki McCray. Her shot banged off the rim into the hands of UConn guard Jennifer Rizzotti who raced down the floor, only to confront Tennessee's best defensive player, Michelle Marciniak. Near the top of the key, Marciniak went for a steal, but Rizzotti zipped past her to score an uncontested layup. Rizzotti's sensational play was the game-breaker, and the Huskies won 70–64. UConn's first national championship capped a perfect 35–0 season. Rizzotti's spectacular play was captured by a *Sports Illustrated* photographer and appeared on the cover of the ensuing issue. Lobo was named the 1995 national player of the year, the first of several that Auriemma recruited to the Storrs campus.

Under the leadership of two very different coaches, Connecticut and Tennessee women's basketball flourished. Pat Summitt had grown up on a family farm in northern Tennessee and brought to her position a strong work ethic that reflected the influence of her hard-working parents and her competitive nature honed by playing a take-no-prisoners form of basketball with her four brothers in a hayloft. While Summitt presented an image of controlled competitiveness, Auriemma exuded an exuberantly aggressive persona that did nothing to hide his Italian heritage. He was born in a rural town in Italy, came to the United States with his parents at age seven, and grew up in the mill town of Norristown, Pennsylvania. He played high school basketball and, after graduation from West Chester University, coached high school basketball before taking an assistant coaching position at Virginia. The personal rivalry between Auriemma and Summitt would be waged during the regular season and the NCAA tournament. That rivalry intensified over the years as the two schools captured 12 of 15 NCAA championships between 1995 and 2010 (UConn 7, Tennessee 5), although overall Tennessee still held a narrow 8–7 lead in total championships won over three decades.

Summitt came roaring back after that stinging loss to UConn in 1995. Freshman Chamique Holdsclaw dazzled sports fans as she led Tennessee to three consecutive NCAA titles. The 6 foot 2 inch forward replaced Lobo as the face of women's basketball. During her junior year, the Lady Vols went undefeated in 39 games, easily capping a magical season with a 93–75 manhandling of Louisiana Tech in the championship game. After that blowout, Bulldog coach Leon Barmore could only shake his head, asserting that Holdsclaw "is the best player ever to play the game."[14] The widely expected fourth consecutive title, however, eluded Tennessee in 1999, largely due to a raft of injuries to several key players. After her final game, Summitt concluded, "I've never had a player like Chamique. I don't think anyone has."[15]

Despite compiling a cumulative 96–9 record in the four seasons after their initial national championship, the Huskies never got past the Elite Eight. Those four years proved to be but prelude to another national championship in 2000. Led by the superb backcourt duo of 5 foot 6 inch Shea Ralph and 5 foot 5 inch Sue Bird, and with the heavy lifting up front done by the super-quick and athletic 6 foot 2 inch Leningrad native Svetlana Abrosimova, the Huskies went 16–0 against their Big East opponents. The Huskies topped off this magical season by once more soundly defeating the team in the championship game that had become their primary rival: Tennessee. This time they did it in convincing fashion, 72–51. After the trophy presentation, the team lifted their coach to their shoulders and carried him triumphantly off the floor as Pat Summitt passively watched.

As the years went by, the personal rivalry that developed between the two coaches steadily intensified. Given the high stakes for which they played, it was perhaps inevitable that their relationship would become strained. Over the years, the outspoken Auriemma was prone to make off-the-cuff comments that he intended to be humorous, but which sometimes struck the listener as having an unnecessary cutting edge. His comments that the Lady Vols were the "Microsoft" of women's basketball, or the "Evil Empire," did not sit well with the folks in Knoxville. Summitt was among understanding friends in the coaching profession as her relationship with him diminished and the slights and stinging comments piled up. Auriemma candidly admitted that probably 90 percent of women coaches "resent me because I'm a man. The other 10% appreciate what I do and are my friends."[16]

Auriemma's occasional rhetorical excesses notwithstanding, the reason for their very public nasty spat that erupted in the summer of 2007 apparently revolved around recruiting.

Throughout her career at Tennessee, Summitt's recruiting territory lay primarily in the South, while Auriemma built his program mining talent from the Northeast and the New York City area. He acknowledged that his major competitor in recruiting had more often than not been Vivian Stringer's Rutgers program, not Tennessee. But upon occasion, they pulled out all stops to sign the same premier athlete.

It is difficult to make judgments about recruiting successes and disappointments because so much remains hidden beneath the surface. Summitt clearly enjoyed one victory when she lured New York City native Chamique Holdsclaw away from Auriemma, but he had won an earlier battle when All-American Shea Ralph of North Carolina selected Connecticut. Her mother had played with Summitt in international competition during the 1970s, and Shea had attended Summitt's summer camps as a youngster. When she called to tell Summitt that she had committed to UConn, the coach was apparently stunned, but quickly wished her well. That apparently was not Auriemma's reaction when he received a similar call from highly recruited Semeka Randall of suburban Cleveland, informing him that she was headed to Knoxville. Randall recalled that he became agitated and challenged her decision point by point; she was in tears when the conversation ended. She also noted wryly that Auriemma never sought to quiet the thunderous "boos" from Huskies fans that greeted her every time she played in Connecticut, saying that in Storrs everyone believed her name to be "Boo Randall."[17]

The long-simmering animosity boiled over when Auriemma invaded the Deep South to recruit a two-time Naismith High School National Player of the Year, Maya Moore. Both he and Summitt wanted to secure the commitment of 6 foot 3 inch Moore, an honors student at Collins Hill High School in Georgia. After the two waged an intense battle in which coaching egos became deeply involved, Moore decided that she wanted to play "up north." As in other instances where she had lost out on a prime recruit, Summitt remained publicly non-committal, but apparently she found this particular setback to be particularly grating. After Moore announced her decision, Tennessee filed a 34-page document with NCAA, and an inquiry was launched but no major violations were uncovered. The issue apparently revolved around a visit Moore and her mother took to the headquarters of ESPN in Bristol, Connecticut during her recruiting visit. The final report concluded that UConn had committed a "secondary" violation. It resulted in a letter of reprimand, which is roughly equivalent to a parking ticket. Connecticut-based sports writers had a field day lambasting Summitt for being, among other things, "the pettiest coach in college sports." For her part, Summitt had no public comment, but in the summer of 2007 the Tennessee Women's Athletic Department refused to renew the regular season series with Connecticut. Auriemma told the *Hartford Courant*, "[Summitt] accused us of cheating in recruiting, but she doesn't have the courage to say it in public." And for good measure: "She hates my guts." Summitt responded to his outburst with a recollection of her rural Tennessee upbringing: "If I ever spoke out like Geno, my dad would probably take me behind the barn and get out the tobacco stick."[18]

Maya Moore more than lived up to expectations, earning All-American honors in each of her four seasons. The Huskies lost to Stanford in the semifinals of the Final Four in her freshman season, but the Huskies romped to the national title in 2009. In 2010, the Huskies went undefeated and won every game by 10 points or more until edging Stanford in the championship game 54–47. Auriemma now had seven national championships, just one

Figure 15.1   Maya Moore of Connecticut drives to the basket against Rutgers in a Big East Conference game in Hartford on February 3, 2009. Moore was the latest of a large number of All-Americans who played for the Huskies coached by Geno Auriemma and helped capture seven national championships between 1995 and 2010. *Image © Gary Hamilton/Icon SMI/Corbis*

shy of his long-time rival Pat Summitt. In the ensuing 2010–11 season, in a rebuilding year, the Huskies ran their consecutive win streak to 89 before being decisively defeated by Stanford on the road.

The rivalry generated considerable national interest in women's basketball, but many observers wondered if the annual battle for supremacy between the same two teams was good for the overall competitive balance of women's basketball. Many also lamented the cessation of their annual regular season game. Coach Jim Foster of Ohio State said it well: "The timing of it was advantageous for the game's growth … There are other good games taking place that aren't touted, and maybe now some of them will surface. As for UConn and Tennessee, now they'll just meet in the NCAA tournament – if they're fortunate."[19]

Billie Jean Sparks a Revolution

It was inevitable that the gathering social and political storm that came to be called the women's rights movement would spill over into the major professional sports in which it participated. The drive for equal treatment by the Ladies Professional Golf Association and within the United States Tennis Association (USTA) was a long and difficult struggle.

During the 1960s, the male-dominated United States Tennis Association held tournaments for both men and women, but the women were given short shrift. Fewer tournaments were held for women than for men, and at those major tournaments, such as the US Open, where men and women both competed for championships, the prize money for the men was four or five times higher than for the women. Seldom did the women get to play on center court, except for semifinals and finals matches, and their locker rooms were reportedly smaller and less well appointed. Most women players accepted this pattern of discrimination without protest, but not the top woman player of the era, Billie Jean King. Born in 1943 to working-class parents, King grew up in Long Beach where she learned to play tennis on the city's public courts. After she won several junior tournaments, she received instruction from pioneering woman tennis star, Alice Marble. At age 18, she had already enjoyed top junior rankings and won her first match at Wimbledon.[20]

By 1965, King was the top-ranked American woman tennis player, popular with fans for her aggressive, attacking style. In 1966, she defeated Maria Bueno for the Wimbledon title, and followed up in 1967 with her first of four US Open championships. During more than a decade as a leading player, King won 72 tournaments, and despite the relatively low women's prize money, she managed to win more than $2 million during her professional career. She won six Wimbledon singles titles, along with 14 other Wimbledon championships in doubles and mixed doubles. Her success was all the more remarkable because of several surgeries she had to endure to repair chronic knee problems. During the 1970s, the battles she had with the rising young star Chris Evert did much to stimulate widespread interest in women's tennis.

King was never shy on or off the court. She assumed the leadership of women's professional tennis, and during the late 1960s began to criticize the male-dominated USTA for its discriminatory policies. In 1970, she created headlines when she called a press conference to denounce the fact that as the Italian Open champion she received a prize of just $1,500, while the male champion earned $12,500. In 1972, Australian Stan Smith walked away from Wimbledon with $12,500 and King just $4,800, and later that same year, she earned $10,000 by winning the US Open, but her male counterpart, Ilie Năstase, cashed a check for $25,000. As president of the new organization she had helped establish, the Women's Tennis Association, King suggested a boycott might be the likely solution. Her outspoken leadership had its effect, and no boycott was forthcoming, but the disparity in prize money was steadily reduced. Throughout 1973, the total amount of prize money paid to women on the tour totaled $900,000, but 20 years later that had grown, along with the popularity of the women's game, to more than $25 million.[21]

King's dual role as the top woman player in the world and the outspoken advocate of improved conditions for women's tennis made her the logical target of self-styled tennis hustler Bobby Riggs. Born in 1918, Riggs had enjoyed considerable success in his tennis career, including winning the 1939 Wimbledon and US Open titles. What should have been his best years were wiped out by tournament cancellations during the war; in the late 1940s, he played the best of the day – Don Budge, Pancho Gonzales, and Jack Kramer – but his career was in decline. Long after he left the men's circuit, Riggs continued to earn a living playing exhibition matches, often placing a large side bet on the outcome. Always known as a hustler, Riggs drew national attention to himself when he announced that the demands by King and other women for equal treatment were a sham, stating that he could easily beat any of the top-ranked women despite his 55 years. This was preliminary to his announcement that he had conned some California promoters into putting up $10,000, winner-takes-all, for a match between himself and the outstanding Australian, Margaret Court. Although most experts thought Court, at the top of her game and in great physical condition, would easily defeat Riggs, she played tentatively and permitted a good case of nerves to undercut her normal game. She lost in straight sets, and Riggs crowed long and loud.

Riggs then set his sights on King, who had earlier rejected his challenge. Because Court had been decisively beaten, however, King felt she had no alternative but to respond. She decided that not to play Riggs would hurt the stature of women's tennis. *Time* magazine noted that King was "the personification of the professional female athlete that Riggs loves to taunt." Once the match was scheduled for the Houston Astrodome, the hype machine went into high gear. ABC-TV Sports agreed to dispatch Howard Cosell to cover the event, and the newspapers were filled with pre-match hyperbole. Riggs told the press, "Hell, we know there is no way she can beat me. She's a stronger athlete than me and she can execute various shots better than me. But when the pressure mounts and she thinks about 50 million people are watching on TV, she'll fold. That's the way women are." He even added that his forthcoming victory would "put Billie Jean and all other women libbers back where they belong – in the kitchen and the bedroom."[22]

Many experts agreed and picked Riggs to win the match of the "libber vs the lobber." Famed handicapper Jimmy the Greek set the odds with Riggs an 8–5 favorite. Gene Scott, a ranked tennis player, concurred, giving expression to the many sexist emotions current at the time: "You see, women are brought up from the time they're six years old to read books, eat candy and go to dancing class. They can't compete against men. They're not used to the competition. Maybe it'll change some day. But not now."[23]

On the evening of September 20, 1973, some 35,000 people paid their way into the Astrodome, and ABC estimated its television audience at 50 million. It would be one of the most significant sporting events of the era. *Sports Illustrated* senior correspondent Curry Kirkpatrick aptly described the scene as having "all the conflicting tones of a political convention, championship prizefight, rock festival, tent revival, town meeting, Super Bowl and sick joke." As soon as the match began, however, it was evident that the joke was on

Riggs. From the first few points, King took charge, easily handling the many lobs, drop shots, and other assorted slice-and-dice trick shots that Riggs threw at her. She pounded the ball deep to the corners, took to the net to put away crisp volleys, and won in three easy sets, claiming the winner-takes-all $100,000 prize. "Seldom has there been a more classic example of a skilled athlete performing at peak efficiency in the most important moment of her life," Kirkpatrick concluded. The "battle of the sexes" ended with King noting, "It helped women stand taller."[24]

This bizarre spectacle might have proven little, if anything, but it gave women's tennis a terrific boost in credibility. As King's career faded over the next several years, she was replaced in the limelight by Chris Evert, a stellar baseline player, and the hard-hitting left-handed Martina Navratilova, who defected at the age of 18 from communist Czechoslovakia in 1974 and became a US citizen in 1981. Throughout much of the 1970s and the 1980s, the names of "Chris and Martina" evoked instant images of their many closely contested matches, especially in Grand Slam tournament finals. The contrast in their style of play tantalized tennis fans; Evert seldom rushed the net, preferring to hit her crisp ground strokes from the baseline for winners, while Navratilova's high-energy game of serve and volley provided a sharp contrast.[25]

Figure 15.2   Billie Jean King and Bobby Riggs pose in New York City for a promotional photograph before their famous "battle of the sexes" in the Houston Astrodome in 1973. Their match attracted the largest television audience for tennis in history. King decisively defeated the 55-year-old hustler and self-proclaimed male chauvinist in three straight sets. King's victory set the stage for an upsurge of popularity in women's tennis and is considered an important step in the rise of acceptance of all women's sports. *Image © Bettmann/Corbis*

Navratilova played almost 20 years at the highest level, her dedication to physical fitness setting a new standard for female tennis professionals. After several years when she was overweight and derisively called the "Great Wide Hope" by tennis television commentator Bud Collins, she decided to take her professional career seriously and began a rigorous workout regimen that she supplemented with close attention to her diet. She ran several miles a day and lifted weights while engaging in hours of intense tennis practice. Her regular traveling entourage included a physical trainer and a nutritionist as well as a tennis coach. Navratilova won a total of 18 Grand Slam events and 167 singles tournaments overall, a number that almost surely will never be topped. Evert, possessed of a classic two-handed backhand shot, which she could hit down the line or cross-court with stunning accuracy, won 101 tournaments, of which 16 were Grand Slams (including seven at Roland Garros Stadium outside Paris where the red clay was to her particular liking).

Their competition provided sports fans with a rare view of what true sportsmanship could and should be: fierce competition on the court, mutual admiration and friendship off it. When their last singles match was played in 1987, Navratilova held a narrow 43–37 edge over her rival; theirs was one of the greatest tennis rivalries of all time. "Martina revolutionized the game by her superb athleticism and aggressiveness, not to mention her outspokenness and candor," Evert said upon Navratilova's retirement.

> She brought athleticism to a whole new level with her training techniques – particularly cross-training, the idea that you could go to the gym or play basketball to get in shape for tennis. She had everything down to a science, including her diet, and that was an inspiration to me. I really think she helped me to be a better athlete. And then I always admired her maturity, her wisdom and her ability to transcend the sport. You could ask her about her forehand or about world peace and she always had an answer. She really is a world figure, not just a sports figure.[26]

Viva America! World Cup Winners

Football for Americans means heavy pads, grunting linemen, artistic quarterbacks, and speedy running backs. Above all, it is a game orchestrated and controlled by coaches. Football for the rest of the world means, of course, a free-flowing game in which scoring is low and the cultural significance high. Soccer is a game that most Americans have long ignored, even scorned as dull. Until recent years, few Americans bothered to learn the intricacies of the world's most popular sport: deft footwork, precise timing, and complex defensive and offensive maneuvering. Thus, the spectacular rise to an improbable World Cup victory by the American women's national soccer team in 1999 gave sports fans everywhere reason for good cheer and hope. That the United States had a women's team competing at this rarified level was viewed by most observers as a vindication of the passage of Title IX, 27 years earlier. What that legislation helped produce was a groundswell of youth soccer programs that by the 1990s had produced a pool of talented women from which to build a world-class competitive team. In 1972, when Title IX slipped virtually unnoticed through Congress, only one in every 27 girls participated in any form of organized athletic team activity. By 1999, one in every three girls had such an opportunity. The success of those athletes in turn spawned an enormous base of young female athletes who sought to emulate their achievements. As Donna Lopiano, executive director of the Women's Sports Foundation, said, "People don't realize it takes ten to fifteen years to make a professional athlete."[27]

The march of the American women to the title was followed closely by the American people, feeding off heavy media coverage. That the final rounds of the competition were held in major American stadiums added to the interest, of course, but the existence of youth soccer programs for a quarter-century had led to the formation of an American team with the talent to challenge the world's best. Major corporate sponsors helped ignite interest, and 79,000 wildly enthusiastic fans turned out at the Meadowlands near New York City for the Americans' trouncing of Denmark in the opening round; observers noticed that the lines of young girls at the ice-cream stands were much longer that those of adults at beer concessions. Fans came with their faces painted red, white, and blue, carrying homemade banners and waving American flags. Women's sports in America had come of age.

Many of the American players received heavy media coverage, but public attention focused most intently upon the team's self-effacing star, forward Mia Hamm. The daughter of a military family, Hamm had always demonstrated a penchant for sports. At age 14, she attracted attention for her play on an Olympic developmental soccer team. When the US national team coach Anson Dorrance first saw her outmaneuver older and more experienced players with her deft dribbling and quickness, he was stunned: "This skinny brunette took off like she had been shot out of a cannon," he later commented. At 15, she became the youngest player ever named to the national team, and she followed Dorrance to the University of North Carolina, where he was the head coach. She led the women's team to four consecutive NCAA championships from 1989 through 1992, and by the time she was 25 was recognized as the world's best female soccer player.[28]

At 5 feet 5 inches and 125 pounds, Hamm was not the most imposing player on the field, but her fierce determination and quick reflexes enabled her to rise to the top of her sport. At age 19, she was the youngest player on the US national team that won the world championship in 1991 in China. Hamm emerged as a youthful star on the team, adept at dribbling and ball handling with either foot, using her strength and speed to surprise defenders. But she was also blessed with the innate gift of being able to decoy defenders and goalies when she got near the net. She had the extra sense of how to get the ball past them and into the net. As she explained, "A great finisher can analyze in a split second what the goalie is doing, what surface of the ball to use, and then put the ball in exactly the right spot. It's an ability to slow down time. You don't actually shoot any faster than other players do, but you process a lot more information in the same time." But after saying that, she added her usual self-effacing caveat: "I'm still working on that."[29]

The unexpected world championship in 1991 marked the arrival of the United States as a world soccer power, but when the team returned home they were met by an apathetic nation. Only a few people – family, friends, and a handful of US Soccer Federation members – met the airplane. No television cameras, no throng of cheering fans welcomed the team home. *Sports Illustrated* gave the triumph one brief paragraph notice, and television talk hosts David Letterman and Johnny Carson neglected to call. "No one offered us endorsements, money, or fame," Hamm wrote in her autobiography, but "that is not why we play … Look back at the pictures of all the young faces on that 1991 team, awash with smiles, the glow of a world championship, and athletic glory in its purest form, and it becomes obvious why we play."[30]

By 1999, however, that apathy had turned into national acclaim. Hamm and her teammates had become the center of heavy media coverage. As they powered their way to the final match against China played in Pasadena, Americans followed their games intently. Forty million persons watched the game on television, and a capacity crowd of 92,000, including President Bill Clinton, filled the Rose Bowl, the largest crowd in history to watch a women's athletic event. By this time, Hamm was the world record holder for the number of goals scored in international competition and she had become the symbol of the emergence of the American woman athlete. But unlike so many top male athletes, Hamm refused to talk about herself and her achievements, insisting instead that she was merely part of a great team composed of many star athletes. "People don't want to hear that I'm no better than my teammates," she once groused to a reporter. "They want me to say, 'I'm this or that,' but I'm not. Everything I am I owe to this team."[31]

The championship game against China proved to be all that those who paid up to $1,000 to scalpers hoped for. It was a struggle marked by a relentless Chinese defense pitted against the attacking Americans. Midway through the second half, midfielder Michelle Akers was taken to the locker room suffering from extreme dehydration and a concussion. After the 90 minute regular time had expired, the teams battled through two 15 minute overtime periods, setting up the dramatic penalty-kick shootout anticlimax. It is the type of situation that soccer players hate; the goal tender was now confronted by five free kicks just 12 yards from the goal to decide the match. The American goalie, Briana Scurry, guessed right on the third Chinese kick and made a leaping fingertip stop, setting up the winning goal by Brandi Chastain. When her kick zipped into the corner of the net, giving the United States an improbable 5–4 victory, the large crowd erupted in cheers and the triumph was proclaimed across the land the next morning with front-page headlines.

Although there were plenty of heroes to go around – Chastain, Akers, Scurry, Julie Foudy – it was Hamm who captured the public's imagination. She was soon seen flipping Michael Jordan in a judo move in a popular Nike advertisement to the musical accompaniment of "Anything You Can Do, I Can Do Better." Nike soon thereafter named the largest building on its sprawling Portland campus after her. As Nike CEO Phil Knight explained, "We've had three athletes who played at a level that added a new dimension to their games. That's been Michael Jordan in basketball, Tiger Woods in golf, and Mia Hamm in soccer." Hamm continued to play the game for five more years with the same ferocity and intensity that had propelled her to the top of the sports world. She increasingly devoted her time to her foundation, which supported programs to create opportunities for young women in sports and to foster research in bone marrow disease (which had tragically taken her older brother Garret's life at age 28). Some of the funds that she contributed to her foundation came from her endorsement of a Soccer Barbie doll, which was programmed to say, "I can kick and throw like Mia Hamm." As Hamm explained, "When I was little, Barbie rode around in a red Corvette and lived in a mansion. I sure didn't relate to that. Soccer Barbie is a lot more realistic."[32]

Figure 15.3   Mia Hamm's triumphant soccer career inspired a new generation of young girls to take up the game. In 1999, she and her teammates won the World Cup in dramatic fashion over China, greatly elevating the significance of women's sports and soccer in the eyes of the American public. She is pictured here on the attack in a 2003 match against Sweden. *Image © Paul J. Sutton/Duomo/ Corbis*

The fact that Mia Hamm and her fellow soccer players had captured the imagination of the American people and helped lure hundreds of thousands of youngsters into youth soccer programs was a strong indication of the changes that had occurred within the structure of American sports. Although the enormous power of television kept a national focus on the major male team sports of basketball, football, and baseball, beneath the surface the popularity of participant sports such as youth soccer continued to grow. No one person and no team better symbolized that democratic spirit than Mia Hamm and the US national women's soccer team's capturing of the World Cup before an exulting nation.

"You've Come a Long Way Baby!" Or Have You?

The blizzard of books and articles on the growth in popularity of women's sports is overwhelming, and the immediate conclusion that one might draw from the literature is that women have made great advances in the sports world since passage of Title IX in 1972. As the preceding pages indicate, females have indeed benefited greatly from organized programs linked to educational institutions. Organized youth instructional programs each year give hundreds of thousands of girls opportunities to develop their skills in basketball, soccer, softball, volleyball, swimming, tennis, gymnastics, and golf. These programs feed into high school sports that in turn channel a few elite athletes to college programs with the same financial aid as available to males. When a comparison is made between participation and skill levels in the second decade of the twenty-first century and the status of sports for females in the decades before Title IX, the conclusion has to be that indeed women have come a very long way.

Beyond the realm of sports connected to educational institutions, however, the results have been mixed at best. Consumer preference meant that the women had to compete with male athletes for the attention of the general public, and for their discretionary dollars. Without the mandate of Title IX, market forces take over. Although the growth of women's sports has produced new generations of adult women who appreciate the role that competitive sports has played in their lives, they apparently have not emulated males who are more inclined to become lifelong sports junkies. The content of ESPN only infrequently touches upon women's sports, but one can surmise that this very profitable corporation would readily appeal to that market if an audience existed. No ESPNW has yet to hit the airwaves, although a news report in the autumn of 2010 revealed that the company was exploring the idea of creating an internet blog site aimed at females as an initial step toward the possibility of a new cable network structured for a female audience. ESPN vice president Laura Gentile was candid: "Women see us as their father's brand, or husband's brand, or boyfriend's brand. They recognize it's not theirs." Anecdotal evidence connecting successful women who have risen to top corporate positions with their experiences in competitive sports as a youth have begun to appear in national business publications.[33] Studies have repeatedly indicated that less than a quarter of television viewers who watch sports on television are female. Advertisements that support sports programming are geared to a male audience: automobiles and pickup trucks, beer, shaving lotions, and male sexual performance enhancement drugs.

Repeated efforts to create viable opportunities for women's teams at the professional level have produced more failures than successes. The founding of the Women's Professional Basketball League was announced in 1978 based upon the spirit of Title IX and a few star players. Ann Meyers of USC was the top draft choice, but several top prospects took one look at the proposed $5,000 salary and rejected contract offers. Teams named the Angels, Does, Gems, and Hustle failed to attract either sufficient numbers of ticket buyers or a television contract, and the league folded in 1981. Efforts to establish viable professional leagues for softball, volleyball, soccer, and team tennis (with both male and female members on each team) have received limited support despite all of the best intentions of investors and sponsors.

The most visible effort to establish a women's professional league has been the Women's National Basketball Association (WNBA) that set up shop in 1997 under the protective wing of the highly successful NBA. Founders of the WNBA believed there was sufficient interest in women's basketball as evidenced by the large attendance at the 1996 Olympics in Atlanta to watch the American women win the gold medal. Such interest indicated that a professional women's league could succeed financially. Such top college players as Rebecca Lobo, Sheryl Swopes, and Lisa Leslie were among those drafted by such new teams as the New York Liberty, Houston Comets, and Los Angeles Sparks. By 2000, the league had increased to 16 teams, but several franchises lost their sponsorships and the league contracted to 12 teams for the 2010 season. Despite having won three championships, the Detroit Shock was relocated to Tulsa, and only four of the founding franchises remained in their original location. Salaries for the 11-player rosters did not begin to equate with the NBA. In 2010, each team had a salary cap of $750,000, a total far less than paid to first-round draft choices by the NBA. Although management of these franchises would not reveal the details of their finances, it has been widely presumed that few ever made a profit and only the dedication of investors and the continuing support of Commissioner David Stern of the NBA has keep the league afloat.

The Ladies Professional Golf circuit began under the leadership of Babe Didrikson Zaharias after the Second World War, and slowly built its tournament schedule while offering limited prize money. The growth of a series of talented golfers such as Louise Suggs and Patty Berg during the 1950s and 1960s helped create visibility and credibility. Kathy Whitworth enjoyed a sparkling career during the 1970s; she won 10 majors and 88 LPGA tournaments, and became the first woman golfer to reach a career earnings total of $1 million. Whitworth was replaced atop the tour during the 1980s by Patty Sheehan and Nancy Lopez, and television coverage sparked interest in the LPGA. Many golfing experts consider the Swedish-born resident of Lake Tahoe, Annika Sorenstam, to be the greatest female golfer of all time. She won 72 tour events and 10 majors between 1991 and her retirement in 2008. In 2003, at the top of her game, she was invited to play in the men's Colonial tournament in Dallas amidst a wave of publicity, but finished 88th after two rounds and missed the cut.

During Sorenstam's rise to prominence, however, a perceptible decline in interest in the women's tour occurred. The number of tour events fell each year and by 2011 the tour consisted of only 24 tournaments. Even those events had to scramble to find corporate sponsors. Sorenstam's dominance, and the lack of the rise of a new generation of American golfers who could challenge her, tended to diminish the LPGA tour's appeal to television audiences. Efforts to stimulate renewed interest by the hyping of teenage sensation Michelle Wie, a native of Hawaii, fizzled when she failed to live up to predictions. She turned professional before her 16th birthday and immediately signed lucrative endorsement contracts totaling an estimated $20 million. Wie created considerable controversy by entering a series of men's PGA events when offered sponsors' exemptions, but failed to make the cut in all 11 instances. When she entered the LPGA upon reaching the minimum age of 18, the results were unimpressive. Criticism mounted when she missed cuts or withdrew from several tournaments for alleged physical ailments; it seemed to a growing band of skeptics that she reported injuries when playing poorly. Wie amassed a substantial fortune from endorsements and appearance fees, but the hoopla surrounding her career did nothing to increase interest in the LPGA tour. Some believed her futile attempts to compete with the men and her frequent withdrawals from tournaments actually hurt the credibility of the women's circuit. By the end of 2010, she had won only one LPGA tournament, the 2010 Canadian Women's Open.

The women's professional game that thrived was tennis. Interest in women's tennis was stimulated early on by the stirring play of Billy Jean King and Chris Evert, and then increased during the 1980s when naturalized American citizen Martina Navratilova reached her prime. Lindsay Davenport and several other Americans enjoyed considerable success in the 1990s and competed well against a growing number of talented players from abroad. The sensational play of the Williams sisters, Venus and Serena, during the first decade of the twenty-first century helped maintain strong public interest in women's tennis.

Title IX at Forty

Few Americans had any inkling that Title IX would revolutionize the face of American sports. In retrospect, however, its passage stands as a watershed moment in American history, and not just in the cozy world of organized athletics. It was a critical element in the women's rights movement, and opened up opportunities for millions of girls and young women that they otherwise would not have had. Women's rights advocates have argued that Title IX would have been unnecessary had the Equal Rights Amendment, passed by Congress that same year, been ratified by the required 38 states; that it failed ratification by only three states was indicative of the public's ambivalence regarding women's rights, and its ultimate defeat indicated that the amendment had generated large pockets of opposition.

The same controversy that surrounded the ratification fight over what would have become the 27th amendment to the Constitution was played out in the debate over the meaning and impact of Title IX.[34] Once the Department of Education issued its permanent guidelines in 1979, opposition moved to the federal court system. Opponents gained a pyrrhic victory in the *Grove City* vs *Bell* decision of 1984. By that time the NCAA had included women's sports, and the growth of programs for girls had produced a tidal wave of participation that swept the nation and could not be reversed. The shift in public opinion that now embraced the intrinsic worth of competitive sports for females was confirmed in 1988 when Congress passed the Civil Rights Restoration Act that negated *Grove City*.

The legal phase of the battle was effectively concluded in a case brought by women athletes at Brown University in 1992 after the institution announced it would reduce expenses in its athletic budget by simultaneously dropping two men's and two women's sports. The administration believed that it operated in good faith under Title IX because the same number of athletes of both genders would be deprived of intercollegiate competition. Members of the targeted women's volleyball and gymnastic teams disagreed, and based their legal action upon the fact that the percentage of women athletes remained at just 36 percent of the total number of intercollegiate athletes at Brown. The US district court in Rhode Island agreed, and ordered the two women's programs be reinstated – but not the men's water polo and golf teams – because of the disparity in the overall participation rate. In 1996, the Court of Appeals in Boston upheld the decision, and the following year the US Supreme Court refused to hear the case upon appeal.

The landmark decision in *Cohen* vs *Brown* effectively resolved one of the major arguments that opponents had mounted against Title IX: that the guidelines issued by the Department of Education created a quota system rather than taking into consideration the popular perception that in most educational institutions, substantially more males than females were interested in participation in competitive athletics. Advocates of what had come to be known as "gender equity" were thrilled with the Appeals Court ruling that the participation rate of women athletes at Brown had to be within 2.5 percent of the ratio of total male and female undergraduate enrollment. Meanwhile, the male students whose water polo and golf teams were dropped had to accept that their programs were not going to be restored. Their lament echoed men across the country whose college teams, estimated at more than 400, had been dropped in order to achieve the required legal gender proportionality.

Conservatives railed against *Cohen*, just as they had long protested the threat of Title IX to the status quo. Underlying this protest was the inherent conservative resistance to any type of federal imposition of change upon states and individual citizens. Thus it was not surprising that a leading conservative columnist would view Title IX as another example of liberal activism run amuck. The syndicated and *Newsweek* columnist George Will denounced Title IX as "lunacy," noting that many men had been deprived of participation in those non-revenue-producing sports most vulnerable to cutting: track and field, gymnastics, wrestling, swimming and diving, tennis, volleyball and baseball. Moreover, Will argued, the legislation sought to create "affirmative androgyny" by basing the policy upon the assumption that women are equally interested in competitive sports as males. He argued that "men and women have different interests, abilities, and zeal regarding competition," and that "young men have distinctive needs for hierarchy and organized team activities" that are much greater than found among females.[35]

Will concluded that Congress and the federal courts had created a "train wreck called Title IX." It was significant, however, that he did not reiterate the argument often made by male athletic directors and commonplace on sports talk shows: that football participation rates should not be included in determining proportionality because there was not an equivalent sport for women requiring large numbers of participants and a huge outlay of funds. Nor did he raise the popular (but erroneous) criticism that the law required women be permitted to play on men's teams. Will's attack, however, focused only on university sports, and ignored the immense popularity of junior high and high school sports.

Even Title IX's biggest critics, however, have not attempted to challenge one fundamental fact: the growth of sports programs for young females has changed the cultural landscape in a fundamental way, providing millions of girls opportunities to learn the same important lessons that at one time had been reserved only for their brothers. As Title IX approached its 40th anniversary, no prominent political leader was willing to suggest it be repealed.

16

"Only in America!"

In his stirring inaugural address on January 20, 1961, President John F. Kennedy challenged the American people to conquer "new frontiers." He had many goals in mind, but among the most prominent was to catch and surpass the Soviet Union in the space race. The early success of the Soviet Union in placing a small satellite into orbit around the earth in 1957 was deeply disturbing to the American people because every time Sputnik crossed the United States – it was visible at night – it was a reminder that the Soviets had greater missile expertise than the United States. The United States also had fallen behind the Soviets in international sports competition, as evidenced by the medal count at the 1956 and 1960 Olympics. The Soviet and Eastern bloc men and women clearly were superior to the athletes from the United States.

Early in his administration, Kennedy urged the American people to exercise regularly and to get into better physical condition. The president's implicit message was that the American people had gone soft, a condition not acceptable at a time when the nation was confronted by a resolute Soviet Union. Kennedy encouraged efforts by a presidential advisory committee to improve physical fitness as part of his Cold War strategy. His own family set an example by engaging in aggressive co-ed touch football games that the press covered as if they were postseason bowl games. Several of Kennedy's cabinet members responded to the fitness challenge and participated in highly publicized 50 mile fitness walks.

These two seemingly disparate issues – the space race and physical fitness – came together when test pilot turned astronaut, John Glenn, was selected to be the first American to ride a Mercury capsule in orbital flight around the earth. Glenn appeared to be the perfect incarnation of the fictional Jack Armstrong, the "All-American Boy." The son of middle-class parents, born and raised in the small Ohio town of New Concord, Glenn married his high school sweetheart and in 1942 dropped out of Muskingum College to join the Navy Air Corps. He flew 59

Sports in American Life: A History, Second Edition. Richard O. Davies.
© 2012 John Wiley & Sons, Inc. Published 2012 by John Wiley & Sons, Inc.

missions in the South Pacific, and during the Korean War flew another 63 missions, shooting down three enemy aircraft, and earning five Distinguished Flying Crosses and many other commendations. After the war, he became a Navy test pilot, and in 1957 set a transcontinental record by flying from Los Angeles to New York City in 3 hours and 23 minutes. In 1959, Glenn was one of the seven men selected from among 110 candidates to become an astronaut.

When his selection for the first orbital mission was announced, Glenn immediately became a household name. Media reports emphasized that this trim, athletic 41-year-old kept fit by running several miles each day. Glenn had learned that distance running was instrumental to his physical conditioning. He was an early disciple of US Air Force physician Kenneth Cooper, whose research on heart disease had led him to recommend extended periods of moderate exercise that would elevate the heart rate. Cooper found that an aerobic exercise that elevates the heart rate to 130 beats per minute for 30 minutes or more, three times a week, substantially reduces the heart rate, lowers blood pressure, improves the likelihood of a good night's sleep, stimulates mental acuity, reduces the chances of depression, and in general creates a happier, healthier individual.[1]

When Glenn's Mercury capsule, *Friendship 7*, successfully left the launch pad and pushed beyond the earth's gravitational pull to a height of 192 miles on February 20, 1962, most activity in the United States came to a halt. Americans everywhere followed his voyage with a combination of pride and apprehension. With all three national television networks covering the event, the American people collectively held their breath through the dicey "lift off," and listened intently as Glenn chatted with "mission control" from outer space and calmly took over flying the capsule when a computer failed. After making three orbits of the earth and spending nearly 5 hours aloft, *Friendship 7* returned to earth, splashing down right on target in the Atlantic Ocean. When NASA announced that a Navy ship had picked Glenn up safe and sound, the American people exulted. Because Glenn's life was thought to be endangered due to a loose heat shield designed to prevent incineration during re-entry into the earth's atmosphere, his mission seemed even more heroic.

Safely back on earth, Glenn resumed his daily runs, and millions of Americans joined in. All across America, men and women took to the roads to enjoy the same health benefits that John Glenn and his fellow astronauts had achieved from aerobic exercise. Jogging as well as serious distance running became a national craze. In 1968, Cooper's book *Aerobics* hit the market and became an instant bestseller. In this and several subsequent books, Cooper explained that running was only one means of achieving good cardiovascular results, which could be accomplished by other activities such as swimming, squash, racquetball, aerobic dancing, even speed walking. Conventional wisdom now indicated that an active lifestyle that included vigorous physical activity was essential to good health. If an adult had run through city streets several miles each day during the 1950s, he would have been laughed out of town as some kind of nut. Now the streets and byways of America were filled with runners.

Triumph of the Swoosh

The running and jogging craze became a national phenomenon. By the early 1970s, in cities large and small, charitable organizations held weekend 10,000 meter (6.2 mile) races or shorter "fun runs" that drew hundreds of thousands of runners (and walkers). In the spirit of the 1960s phenomenon of large outdoor rock concerts, promoters introduced the weekend mass run. In Boulder, Colorado, the Memorial Day "Bolder Boulder" 15 kilometer run attracted upwards of 50,000 runners, and in Phoenix, Arizona, a local restaurant held an annual spring 10 kilometer race that saw 20,000 entrants resolutely chugging along the banks of irrigation canals. For years, a small number of runners had annually raced across San Francisco on a Sunday morning in May, beginning in the shadows of the Bay Bridge, traversing the city's steep hills, and ending up at the ocean front in Golden Gate Park. The "Bay to Breakers" race now attracted upwards of 100,000 runners, joggers, and walkers – of all sizes, shapes, and ages – many of whom ran in crazy costumes or tethered together in a unique "centipede" arrangement. The festive atmosphere surrounding the race had the feeling of a mobile rock concert, and it became the largest annual community event in the City by the Bay. On a more serious level, the historic Boston Marathon grew to the point where qualifying times had to be submitted and the number of entries limited to 20,000. The New York Marathon became a popular annual event, drawing 20,000 runners in 1980 and more than 50,000 in 2000. In 1961, the year in which President Kennedy first prodded the American people to get off their couches and into a serious exercise routine, fewer than 200 runners had shown up for the 26 mile (and 385 yard) ordeal.

The craze did not run its course, as many predicted, but sustained itself as an important form of exercise for millions of Americans. Its advantages were simple: it could be done at any time of the day, it could be incorporated into business or vacation trips, it was inexpensive, and it was effective. Aerobic-style running was assimilated into the lifestyle patterns of millions of Americans, and the more dedicated sustained that commitment well past middle age. Runners flocked to sporting goods stores to buy the latest innovation in running shoes, purchased stylish workout gear, carried a heart monitor while they ran, kept a daily log of their times and distances, invested in digital watches to time their runs, and planned their day's activities around workouts. Conversations around the office water cooler or at cocktail parties (where white wine or a designer beer increasingly replaced strong spirits as beverages of choice) frequently included not-so-subtle braggadocio: "I only got in 40 miles this last week," or "I'm training to do my third marathon next month." Those conversations also were replete with references to the benefits of "carbohydrate loading," the positive effect of the release of "endorphins" that produced a "runner's high," the value of "interval training" and "cross-training," how to ward off aggressive dogs (and an occasional petulant automobile driver), the relative merits of competing running shoes, the best vitamin and herbal supplements, and the advantages of this or that magical new nutritional plan.

Aerobic running was the spearhead of a much wider fitness movement that followed in its wake. It was only natural that in the world's leading capitalist nation, entrepreneurs would take note that Americans were ready to invest substantial sums of money in their quest for health and fitness. During the 1970s, a new type of business appeared in American cities – the private health club. Offering a wide range of activities – racquetball, squash, indoor swimming, weightlifting, aerobic dance classes, stationary exercise bicycles, electronic treadmills, and stair-climbing machines – the clubs also provided the upscale amenities of steam baths, whirlpools, saunas, stylish locker rooms, massage therapy, dietary counseling, and a restaurant featuring a juice bar and vegetarian entrées. The new profession of "personal trainer" emerged, providing one-on-one counseling by a "certified health professional" regarding diet and workout strategies – for a hefty fee.

These trends reflected the pioneering work of three physical culturists who preached much the same message, but clearly were ahead of their time. Born in rural Missouri in 1868, Bernarr Macfadden willed himself to survive a "sickly" childhood by following a regimen of physical exercise and a diet heavy in fruits, nuts, and vegetables. By the turn of the century, weightlifting had transformed his scrawny 5 foot 6 inch frame into a block of rippling muscles. Macfadden launched a publicity campaign to sell his lifestyle to the American people, establishing various institutes and fitness camps. Not hesitant to promote himself and his message of "physical culture," Macfadden was part health educator and part carnival huckster. By the 1920s, his personal fortune, derived largely from his publications, lectures, and a chain of "healthatoriums" that offered classes and special spa treatments, was estimated at $20 million. But as he aged Macfadden engaged in increasingly bizarre behaviors. His public advocacy of the joys of sex and his publications that featured men and women scantily attired (to facilitate strenuous physical activity) both titillated and alienated readers. His repeated renunciations of the medical profession amounted to nothing more than ignorance compounded by stubbornness. This one-time fitness advisor to presidents died in 1955 at the advanced age of 87, but not before he had attracted national attention at age 81 by safely parachuting from an airplane – his first of two such publicity-seeking plunges.[2]

Beset by increasing criticisms of his personal life and public behavior, Macfadden lost his public relations edge during the 1920s to bodybuilder Angelo Siciliano, a modest man whose imposing physique appeared with regularity in the popular media. Born in Italy in 1892, Siciliano emigrated to the United States as a child. He was, according to his own narrative, a "97 pound weakling" who once was humiliated while with a female friend on a Long Island beach when a husky lifeguard kicked sand in his face. He thereupon became obsessed with bodybuilding, eventually creating his own workout program that relied upon simple isometric exercises without the use of weights. He won Bernarr Macfadden's "World's Most Beautiful Man" contest in 1920 and became a favorite model for photographers and sculptors, taking the name of Charles Atlas. He packaged his unique muscle-building system into a mail-order course ($29.95 for the complete set of 12 lessons) and sold millions of copies by promoting them in comic book and magazine advertisements depicting his own body development from that of embarrassed skinny kid on the beach to the world's most perfect male specimen. Atlas urged a healthy lifestyle free from alcohol (he'd celebrate personal triumphs with a glass of carrot juice), and when asked, told strangers that the secret to a healthy life was "Live clean, think clean, and don't go to burlesque shows." He continued his daily exercise program into old age – 50 knee bends, 100 sit-ups, and 300 push-ups, and distance running on a Florida beach – and appeared in magazine photographs in his 70s, his muscles still rippling and his impressive physique unchanged. Atlas died of cardiac arrest after a long run at the age of 79 in 1972, just as the national fitness craze was captivating the American public.[3]

In 1936, a young bodybuilder by the name of Jack LaLanne opened one of the nation's first health clubs in Oakland, California, and in 1951 began a 33 year stint on daytime television demonstrating exercises and urging his viewers to join in his workout routines, and (of course) to purchase his assorted exercise equipment and famous "power juicer." He invented exercise machines that utilized pulleys and adjustable weights, and his health clubs expanded to a chain of 200. LaLanne claimed he was the first physical fitness expert who encouraged women to lift weights as a regular component of their exercise program, and he devoted his life to promoting good health through vigorous exercise and a vegetarian diet that included some fish. In 2010 at the age of 96, still deriving much of his daily nutrition from the fruit and eggwhite concoctions he squished in his personal "power juicer," LaLanne was still lifting weights and doing exercises 2 hours each morning before spending another hour swimming laps.[4] He died of respiratory failure brought on by pneumonia on January 23, 2011. That Macfadden, Atlas, and LaLanne lived long and healthy lives gave credence to their basic message of proper diet and vigorous exercise. Those messages, tweaked and modified, would be advanced by an army of health advocates during the latter years of the twentieth century.

All three of these early fitness crusaders walked a well-traveled American entrepreneurial highway. As the fitness craze swept the United States in the 1960s and the 1970s, old-line athletic apparel and equipment companies attempted to respond to the burgeoning new market, but they faced a wave of new competition. Companies armed with alluring new products and compelling advertising strategies entered the fray. The company that proved to be the most agile and adept in setting the standard for the new fitness age began in the Oregon college town of Eugene during the 1960s. Year after year, coach Bill Bowerman's University of Oregon track and field team was one of the nation's best, and he was forever experimenting with equipment as well as exploring new techniques of running and jumping. He wanted to create a lighter running shoe that provided sufficient traction. In one inspired moment, he used his wife's waffle iron to create a revolutionary "waffle" composition sole to which he attached light leather and fabric shoes. In 1964, Bowerman shook hands with one of his former Oregon track athletes, Phil Knight, to create a small shoe manufacturing company, Blue Ribbon Sports. Knight had originally contemplated such a company in a research paper he had written in a seminar while pursuing his MBA at Stanford, in which he pondered whether an American firm could challenge Adidas, the German outfit that dominated the sports shoe market. Bowerman and Knight changed their company's name to Nike, the Greek goddess of victory, and for a mere $35 they commissioned the design of the soon-to-be-ubiquitous "swoosh" as their company's logo. In 1972, sales reached $3 million, and new and more colorful models began to appear with unerring frequency. The first "waffle shoe" appeared in 1974 and sales zoomed. Nike entered the athletic shoe market at the same time the running craze was enveloping the nation. The niche market of running shoes provided the platform for building a Fortune 500 company that would branch out into many sports and leisure activities.

In 1980, Nike went public with a stock offering and immediately became a darling of Wall Street. By this time, Nike had eclipsed its competition and launched an audacious advertising campaign that reflected new trends in modern society. CEO Phil Knight blended the emerging fitness movement with America's obsession with status, style, and innovation. He tied Nike's expanding line of products to charismatic athletes who either flaunted or at least challenged society's norms. When Knight selected the 21-year-old, unproven NBA player Michael Jordan in 1983 to be Nike's spokesman for a revolutionary new form of basketball shoe – the "Air Jordan" with its cushioned pocket of air in the heel – his competitors scoffed. But Jordan's infectious smile, bubbly public personality, and growing stature as an NBA star made the clunky basketball shoe a runaway bestseller. Nike aggressively expanded its product line to encompass a wide range of leisure and sports clothing and equipment. The company likewise hit paydirt in 1996 when it signed the highly touted 21-year-old Tiger Woods to a lucrative endorsement contract. Ten years later it took a similar risk with the 16-year-old golf phenomenon from Hawaii, Michelle Wie. In 1996, Nike reported net profits of over $550 million on $6.5 billion in revenues; in 2004 its net revenues had increased to $14 billion and its profits had grown accordingly. Not bad for a company that began in a small-town Oregon kitchen with a waffle iron and a dream.[5]

The World of Jimmy the Greek

In 1951, the subterranean world of sports gambling burst into public view, and the picture was not a pretty one. The far-reaching college basketball points-shaving scandals ripped at the heart of the credibility of college sports, and the sensational hearings conducted by Senator Estes Kefauver on the influence of organized crime drew close connections between sports gambling and organized crime. Although Kefauver focused attention on a dying institution – illegal horse betting parlors that received race results from distant racetracks by telegraph lines – he also brushed up against the rapidly growing phenomenon of betting on college and professional football, basketball, and baseball. The connections between organized crime and sports gambling seemed all the more ominous because they both were linked to local political machines.

Most of this enterprise was illegal, operating beyond the purview of tax collectors and law enforcement authorities. Federal officials estimated that some 200,000 illegal bookmakers handled wagers that exceeded the annual income of General Motors. The public perception of sports gambling seemed divided. The traditional perception that gambling was a sin was aptly summarized by a Methodist minister in 1963 when he wrote, "Gambling is a moral and social evil that tends to undermine the ethical teachings of our churches and glorifies the philosophy of getting something for nothing."[6] By 1963, however, this traditional viewpoint was rapidly losing its appeal; already 30 states had given their approbation to gambling by legalizing pari-mutuel horse racing – actually, a slick trick by which politicians could increase government revenues without raising taxes. Gambling on other sports, however, had been illegal throughout the United States until the economically troubled state of Nevada legalized wide-open casino gambling in 1931 as a depression-bred effort to increase tourism and raise state revenues.

Legalized sports gambling in Nevada might have begun on a modest basis but by the 1980s it had become a powerful economic force that exerted strong, if often overlooked, influence upon college and professional sports. The enterprise began modestly in a few undistinguished buildings in Las Vegas and Reno, where bookmakers ground out small profits by booking bets on horse races conducted at tracks around the country. Reeking with cigar smoke and stale beer, these "turf clubs" also accommodated clients who wished to bet on baseball, basketball, and football. In 1951, Congress imposed a 10 percent tax on sports wagers other than horse races. This tax had the potential of ending legal sports gambling in Nevada because the rate made it impossible for a bookmaker to turn in a profit.

Club managers used various subterfuges to get around paying the federal tax while accommodating their customers' desires to wager on professional and college team games, but in Nevada, sports gambling remained a relatively small and unobtrusive enterprise.[7]

That reality changed in 1974 when Congress lowered the prohibitive tax rate to just 2 percent. It was now possible for a well-run sports book to consistently turn a profit. Two years later, the Nevada Gaming Control Board voted to permit sports wagering within casinos; soon, plush sports books appeared in the largest casinos, complete with banks of television sets for bettors to watch the fate of their investments being determined at stadiums and ballparks around the country. The days of the dingy turf clubs were numbered. In 1983, Congress further encouraged Nevada's sports books by reducing the federal tax on sports bets to just .25 percent. By 1986, every large hotel-casino in Nevada offered a full-service sports book to their customers.

In 1976, Nevada lost its monopoly on legalized gambling when the state of New Jersey authorized the opening of casinos in Atlantic City, and within a few years every state except Hawaii and Utah had some form of casino gambling. Between 1963 and 1990, 37 states also approved the operation of state lotteries. The newfound embrace of gambling, however, did not extend to sports wagering. The stigma of possible scandals involving games tampered with by gamblers seeking a sure thing prevented its widespread legalization. In 1993, Congress passed legislation that essentially gave Nevada a monopoly on legalized sports action by forbidding other states from entering the field. That did not mean, however, that sports fans in other states could not get down a bet. Illegal bookmakers operated in cities large and small, unregulated and untaxed. Many college campuses even had student bookies operating out of campus hangouts. These individuals, contrary to popular myth, were seldom associated with crime syndicates; rather, they were small operators handling their own cluster of customers. Emulating the Nevada sports books, they adjusted the odds or points spread to generate equal amounts of money on both sides of a contest so that they could earn a profit of about 4 to 5 percent on the money wagered (in gambling lingo, this is called the "juice" or "vig"). With the advent of the world wide web during the 1990s, several hundred offshore internet sports books in the Caribbean, Mexico, England, and Australia posed major competition to the neighborhood bookie; gamblers could now use their credit cards to place bets from their laptop computer.

In 1976, CBS took note of the fact that the National Football League had become a favorite of gamblers. Football was a natural venue for gamblers because a carefully set points spread made every game attractive to bettors. Because a team played only one game per week, interest intensified, giving gamblers time to analyze, ponder, and reflect upon the merits of two teams relative to the points spread. Newspapers published the betting line in the sports pages, and television sports shows, talk radio, and internet sites intensified interest. With an eye toward an emerging trend among football fans, in 1976 CBS-TV introduced the nation's most famous sports handicapper, Demetrius Synodinos, a.k.a. Jimmy "The Greek" Snyder, to its popular Sunday afternoon "NFL Today" show that preceded the professional games of the day. The weekly appearance of the most famous Las Vegas handicapper brought an immediate legitimacy to the craft. CBS and the NFL denied that his presence encouraged fans to bet on NFL games, but his weekly "picks" certainly did nothing to discourage wagering. Each Sunday "The Greek" "released" predictions on the upcoming afternoon games, complete with seeming insightful details and crisp analysis, all delivered with an assurance that his prediction was a sure thing. As Snyder's segment segued to a commercial, gamblers all across America rushed to their telephones to get down a bet; bookies monitored the show and made adjustments in their betting lines to compensate for the response to Snyder's opinions.[8]

Snyder began his gambling career as a teenager during the Depression years of the 1930s in his hometown of Steubenville, Ohio. Before the Second World War, he moved to Florida, where he showed proficiency in picking winning horses. During the 1940s, he relocated to New York City, where he became known as a "high-roller," someone who bets heavily on sporting events. His high profile led to police and FBI surveillance and attention by the Kefauver Committee. Like many professional East Coast gamblers, he relocated to Las Vegas in the late 1950s where he could openly ply his trade. In 1963, Snyder began writing a weekly sports-betting column for the *Las Vegas Sun* that became widely syndicated. He formed a handicapping service and a public relations firm, all the while promoting himself as the nation's top odds-maker and handicapper. He often referred to himself as the "Wizard of Odds."[9]

The rapid growth of sports wagering contributed substantially to the growing popularity of mainstream team sports in contemporary America, and Snyder rode that cresting wave to national prominence and celebrity. Sports gambling grew exponentially during the late twentieth century. In 1980, it was estimated by federal officials that somewhere in the neighborhood of $10 billion was wagered illegally each year, but with the growth of televised sports and the decline in anti-gambling sentiment, that figure rose to $90 billion by 1995. The biggest single sporting event for gamblers was the Super Bowl. In 2000, federal officials estimated that the American people bet more than $1 billion on the Super Bowl. Of that amount, about $80 million – or less than 10 percent – was channeled through the legal sports books in Nevada; the rest was wagered in defiance of federal and state anti-gambling laws, some of it in small office pools. In Nevada, Super Bowl Sunday was the single largest event at the state's approximately 100 sports books, when they took about $75 million in bets; over the year they handled more than $3 billion in sports wagers. The four-week NCAA men's basketball tournament produced the second-largest betting event. However, the sports books cranked out a profit on a daily basis with off-track horse racing and the daily flow of games throughout the year. In fact, there was only one day each year in which sports books did not have a new contest upon which gamblers could get down a bet: the Monday before the annual July All-Star baseball game. Even on Christmas Day, in Las Vegas and on the streets of American cities, there were bookies eager to accept their action on basketball and football games.

The Tragedy of Pete Rose

The fact that even experienced sports gamblers can and do lose money – lots of it – was made patently clear by the example of Cincinnati Reds player-manager Pete Rose. When he dropped a bloop single into left field on September 11, 1985, for his 4,192nd base hit, eclipsing the record set decades earlier by Ty Cobb, Rose seemed to be on the fast track to the Hall of Fame. Rose's insatiable quest to bet on sports, including baseball games in which he was involved, derailed his express trip to Cooperstown. A blue-collar player of limited natural ability who drove himself to succeed, Rose's frenetic style of play, highlighted by his furious head-first slides, had earned him the popular nickname of "Charlie Hustle." But when baseball commissioner A. Bartlett Giamatti announced in August 1989 that Rose had agreed to a lifetime ban following allegations that he had broken organized baseball's cardinal rule prohibiting anyone associated with a major-league team from betting on baseball, the sports world was stunned. By placing Rose on baseball's ineligible list, Giamatti ensured that he could not be nominated for membership in the Hall of Fame.[10]

It was a most curious agreement, because Rose had not admitted that he had bet on baseball. He did, however, accept a severe punishment as if he had. In announcing the agreement, Giamatti proceeded to inform a press conference that while he was relieved that this meant "a sorry end to a sorry episode," it was ultimately "a disgrace to the game." Referring to a 1,200-page report by private investigator John Dowd which guided his decision, the commissioner left no doubt as to his take on the situation: "In the absence of a formal hearing and therefore in the absence of evidence to the contrary, I am confronted by the factual record of Mr. Dowd. On the basis of that, yes, I have concluded he [Rose] bet on baseball."[11]

Rose and his attorney apparently had been led to believe that Rose would be barred from the game for only a year or so. When that assumption, and a serious misperception or miscalculation on their part, proved in error, baseball's all-time hit leader proceeded to campaign vigorously to have Giamatti's decision reversed, proclaiming at every opportunity that he had never bet on baseball. He continued his denial for the next 15 years – telling anyone who would listen that he had been railroaded. However, skeptics wondered why Rose had agreed to such a settlement if he was innocent. Ultimately, the truth came out. Apparently, after years of futility, Rose came to believe that if he confessed and apologized, Commissioner Bud Selig would lift the suspension and he could once more seek employment in baseball as a coach or manager and have his name placed on the Hall of Fame ballot. Thus, in early 2004, Rose published a slapdash memoir in which he recanted his denials, although positing a series of dubious physiological and psychological problems to explain away his betting problem and his subsequent campaign of lies and deception. Rose's version of events suggests he was possessed by demons beyond his control. Everyone, it seemed, was to blame but himself. But after 300 tortured pages in his soap-opera-style *mea culpa*, Rose finally admitted that he had been persistently lying about his gambling problem for almost two decades. Now, he confessed that during the time he managed the Reds he bet on games "about four or five times a week," in defiance of baseball's best-known rule. As if it mattered, he self-righteously emphasized that he had never bet against the Reds and that "I never made any bets from the clubhouse." Sports journalists overwhelmingly condemned Rose's duplicity, and the millions of fans who had believed his version of the truth felt betrayed, or worse. Contrary to his hopes in releasing the book, his Hall of Fame hopes took on even greater odds. In 2007, during an ESPN radio interview with Dan Patrick, he admitted to betting on many Reds games but only to win, never to lose. He also said, "I bet on my team every night," a statement that was quickly challenged for its veracity by leading sportswriters.[12]

Rose's self-serving book and subsequent oral confession did little to rehabilitate his image with sports fans. It took him 15 years to come clean with his many gullible supporters. Now the nickname of "Charlie Hustle" had taken on a new and distorted meaning, and Rose's hopes of being reinstated into baseball's good graces remained firmly mired in the mess he created. When, or if, Commissioner Selig or his successors might lift the ban remained one of baseball's mysteries. Rose certainly did not enhance his chances by making his confession in a superficial "autobiography." It seemed to his growing band of cynical critics that Pete Rose had elected to write the book not so much as a means to come clean but primarily to hustle a few book royalty checks.

Rose's gambling problems, however depressing, nonetheless underscored the fact that organized baseball had in fact been successful in eliminating the scourge of fixed games following the debacle of the 1919 World Series. College basketball had not been so lucky. After the devastating revelations of points shaving in 1951 that saw 33 players arrested, the NCAA and college officials claimed that the problem had been solved. But in 1961 a second scandal was revealed by New York district attorney Frank Hogan. This proved to be a bigger scandal than the one before: Hogan indicted 49 players from 27 colleges. At least 67 games had been subject to points-shaving efforts during 1957–61. The central figure this time was a product of the streets and playgrounds of New York City and a former Columbia University All-American forward, Jack Molinas, who had become a budding star in the NBA until he was banished for life in 1954 for gambling on his own team, the Fort Wayne Zollner Pistons. In 1963, Hogan nailed Molinas – now possessed of a law degree and a member of the New York State Bar – when Molinas instructed an accused player, Billy Reed of Bowling Green State University, how to lie to the grand jury. Reed, however, had already cut a deal with Hogan and was wearing a recording device. Molinas went to jail for four years for suborning perjury, but – just like 10 years earlier – college basketball's new scandal faded from public view with incredible speed. Sportswriters, it seemed, were not interested in keeping the story alive; perhaps they, like basketball fans, were weary of scandal and wanted to move on.[13]

During the 1980s, gambling problems once again hit the headlines when former Ohio State All-American quarterback Art Schlichter was kicked out of the National Football League for repeated violations of its anti-gambling policies. Schlichter, it seemed, was unable to overcome his desire to bet heavily on football and other sports, his life ultimately ruined by what *Sports Illustrated* called "a textbook case of a man's promise destroyed by gambling." Long after being banished from professional football, he ended up in prison on various charges of credit card fraud, writing bogus checks, and theft, all crimes stemming from his gambling debts.[14] In 1985, scandal once again touched college basketball when it was revealed that a top Tulane University player had shaved points in return for drugs – a modern twist on an old story. That same year it was revealed that in 1979 a notorious New-England-based gambler, Richard "The Fixer" Perry, who had been convicted of fixing horse races, had also bribed a Boston College basketball player to dump games. In 1994 a Northwestern running back even fumbled near the goal line to make certain that his team would not cover a points spread upon which he had money wagered.

Figure 16.1 Pete Rose, shown here in one of his signature head-first slides, was headed for the Hall of Fame until he was derailed by his gambling habit that led him to break baseball's cardinal rule against betting on baseball games. Curiously, Rose accepted a lifetime ban by Commissioner Bart Giamatti in 1989, but steadfastly maintained his innocence until 2004. Whether the man who broke Ty Cobb's career hit record would ever become eligible to be voted into the Hall of Fame remained an open question more than 20 years after Giamatti announced the ban. *National Baseball Hall of Fame Library, Cooperstown, NY, USA © NBL*

It was not surprising, with the early rumors about Pete Rose hitting the streets along with a flurry of other gambling issues, that the leading sports magazine of the time, *Sports Illustrated*, would feel compelled to examine the influence of gambling on sports. In 1986, the magazine weighed in with a lengthy issue devoted to sports gambling in which the editors made clear that they believed the practice posed a major threat to the integrity of the entire enterprise:

> Most Americans tend to view such wagering as a naughty-but-nice diversion. Yet from the Black Sox scandal of 1919 to the Tulane basketball fixes of last season, nothing has done more to despoil the games Americans play and watch than widespread gambling on them. As fans cheer their bets rather than their favorite teams, dark clouds of cynicism and suspicion hang over games, and the possibility of fixes is always in the air.[15]

The Demise of Boxing

As the debate over sports gambling unfurled during the late twentieth century, it was curious that the sport most often suspected of nefarious influence by gamblers was virtually ignored. That oversight suggests that the "manly art" of pugilism, which had always existed on the fringes of respectability, had fallen into such public disfavor that it was in danger of becoming completely irrelevant. Except for a few high-profile championship bouts, few sports fans paid much attention. That was because by the late twentieth century, it had become little more than the mind-numbing burlesque and charade that was professional wrestling. Controlled by three rival international organizations of questionable origin and authority, beset by conniving and untrustworthy promoters, dogged by professional medical commentaries insisting it was too dangerous to be labeled a sport, beset with a welter of confusing weight classifications such as "cruiser weight" and "junior heavyweight," boxing had careened close to becoming a caricature of its former self. Additionally, boxing had long existed under the cloud of suspicion that fighters would "take a dive" at the behest of influential gamblers. Actually, this state of affairs was not much out of the ordinary for boxing, because the enterprise had always been viewed with suspicion as a brutal blood sport that debased the human condition and was run by individuals of dubious virtue.

Although he was arguably the first bona fide sports star in America, heavyweight John L. Sullivan often had to ply his craft in out-of-the-way places to avoid the long arm of the law. At the turn of the twentieth century, the only state that openly permitted prizefighting was Nevada. The negative image of boxing changed substantially with the legalization of the sport in many states during the 1920s when Jack Dempsey and Gene Tunney stirred widespread excitement. Million-dollar gates, radio broadcasts live from ringside, and heavy media attention created a new and more positive image for the sport. During the next half-century, boxing enjoyed its heyday, as leading boxers such as Joe Louis, Sugar Ray Robinson, Jersey Joe Wolcott, Jake LaMotta, Rocky Marciano, and Kid Gavilan provided plenty of excitement and newsworthy action in and out of the square "ring." Even then a distasteful aura still hovered over the sport. Allegations of fixed fights, rumours of close connections between fight promoters and organized crime syndicates, and an occasional death in the ring tended to remind observers that boxing had never quite escaped its questionable historical legacy.

The demise of the sport began in the 1950s, when the boxing game was grossly distorted by the machinations of commercial television, but that fact was largely overlooked due to the excitement produced by the charismatic Muhammad Ali. But Ali's powerful presence and huge box office draw merely masked the problems confronting the sport, and when he departed in 1980, the game fell into a prolonged decline. The lack of a strong, ethical organization to monitor the fight game lay at the heart of boxing's problems. The United States Congress failed to establish a national regulatory body despite repeated calls for such a body. State boxing commissions were typically run as tight little political fiefdoms and demonstrated a greater interest in assisting promoters to arrange profitable fights than in monitoring the integrity of the sport. Consequently, over the years several different international bodies claimed they were the legitimate organization to supervise the business and monitor the physical and financial wellbeing of professional boxers. The result was that the casual fan was confused by a proliferation of weight divisions and by multiple champions claiming titles. Public interest became dulled by a lack of charismatic fighters.

Not surprisingly, money lay at the root of boxing's evils. Most young men who opted for a professional boxing career were poor and minimally educated; many had experienced encounters with law enforcement. They saw the sport as their main opportunity to escape difficult social and economic circumstances. But even those few who managed to rise to the top of the profession more often than not found themselves somehow shorn of their large payoffs by unscrupulous managers and promoters. News reports that a prominent ex-boxer was broke and simultaneously in trouble with the Internal Revenue Service were not uncommon.

Boxing's image always suffered from its sheer brutality. It is the only major sport in which the basic intent is to inflict serious physical harm upon one's opponent. The most exciting moment is the knockout, which results when a boxer suffers a concussion sufficient to render him unconscious. Over the years, comedians have made light of the "punch-drunk" ex-pugilist, but such a condition is a very real and very serious medical problem. Officially called "chronic encephalopathy," it results from the brain absorbing small injuries over an extended period of time, with the end result being a loss of memory, uncontrollable tremors, and general physical debilitation. That Muhammad Ali exhibited precisely those symptoms within a few years after retiring following a 20-year professional career should have come as no shock to anyone closely associated with the dark side of boxing.[16]

This has been known as an incontrovertible medical fact for more than a half-century, but all reform proposals by the American Medical Association to prevent such injuries have been ignored. Between 1945 and 2005, some 120 Americans died from blows received in the ring. Most of these deaths occurred in low-profile situations, but a few instances produced considerable negative publicity. Among these was the death of Charlie Mohr, a University of Wisconsin middleweight who died in the spring of 1960 while defending his NCAA championship. In this instance, the required protective headgear did not prevent massive bleeding, and Mohr's death led to the NCAA dropping boxing as an intercollegiate sport. In 1962, a popular welterweight, Benny "Kid" Paret, was killed by the punches of Emile Griffith in a championship bout. Known for his ability to absorb punishment, Paret had been knocked out twice the previous year, a fact that many believed made him susceptible to a fatal punch even though an electrocardiogram before the fight revealed no brain damage. In 1963, a club fighter by the name of Davey Moore was killed in a Los Angeles bout, but it was revealed that, desperate for money, he had lied to authorities about underlying health problems.[17]

On November 13, 1982, in a lightweight championship bout in Las Vegas, an overmatched Korean boxer, Duk Koo Kim, never regained consciousness after absorbing a horrendous beating for 14 rounds at the hands of champion Ray "Boom Boom" Mancini. Showing enormous fortitude, if not good sense, Kim had gained the admiration of the ringside television announcer, who said as the final and fatal round began, "Duk Koo Kim. You may not have heard of him before – but you will remember him today. Win or lose." Kim collapsed to the canvas in that round, and he died four days later in a Las Vegas hospital of cerebral edema – swelling of the brain. Promoters paid his pregnant widow his guaranteed purse of $20,000.[18]

The fact that Kim died from injuries sustained in a nationally televised championship fight brought considerable, if fleeting, attention to the brutality of the sport. State boxing commissions went into defensive mode, reviewing their policies amid a flurry of critical magazine articles and newspaper opinion columns. Ultimately, the Congressional Subcommittee on Commerce, Transportation and Tourism conducted the obligatory hearings. Congressman James J. Florio of New Jersey, who chaired the hearings, stated, "Our ultimate conclusion is that there has to be some degree of uniformity with regard to boxing across the nation. We have to spell out Federal standards that have to be adhered to by the states in order for boxing to take place." Pledging himself to introduce legislation to require a national database on boxers' physical condition (which subsequently was shelved), Florio said, "People keep saying, 'What does the boxing profession think of the controversy?' Well, the answer is: There is no boxing profession. It's not a system, it's a non-system, and it's getting worse."[19]

Iron Mike and the King of Boxing

Central to boxing's decline was promoter Don King. His meteoric rise to international boxing prominence began shortly after he was released from an Ohio prison in 1971 where he had served four years on manslaughter charges. Within four years of leaving prison, King had shrewdly finagled himself to the top of the boxing promotion business where he reigned for the next quarter-century. As head of Don King Productions, he wheeled and dealed with sponsors, fighters, managers, and boxing commissions, raking in hundreds of millions of dollars in profits.

Born in Cleveland in 1931, King grew up on that city's tough east side. By the time he was in his early 20s, he had become a leading numbers operator, using a small tavern as cover for his illegal but lucrative business. In 1954, he shot and killed a man in an altercation over a numbers payoff but successfully pleaded self-defense. In 1966, he killed his second man, a small-time Cleveland gambler and racketeer, during an altercation over $600 that King said the man owed him from a wager. According to witnesses, the 240 pound King brutally beat Sam Garrett to death outside a tavern in broad daylight, repeatedly kicking the much smaller and sickly man (who had recently undergone kidney surgery) long after he had lost consciousness. King was convicted of second-degree murder, a crime punishable with up to life in prison. The presiding judge, however, with no one present in his office and without informing the prosecutor, inexplicably reduced the sentence to manslaughter. King served what most observers felt was a very light sentence – four years.[20]

Just three years after leaving prison, King thrust himself upon the world when he promoted the famous "Rumble in the Jungle" championship fight in 1974 between Muhammad Ali and George Foreman. By capitalizing on the new technology of making the fight available to cable television subscribers, King was able to offer a historic (for the time) $1 million purse that the two fighters split. In 1975, he followed up with the "Thrilla in Manila," the epic brawl between Ali and Joe Frazier. During the late 1970s, Ali was the central player in King's domination of the sport, but when age took its toll on Ali, King quickly moved to sign top heavyweight prospects Larry Holmes, Ken Norton, and the Spinks brothers, Leon and Michael, to contracts that gave him exclusive rights to promote their fights. In addition, his stable of fighters included one of the most popular of all fighters of the time, the handsome, flashy welterweight Sugar Ray Leonard. Within a decade, King had magically transformed himself from convicted felon into one of the most famous and richest men in America. Don King had an innate sense of how to exploit his natural flamboyance into creating an image of himself as black America's version of Horatio Alger. He loved to talk about himself and his financial success using the phrase, "Only in America," and his publicity machine repeatedly related how he had vowed while in prison to become a law-abiding and hard-working citizen.[21]

In 1985, a promising new boxer appeared on the scene, to whom King was ineluctably drawn. That boxer was the 19-year-old Mike Tyson. Born to an unmarried New York City welfare recipient, Tyson grew up in one of the nation's most notorious slums, the Brownsville section of Brooklyn. Raised in an environment of pervasive poverty, crime, drugs, and violence, Tyson was prone to breaking the law and was quick to use his fists. By age 12, he had been arrested 40 times and landed in a juvenile detention center, where a physical education instructor sought to control his rage and elevate his poor self-image by teaching him to box. By 1979, Tyson had shown so much promise that he was introduced to the famed trainer Cus D'Amato, who provided advanced instruction. In 1981, Tyson won the Junior Olympics; his powerful blows and seething anger quickly became legendary in the boxing circles of New York City. He won his first professional fight in 1985 over Hector Mercedes in a 91 second knockout and proceeded to win 14 more consecutive fights by knockout. At the age of just 22, on November 22, 1986, he won the World Boxing Commission's version of the heavyweight title over Trevor Berbick, and early in 1987 defeated James "Bonecrusher" Smith for the World Boxing Association title. Later that same year, he won a unanimous decision over Tony Tucker in Las Vegas to take the International Boxing Federation title, thereby consolidating his domination of all three versions of the title. The following year, he knocked out Michael Spinks and walked away with the largest purse up to that time in the history of boxing, $21 million.[22]

Don King envisioned the man now known as Iron Mike as the linchpin to his economic future. But Tyson was forever teetering on the edge of self-destruction. His reputation for violent behavior spiraled out of control in September 1988. He was involved in a brutal late-night fight outside a nightclub, and then it was reported in New York newspapers that he had attempted suicide by intentionally driving his BMW into a tree. Media reports indicated that Tyson was under psychiatric treatment for manic depression. Later that same month, while in Moscow with his wife of several months, actress Robin Givens, he reportedly physically attacked her and then attempted to commit suicide by downing a hefty combination of an anti-depressant drug and vodka. At one point, he chased Givens through the hotel lobby, then stood atop a hotel balcony and threatened to jump off. To casual observers, Tyson had become a bona fide sociopath with powerful fists.[23]

Tyson's erratic behavior continued. He also approached his training lackadaisically, and his development as a boxer essentially stopped. In February 1990, King sought an easy payday by promoting a championship fight in Tokyo with journeyman Buster Douglas.

It seemed like a typical Don King promotion, a terrible mismatch that he promoted shamelessly and from which his company earned millions of dollars in pay-per-view television rights. The fight was considered such a mismatch that several Las Vegas sports books refused to put it on their board, and those that did offered it at the staggering odds of 42–1. Overconfident, Tyson barely went through the motions in training and never seemed to realize that he was in a championship bout when the bell rang. From the beginning Douglas controlled the fight. In round 10, the challenger caught the champion on the jaw with a flurry of punches. Tyson went down, wobbled to his feet, then pitched forward again for the count. It was, to say the least, a stunning upset.[24]

Things continued to go downhill for Tyson, and along with him went the tarred image of boxing. In 1992, Tyson was accused of raping an 18-year-old beauty pageant contestant in an Indianapolis hotel, and an Indiana jury found him guilty. As the doors of the Indiana State Prison swung shut, it was reported that Tyson was nearly broke; somehow he had managed to divest himself of the estimated $77 million he had earned during his seven-year professional career. As writer Jack Newfield, well known for his antipathy for Tyson's manager, commented, "Under Don King's tutelage, Mike Tyson lost his crown, lost his money, and lost his freedom."[25]

Within two years following his release from prison in 1995, Tyson had regained the WBC and WBA crowns with technical knockout wins over Bruce Seldon and Frank Bruno. Then, on November 9, 1996, his skills now obviously diminishing and the effects of his frenetic lifestyle catching up with him, Tyson lost his WBA crown in an 11-round technical knockout to Evander Holyfield in Las Vegas. The following June, King arranged a lucrative rematch, but Holyfield dominated the bout from the beginning. It was clear that Tyson no longer was the powerful, much-to-be-feared fighter. What unfolded that evening in Las Vegas stunned everyone present and would become a permanent, if bizarre, part of boxing lore. The demons that afflicted Tyson were obviously at work that night when in a first-round clinch he chomped down on Holyfield's ear. After receiving a stern warning from referee Mills Lane, in the third round Tyson proceeded to bite off a 1 inch chunk of Holyfield's ear. The shocked veteran referee summarily disqualified the now irreparably tarnished Iron Mike. Sportswriters excoriated him for weeks. More importantly, the Nevada Boxing Commission fined him $3 million and suspended him for a year. The reputation of boxing had sunk to an all-time low.

In 1999, Tyson's problems continued when he got into a fracas along a Maryland highway with two men whose car had collided with his; as a result he spent another nine months in prison. Upon his release, the aging boxer vainly attempted to put together several big paydays, but he was no longer the fearsome Iron Mike. In 2001, he filed for bankruptcy, and his boxing career ended with a knockout at the hands of journeyman Danny Williams in Louisville in June 2004.

Undeterred by his break with his biggest meal ticket, Don King continued to promote fights. Despite an avalanche of complaints by his former clients that he had ripped them off, promising young boxers continued to sign on with Don King Productions, eager to earn one of the million-dollar payouts for which King was famous. As former heavyweight champion Larry Holmes said: "I make more money with Don King stealing from me than from 100 other promoters."[26] Such was the sorry state of boxing.

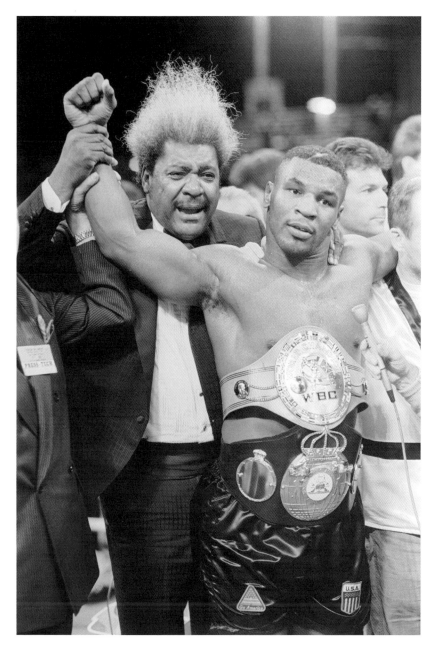

Figure 16.2   Promoter Don King congratulates Mike Tyson after he won a unanimous decision over James "Bonecrusher" Smith in Las Vegas in 1987. King made millions of dollars from promoting championship fights and exploiting the potential of pay-for-view television. Tyson's many personal problems became a sad metaphor for the dizzying decline of the appeal of boxing during the latter decades of the twentieth century. *Image © Bettmann/Corbis*

Whatever It Takes

In 1973, Harold Connolly, the 1956 American Olympic gold medalist in the hammer throw, told a US Senate committee, "The overwhelming majority of athletes I know would do anything, and take anything, short of killing themselves to improve athletic performance."[27] Connolly spoke at a time when sports administrators and fans were just beginning to perceive the impact of performance enhancing substances used by athletes to improve body mass and strength. Originally, the controversy focused on the use of anabolic steroids to increase muscle mass, but as the years passed a large and varied number of substances were developed by clandestine scientists who were in cahoots with trainers and athletes. The science of identifying and determining illegal sports "doping" required the expertise of research scientists and physicians. Even those individuals who devoted their careers to finding ways to determine when an athlete had violated established rules had to admit that they themselves believed the use of some sophisticated substances could be "masked" to avoid detection. Other newly developed drugs were immune to identification because no one except a few conspirators even knew of their existence.

The term "doping" is derived from the Dutch *dop*, which was a special type of brandy that had a stimulating effect and which was made from grape skins found only in South Africa. By the late nineteenth century the term *dope* was used to describe substances given to race horses and racing greyhound dogs – normally a narcotic mixture of opium – intended to impair their performance so that gamblers betting on a long shot could enjoy a big payday. During the latter part of the twentieth century, "doping" became a generic term to describe the use of any substance that would improve performance in the world of sports.[28] Leaders in the world of international sports competition first became concerned in the 1960s when female athletes from Iron Curtain countries exhibited unusual strength and masculine traits such as heavy musculature development, deep voices, and facial hair. However, the use of performance enhancing substances can be traced to the late nineteenth century when Belgian bicycle racers were found to be taking a potion of sugar tablets soaked in ether, French riders quaffed heavy doses of caffeine, and British cyclists inhaled pure oxygen while using brandy to wash down a mixture of strychnine, heroin, and cocaine. By 1900, boxers in England and America were believed to drink a combination of strychnine and alcohol before, and during, a bout. As early as the 1904 Olympics, evidence of doping startled officials when an American marathon runner, Thomas Hicks, nearly died mid-race after he downed a mixture of eggwhites and strychnine. Following the Second World War, stimulants such as amphetamines became popular, especially with cyclists. In 1960, at the Rome Olympics, several cyclists had to be given emergency treatment following their excessive stimulant use, and a Danish rider died. The victims had reportedly suffered extreme dehydration brought on by the presence of massive quantities of amphetamines in their system. In 1967, one of the world's leading cyclists, Tommy Simpson of Great Britain, died during the Tour de France. An autopsy revealed that he died from an overdose of amphetamines.[29]

The widespread popularity of recreational drugs during the rebellious years of the 1960s fused with a growing awareness by world-class athletes that certain substances improved their performances. As sports physician Robert O. Voy wrote in 1991, "There are probably gold medal winners and world record holders from the United States who would never have even come near the winner's podium had it not been for their use of performance enhancing substances."[30] As usage became increasingly widespread, many athletes came to the conclusion that in order to keep pace with their competition – whether to win an Olympic medal or simply to make the starting lineup of a college football team – they had to endanger their health and reputation by using banned substances to improve performance. Injured athletes found that certain banned substances increased recovery time. As Dr Voy observes, "What's worse, I also know, after working elbow-to-elbow with elite-level athletes, that many drug users do not *want* to use drugs but feel they *have* to stay even with everyone else."[31] American Olympic weightlifter, Ken Patera, laconically commented to the press in 1971 after he lost to a Russian superheavyweight lifter at the Pan American games: "The only difference between me and [Vasily Alexeev] was that I couldn't afford his drug bill. When I hit Munich [for the 1972 Olympics], I'll weigh in at about 340, or maybe 350. Then, we'll see which are better – his steroids or mine."[32] In Munich, Patera apparently learned that Alexeev's druggist was better: the Russian took the gold.

During the late twentieth century, as understanding about the use of steroids became commonplace, most sports executives and fans were bewildered by the news. The names of the substances were foreign to nearly everyone, their dangers unknown, and their users protected by various player union contracts. Colleges and high schools found that testing was prohibitively expensive and that various legal protections – including a constitutional ban on unwarranted search and seizure – made a comprehensive prohibition against their use impossible. The typical response by fans, coaches, athletic directors, and sports journalists was to ignore the problem, hoping it would simply go away. Unfortunately, this "see no evil, hear no evil" policy placed many athletes at risk.

Initially, there was a great deal of disagreement about the actual ability of steroids to produce muscle mass and strength. It was not until the mid 1980s that a reliable body of scientific evidence had been developed. By then, scientists had not only confirmed what users had known for years, but could also now say with certainty, that usage could result in serious physical harm. On one level, chemically induced growth produces greater stress on joints and limbs, creating muscle tightness and thereby the potential for injury (such as recurring pulled hamstring muscles). Male athletes who took popular substances such as Dianabol (popularly called "D-bol") exposed themselves to many serious health risks, including arterial sclerosis, high blood pressure, liver disease and heart disease, prostate cancer, sterility, and – as often emerged as the first symptom of heavy usage – psychological changes that sometimes produced violent behavior. Women risked damage to their reproductive organs, high blood pressure, irregular menstruation, severe depression, and irreversible physical changes that included masculine features, excessive hair growth on the body and face, and a deepened voice.

The athletes were far ahead of athletic administrators in their knowledge of steroids . By the mid 1960s, the use of anabolic steroids – synthetic male hormones – became almost a *sine qua non* for world-class weightlifters and among weight throwers in track and field. The team physician for the 1968 American Olympic track team was later quoted as saying, "I don't think it is possible for a weight man to compete internationally without using anabolic steroids … All the weight men on the Olympic team had to take steroids. Otherwise they would have been out of the running." Sprinters also learned that a steroid such as Dianabol enhanced their explosiveness off the starting blocks. At the Mexico City Games in 1968, insiders discovered that discussions over steroid use by Americans and athletes from other countries was not over the moral issue of taking such drugs but about which substances were the most effective. The 1968 American decathlon gold medalist and the recipient of the prestigious Sullivan Award by the American Amateur Union, Bill Toomey, readily admitted to using drugs to enhance his performance at Mexico City.

As a result of the subsequent rise in new world records, news of the epidemic could not be contained. John Hendershott, editor of *Track and Field News*, sarcastically commented that anabolic steroids were the new "breakfast of champions," and journalist Bil Gilbert published a revealing series in *Sports Illustrated* in 1969 in which he described widespread usage and called for prohibition of anabolic steroids.[33] It would not be until 1980 that the International Olympic Committee began to impose prohibitions on the use of performance enhancing substances and instituted modest testing procedures. The American Olympic Committee and the NCAA, two primary guardians of the integrity of American sports, were likewise lethargic in their response.

Professional football players, especially linemen and linebackers, were quick to take note. Although it was not commonly known until much later, the use of anabolic steroids became rampant in the National Football League during the 1970s. Various estimates indicated that more than 50 percent of all players at least experimented with their use and that 75 percent of linemen and linebackers were regular consumers. Gilbert's 1969 articles had intimated widespread usage encouraged by strength coaches and team physicians. In 1991, Steve Courson, an offensive lineman for the Pittsburgh Steelers and Tampa Bay Buccaneers from 1977 until 1984, stunned league officials and football fans with his candid recollection of heavy steroid use that began when he was a freshman at the University of South Carolina in 1973. Of his days in Pittsburgh, Courson commented that not only did half of his teammates use steroids but "an even greater number" took amphetamines before a game. These powerful stimulants were readily available in the Steelers locker room in large cookie jars, from which "interested players could scoop up however many pills they wanted." Courson later recalled that the combination of steroids and amphetamines greatly increased his and his teammates' aggression, and they would seek to "take an edge off" the "roid rage" after games and practices by smoking marijuana.[34]

Courson recalled that locker room talk frequently revolved around the relative merits of the many drug combinations available to them. "We sounded like a bunch of pharmacists talking shop," he recalled.[35] The strongly worded warnings by physicians about the dangers of steroid use were not exaggerated. By age 36, Courson's career came to a crashing halt when he was diagnosed with a serious heart condition complicated by other serious maladies. After he became the first NFL player to speak openly about steroid usage, the NFL sought to impose damage control, issuing a flurry of conflicting and self-serving press releases. Courson's head coach at Pittsburgh, Chuck Noll, testified to a congressional committee that he had never ordered, authorized, or even recognized any use of such substances during his 30 years in the NFL.[36]

Athletes also participated in the more common drug culture, but most sports fans were oblivious to this fact. That changed in June 1986 when two high-profile athletes died of cocaine overdoses within three days of each other. Len Bias was a talented All-American basketball player at the University of Maryland, and after his senior year was the first-round draft choice of the Boston Celtics, a championship team that envisioned him as the player who would eventually replace forward Larry Bird as the team's superstar. General Manager Red Auerbach believed he had secured the most promising player of the decade, and many basketball experts considered that the 6 foot 8 inch forward had the potential to equal Michael Jordan as an all-around performer.

The circumstances surrounding Bias's death remain unclear, but he apparently used cocaine the night he returned from Boston after signing a lucrative Celtics contract and being introduced by an exuberant Red Auerbach to the New England media. Back in College Park, Maryland, he visited with friends in a dormitory and then left for an unknown destination. About 6 a.m., he returned to the campus, where he suffered a massive seizure and shortly thereafter died in a hospital emergency room. The autopsy revealed he died of a heart attack brought on by an overdose of cocaine. Subsequent investigations revealed that Bias was not a first-time user, but had been living with a drug problem for several years.[37] Two days after Bias died on the East Coast, Cleveland Browns defensive back Donald Rogers died from a heart attack in Sacramento. An autopsy indicated that the attack was also caused by cocaine. Together, the two tragedies forced a major reassessment of drug education in college and professional sports.

The deaths of these two elite athletes also stimulated extensive media coverage. Sports pages were filled with anguished columns, and many popular sports figures were seen on television urging young athletes to "Just say no" to drugs. But as the furor over the two deaths receded into the background, repeated stories of top professional athletes and their drug usage indicated that "Just say no" was not working. The flame-throwing Los Angeles Dodgers left-handed pitcher Steve Howe became a poster boy for the problem when he was arrested seven times for violating drug laws and suspended four times from organized baseball, including two "lifetime suspensions." Dexter Manley, star defensive tackle of the Washington Redskins, and New York Knicks star forward Michael Richardson, were suspended permanently by their leagues for repeat offenses. The gold medal winner of the 100 meter sprint at the 1988 Seoul Olympics, Canadian sprinter Ben Johnson, had surprised track experts when he blew by the favored American Carl Lewis to set a world record that prompted the press to call him "The World's Fastest Human." But fame is often fleeting, and in Johnson's case extremely so. He had his gold medal taken away and his record time erased from the record books when he tested positive to the use of Stanozolol after the race. Not only did Johnson have his career ended, but he lost an estimated $15 million in potential product endorsements.

Football, because of its emphasis upon speed, strength, and bulk, became the center of attention. Ambivalence characterized much of the reaction by college and professional teams. After all, the hard-hitting 240 pound linebacker or the hole-opening blocker were often singled out by sportswriters for their raw physical power. The implications of steroid use, however, were brought into sharp focus in 1992, with the agonizing death of former All-Pro defensive end Lyle Alzado. Near death from a rare form of brain cancer, Alzado went public and attributed his disease to more than 20 years of taking steroids and human growth hormones. He had begun his college football career as an undersized defensive lineman at Yankton College in South Dakota in 1969, but after being introduced to anabolic steroids his weight zoomed to 240 pounds. Not only did he put on immense muscle mass, but his strength and speed also increased. His growth in physical strength was accompanied by a simultaneous growth in his penchant for aggressive behavior. "I outran, outhit, outanythinged everybody," he recalled. "I was taking steroids and I saw that they made me play better and better."

Alzado's ferocity and fearlessness made him a fourth-round draft choice by the Denver Broncos. Now weighing 300 pounds, he spent 15 years in the National Football League, receiving several All-Star team recognitions, and concluded his career with the Oakland

Raiders. In 1984, he was the defensive star when the Raiders handily defeated the Washington Redskins in the Super Bowl. But his steroid-driven career exacted an enormous price. At age 41, he suffered from severe depression and had to deal with periodic dizziness, fainting spells, and intense headaches. In 1991, he was diagnosed with an unusual form of brain lymphoma. Although his physicians would not categorically state that his illness resulted from steroid use, Alzado flatly told the world in a *Sports Illustrated* article a few weeks before his death that in his own mind, this was the case:

> I started taking anabolic steroids in 1969 and never stopped. It was addicting, mentally addicting. Now I'm sick, and I'm scared. Ninety percent of the athletes I know are on the stuff. We're not born to be 300 lbs or jump 30′. In all the time I was taking steroids, I knew they were making me play better. I became very violent on the field and off it. I did things only crazy people do. Once a guy sideswiped my car and I beat the hell out of him. Now look at me. My hair's gone, I wobble when I walk and have to hold on to someone for support, and I have trouble remembering things. My last wish? That no one ever dies this way.[38]

Although much of the news regarding performance enhancing drugs revolved around football, cycling, weightlifting, and track and field, organized baseball encountered a serious public-relations dilemma following the 1998 season in which Sammy Sosa of the Chicago Cubs and Mark McGwire of the St Louis Cardinals engaged in a home run derby that saw McGwire ultimately hit 70 home runs and Sosa 66. Both sluggers easily passed Roger Maris's record of 61 set in 1961. Fans packed the stadiums to watch McGwire and Sosa swing for the fences. Their competition resulted in a friendly rivalry between the two men that the media loved, and their exploits did much to bring fans back to the game after the disastrous work stoppage of 1994. However, reports that McGwire was using androstenedione – a form of testosterone supplement popularly called "andro" – caught the attention of baseball writers. At the time, the supplement was not banned by the federal government or by organized baseball, but its ability to increase muscle mass and strength was well established. It was also widely rumored, but never proven, that Sosa's sudden-found extra power also resulted from something more than good diet and weight training.

McGwire never attempted to hide the fact that he was taking "andro." Large containers of the substance were visible on his Busch Stadium locker shelf. The active ingredient in androstenedione is a natural chemical substance that enables the body to produce more testosterone than normal. It is by scientific or legal definition not a steroid but rather an "androgen" – a steroid precursor – that produces a change of chemical reactions in the body that promote the production of testosterone. At the time McGwire was taking andro and swatting baseballs over distant fences, it was not an illegal substance according to the Federal Drug Administration. But when reporters began to explore McGwire's use of andro, many fans and most baseball experts took exception, arguing that he was unfairly setting a major-league record with a substantial boost from chemicals. McGwire was candid in his response, noting that the substance was purchased legally and that it was not banned. He was playing within the rules. "Everything I've done is natural," he plaintively said. And, more ominously, "Everybody that I know in the game of baseball uses the same stuff I use."[39]

It was not until 2003 that the FDA issued a ruling making androstenedione a banned substance. Ever since its introduction to the market in the mid 1990s, as a steroid precursor and not the steroid itself, drug and health food companies had marketed it as a dietary supplement. In April 2003, when the head of the major-league players' union, Donald Fehr, refused to support a ban on andro before a Senate subcommittee, US Senator John McCain threatened punitive legislation. A visibly upset McCain told Fehr that he and his union were "aiding and abetting cheaters" and that if organized baseball did not act swiftly, Congress would. That the NFL had banned the substance in 1999 only added to baseball's besmirched image. Baseball finally made its ban effective for the 2004 season, and home run production slipped noticeably in subsequent seasons.

American sports officials at all levels wrestled, inconclusively and uneasily, with the many legal and scientific vagaries of performance enhancing substances. In 2004, the *San Francisco Chronicle* published a front-page exclusive story that reported on sealed federal grand jury testimony taken a year earlier, at which time the leading All-Star slugger and first baseman of the New York Yankees, Jason Giambi, admitted to taking a new generation of steroids for which there was no test. That Giambi had gained an estimated 30 pounds of muscle between 2000 and 2003 had not been lost on reporters, but until the story leaked to the press he had adamantly denied using any illegal substance. He had fallen victim to a mysterious severe stomach ailment that sidelined him for the latter half of the 2004 season and seemed to link him to steroids. His leaked grand jury testimony confirmed those suspicions.[40]

Like many athletes before him, Giambi had willingly and knowingly risked his health, perhaps his life, in the quest for an edge on his competition – or, given the perception that many other baseball players were also using, perhaps he was merely attempting to stay even with his competition. The American penchant for winning at all costs was once more on the front page for all to contemplate.

Under a Cloud: Barry Bonds Chases Hank Aaron

When Jason Giambi was forced to tell the truth to a federal grand jury, he was assured that his comments would be kept sealed and, in return for his testimony against a San Francisco drug company, would be exempt from federal prosecution. But someone leaked the testimony, and Giambi had to confront the reality of his steroid use in public.

The ethical dilemma that Giambi faced, however, was not as complex as that which confronted star San Francisco Giants outfielder Barry Bonds, one of baseball's all-time great players who was caught up in the same federal grand jury investigation. Giambi admitted using steroids over a three-year period, including injecting himself with the steroid Deca Durabolin as well as administering a new and undetectable synthetic steroid, THG (tetrahydrogestrinone), which is absorbed through the skin. In his testimony before the same grand jury, Bonds admitted using supplements and a cream provided by his personal trainer but contended that they were harmless herbal compounds.[41]

The son of star outfielder Bobby Bonds, who played for the Giants and six other major-league teams over 14 seasons, Barry entered the National League in 1986 after being drafted by the Pittsburgh Pirates. He established himself as a talented contact hitter and left fielder and became a perennial All-Star. Acquired by the San Francisco Giants in 1993 as a free agent, Bonds signed the most lucrative contract in baseball history up to that time and proceeded to establish unquestioned Hall of Fame credentials. At the end of his 15th _ major-league season, he had a career batting average of slightly over .300 and 494 home runs. In only four seasons up to this point had Bonds hit more than 40 home runs, with his career high of 49 occurring in 2000.

At the age of 37, when professional ballplayers are normally well into their declining years, Bonds unleashed a burst of unusual power for someone his age. Playing in the new Pac Bell Park in San Francisco in 2001, where the distances to the outfield fence are long and the winds blow in from right field off San Francisco Bay, Bonds proceeded to eclipse the single-season 70 home run record established in 1998 by Mark McGwire, ending the season with 73. His bulked-up body was evident to any casual observer. The one-time slender, lithe athlete had late in his career developed a large, imposing, powerful frame that enabled him to launch tape-measure home runs into the waters of McCovey Cove beyond the distant right-field bleachers. Bonds attributed his increased size and strength to his rigorous year-round physical conditioning program and a carefully regimented diet supplemented by vitamins provided by his personal trainer, Greg Anderson. Widespread whispers that Bonds had transformed himself by the use of steroids and human growth hormones were categorically denied.

During the next three seasons, Bonds continued his home run barrage, long after his 40th birthday. By the end of the 2005 season, he had hit a career 703 home runs, just 11 behind Babe Ruth's record, and well within hailing distance of the 755 set by Henry Aaron in 1973. While Bonds hit 45 home runs the year he turned 40, Aaron had struggled to hit 16. Bonds had somehow managed to hammer 209 home runs between his 37th and 40th birthdays – a feat that produced incredulity. Then came revelations of his testimony to a federal grand jury admitting use of substances he called "the cream" and "the clear," that were allegedly produced by the Bay Area Laboratory Company (BALCO). The grand jury had opened its investigation into BALCO – leading to the secret testimony of Giambi, Bonds, and several other premier athletes – only after the testing laboratory in Los Angeles used by the United States Olympic Committee had received anonymously a syringe filled with a substance unknown to all testing laboratories. It apparently had come from an unknown track and field coach who had reason to suspect that new and unknown synthetic steroids were being used by world-class track athletes.

One of those was sprinter Marion Jones, who won five medals at the 2000 Olympics. She was sentenced to six months in prison for lying to the federal grand jury about her usage and forfeited her medals. She confessed to having used tetrahydrogestrinone, one of the substances that Bonds was alleged to have used. Speculations also swirled around the role played in this drama by Greg Anderson, Bonds's personal trainer, when he refused on two separate occasions to testify before the grand jury and was sentenced to jail by a federal judge.

For years, the leadership of the baseball players' union and the leaders of organized baseball had danced around the issue of performance enhancements. Now, faced with an angry US Senate committee headed by Senator John McCain and buffeted by the startling revelations of the BALCO investigation, a new drug-testing policy was rushed into being for the 2005 season, calling for year-round unannounced testing with a 10 day unpaid suspension for an initial offense escalating to a year's suspension after four positive tests. While sports commentators felt that this was a positive development, given the prior years of relentless stonewalling by the players' union, most journalists and public officials contended that it was too little, much too late. The initial 10 day suspension drew caustic commentary and many a cynic pointed to the fact that both the NFL and the NBA had passed more stringent policies years earlier, and that the US Olympic Committee was routinely banning athletes from competition for two years or more if they tested positive for the first time.

The BALCO episode was clearly the most direct and damaging hit that any American professional sport took on the steroid issue up to that time. Its biggest star – arguably one of the greatest players in the history of the game – had been implicated. Dr Charles Yesalis, a Penn State professor of health policy and coauthor of the authoritative book, *The Steroids Game* (1998), placed the BALCO development into an ironic but compelling context: "I haven't seen anything that shows me the fans really care," he told a reporter. "Baseball just had a stellar year, and if your IQ was at or near room temperature you didn't need to hear Jason Giambi's testimony to know these guys are using drugs." In comparing the recent exploits by Mark McGwire, Ken Caminiti, Gary Sheffield, Sammy Sosa, and Barry Bonds, among the most notable sluggers, Yesalis conceded, "they are breaking records, but I'm outraged." But he sadly acknowledged that most fans did not share his anger. In an all-consuming entertainment age, he said with a heavy dose of sarcasm: "Why should you draw a distinction between athletes who do and don't use drugs? Using drugs makes the athletes more entertaining. The ball goes out of the park more often."[42]

In spring 2005, the US House of Representatives held public hearings on steroid use. Mark McGwire's awkward, non-responsive comments severely damaged his public image. Only the most generous did not come away from hearing McGwire's testimony believing he had not taken substances far more powerful than andro while assaulting baseball's home run records. At those same hearings, one of only seven major-league players in history to make 3,000 base hits, 40-year-old Baltimore Orioles first baseman Rafael Palmeiro, emphatically told the congressional committee under oath, "I have never used steroids. Period." He dramatically jabbed his finger in the air for added emphasis. Four months later Palmeiro was suspended by major-league baseball for testing positive to a "serious steroid." Pundits now were forced to question just how many hits this discredited potential Hall of Fame player might have made if he had not used illegal substances. Was this a first-time situation, or had he used them for years? A cloud of suspicion hovered over the long-time popular player, and it seemed likely to remain there long into his post-baseball life.

In spring 2006, Barry Bonds continued his home run drive under a very dark cloud created by a devastating book written by two highly respected investigative journalists.[43] This book presented what most knowledgeable observers believed to be overwhelmingly conclusive evidence that Bonds' late-career home run bonanza was the result of use of steroids. Record holder Henry Aaron had already publicly distanced himself as Bonds approached his record of 755 home runs. Aaron had publicly spoken out against steroid use as "cheating" long before Bonds went on his homer binge. Aaron refused to accept a lucrative offer from a television network to travel with the Giants so as to be present when the mark was broken. Although fans in San Francisco enthusiastically cheered Bonds's run at the record, he was roundly jeered by baseball fans everywhere else he played. Among serious baseball fans and journalists, his achievement produced an ambivalence that was palpable.[44]

When Bonds broke Aaron's record on August 7, 2007, fans in San Francisco celebrated, but everywhere else throughout the world of baseball there was profound uncertainty, even sadness. Sports sociologist Harry Edwards perhaps best captured the sense of the nation when he said: "For the first time, the standard-bearer and the record holder have been separated. Henry Aaron, Roger Maris, these are the standard-bearers. Mark McGwire, Barry Bonds, these are the record-holders. For the first time ever, the standard of excellence and the record-holder are totally different people."[45]

Four months after he surpassed Henry Aaron in the record books, Bonds was indicted by a federal grand jury for perjury. His trial was repeatedly postponed by legal maneuvering, but was scheduled to begin in a San Francisco federal court in March of 2011 as the questions repeatedly asked of McGwire and Bonds – and other standouts of their generation – was whether or not they deserved election into the Hall of Fame in Cooperstown.

17

The Democratization of Sports

In the decades following the Second World War, the United States enjoyed a sustained and unparalleled period of economic growth. Powerful scientific and technological innovations transformed American life. Life expectancy increased substantially and the population rose from 140 million in 1940 to 308 million in 2010. Although industrial production remained high – despite strong competition from modern Asian and European countries – the greatest increase in economic activity occurred in the service and high-tech areas. Following a sobering downturn in traditional "Rust Belt" heavy industry during the 1970s, a stunning "new economy" took hold during the 1980s, spurred by biotechnology and computer science. New patterns of immigration led to a significant increase in racial, ethnic, and religious diversity. All of these forces contributed to a growing tenor of egalitarianism and democracy in the ebb and flow of everyday American life; those sensibilities were played out in the recreational activities and games in which the American people took part, and the sporting contests that they watched.

Community Cauldron: High School Sports

The growth of organized youth sports during the years after the Second World War was one important manifestation of the nation's growing affluence. Not only did families have more time and more money to devote to recreation, but parents believed competitive sports taught lessons essential for the development of children. Some optimistic parents even calculated that, if properly coached and trained, their child could eventually receive a college athletic scholarship. During the early decades of the twentieth century, physical education pioneer Luther Gulick and his followers established the importance of competitive sports in helping young people to grow and develop into healthy, physically fit young adults who also

Sports in American Life: A History, Second Edition. Richard O. Davies.
© 2012 John Wiley & Sons, Inc. Published 2012 by John Wiley & Sons, Inc.

understood the importance of good citizenship and moral leadership. The foundation of the large and pervasive American sports culture of recent years – youth and public school sports programs – was based upon the competitive, winning model. Proper attention was paid, of course, to the importance of good sportsmanship, but the underlying message was "compete to win."

By the 1920s, state athletic associations were conducting statewide championships in basketball, track and field, and baseball. Various systems were devised to determine state champions in football, such as holding statewide ballots by coaches and journalists or conducting postseason playoffs. High school sports were of great importance everywhere, but they seemed to have an elevated role in small cities and towns where social life revolved around the activities of the only high school in town. Intense political and economic rivalries that had developed over the passing of the years between neighboring towns were naturally played out when their high school teams met on field or court.

The power of a high school team to galvanize a community has been demonstrated in many settings. One of the most dramatic examples occurred in 1954 in Indiana, a state in which boys' basketball enjoyed a special place in the grand order of things. The state athletic association did not divide schools into several divisions based on enrollment. Instead, all schools, large and small, competed in a single division. Over the years, in the state tournament in which all teams were entered, a few "miracle" teams from small rural schools had pulled off an occasional upset over a large urban school. However, the four finalists that made it to the championships in Indianapolis invariably represented urban schools with large enrollments. However, 1954 proved to be a special year, when the tiny school from the farming town of Milan (pop. 987), located in the rolling hills of the southeastern corner of the state, powered its way through the sectional and regional tournaments to reach the state finals played in Butler University's cavernous field house in Indianapolis.

It was truly a David versus Goliath story – 773 teams had entered in the tournament – and the state's basketball fans were enthralled by the appearance of this team of farm boys from a small town. The tallest player on the team was 6 foot 1 inch center Gene White, and the team's leader was sharpshooting 5 foot 11 inch forward Bobby Plump. Plump had spent countless hours practicing his favorite jump shot on a hoop nailed above the barn door. Although the Milan Indians came into the tournament with a 20–2 record, statewide ranking polls did not give them any mention. At Indianapolis, the Indians encountered one of the state's top-ranked teams, the powerful Tigers from Crispus Attucks High School in Indianapolis, a team led by future All-American and NBA Hall of Fame player Oscar Robertson. But Plump hit nine of 13 shots to lead Milan to a 13-point victory, and on Saturday night the "little team that could" squared off for the state championship against top-seeded and heavily favored Muncie Central.[1]

The Muncie Bearcats represented a school with a rich basketball tradition that boasted of a starting five averaging 6 feet 4 inches. With 15,000 fans crammed into Butler field house and an estimated 2 million people watching on a statewide television network, Milan coach Marvin Wood employed a slowdown offense he called the "cat and mouse." The Indians refused to run with the bigger and faster opponents, and passed the ball for minutes before taking a wide-open shot; and as the game unfolded the teams traded the lead several times. The score was tied at 26–26 as the fourth quarter began, and following Wood's instructions,

Plump stood improbably at midcourt holding the ball for more than 5 minutes, while the Bearcats refused to come out of their zone defense. With just 18 seconds remaining in the game and the score tied at 30–30, the Bearcats had moved into a man-to-man defense. Plump moved off a screen, dribbled into the key, and calmly released a 15 foot jump shot. It was just the same shot he had practiced thousands of times. As the buzzer sounded, the ball nestled softly into the net. In that very instant, one of Indiana's greatest sports legends was born. "Bobby Plump overwhelmed Indiana," the *Indianapolis Star* reported. "No other high school player ever had a season like the one he has just completed. He completely captured the heart of Indiana's basketball fans, a discriminating audience, which chooses its heroes carefully and treasures them forever."[2] The "Milan Miracle" became the basis for the popular 1986 motion picture *Hoosiers*, although Indiana basketball purists were quick to point out many discrepancies between reality and the Hollywood version.

Future Milan teams never could repeat what that special team of 1954 had accomplished, but in larger communities some high school teams have enjoyed a winning tradition extending over decades. One of the most prominent such programs has been the football team from Washington High School in Massillon, Ohio.

In 1932, a young graduate from Miami University took over the head coaching duties at Massillon's only high school. Between 1935 and 1940, Paul Brown's Tigers won 58 of 60 games and claimed six consecutive state championships. Brown, who went on to a storied coaching career at Ohio State and the National Football League, established a tradition that continues to the present day. He created the Tiger Booster Club to raise funds and provide community support, and installed his offensive and defensive schemes throughout a network that extended downward to the junior varsity, freshman, and junior high teams, even to the touch football games played between elementary schools. When players arrived at Washington High from the city's three junior high schools, they were already well versed in his system.

Located in the industrial belt of northeastern Ohio, Massillon and its 30,000 residents relied upon the presence of a large steel plant. It was the epitome of the tough blue-collar town, and its attitude was revealed through the tenacity of its football teams. The winning tradition continued after Brown left for greater opportunities, and over the years, the Tigers claimed 23 state football championships as determined by a statewide poll of sportswriters, and sent hundreds of players off to major college teams, of whom 16 became All-Americans and several starred in the National Football League. Six of its head coaches left to take college head coaching positions, and as the winning seasons piled one upon the other, community commitment intensified. The booster club grew to 3,000 paying members by 1980, and the team played in 22,000-seat Paul Brown Stadium. The Tigers were among the first high school teams to play on artificial turf, and players were expected to follow a prescribed year-round training regimen in a well-equipped weight room.

On game days, the town's main streets were lined with orange and black banners. Handwritten signs urging the team to victory were posted in storefront windows. Young boys in Massillon were raised with the expectation that they would contribute to the team; each new baby boy left the local hospital with his first worldly possession, an orange and black miniature football, a gift of the Tigers Boosters. Parents frequently held their boys back one year in elementary school so they would be more fully developed physically for their senior season. For girls, positions on the cheer squad and drill team were the focus of intense competition, and the Tiger Swing Band was considered one of the most accomplished in the state. Visitors to town could tour the Tiger Football Museum, and the website is the equal of most university athletic programs.

In 1985, Washington High won its 600th game, becoming the first high school team in the United States to achieve that level of success, and at the end of the 2010 season the Tigers' overall record stood at 796 wins, 240 losses, and 35 ties. The Tigers have played their way into the state Final Four playoffs 17 times since the system was initiated in 1972 but without ever claiming a state championship via the playoff system. Between 1921 and 2010, the school had endured only four losing seasons, with two back-to-back 4–6 seasons occurring in 2003 and 2004. Competition from other equally well-funded programs across the state of Ohio had caught up with the Tigers, and the last state championship in 1970 (decided by an Associated Press poll) is now a distant memory. But the dedication of the people of "Touchdown Town" did not waver despite the uncustomary three or four losses a season. A family steeped in the city's football culture provided the funds to construct a $3 million state-of-the-art sports medicine complex in 2008, and the following year an indoor practice facility with a full 100 yard football field was constructed. Mike Brown, the son of the founder of this tradition and owner of the NFL Cincinnati Bengals, ruefully commented upon visiting the sparkling new facility: "Massillon High School is ahead of us. We don't have one."

In 1999, Massillon football was the topic of a documentary film shown as a feature in many American theaters. *Go Tigers! A Team's Fate, A Town's Future* revealed a community obsessed with its football team, where sagging Rust Belt economic woes had prompted voters to turn down three consecutive bond issues to bail out a school district bordering on bankruptcy. Nonetheless, the team had sparkling new uniforms, nine assistant coaches, a full-time trainer, and a sports information director. As the season's final regular season game against traditional archrival Canton McKinley High loomed, the film's director indicated that unless the Tigers won the big game, the fourth tax levy vote was probably doomed. They did win – and the bond issue passed by a narrow majority. The observation of a visiting journalist in 1965 still rang true in 2005: "If you are a member of the solid blue collar class in Massillon the odds are that you are also an official booster of football." He also noted that, "visiting teams are crushed before the kickoff by the Tigers' record, confidence, spirit, the town's booster pride and noise, their conditioning and training."[3]

Observers have long believed that similar patterns of obsession with high school football could be found in Pennsylvania, Texas, and in fact throughout much of the South. In 1990, the special obsession produced by high school football in Texas was revealed when the *Philadelphia Inquirer* reporter, H. G. "Buzz" Bissinger, published his bestselling book based upon a full year spent in Odessa, Texas, observing the community-wide obsession with Permian Basin High School football. In *Friday Night Lights*, Bissinger described an "intensity more than I could have imagined," where the pressure to win was inexorable, extravagant football expenditures and minimal academic budgets were accepted, and players skated through their academic courses with little effort. The Panthers played in a modern 20,000-seat stadium, complete with artificial turf, a large press box, bright lighting, and a modern scoreboard. For games in distant Dallas, the team traveled by chartered jet. The players basked in the adulation of the adults in the community, and within the social structure of the school, players were the exalted ones. Bissinger described impressionable teenagers being subjected to intense community pressure to "win state," with their coaches under siege to win every game.[4]

Bissinger's candid narrative shocked many readers. "It became obvious that these kids held the town on their shoulders," he wrote. According to one disillusioned parent:

> Athletics lasts for such a short period of time … But while it lasts, it creates this make-believe world where normal rules don't apply. We build this false atmosphere. When it's over and the harsh reality sets in, that's the real joke we play on people … Everybody wants to experience that superlative movement, and being an athlete you can have that. It's Camelot for them. But there's life after [football].[5]

And that life, Bissinger reported afterward, was often fraught with disillusion.

The increased profiles of high school football and basketball were greatly intensified by the national recruiting efforts of major college teams, encouraged by a host of state and regional publications that described the talents of top high school players for the benefit of interested coaches/recruiters. The national newspaper, *USA Today*, created a new level of expectation with its national rankings of high school football, basketball, and baseball teams, and ESPN gained ratings with telecasts of meetings of top football teams. The emergence of the internet created a plethora of websites devoted to recruiting, thus turning recruiting seasons into further competition between high-profile college programs.

Youth Sports

Increased emphasis on channeling young boys and girls into structured youth sports programs – with the tendency to force a young athlete to concentrate upon one sport very early in their development – has generated considerable attention from child development specialists in the past few decades. The issues are many and complex, but essentially many parents believe that such programs are important for their youngsters' development. As of 2010, an estimated 12 million youths between the ages of seven and 13 take part annually in adult-supervised competitive team-oriented programs in football, basketball, softball, hockey, soccer, and baseball. In addition to this, hundreds of thousands of preteens and teenagers are enrolled in costly instructional programs for individual performance sports, such as gymnastics, ice skating, skiing, swimming, golf, and tennis. In many cities, for-profit instructional services offer youngsters individualized instruction.

Organized team play for youths was virtually unheard of until the YMCA began to field teams late in the nineteenth century. Following the Second World War, however, conditions were just right for such programs to flourish. Postwar prosperity put discretionary income in the hands of parents who wanted to provide their children with opportunities that they had been denied growing up in a time of depression and war. Lurking behind the youth movement were Cold War fears of communist subversion, as well as the informal social and economic power exerted within American society by large corporations. Parents wanted to instill in their offspring the values they deemed necessary to survive and succeed in this conflicting time: competition, patriotism, acceptance of authority, discipline, and the importance of cooperation and teamwork. In the age of the "organization man," parents wanted to instill in their children the values of working within a group, interacting effectively with others, and accepting authority – precisely those interpersonal skills that they believed would enable them to succeed as adults within large corporate or governmental organizations. It has often been said that in America, access to the boardroom of major corporations is a journey that begins in the locker room. Whether consciously or unconsciously, parents of the postwar era sought a controlled environment in which their children would learn the skills that would enable them to succeed as adults – long after their playing days were over. For them, future professional and business success indeed would grow out of the many lessons learned in sports.

The result was the popularity of Little League Baseball, Bobby Sox Softball, and Pop Warner Football. Little League Baseball set the standard. Founded in Williamsport, Pennsylvania in 1939 by factory worker Carl Stotz, the program expanded rapidly across the United States following the end of the Second World War. By 1950, more than a million boys age nine to 12 participated. The organization soon had leagues in Canada, Europe, Latin America, and the Far East. In 1948, it held its first Little League World Series in Williamsport, and the 1953 championship game was described on ABC radio by Howard Cosell. Ten years later, Roone Arledge televised the finals on his "Wide World of Sports" on ABC-TV. Growth continued, and by 1980 there were more than 16,000 local leagues serving some 2.5 million youths. The pattern of growth leveled out during the late twentieth century, but more than 3 million young boys (and a sprinkling of girls) participated each year in Little League.[6]

Emphasis was upon adult control, with each local league governed by a commissioner who enforced the rules and policies established at the international administrative offices in Williamsport. The emphasis was upon emulating the atmosphere in which major-league teams operated. Before the season began, players "tried out," were evaluated by coaches, and were "drafted" to teams. Players not drafted were deemed "free agents" and could be signed by any team willing to take them on. Standardized uniforms were issued, with teams normally assigned names emulating the major leagues (Tigers, Cubs, Twins, Astros, etc.); practices were conducted several times a week; team strategies were taught by the coaches; and games were played in miniature stadiums complete with outfield fences, manicured grass infields, dugouts, scoreboards, a public-address announcer, and bleachers from which family members could watch. At season's end, a league "all-star" team was selected to enter a district tournament with the distant goal of being one of a handful of teams to move through state and regional tournaments in order to qualify for the Little League World Series in August.

While various informal polls taken by this author over the years indicate that a vast majority of Little League graduates look back on their experience as a positive one, the idea of establishing adult supervision over youthful play produced many skeptics. The litany of criticisms are familiar: the preteen years, it is frequently said, are a time when children should learn to organize their own play and not have the spontaneity of play subverted by meddling, if well-meaning, adults. Although Little League literature emphasizes the primary goals of participation and learning, in reality many coaches play the best players in the most important positions, stationing the least adept for the humiliating minimum number of required innings in right field where few balls are likely to be hit. The pressure to win sometimes places players under emotional stress, and parents and other onlookers often exhibit antisocial behavior, loudly criticizing the umpires, the coaches, even the young players. The national news occasionally reports a physical attack by an angry parent upon an umpire, and many leagues have had to deal with verbal assaults on the coach by irate parents who believed the coach did not appreciate their child's ability. Over the years, some leagues have required parents to attend a preseason clinic that teaches the basics of good sportsmanship and proper fan behavior.

Former major-league pitcher Jim Brosnan, writing in 1963, summarized the case against Little League and, implicitly, other adult-supervised youth programs. He complained that the organization "is rapidly becoming a status symbol replete with too much aggressiveness, competitiveness, and emphasis upon winning. It is not a world the kids make." He found the "draft" repulsive: "Putting a price on a boy's ability is obviously adult business." He found from personal observation that many coaches did more damage than good: the coaches "are usually on the lower part of the sociological curve, guys who can't quite make it in their business, marriage, or social life. So they take it out on the kids." That Little League required the maintenance of team won–lost records and standings, selected postseason "all-stars," and sponsored a set of elimination tournaments resulting in a World Series, Brosnan contended, was an absurdity that contradicted the organization's professions about the primacy of participation rather than victory. "Preadolescents are immature and can't be expected to live up to the physical and emotional guidelines of older children – parents included. Winning games should not be given the importance that exists in the Little League age group."[7]

Brosnan's critique, and others like it, had no discernible impact, and parents found in the program much to like. Some parents even envisioned that their youngsters would someday be like Joey Jay, a pitcher who was the first of many Little Leaguers to progress to playing in the major leagues. In 1955, Jay signed a contract with a hefty $20,000 signing bonus with the Milwaukee Braves and enjoyed a lengthy major-league career, complete with All-Star Game appearances. A visitor to the Little League Museum in Williamsport is confronted with a large exhibit that features former Little Leaguers who became major-league stars.

Founded in 1929, Pop Warner Football, with approximately 350,000 players in 2010, has never approached the size or impact of Little League, but it nonetheless offers a national program including postseason tournaments. Its critics are even harsher than those of Little League, contending that preadolescent boys are not prepared to handle the physical shocks of tackling and blocking. Critics are especially harsh in their treatment of coaches who revel in the physical aspects of the game and conduct ruthless practice sessions, supposedly in emulation of well-known college or professional coaches. Pop Warner games, of course, include young boys in full pads knocking each other around while coaches direct the action from the sidelines. Uniformed referees blow their whistles and throw their penalty flags while squads of young girls lead organized cheers. Each December, teams from around the country that have won their regional tournaments convene at Disney World in Orlando for championship "bowl games."[8]

With some parents willing to spend substantial sums on their child's athletic development, a cottage industry developed in urban areas that featured year-round instructional programs in such mainline sports as basketball, baseball, softball, volleyball, tennis, and gymnastics. Among the most extensive were programs for young girls in gymnastics, ice skating, and swimming. Over the years, the more adept girls are encouraged to move into intensive advanced programs, complete with regional and national competitions that lead, in some instances, to college scholarships. It was out of this structured program that America's female world-class gymnasts emerged – highly skilled athletes, often no more than 15 or 16 years of age. In order to achieve this pinnacle of success, parents sometimes have to neglect their daughter's education and social development and have her live apart from her family to be near a nationally acclaimed coach. There she is expected to adhere to rigid diets, put in many hours of arduous training each day, and generally not have the opportunities of a normal teenage social life. Many promising gymnasts, of course, also suffer severe injuries in the process.

In her revealing book on the training of America's elite gymnasts and figure skaters, journalist Joan Ryan describes the heavy sacrifices required of elite female athletes who have aspirations of international competition. Because of the influence of television, American viewers focused on American gymnasts during the Summer Olympics and on figure skaters during the Winter Olympics. For those few athletes who win gold medals, the reward is great: product endorsements, speaking engagements, special exhibitions, and television talk show appearances, all of which produce substantial income.[9]

But the long trail leading to such heights is fraught with dangers and littered with disappointed, disillusioned, even clinically depressed young women. Ryan details a sordid story of eating disorders brought on by expectations that women gymnasts must weigh below 100 pounds in order to perform at the highest level. This expectation sometimes has to be achieved by following a diet of 1,000 calories a day. If the girls were permitted to develop naturally into young women, their breasts and hips would preclude their performing the physical tasks demanded of Olympic champions. In 1976, the average age of the American Olympic gymnastics team was 18 and the girls averaged 106 pounds; by 1992, the team average had fallen to 16 years of age and the girls averaged just 83 pounds each.

Such unrealistic and debilitating demands, Ryan charges, result in stunted growth, the postponement of puberty, weakened bone structure, and psychological disorders. She concludes, "Our national obsession with weight, and our glorification of thinness, have gone completely unchecked in gymnastics and figure skating." The result, Ryan charges, is nothing less than "child abuse," with much of the blame falling "on the coaches and parents … Child labor laws prohibit a thirteen-year-old from punching a cash register for forty hours a week, but that same child can labor for forty hours or more inside a gym or an ice skating rink without drawing the slightest glance from the government." Her research into the two sports revealed: "there have been enough suicide attempts, enough eating disorders, enough broken bodies, enough regretful parents and enough bitter young women to warrant a serious re-evaluation of what we're doing in this country to produce Olympic champions."[10]

Ever since it became a sport of importance during the 1970s, women's professional tennis has seen many a child prodigy rise rapidly to the top of the ratings, only to suffer from debilitating injuries or psychological burnout. Despite career-ending injuries to outstanding players by the time they reach voting age, such as Andrea Jaeger and Tracy Austin, parents have repeatedly enrolled their sons and daughters in programs designed to produce national junior champions, with an eye toward a professional career. Capitalizing upon that parental urge was Nick Bollettieri. In 1980, he opened his Bollettieri Tennis Academy in Bradenton, Florida, and soon top teenage players were living away from home in order to perfect their tennis skills. Among his former star pupils were high-profile tour professionals Andre Agassi, Monica Seles, Anna Kournikova, Tommy Haas, Jim Courier, and Maria Sharapova.[11]

Bollettieri later merged his program with a leading sports management company, which expanded the curriculum to several sports. By 2000, a sports and educational campus offered specialized instruction year-round in baseball, basketball, soccer, and golf as well as tennis. In 2010, the International Management Group (IMG) academy had some 650 full-time students enrolled. From September through May, the students attended academic classes and then engaged in their individual sport at least four hours a day, six days a week, participated in rigorous physical conditioning, and learned behavioral concepts to improve individual performance.[12]

The IMG program mirrored a trend across the United States whereby prospective top athletes at an early age are channeled by parents and coaches into concentrating their efforts on a single sport. The theory is that competition for team slots is so intense at large high schools that only a year-round commitment to one sport can assure a place on the team. The result often is that, as early as the seventh or eighth grade, prospective high school athletes select one sport upon which to concentrate, spending much of their free time working on their skills in various private settings under the supervision of tutors or clinic instructors. Summers for these aspiring athletes (and their parents) are given over to attending specialized camps and playing on club teams in competitive leagues. The pressure for excellence has led to the creation of these teams – hockey, soccer, softball, volleyball, basketball, and wrestling, for example – hiring professional coaches rather than relying on the skills of volunteers. Teams in the 10–16 age bracket might enter several tournaments each year, entailing long trips to compete in high-level competitions that bring together teams from many states.

The pressure to specialize in one sport, of course, is a byproduct of the emphasis placed on winning. Such pressure has naturally been interpreted by various experts as both good and bad, depending on the psychological makeup of the individual. What cannot be disputed, however, is that organized play has replaced unorganized, spontaneous play by youngsters. Instead, the organizing, coaching, and specialized athletic tutoring of young athletes has become a profitable new industry in the United States. IMG is only the most visible example of what has become a substantial enterprise. Left to their own devices, children are natural cross-trainers, dabbling in many sports and related activities. But the growth of organization and adult supervision has undercut spontaneity. Many experts decry the overemphasis at an early age upon concentration on one sport. "We've got tennis kids who can't hop, skip or jump," laments David Donatucci of the IMG Performance Institute: "We've got golfers who if you threw them a ball, they'd duck – basketball players who can't swing a baseball bat. We've got some kids who are really good at their sports, but if you looked closer, you'd be surprised at how unathletic they really are."[13]

Golf's Golden Age: Arnie, the Super Mex, and the Golden Bear

The importance parents placed upon getting their children into the "right" sports program in part reflected the growth of televised sports and the big dollar signs it dangled before the public. This led to the emergence of celebrity status for standouts in sports that heretofore received only limited attention. Following the Second World War, golf and tennis, for example, underwent fundamental changes in their images, becoming new examples of how the democratizing spirit of sports was taking hold. After the spectacular reign of Bobby Jones during the 1920s, professional golf went into the doldrums until after the war. Babe Didrikson Zaharias went on a tear on the limited women's circuit, but only the most dedicated of golf fans paid much attention. Following the war, men's golf was dominated by Ben Hogan and Sam Snead, who engaged in epic duels in major tournaments. "Slammin' Sammy" was known for his long drives off the tee, and between 1942 and 1955 he won seven Grand Slam events while compiling a career number of 81 PGA tournament victories. Famous for his graceful, natural golf swing, Snead is unfortunately remembered as one of the all-time great golfers who never managed to win the US Open. Throughout his lengthy career, Snead played in 37 Opens, and although he came close several times, never closed the deal.

Ben Hogan was born in Texas in 1912 and raised in near-poverty by his widowed mother. He began caddying at age 12 to help with his family's finances. The slender 5 foot 7 inch, 135 pound Hogan joined the PGA tour in 1938 and by the eve of the Second World War had become a player who exhibited every indication of future greatness. After returning from military service, "Bantam Ben" became the leading golfer of his era on the strength of his dedication and endless practice. Not a natural golfer – he frequently said there was no such thing – he simply willed himself to become better by long daily practice sessions. When his finely honed swing was called "natural" by admirers, he muttered, "There is nothing natural about a golf swing."[14] In 1948, Hogan won the US Open and seemed destined for the same golfing pantheon as Bobby Jones.

That potential was nearly snuffed out on February 2, 1949, when his automobile was hit head-on by a Greyhound bus on a foggy West Texas highway. He saved his wife's life by throwing his body across hers at impact but suffered life-threatening injuries, including broken ribs and a crushed pelvis. Rushed to an El Paso hospital, he nearly died from blood clots that formed following surgery to repair his broken bones; doctors had to tie off veins in his legs to prevent clots from reaching his heart.

Golfing experts believed that he would never play professionally again, but Hogan was determined to return to the tour. He played his first tentative round in December of the same year as the accident, and the following summer, with his legs wrapped in elastic stockings, he won another US Open in dramatic fashion in a three-way playoff with George Fazio and Lloyd Mangrum. In 1951, Hogan won a second consecutive Open championship at Oakland Country Club in Michigan. Despite having to fight constant leg pain and numbing fatigue as a result of the accident, in 1953 at the age of 41 he enjoyed his best year, winning his only British Open and Masters along with his fourth US Open.[15]

Although Hogan is considered one of golf's greatest players, his reserved personality and lack of charisma never made him a popular champion. All business on the course and withdrawn off it, Hogan was greatly respected as an exceptional golfer, but he never received public adulation. Hogan approached his golf with analytical precision, played round after round without a smile erasing the steady grim visage of concentration, and changed golf forever with his intense approach that combined endless practice with a seriousness of purpose and attention to even the most minute nuances of the game. Even his books on how to play the game (especially *Five Lessons: The Modern Fundamentals of Golf*, 1957) were laden with detailed, highly technical language that left most weekend golfers more confused than enlightened. For this intense man, golf was a tough business, never a game.

Perhaps Hogan's public persona explains the enthusiastic, even exuberant embrace with which golf fans greeted a newcomer to the tour whose enthusiasm for the game was infectious. Arnold Palmer arrived just as Hogan and Snead began the inevitable decline in their game as they approached the age of 50. A native of the small town of Latrobe, located 30 miles east of Pittsburgh, Palmer grew up working on the nine-hole golf course where his father was combination greens keeper, teaching professional, and clubhouse manager. Palmer carried 175 pounds on a husky 5 foot 11 inch frame appropriate for a college halfback. He smacked the ball with unusual ferocity out of a cramped, unconventional swing that probably made the stylistic Snead and perfectionist Hogan cringe. He lunged at the ball with a curious swipe that was part home run swing and part hockey slapshot; nonetheless, Palmer hit the ball with a raw power seldom seen on the tour. After hitting the ball long off the tee, he characteristically walked at a rapid pace down the fairway, puffing on a cigarette, and talking rapidly to his caddy. He then quickly lined up his next shot, tossed his cigarette aside with a flourish, and with a minimum of pre-shot ritual, smacked his next shot. Once on the green, unlike many professionals, he spent a minimum amount of time reading the line. Then he hunched over the ball in a uniquely familiar but unorthodox style, his body language indicating he was superbly confident that the ball was going into the cup.[16]

Palmer's every motion and expression told the gallery that he loved to play the game. He seemed to relish a situation where he had to make a difficult shot under extreme pressure on the last day of a major tournament. His come-from-behind "charges" – often built around a stirring shot out of a bad lie – became a part of his appeal. Palmer brought an air of excitement to the game never before witnessed, thereby helping popularize golf with the American people more than any other individual in the history of the game.[17]

Palmer came late to the professional tour. After playing collegiate golf for three years at Wake Forest College and serving three more in the Coast Guard, he did not turn professional until 1955 at the relatively advanced age of 25. He immediately became a favorite of the gallery. Between 1955 and 1973, Palmer won 60 PGA events including seven majors, and during the 1980s he won 10 tournaments on the seniors tour. Although his overall record falls somewhat short of other top players, he undoubtedly was the most popular golfer of the twentieth century. Very long (if not always straight) off the tee and sensational on the green, especially in high-pressure situations, Palmer popularized the game for the average American. His charisma was infectious, and the galleries that followed him were enormous. Unlike the reserved crowds of an earlier day, his fans were loud and exuberant, urging him onward. "Charge!" they'd shout as he began one of his patented final rounds seeking to overcome the targeted leader. Dubbed "Arnie's Army," his legions of fans transformed the culture of American golf, stripping away its elitist pretensions. In 1981, when Palmer left the PGA circuit to join the seniors tour, one close observer attempted to pinpoint the Palmer mystique:

> There's no word or phrase that quite describes what it is that Palmer transmits to the galleries. He is one of a kind – different and special. He keeps reinventing the game of golf. Maybe someday he will invent a way to describe himself and what he does to the multitudes of people who come out to watch him.[18]

Some like to say that Palmer saved golf from stultifying boredom, while others argue that he changed it forever by democratizing the sport. Beyond question, one of Palmer's most important contributions was that he lured to the game millions of fans who had never before paid much attention. Wherever he played, his supporters came out to cheer as part of the volunteer "Army." Television ratings soared, especially when Palmer was in contention on the last day of a big tournament.

Arnold Palmer popularized golf for middle-class and blue-collar America, and as a result of his widespread fame, a new and decidedly larger group of men and women took up the game. Just as Palmer's game began to slip slightly in the late sixties, he had to make room for two younger rivals. One was a stocky Mexican American from Dallas, Lee Trevino. The exuberant, seemingly carefree Trevino arrived at the top echelon of professional golf in a way that simply shouted, "The American Dream." Born to a single parent in 1939, he was raised by his mother who squeezed out a living as a domestic worker. They lived in a wooden shack that lacked electricity or plumbing. Even as a youngster, Trevino found a way to take advantage of his circumstances. His family's modest dwelling stood near a suburban Dallas golf course, and he searched for errant balls for resale. By the time he was 16, playing on public courses, Trevino carried a handicap of two. When he returned to Dallas in 1960 after a four-year stint in the Marines, he hustled games at public courses, making money on side bets. He learned that players better than he would often choke when money was on the line. Possessed of excellent feel for a golf club, he began to challenge (and distract) opponents by promising to play right-handed with left-handed clubs. Then he taught himself to play an entire course with a taped quart-size bottle; he later claimed that he never lost a bet during a three-year stint playing with the bottle.[19]

Trevino was self-taught and super-confident in his skills. "I'll tell you what pressure is," he once remarked. "It's playing a big guy for five bucks and you only have two in your pocket." In 1966, he entered and won the Texas Open and then began to play on the PGA tour, winning $20,000 his first year. Encouraged by that seemingly enormous income, Trevino played well in 1967 and was named PGA Rookie of the Year. In 1968 he won $50,000 in early tournaments and was marked as a future star, a promise that he fulfilled at the US Open in Rochester in June when he blistered the course to tie the record of 275 while holding off challenges from Jack Nicklaus and Bert Yancey. His greater triumph, however, was the bond he established in that tournament with the fans. They cheered his every shot and engaged in continuous back-and-forth commentary with the animated golfer that prompted many a laugh. Shouts of "Whip the Gringo!" came out of the predominantly Anglo gallery, and indeed he did. With Arnold Palmer shooting an uncharacteristic 301 for a 59th-place finish, Arnie's Army seemed to morph into "Lee's Fleas." Still, many sportswriters considered Trevino's victory a lucky moment, at least until he won the Hawaiian Open later in the year. He went on to have a solid year in 1969 by winning the Tucson Open and more than $100,000. In 1970, although winning just one tournament, he nonetheless ended the year as the leading money winner on the tour with $157,000 in prize money. With those hefty purses deposited in his bank, Trevino cracked, "You can call me a Spaniard now. Who ever heard of a rich Mexican?"[20]

In 1971, Trevino was at the top of his game, and in the space of just 23 days he won three tournaments: the US Open for a second time, the British Open, and the Canadian Open. At season's end, the awards came pouring in to the exuberant man who made galleries laugh and cheer. He was named the PGA Player of the Year. Long before the word "diversity" had entered the American political lexicon, the gifted sportswriter Dan Jenkins had early captured the importance of Trevino as a symbol of racial and ethnic achievement. Touching upon the cultural significance of Trevino's arrival at the top of the leader board, Jenkins lauded the "Super Mexkin": "There he was out in the midst of all of that US Open dignity with his spread-out caddy-hustler stance and his short, choppy public-course swing, a stumpy little guy, tan as a tamale, pretty lippy for a nobody, and, yeah, wearing those red socks."[21] In naming him its Sportsman of the Year for 1971, *Sports Illustrated* noted that Trevino had "added a new dimension" to the staid sport of golf because he was "a common man with an uncommon touch."[22]

While Palmer and Trevino made golf fashionable among the American working and middle classes – the number of weekend hackers increased during the 1960s and the 1970s by several million – the greatest golfer of the era never quite connected with the general public, at least not until the autumn years of his playing career. Jack Nicklaus's achievements, however, clearly overshadowed Hogan, Palmer, and Trevino, as well as the best of the foreign players, Gary Player. In a career that spanned four decades of serious competition – he won his last major at the 1986 Masters at the age of 46 – Jack Nicklaus won a record-setting 18 major tournaments among the 70 tour championships he captured. He was the leading money winner on the tour eight times and runner-up six times. The PGA named him its Golfer of the Year on five occasions. Nicklaus was known for the length and accuracy of his high fade drives off the tee, his ability to hit his irons with the precision of Ben Hogan, and, once on the green, his unerringly accurate putting, especially in clutch situations.[23]

From the time Nicklaus appeared on the national scene, he demonstrated a rare combination of strength and finesse. A cautious player who always played the percentages, Nicklaus crafted each shot with the intent of minimizing errors and maximizing his opportunity to score. When compared to the electrifying Palmer and Trevino, his cautious, calculated, cerebral style of play never resonated with fans. Early in his career, as he began to challenge Palmer, he was frequently criticized by fans for his aloofness and detached style of play.[24]

Over the years, Nicklaus learned to ignore the many sharp comments, even boos, that came from Arnie's Army, who disliked him for knocking their hero off his pedestal. As Frank Deford wrote long after the chill between the two highly competitive men had waned, "No matter how badly Nicklaus beat Palmer, he didn't win affection. Esteem, respect, admiration – yes. But affection? No."[25] His consistently excellent play slowly won over the fans, who began to call him the "Golden Bear" after his blond mop of hair and large physique. When he stomped the field at the Open in 1965 and won by a shocking nine strokes, even Bobby Jones could only watch in awe: "He plays a kind of game with which I am not familiar," the former Grand Slam champion ruefully commented.[26]

Born and raised in Columbus, Ohio, Nicklaus had access to the venerable Scioto Country Club at an early age where he was mentored by former tour player and renowned golfing instructor, Jack Grout. Nicklaus was an all-around athlete in high school, starring in basketball, football, and track, but his major talent was smacking a golf ball long and straight; he was routinely driving 275 yards from the tee when he entered his teens. At age 13, he scored a 69 from the back tees at Scioto, a distance of 7,095 yards. His parents poured substantial money into his golfing education, and at age 16 he rewarded them by shooting a 64 in the first round of the Ohio Open and went on to win the tournament over a field of top adult amateurs and professionals. As a junior and senior high school student in Columbus, he won 15 junior tournaments. At age 17, he qualified for the US Open, and in 1959 became the youngest player in 50 years to win the US Amateur Championship. In 1960, while still an amateur, he finished just two strokes behind Arnold Palmer at the memorable US Open tournament at Cherry Hills in Denver.

Although Lee Trevino correctly observed that the one-iron was the most difficult club to use, it was one of Nicklaus's favorite clubs, especially at crunch time. At Baltusrol in the 1967 US Open, he hit his one-iron into a brisk wind 238 yards onto the green, close enough to sink his putt. That magnificent shot under extreme pressure enabled him to eclipse the 276 course record set in 1948 by Ben Hogan. In 1972, he assured his US Open victory at Pebble Beach when he hit the ball 250 yards onto the 17th green, and at the 1975 Masters he drilled a one-iron shot 246 yards to the 15th green to give him a one-stroke advantage over Tom Weiskopf and Johnny Miller. Many considered this the single best shot of his career. It was thus only fitting that he won his 18th and final major – the 1986 Masters – by making an eagle on the 15th hole and birdies on the next two to edge Greg Norman and Tom Kite by a single stroke.[27] In a fitting testimony to Nicklaus's lifetime achievement, Tiger Woods frequently said that his major career goal was to exceed Nicklaus's 18 major championships. At a celebration of the first 100 years of American golf in 1988, a distinguished panel of journalists and golfers voted the Golden Bear the "Golfer of the Century."

The Comeback Kids

For nearly a century, serious bicycle racing was one of the least popular of America's many so-called minor sports. No one paid much attention to the few stage races that were held each year – such as the Coors International Bicycle Classic or the World Professional Road Race – until two Americans surprisingly came to dominate a sport that the French take as seriously as Americans do their baseball and football. Not only did the amazing exploits of Greg LeMond and Lance Armstrong reveal inner strength to overcome life-threatening crises, but they also came to dominate the sport and the event that the French have long considered to be their special sports event – the Tour de France. When it comes to real-life

Figure 17.1   Two of golf's greatest players line up a putt during the 1973 Ryder Cup in St Louis. Arnold Palmer (standing) helped make golf a mainstream sport with his enthusiastic style of play and dramatic "charges" on the final day of major tournaments. Jack Nicklaus, who set a new standard with 18 major tournament victories between 1962 and 1986, was voted the top golfer of the twentieth century. *Image © Bettmann/ Corbis*

stories of individuals overcoming extreme hardship or misfortune to accomplish great things, the American people cannot hear enough.

Greg LeMond made headlines in 1986 when he became the first American ever to win the Tour de France. He began his riding career as a teenager in Reno in 1976 and became so wrapped up in his training that he withdrew from high school. One of his favorite stories is of a teacher who admonished him for skipping class to train on the vast open expanses of Nevada highways: "Greg, you'll never make anything of yourself riding a bike." He won the Junior World Championship in Buenos Aires 1979, and two years later turned professional and competed well on the European circuit. He became the first American ever to finish in the top three in his first Tour de France in 1983. Two years later, he finished the 2,500 mile race in second place. He rode on a team that featured the popular French rider, Bernard Hinault, but tensions over team and personal goals led to a much-publicized disagreement in which each rider felt betrayed by the other. Thereafter, the more than 20 million Frenchmen who lined the roads for the Tour did not know whether to cheer or jeer the American. After all, this upstart American was threatening to win their equivalent of the Super Bowl.[28]

LeMond's first Tour de France championship ride in 1986 was cheered, of course, but more than anything else it was considered a rare anomaly. LeMond missed the next two years of racing after he was accidentally hit in the back by a shotgun blast triggered by his brother-in-law while hunting wild turkey in northern California. Emergency surgery saved his life, but several pellets remained in his abdomen. During his slow recovery, he had to undergo an emergency appendectomy and then leg surgery for a serious infection.

While knowledgeable cycling people believed that his racing days were over – no sport is more demanding on the body for such an extended period of time than multistage, multiday road racing – LeMond returned to his vigorous training regimen and surprised the world when he won the 1989 Tour de France. He did so in dramatic fashion, taking the lead in the 2,000 mile race only in the final moments of the last stage through the streets of Paris, edging out the home-country favorite and two-time champion Laurent Fignon. Only a supreme effort bolstered by fierce determination enabled the 28-year-old American to make up a seemingly insurmountable 50 second lead on the final stage into Paris. Riding at a record speed averaging 34 miles per hour, the fastest ever for a time trial stage in the Tour, he edged out Fignon by a mere 8 seconds. It was the closest finish in the history of the tour. LeMond repeated as champion again in 1990, but he was soon thereafter afflicted with a rare disease that reduces the ability of the muscles to burn sufficient protein. He retired from racing in 1994.[29]

The ambivalent feelings that the French people displayed when the Americans hijacked their national sport turned into downright obnoxious behavior when a brash, blunt, and arrogant Texan, Lance Armstrong, began his almost incomprehensible feat of winning seven straight Tour de France races beginning in 1999. This accomplishment proved to be too much for French cycling fans, who not only saw their top racers fall far behind the American, but also suffered the terrible embarrassment of having one of their best, Richard Virenque, disqualified for doping. As Armstrong piled up his impressive string of victories, French fans insinuated that he had to be benefiting from banned substances. Otherwise, how could he sustain his incredible charges up the steep mountain roads where he picked up valuable minutes on the *peloton* (the pack)?[30] Even after he retired for the first time in 2005 after victory number seven, various French publications sought in vain to besmirch his incredible achievement.

Armstrong's many supporters and associates said that his unprecedented domination of the world's greatest stage race was a combination of personal determination, a passion for exhaustive workouts, and the miracles of modern medicine. Born in Plano, Texas, in 1971, he became a local legend as a teenager for his domination of triathlons, winning at age 17 the national sprint triathlon (1,000 meter swim, 15 mile bike ride, 3 mile run). He then decided to concentrate on biking full-time, moved to Austin, and soon achieved international notice. In 1991, he won the US National Amateur and in 1993, having turned professional, won $1 million by capturing the American triple crown; that same year, he also won a stage of the Tour de France, the youngest rider ever to do so. His dedication to long, punishing workouts had already become the talk of the international racing set, but so too was his expressive character that contrasted with the traditional bland personalities that had dominated racing.

Armstrong was incredibly blessed with inherent physical attributes that contributed to his success as a cyclist. Tests taken when he was 16 at the Cooper Clinic in Dallas, home to the aerobics movement, revealed that he had an almost superhuman capacity to absorb and utilize oxygen, and that his propensity for producing lactic acid – the substance that causes the burning sensation in one's lungs and legs when winded or fatigued – was incredibly low. Journalist Alan Shipnuck summarized Armstrong's public persona after he captured the Tour du Pont: "Armstrong's bionic legs, savvy in the saddle, and steel will may have dazzled his competitors, but it is his charisma and matinee-idol good looks that charmed the two-million plus fans."[31]

On the first day of October, 1996, everything seemingly was breaking Armstrong's way. He had signed a $1 million endorsement deal with Nike and a $2 million contract to ride with the French Cofidis cycling team. Armstrong seemed destined for fame and fortune. Incredibly strong and with unmatched endurance, Armstrong now set his sights on winning the big one – the 1997 Tour de France – exuding all of the confidence of a 25-year-old athlete possessed of enormous strength and endurance: "I was a world-class athlete with a mansion on a riverbank, keys to a Porsche, and a self-made fortune in the bank. I was one of the top riders in the world and my career was moving along a perfect arc of success." He felt "bullet proof."[32]

That euphoric, even cocky, attitude changed the next day. On October 2, 1996, Armstrong was diagnosed with advanced stage-three testicular cancer. He immediately underwent surgery to remove a cancerous testicle, but tests revealed that the disease had metastasized to his lungs and brain. A team of oncology physicians told Armstrong that he had 14 tumors that threatened his life. His chances of survival were not good. His physicians put him on a program of aggressive chemotherapy and radiation that stretched over three months. During this grueling ordeal, he lost 15 pounds of muscle (his body fat was measured at just 2 percent), but between treatments in the hospital, despite his weakened condition, he continued to ride his bike, often struggling to complete just a few miles. His treatments, however, proved effective, and by the summer of 1997 tests revealed no signs of malignancy.

Armstrong returned to riding. By January 1998, he was once more logging between 600 and 700 miles a week. The loss of weight, he discovered, had made him both leaner and lighter, producing a body perfectly suited for the steep climbs of the French Alps that are a crucial part of each Tour de France. An exercise physiologist who tested Armstrong found that he had gained 6 percent of power despite the loss of 15 pounds of muscle. The reason was simple: he spent many months preparing for the Tour de France by riding between 5 and 7 hours a day up and down the steep Pyrenees, always putting in a minimum of 30 hours of these arduous workouts each week. Physiologist Ed Coyle put Armstrong's superior strength into perspective when he said that he could ride a bike at the high rate of

32 mph for a full hour's time, whereas the average well-conditioned college-age male could keep up that pace for only 45 seconds: "For the first 10 seconds they're great. After about 20 seconds they think they're gonna die. After 40 seconds they throw up."[33]

When Armstrong's illness was first announced, the Cofidis team decided not to renew his contract, and so the once-again healthy Armstrong signed with a team sponsored by the United States Postal Service. His return to the Tour was vindication of his bravery in fighting his cancer with the most aggressive treatment possible and a vivid testimony to his tenacity in regaining a level of competitive fitness. When he won the first stage of the race, the short 8 kilometer Prologue time trial, leaving the Cofidis team in his wake as he proudly donned the *maillot jaune* – the yellow jersey that signifies the Tour leader – he readily admitted that he enjoyed immensely that moment of personal revenge. He then proceeded to stun the world with his endurance, and in the crucial mountain stage where even the greatest of riders have been reduced to absolute exhaustion, Armstrong pulled ahead of the *peloton* by a startling 6 minutes. His performance was almost beyond comprehension, prompting one journalist to write in awe, "It was so remarkable that everything we thought we knew about human athletic achievement needs to be reconsidered." Upon returning to the United States, he was invited to the White House where Vice President Al Gore said, "You captured the eyes of the nation and the hearts of the entire world."[34]

Armstrong's achievement naturally produced suspicions that he was doping. As he sped through the mountains in 1999, eclipsing long-established records, the speculation and insinuation in the French press began. Some articles even speculated that his chemotherapy, which had produced severe nausea for three months and shrunk his muscular body by 15 pounds, had somehow mysteriously given him some secret drugs that enhanced performance! He has flatly denied ever using such substances and has been tested hundreds of times with always a negative result. French racing officials, frustrated that an American – of all foreigners! – dominated their national sport, have gone the extra mile in attempts to implicate Armstrong for using drugs; of course, the sport has been rife with such activities for years and those allegations were to be expected. Armstrong has attempted to meet his skeptical French critics halfway: he learned to speak French and purchased a house in the French countryside to facilitate his pre-race training. During races, he was constantly barraged by angry cries from French fans hollering "Dope! Dope," but he said such taunts only inspired him to pedal faster.[35]

In retrospect, Armstrong realized that the attacks were part of the larger cultural and political divide between the American and French cultures: "I lived in France, and I love the country." He took special note of the fact that after a massive drug scandal during the 1998 Tour, in which he did not participate, many top non-French riders did not train in France for fear of police surveillance:

> Not me. While other riders were afraid of being harassed by the police or investigated by the governmental authorities, I trained there every day. France was the most severe place in the world to be caught using a performance enhancer, but I did all my springtime racing in France, and conducted my entire Tour preparation there. Under French law, the local police could have raided my house whenever they wanted. They didn't have to ask, or knock … If I was trying to hide something, I'd have been in another country.

But even his residency did not assuage the criticism. "Nothing works," he once sighed. "They told me to speak French. Told me to smile, sign autographs. Didn't work. It's just not going to happen."[36]

In 2008, Armstrong announced that he was returning to competitive racing in order to publicize his foundation's crusade against cancer. His appearance in races around the globe stimulated plenty of media attention, and a revival of doping allegations. He managed a third-place finish in the 2009 Tour de France, and in 2010 suffered several crashes and finished in 23rd place. He thereupon announced his second and permanent retirement and defended his integrity by asserting that he was the "most tested athlete in the world." His credibility remained in question, however, when the American cyclist Floyd Landis accused Armstrong of doping. Landis had been a Postal Service teammate and had won the 2006 Tour de France; however, he was later stripped of his title for testing positive. In August of 2009, a Los Angeles federal grand jury began probing the conflicting and confusing web of evidence and new (and resurrected) allegations made about Armstrong's alleged doping between 1999 and 2005. Because these years included those when his team was sponsored by the United States Postal Service, he faced possible indictments on charges of racketeering, drug trafficking, money laundering, and defrauding the federal government. With the controversy still raging after his permanent retirement in 2010, and with a federal grand jury looking into the charges, Lance Armstrong's legacy remained an open question.

Although Greg LeMond and Lance Armstrong became famous Americans, treated like conquering heroes when they returned from their triumphs in France, the sport of bicycle racing enjoyed only a moderate boost in the United States. Significantly, *Sports Illustrated* selected LeMond for its prestigious Sportsman of the Year award in 1989 and Armstrong in 2001. But for deep-seated cultural reasons, bicycle racing never became more than a niche sport in the United States, attracting a relatively small but enthusiastic number of participants. Although the Tour de France received substantial coverage when the Americans were in contention, bicycle racing within the United States normally existed far below the radar screen of the media. Nonetheless, an estimated 12 million Americans, mostly between the ages of 18 and 50, had taken up biking in a serious fashion by the onset of the twenty-first century, donning the colorful outfits, shaving their legs (to prevent painful treatment if the rider should fall and scrape the skin), wearing aerodynamic helmets, and riding long distances with their local biking clubs, perhaps entering races on weekends. Perhaps some have been inspired by the example of LeMond and Armstrong, but most have taken up the sport as an enjoyable and effective means of physical conditioning. One never sees an overweight biker whiz by.

"Sidewalk Surfing" and the Rise of "X-treme" Sports

The anti-establishment impetus that was unleashed during the 1960s had a profound impact upon sports and recreation in the United States. Rebellious youth created a new ethos of anti-establishment attitudes that questioned middle-class conventions. Unkempt long hair and grungy clothes challenged the "straight" nature of their parents' generation, as did use of marijuana (and sometimes more powerful drugs), the loosening of sexual practices, and powerful messages of protest and alienation proclaimed by folk and rock musicians. The counterculture had its roots in the civil rights and anti-war movements, but it also claimed close intellectual moorings with the Beat Generation writers of the 1950s. The rebellion thrived upon the messages of a vanguard of artists who took their place in a long tradition of American protest that expressed dissident ideas through the medium of music. The movement sought to "empower" marginalized groups and social outcasts, and to push back against efforts to repress the complex movement.

Emphasis upon individual expression and clarion calls to "do your own thing" led to innovations in sports and recreation. The new emphasis tended to be upon those activities that encouraged individual activity rather than those requiring involvement with a group or team. Established sports and recreations like running, tennis, handball, golf, weightlifting, squash, cycling, skiing, and swimming gained millions of new adherents.

True to the spirit of individualism, sports innovations during the sixties invited participants to break free from conventional activities and encouraged them to explore new possibilities. Many youths tended to shun the rigors of football or the tedium of baseball practice conducted under the supervision of adults, and embraced instead activities that were distinctly identified with the counterculture. These activities were tagged with various names: "alternative sports," "action sports," "lifestyle sports." By the onset of the twenty-first century, they had gained millions of participants and often were lumped together under the term "extreme sports."[37]

Among the sports that grew "from the bottom up" were skateboarding and snowboarding. These new activities gained widespread acceptance among independent-minded youth. What distinguished these new innovations is that they were established and grew free from the clutch of organized sports, drawing participants through underground and informal social networks. Efforts to create rules and organized competitions were met with a tide of passive resistance. In many communities, efforts were made by local government officials to curb or even forbid the new generation of enthusiasts from engaging in these activities, somehow considered out-of-bounds. Just as traditionalists denounced the protest-laden folk and rock music of such artists as the Grateful Dead, Bob Dylan, and the Beatles, those who considered themselves defenders of the established order urged local officials to ban skateboarders from public places.

Skateboarding had its roots in the surfing tradition that had attracted a small but dedicated group of enthusiasts to southern Californian beaches ever since the first primitive wooden boards had been imported from Hawaii early in the twentieth century. During the 1950s, the possibilities of "surfing" downhill on streets and sidewalks produced crude wooden decks that were placed upon traditional metal roller skate wheels. These contraptions were unwieldy and led to many a fall; impact with the "concrete waves" often produced injuries. Because the equipment proved inadequate, the infant sport lost much of its appeal. But it had gained a foothold, even penetrating the Midwest – Oklahoma City in particular. Significantly, the first copies of *SkateBoarder* hit the stands in 1964 amidst the heights of the social protest movement.[38]

The nascent activity of "sidewalk surfing" was revived with a rush in the 1970s when urethane wheels were attached to composition boards with adhesive surfaces. Manufacturers produced an exciting new product and specialized "board shops" soon were selling colorful decks to a rapidly expanding market of young enthusiasts. Innovations by manufacturers produced boards that were meant to be ridden hard, low, and fast. The sport took hold, and made quantum leaps in participation levels when low-to-the-ground skateboarding maneuvers were created. Adhesive surfaces made it possible for riders seemingly to defy gravity by propelling their board into the air while maintaining contact until landing. Leading in the development of these daring maneuvers was Florida teenager Alan "Ollie" Gelfand, who popularized the "Ollie Air" maneuver in which the skateboarder propels himself into the air and, while maintaining contact with the board, does a 360 degree twist and lands intact. In San Diego, another teenager, Tony Hawk, helped popularize the sport and used skateboarding as entrée into an acting career.[39]

One feature of skateboarding was that it could be practiced on most any hard surface. Among the most popular surfaces were sloped parking lots and side streets, but empty swimming pools – the result of a prolonged drought in southern California and an economic recession – had a special attraction. The famed Z-Boys who took up the sport in the southern California beach communities of Santa Monica, Ocean Park, and Venice Beach became the center of attraction for the new sport. The initial relationship between skateboarding and water surfing was readily evident because this pioneering group of skateboarders had already become proficient on the ocean waves. The area in which they developed their skateboard moves was known as "Dogtown." This diverse urban area of small shops, bars, and apartments offered plenty of paved sloping and banked surfaces. It was here that Jeff Ho and Skip Engblom established Zephyr Productions in 1971 and began designing and manufacturing surfboards; they later moved into skateboards. They expanded their business to produce colorful boards that featured graffiti symbols prominent in the multiethnic neighborhood. The Zephyr skateboarding "team" pioneered in developing moves that spread quickly across the country. Their exploits were captured in Stacy Peralta's prize-winning documentary film, *Dogtown and Z-Boys: A Film about the Birth of the Now* that was released in 2001. As the documentary makes clear, the Z-Boys worked very hard to develop their trademark moves. Good old-fashioned American hard work and competitiveness underpinned the work of the Z-Boys. They established the standards for the emerging sport.[40]

The release of a fictionalized version of the Z-Boys in 2005, *The Lords of Dogtown* by Sony Pictures, symbolized the passage of skateboarding from rogue activity into a phenomenon tacitly accepted by mainstream America. One of the most prominent of the original Z-Boys, Tony Alva, operated a flourishing business in Oceanside where he produced his own brand of boards designed for both surf and turf. True to his Dogtown roots, this free-spirited entrepreneur continued surfing and skating on a regular basis.

The unconventional nature of the new sport produced a conservative pushback. Early efforts to ban boards from public places proved unenforceable but many a confrontation between law enforcement and teenage boarders occurred. The sport took on a distinctly edgy, anti-establishment attitude as free-spirited boarders whizzed by startled pedestrians on a busy sidewalk or zipped across a street in front of surprised motorists. Often the skateboarders wore clothing that shouted "rebellion." The popularity of the grunge clothing fad of the early 1990s became *de rigueur* for most skateboarders: baggy denim pants, worn low on the hips, and disheveled oversized flannel shirts or tie-dyed T-shirts. This fashion was often accented by stringy hair and a few tattoos and body piercings. Physical appearances added to mainstream public identification of skateboarding with a roguish image of alienation and the flaunting of accepted social norms. After years of efforts to banish skateboarders from public places failed, pragmatic city recreation directors decided to build skateboarding venues in public parks that greatly reduced the level of generational conflict.

In 1964, the first issue of *SkateBoarder* editorialized: "We predict a real future for the sport – a future that could go as far as the Olympics. It's a much more 'measureable' sport than surfing and therefore lends itself more to competition."[41] Efforts to create national and international governing bodies to establish rules for competition, however, came and went, and standardization occurred at a glacial pace – with vertical jumping competitions the most popular. These were popularized by construction of hard-surfaced "halfpipe" ramps with winners being determined by how high they could fly above the edge of the ramp, execute spins, and land safely back within the confines of the halfpipe.

As skateboarding spread worldwide, suggestions that it be made an Olympic event appeared, but such efforts always came up against the inherently rebellious nature of the sport. It had begun as a quasi-underground expression of rebellion, and many of its adherents preferred to keep it that way. If skateboarding became an Olympic sport, many of its enthusiasts asked, would it lose its renegade appeal, be subjected to rules and regulations, and thereby be co-opted by the establishment?

Similar issues surrounded the rapid development of snowboarding after the first snowboards were introduced at the nation's ski resorts during the 1960s. Many a confrontation occurred when traditional skiers protested. Eventually snowboarders were grudgingly accepted by skiers, and their appearance became commonplace by the mid 1980s as a truce fell over the nation's slopes. Much of the conflict seemed to grow out of perceived indifference by snowboarders to established skiing etiquette. Once again, the preference of many snowboarders for the grunge clothing style offended style-minded skiers. In the case of snowboards, however, traditional capitalistic impulses prevailed because ski resort operators found it expedient to sell lift tickets to the snowboarders. By 2010, an estimated 7 million snowboarders hit the slopes each winter, with more than half of those enthusiasts thought to be under the age of 21.

The fact that snowboarding became an official sport at the 1998 Winter Olympics in Japan attests to its acceptance. Two women's and two men's events were held at Nagano. The competition made for stirring television coverage and did much to stimulate the popularity of competitive snowboarding. The sport's first superstar was American Shaun White, whose daring high-flying exploits in the halfpipe event won him gold medals at the 2006 and 2010 Winter Games. In 2010, on Vancouver's Cypress Mountain, the 24-year-old California native became an international sensation as he outdistanced his competition when he successfully completed what he called his daring, high-flying "Double McTwist" that dazzled television audiences around the globe. The triumph of board culture was made complete when the American skateboarding team competed in baggy blue denim pants and oversized red and white flannel shirts.[42]

The commercial appeal of snowboarding and skateboarding produced multimillion-dollar sales in equipment each year. A similar commercial success accompanied the rapid growth in popularity of the mountain bike. This sturdy design construction was introduced in the mid 1970s, and within a few years sales exceeded those of conventional thin-tire road racing bikes. The mountain bike appealed to all ages. It was the product of the ingenuity of biking enthusiasts from northern California, who modified traditional bicycle design to encourage off-road biking. Extra sturdy frames, fat tires and multiple gears enabled riders to traverse bumpy dirt trails and climb steep hills. Just as women riders in the late nineteenth century embraced bicycles because they provided a new sense of freedom and independence, so too did active Americans of all ages take to their mountain bikes to ride free of traffic. By 2010, an estimated 55 million Americans rode mountain bikes.[43]

These trends in recreation did not go unnoticed. In 2005, a *New York Times* article concluded that what had once been a counterculture endeavor had gone mainstream. Looking specifically at young skateboarders donning safety helmets to hit the sidewalks in suburban neighborhoods, Damien Cave noted, "What began as a marginalized activity, prohibited by many communities and embraced by early skaters for its go-to-hell attitude, has morphed into a mainstream youth sport dominated by doting parents and rules about safety." Even seven-time Tour de France winner Lance Armstrong appeared in advertisements astride an expensive mountain bike, and President George W. Bush frequently rode his mountain bike with wild abandon at his Texas ranch, much to the delight of journalists, while he forced secret service agents to pedal much faster than they desired. Perhaps most significant was that city governments had made peace with skateboarders. More than 2,500 skateboard parks, featuring ramps and miniature halfpipes, had been constructed by municipal parks and recreation departments.[44]

The growing popularity of these new sports was recognized when commercial television network ESPN introduced the X-Games in 1995. The made-for-television competitions were a clever effort to take commercial advantage of the growing interest in skateboarding and snowboarding, along with other lesser-known "extreme" sports. The programming was specifically aimed at younger viewers and attracting new advertising revenue streams. The Winter X-Games were held every year in February at major ski resorts, and attracted competitors from around the world. In addition to snowboarding, snowmobiling and skiing events were featured. The Summer X-Games featured a variety of crosscountry motorcycle racing events (motocross) and various men's and women's skateboarding events.

The anti-establishment sentiment that provided the underlying appeal of these "extreme" sports also contributed to the growth of a multimillion-dollar entertainment business. Mixed Martial Arts (MMA) was created for cable television networks in the mid 1990s. The new sport blended the over-the-top hype of professional wrestling with blatant exploitation of the imagery of unrestrained violence. The crass pandering to those who revel in blood and gore proved to be a winning concept. After some early setbacks that required strategic reconfiguring of the format, MMA grew in popularity to the point that it became an established niche sport. Some observers even suggested that the appeal of MMA equaled that of traditional boxing. Unlike professional wrestling, which has not been considered a sport because of its reliance upon scripted "bouts," MMA gained millions of enthusiasts because its fights were competitive contests, but it proved unable to attract sustained coverage from the established sports media.

The first "ultimate fighting" card was offered in Denver in November 1993. Its promoters initially considered it to be a one-time event. About 3,500 curious spectators showed up to watch a series of bouts that featured men with various forms of combat expertise. Spectators filing into McNichols Arena were told that there were no rules governing the mayhem promised, other than the combatants were given a no-holds-barred license to overpower their opponents. Promotional materials suggested that knockouts would be frequent, and even held out the prospect of far more ominous outcomes. The possibility of plenty of spilled blood was prominently mentioned. No one present that night could have imagined that within 15 years, MMA and "ultimate fighting" would become firmly established in American popular culture, packing large arenas and drawing hundreds of thousands of fans willing to pay substantial fees to watch on closed-circuit television. Eventually, MMA contestants included boxers, wrestlers, karate fighters, kick boxers, and sumo wrestlers.

Several of the bouts in Denver produced a chorus of boos as contestants ended up in interminable embraces, squirming about on the mat with little discernible action or violence. Other contests, however, lived up to the promise of mayhem when a kick boxer pulled out a large clump of hair from his opponent, and another fighter sank his teeth into an opponent's foot. The victim's spontaneous reaction pulled two teeth from the assailant's mouth and left them embedded in his foot! The promise of brutality truly occurred when a kick boxer broke an unsuspecting foe's ankle with a powerful heel hook, an injury the inexperienced referee did not recognize. While the victim flailed around on the mat in anguish, the inspired crowd screamed for more. The kick boxer later said, "They were mad at me. Can you believe it? I broke the guy's ankle and they wanted more." Journalist Jon Wertheim uncharitably described the crowd as consisting largely of "heavy-duty white trash, the curious, and the bloodthirsty," but as the sport became established it attracted spectators from a wide range of socioeconomic groups.[45]

The concept of no-holds-barred combat was an inspired one, at least from the perspective of promoters and cable television executives who grasped the inherent commercial promise of a new blood sport. Matches were soon staged that permitted all forms of bare-knuckle punching, kicking, jiu-jitsu, wrestling, and throwing. Historians were reminded of the savagery of the traditional "rough-and-tumble" eye-gouging affairs of the pre-Civil War Appalachian region (although MMA rules prohibited eye gouging). Promoters added an inspired image-laden touch when they pitted contestants against each other within the confines of what became known as The Octagon: a grotesque eight-sided chainlink cage rather than the traditional 20 × 20 foot boxing ring. According to early press releases, "There are no rules!" Contestants, they proclaimed, would battle until "knockout, submission, doctor's intervention, or death." Initially, the sanctioning body that took the name Ultimate Fighting Championship (UFC) permitted kicking an opponent who was down, hitting the groin, and choking. One standard tactic was to pin an opponent to the mat and slug him with the other hand. Fans were apparently attracted by the announcement that referees were prohibited from stopping a bout. (In reality the referee was instructed to halt a contest when a contestant was considered unable to defend himself or unwilling to concede.)

Just as the new blood sport was gaining popularity as a pay-per-view cable television attraction, it was temporarily sidetracked by a prominent fan of traditional boxing, Senator John McCain of Arizona. After viewing videotapes of several contests he angrily denounced ultimate fighting as a degrading form of "human cockfighting." He apparently took too literally the over-exaggerated promotional claims that "death" might occur to a combatant at any moment. McCain sent letters to state boxing commissions demanding that the sport be abolished. Promoters were quick to modify the rules to mollify the senator and future presidential candidate, creating a baseline rule that protection of the health of the contestants was essential.[46]

The promotional hype borrowed heavily from professional wrestling and included the blaring of rock music before matches, but the idea that the fighters were prepared for the possibility of death every time they entered The Octagon was subtly squashed. Weight classes were established, choking and other gruesome tactics were banned, and small gloves were placed on the bare fists to reduce the number of bloody cuts and scrapes. (The gloves were designed not to protect the recipient of blows, but to prevent fingers from being broken.) Five-minute rounds became the norm. Death, however, did occur on two separate occasions. In 2007 and 2008, contestants died of brain hemorrhages following knockouts; MMA supporters quickly pointed out that 120 deaths occurred in professional boxing between 1950 and 2010.

The appeal of a "full-contact sport" that incorporated many combat formats pushed the limits of what a civilized society might permit under the guise of sporting competition, perhaps, but it was a logical outgrowth of the needs of commercial television to continually find new ways to lure viewers. In 2005, the sport gained a level of unofficial sanction when the United States Army began to hold MMA championships. By that time, however, most state boxing commissions had voted to permit bouts and the sport had spread across the globe. Like other "X-treme" sports, ultimate fighting had gone mainstream.

Epilogue

During the latter half of the twentieth century the American people expanded and refined their roles as participants, dedicated fans, and casual spectators. New forms of mass media greatly expanded the seeming importance of sports. Television extended to the American public unprecedented opportunities to watch college and professional games. New customs and rituals naturally took hold; health clubs and city recreational programs encouraged participation of people of all ages in a myriad of individual and team activities. Sports betting, fostered by the influence of Las Vegas and the internet, grew to an immense (but unknown) size and influence, and in a new twist to the American penchant for gambling, fantasy leagues attracted millions of weekend wannabe "sports executives" who created their own dream teams, drafting, buying, and selling players at will. Sports bars and restaurants, mixing alcohol and casual food fare with a bank of television sets, became entertainment fixtures in communities large and small. ESPN and its several imitators provided national and regional sports coverage in repetitive and excessive detail, while national radio network gossip and sports talk shows fanned the fires with news, analysis, and commentary, information and ideas that were turned into white heat by local stations devoted exclusively to sports talk. By the twenty-first century, these more traditional forms of communications were further supplemented (or subverted) by an endless array of internet sites providing tidbits of sports information that featured endless rounds of second-guessing, rumors, and wild speculation.

Americans are not just spectators; millions are also fans of their favorite professional or college teams. Spectators watch sports for their entertainment value, sometimes in person but much more often by clicking their television remote control. When the game is over the casual spectator moves on to other entertainment, but the true sports fan – passionately committed to the fortunes of one team – is left consumed with a sense of either elation or dejection. Fan(atic)s have their own special personal bond with one team; more often than

Sports in American Life: A History, Second Edition. Richard O. Davies.
© 2012 John Wiley & Sons, Inc. Published 2012 by John Wiley & Sons, Inc.

not it is the team that they embraced as a child because that was the team their father rooted for. Being a true lifelong fan is much like belonging to a political party: it is almost tribal in its meaning, the bonds are often strained but never broken, and loyalty is unquestioned even during the depressing depths of the inevitable losing seasons. In my native state of Ohio, for example, an estimated 25 percent of the 13 million residents on a given autumn Saturday closely monitor the fate of the Ohio State University Buckeyes on television or radio. On home-game days, 100,000 ticket-holders, bedecked in their scarlet and gray outfits, jam Ohio Stadium located along the picturesque Olentangy River on the edge of the sprawling Columbus campus. Coaches at Ohio State have come and gone over the years, but the one true measurement of their tenure has been how many times they defeated rival Michigan in the Big Game, a tradition that began in 1897 and one that shows no indication of ending anytime in the new century. During the days leading up to game-day Saturday, Buckeye fans follow the latest injury reports and news bulletins regarding the team's practices. Journalistic assessments of the opposition are read with the utmost seriousness. Internet sites are probed for even more detail, along with confident predictions and the wildest of rumors. Everyone in Ohio, it seems, is smarter than the coach, especially when it comes to picking the starting quarterback or second-guessing a crucial play call. Sundays are given over to a detailed review of the previous day's game; blowout victories produce little joy but plenty of criticism for style points; defeats lead to anguished wailing and infinite criticism of the head coach, even of the university president for picking such a dumb lout. Following the near-inevitable trip to a postseason bowl game after yet another winning season, OSU fans intently follow the news of the midwinter recruiting wars, and 40,000 turn out for the annual inter-squad game that ends the ritual of spring practice. By June, Buckeye fans are awaiting the arrival of the annual college football preseason magazines and their assessments of the college teams. Opening game kickoff is just around the corner.

Every major college football and basketball team has its diehard loyal fans, and the same is true of professional teams. In certain instances, as with the Green Bay Packers, the team becomes not only a community treasure, but one that is shared with the entire state, in this case Wisconsin. Fans everywhere worry before each upcoming contest, cheer loudly during the game, grouse about every fumble and incomplete pass, and suffer temporary depression after the inevitable losses. Defeat at the hands of the traditional rival in the Big Game – e.g., UCLA–USC, Florida–Florida State, Oregon–Oregon State, Alabama–Auburn, Texas–Oklahoma – is unthinkable but somehow the dejected fans manage to live to cheer another day.

Journalist Warren St John explored the phenomenon of the super-fan in his book about the dedicated thousands who travel far and wide in an unorganized armada of crimson-bedecked recreational vehicles that converge upon the site of the University of Alabama football game each autumn weekend for 48 hours of serious tailgating. The dedication to the Crimson Tide cause of these individuals is striking. During the 1999 season, St John encountered many Alabama fans that had seldom (if ever) missed a game for 25 years or more. During the season, he met a funeral parlor director who offers (with many takers) specially designed Crimson Tide caskets, tastefully bedecked in crimson and white, complete with the block A letter inscribed inside the lid. Another fan, carrying an electronic pager linking him to a Nashville hospital where he hoped to receive a heart transplant, defied instructions and traveled far beyond permitted distances to watch his favorite team play. He said he would rather risk missing his transplant operation than miss the Tide's game! St John also related one conversation with a quiet gray-haired couple in their 60s who proudly confessed they had not missed an Alabama game for 15 years:

> So the reporter idly asks what sort of things they've given up in pursuit of the Tide. Let's see, the man said in a soft Southern drawl. We missed our daughter's wedding. You what? We told her, just don't get married on a game day and we'll be there, hundred percent, and she went off and picked the third Saturday in October which everybody knows is when Alabama plays Tennessee, so we told her, hey, we got a ball game to go to. We made the reception – went there soon as the game was over.[1]

Studies by psychologists and sociologists have contributed to our understanding of the dedicated sports fan.[2] These studies suggest that the decline in the durability of the American family and the rise of a mobile population has prompted many Americans to seek a new form of social and community identification by closely associating themselves with a particular team. Urbanization, technology, and geographical mobility have undercut traditional societal bonds, and so many individuals have found it reassuring to align themselves with a group of strangers who also accept the same symbols – logo, mascot, coach, players, fight song, team colors. Most often that allegiance is to a single team, but it can also be a statewide identification with a sport, such as high school basketball in Indiana or football in Texas. In a few instances the phenomenon has extended to the entire United States, as evidenced by the widespread adulation expressed over the 1980 US Olympic hockey team and the 1999 women's World Cup soccer team.

Although academics have posited many theories, often couched in humanist, Marxist, or feminist perspectives, the truth is that even the most dedicated ("rabid") fan puts his or her team loyalty into a healthy perspective. For the great majority of fans, as Warren St John discovered in the makeshift RV city that magically coalesces for Alabama football games, the pleasure gleaned from the process temporarily removes the individual from the daily pressures of everyday life, providing an emotional "time out." Individuals get an opportunity for personal renewal by immersing themselves in a pleasurable social activity with like-minded individuals who come from a wide variety of backgrounds (many are not even Alabama alumni). Victory, of course, is eminently better than defeat, but everyone knows that after every loss there is always another game to be played, another season around the corner that promises glorious victories yet to be won.

Over the years, many students and friends have asked my predictions on what the future of American sports holds in the twenty-first century. Historians, perhaps, are not good prognosticators since their eyes are firmly set upon the past, but they are good readers of long-term trends, and the prominent ones that I foresee have been discussed in detail in the preceding pages. It seems likely that participation in games and sports will increase among people of all ages in the future. In an effort to reverse the distressing national trend toward obesity, more and more Americans will join in the exercise phenomenon, encouraged not only by government agencies, employers, and their personal physicians, but also by the vast amount of monies spent on advertising by health clubs and sporting goods companies. The popularity of youth sports will continue to provide an important facet in the lives of most families with children, especially those with parents who understand the importance of exercise and competition in the physical and social development of their children. In particular, the number of girls and women who compete in organized sports will continue to grow, demonstrating that Congress's enactment of Title IX in 1972 was a fortuitous act of statesmanship.

Because of the pervasive influence of television, the most popular spectator sports will remain as they are today: football, baseball, and men's basketball will constitute the "big three." Those games have such a long and rich tradition that it would take cataclysmic events to reduce their importance in the grand scheme of things. Big-time college athletics has become an enormous economic dynamo that will not shrink. Renewed efforts at reform (emulating the Carnegie and Knight commissions) will come and go, but have little impact upon the well-entrenched power structure that controls the enterprise. It is possible that the number of universities and colleges willing to pay the high cost of competing in Division I-A football will slowly dwindle, but other schools may opt to take their place in quest of increased public recognition. Several "mid-major" football conferences, such as the Mid-American, Sun Belt, and Western Athletic, may be forced to retreat to a lower division, or perhaps create their own version of the Bowl Championship Series, so that they can realistically compete for a national championship. Despite its inherent inequities and failings, the current Bowl Championship Series, dominated by six self-anointed conferences, will likely continue in some form for many years, postponing as long as possible the establishment of a postseason playoff that nearly every football fan wants. Professional baseball will continue to attract plenty of attention and attendance, but the game's relative lack of action makes for bland television fare, and that will prevent it from ever regaining its perch as the most popular sport in America. Stock car racing, which has enjoyed a significant rise in popularity in the past 30 years, will continue to enjoy its national stature as it builds racetracks outside the South. NASCAR will continue to grow unless it proves unable to control its internal operations or prevent the creation of a rival circuit. The so-called niche sports – hockey, soccer, tennis, golf – will continue to enjoy their current levels of popularity with small segments of the population, but will never rise to challenge the big three (or big four if NASCAR can sustain its current growth rate).

Sports at all levels will have to deal with repeated threats to their integrity. The growth of internet sport gambling sites poses a serious problem that seems impervious to government regulation; the potential for fixed games will increase as a result. In some instances, the interest in gambling (such as with the fantasy leagues) can supersede the importance of the games themselves. Similarly, the ability of illicit drug makers to stay ahead of the testing laboratories will mean that the integrity of games will be increasingly compromised unless effective measures are mounted to counter the rise in use of illegal substances. The recurring incidents of lawlessness by male athletes – heavily reported by the national media – will remain a nagging problem for sports officials. Violent and antisocial behavior by leading athletes produces dramatic headlines that are usually soon forgotten, but until American society can find ways to curb similar behavior among the population in general, the news media will continue to report upon a tedium of physical assaults, the occasional use of firearms, and drug abuse by athletes.

I have little hope that the shame of intercollegiate athletics – especially recruiting violations, academic fraud, and financial excesses – will end. The NCAA and its campus clients – the athletic directors and coaches – have created a lucrative, closed world unto themselves within the realm of higher education; the overweening influence of money generated from the box office and television rights will prove too great an obstacle for any substantive reform effort to be successful. With the pots of money getting ever larger, the incentives to cheat in recruiting and in determining eligibility are likely to increase proportionately.

Such weighty matters, however, pale in comparison to the many benefits sports provide the average American. During the past decade my wife and I have taken to the roads of America, ostensibly in search of information for my other academic research interest in the history of the evolving role of small towns, but our travels have also impressed upon me the pervasive influence of sports. Visits to hundreds of college and university campuses reveal the centrality of sports to those educational institutions, with large football stadiums and basketball arenas dominating the campus landscape. At an upscale restaurant in Columbus in May, the band breaks out into the Buckeye fight song, "Across the Field," and in New England, it seems that every other child and adult is wearing a Red Sox cap. In rural Florida, while enjoying a leisurely lunch at a local spot festooned with stock car memorabilia, we witness a near-brawl break out among several young men, seemingly over differing opinions on the proper carburetor settings. All across the land, in the Dakotas or in Texas, in Oregon or in Tennessee, the local newspapers and radio air waves are filled with local sports news and information, and in the evenings the skies are alive with the lights of adult softball and youth baseball fields. Far into the night the quiet of our downtown St Louis hotel in February is punctured by the raucous sounds of several hundred Detroit Red Wing fans who arrived en masse on Thursday in preparation for a Sunday afternoon face-off with the St Louis Blues, and a revisit to that same hotel in June found us surrounded by thousands of red-shirted Cardinal fans in town for the weekend intra-league series with the Yankees; most of those happy folk with whom we talked had driven in excess of 150 miles to take in a mid-season game.

And so it goes throughout the United States, where sports have become an integral aspect of the daily ebb and flow of American life. As has oft been written, America is truly a land of many contrasts and cultures. From Miami to Seattle, from San Diego to Boston, sports provide a common thread, even a common language, for a diverse people and a far-flung nation made up of many peoples, cultures, regions, and locales. To understand America, as the French scholar and writer Jacques Barzun once wrote, foreigners must first learn the language and culture of baseball. His oft-quoted observation was an exaggeration undoubtedly, but he was definitely onto something. To paraphrase and expand his comment, to understand America, its history and its present, it would be wise to appreciate and recognize the centrality of sports.

Notes

Preface

1 Richard O. Davies, *America's Obsession: Sports and Society since 1945* (Fort Worth, TX: Harcourt Brace, 1994).

2 See the *Journal of Sport History* published by the North American Society for Sport History. For the early histories and related studies of the broad expanse of American sports history and American society's embrace of sports, see Foster Rhea Dulles, *America Learns to Play: A History of Popular Recreation, 1607–1940* (New York: Appleton-Century, 1940); John R. Betts, *America's Sporting Heritage, 1850–1950* (Reading, MA: Addison-Wesley, 1974); John A. Lucas and Ronald A. Smith, *Saga of American Sports* (New York: Lea and Febiger, 1978); James A. Michener, *Sports in America* (New York: Random House, 1976); Benjamin G. Rader, *American Sports: From the Age of Folk Games to the Age of Televised Sports* (Englewood Cliffs, NJ: Prentice Hall, 1983; 6th edn, 2009); Douglas Noverr and Lawrence E. Ziewacz, *The Games They Played: Sports in American History* (Chicago: Nelson-Hall, 1988); Elliott J. Gorn and Warren Jay Goldstein, *A Brief History of American Sports* (New York: Hill and Wang, 1993); and Steven A. Riess, *Major Problems in American Sport History* (Boston: Houghton Mifflin, 1997). Three authors provide a global perspective on

the history of sports: Richard D. Mandell, *Sport: A Cultural History* (New York: Columbia University Press, 1984); William J. Baker, *Sports in the Western World* (Totawa, NJ: Rowman and Littlefield, 1982); and Allen Guttmann, *Sports: The First Five Millennia* (Amherst, MA: University of Massachusetts Press, 2004). Students might begin their study of the phenomenon of American sports with Michael Mandelbaum's thought-provoking *The Meaning of Sports: Why Americans Watch Baseball, Football, and Basketball and What They See When They Do* (New York: Public Affairs, 2004).

3 Warren Goldstein, *Playing for Keeps: A History of Early Baseball* (Ithaca, NY: Cornell University Press, 1989); Goldstein, "Thirty Years of Baseball History: A Player's Notes," *Reviews in American History* (December, 2010), pp. 759–70.

4 Elliott J. Gorn and Michael Oriard, "Taking Sports Seriously," *Chronicle of Higher Education* (March 24, 1995).

1 The Emergence of Organized Sports, 1607–1860

1 Bruce C. Daniels, *Puritans at Play: Leisure and Recreation in Colonial New England* (New York: St Martin's, 1995).

Sports in American Life: A History, Second Edition. Richard O. Davies.
© 2012 John Wiley & Sons, Inc. Published 2012 by John Wiley & Sons, Inc.

2 Ibid., pp. 168–9.

3 T. H. Breen, "Horses and Gentlemen: The Cultural Significance of Gambling Among the Gentry of Virginia," *William and Mary Quarterly* (1977), pp. 239–57.

4 Ibid., pp. 242–7.

5 For a useful summary of the Southern sporting life, see Elliott Gorn and Warren Goldstein, *A Brief History of American Sports* (New York: Hill and Wang, 1993), pp. 17–30; see also Nancy L. Struna, *People of Prowess: Sport, Leisure, and Labor in Early Anglo-America* (Urbana, IL: University of Illinois Press, 1996), pp. 96–164.

6 Gorn and Goldstein, pp. 17–37.

7 Breen, p. 245.

8 Ibid., pp. 241–54.

9 Ibid., p. 251.

10 Elliott J. Gorn, "'Gouge and Bite, Pull Hair and Scratch': The Social Significance of Fighting in the Southern Back Country," *American Historical Review* (February, 1985), pp. 18–43, citation pp. 21–2.

11 For a detailed analysis of the important social role taverns played in colonial America see Struna, pp. 143–64.

12 Gorn, p. 42.

13 Ibid., p. 20.

14 Struna, p. 163.

15 Gorn and Goldstein, pp. 53–4.

16 Melvin L. Adelman, *A Sporting Time: New York City and the Rise of Modern Athletics, 1820–70* (Urbana, IL: University of Illinois Press, 1986), pp. 42–3.

17 "Rules and Regulations Approved and Adopted by the New York Jockey Club" (September 13, 1842), *American Periodicals Online, 1740–1900,* pp. 586–92.

18 Gorn and Goldstein, p. 54.

19 Adelman, pp. 34–8.

20 Ibid., pp. 43–4.

21 Peter Levine, *American Sport: A Documentary History* (Englewood Cliffs, NJ: Prentice-Hall, 1989), pp. 18–26.

22 Dwight Akers, *Riders Up: The Story of American Harness Racing* (New York: Putnam, 1938), p. 30.

23 Akers, p. 93.

24 Adelman, pp. 55–73.

25 Adelman, p. 61; Akers, pp. 30–2.

26 Gorn and Goldstein, p. 77.

27 Akers, pp. 48–53.

28 Steven Riess, *City Games: The Evolution of American Urban Society and the Rise of Sports* (Urbana, IL: University of Illinois Press, 1989), p. 40; A. D. Turnbull, *John Stevens* (New York: Century, 1928), p. 510; Adelman, p. 212.

29 Adelman, pp. 213–14.

30 Ibid., pp. 214–20.

31 Ibid., pp. 189–93.

32 Ibid., pp. 192–7.

33 Ibid., pp. 197–8.

34 John Dizikes, *Sportsmen and Gamesmen* (Boston: Houghton Mifflin, 1981), p. 106.

35 Dizikes, pp. 106–10; Adelman, p. 212.

36 Dizikes, pp. 114.

37 Ibid., p. 117.

38 Elliott J. Gorn, *The Manly Art: Bare-Knuckle Prize Fighting in America* (Ithaca, NY: Cornell University Press, 1986), pp. 60–4.

39 Ibid., p. 77.

40 Ibid., pp. 71–81.

41 Ibid., p. 79.

42 Ibid., pp. 81–97; Adelman, pp. 231–2.

43 Jon Sternglass, *First Resorts: Pursuing Pleasure at Saratoga Springs, Newport and Coney Island* (Baltimore: Johns Hopkins University Press, 2001), pp. 147–55.

44 David Block, *Baseball Before We Knew It: A Search for the Roots of the Game* (Lincoln, NE: University of Nebraska Press, 2005), p. 161. See also Harold Seymour, *Baseball: The Early Years* (New York: Oxford University Press, 1960), pp. 8–11; Albert Spalding, *America's National Game* (New York: American Sports, 1911), pp. 19–26. For the most detailed and authoritative examination of the early history of baseball, see John Thorn, *Baseball in the Garden of Eden: The Secret History of the Early Game* (New York: Simon and Schuster, 2011).

45 John P. Rossi, *The National Game: Baseball and American Culture* (Chicago: Dee, 2000), pp. 5–7; Geroge B. Kirsch, *Baseball and Cricket: The Creation of American Team Sports, 1838–72* (Urbana, IL: University of Illinois Press, 1989), pp. 58–73.

46 Seymour, pp. 15–20; David Q. Voigt, *American Baseball: From the Commissioners to Continental Expansion* (Norman, OK: University of Oklahoma Press, 1970), pp. 15–17.

47 Seymour, pp. 15–20; Benjamin Rader, *Baseball: A History of America's Game* (Urbana, IL: University of Illinois Press, 1992), pp. 58–73.

48 Rossi, pp. 3–10.

49 Melvin J. Adelman, "The Early Years of Baseball," in S. W. Pope, ed., *The New American Sports History* (Urbana, IL: University of Illinois Press, 1997), pp. 58–87.

2 Baseball: "This Noble and Envigorating Game"

1   Kenneth S. Robson, ed., *A Great and Glorious Game: Baseball Writings of A. Bartlett Giamatti* (Chapel Hill, NC: Algonquin, 1998), p. 7.

2   Edward Pessen, "Life, Baseball, and the Intellectuals," *Reviews in American History* (March, 1992), pp. 111–16, citation p. 112; Charles C. Alexander, *Our Game: An American Baseball History* (New York: Holt, 1991), pp. 3, 112.

3   Harold Seymour, *Baseball: The Early Years* (New York: Oxford University Press, 1960), pp. 8–11; Albert Spalding, *America's National Game* (New York: American Sports, 1911), pp. 19–26.

4   Alexander, pp. 11–12.

5   David Q. Voigt, *American Baseball: From the Commissioners to Continental Expansion* (Norman, OK: University of Oklahoma Press, 1970), pp. 15–17; Steve Gelder, "Their Hands Are All Playing: Business and Amateur Baseball, 1845–1917," *Journal of Sport History* (spring, 1984), pp. 5–27.

6   Joseph Amato, *The Decline of Rural Minnesota* (Marshall, MN: Crossings, 1960), pp. 49–55; Lewis Atherton, *Main Street on the Middle Border* (Bloomington, IN: Indiana University Press, 1954), pp. 200–2.

7   Allen Guttmann, *From Ritual to Record: The Nature of Modern Sports* (New York: Columbia University Press, 1978), pp. 96–7.

8   Melvin Adelman, *A Sporting Time: New York City and the Rise of Modern Athletics, 1820–70* (Urbana, IL: University of Illinois Press, 1986), pp. 165–6.

9   Alexander, p. 14; Adelman, pp. 170–2; John P. Rossi, *The National Game: Baseball and American Culture* (Chicago: Dee, 2000), pp. 15–17; Seymour, pp. 56–8.

10 Benjamin Rader, *Baseball: A History of America's Game* (Urbana, IL: University of Illinois Press, 1989), pp. 25–8; Alexander, p. 19.

11 Seymour, p. 58.

12 Ibid., pp. 56–8; Alexander, p. 23.

13 Alexander, p. 23.

14 Seymour, p. 61.

15 Jules Tygiel, *Past Time: Baseball as History* (New York: Oxford University Press, 2000), p. 17.

16 Alexander, p. 10.

17 Tygiel, pp. 18–19.

18 Ibid., p. 23.

19 Ibid., p. 23.

20 Ibid., p. 19.

21 Adelman, pp. 175–6; Tygiel, pp. 15–34.

22 Warren Jay Goldstein, *Playing for Keeps: A History of Early Baseball* (Ithaca, NY: Cornell University Press, 1989), pp. 35–7.

23 Rader, pp. 18–20; Ian Tyrrell, "The Emergence of Modern American Baseball, 1850–80," in Richard Cashman and Michael McKernan, eds, *Sports in History* (Brisbane: University of Queensland Press, 1979), pp. 205–26, citation p. 219.

24 Richard O. Davies and Richard G. Abram, *Betting the Line: Sports Wagering in American Life* (Columbus, OH: Ohio State University Press, 2001), pp. 18–20; Rader, pp. 19–20.

25 Alexander, pp. 18–21; Rader, pp. 26–8.

26 Tyrrell, p. 222.

27 Stephen Freedman, "The Baseball Fad in Chicago, 1865–1870," *Journal of Sport History* (summer, 1978), pp. 42–64.

28 Rader, p. 29.

29 S. W. Pope, ed., *The New American Sports History* (Urbana, IL: University of Illinois Press, 1997), pp. 64–5; Rader, p. 43.

30 J. E. Findling, "The Louisville Grays' Scandal of 1877," *Journal of Sport History* (summer, 1976), pp. 176–87.

31 R. Jake Sudderth, "Albert Goodwill Spalding," in Arnold Markoe, ed., *Scribner Encyclopedia of American Lives: Sports Figures* (New York: Scribner, 2002), vol. 2, pp. 382–4.

32 Alexander, pp. 34–45; Rader, pp. 41–55.

33 Ronnie D. Lankford, Jr, "Michael Joseph 'King' Kelly," in *Scribner Encyclopedia*, vol. 1, pp. 509–11.

34 Alexander, p. 47.

35 Rader, pp. 32–4; Alexander, pp. 48–9.

36 Seymour, pp. 135–88; Rader, pp. 47–52.

37 Alexander, pp. 36–58.

38 Alexander, pp. 49–52; Rader, pp. 51–2.

39 Seymour, pp. 334–5; Rossi, pp. 34–5; Alexander, pp. 49–52.

40 Seymour, pp. 221–39; Alexander, pp. 53–8.

41 Spalding, p. 280.

42 Ibid., p. 281.

43 Seymour, p. viii.

3   The Formative Years of College Football

1   Michael Oriard, *Reading Football: How the Popular Press Created an American Spectacle* (Chapel Hill, NC: University of North Carolina Press, 1993), pp. 44–5.

2   Oriard, pp. 45–6; John Stuart Martin, "Walter Camp and His Gridiron Game," *American Heritage* (October, 1961), pp. 50–5; Elliott J. Gorn and Warren Jay Goldstein, *A Brief History of American Sports* (New York: Hill and Wang, 1993), pp. 154–62.

3   John Sayle Watterson, *College Football: History, Spectacle, Controversy* (Baltimore: Johns Hopkins University Press, 2000), pp. 18–25.

4   Martin, pp. 77–9.

5   Oriard, pp. 25–56.

6   Scott A. McQuilkin and Ronald A. Smith, "The Rise and Fall of the Flying Wedge," *Journal of Sport History* (spring, 1993), pp. 57–64, citation p. 59.

7   Ronald A. Smith, *Sports and Freedom: The Rise of Big-Time College Athletics* (New York: Oxford University Press, 1988), pp. 88–98; Watterson, pp. 13–14.

8   Watterson, pp. 58–60.

9   Robin Lester, *Stagg's University: The Rise, Decline, and Fall of Big-Time Football at Chicago* (Urbana, IL: University of Chicago Press, 1995), p. 2; Watterson, p. 114.

10 Watterson, pp. 27–63.

11 Ibid., pp. 28, 36.

12 Lester, pp. 7–14.

13 Ibid., pp. 18–19.

14 Ibid., p. 26.

15 John U. Bacon, "Fielding Yost and Building a Sports Empire," *Michigan History Magazine* (September, 2000), pp. 29–33.

16 Lester, pp. 125–63.

17 Oriard, pp. 57–8.

18 Murray Sperber, *Shake Down the Thunder: The Creation of Notre Dame Football* (New York: Holt, 1993), p. 23.

19 University of Missouri Alumni Affairs Office.

20 Sperber, pp. 79–81.

21 Martin, p. 51.

22 W. Bruce Leslie, *Gentlemen and Scholars: College and Community in the Age of the University* (Pennsylvania State University Press, 1992), p. 109.

23 "President Eliot's Report," *Harvard Graduate Magazine* (1895), p. 869.

24 Ibid., p. 869.

25 Watterson, pp. 27–9.

26 Ibid., p. 28.

27 Ibid., pp. 27–9.

28 Lester, p. 65.

29 Watterson, pp. 64–9.

30 Ibid., pp. 68–74; H. W. Brands, *T. R. The Last Romantic* (New York: Basic, 1997), p. 553.

31 Watterson, pp. 68–74; Brands, p. 553.

32 Watterson, p. 72.

33 Ibid., p. 79; "Athletic Leader Will Be Missed," *New York Times* (September 1, 1912).

34 Watterson, pp. 120–40.

35 Sally Jenkins, *The Real All-Americans; The Team that Changed a Game, A People, a Nation* (New York: Doubleday, 2007), pp. 1–7, 280–6; Bill Crawford, *All American: The Rise and Fall of Jim Thorpe* (New York: Wiley, 2005), p. 188.

36 Sperber, pp. 37–40.

4   The Modernization of American Sports, 1865–1920

1   Frank Luther Mott, *A History of American Magazines* (Cambridge, MA: Harvard University Press, 1938), pp. 331–7.

2   Gene Smith, "A Little Visit to the Lower Depths via the *National Police Gazette*," *American Heritage* (October, 1972), pp. 65–73.

3   Guy Reed, "Richard Fox, John L. Sullivan, and the Rise of Modern American Prizefighting," *Journalism History* (summer, 2001), pp. 73–86.

4   Michael T. Isenberg, *John L. Sullivan and His America* (University of Illinois Press, 1988), pp. 102–13; James A. Cox, "The Great Fight: 'Mr. Jake' vs. John L. Sullivan," *Smithsonian* (December, 1984), pp. 153–68, citation p. 158.

5   Cox.

6   Isenberg, pp. 271–80; Cox, pp. 164–6.

7   Jeffrey T. Sammons, *Beyond the Ring: The Role of Boxing in American Society* (Urbana, IL: University of Illinois Press, 1988), pp. 10–12; Isenberg, pp. 276–9.

8   Isenberg, pp. 281–99.

9   Elliott J. Gorn, *The Manly Art: Bare-Knuckle Fighting in America* (Ithaca, NY: Cornell University Press, 1986), pp. 238–47; Arnold Fields, *James L. Corbett* (Jefferson, NC: McFarland, 2001), pp. 53–63.

10 *New York Times* (November 12, 1922), p. 19.

11 James M. Mayo, *The American Country Club: Its Origins and Development* (New Brunswick, NJ: Rutgers University Press, 1998), pp. 7–13.

12 Bob Considine and F. R. Jarvis, *The First One Hundred Years: A Portrait of the NYAC* (New York: Macmillan, 1969).

13 Quoted in *Sports Illustrated* (Fiftieth Anniversary Insert, July 14, 2003); see also Elliott J. Gorn and Warren Goldstein, *A Brief History of American Sports* (New York: Hill and Wang, 1993), pp. 135–7.

14 Benjamin G. Rader, *American Sports: From the Age of Folk Games to the Age of Televised Sports* (Upper Saddle River, NJ: Prentice Hall, 2004), p. 79.

15 Mayo, pp. 63–4.

16 Ibid., p. 85.

17 Robert J. Moss, *Golf and the American Country Club* (Urbana, IL: University of Illinois Press, 2001), p. 3.

18 Mayo, pp. 83–4.

19 Ibid., p. 85.

20 John Levi Cutler, *Gilbert Patten and his Frank Merriwell Saga* (Orono, ME: University of Maine Press, 1934).

21 Gail Bederman, *Manliness and Civilization: A Cultural History of Gender and Race in the United States, 1880–1917* (Chicago: University of Chicago Press, 1995), pp. 14, 84–8.

22 Gorn and Goldstein, p. 90.

23 Thomas W. Higginson, "Saints and Their Bodies," in Steven Riess, ed., *Major Problems in American Sport History* (Boston: Houghton Mifflin, 1997), pp. 82–95; Gorn and Goldstein, p. 91.

24 Clifford Putney, *Muscular Christianity: Manhood and Sports in Protestant America, 1880–1920* (Cambridge, MA: Harvard University Press, 2001), pp. 64–72.

25 Ibid., pp. 153–61.

26 Ibid., pp. 9–126.

27 Roosevelt to Camp, March 11, 1895, in H. W. Brands, ed., *The Selected Letters of Theodore Roosevelt* (New York: Cooper Square, 2001), p. 99.

28 Theodore Roosevelt, "Value of an Athletic Training," *Harper's Weekly* 37 (December 23, 1893), quoted in Gorn and Goldstein, p. 146.

29 "The American Boy," in *The Strenuous Life: Essays and Addresses* (New York: Century, 1902), pp. 155–64.

30 Joseph B. Oxendine, *American Indian Sports Heritage* (Champaign, IL: Human Kinetics, 1988), pp. 203–37; Bill Crawford, *All American: The Rise and Fall of Jim Thorpe* (New York: Wiley, 2005); Robert W. Wheeler, *Jim Thorpe: The World's Greatest Athlete* (Norman, OK: University of Oklahoma Press, 1979).

31 Kate Buford, "Jim Thorpe," in Arnold Markoe, ed., *Scribner Encyclopedia of American Lives: Sports Figures* (Scribner, 2002), vol. 2, p. 428.

32 Crawford, p. 204.

33 Grace Naismith, "Father Basketball," *Sports Illustrated* (January 31, 1955), p. 65.

34 John Devaney, *The Story of Basketball* (New York: Random House, 1976), p. 12.

35 Alexander Wolff, "The Olden Rules," *Sports Illustrated* (November 25, 2003), insert; Keith Myerscough, "The Game with No Name," *International Journal of History of Sport* (April, 1995), pp. 137–52.

36 Mike Douchant, *Encyclopedia of College Basketball* (New York: Gale, 1995), p. 5.

37 Gorn and Goldstein, pp. 169–77.

5   Baseball Ascendant, 1890–1930

1   Charles C. Alexander, *Our Game: An American Baseball History* (New York: Holt, 1991), pp. 58–83; Benjamin G. Rader, *Baseball: A History of America's Game* (Urbana, IL: University of Illinois Press, 1992), pp. 61–9; John P. Rossi, *The National Game: Baseball and American Culture* (Chicago: Dee, 2000), pp. 51–8; Charles C. Alexander, *John McGraw* (Lincoln, NE: University of Nebraska Press, 1988), pp. 32–81.

2   Harold Seymour, *Baseball: The Early Years* (New York: Oxford University Press, 1960), p. 290.

3   Rossi, pp. 56–7; Alexander, *Our Game*, pp. 68–9; Eugene C. Murdock, *Ban Johnson: Czar of Baseball* (Westport, CT: Greenwood, 1982), pp. 26–7.

4   Rossi, p. 57.

5   Murdock, pp. 18–48.

6   Alexander, *Our Game*, pp. 76–83; Murdock, pp. 43–66.

7   Harold Seymour, *Baseball: The Golden Age* (New York: Oxford University Press, 1971), pp. 8–14; Alexander, *Our Game*, pp. 76–83; Murdock, pp. 43–66.

8   Rader, pp. 70–81; Seymour, *The Early Years*, pp. 307–24.

9   Louis P. Masur, *Autumn Glory: Baseball's First World Series* (New York: Hill and Wang, 2003), p. 220.

10 Murdock, pp. 82–98.

11 Frank Deford, *The Old Ball Game: How John McGraw, Christy Mathewson, and the New York Giants Created Modern Baseball* (New York: Grove, 2005), p. 122.

12 Reed Browning, *Cy Young: A Baseball Life* (Amherst, MA: University of Massachusetts Press, 2000).

13 Ty Cobb, *My Life in Baseball: The True Record* (Lincoln, NE: University of Nebraska Press, 1993), p. 65.

14 Charles C. Alexander, *Ty Cobb* (New York: Oxford University Press, 1984), pp. 5, 240.

15 Seymour, *The Early Years*, p. 290.

16 Frank Deford, "Giants Among Men," *Sports Illustrated* (August 25, 2003), p. 61.

17 Alexander, *John McGraw*, pp. 7–8.

18 Rossi, pp. 61–8; Connie Mack, *My 66 Years in the Big Leagues* (Philadephia: Winston, 1950).

19 William C. Kashatus, "Connie Mack," in Arnold Markoe, ed., *Scribner Encyclopedia of American Lives: Sports Figures* (New York: Scribner, 2002), vol. 2, p. 90.

20 Jules Tygiel, *Past Time: Baseball as History* (New York: Oxford University Press, 2000), pp. 35–63; Rader, pp. 90–1.

21 Rader, p. 101.

22 Murdock, pp. 108–18; Alexander, *Our Game*, pp. 102–7; Seymour, *The Golden Age*, pp. 169–234.

23 Alexander, *Our Game*, pp. 102–7; Murdock, p. 118.

24 Rader, pp. 110–11; Alexander, *Our Game*, p. 135.

25 Seymour, *The Golden Age*, pp. 235–55; Murdock, pp. 119–31.

26 Rader, pp. 102–3; Alexander, *Our Game*, pp. 108–13.

27 Much has been written about the 1919 World Series and its aftermath. The best source is Eliot Asinof, *Eight Men Out: The Black Sox and the 1919 World Series* (New York: Holt, 1987). See also the detailed narrative in Seymour, *The Golden Age*, pp. 274–310, and the concise summary by Alexander in *Our Game*, pp. 115–29. For a perspective from the business of sports gambling, see Richard O. Davies and Richard G. Abram, *Betting the Line: Sports Wagering in American Life* (Columbus, OH: Ohio State University Press, 2001), pp. 18–28.

28 Murdock, pp. 188–9.

29 Alexander, *Our Game*, p. 124; Seymour, *The Golden Age*, p. 293.

30 Alexander, p. 124.

31 Leo Katcher, *The Big Bankroll: The Life and Times of Arnold Rothstein* (New York: Da Capo, 1994), pp. 144–5.

32 Seymour, *The Golden Age*, p. 330.

33 The best biographies of Ruth are Robert Creamer, *Babe: The Legend Comes to Life* (New York: Simon and Schuster, 1974), and Marshall Smelser, *The Life that Ruth Built* (Lincoln, NE: University of Nebraska Press, 1975).

34 Dan Shaughnessy, *The Curse of the Bambino* (New York: Dutton, 1990).

35 Creamer, p. 273.

36 Tygiel, p. 85.

37 Smelser, pp. 366–7.

38 Creamer, p. 440.

39 Ibid., p. 397.

40 Lee Lowenfish, *Branch Rickey: Baseball's Ferocious Gentleman* (Lincoln, NE: University of Nebraska Press, 2007); Murray Polner, *Branch Rickey: A Biography* (New York: Atheneum, 1982); Tygiel, pp. 87–115.

41 Tygiel, p. 94.

42 Alexander, *Our Game*, pp. 143–5; Tygiel, pp. 93–4.

43 Murdock, p. 207.

44 Seymour, *The Golden Age*, p. 460.

6   Playing Nice: Women and Sports, 1860–1945

1   Dudley A. Sargent, "Are Athletics Making Girls Masculine? A Practical Answer to a Question Every Girl Asks," *Ladies' Home Journal* (March 12, 1912), in Jean O'Reilly and Susan K. Cahn, eds, *Women and Sports in the United States: A Documentary Reader* (Boston: Northeastern University Press, 2007), pp. 56–9.

2   Catharine Beecher, "Letters to the People on Health and Happiness," in Steven A. Riess, ed., *Major Problems in American Sport History* (Boston: Houghton Mifflin, 1987), p. 172.

3   Clifford Putney, *Muscular Christianity: Manhood and Sports in Protestant America, 1880–1920* (Cambridge, MA: Harvard University Press, 2001) pp. 64–72.

4   Ibid., pp. 153–61.

5   Susan K. Cahn, *Coming on Strong: Gender and Sexuality in Twentieth-Century Women's Sports* (New York: Free, 1994), p. 7.

6 Frances E. Willard, *A Wheel within a Wheel: How I Learned to Ride the Bicycle* (New York: Revel, 1895), pp. 54–5. Susan B. Anthony is quoted in Willard.

7 Patricia Marks, *Bicycles, Bangs, and Bloomers: The New Woman in the Popular Press* (Lexington, KY: University Press of Kentucky, 1990), p. 193.

8 Richard O. Davies, *Main Street Blues: The Decline of Small-Town America* (Columbus, OH: Ohio State University Press, 1998), p. 110.

9 Senda Berenson, *Basketball for Women* (New York: American Sports, 1903), pp. 36–9.

10 Agnes Rogers, "The Undimmed Appeal of the Gibson Girl," *American Heritage* (December, 1957), pp. 80–98; Frederick Platt, "The Gibson Girl," *Art and Antiques* (November, 1981), pp. 112–17.

11 Elliott J. Gorn and Warren Goldstein, *A Brief History of American Sports* (New York: Hill and Wang, 1993), p. 146.

12 Ibid., p. 146.

13 Allen Guttmann, *Women's Sports: A History* (New York: Columbia University Press, 1991), pp. 135–42.

14 Ina Gittings, "Why Cramp Competition?" *Journal of Health and Physical Education* (January, 1931), pp. 10–12, 54, citation p. 10.

15 Ibid., p. 54.

16 Cahn, pp. 32–6; Will Grimsley, *Tennis: Its History, People and Events* (Englewood Cliffs, NJ: Prentice-Hall, 1971), pp. 140–50.

17 Joseph Severo, "Obituary of Gertrude Ederle," *New York Times* (December 1, 2003), p. A23.

18 Ibid.

19 Cahn, pp. 32–3.

20 Susan E. Cayleff, *Babe: The Life and Legend of "Babe" Didrikson Zaharias* (Urbana, IL: University of Illinois Press, 1995), p. 81; Gene Schoor, *Babe Didrikson: The World's Greatest Woman Athlete* (Garden City, NY: Doubleday, 1978); William O. Johnson and Nancy P. Williamson, *"Whatta-Gal": The Babe Didrikson Story* (Boston: Little, Brown, 1977).

21 Cayleff, p. 88; Schoor, p. 96.

22 Cahn, p. 216.

23 Ibid.

24 Cindy Himes, "The Female Athlete in America, 1860–1940" (PhD dissertation, University of Pennsylvania, 1986), quoted in Cayleff, p. 261.

25 Gai Ingham Berlage, *Women in Baseball: The Forgotten History* (Westport, CT: Praeger, 1994), Susan E. Johnson, *When Women Played Hardball* (Seattle: Seal, 1994); Jennifer Ring, *Stolen Bases: Why American Girls Don't Play Baseball* (Urbana, IL: University of Illinois Press, 2009).

26 Susan Cahn, "No Freaks, No Amazons, No Boyish Bobs," *Chicago History Magazine* (spring, 1989), p. 30.

7 "An Evil To Be Endured": Sports on Campus, 1920–1950

1 Walter Byers, *Unsportsmanlike Conduct: Exploiting College Athletes* (Ann Arbor, MI: University of Michigan Press, 1995), pp. 44–5.

2 Andrew Zimbalist, *Unpaid Professionals: Commercialism and Conflict in Big-Time College Sports* (Princeton, NJ: Princeton University Press, 1999), p. 3.

3 Robin Lester, *Stagg's University: The Rise of Big-Time College Athletics* (Urbana, IL: University of Illinois Press, 1995), p. 191.

4 Ronald A. Smith, *Sports and Freedom: The Rise of Big-Time College Athletics* (New York: Oxford University Press, 1988), pp. 172–4.

5 Smith, p. 157.

6 Andrew Miracle and C. Roger Rees, *Lessons of the Locker Room: The Myth of School Sports* (Amherst, NY: Prometheus, 1994), pp. 29–55.

7 John Sayle Watterson, *College Football: History, Spectacle, Controversy* (Baltimore: Johns Hopkins University Press, 2000), p. 157.

8 Watterson, p. 15.

9 Lester, pp. 128–31.

10 Red Grange and Ira Morton, *The Red Grange Story: An Autobiography* (Urbana, IL: University of Illinois Press, 1993).

11 Watterson, pp. 152–5.

12 Charles Fountain, *Sportswriter: The Life and Times of Grantland Rice* (New York: Oxford University Press, 1993), p. 209.

13 Watterson, p. 154.

14 Murray Sperber, *Shake Down the Thunder: The Creation of Notre Dame Football* (New York: Holt, 1993), p. 185.

15 Ray Robinson, *Rockne of Notre Dame: The Making of a Football Legend* (New York: Oxford University Press, 1999), pp. 39–48; Sperber, pp. 37–42.

16 Robinson, p. 62.

17 Sperber, pp. 105–13.

18 John A. Lucas and Ronald A. Smith, *Saga of American Sport* (Philadelphia: Lea and Febiger, 1978), p. 316.

19 Sperber, p. 182.

20 Ibid., pp. 182–8.

21 John R. Thelin, *Games Colleges Play: Scandal and Reform in Intercollegiate Athletics* (Baltimore: Johns Hopkins University Press, 1994), pp. 90–6.

22 Elliott J. Gorn and Warren Jay Goldstein, *A Brief History of American Sports* (New York: Hill and Wang, 1993), p. 232.

23 Watterson, p. 161.

24 Ibid., pp. 161–2.

25 Howard J. Savage, *American College Athletics* (New York: Carnegie Foundation, 1929); Watterson, p. 165; Gorn and Goldstein, p. 232.

26 Thelin, p. 94.

27 Murray Sperber, *Onward to Victory: The Crises That Shaped College Sports* (New York: Holt, 1998), pp. 285–6.

28 Sperber, *Onward to Victory*, p. 286.

29 Sperber, *Onward to Victory*, pp. 294–326; Richard O. Davies, *America's Obsession: Sports and Society since 1945* (Fort Worth, TX: Harcourt Brace, 1994), pp. 18–27.

30 Richard O. Davies and Richard G. Abram, *Betting the Line: Sports Wagering in American Life* (Columbus, OH: Ohio State University Press, 2001), pp. 51–60; Charles Rosen, *The Scandals of '51: How the Gamblers Killed College Basketball* (New York: Seven Stories, 1999), p. 26; Sperber, *Onward to Victory*, pp. 286–7.

31 Davies, pp. 24–5.

32 *New York Times* (March 29, 1996), p. B-22.

33 Clair Bee, "I Know Now Why They Sold Out to Gamblers," *Saturday Evening Post* (February 2, 1952), pp. 26–7; Davies, p. 22.

8 Sports in an Age of Ballyhoo, Depression, and War, 1920–1945

1 John Roberts Tunis, "Changing Trends in Sports," *Harper's Magazine* (December, 1934), pp. 75–86.

2 Mark Inabinett, *Grantland Rice and His Heroes: The Sportswriter as Mythmaker in the 1920s* (Knoxville, TN: University of Tennessee Press, 1994), p. 14.

3 Inabinett, p. 3.

4 Lynn Dumenil, *The Modern Temper: American Culture and Society during the 1920s* (New York: Hill and Wang, 1995), p. 78; Murray Sperber, *Onward to Victory: The Crises that Shaped College Sports* (New York: Holt, 1998), p. 30.

5 Inabinett, p. 2.

6 Ibid., p. 42.

7 Tony Silvia, *Baseball over the Air: The National Pastime on the Radio and in the Imagination* (Jefferson, NC: McFarland, 2007), provides a comprehensive survey of the impact of radio upon baseball; Ronald A. Smith, *Play-by-Play: Radio, Television, and Big-Time College Sport* (Baltimore: Johns Hopkins University Press, 2001), pp. 25, 42–6; Charles Fountain, *Sportswriter: The Life and Times of Grantland Rice* (New York: Oxford University Press, 1993), pp. 195–6.

8 Smith, pp. 24–8.

9 Herbert Warren Wind, *The Story of American Golf: Its Champions and Championships* (New York: Knopf, 1975), pp. 70–82.

10 Ibid., pp. 118–32.

11 Ibid., pp. 133–64.

12 Inabinett, p. 57.

13 Ibid., p. 61.

14 Frank Deford, *Big Bill Tilden: The Triumphs and the Tragedy* (New York: Simon and Schuster, 1976), pp. 13–58; Al Silverman, *Sports Titans of the Twentieth Century* (New York: Putnam, 1968), pp. 136–53; Inabinett, pp. 63–73.

15 Deford, pp. 17–18.

16 Charles Samuels, *The Magnificent Rube: The Life and Gaudy Times of Tex Rickard* (New York: McGraw-Hill, 1957).

17 Randy Roberts, *Jack Dempsey: The Manassa Mauler* (Baton Rouge, LA: Louisiana State University Press, 1979).

18 Ibid., p. 189.

19 Ibid., p. 143.

20 William Nack, "The Long Count," *Sports Illustrated* (September 22, 1997), pp. 72–84; Roberts, pp. 212–35.

21 Nack, p. 23.

22 This section relies heavily upon Charles C. Alexander, *Breaking the Slump: Baseball in the Depression Era* (New York: Columbia University Press, 2002). Also useful are John P. Rossi, *The National Game: Baseball and American Culture* (Chicago: Dee, 2000), pp. 21–44, and Benjamin G. Rader, *Baseball: A History*

of America's Game (Urbana, IL: University of Illinois Press, 1992), pp. 136–41.

23 Alexander, p. 89.

24 Lynn Hoogenboom, "Jay Hanna 'Dizzy' Dean," in Arnold Markoe, ed., *Scribner Encyclopedia of American Lives: Sports Figures* (New York: Scribner, 2002), vol. 1, p. 221.

25 Alexander, pp. 94–6.

26 Ibid., p. 183.

27 Lou Cannon, *Governor Reagan: His Rise to Power* (New York: Public Affairs Press, 2003), p. 45; for a detailed analysis of the art of recreation of games by radio announcers, see the intriguing discussion in Silvia, pp. 35–55.

28 Alexander, p. 101.

29 Ibid., p. 271.

30 See Richard Ben Cramer, *Joe DiMaggio: The Hero's Life* (New York: Simon and Schuster, 2000), and Leigh Montville, *Ted Williams: Biography of an American Hero* (New York: Broadway, 2004). Novelist John Updike happened to attend Williams's final game in 1960 and recounted that day in a classic essay, "Hub Fans Bid Kid Adieu," *New Yorker* (October 16, 1060).

31 Alexander, p. 271.

32 Laura Hillenbrand, *Seabiscuit: An American Legend* (New York: Random House, 2001).

33 Ibid., p. 93.

34 Ibid., p. 324.

35 Rossi, p. 142.

9 America's Great Dilemma

1 Gunnar Myrdal, *An American Dilemma: The Negro Problem and Modern Democracy* (New York: Harper & Row, 1944).

2 Michael E. Lomax, "Black Entrepreneurship in the National Pastime," in Patrick B. Miller and David K. Wiggins, eds, *Sport and the Color Line: Black Athletes and Race Relations in Twentieth-Century America* (New York: Routledge, 2004), pp. 24–43.

3 Michael T. Isenberg, *John L. Sullivan and His America* (Urbana, IL: University of Illinois Press, 1988), p. 301; Richard Hoffer, "The Great Black Mark," *Sports Illustrated* (July 5, 2010), p. 14.

4 Randy Roberts, *Papa Jack: Jack Johnson and the Era of White Hopes* (New York: Free, 1983), pp. 3–53.

5 Roberts, p. 18; David K. Wiggins and Patrick B. Miller, eds, *The Unlevel Playing Field: A Documentary History of the African American Experience in Sport* (Urbana, IL: University of Illinois Press, 2003), pp. 58–63.

6 Several popular accounts of the "Fight of the Century" contain excellent photographs and detailed accounts. See: Robert Greenwood, *Jack Johnson vs. James Jeffries: The Prize Fight of the Century* (Reno: Bacon, 2004); Ray Hagar and Guy Clifton, *Johnson–Jeffries: Dateline Reno. The Fight of the Century as Told through the Pages of Reno's Newspapers* (Reno: Reno Gazette Journal, 2010); and Steven Frederick, *The Last Great Prize Fight: Johnson vs. Jeffries* (San Francisco: Creative Commons, 2010).

7 Jeffrey T. Sammons, *Beyond the Ring: The Role of Boxing in American Society* (Urbana, IL: University of Illinois Press, 1988), pp. 34–40; Thomas R. Hietala, *The Fight of the Century: Jack Johnson, Joe Louis, and the Struggle for Racial Equality* (Armonk, NY: Sharpe, 2002), pp. 29–39; Roberts, pp. 54–84.

8 Roberts, pp. 85–101; Hoffer, pp. 14–15.

9 Wiggins and Miller, p. 74.

10 Hietala, p. 46.

11 Jules Tygiel, *Past Time: Baseball as History* (New York: Oxford University Press, 2000), p. 117.

12 Robert Peterson, *Only the Ball Was White: A History of Legendary Black Players and All-Black Professional Teams* (New York: Oxford University Press, 1992); and Neil Lanctot, *Negro League Baseball: The Rise and Ruin of a Black Institution* (Philadelphia: University of Pennsylvania Press, 2004).

13 Eric Enders, "Rube Foster," in Arnold Markoe, ed., *Scribner Encyclopedia of American Lives: Sports Figures* (New York: Scribner, 2002), vol. 1, p. 292.

14 Peterson, pp. 103–15; Enders, pp. 291–3; Charles C. Alexander, *Our Game: An American Baseball History* (New York: Holt, 1991), pp. 151–5; Benjamin G. Rader, *Baseball: A History of America's Game* (Urbana, IL: University of Illinois Press, 1992), pp. 142–50; Wiggins and Miller, pp. 92–5.

15 Charles C. Alexander, *Breaking the Slump: Baseball in the Depression Era* (New York: Columbia University Press, 2002), pp. 204–38.

16 Peterson, pp. 91–5.

17 Larry Tye, *Satchel: The Life and Times of an American Legend* (New York: Random House, 2009); Peterson, pp. 129–49; Alexander, *Breaking the Slump*, pp. 211–38; Wiggins and Miller, pp. 95–8.

18 Alexander, *Our Game*, p. 181; Timothy M. Gay, *Satch, Dizzy, & Rapid Robert: The Wild Saga of Interracial Baseball before Jackie Robinson* (New York: Simon and Schuster, 2010), pp. 4, 105.

19 Lanctot, pp. 365, 395.

20 William J. Baker, *Jesse Owens: An American Life* (New York: Free, 1986).

21 Chris Mead, *Champion: Joe Louis, Black Hero in White America* (New York: Scribner, 1985), p. x.

22 Heitala, pp. 150–90; Joe Louis with Edna and Art Rust, Jr, *Joe Louis: My Life* (New York: Harcourt Brace Jovanovich, 1978). See especially Randy Roberts, *Joe Louis: Hard Times Man* (New Haven, CT: Yale University Press, 2010).

23 Mead, p. 6.

24 Ibid., p. 6.

25 Gerald Astor, *"And a Credit to his Race": The Hard Life and Times of Joseph Louis Barrow, a.k.a. Joe Louis* (New York: Saturday Review Press, 1974).

26 Mead, pp. 128, 134; Lewis Erenberg, *The Greatest Fight of Our Generation: Louis vs. Schmeling* (New York: Oxford University Press, 2006); David Margolick, *Beyond Glory: Joe Louis vs. Max Schmeling, and a World on the Brink* (New York: Knopf, 2005).

27 Mead, p. 295.

28 Arnold Rampersad, *Jackie Robinson: A Biography* (New York: Knopf, 1997), p. 120.

29 Rampersad, p. 120.

30 Jules Tygiel, *Baseball's Great Experiment: Jackie Robinson and His Legacy* (New York: Oxford University Press, 1983), provides the most authoritative account of the role of Branch Rickey and Jackie Robinson in breaking baseball's color line. See also Joseph Dorinson and Joram Warmund, eds, *Jackie Robinson: Race, Sports, and the American Dream* (Armonk, NY: Sharpe, 1998); and John R. M. Wilson, *Jackie Robinson and the American Dilemma* (New York: Longman, 2010).

31 Harvey Frommer, *Rickey and Robinson* (New York: Macmillan, 1982), pp. 80–130.

32 Joseph Dorinson, "Jack Roosevelt Robinson," in *Scribner Encyclopedia*, vol. 2, p. 290.

33 Tygiel, *Past Time*, p. 111.

34 Rampersad, pp. 172–3.

35 Ibid., p. 173.

36 David Halberstam, *October 1964* (New York: Fawcett, 1995), p. 55.

37 Tygiel, *Baseball's Great Experiment*, pp. 285–302.

38 Ibid., p. 302.

39 Will Grimsley, *Tennis: Its History, People and Events* (Englewood Cliffs, NY: Prentice Hall, 1971), p. 165.

40 Ibid., p. 161.

41 Arthur Ashe and Arnold Rampersad, *Days of Grace* (New York: Knopf, 1993).

42 Grimsley, p. 124.

43 *Life*, November 5, 1951.

44 Charles H. Martin, "Racial Change and 'Big-Time' College Football in Georgia: The Age of Segregation, 1892–1957," *Georgia Historical Quarterly* (fall, 1996), pp. 532–62.

45 Martin, "Racial Change," p. 554; see also Martin, "Integrating New Year's Day: The Racial Politics of College Bowl Games in the American South," *Journal of Sport History* (autumn, 1997), pp. 358–77.

46 Charles H. Martin, "The Rise and Fall of Jim Crow in Southern College Sports: The Case of the Atlantic Coast Conference," *North Carolina Historical Review* (July, 1999), pp. 253–84.

47 Charles H. Martin, "Jim Crow in the Gymnasium: The Integration of College Basketball in the American South," *International Journal of the History of Sport* (April, 1993), pp. 68–86.

48 Randy Roberts and James Olson, *Winning Is the Only Thing: Sports in America since 1945* (Baltimore: Johns Hopkins University Press, 1989), p. 45.

49 "Texas Western Tamed Wildcats in NCAA," *New York Times* (March 21, 1966), p. 44; Frank Deford, "Go-Go with Bobby Joe," *Sports Illustrated* (March 28, 1966), pp. 26–9.

10 Television Changes the Image of American Sports

1 Tex Maule, "The Best Football Game Ever Played," *Sports Illustrated* (January 5, 1959), pp. 8–11; John F. Steadman, *The Greatest Football Game Ever Played: When the Baltimore Colts and the New York Giants Faced Sudden Death* (New York: Press Box, 1988); Mark Bowden, *The Best Game Ever: Giants vs. Colts, 1958, and the Birth of the Modern NFL* (New York: Atlantic Monthly Press, 2008), p. 208.

2 Bowden, pp. 1–18; Maule, p. 9; Randy Roberts and James Olson, *Winning Is the Only Thing* (Baltimore: Johns Hopkins University Press, 1989), p. 111; Arthur Daley, "Overtime at the Stadium," *New York Times*

(December 29, 1958), p. 25; Robert W. Peterson, *Pigskin: The Early Years of Pro Football* (New York: Oxford University Press, 1997), pp. 202–3.

3   Phil Patton, *Razzle-Dazzle: The Curious Marriage of Television and Professional Football* (Garden City, NY: Dial, 1984), pp. 7–16.

4   William O. Johnson, Jr, *Super Spectator and the Electric Lilliputians* (Boston: Little, Brown, 1971), pp. 39–46; Benjamin G. Rader, *In Its Own Image: How Television Has Transformed Sport* (New York: Free, 1984), pp. 17–18.

5   Ron Powers, *Supertube: The Rise of Television Sports* (New York: Coward-McCann, 1984), pp. 31–2; Ronald A. Smith, *Play-by-Play: Radio, Television, and Big-Time College Sports* (Baltimore: Johns Hopkins University Press, 2001), p. 51.

6   Rader, p. 79; Charles C. Alexander, *Our Game: An American Baseball History* (New York: Holt, 1991), pp. 222–3; Powers, pp. 70–6.

7   Alexander, pp. 217–45; Rader, pp. 47–64; Neil J. Sullivan, *The Minors: The Struggles and the Triumphs of Baseball's Poor Relation from 1876 to the Present* (New York: St Martin's, 1990), pp. 97–105.

8   Alexander, pp. 216–77.

9   Jeffrey T. Sammons, *Beyond the Ring: The Role of Boxing in American Society* (Urbana, IL: University of Illinois Press, 1988), p. 149; at the same time, professional wrestling enjoyed a brief period of popularity, but the semi-scripted matches soon lost their allure as the viewing audiences became more sophisticated.

10 Arthur Daley, "Is Boxing on the Ropes?" *New York Times Magazine* (January 31, 1954), pp. 19ff; John Lardner, "So You Think You See the Fights on TV!" *Saturday Evening Post* (May 2, 1954), pp. 144–6.

11 Daley, "Is Boxing on the Ropes?" p. 19.

12 Johnson, pp. 91–6; Roberts and Olson, pp. 103–8; Lardner, pp. 145–6; Sammons, p. 150.

13 Daley, "Is Boxing on the Ropes?" p. 22.

14 Sammons, pp. 151–77.

15 Peterson, *Pigskin: The Early Years of Pro Football* (New York: Oxford University Press, 1997), pp. 151–63.

16 Rader, pp. 83–9.

17 Tex Maule, "The Infighting Was Vicious," *Sports Illustrated* (February 8, 1960), pp. 50–2.

18 David Harris, *The League: The Rise and Decline of the NFL* (New York: Bantam, 1986).

19 Johnson, p. 124.

20 Ibid., pp. 125–6.

21 Roberts and Olson, p. 113.

22 Powers, pp. 145–6; Smith, pp. 105–6.

23 Bert Randolph Sugar, *The Thrill of Victory: The Inside Story of ABC Sports* (New York: Hawthorn, 1978), pp. 86–130.

24 Ibid., p. 121.

25 Rader, p. 93; Harris, pp. 16–17.

26 Patton, pp. 113–19; Rader, pp. 96–9.

27 Powers, pp. 182–7; Patton, pp. 105–12.

28 Marc Gunther and Bill Carter, *Monday Night Mayhem: The Inside Story of ABC's Monday Night Football* (New York: Beech Tree, 1988); Howard Cosell with Peter Bonventre, *I Never Played the Game* (New York: Morrow, 1985).

29 Michael Freeman, *ESPN: The Uncensored History* (Dallas: Taylor, 2000), p. 80.

30 "An All-Sports Network," *Newsweek* (November 12, 1979), p. 124; Freeman, p. 80.

31 Bill Rasmussen, *Sports Junkies Rejoice! The Birth of ESPN* (Hartsdale, NY: QV, 1983), pp. 76–82, 122–215; Freeman, pp. 70–95.

32 Richard Sandomir, "Happy Birthday to Us," *New York Times* (September 7, 2004), p. 31.

33 Richard Sandomir, "Disney's ESPN Unit Buying Classics Sports Programmer," *New York Times* (September 4, 1997), p. D7; Freeman, pp. 213–36.

34 Freeman, pp. 111–94; William O. Johnson, "High on Cable," *Sports Illustrated* (August 17, 1981), pp. 28–40; "ESPN's 10-Year Journey to the Top," *New York Times* (September 18, 1989), p. D8.

35 Richard Sandomir, "At ESPN, the Revolution was Televised," *New York Times* (September 7, 1999), p. D1; Freeman, pp. 195–212.

36 Freeman, pp. 269–92.

11   College Sports in the Modern Era

1   Allen L. Sack and Ellen J. Staurowsky, *College Athletes for Hire: The Evolution and Legacy of the NCAA's Amateur Myth* (Westport, CT: Praeger, 1998), pp. 99–100.

2   John Tunis, "Dying for Dear Old Mazuma," *The Outlook* (November 27, 1929), p. 506.

3   Murray Sperber, *College Sports, Inc.: The Athletic Department vs. the University* (New York: Holt, 1990).

4 Walters Byers, *Unsportsmanlike Conduct: Exploiting College Athletes* (Ann Arbor, MI: University of Michigan Press, 1995). For a detailed treatment of the history of the ethical issues involved in big-time college sports, see Ronald A. Smith, *Pay for Play: A History of Big-Time College Athletic Reform* (Urbana, IL: University of Illinois Press, 2011).

5 Gallico, quoted in John Sayle Watterson, *College Football: History, Spectacle, Controversy* (Baltimore: Johns Hopkins University Press, 2000), p. 199; see also Paul Gallico, "Hero Poison," *American Magazine* (November, 1934), pp. 55ff; and "Beware of the Athlete's Head," *Readers Digest* (October, 1936), pp. 11–14; John Tunis, "Whose Game Is It?" *The Outlook* (November 3, 1929), pp. 424–5; "What Price Football?" *American Mercury* (October, 1939), pp. 267–72; and "Dying for Dear Old Mazuma"; Francis Wallace, "This Football Business," *Saturday Evening Post* (September 28, 1929), pp. 10–11ff; and "I Am a Football Fixer," *Saturday Evening Post* (October 31, 1936), pp. 16–17ff; and Sol Metzger, "The Football Fallacy," *Saturday Evening Post* (November 8, 1930), pp. 28–30ff.

6 John R. Thelin, *Games Colleges Play: Scandal and Reform in Intercollegiate Athletics* (Baltimore: Johns Hopkins University Press, 1994), pp. 101–3.

7 Thelin, p. 169; Byers, pp. 69–75.

8 Thelin, pp. 98–154.

9 Byers, p. 61; Don Yeager, *Undue Process: The NCAA's Injustice for All* (Champaign, IL: Sagamore, 1991), p. 13.

10 Ronald A. Smith, *Play-by-Play: Radio, Television, and Big-Time College Sport* (Baltimore: Johns Hopkins University Press, 2001), p. 67.

11 Michael Oriard, *Bowled Over: Big-Time College Football from the Sixties to the BCS Era* (Chapel Hill, NC: University of North Carolina Press, 2009), pp. 133–41.

12 Andrew Zimbalist, *Unpaid Professionals: Commercialism and Conflict in Big-Time College Sports* (Princeton, NJ: Princeton University Press, 1999), pp. 149–72; Murray Sperber, *Beer and Circus: How Big-Time College Sports Is Crippling Undergraduate Education* (New York: Holt, 2000), pp. 71–80.

13 Hayes is the subject of numerous books, all of which follow a familiar pattern of praise tempered by mild criticisms for some of his more notorious excesses. See Robert Vare, *Buckeye: A Study of Coach Woody Hayes and the Ohio State Football Machine* (New York:

Harpers, 1974); Jerry Brondfield, *Woody Hayes and the 100-Yard War* (New York: Random House, 1974); and John Lombardo, *A Fire to Win: The Life and Times of Woody Hayes* (New York: St Martin's Griffin, 2005).

14 Richard O. Davies, *Rivals! The Ten Greatest American Sports Rivalries of the 20th Century* (Malden, MA: Wiley-Blackwell, 2010).

15 Mickey Herskowitz, *The Legend of Bear Bryant* (New York: McGraw-Hill, 1987) is an uncritical biography. More balanced is Keith Dunnavant, *Coach: The Life of Paul "Bear" Bryant* (New York: Simon and Schuster, 1996).

16 Dunnavant, pp. 159–77, is convinced of Bryant's innocence; James Kirby, *Fumble: Bear Bryant, Wally Butts, and the Great College Football Scandal* (New York: Harcourt, 1986), reaches a similar conclusion but says that trial lawyers left important questions unanswered.

17 Sperber.

18 For example, see Thelin, *Games Colleges Play*; Yeager, *Undue Process*; Rick Telander, *The Hundred Yard Lie: The Corruption of College Football and What We Can Do To Stop It* (New York: Simon and Schuster, 1989); Charles Thompson and Allen Sonnenschein, *Down and Dirty: The Life and Crimes of Oklahoma Football* (New York: Carroll and Graff, 1990); David Whitford, *A Payroll to Meet: A Story of Greed, Corruption, and Football at SMU* (New York: Macmillan, 1989); David Wolf, *Foul! The Connie Hawkins Story* (New York: Holt, Rinehart and Winston, 1972); Alexander Wolff and Armen Keteyian, *Raw Recruits: The High Stakes Game Colleges Play to Get their Basketball Stars – And What It Costs to Win* (New York: Pocket, 1990); Richard O. Davies, *America's Obsession: Sports and Society since 1945* (Fort Worth, TX: Harcourt Brace, 1994), p. 203.

19 Yeager, *Undue Process*.

20 Whitford, *A Payroll to Meet*.

21 For different perspectives on Tarkanian, see Richard O. Davies, "Jerry Tarkanian: Nevada's Special Rebel," in Davies, *The Maverick Spirit: Building the New Nevada* (Reno, NV: University of Nevada Press, 1999), pp. 248–70; Byers, pp. 204–11; Jerry Tarkanian and Terry Pluto, *Tark: College Basketball's Winningest Coach* (New York: McGraw-Hill, 1988); and Don Yeager, *Shark Attack: Jerry Tarkanian and His Battle with the NCAA and UNLV* (New York: Harper Collins, 1992).

22 Davies, "Jerry Tarkanian," p. 269.

23 Oriard, p. 141.

24 Zimbalist, pp. 96–7; Smith, *Play-by-Play*, pp. 162–7.

25 Smith, *Play-by-Play*, pp. 162–7.

26 *Report of the Knight Commission*, March, 1991.

27 Arthur Fleisher et al., *The National Collegiate Athletic Association: A Study in Cartel Behavior* (Chicago: University of Chicago Press, 1992), p. 160.

28 Knight Commission, *A Call to Action: Reconnecting College Sports and Higher Education*, June 2001.

29 Ibid.

12 Play for Pay

1 *Time* (August 1, 1969), p. 41.

2 Joe Posnanski, "Modell Doesn't Get It," *Kansas City Star* (January 22, 2001).

3 Ibid.

4 Mark S. Rosentraub, *Major League Losers: The Real Costs and Who's Paying for It* (New York: Basic, 1997), pp. 242–81; Michael N. Danielson, *Home Team: Professional Sports and the American Metropolis* (Princeton, NJ: Princeton University Press, 1997), pp. 3–6.

5 Posnanski.

6 Danielson, pp. 67, 120–5; Dave Anderson, "Twelve Vans to Indianapolis," *New York Times* (March 30, 1984), p. 23.

7 *New York Times* (November 26, 1995), p. F6.

8 Danielson, pp. 105–8.

9 Ibid., p. 110.

10 Neil Sullivan, *The Dodgers Move West* (New York: Oxford University Press, 1987), pp. 20–106; Michael D'Antonio, *Forever Blue: The True Story of Baseball's Most Controversial Owner, and the Dodgers of Brooklyn and Los Angeles* (New York: Riverhead, 2009), pp. 227–53.

11 Sullivan, p. 188.

12 Charles Alexander, *Our Game: An American Baseball History* (New York: Holt, 1991), pp. 246–9.

13 Andrew Zimbalist, *Baseball and Billions: A Probing Look inside the Big Business of Our National Game* (New York: Basic, 1992), pp. 123–46; *New York Times* (May 2, 2004), p. B6; Ken Belson, "As Teams Abandon Stadiums the Public is Left with the Bill," *New York Times* (September 8, 2010), pp. 1ff.

14 Benjamin G. Rader, *Baseball: A History of America's Game* (Urbana, IL: University of Illinois Press, 1992), pp. 189–97.

15 Marvin Miller, *A Whole Different Ball Game: The Sport & Business of Baseball* (New York: Birch Lane, 1991), pp. 174–202, citations p. 194; Zimbalist, pp. 18–22; Richard O. Davies, *America's Obsession: Sports and Society since 1945* (Fort Worth, TX: Harcourt Brace, 1994), pp. 129–43.

16 Gerald Scully, *The Business of Major League Baseball* (Chicago: University of Chicago Press, 1989), pp. 37–9: Zimbalist, pp. 21–2.

17 Scully, p. 37.

18 Zimbalist, pp. 75–104.

19 Scully, pp. 39–43; Zimbalist, pp. 23–7.

20 Tom Verducci, "In the Strike Zone," *Sports Illustrated* (August 1, 1994), pp. 26ff; "Brushback," *Sports Illustrated* (April 10, 1995), pp. 60–7.

21 John P. Rossi, *The National Game: Baseball and American Culture* (Chicago: Dee, 2000), pp. 205–8.

22 Bob Costas, *Fair Ball: A Fan's Case for Baseball* (New York: Broadway, 2000), pp. 91–104.

23 David Maraniss, *When Pride Still Mattered: A Life of Vince Lombardi* (New York: Simon and Schuster, 1999); Michael MacCambridge, *America's Game: The Epic Story of How Pro Football Captured a Nation* (New York: Random House, 2004), pp. 231–47.

24 David Harris, *The League: The Rise and Decline of the NFL* (New York: Bantam, 1986), pp. 542–8; MacCambridge, pp. 356–72.

25 Ibid.

26 Glenn Dickey, *Just Win, Baby: Al Davis and His Raiders* (New York: Harcourt Brace, 1991).

27 Harris, pp. 413–594; MacCambridge, pp. 345–7.

28 Terry Pluto, *Loose Balls: The Short, Wild Life of the American Basketball Association* (New York: Simon and Schuster, 1990).

29 Stephen Fox, *Big Leagues: Professional Baseball, Football, and Basketball in National Memory* (New York: Morrow, 1994), pp. 430–2; Richard O. Davies, *Rivals! The Ten Greatest American Sports Rivalries of the 20th Century* (Malden, MA: Wiley-Blackwell, 2010), pp. 130–55.

30 David Halberstam, *Playing for Keeps: Michael Jordan and the World He Made* (New York: Random House, 1999).

31 Walter LaFeber, *Michael Jordan and the New Global Capitalism* (New York: Norton, 2002).

32 Mark D. Howell, *From Moonshine to Madison Avenue: A Cultural History of the NASCAR Winston Cup Series* (Bowling Green, OH: Bowling Green State University Popular Press, 1997), p. 15.

33 Ibid.

34 Daniel S. Pierce, *Real NASCAR: White Lightning, Red Clay, and Big Bill France* (Chapel Hill, NC: University of North Carolina Press, 2010); Scott Crawford, "William France," in Arnold Markoe, ed., *Scribner Encyclopedia of American Lives: Sports Figures* (New York: Scribner, 2002), vol. 1, pp. 298–300; Joe Menzer, *The Wildest Ride: A History of NASCAR* (New York: Touchstone, 2001), pp. 57–76.

35 www.hickoksports.com/biograph/francebill.shtml.

36 Howell, p. 32; Pierce, pp. 212–19.

37 Howell, p. 32.

38 Tom Wolfe, "The Last American Hero is Junior Johnson. Yes!" *Esquire* (March, 1965), pp. 68ff.

39 Menzer, pp. 197–200.

40 Ibid., pp. 160–3; Pierce, pp. 238–42.

41 Menzer, p. 161.

13 Do You Believe in Miracles?

1 Jamie Fitzpatrick, "Miracle on Ice," www.proice-hockey.com.

2 www.brainyquote.com/decoubertin.

3 Allen Guttmann, *The Olympics: A History of the Modern Games* (Urbana, IL: University of Illinois Press, 1992), p. 12; see also David C. Young, *The Olympic Myth of Greek Amateur Athetics* (Chicago: Ares, 1985).

4 Allen Guttmann, *The Games Must Go On: Avery Brundage and the Olympic Movement* (New York: Columbia University Press, 1984), pp. 62–81; Guttmann, *The Olympics*, pp. 53–71.

5 Guttmann, *The Olympics*, pp. 85–102.

6 Randy Roberts and James Olson, *Winning Is the Only Thing: Sports in America since 1945* (Baltimore: Johns Hopkins University Press, 1989), p. 13.

7 William O. Johnson, *All That Glitters Is Not Gold: The Olympic Games* (New York: Putnam, 1972), pp. 223–4; Benjamin G. Rader, *In Its Own Image: How Television Has Transformed Sports* (New York: Free, 1984), p. 158.

8 Richard Espy, *The Politics of the Olympic Games* (Berkeley, CA: University of California Press, 1979), p. 38.

9 Guttmann, *The Games Must Go On*, pp. 82–131.

10 Ibid., p. 116.

11 Ibid., p. 162.

12 Wilma Rudolph, *Wilma: The Story of Wilma Rudolph* (New York: New American Library, 1977); Katharine Britton, "Wilma Glodean Rudolph," in Arnold Markoe, ed., *Scribner Encyclopedia of American Lives: Sports Figures* (New York: Scribner, 2002), vol. 2, pp. 308–10.

13 Ron Powers, *Supertube: The Rise of Television Sports* (New York: Coward-McCann, 1984), p. 18; Jim Spence, *Up Close and Personal: The Inside Story of Network Television Sports* (New York: Atheneum, 1988), p. 42.

14 Powers, pp. 204–20; Rader, pp. 157–63.

15 Guttmann, *The Olympics*, pp. 130–2; Guttmann, *The Games Must Go On*, pp. 243–5.

16 Guttmann, *The Games Must Go On*, p. 245.

17 Johnson, pp. 262–3.

18 Ibid., p. 270.

19 Guttmann, *The Olympics*, pp. 138–40; John Kiernan, Arthur Daley, and Pat Jordan, *The Story of the Olympic Games, 776 BC to 1976* (Philadelphia, Lippincott, 1977), pp. 378–80; Roberts and Olson, pp. 190–3.

20 Bruce Lowitt, "Terrorists Turn '72 Munich Olympics into Bloodbath," *St Petersburg Times* (December 29, 1999).

21 Powers, p. 214.

22 Guttmann, *The Games Must Go On*, p. 254.

23 Guttmann, *The Olympics*, pp. 127–8; Kiernan et al., pp. 484–6.

24 Roberts and Olson, p. 205.

25 David Marc, "Carl Lewis," in *Scribner Encyclopedia*, vol. 2, pp. 39–41.

26 Adriana Tomasino, "Mary Lou Retton," in *Scribner Encyclopedia*, vol. 2, pp. 262–3.

27 Kenneth Reich, *Making It Happen: Peter Ueberroth and the 1984 Olympics* (Santa Barbara: Capra, 1986).

28 Rader, p. 15e6; Kiernan, pp. 518–19; Sabine Louissaint, "Bruce Jenner," in *Scribner Encyclopedia*, vol. 1, pp. 467–8.

29 www.nba.com/dreamteam.

14 The Persistent Dilemma of Race

1 Michael Oriard, *Bowled Over: Big-Time College Football from the Sixties to the BCS Era* (Chapel Hill, NC: University of North Carolina Press, 2009), pp. 15–124. To compare the team photographs of the Notre Dame squads of 1969 and 1971 (p. 51) is to see the rapid change in racial composition in one major college football program.

2   Michael MacCambridge, *America's Game: The Epic Story of How Pro Football Captured a Nation* (New York: Random House, 2004), pp. 167–9.

3   John Sayle Watterson, *College Football: History, Spectacle, Controversy* (Baltimore: Johns Hopkins University Press, 2000), pp. 308–31; Randy Roberts and James Olson, *Winning Is the Only Thing: Sports in America since 1945* (Baltimore: Johns Hopkins University Press, 1989), pp. 185–6.

4   David W. Zang, "The Greatest: Muhammad Ali's Confounding Character," in Patrick Miller and David K. Wiggins, eds, *Sport and the Color Line* (New York: Routledge, 2004), pp. 289–303.

5   Muhammad Ali with Richard Durham, *The Greatest: My Own Story* (New York: Random House, 1975), pp. 17–19.

6   Thomas Hauser, *Muhammad Ali: His Life and Times* (New York: Touchstone, 1991), pp. 56–80.

7   Ibid., pp. 81–112; Jeffrey T. Sammons, *Beyond the Ring: The Role of Boxing in American Society* (Urbana, IL: University of Illinois Press, 1988), pp. 193–7.

8   Hauser, pp. 104, 147.

9   Roberts and Olson, p. 170.

10 Hauser, p. 139; Roberts and Olson, pp. 173–4.

11 Sammons, pp. 200–4; Hauser, pp. 171–202.

12 *New York Times* (April 30, 1967), p. 19; "Muhammad Ali Loses His Title to the Muslims" (April 20, 1967), p. F-8; "As the Judge Threw the Book at Muhammad," *Sports Illustrated* (July 3, 1967), pp. 18–19; "Decision for Allah," *Newsweek* (July 12, 1967), pp. 61–3; Roberts and Olson, pp. 171–2.

13 Hauser, p. 166.

14 Ibid., p. 167.

15 Sammons, pp. 207–19; Hauser, pp. 463–515.

16 Harry Edwards, *The Revolt of the Black Athlete* (New York: Free, 1969), p. 43.

17 Harry Edwards, "What Happened to the Revolt of the Black Athlete? 1968 and Today," *Colorlines* (summer, 1998), pp. 12–15, citation p. 16, recorded December 16, 1967.

18 Edwards, "What Happened?"

19 Roberts and Olson, p. 175.

20 Newell G. Bringhurst, *Saints, Slaves, and Blacks: The Changing Place of Black People within Mormonism* (Westport, CT: Greenwood, 1981), pp. 181–3.

21 See Roberto Regalado, *Viva Baseball: Latin Major Leaguers and Their Special Hunger* (Urbana, IL: University of Illinois Press, 1998); Adrian Burgos, Jr, *Playing America's Game: Baseball, Latinos, and the Color Line* (Berkeley, CA: University of California Press, 2007).

22 Charles C. Alexander, *Our Game: An American Baseball History* (New York: Holt, 1991), pp. 151–2.

23 David Maraniss, *Clemente: The Passion and Grace of Baseball's Last Hero* (New York: Simon and Schuster, 2006), p. 2.

24 Ibid., p. 71.

25 Ibid., p. 160.

26 Douglas Kellner, "The Sports Spectacle, Michael Jordan and Nike," in Miller and Wiggins, pp. 305–26.

27 Edwards, "What Happened?"

28 Howard Bryant, *The Last Hero: A Life of Henry Aaron* (New York: Pantheon, 2010), provides a thoughtful and richly researched biography of the man who broke Babe Ruth's record. See also Hank Aaron with Lonnie Wheeler, *I Had a Hammer: The Hank Aaron Story* (New York: HarperCollins, 1991), pp. 315–20.

29 Bryant, p. 395.

30 Aaron and Wheeler, p. 328.

31 Bryant, p. 515.

32 Martin Kane, "An Assessment of 'Black is Best,'" *Sports Illustrated* (January 18, 1971), pp. 73–83.

33 Harry Edwards, "The Sources of the Black Athlete's Superiority," *The Black Scholar* (November, 1971), pp. 32–41.

34 Harry Edwards, *The Sociology of Sport* (Homewood, IL: Dorsey, 1973), p. 194.

35 Ibid., p. 194; see also Harry Edwards, "The Myth of the Racially Superior Athlete," *Intellectual Digest* (March, 1972), pp. 58–60.

36 Quoted in Edwards, "The Sources," pp. 39–40.

37 Alexander, pp. 350–1; Roger Kahn, *Into My Own: The Remarkable People and Events that Shaped My Life* (New York: St Martin's, 2006), pp. 274–5.

38 Richard O. Davies, "The Age of Jimmy the Greek: Sports Wagering in Modern America," *Nevada Historical Society Quarterly* (Spring, 1999), pp. 21–45.

39 Jay J. Coakley, *Sport in Society* (New York: McGraw-Hill, 7th edn, 2001), p. 246.

40 This viewpoint is cogently expressed by prominent sports historian Ronald A. Smith in a review essay published in *Journal of Sport History* (summer, 2007), pp. 308–11.

41   David Owen, *The Chosen One: Tiger Woods and the Dilemma of Greatness* (New York: Simon and Schuster, 2001), p. 194.

42   Gary Smith, "The Chosen One," *Sports Illustrated* (December 23, 1996), pp. 28–52.

43   John Garrity, "Open and Shut," *Sports Illustrated* (June 26, 2000), p. 63.

44   Frank Deford, "Better than Imagined," *Sports Illustrated* (December 18, 2000), p. 91.

45   Steve Rushin, "Grand Stand," *Sports Illustrated* (July 31, 2000), pp. 52–61.

46   Associated Press, June 16, 2008.

47   Julianne Cicarelli, "Venus Ebony Starr Williams," in Arnold Markoe, ed., *Scribner Encyclopedia of American Lives: Sports Figures* (New York: Scribner, 2002), vol. 2, pp. 503–5.

48   "Never Too Young for Tennis Millions," *New York Times* (November 10, 1993); S. L. Price, "Venus Envy," *Sports Illustrated* (September 10, 1999), pp. 35–6.

49   *New York Times* (September 10, 1999), p. D4.

50   Price, pp. 35–6.

51   *New York Times* (March 1, 1999), p. D1; S. L. Price, "Father Knew Best," *Sports Illustrated* (September 20, 1999), pp. 40–3.

52   L. Jon Wertheim, "The Serena Show," *Sports Illustrated* (May 26, 2003), pp. 38–41; Wertheim, "Go in Style," *Sports Illustrated* (March 22, 2004), pp. 113–15.

53   Wertheim, "The Serena Show."

54   Cicarelli, p. 504.

15   Playing Nice No Longer: Women's Sports, 1960–2010

1   Quoted in Richard O. Davies, *America's Obsession: Sports and Society since 1945* (Fort Worth, TX: Harcourt Brace, 1994), p. 171.

2   Allen L. Sack and Ellen J. Staurowsky, *College Athletes for Hire: The Evolution and Legacy of the NCAA's Amateur Myth* (Westport, CT: Praeger, 1998), pp. 111–16; for an overview of women's sports, see Ying Wushanley, *Playing Nice and Losing: The Struggle for Control of Women's Intercollegiate Athletics, 1960–2000* (Syracuse: Syracuse University Press, 2004); Susan K. Cahn, ed., *Coming on Strong: Gender and Sexuality in Twentieth-Century Women's Sports* (New York: Free, 1994); and Jean O'Reilly and Susan K. Cahn, *Women and Sports in the United States: A Documentary Reader* (Boston: Northeastern University Press, 2007).

3   Walter Byers, *Unsportsmanlike Conduct: Exploiting College Athletes* (Ann Arbor, MI: University of Michigan Press, 1995), p. 243.

4   Cahn, pp. 250–6.

5   Byers, p. 243; Cahn, p. 255.

6   Cahn, pp. 255–7; Wushanley, pp. 126–59.

7   Byers, p. 245; Murray Sperber, *College Sports, Inc.: The Athletic Department vs. the University* (New York: Holt, 1990), p. 322.

8   Sack and Staurowsky, pp. 111–26.

9   Cahn, pp. 278–9.

10   For an overview of women's basketball, see Pamela Grundy and Susan Shackelford, *Shattering the Glass: The Remarkable History of Women's Basketball* (New York: New, 2005).

11   Pat Summitt with Sally Jenkins, *Reach for the Summit* (New York: Broadway, 1998); Randy Moore, *Tennessee Lady Volunteers* (Guilford, CT: Globe Pequot, 2005).

12   Moore, p. 101.

13   Geno Auriemma with Jackie MacMullan, *Geno: In Pursuit of Perfection* (New York: Warner, 2006).

14   Moore, p. 133.

15   Ibid., p. 139.

16   Auriemma, pp. 265–71; Frank Deford, "Geno Auriemma + Diana Taurasi = Love, Italian Style," *Sports Illustrated* (November 24, 2003), pp. 124–33.

17   Richard Kent, *Lady Vols and UConn: The Greatest Rivalry in Women's Basketball* (Nashville, TN: Cumberland House, 2007), pp. 86–8, 106.

18   Kent, pp. 104–9; *New York Times* (April 8, 2008), p. C16.

19   Lori Riley, "Did Season Suffer without UConn–Tennessee?" *Hartford Courant* (April 4, 2008).

20   Billie Jean King, *Billie Jean* (New York: Harper and Row, 1974); Karen Gould, "Billie Jean Moffitt King," in Arnold Markoe, ed., *Scribner Encyclopedia of American Lives: Sports Figures* (New York: Scribner, 2002), vol. 1, pp. 517–19.

21   Frank Deford, "Mrs. Billie Jean King!" *Sports Illustrated* (May 19, 1975), pp. 71–82.

22   *New York Times* (August 3, 1973), p. 61; Pete Axthelm, "The Battle of the Sexes," *Newsweek* (September 24, 1973), pp. 82–5.

23   *New York Times* (July 12, 1973), p. 41.

24   Curry Kirkpatrick, "There She Is: Ms America," *Sports Illustrated* (October 1, 1973), pp. 30–2.

25 Johnette Howard, *The Rivals. Chris Evert vs. Martina Navratilova: Their Epic Duels and Extraordinary Friendship* (New York: Broadway, 2005); Martina Navratilova with George Vecsey, *Martina* (New York: Fawcett Crest, 1985); Chris Evert Lloyd with Neil Amdur, *Chrissie: My Own Story* (New York: Simon and Schuster, 1982).

26 Curry Kirkpatrick, "The Passion of a Champion," *Newsweek* (November 14, 1994), p. 58.

27 Sara Hammel and Anna Mulrine, "They Got More than Just a Game," *US News and World Report* (July 12, 1999), p. 54.

28 Mark Starr, "Keeping Her Own Score," *Newsweek* (June 21, 1999), p. 60; Mia Hamm, *Go for the Goal: A Champion's Guide to Winning in Soccer and Life* (New York: HarperCollins, 2000), pp. 3–24.

29 Starr, p. 62.

30 Hamm, pp. 208–9.

31 Mark Starr and Martha Brant, "It Went Down to the Wire … and Thrilled Us All," *Newsweek* (July 19, 1999), p. 53.

32 Starr, p. 61.

33 Michael Hiestand, "ESPN Aims for Female Audience," *USA Today* (October 20, 2010).

34 For a detailed presentation of the 40-year struggle within one university produced by the passage of Title IX, see an informative and detailed oral history that draws upon more than 50 interviews with participants: Alicia Barber, Mary A. Larson, and Allison Tracy, eds, *We Were All Athletes: Women's Athletics and Title IX at the University of Nevada* (Reno, NV: University of Nevada Oral History Project, 2011).

35 George Will, "The Train Wreck Called Title IX," *Newsweek* (May 27, 2002).

16 "Only in America!"

1 Kenneth Cooper, *Aerobics* (New York: Bantam, 1968).

2 Robert Ernst, *Weakness Is a Crime: The Life of Bernarr Macfadden* (Syracuse: Syracuse University Press, 1991); Mary Macfadden and Emile Gauvreau, *Dumbbells and Carrot Strips: The Story of Bernarr Macfadden* (New York: Holt, 1953); Clement Wood, *Bernarr Macfadden: A Study in Success* (New York: Beekman, 1974).

3 Jonathan Black, "Muscle Man," *Smithsonian* (August, 2009), pp. 64–71.

4 Patrick Perry, "Jack LaLanne: Fit For Life," *Saturday Evening Post* (November, 2000), pp. 38ff.

5 H. W. Brands, "Just Do It," in *Masters of Enterprise: Giants of American Business. From John Jacob Astor and J. P. Morgan to Bill Gates and Oprah Winfrey* (New York: Free, 1999), pp. 256–66; Timothy Egan, "The Swoon of the Swoosh," *New York Times* (September 13, 1998); Aaron Frisch, *The Story of Nike: Built for Success* (North Mankato, MN: Smart Apple Media, 2004). For Bill Bowerman's role in creating Nike, see Kenny Moore, *Bowerman and the Men of Oregon* (Kutztown, PA: Rodale, 2006).

6 Quoted in Jimmy Breslin, "In Defense of Gambling," *Saturday Evening Post* (January 5, 1963), p. 12.

7 Richard O. Davies, "Only in Nevada: Nevada's Unique Experiment with Legalized Sports Gambling, 1931–2000," *Nevada State Historical Society Quarterly* (spring, 2001), pp. 3–19; Richard O. Davies and Richard G. Abram, *Betting the Line: Sports Wagering in American Life* (Columbus, OH: Ohio State University Press, 2001), pp. 140–2.

8 Richard O. Davies, "The Age of Jimmy the Greek: Sports Wagering in Modern America," *Nevada State Historical Society Quarterly* (spring, 1999), pp. 21–45.

9 Jimmy Snyder, *Jimmy the Greek: By Himself* (Chicago: Playboy, 1975); Ginger Wadsworth with Jimmy Snyder, *Farewell Jimmy the Greek: Wizard of Odds* (Austin, TX: Eakin, 1997).

10 Michael Y. Sokolove, *Hustle: The Myth, Life, and Lies of Pete Rose* (New York: Simon and Schuster, 1990).

11 James Reston, Jr, *Collision at Home Plate: The Lives of Pete Rose and Bart Giamatti* (Lincoln, NE: University of Nebraska Press, 1991), pp. 306–8.

12 Pete Rose, *My Prison without Bars* (Emmaus, PA: Rodale, 2004), p. 316; Murray Chass, "Truth is Revealed in Bets Pete Rose Didn't Make," *New York Times* (March 16, 2007).

13 Charley Rosen, *The Wizard of Odds: How Jack Molinas Almost Destroyed the Game of Basketball* (New York: Seven Stories, 2001).

14 "Unartful Dodger," *Sports Illustrated* (May 29, 2000), pp. 28–9.

15 John Underwood, "The Biggest Game in Town," *Sports Illustrated* (March 10, 1986), pp. 30–1.

16 David Noonan, "Boxing and the Brain," *New York Times* (June 12, 1983), pp. 40ff.

17 Robert H. Boyle and Wilmer Ames, "Too Many Punches, Too Little Concern," *Sports Illustrated* (April 11, 1983), pp. 44–67; Charles Leerhsen, "The AMA Tries to KO Boxing," *Newsweek* (December 17, 1984), p. 67.

18 Fred Bruning, "Shake Hands and Come Out Killing," *Macleans* (December 13, 1982), p. 13.

19 Noonan, p. 42.

20 Jeffrey T. Sammons, *Beyond the Ring: The Role of Boxing in American Society* (Urbana, IL: University of Illinois Press, 1988), pp. 219–21.

21 Gloria Cooksey, "Don(ald) King," in Arnold Markoe, ed., *Scribner Encyclopedia of American Lives: Sports Figures* (New York: Scribner, 2002), vol. 1, pp. 519–20.

22 For several perspectives on Tyson and his career, see Daniel O'Connor, ed., *Iron Mike: The Mike Tyson Reader* (New York: Thunder's Mouth, 2002).

23 Jack Newfield, *Only in America: The Life and Crimes of Don King* (New York: Morrow, 1995), pp. 266–72.

24 Ibid., p. 288.

25 Joyce Carol Oates, "Rape and the Boxing Ring," *Newsweek* (February 24, 1992), pp. 60–1; William Nack, "A Crushing Verdict," *Sports Illustrated* (September, 1992), pp. 22–3; Newfield, p. 293.

26 Newfield, pp. 132–8.

27 Tom Donahoe and Neil Johnson, *Foul Play: Drug Abuse in Sport* (New York: Blackwell, 1986), p. 1.

28 Robert Voy, *Drugs, Sport, and Politics* (Champaign, IL: Human Kinetics, 1991), p. 307. See also Rob Beamish and Ian Ritchie, *Fastest, Highest, Strongest: A Critique of High-Performance Sport* (New York: Routledge, 2006).

29 Voy, pp. 16–18.

30 Ibid., p. xv.

31 Ibid.

32 Ibid.

33 Michael S. Bahrke and Charles E. Yesalis, *Performance-Enhancing Substances in Sport and Exercise* (Champaign, IL: Human Kinetics, 2002), pp. 7–8; Bil Gilbert, "Drugs in Sports," *Sports Illustrated* (June 23, June 30, July 7, 1969).

34 Steve Courson, *False Glory. Steelers and Steroids: The Steve Courson Story* (Stamford, CT: Longmeadow, 1991), pp. 49–55.

35 Ibid., p. 55.

36 Ibid., pp. 55–9.

37 C. Fraser Smith, *Lenny, Lefty, and the Chancellor: The Len Bias Tragedy and the Search for Reform in Big-Time College Basketball* (Baltimore: Bancroft, 1992).

38 By Lyle Alzado, as told to Shelly Smith, "I'm Sick and I'm Scared," *Sports Illustrated* (July 8, 1991), pp. 20–4.

39 David Markel, Noah Kaplan, and Michael Fishel, "The Andro Debate," www.angelfre.com/tx2/andro.

40 Bill Saporito, "How Pumped Up Is Baseball?" *Time* (December 17, 2004), pp. 34–5.

41 Rick Reilly, "No Doubt About It," *Sports Illustrated* (December 12, 2004), p. 118.

42 "Drug Free Sports Might Be a Thing of the Past," Associated Press (December 27, 2004).

43 Mark Fainaru-Wada and Lance Williams, *Game of Shadows: Barry Bonds, BALCO, and the Steroids Scandal that Rocked Professional Sports* (New York: Gotham, 2006).

44 Jerry Adler, "Toxic Strength," *Newsweek* (December 26, 2004), pp. 45–52.

45 Howard Bryant, *The Last Hero: A Life of Henry Aaron* (New York: Pantheon, 2010), p. 514.

17   The Democratization of Sports

1 Richard O. Davies, *America's Obsession: Sports and Society since 1945* (Fort Worth, TX: Harcourt Brace, 1994), pp. 103–9.

2 Bobby Plump, with Marty Pieratt and Ken Honeywell, *Bobby Plump: Last of the Small Town Heroes* (Indianapolis: Good Morning, 1997).

3 Christopher Davis, "Go Massillon Go!" *Esquire* (December, 1965), pp. 206–7.

4 H. G. Bissinger, *Friday Night Lights: A Town, A Team, and a Dream* (Reading, MA: Addison-Wesley, 1990), p. xiii.

5 Bissinger, p. xiv.

6 Lewis Yablonsky and Jonathan Brower, *The Little League Game: How Kids, Coaches, and Parents Really Play It* (New York: Times, 1979); Bill Geist, *Little League Confidential: One Coach's Completely Unauthorized Tale of Survival* (New York: Macmillan, 1992); Lance and Robin Van Auken, *Play Ball: The Story of Little League Baseball* (University Park, PA: Pennsylvania State University Press, 2001).

7 Jim Brosnan, "Little Leaguers Have Big Problems – Their Parents," *Atlantic* (March, 1963), pp. 117–20.

8 Andrew Powell, *We Own This Game: A Season in the Adult World of Youth Football* (New York: Atlantic

Monthly, 2003); M. J. Stuart et al., "Injuries in Youth Football," *Mayo Clinic Proceedings* (2002), pp. 317–22.

9   Joan Ryan, *Little Girls in Pretty Boxes: The Making and Breaking of Elite Gymnasts and Figure Skaters* (New York: Doubleday, 1995).

10 Ibid., pp. 13–15.

11 Davies, pp. 124–6.

12 Michael Sokolove, "Constucting a Teen Phenom," *New York Times Magazine* (November 28, 2004), pp. 80–5.

13 Ibid., p. 84.

14 James Dodson, *Ben Hogan: An American Life* (New York: Doubleday, 2004).

15 "A Champion Proves They Can Come Back," *Life* (January 23, 1950), pp. 21–3; "Little Ice Water," *Time* (January 10, 1949), pp. 52–6; "Out for Greatness," *Newsweek* (July 20, 1953), pp. 80–1.

16 Ian O'Connor, *Arnie and Jack: Palmer, Nicklaus and Golf's Greatest Rivalry* (Boston: Houghton Mifflin, 2008); Thomas Hauser, *Arnold Palmer: A Personal Journey* (San Francisco: Collins, 1994); Ray Cave, "Sportsman of the Year: Arnold Palmer," *Sports Illustrated* (January 9, 1961), p. 25.

17 Cave, pp. 23–31.

18 Alfred Wright, "The Trouble with Leading an Army," *Sports Illustrated* (June 30, 1962), pp. 16–20; "Win or Lose: Arnie Draws," *Sports Illustrated* (July 17, 1981), p. 47.

19 "Golf: The Man and the Myth," *Time* (June 28, 1968), p. 76; Martin Sherwin, "Lee Buck Trevino," in Arnold Markoe, ed., *Scribner Encyclopedia of American Lives: Sports Figures* (New York: Scribner, 2002), vol. 2, pp. 438–9.

20 Dan Jenkins, "Lee Trevino, Fleas and All," *Sports Illustrated* (June 8, 1970), pp. 70–1; "Lee Trevino, Cantinflas of the Country Clubs," *Time* (July 19, 1971), p. 48.

21 Jenkins, p. 71.

22 Curry Kirkpatrick, "A Common Man with an Uncommon Touch," *Sports Illustrated* (December 20, 1971), pp. 34–9.

23 Richard O. Davies, *Rivals! The Ten Greatest Sports Rivalries of the 20th Century* (Malden, MA: Wiley-Blackwell, 2010), pp. 107–29; Jack Nicklaus with Ken Bowden, *Jack Nicklaus: My Story* (New York: Simon and Schuster, 1997).

24 "Prodigious Prodigy," *Time* (June 29, 1962), pp. 38–42.

25 Frank Deford, "Still Glittering after All These Years," *Sports Illustrated* (December 25, 1978), p. 34.

26 Martin Sherwin, "Jack William Nicklaus," in *Scribner Encyclopedia*, vol. 2, pp. 188–90.

27 Rick Reilly, "Day of Glory for a Golden Oldie," *Sports Illustrated* (April 21, 1986), pp. 18–25; Pete Axthelm, "From Fat Boy to Legend," *Newsweek* (April 28, 1986), pp. 26–32.

28 Samuel Abt, *LeMond: The Incredible Comeback of an American Hero* (New York: Random House, 1990); Franz Lidz, "Vive LeMond," *Sports Illustrated* (July 31, 1989), pp. 12–17; Alexander Wolff, "Tour de Courage," *Sports Illustrated* (August 5, 1991), pp. 2–31.

29 E. M. Swift, "An American Takes Paris," *Sports Illustrated* (August 6, 1986), pp. 12–17; Greg LeMond, *Greg LeMond's Complete Book of Bicycling* (New York: Putnam, 1987), pp. 9–40.

30 Austin Murphy, "Magnifique!" *Sports Illustrated* (August 6, 2001), pp. 34–9; Kelli Anderson, "King of the Hill," *Sports Illustrated* (August 5, 2002), p. 38.

31 Alan Shipnuck, "Tour de Armstrong," *Sports Illustrated* (May 20, 1996), pp. 48–50.

32 Lance Armstrong, *It's Not About the Bike: My Journey Back to Life* (New York: Berkeley, 2001), p. 4.

33 Rick Reilly, "Sportsman of the Year: Lance Armstrong," *Sports Illustrated* (December 16, 2002), p. 56.

34 Timothy Kringer, "Lance Armstrong," in *Scribner Encyclopedia*, vol. 1, p. 41; Richard Hoffer, "Tour de Lance," *Sports Illustrated* (July 6, 1999), p. 27; Selena Roberts and David Epstein, "The Case Against Lance Armstrong," *Sports Illustrated* (January 24, 201), p. 59.

35 Armstrong, p. 38.

36 Armstrong, p. 248.

37 The best secondary source for this phenomenon is David Kent Sproul, "Post-Modern Cowboys: The Transformation of Sports in the Twentieth Century" (unpublished doctoral dissertation, University of Nevada, Las Vegas, August, 2005).

38 Michael Brooke, *The Concrete Wave: The History of Skateboarding* (Toronto: Warwick, 1999); Sproul, pp. 135–46.

39 Brooke, pp. 46–57.

40 Sproul, pp. 169–230.

41 John Severson, "Sidewalk Surfing?" *Skateboarder* (winter, 1964), p. 7.

42 David Wallechinsky and Jaime Loucky, eds, *The Complete Book of the Winter Olympics, 2010 Edition*

(London: Aurum, 2010); John Branch, "White Takes Gold in Snowboard Halfpipe," *New York Times* (February 12, 2006), p. 27.

43   Sproul, pp. 231–68.

44   Damien Cave, "Dogtown, USA," *New York Times* (June 12, 2005), p. 6.

45   L. Jon Wertheim, *Blood in the Cage: Mixed Martial Arts, Pat Miletich, and the Furious Rise of the UFC* (Boston: Houghton Mifflin Harcourt, 2009), p. 58.

46   Wertheim, pp. 98–102.

Epilogue

1   Warren St John, *Rammer Jammer Yellow Hammer* (New York: Three Rivers, 2004), p. 10.

2   For a useful analysis of the studies of spectator and sports fan behavior, see Daniel L. Wann, Merrill J. Melnick, Gordon W. Russell, and Dale G. Pease, *Sports Fans: The Psychology and Social Impact of Spectators* (New York: Routledge, 2001).

Index

Sports in American Life: A History, Second Edition, Richard O. Davies
© 2012 John Wiley & Sons, Inc. Published 2012 by John Wiley & Sons, Inc.